Handbook of Child Sexual Abuse

Handbook of Child Sexual Abuse

Identification, Assessment, and Treatment

Edited by

Paris Goodyear-Brown

WILEY

John Wiley & Sons, Inc.

Library of Congress Cataloging-in-Publication Data:
Handbook of child sexual abuse: identification, assessment, and treatment/edited by Paris Goodyear-Brown.
    p. cm.
  Includes bibliographical references and index.
  ISBN 978-0-470-87729-6 (cloth); 978-1-118-08228-7 (ePub); 978-1-118-08264-5 (eMobi); 978-1-118-08292-8 (ePDF)
   1. Child sexual abuse. 2. Child sexual abuse—Psychological aspects. 3. Sexually abused children—Rehabilitation. I. Goodyear-Brown, Paris.
  HV6570.H356 2011
  362.76—dc22
                                                                                    2011010996

In memory of my grandmother, Marie Theresa Varricchio Turco, who taught me how to be tough and generous, and who never stopped trying to feed me.

Contents

Preface

THE IDEA FOR this volume began, as many good things do, over a meal. I had just given a couple of talks at a multidisciplinary conference on child sexual abuse, had attended another talk and was enjoying dinner with colleagues. As we discussed the information that had been shared in the final talk and dissected it, debating it through the lenses of our various disciplines, I found myself intrigued, engaged, and enjoying myself immensely. Here were the latest ideas of researchers and clinicians, forensic interviewers and law enforcement professionals, caseworkers and victim advocates, all of whom are leaders in their respective fields, doing the work of helping children who have been sexually victimized. I wanted to capture and share with others the dialogue that bounced from emerging practice trends to the challenges of working within existing systems to the rigors of ongoing research to the nuances of individualized treatment.

The goal of these kinds of discussions, in my mind, is the refinement of thought. This refinement of thought occurs on the individual level, often in the form of paradigm shifts; it seeps into one's professional life, influences others, becomes pragmatized in agency policies, and ultimately shapes the societal response to the problem at hand: in this case, child sexual abuse.

This handbook is the most comprehensive volume on child sexual abuse to date and offers a snapshot of the state of the field as it stands today. As such, it is intended to aid the refinement of our thoughts, to help increase our mutual understanding as we approach this critically important issue together, and to help shape society's approach to child sexual abuse.

The field of child sexual abuse has experienced an explosion of research, literature, and treatment methods over the past 30 years. The contributing authors, many of whom are pioneers in their respective specialties, lend their expertise to a volume that combines the latest research with a wealth of clinical experience. When appropriate, outcome data is shared and augmented with clinical case examples and specific strategies for impacting change.

As I wrestled through my own contributions to this volume and edited chapter after chapter of collegial writings, immersing myself in the language of child sexual abuse, I was struck anew by the way our words—the way we talk about a thing—influence the way we think about that thing. As language evolves, so does culture. For example, teenagers who have historically been referred to as juvenile sex offenders are discussed in this volume as adolescents with illegal sexual behavior. The language choice here is meant to influence a societal reconceptualization of this group as developmentally distinct from adult offenders and in need of different kinds of assessment and treatment. Another intentional distinction is offered between children who have sexual behavior problems that occur comorbidly with a history of sexual abuse and those who have these same behaviors in the absence of documented abuse. The traditional argument has been that if a child is sexually acting out, that child must have been sexually abused. Modern assessment and treatment methods are disproving this view and providing targeted intervention strategies for differing etiologies. Most provocatively, this volume offers a distinction between the event of child sexual abuse and the potential symptomatology and treatment that may be necessary. Our society tends to look on those who have been sexually abused as damaged goods, as pathologically scarred. The research suggests, however, that at least 30% of survivors are asymptomatic. Does this mean that these children suffer no adverse consequences or that we simply have not found a measurement tool to quantify these consequences? This volume is certainly not meant to provide a definitive answer to this question, but certainly attempts to further the dialogue on this issue.

The handbook is divided into several sections and can be used as a primer for professionals new to the field, as a topic-specific aid to seasoned professionals and as a reference guide for all. The first section of the book tackles definitional and epidemiological issues and the effects of child sexual abuse, both short term and into adulthood. Chapters on neurobiological implications of abuse and the long-term physiological effects of trauma help to frame the potential implications of early sexual victimization.

The second section of the handbook begins with a description of the various professionals who may become involved when an allegation of sexual abuse has been made. Representatives from each professional discipline offer guidelines about their roles in cases of child sexual abuse (CSA) with a view to how multidisciplinary team members can collaborate most effectively. A chapter on forensic interviewing guidelines is followed by chapters on the comprehensive assessment of children referred with alleged sexual abuse histories and considerations in providing developmentally sensitive assessment.

The third section of the handbook covers treatment options for children who have traumagenic symptoms as a response to their sexual victimization. The case for evidence-based practice is made and then followed by chapters that explicate the most rigorously researched treatments for traumatized children. Other promising treatments that incorporate expressive therapies such as play, art, and bibliotherapy are detailed and a format for group therapy is offered. Two dyadic treatments, each of which can enhance the positive relationship between the nonoffending parent and CSA survivor, are also outlined.

The fourth section covers a range of information, including treatment considerations for adolescents who have been sexually abused, adolescent survivors who engage in self-injurious behaviors, and adolescents who engage in illegal sexual behavior. Cultural issues in intervention and prevention of child sexual abuse are explored and guidelines are provided for enhancing multicultural competencies. Secondary trauma and vicarious traumatization are also given attention as they are real concerns for any helping professional routinely involved with child sexual abuse cases. The handbook wraps up with a chapter that offers an ecological approach for the prevention of CSA.

It is my hope that this handbook equip those on the frontlines in the battle against CSA not merely with the knowledge that can be culled from the breadth of empirical information, intervention models, and case conceptualizations offered in this volume, but also with renewed vision for the importance of the role played by each helping professional in the shaping of our culture and the healing of our children.

Paris Goodyear-Brown

Acknowledgments

I WANT TO BEGIN by thanking the chapter authors, most of whom are in high demand and overextended, for giving the gift of their time, knowledge, and energy to this project. A volume like this is only as strong as the authors represented in it and this book is stronger because of each of you.

Special thanks to Jim Campbell and Marilyn Grundy for helping me think through the best authors for various material and for playing the role of liaison when necessary. Thanks to Kara Borbely at John Wiley & Sons, who tirelessly kept the streams of communication flowing throughout the project and to the rest of the editorial staff.

Thanks to Toni Goodyear, for serving as sounding board and informal editor throughout.

Special thanks to Pam Paxton for loving my children like they were your own when I needed to steal away to write or edit, and thanks to my children, Sam, Madison, and Nicholas, for filling me back up when I was emptied out.

Thanks to my husband for always looking in the same direction with me, and sometimes showing me the view from further down the road. Last but certainly not least, thanks to all the children and families who have graced my office with their journeys toward recovery.

About the Editor

Paris Goodyear-Brown, MSW, LCSW, RPT-S, is a Licensed Clinical Social Worker and a Registered Play Therapist-Supervisor with 17 years of experience in treating abused and traumatized children. She holds a clinical appointment with Vanderbilt University; has served as adjunct professor and/or guest lecturer for several universities in middle Tennessee; sees clients in an outpatient setting; provides training, consultation, and supervision to mental health agencies across the country; and has an international reputation as a dynamic speaker on child therapy topics. She is best known for developing evidence-informed, play-based interventions that are used to treat a range of issues related to child psychopathology. She is the creator of the Flexibly Sequential Play Therapy (FSPT) model for treating traumatized children, co-creator of Nurturing Engagement for Attachment Repair (NEAR) and co-investigator on a grant to pilot this protocol with children who have experienced caregiver disruptions and engage in externalizing behaviors. Her clinical and research interests include the treatment of child trauma (particularly child sexual abuse), attachment disturbances, and other clinical presentations of anxiety. She has received the APT award for Play Therapy Promotion and Education. She is the author of multiple books, chapters, and articles related to child therapy, including *Play Therapy with Traumatized Children: A Prescriptive Approach, The Worry Wars: An Anxiety Workbook for Kids and their Helpful Adults, Digging for Buried Treasure: 52 Prop-Based Interventions for Treating the Problems of Childhood* (Volumes 1 and 2), and a bibliotherapy resource entitled *Gabby the Gecko*.

Contributors

Robbie Adler-Tapia, PhD
Psychologist
EMDRIA Therapist Certified in
    EMDR
EMDRIA-Approved Consultant
    and Specialty Trainer
EMDR Institute Facilitator
EMDR/HAP Trainer
Tempe, Arizona

Bonnie Beneke, LCSW
Executive Director of Tennessee
    Chapter of Children's Advocacy
    Centers
Nashville, Tennessee

Dawn Blacker, PhD
Assistant Director MH
    Services/Training Director
CAARE Diagnostic and
    Treatment Center
Dept. of Pediatrics
UC Davis Children's
    Hospital
Sacramento, California

Barbara L. Bonner, PhD
CMRI/Jean Gumerson Endowed
    Chair
Director, Center on Child Abuse
    and Neglect
Professor of Pediatrics

University of Oklahoma Health
    Sciences Center
Oklahoma City, Oklahoma

Sue C. Bratton, PhD
Professor and Director,
    Center for Play Therapy
University of North Texas
Denton, Texas

Lorena Burris, PhD
Research Associate
Center on Child Abuse
    and Neglect
University of Oklahoma Health
    Sciences Center
Oklahoma City, Oklahoma

Peggy L. Ceballos, PhD
Assistant Professor
University of North Carolina
    at Charlotte
Charlotte, North Carolina

Mark Chaffin, PhD
Professor of Pediatrics
Center on Child Abuse and
    Neglect
University of Oklahoma Health
    Sciences Center
Oklahoma City, Oklahoma

Judith Cohen, MD
Center for Traumatic
    Stress in Children and Adolescents

Allegheny General Hospital
Drexel University College of
  Medicine
Pittsburgh, Pennsylvania

Mary B. Costas, Ph.D.
Private Practice
Ft. Worth, Texas

Abbe Fath, MSSW, LCSW
Nashville Children's Alliance
Nashville, Tennessee

Monica M. Fitzgerald, Ph.D.
Assistant Professor
University of Colorado-Denver
Kempe Center for the
  Prevention and
  Treatment of Child Abuse
  and Neglect
Dept. of Pediatrics, SOM
Gary Pavilion, Children's
  Hospital
Aurora, Colorado

Lisa Aronson Fontes, Ph.D.
University without Walls,
  University of Massachusetts,
  Amherst
Hadley, Massachusetts

Linda Cordisco Steele, M.Ed., LPC
National Children's Advocacy
  Center
Huntsville, Alabama

**Rachel Cook Freeman, MSSW,
  LCSW**
Vice President, Clinical Services
Sexual Assault Center
Nashville, Tennessee

**Richard L. Gaskill, Ed.D., LCP,
  LCPC, RPT-S**
Lecturer Wichita State University
Sumner Mental Health Center
Wellington, Kansas

Eliana Gil, Ph.D.
Gil Center for Healing and Play
Fairfax, Virginia

**Paris Goodyear-Brown, MSSW,
  LCSW, RPT-S**
Adjunct Instructor of Psychiatric
  Mental Health, Vanderbilt
  University
Paris and Me, Inc.: Counseling
  for Kids
Brentwood, Tennessee

Deanne Ginns-Gruenberg, MA
Director of Mental Health
  Resource Acquisitions
Self-Esteem Shop
Royal Oak, Michigan

C. Curtis Holmes, Ph.D.
Licensed Psychologist
Warner Robins, Georgia

**Kathleen Kendall-Tackett, Ph.D.,
  IBCLC**
Clinical Associate Professor
Dept. of Pediatrics
Texas Tech University School
  of Medicine
Amarillo, Texas

Maureen C. Kenny, Ph.D.
Professor and Director of the
  Graduate Program in
  Counselor Education

Dept. of Educational and
  Psychological Studies
Florida International University
Miami, Florida
Program Director of KLAS:
  Kids Learning About Safety
College of Education
Miami, Florida

Garry L. Landreth, Ph.D.
Regents Professor
University of North Texas
Denton, Texas

Liana Lowenstein, MSW
Private Practice
Toronto, Ontario

**Cathy Malchiodi, PhD, LPCC,
LPAT, ATR-BC**
National Institute for Trauma
  and Loss in Children
Louisville, Kentucky

**Sharon A. McGee, MS, LPC,
LMFT, RPT-S**
Private Practice
Montgomery, Alabama

Michele M. Many, MSW, LCSW
Dept. of Psychiatry
Louisiana State University
  Health Sciences Center
New Orleans, Louisiana

Lori Myers, MSSW, LCSW
Sexual Assault Center
Nashville, Tennessee

Joy D. Osofsky, Ph.D.
Depts. of Pediatrics and
  Psychiatry

Louisiana State University
  Health Sciences Center
New Orleans, Louisiana

Bruce D. Perry, MD, Ph.D.
Senior Fellow
Child Trauma Academy
Houston, Texas
Adjunct Professor
Dept. of Psychiatry and Behavioral
  Sciences
Feinberg School of Medicine
Northwestern University
Chicago, Illinois

Carol A. Plummer, Ph.D., ACSW
Associate Professor, Myron B.
  Thompson School of Social
  Work, University of Hawaii
  Research Affiliate, Consuelo
  Foundation
Henke Hall
Honolulu, Hawaii

Benjamin E. Saunders, Ph.D.
Professor and Associate Director
National Crime Victims Research
  and Treatment Center
Dept. of Psychiatry and Behavioral
  Science
Medical University of South
  Carolina
Charleston, South Carolina

Susan R. Schmidt, Ph.D.
Assistant Professor of Research
Center on Child Abuse and
  Neglect
University of Oklahoma Health
  Sciences Center
Oklahoma City, Oklahoma

Carolyn Settle, MSW, LCSW
EMDRIA Therapist Certified
  in EMDR
EMDRIA-Approved Consultant
  and Specialty Trainer
EMDR Institute Facilitator
EMDR/HAP Trainer
Scottsdale, Arizona

Francine Shapiro, Ph.D.
Mental Research Institute
Palo Alto, California

Janine Shelby, Ph.D., RPT-S
Assistant Professor
Dept. of Psychiatry
Geffen School of Medicine,
  UCLA
Child and Adolescent Psychiatry
Harbor-UCLA Medical Center
Torrance, California

Jane F. Silovsky, Ph.D.
Associate Professor
Center on Child Abuse and Neglect
University of Oklahoma Health
  Sciences Center
Oklahoma City, Oklahoma

Lisa M. Swisher, Ph.D.
Clinical Assistant Professor
Center on Child Abuse and
  Neglect
University of Oklahoma Health
  Sciences Center
Oklahoma City, Oklahoma

Keegan R. Tangeman, Psy.D.
Child and Adolescent
  Psychiatry

Harbor-UCLA Medical Center
Torrance, California

Alanna Truss, Ph.D.
Clinical Psychologist, Dept.
  of Psychiatry, Vanderbilt
  University
Vanderbilt Center of Excellence
  for Children in State
  Custody
Vanderbilt Psychiatry
Nashville, Tennessee

Anthony J. Urquiza, Ph.D.
Director, Mental Health Services
  and Clinical Research
CAARE Diagnostic and
  Treatment Center
Dept. of Pediatrics
UC Davis Children's Hospital
Sacramento, California

Patti van Eys, Ph.D.
Assistant Professor of Psychiatry,
  Vanderbilt University
Vanderbilt Center of Excellence
  for Children in State
  Custody
Vanderbilt Psychiatry
Nashville, Tennessee

Jimmy Widdifield Jr., MA, LPC
Developmental Pediatric
  Counselor
Center on Child Abuse and
  Neglect
University of Oklahoma Health
  Sciences Center
Oklahoma City, Oklahoma

Sandy K. Wurtele, Ph.D.
Professor, Dept. of Psychology
Chair, UCCS Institutional
 Review Board for Human
 Subjects
Director, Undergraduate Studies
 in Psychology
University of Colorado at
 Colorado Springs
Colorado Springs, Colorado

Arye Zacks, BA
Modiin, Israel

SECTION I

IDENTIFICATION

CHAPTER 1

Child Sexual Abuse

The Scope of the Problem

PARIS GOODYEAR-BROWN, ABBE FATH, and LORI MYERS

INTRODUCTION

THE PROBLEM OF child sexual abuse is one riddled with complexity. To have a sexually victimized child give a clear disclosure that is replicated in a forensic interview process, proven in a court of law, and ultimately results in both physical and felt safety for the child client is a hope held by the myriad helping professionals involved in these cases. When the victimization is of a grossly criminal nature, people are quick to term it child sexual abuse (CSA). However, many of the cases that come across the desks of those on the front lines are much more nebulous and require a nuanced view toward identification, assessment, and treatment.

The difficulty begins with definition: What constitutes child sexual abuse? What is the age of consent? What services should be offered to survivors? What consequences are administered to perpetrators? What is considered normal sexual behavior? Abnormal? Abusive? More specific questions, such as: "How much older must the older of two sexually inappropriate children/teenagers be for a discrete sexual act to be called abuse?" The answers to these questions and ones even more basic, including how we define the terms *perpetrator* and *victim*, are socially constructed and therefore changeable as societal norms ebb and flow (Barnett, Manly, & Cicchetti, 1993; Bradley & Lindsay, 1987).

DEFINITION

Where do we begin, as a culture, to determine when a child is being or has been sexually abused? The federal legislation that most closely addresses issues related to child sexual abuse is the Child Abuse Prevention and Treatment Act (CAPTA), originally enacted in 1974. The Keeping Children and Families Safe Act of 2003 amended and reauthorized this act. This document defines sexual abuse as:

> the employment, use, persuasion, inducement, enticement, or coercion of any child to engage in, or assist any other person to engage in, any sexually explicit conduct or simulation of such conduct for the purpose of producing a visual depiction of such conduct; or the rape, and in cases of caretaker or inter-familial relationships, statutory rape, molestation, prostitution, or other form of sexual exploitation of children, or incest with children
> —*United States Code: Title 42-chapter 67. Report concerning voluntary reporting system/LII/Legal Information Institute*

Although every state has laws against child sexual abuse, specific definitions vary from state to state and sexual abuse is not always explicitly addressed as separate from physical abuse. For the purposes of this text, sexual abuse will be defined as any sexual activity involving a child in which the child is unable or unwilling to give consent (Berliner, 2011; Berliner & Elliott, 2002; Finkelhor, 1979). The age of consent varies in the literature and although many states put the age of consent at 18 years of age, some states define it as much younger. In Tennessee, for example, the kinds of criminal charges brought in cases of sexual abuse are determined by the age of the minor, with children under 13 most easily meeting the legal definition of child sexual abuse (Child Gateway document).

Sexual abuse extends to both contact and noncontact activities that result in the sexual gratification of an adult or a significantly older or more mature child/adolescent. Activities that fall under the umbrella of child sexual abuse include touching or fondling of genitals, oral acts involving genitalia, penetration, sexual exploitation of the child for material gain (prostitution, child pornography), voyeurism, exhibitionism, and exposure to sexually explicit talk or materials. Any act that involves coercion, force, or the threat of force can be categorized as child sexual abuse. When one child is older or developmentally more mature than the other child participating in sexual activity, the first child may coerce the younger simply by nature of his positional authority. When one child is physically bigger, even if the age discrepancy is minimal, the smaller child may feel threatened and acquiesce to inappropriate sexual activity. If an older child controls resources to which a younger child wants access, an unspoken form of coercion may be at work. Even hierarchical differences in social standing within a peer group may arguably add to the coercive nature of a sexual encounter. The purpose of highlighting these various forms of coercion among youth is not to characterize the instigator as an "offender" or "perpetrator" by adult standards, but rather to call attention to the fact that the younger child's experience may result in a posttraumatic stress reaction or have components of the sequelae often reported by other CSA victims. In addition to these criteria, an argument can be made that any sexual behavior involving a child that results in the premature activation of that child's sexual development qualifies as abuse. When the sexual behavior of an adult or older child/teen activates a developmentally inappropriate stimulation of the sexual self of a child, the behavior can be termed *abusive*.

Taking the political and/or clinical definitions of sexual abuse and applying them to actual cases becomes significantly messier. Following are some clinical examples of cases where CSA was a potential issue.

A school teacher goes to her principal very concerned because one of her 1st grade students has been exposing himself to classmates. School is concerned as the child has recently been reunified with his biological mother who has a reported history of substance abuse and prostitution. School is unclear who has access to the child while in mom's care.

A mother contacts a therapist known for her expertise in child sexual abuse and says that her almost-3-year-old was recently left in the care of mother's adult nephew. Mother states that since this time, her daughter has been excessively clingy, fearful, and is not sleeping well. Mother reports that her child has stated, "Brandon hurt bootie," but mother has been unable to elicit further information.

A mother calls the Department of Children's Services in a frenzied state and tells the person on the phone that her son has been sexually abused. The mother states that upon her 9-year-old son's return from camp he has been masturbating frequently and looking at pornographic material on the Internet. She has asked that her son not "play with himself" in public but he continues to masturbate in the common areas of the home.

A therapist receives a call from an anxious and angry father. The father tells the therapist that he has recently remarried and his wife has a 17-year-old son that lives with the family every other weekend. His 15-year-old daughter has started dressing "like a slut" and has started hanging out with a group of teenagers that have a reputation for being sexually active. The father is concerned that something might have happened between his daughter and stepson while they were alone together in the house.

These above case excerpts highlight a range of presentations of sexual concerns. Helping professionals can often feel overwhelmed by both the nebulous nature of clients' sexual concerns and the intense anxiety that is often being experienced by one or more of the child's caregivers at the time that help is sought. The members of each professional discipline involved with CSA cases feel pressure to find definitive answers for families. Furthermore, both caregivers and helping professionals can feel overwhelmed by the number of people that can be involved in cases of child sexual abuse. See Chapter 4 for an in-depth exploration of the various roles of helping professionals involved with cases of child sexual abuse.

DISCLOSURE

Disclosure of CSA is becoming more commonly and appropriately thought of as a process versus an event (Alaggia, 2004; Goodyear-Brown, 2010; Summit, 1983). Much like other aspects of CSA, the disclosure process is not often neat, concise, and orderly. On the contrary, it is more likely to be messy, convoluted, and peppered with ambiguity. Estimated rates of disclosure are dependent on what constitutes a "disclosure" (telling anyone versus telling a professional involved in the investigation of the allegation). Another important consideration is the discrepancy between the incidents of CSA actually reported to authorities and the CSA that was either never disclosed or disclosed to someone but not reported to authorities at any point (Finkelhor, 1979; Finkelhor, Hotaling, Lewis, & Smith, 1990). Less than 10% of child sexual abuse is reported to authorities (Lyon & Ahern, 2011). More than one-third of suspected CSA victims fail to disclose their abuse (Lamb, Hershkowitz, Orbach, & Esplin, 2008) and some victims may choose to remain silent well into adulthood (Alaggia, 2004; Alaggia & Kirshenbaum, 2005; Finkelhor et al., 1990; Finkelhor, 1979; Summit, 1983). Delays and nondisclosure seem to be related to the level of relationship that the child has with the perpetrator, where closer relationships lead to a greater likelihood of nondisclosure (Hershkowitz, Horowitz, & Lamb, 2005; Hershkowitz, 2006; Pipe et al., 2007).

The Child Sexual Abuse Accommodation Syndrome (CSAAS), which delineates five categories: secrecy; helplessness; entrapment and accommodation; delayed; conflicted and unconvincing disclosure; and retraction, helps to illustrate the multiplicity of paths that children may take towards disclosure (Summit, 1983). Although this conceptualization of accommodation has come under recent criticism (Bradley & Wood, 1996; London, Bruck, Ceci, & Shuman, 2005), an analysis of the research does support the phenomenon of nondisclosure and recantation.

Disclosure may be purposeful, accidental, elicited or prompted, behavioral, triggered, and purposely withheld (Alaggia, 2004). There are multiple factors that influence a victim's decision to disclose abuse and navigate the resulting fallout. Family dynamics and roles, intrafamilial communication patterns and social isolation (Alaggia & Kirshenbaum, 2005), gender (Alaggia, 2004; Finkelhor et al., 1990; Summit, 1983), developmental level (Goodman-Brown et al., 2003; Staller & Nelson-Gardell, 2005), relationship to the perpetrator (Goodman-Brown et al., 2003; Hershkowitz, Lanes, & Lamb, 2007); expected or actual support (or lack thereof) by the nonoffending caregiver (Alaggia, 2004; Hershkowitz et al., 2007; Staller & Nelson-Gardell, 2005), perceived responsibility for the abuse (Goodman-Brown et al., 2003; Staller & Nelson-Gardell, 2005) and awareness of potential negative consequences (Goodman-Brown et al., 2003; Staller & Nelson-Gardell, 2005; Summit, 1983) have all been studied as elements contributing to likelihood and timing of disclosure.

A known perpetrator, multiple incidents and severity of CSA, increased age, gender of the victim, anticipated or actual nonsupportive caregiver, potential negative consequences and additional dysfunction within the home decrease the probability of any type of disclosure, timely or not (Alaggia, 2004; Finkelhor et al., 1990; Goodman-Brown et al., 2003; Hershkowitz et al., 2007; Staller & Nelson-Gardell, 2005; Summit, 1983). An older child is more likely to have the capacity to imagine all the possible outcome scenarios that may result from the decision to disclose and therefore may be more cautious than a younger child about telling (Staller & Nelson-Gardell, 2005). Males are considered less likely to disclose CSA than females (Finkelhor, 1979; Finkelhor et al., 1990), although more research is warranted regarding the disclosure dynamics of male victims.

Recantation may be a defense attorney's realized dream and potentially a prosecutor's nightmare, but in actuality it is an anticipated part of the disclosure process. A child's recant can be the result of multiple factors and its presence is documented in various studies when there is corroboration, including physical evidence, to substantiate the initial allegation of CSA (Shapiro Gonzalez, Waterman, Kelly, McCord, & Oliveri, 1993; Hershkowitz, Lanes, & Lamb, 2007; Malloy, Lyon, & Quas, 2007). Children may be more likely to recant if they are 9 years old and older, if the alleged perpetrator is known, if more than one incident has occurred, and if the child has perceived the parent's response as anxious (Hershkowitz et al., 2007).

Finally, children risk a tremendous amount when they make a disclosure. The way in which the disclosure is met by those closest to the child can make a significant impact on the long-term adverse effects of abuse. Negative reactions appear to lead to more adverse long-term effects (Bernard-Bonnin, Hebert, Daignault, & Allard-Dansereau, 2008; Leifer, Shapiro, & Kassmen, 1993; Mannarino & Cohen, 1997), whereas support from nonoffending caregivers leads to better long-term mental health outcomes.

BEHAVIORAL INDICATORS THAT A CHILD MAY HAVE EXPERIENCED SEXUAL ABUSE

As the phenomenon of CSA has gained increasing public attention in recent years, parents, teachers, and other adults who care for children want to know what to look for; what indicators raise the red flag for potential sexual abuse. Behavior is a child's primary form of communication. When children do not have the words or ability to verbally communicate trauma they begin to "act out," have psychosomatic symptoms, or show their trauma through behavioral indicators. Many of the behaviors that may indicate CSA are also exhibited in nontrauma situations, so all must be noted with caution. Professionals are trained to look for sudden emotional or behavioral changes (Hibbard & Hartman, 1992; Wells, McCann, Adams, Voris, & Dahl, 1997), clinginess or fear of being alone (Bernet, 1997; Herbert, 1987; Hibbard & Hartman, 1992; O'Keefe, 2004; Wells et al., 1997), sleep disturbances including nightmares (Bernet, 1997; Hibbard & Hartman, 1992; McClain et al., 2000; O'Keefe, 2004; Wells et al., 1997), school disturbances including learning difficulties, poor concentration and declining grades (Hibbard & Hartman, 1992; McClain et al., 2000; O'Keefe, 2004), enuresis and encopresis (Bernet, 1997; McClain et al., 2000; O'Keefe, 2004), aggression (McClain et al., 2000; O'Keefe, 2004), social withdrawal (Herbert, 1987; Wells et al., 1997), depression and suicidal ideations (Bernet, 1997; Hibbard & Hartman, 1992; McClain et al., 2000; O'Keefe, 2004; Wells et al., 1997), eating disturbances (Bernet, 1997; McClain et al., 2000; O'Keefe, 2004), anxiety (Bernet, 1997; Herbert, 1987; Hibbard & Hartman, 1992; Wells et al., 1997) and sexual behaviors (Bernet, 1997; Herbert, 1987; McClain et al., 2000; O'Keefe, 2004; Wells et al., 1997). Any of these behaviors, taken on their own, might have any number of causes. The presence of several indicators in the absence of other explanations is cause for further assessment.

PREVALENCE AND INCIDENCE

Definitions of child maltreatment, including definitions of child sexual abuse, are socially constructed and are therefore prey to the vagaries of the current sociocultural climate. This lack of definitional consensus combined with the complexities of polyvictimization makes it difficult to gather even basic statistics such as prevalence and incidence (Cicchetti & Toth, 1995; Wynkoop, Capps, & Priest, 1995). Incidence refers to the number of new occurrences of an event within a certain time frame. Because sexual abuse is rarely reported immediately, incidence is difficult to measure (Finklehor, Hotaling, Lewis, & Smith, 1990). The Juvenile Victimization Survey (Finkelhor, Ormrod, Turner, & Hamby, 2005) was used to assess the interrelatedness of various types of victimization within a national survey. Sexual victimization was experienced by one out of every 12 survey participants (ages 2 to 17) in the study year. Prevalence measures the overall number of cases within a specific time frame. Many dynamics converge to make prevalence rates difficult to pin down. The diversity of ways in which sexual abuse is defined for research purposes contributes to this difficulty in standardization. The areas of variability include the age used to define childhood, the age difference between the perpetrator and the victim, and the specific type of sexual abuse being measured (Pereda, Guilera, Forns, & Gomez-Benito, 2009).

Data-collection tools are inadequate and have been repeatedly criticized. In 1985, Whitcomb highlighted the fact that the FBI Uniform Crime Report did not categorize sexual assault by victim age, making it impossible to discern the number of reported cases that constitute child sexual abuse. In 1995, Wynkoop, Capps, and Priest commented on the continued elusiveness of epidemiological information, highlighting the fact that, historically, most reporting instruments did not separate sexual abuse from other forms of abuse. Fifteen years later the reports of incidence and prevalence continue to vary widely across the literature. Even the National Criminal Victimization Survey (NCVS), the largest national survey of annual incidence of crime may underestimate actual incidence rates (Kilpatrick, 2004; Kilpatrick, McCauley, & Mattern, 2009). The worldwide estimate of prevalence derived from three decades of research ranges from 11% to 32% for females and 4% to 14% for males (Sapp & Vandeven, 2005). In 2008 there were 69,184 reported victims of CSA in the United States alone (U.S. Department of Health and Human Services, 2010). However, the number of reports made to child abuse authorities has decreased significantly, with some states showing as much as a 39% decline in substantiated reports between the years of 1992 and 1999 (Jones, Finkelhor, & Kopiec, 2001).

MULTIPLE FORMS OF VICTIMIZATION

The need for a nuanced approach to CSA stems in part from our growing understanding of the complex nature of child maltreatment. Many children with a history of sexual abuse may also have been exposed to other forms of maltreatment and/or environmental chaos. The polyvictimization of these children, which may include physical abuse, intrafamilial violence, exposure to community violence, complicate both the identification and the treatment dynamics of work with this population (Finkelhor, Ormrod, Turner, & Hamby, 2005).

The Adverse Childhood Experiences Study (Felitti et al., 1998) looked at a person's trauma exposure and household dysfunction in childhood and the relationship of these dynamics to adult health-risk behavior and disease using data from 9,508 respondents. As the number of ACE exposures increased so did lifelong health risks. Dong, Anda, Dube, Giles, and Felitti (2003) conducted a study involving 18,175 responding adult subjects evaluating the relationship between child sexual abuse and the other nine Adverse Childhood Experiences (ACEs). Twenty-one percent of the respondents reported a history of CSA and the findings included a strong correlation between the CSA of this group and the other nine ACEs. Additionally, the respondents who reported multiple CSA experiences, more severe CSA, or multiple and intrafamilial perpetrators were also more likely to have reported multiple ACEs. CSA was most often concurrent with other negative childhood experiences such as physical abuse, physical violence against the mother, mental illness in household, neglect, household substance abuse, and so on, and not commonly identified as the only ACE. Children who are sexually victimized once are likely to be sexually victimized again, with as many as 75% of children in clinical samples experiencing multiple episodes of sexual victimization (Conte & Schuerman, 1987; Elliot & Briere, 1994; Ruggiero, McLeer, & Dixon, 2000).

Briere and Elliott (2003) surveyed a geographically diverse sample of the general population and found a 21% overlap in the number of people who had experienced both physical and sexual abuse, while other researchers have concluded that physical abuse was a noteworthy predictor of child sexual abuse across childhood (Fleming, Mullen, & Bammer, 1997). The more we understand about the overlap between various forms of maltreatment, the argument that we may indeed "underestimate the burden of victimization that young people experience" (Finkelhor, Ormrod, Turner, & Hamby, 2005, p. 5) is strengthened.

RISK FACTORS

Childhood sexual abuse is a pervasive problem, affecting people across lines of gender, race, culture, religion, geographic area, and socioeconomic class. The third national incidence study of child abuse and neglect (Sedlak & Broadhurst, 1996) states that from age 3, children are consistently vulnerable to CSA. However, females are at higher risk for CSA than males (Berliner, 2011; Gault-Sherman, Silver, & Sigfusdottir, 2009). Gault-Sherman and colleagues (2009) found that females were approximately three times more likely to fall victim to CSA than males and more likely to develop depressed mood and general anxiety; 86.5% of the females with CSA identified an intrafamilial perpetrator, which was also the case for 95.9% of the males with CSA.

According to surveys from the general population, 6% to 16% of offenders were parental figures and up to one third of the cases of CSA were perpetrated by a relative. A comparatively small number of offenders (5% to 15%) were strangers (Berliner & Elliott, 2002). The remaining group is comprised of people known to the child (Berliner, 2011).

Low socioeconomic status, while an important risk factor in other forms of abuse, has not been proven to be a significant risk factor for sexual abuse (Berliner & Elliott, 2002; Finkelhor, 1993; Putnam, 2003). Race and ethnicity also appear to have little impact on a child's risk for sexual abuse, although the resulting symptom constellation may manifest differently based on these variables (Mennen, 1995; Shaw, Lewis, Loeb, Rosado, & Rodriguez, 2001).

Substance abuse is identified as another risk factor, as it can cause impairment of thought, ability, judgment, and capability to protect (Goldman, Salus, Wolcott, Kennedy, & Office on Child Abuse and Neglect [HHS], 2003). A parent's substance abuse problem can be seen as increasing the risk for various forms of maltreatment, including sexual abuse. One study found intrafamilial sexual abuse occurred more frequently when an alcoholic father was present and extrafamilial sexual abuse occurred more frequently when an alcoholic mother was present or the mother was deceased (Fleming, Mullen, & Bammer, 1997).

FAMILY STRUCTURE

The Fourth National Incidence Study of Child Abuse and Neglect, Report to Congress (NIS-4; Sedlak et al., 2010) examined family structure as a potential risk factor for child maltreatment using data collected in 2005 and 2006. Across maltreatment groups, children living with married biological parents had the lowest maltreatment rate collectively. Children who lived with a single parent with a live-in partner had more than eight times the maltreatment rate of those living with married biological parents and were 10 times more likely to be abused. Goldman, Salus, Wolcott, Kennedy, and the Office on Child Abuse and Neglect (HHS; 2003) found that only 31% of CSA survivors lived with both biological parents, whereas 27% lived with a stepfather or mother's boyfriend.

The presence of a stepfather has long been conceptualized as a risk factor as has living without the mother, even for a short time (Friedrich, 1990). Finkelhor (1979) found that, in addition to the risk factors mentioned earlier, several risk factors were specific to maternal dynamics including: maternal distance, mom's educational achievement (lacking a high school diploma), and a punitive stance on sexuality from mom. Lack of physical paternal affection, extremely low annual household income and a lack of friendships (two or fewer friendships in childhood) were also risk factors. These risk factors were characterized as cumulative. A child's vulnerability to CSA increased by between 10% and 20% with each additional dynamic (Finkelhor, 1979).

OFFENDER DYNAMICS

Another important data set includes perpetrators of CSA and their input regarding factors that potentially put children at risk. Elliott, Browne, and Kilcoyne (1995) interviewed 91 child sex offenders regarding their selection of victims using a semi-structured questionnaire. Characteristics that the interviewed offenders identified as risk factors for children included a perception that a child had low self-esteem or a lack of self-confidence, had family problems, was overly trusting of others, had little supervision, or was isolated. The offender's subjective perception of the child as pretty and/or provocatively dressed, young and small also influenced the choice of victim. Of note, the offenders showed a 90% consistency rate regarding their answers to interview questions.

INTERGENERATIONAL TRANSMISSION OF ABUSE

Multigenerational cycles of abuse may increase risk of maltreatment, as how one was parented will likely play a significant role in his or her own future parenting style (Goldman, Salus, Wolcott, Kennedy, & the Office on Child Abuse and Neglect [HHS], 2003). This can, however, be observed at both extremes, as there are adult survivors of child maltreatment that continue this cycle with their own children and certainly those adult survivors who break this cycle. Although Oates, Tebbutt, Swanston, Lynch, and O'Toole (1998) found that children who experienced sexual abuse did not vary on measures of depression, self-esteem, and behavior regardless of whether their mothers were survivors of sexual abuse, existing studies of intergenerational issues do not separate one form of abuse from another, so there is little data specific to intergenerational patterns in CSA transmission (Putnam, 2003).

THE IMPACT OF MASS MEDIA

If the definition of child sexual abuse holds an adult culpable for exposing a child to sexually explicit material, then there is an argument to be made for the culpability of the mass media in putting all children further at risk for CSA. The objectification of the physical body, the pervasiveness of sexually thematic material, and the frequent combination of sex and aggression in the media set the stage for unhealthy perceptions of sexuality.

According to the Nielsen's A2/M2 Three Screen Report for the second quarter of 2009, children and teenagers are watching an average of 101 hours of television per month. The sexualized messages that are prevalent in mainstream media have continued to increase in the past few years. According to Ward (1995) 11.5% of the messages coded from television involved sexually objectifying comments, the majority of which were focused at women. The sexual speech on prime-time comedies coded by Lampman and colleagues (2002) found that 23% of behavior involved leering, ogling, staring, and catcalling of female characters, and 16.5% of the sexualized speech referred to nudity or body parts.

This sexual socialization (Ward, 2003), including the focus on the attractiveness of one's physical body, has never been more highlighted than in the current group of television programs given over to beauty pageants for children. For these glitzy pageants, children as young as 2 are coached on how to capitalize on their physical attractiveness. The molding process may include fake eyelashes, fake tans, fake hair, and even fake teeth. The intention is to make the children look older than they are. Children's beauty is judged in part on how they look in a swimsuit. Children are directed to both move suggestively and dress revealingly. One young child presented on stage wearing a replica of Madonna's gold-cone corset; another dressed as Michael Jackson performed his famous crotch grab. In one memorable episode, a distressed father of a 7-year-old cringes as he compares his daughter's pageant costume to a "dominatrix outfit."

What is more startling still is the response from the audience when these children walk across stage in these costumes and during these performances. Positive audience and judge responses could have a direct effect on self-worth. Primarily reinforcing a child's physical attributes may contribute to susceptibility to further objectification throughout his or her development. A 2007 APA study looking at the sexualization of girls identified a link between the early emphasis on physical appearance with eating disorders, low self-esteem, and depression.

One of the most troubling double standards encouraged by the media is the characterization of sexual activity between boys with adult women and girls with adult males. Boys are more likely to be victimized by women than their female peers, with 20% of boys and 5% of girls being motested by women perpetrators (Finkelhor & Russell, 1984) and yet many current storylines involve underage males having satisfying, even coveted, sexual encounters with adult women.

ASYMPTOMATIC CHILDREN: JUST HOW BAD IS IT?

A child who has been sexually abused is damaged goods, or so goes the assumption of many segments of our modern culture. An analysis of the research offers us a much more hopeful view, one that counters the belief that sexually abused children are tainted for life. Kendall-Tackett, Williams, and Finkelhor (1993) reviewed 45 studies and concluded that approximately one-third of the children with CSA histories showed no symptoms. Finkelhor and Berliner (1995) evaluated children who had been sexually abused and found that up to 40% of those children were asymptomatic.

Rind, Tromovitch, and Bauserman (1998) conducted a meta-analysis of almost 60 studies based on college samples and looked at the history of sexual abuse and family environment. They found that the students with a history of CSA were minimally less well-adjusted than their peers and that most of these adjustment difficulties were due to family environment. This finding is supported by our current understanding that sexual abuse survivors often come from homes that are highly chaotic or manifest dysfunction on a range of other levels.

What could account for this level of psychological resiliency? According to Kinnally and colleagues (2009), positive social support is associated with a lower risk for adverse mental health issues. A combination of familial support, a positive social support network, and inherent resiliencies can be protective factors for children who have experienced CSA and can ameliorate the possible emotional effects of childhood sexual abuse.

POSTTRAUMATIC STRESS DISORDER

The most common diagnosis given to children who have documented histories of sexual abuse is posttraumatic stress disorder (PTSD) (Berliner & Elliott, 2002; Kendall-Tackett, Williams, & Finkelhor, 1993; McLeer et al., 1998; Putnam, 2003; Ruggiero, McLeer, & Dixon, 2000). PTSD symptom clusters include avoidance and/or numbing behaviors, hyperarousal symptoms, and reexperiencing parts of the trauma. Subsets of these symptom constellations are reported by many sexually abused children (McLeer, Deblinger, Henry, & Orvaschel, 1992; McLeer et al., 1998; Wolfe,

Gentile, & Wolfe, 1989). More than 30% of children with CSA histories meet the diagnostic criteria for PTSD (Berliner & Elliott, 2002).

The proposed diagnosis of developmental trauma disorder (van der Kolk, 2005) may be a more appropriate conceptualization for post-traumatic, symptomatology in children as it more thoroughly captures the developmentally determined sequelae of symptoms in children who have experienced extensive trauma. When children experience chronic trauma, it impairs their neurobiological development and capacity to cohesively integrate sensory, emotional, and cognitive information. Developmental Trauma disorder takes into account children's "triggered dysregulation in response to traumatic reminders, stimulus generalization, and the anticipatory organization of behavior to prevent the recurrence of the trauma effects" (van der Kolk, 2005, p. 406).

SEXUAL BEHAVIOR PROBLEMS

Sexual behavior problems (SBP) appear to be a specific effect of CSA. Compared to physically abused children, clinical populations, and normative samples, children with a history of CSA more frequently engage in inappropriate or aggressive sexual behaviors (Friedrich, Beilke, & Urquiza, 1987; Friedrich et al., 1991; Gale, Thompson, Moran, & Sack, 1988; Goldston, Turnquist, & Knutson, 1989; Kolko, Moser, & Weldy, 1988). Chapter 18 provides additional information on this specific set of sequalae and current treatment approaches for SBP.

EMOTIONAL EFFECTS

A variety of negative emotional effects have been reported by children who have experienced sexual abuse. The myriad presentations of sexually abused children make it difficult to pinpoint a "syndrome" or "cluster" of emotional symptoms specific to CSA. The emotional effects that appear to occur most frequently include depression and anxiety (Briere & Elliott, 2003; Caffo, Forresi, & Lievers, 2005; Cohen, Mannarino, & Deblinger, 2006; Kolko, Moser, & Weldy, 1988; Lev-Wiesel, 2008; Maniglio, 2009; Putnam, 2003; Sapp & Vandeven 2005; van der Kolk, 2005). Survivors of sexual abuse are five times more likely to be diagnosed with at least one anxiety disorder than their peers (Berliner & Elliot, 2002). The severity of psychological and behavioral symptoms increases with the severity of the victimization (Boney-McCoy & Finkelhor, 1996; Gidycz & Koss, 1989).

Numerous studies have shown depression and dysthymia to have a strong association with CSA (Hornor, 2010; Lanktree, Briere, & Zaidi, 1991; Putnam, 2003; Wozencraft, Wagner, & Pellegrin, 1991). Women with a history of CSA are three to five times more likely to develop depression than the general population (Putnam, 2003). Fergusson, Lynskey, and Horwood (1996a, 1996b) report that children with noncontact CSA or CSA not involving intercourse are 4.6 times more likely to develop major depression and 8.1 times more likely if the abuse involved intercourse. Depressive disorders often occur in conjunction with PTSD (Cohen et al., 2006) and given the aforementioned rates of PTSD in this population, depression is often comorbidly diagnosed. Suicidal ideation and suicide attempts are also associated with CSA (Brodsky et al., 2008).

Depression manifests in children as anhedonia, pathological guilt, social withdrawal, complaints of fatigue, impairment in school functioning, and low self-esteem. Sexually abused youth have produced lower scores relating to low self-esteem than their physically abused or nonabused peers (Cavaiola & Schiff, 1989) with low self-esteem being related to the severity of abuse (Stern, Lynch, Oates, O'Toole, & Cooney, 1995). Of particular note is the finding that children whose abuse was incestuous in nature struggled more with self-acceptance than the other groups (Cavaiola & Schiff, 1989).

SUBSTANCE ABUSE

Much has been documented on the possible link between experienced trauma and substance abuse or addiction. CSA in girls has been linked with an increased risk of moderate to high substance abuse (Shin, Hong, & Hazen, 2010). No such association was shown for boys. Poly-substance abuse was reported at a rate of around five times that of females without a CSA history. Males who have experienced both physical and sexual abuse have a significantly increased likelihood of illicit drug use when compared to females with the same maltreatment history (Moran, Vuchinich, & Hall, 2004). A history of sexual assault puts adolescents at increased risk for substance abuse and an earlier onset of substance use for those adolescents with a victimization history as compared to their nonvictimized peers (Duncan et al., 2008; Kilpatrick et al., 2000). A PTSD diagnosis also was shown to increase substance use, specifically marijuana and hard drugs. CSA is associated with increased rates of lifetime alcohol use and lifetime diagnosis of dependency (Moran, Vuchinich, & Hall, 2004; Sartor et al., 2007).

EATING DISORDERS

Wonderlich and colleagues (2000) found that children with a CSA history were more likely than the nonabused children to display food restriction when emotionally disturbed, have weight dissatisfaction, pursuit of what they idealized as a thin body, and increased purging behavior.

Van Gerko, Hughes, Hamill, and Waller (2005) examined associations between a CSA history and the eating attitudes and behaviors of 299 women who met the *Diagnostic and Statistical Manual of Mental Disorders*, fourth edition, text revised (*DSM-IV-TR*; American Psychological Association, 2000) criteria for an eating disorder. Those participants with a history of CSA had significantly higher levels of purging behavior than their nonabused peers. Also reported were higher levels of shape concerns. These studies support the possibility that CSA may contribute to eating pathology, especially purging behaviors and body image disturbance, when combined with various other social, genetic, familial, and developmental factors thought to play a part in the development of eating disorders (Lock, 2009).

Ackard, Neumark-Sztainer, Hannan, French, and Story (2001) found that girls who experienced both physical and sexual abuse were four times more likely to participate in bingeing and purging than the nonabused girls, while boys were more than eight times as likely to engage in these behaviors when compared with the nonabused boys. This association was not found for girls with CSA alone. This finding gives weight to the argument that polyvictimization leads to more harmful effects. Corstorphine, Waller, Lawson, and Ganis (2007) examined the relationship between trauma and multi-impulsivity. These researchers found that of the participants who met criteria for various eating disorders, CSA was the only form of childhood trauma reliably and positively associated with multi-impulsivity.

Body dissatisfaction is associated with depression, decreased self-esteem, and eating disorders (Brannan & Petrie, 2008; Grossbard, Lee, Neighbors, & Larimer, 2009). Eating disorders are associated with risk factors of depression and low self-esteem (Mayer, Muris, Meesters, & Zimmerman van Beuningen, 2009). CSA is also associated with depression and decreased self-esteem, so the connection between body dysmorphia, CSA and eating disorders warrants further study.

When assessing the physical, emotional, and developmental damage CSA can wreak, the damage to children developing perceptions of their physical bodies should not be underestimated. Feelings of shame and helplessness paired with an actual crime against the body may predispose children to negative evaluations of their physical bodies, including Body Dysmorphic Disorder (American Psychiatric Association, 2000). The National Eating Disorders Association (2004) notes that for those with eating disorders, food and its control can be used in attempt to regulate overwhelming feelings or emotions.

Another Way of Conceptualizing the Effects of CSA

Finkelhor and Browne (1985) conceptualized the emotional and cognitive ramifications of CSA by examining sexual abuse as a variety of different effects as opposed to a disorder or syndrome. They developed four traumagenic dynamics, which include traumatic sexualization, betrayal, stigmatization, and powerlessness/disempowerment. Traumatic sexualization is the process by which a child's sexuality is inappropriately or dysfunctionally shaped by the sexual abuse. Betrayal occurs with the realization that a person the child is dependent on has caused them harm. Stigmatization manifests in the negative cognitions that children believe about themselves and the world around them. It can become incorporated in the child's sense of self and beliefs about his or her self-worth. Powerlessness/disempowerment is created when the child's will, desire, and sense of efficacy are eroded throughout the abuse experience. Finkelhor and Browne (1985) argue that these four dynamics account for the main effects of trauma in child sexual abuse.

Long-Term Effects of Childhood Sexual Abuse on Adult Survivors

One of the prevailing methodological issues facing CSA researchers is whether the effects of CSA are causal or correlated with several confounding environmental factors. Several studies reviewed the methodological problems associated with the types of research conducted and discussed the lack of male participants in a majority of studies. Multiple studies utilized clinical samples of participants and few studies utilized a random sampling of the population (Briere & Elliott, 2003; Dilillo, 2001; Fergusson, Boden, & Horwood, 2008; Mullen, Martin, Anderson, Romans, & Herbison, 1996; Tyler, 2002; Vogeltanz-Holm, 2004).

Another difficulty with the existing evidence base is the lack of control for outside factors such as social support, family environment, and socioeconomic status. A few multivariate studies have been conducted in recent years to control for outside effects and to show a causal relationship between the long-term effects and CSA (Boney-McCoy & Finkelhor, 1996; Dinwiddie et al., 2000; Fergusson et al., 1996; Mullen et al., 1993). As the research mounts, however, there is growing consensus about the long-term effects of CSA.

Whether the intensity of the symptoms is mild, moderate, or severe, the effects of CSA in adulthood can be understood as an extension of the short-terms effects found in children (Berliner & Elliott, 2002). It appears that a causal relationship exists between CSA and psychiatric disorders in adulthood (Beitchman et al., 1992; Berliner & Elliott, 2002;

Boney-McCoy & Finklehor, 1996; Briere & Elliott, 2003; Dinwiddie et al., 2000; Dube et al., 2005; Fergusson et al., 1996; Fergusson et al., 2008; Greenfield, 2010; Hornor, 2010; Maniglio, 2009; Mullen et al., 1993; Mullen et al., 1996; Owens & Chard, 2003; Taylor & Harvey, 2010; Tyler, 2002; Vogeltanz-Holm, 2004). Briere and Elliott (2003) looked at the prevalence of sequelae of psychological symptoms within the general population who have experienced CSA. They found that CSA is a significant risk factor for all 10 of the categories listed on the Trauma Symptom Inventory. Those categories are: anxious arousal, depression, anger/irritability, intrusive experiences, defense avoidance, dissociation, sexual concerns, dysfunctional sexual behavior, impaired self-reference, and tension-reduction behavior.

Depression, anxiety, and posttraumatic stress disorder are the predominant long-term disorders found to be associated with the occurrence of CSA. Several of the other ramifications found to result from untreated CSA are the use/misuse of substances in adulthood (Berliner & Elliott, 2002; Dinwiddie et al., 2000; Dube et al., 2005; Fergusson et al., 1996; Fergusson, Boden, & Horwood, 2008; Maniglio, 2009; Mullen et al., 1996; Vogeltanz-Holm, 2004), suicidality (Beitchman et al., 1992; Briere & Elliott, 2003; Dinwiddie et al., 2000; Dube et al., 2005; Fergusson et al., 1996; Fergusson et al., 2008; Greenfield, 2010; Hornor, 2010; Mullen et al., 1996; Tyler, 2002), potentially abusive relationships (Dilillo, 2001; Hornor, 2010), and sexual issues (Beitchman et al., 1992; Berliner & Elliott, 2002; Dilillo, 2001; Mullen et al., 1996). All of the studies reported an increase in effects when the CSA involved intercourse and/or threats and force. There are only a handful of studies that address dissociation, personality disorders, and multiple personality disorder (now termed dissociative identity disorder) and the relationship between those symptoms and CSA (Beitchman et al., 1992; Briere & Elliott, 2003; Lev-Wiesel, 2008; Maniglio, 2009; Owens & Chard, 2003; Putnam, 2003). The research shows confounding results for the relationship between CSA and personality disorders. Few studies have looked at gender differences with regard to the effects of CSA, but those that have support the idea that both male and female survivors of CSA are equally susceptible to long term mental health effects (Baynard, Williams, & Seigel, 2004; Dube et al., 2005). Certainly future research in this area is warranted.

Mullen et al. (1996) found that the women reporting CSA had more significant mental health issues than the other types of abuse survivors. These women reported a history of eating disorders, depression, substance use, attempted suicide, sexual problems, poor self-esteem, and a decline in socioeconomic status. Greenfield (2010) researched the long-term physical health effects of CSA on adults. She conducted a review of the literature based on community samples and found CSA to be a determinant of poor physical adult health, although specific health issues were not targeted. For a more thorough treatment of this topic, read Kathleen Kendall-Tackett (Chapter 3) on the long-term health effects of CSA.

CONCLUSION

This chapter is meant to provide a synopsis of what we know and what we do not know. Child sexual abuse is a complex problem with far-reaching consequences for the individual and for society at large. Definitions, prevalence and incidence data, disclosure patterns, risk factors, the role of the mass media, the short-term psychological, behavioral and emotional effects on child survivors as well as a review of the research regarding mental health outcomes in adulthood were all presented with a view toward defining the scope of the problem of child sexual abuse. It is only then that each of us can examine how we might become a part of the solution.

REFERENCES

Ackard, D. M., Neumark-Sztainer, D., Hannan, P. J., French, S., & Story, M. (2001). Binge and purge behavior among adolescents: Associations with sexual and physical abuse in a nationally representative sample: The Commonwealth Fund survey. *Child Abuse & Neglect, 6,* 771–785.

Alaggia, R. (2004). Many ways of telling: Expanding conceptualizations of child sexual abuse disclosure. *Child Abuse & Neglect, 28,* 1213–1227.

Alaggia, R., & Kirshenbaum, S. (2005). Speaking the unspeakable: Exploring the impact of family dynamics on child sexual abuse disclosures. *Families in Society, 86,* 227–233.

American Psychiatric Association. (2000). *Diagnostic and statistical manual of mental disorders* (4th ed., Text rev.). Washington, DC: American Psychiatric Association.

American Psychological Association, Task Force on the Sexualization of Girls. (2007). *Report of the APA Task Force on the Sexualization of Girls.* Washington, DC: American Psychological Association. Retrieved from www.apa.org/pi/wpo/sexualization.html

Barnett, D., Manly, J. T., & Cicchetti, D. (1993). Defining child maltreatment: The interface between policy and research. In D. Cicchetti, & S. L. Toth (Eds.), *Child abuse, child development, and social policy. Advances in applied developmental psychology* (Vol. 8, pp. 7–74). Norwood, NJ: Ablex.

Baynard, V. L., Williams, L. M., & Seigel, J. A. (2004). Childhood sexual abuse: A gender perspective on context and consequences. *Child Maltreatment, 9,* 223–238.

Beitchman, J. H., Zucker, K. J., Hood, J. E., DaCosta, G. A., Akman, D., & Cassavia, E. (1992). A review of long term effects of child sexual abuse. *Child Abuse & Neglect, 16,* 101–118.

Berliner, L. (2011). Child sexual abuse: Definitions, prevalence and consequences. In J. E. B. Myers (Ed.), *The APSAC handbook on child maltreatment* (3rd ed.). Los Angeles, CA: Sage.

Berliner, L., & Elliott, D. (2002). Sexual abuse of children. In J. E. B. Myers, L. Berliner, J. Briere, C. T. Hendrix, C. Jenny, T. A. Reid (Eds.), *The APSAC handbook on child maltreatment* (2nd ed.). Los Angeles, CA: Sage.

Bernard-Bonnin, A.-C., Herbert, M., Daignault, I. V., & Allard-Dansereau, C. (2008). Disclosure of sexual abuse and personal and familial factors as predictors of post-traumatic stress disorder symptoms in school-aged girls. *Pediatrics & Child Health, 13,* 479–486.

Bernet, W. (1997). Practice parameters for the forensic evaluation of children and adolescents who may have been physically or sexually abused. *Journal of the American Academy Child Adolescent Psychiatry, 36*(3), 423–442.

Boney-McCoy, S., & Finkelhor, D. (1996). Is youth victimization related to trauma and depression after controlling for prior symptoms and family relationships? A longitudinal study. *Journal of Consulting & Clinical Psychology, 64,* 1406–1416.

Bradley, A. R., & Wood, J. M. (1996). How do children tell? The disclosure process in child sexual abuse. *Child Abuse & Neglect, 9,* 881–891.

Bradley, E. J., & Lindsay, R. C. (1987). Methodological and ethical issues in child abuse research. *Journal of Family Violence, 2,* 239–255.

Brannan, M. E., & Petrie, T. A. Moderators of the body dissatisfaction-eating disorder symptomatology relationship: Replication and extension. *Journal of Counseling Psychology, 55,* 263.

Briere, J., & Elliott, D. M. (2003). Prevalence and psychological sequelae of self-reported childhood physical and sexual abuse in a general population sample of men and women. *Child Abuse & Neglect, 27,* 1205–1222.

Brodsky, B. S., Mann, J. J., Stanley, B., Tin, A., Oquendo, M., Birmaher, B. . . . Brent, D. (2008). Familial transmission of suicidal behaviors: Factors mediating the relationship between childhood abuse and offspring suicide attempts. *Journal of Clinical Psychiatry, 69,* 584–596.

Caffo, E., Forresi, B., & Lievers, L. S. (2005). Impact, psychological sequelae and management of trauma affecting children and adolescents. *Current Opinion in Psychiatry, 18*(4), 422–428.

Cavaiola, A. A., & Schiff, M. (1989). Self esteem in abused, chemically dependent adolescents. *Child Abuse & Neglect, 13,* 327–334.

Cicchetti, D., & Toth, S. L. (1995). A developmental psychopathology perspective on child abuse and neglect. *Journal of the American Academy of Child & Adolescent Psychiatry, 35*(5), 541–565.

Cohen, J. A., Mannarino, A. P., & Deblinger, E. (2006). *Treating trauma and traumatic grief in children and adolescents.* New York, NY: Guilford Press.

Conte, J. R., & Schuerman, J. R. (1987). Factors associated with an increased impact of child sexual abuse. *Child Abuse & Neglect, 11,* 201–212.

Corstorphine, E., Waller, G., Lawson, R., & Ganis, C. (2007). Trauma and multi-impulsivity in the eating disorders. *Eating Behaviors, 8,* 23–30.

Dilillo, D. (2001). Interpersonal functioning among women reporting a history of childhood sexual abuse: Empirical findings and methodological issues. *Clinical Psychology Review*, 21(4): 553–576.

Dinwiddie, S., Heath, A. C., Dunne, M. P., Bucholz, K. K., Madden, P. A. F., Sultske, W. S., . . . Martin, N. G. (2000). Early sexual abuse and lifetime psychopathology: A co-twin control study. *Psychological Medicine, 30*, 41–52.

Dong, M., Anda, R. F., Dube, S. R., Giles, W. H., & Felitti, V. J. (2003). The relationship of exposure to childhood sexual abuse to other forms of abuse, neglect, and household dysfunction during childhood. *Child Abuse & Neglect, 27*, 625–639.

Dube, S. R., Anda, R. F., Whitfield, C. L., Brown, D. W., Felitti, V. J., Dong, M., & Giles, W. H. (2005). Long-term consequences of childhood sexual abuse by gender of victim. *American Journal of Preventative Medicine, 28*(5), 430–438.

Duncan, A. E., Sartor, C. E., Scherrer, J. F., Grant, J. D., Heath, A. C., Nelson, E. C., . . . Keenan Bocholz, K. (2008). The association between cannabis abuse and dependence and childhood physical and sexual abuse: Evidence from an offspring of twins design. *Addiction, 103*, 990–997.

Elliott, D., Browne, K., & Kilcoyne, J. (1995). Child sexual abuse prevention: What offenders tell us. *Child Abuse & Neglect, 19*, 579–594.

Felitti, V. J., Anda, R. F., Nordenberg, D., Williamson, D. F., Spitz, A. M., Edwards, V., . . . Marks, J. S. (1998). Relationship of childhood abuse and household dysfunction to many of the leading causes of death in adults: The Adverse Childhood Experiences (ACE) Study. *American Journal of Preventative Medicine, 14*, 245–258.

Fergusson, D., Lynskey, M., & Horwood, L. (1996a). Childhood sexual abuse and psychiatric disorder in young adulthood, II: Psychiatric outcome of childhood sexual abuse. *Journal of the American Academy of Child & Adolescent Psychiatry, 35*, 1365–1374.

Fergusson, D., Lynskey, M., & Horwood, L. (1996b). Childhood sexual abuse and psychiatric disorder in young adulthood, I: prevalence of sexual abuse and factors associated with sexual abuse. *Journal of the American Academy of Child & Adolescent Psychiatry, 35*, 1355–1364.

Fergusson, D. M., Boden, J. M., & Horwood, L. J. (2008). Exposure to childhood sexual and physical abuse and adjustment in early adulthood. *Child Abuse & Neglect, 32*, 607–619.

Finkelhor, D. (1979). *Sexually victimized children.* New York, NY: Free Press.

Finkelhor, D. (1993). Epidemiological Factors in the Clinical Identification of Child Sexual Abuse. *Child Abuse & Neglect, 17*, 67–70.

Finkelhor, D., & Berliner, L. (1995). Research on the treatment of sexually abused children. *Journal of the American Academy of Child and Adolescent Psychiatry, 34*, 1408–1423.

Finkelhor, D., & Browne, A. (1985). The traumatic impact of child sexual abuse: A conceptualization. *Journal of Orthopsychiatry, 55*(4), 530–541.

Finkelhor, D., & Russell, D. E. H. (1984). Women as perpetrators: Review of the evidence. In D. Finkelhor (Ed.), Child sexual abuse: New theory and research (pp. 171–185). New York, NY: Free Press.

Finkelhor D., Hotaling G., Lewis, I. A., & Smith, C. (1990). Sexual abuse in a national survey of adult men and women: Prevalence, characteristics, and risk factors. *Child Abuse & Neglect, 14,* 19–28.

Finkelhor, D., Ormrod, R., Turner, H., & Hamby, S. L. (2005). Measuring poly-victimization using the juvenile victimization questionnaire. *Child Abuse & Neglect, 29,* 1297–1312.

Finkelhor, D., Ormrod, R., Turner, H., & Hamby, S. L. (2005). The victimization of children and youth: A comprehensive, national survey. *Child Maltreatment: Journal of the American Professional Society on the Abuse of Children, 10*(1), 5–25.

Fleming, J., Mullen, P., & Bammer, G. (1997). A study of potential risk factors for sexual abuse in childhood. Child Abuse & Neglect, *21,* 49–58.

Friedrich, W. N. (1990). *Psychotherapy of sexually abused children and their families.* New York, NY: Norton.

Friedrich, W. N. (1993). Sexual victimization and sexual behavior in children: A review of recent literature. *Child Abuse & Neglect, 17*(1), 59–66.

Friedrich, W. N., Beilke, R. L., & Urquiza, A. J. (1987). Children from sexually abusive families: A behavioral comparison. *Journal of Interpersonal Violence, 2*(4), 391–402.

Gale, J., Thompson, R. J., Moran, M. A., & Sack, W. H. (1988). Sexual abuse in young children: Its clinical presentations and characteristic patterns. *Child Abuse & Neglect, 12*(2), 163–170.

Gault-Sherman, M., Silver, E., & Sigfusdottir, I. D. (2009). Gender and the associated impairments of childhood sexual abuse: A national study of Icelandic youth. *Social Science & Medicine, 69,* 1515–1522.

Gidycz, C. A., & Koss, M. P. (1989). The impact of adolescent sexual victimization: Standardized measures of anxiety, depression, and behavioral deviancy. *Violence and Victims, 4*(2), 139–149.

Gil, E. (2006). *Helping abused and traumatized children: integrating directive and non-directive approaches.* New York, NY: Guilford Press.

Goldman, J., Salus, M. K., Wolcott, D., Kennedy, K. Y., & the Office on Child Abuse and Neglect (HHS). (2003). *A coordinated response to child abuse and neglect: The foundation of practice.* Washington, DC. Retrieved from www.childwelfare.gov

Goodman-Brown, T. B., Edelstein, R. S., Goodman, G. S., Jones, D. P. H., & Gordon, D. S. (2003). Why children tell: A model of children's disclosure of sexual abuse. *Child Abuse & Neglect, 27,* 525–540.

Goodyear-Brown, P. (2010). *Play therapy with traumatized children: A prescriptive approach.* Hoboken, NJ: John Wiley & Sons.

Greenfield, E. A. (2010). Child abuse as a life-course determinant of adult health. *Maturitas, 66,* 51–55.

Grossbard, J. R., Lee, C. M., Neighbors, C., & Larimer, M. E. (2009). Body image concerns and contingent self-esteem in male and female college students. *Sex Roles, 3–4,* 198–208.

Haas, H. L., & Clopton, J. R. (2001). Psychology of an eating disorder. In J. J. Robert-McComb (Ed.), *Eating disorders in women and children: Prevention, stress management, and treatment* (pp. 39–48). Boca Raton, FL: CRC Press.

Herbert, C. (1987). Expert medical assessment in determining probability of alleged child sexual abuse. *Child Abuse & Neglect, 11*, 213–221.

Hershkowitz, I. (2006). Delayed disclosure of child abuse victims in Israel. *American Journal of Orthopsychiatry, 76*, 444–450.

Hershkowitz, I., Horowitz, D., & Lamb, M. E. (2005). Trends in children's disclosure of abuse in Israel: a national study. *Child Abuse & Neglect, 29*, 1203–1214.

Hershkowitz, I., Lanes, O., & Lamb, M. E. (2007). Exploring the disclosure of child sexual abuse with alleged victims and their parents. *Child Abuse & Neglect, 31*, 111–123.

Hibbard, R. A., & Hartman, G. L. (1992). Behavioral problems in alleged sexual abuse victims. *Child Abuse & Neglect, 16*, 755–762.

Hornor, G. (2010). Child sexual abuse: Consequences and implications. *Journal of Pediatric Health Care, 24*, 358–364.

Jones, L. M., Finkelhor, D., & Kopiec, K. (2001). Why is sexual abuse declining? A survey of state protection administrators. *Child Abuse & Neglect, 25*, 1139–1158.

Kendall-Tackett, K., Williams, L., & Finkelhor, D. (1993). Impact of sexual abuse on children: A review and synthesis of recent empirical studies. *Psychological Bulletin, 113*, 164–180.

Kilpatrick, D. G. (2004). What is violence against women: Defining and measuring the problem. *Journal of Interpersonal Violence, 19*, 1209–1234.

Kilpatrick, D. G., McCauley, J., & Mattern, G. (2009, September). Undertanding national rape statistics. VAWnet Applied Research Forum. Available at www.vawnet.org

Kinnally, E. L., Huang, Y., Haverly, R., Burke, A. K., Galfalvy, H., Brent, D. P., . . . & Mann, J. J. (2009). Parental care moderates the influence of MAOA-uVNTR genotype and childhood stressors on trait impulsivity and aggression in adult women. *Psychiatric Genetics, 19*, 126–133.

Kilpatrick, D. G., Acierno, R., Saunders, B., Resnick, H. S., & Best, C. L. (2000). Risk factors for adolescent substance abuse and dependence: Data from a national sample. *Journal of Consulting & Clinical Psychology, 68*, 19–30.

Kolko, D. J., Moser, J., & Weldy, S. R. (1988). Behavioral/emotional indicators of sexual abuse in psychiatric inpatients: A controlled comparison with physical abuse. *Child Abuse & Neglect, 12*, 529–541.

Kolodny, N. J. (2004). *The beginner's guide to eating disorders recovery.* Carlsbad: CA. Gurze Books.

Lamb, M. E., Hershkowitz, I., Orbach, Y., & Esplin, P. W. (2008). *Tell me what happened: Structured investigative interviews of child victims and witnesses.* London: Wiley.

Lampman, C., Rolfe-Maloney, B., David, E. J., Yan, M., McCermott, N., & Winters, S. (2002, Fall). Messages about sex in the workplace: A content analysis of primetime television. *Sexuality & Culture, 6*, 3–21.

Lanktree, C., Briere, J., & Zaidi, L. (1991). Incidence and Impact of sexual abuse in a child outpatient sample: The role of direct inquiry. *Child Abuse & Neglect, 15*, 447–453.

Leifer, M., Shapiro, J. P., & Kassem, L. (1993). The impact of maternal history and behavior upon foster placement and adjustment in sexually abused girls. *Child Abuse & Neglect, 17*, 755–766.

Lev-Wiesel, R. (2008). Child sexual abuse: A critical review of intervention and treatment modalities. *Children & Youth Services Review, 30,* 665–673.

Lock, J. (2009). Eating disorders in children and adolescents. *Psychiatric Times, 26,* 35–38.

London, K., Bruck, M., Ceci, S. J., & Shuman, D. W. (2005). Disclosure of child sexual abuse: What does the research tell us about the ways that children tell? *Psychology, Public Policy, & Law, 11,* 194–226.

Lyon, T. D., & Ahern, E. C. (2011). Disclosure of child sexual abuse. In J. E. B. Myers (Ed.), *The APSAC handbook on child maltreatment* (3d. ed., pp. 233–252). Newbury Park, CA: Sage.

Malloy, L. C., Lyon, T. D., & Quas, J. A. (2007). Filial dependency and recantation of child sexual abuse allegations. *Journal of the American Academy of Child & Adolescent Psychiatry, 46,* 162–170.

Maniglio, R. (2009). The impact of child sexual abuse on health: A systematic review of reviews. *Clinical Psychology Review, 29,* 647–657.

Mannarino, A. P., & Cohen, J. A. (1997). Family-related variables and psychological symptom formation in sexually abused girls. *Journal of Child Sexual Abuse, 5,* 105–120.

Mayer, B., Muris, P., Meesters, C., & Zimmerman van Beuningen, R. (2009). Brief report: Direct and indirect relations of risk factors with eating behavior problems in later adolescent females. *Journal of Adolescence, 32,* 741.

McClain, N., Girardet, R., Lahoti, S., Cheung, K., Berger, K., & McNeese, M. (2000). Evaluation of sexual abuse in the pediatric patient. *Journal of Pediatric Health Care, 14,* 93–102.

McLeer, S. V., Deblinger, E., Henry, D., & Orvaschel, H. (1992). Sexually abused children at high risk for posttraumatic stress disorder. *Journal of the American Academy of Child & Adolescent Psychiatry, 31,* 875–879.

McLeer, S. V., Dixon, J. F., Henry, D., Ruggiero, K., Escovitz, K., Niedda, T., & Scholle, R. (1998). Psychopathology in non-clinically referred sexually abused children. *Journal of the American Academy of Child & Adolescent Psychiatry, 37,* 1326–1333.

Mennen, F. E. (1995). The relationship of race/ethnicity to symptoms in childhood sexual abuse. *Child Abuse & Neglect, 19,* 115–124.

Moran, P. B., Vucinich, S., & Hall, N. K. (2004). Associations between types of maltreatment and substance use during adolescence. *Child Abuse & Neglect, 28,* 565–574.

Mullen, P. E., Martin, J. L., Anderson, J. C., Romans, S. E., & Herbison, G. P. (1993). Childhood sexual abuse and mental health in adult life. *British Journal of Psychiatry, 163,* 721–732.

Mullen, P. E., Martin, J. L., Anderson, J. C., Romans, S. E., & Herbison, G. P. (1996). The long term impact of the physical, emotional, and sexual abuse of children: A community study. *Child Abuse & Neglect, 20*(1), 7–21.

National Eating Disorders Association. (2004). Factors that may contribute to eating disorders. www.NationalEatingDisorders.org Retrieved from www.nationaleatingdisorders.org/uploads/file/information-resources/Factors%20that%20may%20Contribute%20to%20Eating%20Disorders.pdf

Nielsen A2/M2 Three Screen Report. (2009). http://blog.nielsen.com/nielsenwire/wp-content/uploads/2009/09/3ScreenQ209_US_rpt_090209.pdf

O'Keefe, M. (2004). A case of suspected child sexual abuse. *Journal of clinical forensic medicine*, *11*, 316–320.

Otes, R. K., Tebbutt, J., Swanston, H., Lynch, D. L., & O'Toole, B. I. (1998). Prior childhood sexual abuse in mothers of sexually abused children. *Child Abuse & Neglect*, *22*, 1113–1118.

Owens, G. P., & Chard, K. M. (2003). Comorbidity and psychiatric diagnoses among women reporting child sexual abuse. *Child Abuse & Neglect*, *27*, 1075–1082.

Pereda, N., Guilera, G., Forns, M., & Gomez-Benito, J. (2009). The international epidemiology of child sexual abuse: A continuation of Finkelhor (1994). *Child Abuse & Neglect*, *33*, 331–342.

Pipe, M.-E., Lamb, M. E., Orbach, Y., Sternberg, K. J., Stewart, H., & Esplin, P. W. (2007). Factors associated with nondisclosure of suspected abuse during forensic interviews. In M.-E. Pipe, M. E. Lamb, Y. Orbach, & A. C. Cederborg (Eds.), *Child sexual abuse: Disclosure, delay and denial* (pp. 77–96). Mahwah, NJ: Lawrence Erlbaum.

Putman, F. W. (2003). Ten-year research update review: Child sexual abuse. *Journal of the American Academy of Child & Adolescent Psychiatry*, *42*, 269–278.

Rind, B., Tromovitch, P., & Bauseman, R. (1998). A meta-analytic examination of assumed properties of child sexual abuse using college samples. *Psychological Bulletin*, *124*, 22–53.

Ruffolo, J. S., Phillips, K. A., Menard, W., Fay, C., & Weisberg, R. B. (2006). Comorbidity of body dysmorphic disorder and eating disorders: Severity of psychopathology and body image disturbance. *International Journal of Eating Disorders*, *39*, 11–19.

Ruggiero, K. J., McLeer, S. V., & Dixon, J. F. (2000). Sexual abuse characteristics associated with survivor pathology. *Child Abuse & Neglect*, *24*, 951–964.

Sapp, M. V., & Vandeven, A. M. (2005). Update on childhood sexual abuse. *Current Opinion in Pediatrics*, *17*, 258–264.

Sartor, C. E., Lynskey, M. T., Bucholz, K. K., McCutcheon, V. V., Nelson, E. C., Waldron, M., & Heath, A. C. (2007). Childhood sexual abuse and the course of alcohol dependence development: Findings from a female twin sample. *Drug & Alcohol Dependence*, *89*, 139–144.

Schafer, I., Teske, L., Schulze-Thusing, J., & Hormann, K. (2010). Impact of childhood trauma on hypothalamus-pituitary-adrenal axis activity in alcohol-dependent patients. *European Addiction Research*, *16*, 108.

Sedlak, A. J., & Broadhurst, D. D. (1996). Executive summary of the third national incidence study of child abuse and neglect. U.S. Department of Health and Human Services. Retrieved from www.childwelfare.gov

Sedlak, A. J., Mettenburg, J., Basena, M., Petta, I., McPherson, K., Greene, A., & Li, S. (2010). *Fourth National Incidence Study of Child Abuse and Neglect (NIS-4): Report to Congress*. Washington, DC: U.S. Department of Health and Human Services, Administration for Children and Families.

Shapiro Gonzalez, L., Waterman, J., Kelly, R. J., McCord, J., & Oliveri, M. K. (1993). Children's patterns of disclosures and recantations of sexual and ritualistic abuse allegations in psychotherapy. *Child Abuse & Neglect, 17,* 281–289.

Shaw, J., Lewis, J., Loeb, A., Rosado, J., & Rodriguez, R. (2001). A comparison of Hispanic and African-American sexually abused girls and their families. *Child Abuse & Neglect, 25,* 1363–1379.

Shin, S. H., Hong, H. G., & Hazen, A. L. (2010). Childhood sexual abuse and adolescent substance use: A latent class example. *Drug and Alcohol Dependence, 109,* 226–235.

Staller, K. M., & Nelson-Gardell, D. (2005). "A burden in your heart": lessons of disclosure from female preadolescent and adolescent survivors of sexual abuse. *Child Abuse & Neglect, 29,* 1415–1432.

Stern, A. E., Lynch, D. L., Oates, R. K., O'Toole, B. I., & Cooney, G. (1995). Self esteem, depression, behavior and family functioning in sexually abused children. *Journal of Child Psychology & Psychiatry, 36,* 1077–1089.

Summit, R. C. (1983). The child sexual abuse accommodation syndrome. *Child Abuse & Neglect, 7,* 177–193.

Taylor, J. E., & Harvey, S. T. (2010). A meta-analysis of the effects of psychotherapy with adults sexually abused in childhood. *Clinical Psychology Review, 30,* 517–535.

Tyler, K. A. (2002). Social and emotional outcomes of childhood sexual abuse: A review of recent research. *Aggression and Violent Behavior, 7,* 567–589.

U.S. Department of Health and Human Services. (1998). *Child maltreatment 1996: Reports from the states to the national child abuse and neglect data system.* Washington, DC: U.S. Government Printing Office.

van der Kolk, B. A. (2005). Developmental trauma disorder. *Psychiatric Annals, 35* (3), 401–408.

Van Gerko, K., Hughes, M. L., Hamill, M., & Waller, G. (2005). Reported childhood sexual abuse and eating-disordered cognitions and behaviors. *Child Abuse & Neglect, 29,* 375–382.

Vogeltanz-Holm, N. D. (2004). Childhood sexual abuse and risk for adult psychopathology. *International Encyclopedia of the Social and Behavioral Sciences,* 1712–1716.

Vogeltanz, N. D., Wilsnack, S. C., Harris, T. R., Wilsnack, R. W., Wonderlich, S. A., & Kristjansen, A. F. (1999). *Child Abuse & Neglect, 23,* 579–592

Ward, L. M. (1995). Talking about sex: Common themes about sexuality in the prime-time television programs children and adolescents view most. *Journal of Youth & Adolescence, 24,* 595–615.

Ward, L.M. (2003). Understanding the role of entertainment in the sexual socialization of American youth: A review of empirical research. *Developmental Review, 23*(3), 347–388.

Wells, R., McCann, J., Adams, J., Voris, J., & Dahl, B. (1997). A validational study of the structured interview of symptoms associated with sexual abuse (SASA) using three samples of sexually abused, allegedly abused and nonabused boys. *Child Abuse & Neglect, 21*(12), 1159–1167.

Wolfe, V. V., Gentile, C., & Wolfe, D. A. (1989). The impact of sexual abuse on children: A PTSD formulation. *Behavior Therapy, 20*, 215–228.

Wonderlich, S. A., Crosby, R. D., Mitchell, J. E., Roberts, J. A., Haseltine, B., DeMuth, G., & Thompson, K. M. (2000). Relationship of childhood sexual abuse and eating disturbances in children. *Journal of the American Academy of Child & Adolescent Psychiatry, 39*, 1277–1283.

Wozencraft, T., Wagner, W., & Pellegrin, A. (1991). Depression and suicidal ideation in sexually abused children. *Child Abuse & Neglect, 15*, 505–510.

Wynkoop, T., Capps, S. C., & Priest, B. J. (1995). Incidence and prevalence of child sexual abuse: A critical review of data collection procedures. *Journal of Child Sexual Abuse, 4*(2), 49–67.

CHAPTER 2

Child Sexual Abuse, Traumatic Experiences, and Their Impact on the Developing Brain

RICHARD L. GASKILL and BRUCE D. PERRY

INTRODUCTION

THE U.S. DEPARTMENT of Health and Human Services documented that 3 million children were allegedly maltreated in 2007. Of these cases, more than 50,000 were suspected to have been sexually abused. The sexually abused children in the summary report were more likely female than male and 20% were under 8 years at the time of the assault. Forty percent of the assaults were perpetrated by family members ("Statistics Surrounding Child Sexual Abuse," 2008). It has been estimated that, in the United States alone, there are 39 million survivors of childhood sexual abuse ("Statistics Surrounding Child Sexual Abuse," 2008). The magnitude of this problem is enormous when one realizes child sexual abuse is just one of many co-occurring maladies in children's lives.

Child sexual abuse has commonly been viewed as if it were an isolated traumatic event, but nothing could be further from the truth. In fact, childhood sexual abuse seldom occurs as an isolated event. Rather, sexual abuse is more likely one adverse event coexisting among a host of other adverse circumstances in a child's life (Anda et al., 2006). Among the concomitant stressful events are physical and emotional abuse; parental psychiatric history; parental history of legal involvement; foster care; mental illness of a parent; parental marital discord; family history of violence; and alcohol and drug use in the family. Evidence from neurobiology and epidemiology research suggests these early life adverse experiences cause long-term changes in multiple brain systems (Anda et al., 2006). Worse, increasing frequencies of early adverse childhood experiences in a child's life were highly correlated with enduring brain dysfunction and were also linked to deleterious effects on health and quality of life (Anda et al., 2006).

Van der Kolk (2001) found that the majority of people seeking care for trauma resulting from maltreatment suffered from multiple psychological problems between 75% and 98.6% of the time. This apparent comorbidity of psychopathology became a destructive experience impacting the developing child, increasing risk of emotional, behavioral, academic, social, and physical problems throughout the child's life span (Anda et al., 2006; Perry & Pollard, 1997, 1998; Spinazzola, Blaustein, & van der Kolk, 2005). Among the comorbid neuropsychiatric diagnoses associated with childhood trauma are major depression, dissociative disorder, oppositional defiant disorder, conduct disorder, dysthymia, obsessive-compulsive disorder, phobic disorder, PTSD, substance abuse, borderline personality disorder, attention deficit and hyperactivity disorder, various developmental disorders, schizophrenia, and ultimately nearly all *DSM IV* diagnoses (Perry, 2008). This observation leads trauma researchers to include sexual abuse as only one of a host of traumatic childhood experiences comprising a larger complex web of child maltreatment contributory to long-term dysfunctional emotional, behavioral, cognitive, social, and physical development, and health outcomes (Anda et al., 2006; Perry, 2008; Perry & Pollard, 1998; Spinazzola et al., 2005; van der Kolk, 2001, 2006). Perry and Pollard (1998) claimed that more than 8 million children suffer from a trauma-related neuropsychiatric disorder at any given moment. This chapter addresses child sexual abuse as one of a number of adverse events included in the evolving neurobiological view of complex childhood maltreatment (van der Kolk, 2001). Further, due to the negative impact of child maltreatment on specific low brain structures and the historical neglect of remediation for such trauma, treatment discussions focus on child maltreatment from a neurobiological perspective. Although the neurobiological view of trauma offers enormous advances in treatment design it does require a fundamental familiarity with a few basic brain development principles.

HUMAN BRAIN DEVELOPMENT

The human brain is a surprisingly dynamic structure, mediating not only life-support functions, but also those functions that make us most human (Lehrer, 2009). Unlike our heart, lungs, or most other organs, the brain constructs itself through an extraordinary interaction of genetics and experience. All we are and all we will become—our hopes, our dreams, our knowledge, our relationships and our emotional health—depend on the successful development of the brain. As human beings we are not fast, large, strong, nor do we have sharp teeth or claws compared to many other creatures of the earth. Instead, our survival is largely contingent on the unique properties of our brain. Unlike any other species on the earth, we sense, perceive, process, store, and act on information from both external and internal environment in evolutionarily profound ways. To accomplish this feat, the brain has evolved an efficient, predictable, and hierarchical process of development and organization. Understanding this organization and essential brain processes holds valuable keys to successful treatment of maltreated children.

The human brain develops and organizes in a systematic and hierarchical fashion beginning very early in utero. First driven by genetics and later by experience, the brain is constructed through the interplay between nature and nurture. Because of this interaction between nature and nurture, the brain will become uniquely designed to support the survival of the young child in the world he or she experiences. This organizational process was first conceptualized as being from the bottom up in the early nineteenth century (Jackson, 1958). Maturation and development of the human brain recapitulates evolution, with brainstem and diencephalon regions developing first (Lehrer, 2009). These lower brain regions organize and develop early in utero and will continue in a systematic and predictable fashion, being functional before preschool. As is the case with most developmental processes, those organs or systems that will be required for survival develop first.

Lower brain regions, brainstem and diencephalon, develop early as they control basic life-support functions such as respiration, heart rate, blood pressure, and other critical activities. Higher brain regions develop later and more slowly than the lower brain areas as they are less critical to survival immediately after birth. The higher brain regions of the limbic and cortex areas mediate intricate functions of thinking and emotional regulation. As each of these areas develop and mature they become more sophisticated and efficient in function. The child will progressively display each new skill, called *developmental milestones*, as the various parts of the brain mature, becoming fully functional by puberty (Lehrer, 2009). The various brain regions connect within each region and between regions to form a massive neural network making the transfer of information possible (Perry, 2006). This information can then be perceived, processed, and integrated into various other parts of the brain, creating a huge array of brain functions greatly enhancing our ability to survive through successful management of our relationships and environment (MacLean, 1990; Perry, 2006; van der Kolk, 2006).

ORDER OF PROCESSING

The traditional view of the brain has been one of sequentially processing incoming sensory information beginning at the brainstem (bottom) through the diencephalon, limbic system, and finally the cortex (Jackson, 1958; MacLean, 1990). This model of neural processing implies that the ultimate capacity of integration and processing resides with the cortex, giving the human the capability to manage or cope with the environment. Jackson (1958) believed that the higher brain functions were able to inhibit and control the lower more primitive brain regions. In this dated view, the cortex logically analyzed incoming information and made rational decisions about responses, which were then put into action. The lower brain regions took over only when the higher regions were rendered functionless. This view attributed absolute executive control of the brain to the cortex (Lehrer, 2009). The belief in the superiority of reason to quell emotional impulses dates back to Plato, Descartes, and even Freud (Lehrer, 2009). For most of the twentieth century this notion has prevailed philosophically and is a central tenet in most therapeutic approaches. In fact, under normal conditions the executive and symbolizing capacities of the prefrontal cortex are capable of modifying the more primitive, lower brain region's impulses by inhibiting, organizing, and modulating those autonomic responses (Lehrer, 2009; van der Kolk, 2006). However, research has now demonstrated that it is only partially true and under certain conditions totally erroneous (Perry, 2006, 2008; Perry & Pollard, 1998; van der Kolk, 2006). It is now known that the lower brain regions (brainstem and diencephalon) are capable of functional changes in autonomic excitability and numerous homeostatic states in response to environmental influences without and independent of cortex involvement (Lehrer, 2010; Miller, 1969).

MULTILEVEL RESPONDING

To appreciate the significance of the multilevel responding capacity in the brain, it is instructive to trace neural pathways from the brainstem to the cortex. Perry and Pollard (1998) described the course of sensory input from both the internal environment (blood glucose, arterial pressure, CO_2 levels) and external environment (visual, auditory, tactile, olfactory, and gustatory) as generally traveling first from the peripheral nervous system (PNS) to the spinal cord. Once the impulse reached the spinal cord, sensory information initially entered the brain at the lower, regulatory, and motor areas of the brainstem and into the diencephalon. Neural activity entered the low brain regions as separate, preconscious impulses; unavailable to conscious awareness or verbalization. Even at this level, sorting, integrating, interpreting, storing, and responding began. As the primary sensory signals were processed and reprocessed through sensory association centers, co-occurring signals become connected (Perry, 2006). It is now known that most sensory processing occurs outside of conscious awareness. Only novel, significant, or threatening information is passed onto higher brain levels for further attention (van der Kolk, 1994).

Contrary to cortex superiority models, each brain level interprets stimuli matching it to stored, previous patterns of activation, and initiates a response. As the neural activity is transmitted to higher, more complex areas (limbic and cortical), more intricate cognitive associations are made, allowing interpretation of the experience. The patterns of neural activity are again matched against previously stored patterns of activation and placed in conscious memory (Perry, 2006; van der Kolk, 2006). The neural event can now be categorized, contextualized, understood, stored, and recalled consciously within a larger perceptual or cognitive framework (Perry, 2006; van der Kolk, 2006). This is a truly remarkable mental ability of the human brain. It is at this level of processing that neuronal activity first results in conscious emotional sensations (Perry, 2008; Perry & Pollard 1998; van der Kolk, 2006).

THREAT ASSOCIATIONS

As these sensory stimuli are matched and sorted, signals that are associated with previously identified threat or unknown potential threat trigger an initial alarm response at the most primitive levels of the brain. This alarm response activates neuronal activity in key brainstem and diencephalon nuclei, which contain neurotransmitters (Perry, 2006; van der Kolk, 2006). The fact that sensory input can automatically stimulate hormonal secretions and influence the activation of brain regions involved in attention and memory points to the limitations of conscious control over our actions and emotions. This is particularly relevant in understanding and treating traumatized individuals. It explains why trauma survivors are prone to display irrational, subcortically initiated responses that might be irrelevant, unproductive, or even harmful in the current context (van der Kolk, 2006).

This initial threat response initiates brainstem and midbrain activity, triggering immediate responses to the perceived threat, in near reflexive or Pavlovian fashion (van der Kolk, 1994). Responses at this level of brain function occur long before the signals reach higher cortical areas to be interpreted and ultimately acted on. This process has remarkable survival value as the low brain is making critical decisions for safety and survival when waiting for more detailed and analytical decisions would be detrimental (Lehrer, 2009; Perry, 2006, 2008; van der Kolk, 2006). Obviously, such immediate responses suggest that the lower brain regions are able to compare old patterns associated with threat to patterns just perceived. Perry (2006) calls these associations state memory. This nonverbal, illogical, unconscious association resulting in alarm activation occurs before complete processing and interpretation is completed by the cortex (Perry, 2006). It should also be noted that the cortex is easily overwhelmed. Under stress, the lower brain regions simply take over and shut down higher cortical regions. The cortex is in many ways a puny organ (Lehrer, 2009; van der Kolk, 2006).

Van der Kolk (2006) states that the rational brain (cortex), while able to organize feelings and impulses, does not seem to be particularly well equipped to abolish emotions, thoughts, and impulses. Neural imaging of humans in highly emotional states reveals that intense emotions of fear, sadness, anger, and happiness cause increased activation of sub cortical brain regions and significant reduction in blood flow in various areas in the frontal lobe (van der Kolk 2006). Van der Kolk (1994) also points out that traumatic experiences activate brain regions that trigger intense emotions and decrease activation of the central nervous system (CNS) regions involved in integration of sensory input, motor output, attention, memory, memory consolidation, modulation of physiological arousal, and the ability to communicate with words. Sympathetic nervous system arousal is greatly mobilized preparing the body for a physical fight or flight response. Nearly two-thirds of traumatized children show such symptoms resulting from increased adrenergic activity (van der Kolk, 2006). Physiological responses commonly involved include: stimulated sweat glands, inhibition of gastro-intestinal processes, increased cardiac activity, increased blood pressure, increased respiration, anxiety, or hypervigilance (Hopper, Spinazzola, Simpson, & van der Kolk, 2006). Finally, such intense responses to stressful experiences decrease the child's ability to organize a modulated behavioral reaction and to be engaged in the present (Hooper et al., 2006; Perry, 2008; van der Kolk, 2006).

Perry (2008) pointed out, from a neurobiological point of view, excessive or protracted traumatic experiences unmistakably cause profound alterations in the regulation and functioning of many bodily systems. This in turn can result in new dysfunctional brain patterns influencing the organization and function of higher brain areas. This results in compromised function and ultimately psychopathology. Experience, positive or negative, becomes the neural architecture of the child's brain (Perry, 2008).

STATES BECOME TRAITS

Finally, as has been previously alluded to, brain development is profoundly guided by experience. The sequential nature of neural development and brain function is heavily directed by and modified by the child's interaction with the environment. In a positive sense, the ability to create an internal representation of the external world or internal world through repeated activation is a useful memory and learning tool (Perry & Hambrick, 2008). This means that the greater the frequency of activation of a neural system, the more permanent the neural state becomes. Perry and Hambrick (2008) described neurons and neuronal networks as literally being modified through repeated experiences in what they called an activity or use-dependent process.

Just as the use-dependent process can create positive learning and memory, so can it create negative learning and memory due to neglect, trauma, or chaos. The precortical associations in the case of trauma or neglect are between sensory cues and the autonomic responses of threat. These subcortical signals are capable of eliciting a fear response, altering emotions, behaviors, and physiology. In the case of neglect, the neural system gets so little stimulation that neural systems fail to form and neurons atrophy and disappear. Sadly, these changes can become permanent (Perry, 2006).

Physiological arousal in general triggers trauma related memories, while conversely, trauma related memories precipitate generalized physiological arousal. Studies have demonstrated how the response to potent environmental stimuli (unconditional stimuli) becomes a conditioned reaction. After repeated aversive stimulation, intrinsically nonthreatening cues associated with the trauma (conditional stimuli) become capable of eliciting the defensive reaction by themselves (conditioned response) in a classical Pavlovian fashion (van der Kolk, 1994). The eliciting cue can be any sensory experience that becomes associated with the trauma. It could be eye contact, a smile, a smell, or a gesture (Perry, 2006; van der Kolk, 2006). Much of the resulting dysfunctional relational interaction will be beyond the awareness and understanding of the developing child or youth (Perry, 2006). If the traumatic experiences create a use-dependent state powerful enough, profound regressive changes will be noted in the child's thinking, behavior, and perceptions. Perry and Pollard (1998) described these changes as primitive brainstem driven behavior.

Trauma induces a total brain response. All parts of the brain will be affected by the survival reaction. Cortex, limbic, diencephalon, and brainstem will all create altered memories based on the traumatic experience.

The brain's prior homeostatic state memories will be changed cognitively, emotionally, motorically, and physiologically (Perry & Pollard, 1998). Children experiencing such alterations often express these alterations through academic problems, emotional or relational problems, sensory-motor problems, or core physiological problems. These difficulties will also result in the child having great difficulty benefiting from therapies using cognitive methods, language, or therapeutic relationships as remedial interventions (Perry, 2006; van der Kolk, 2006).

INCREASED VULNERABILITY OF CHILDHOOD

The brain's response to threat is well documented, but the incomplete neural developmental architecture of the child's brain presents additional concerns for treatment of traumatized children (Perry & Pollard, 1998; van der Kolk, 2006). Perry and Pollard (1998) pointed out that adults sometimes believe and speak of children as being resilient to traumatic events because of their young age. In these cases, adults perceive children as possessing qualities that insulate or protect them from the disorganizing impact of psychosocial maltreatment. To the contrary, nearly 20 years of research in child maltreatment has made it abundantly clear that this is not the case. In fact, children are much more vulnerable to trauma during early development than during later development (Perry & Pollard, 1998).

An uncomfortable reality of sequential brain development is that the organizing, sensitive brain of an infant or young child is more malleable to experience than the mature brain. Although traumatic experience may negatively affect the function of an adult, this same experience literally becomes the neural organization for an infant or child's brain (Perry, 2006). This explains why the beneficial effect of psychotherapy was primarily found in adult-onset trauma survivors. Seventy-five percent of the adults achieved asymptomatic ratings while only 33.3% of the child onset survivors achieved asymptomatic status (van der Kolk et al., 2007). This is not surprising given the child's immature neural developmental status versus the adults more mature neurological state. The result of child-onset trauma is that the brain becomes poorly developed and functionally disorganized, rendering the child less able to intellectually, verbally, or emotionally respond to normal experiences let alone traumatic ones. Perry and Pollard (1998) continued by pointing out that although the young child will be unable to effectively respond to the trauma, the child is still capable of experiencing a fear-induced startle response, emotional distress, or any age-appropriate reactivity in response to a traumatic experience. What the child cannot do is understand, symbolize, or verbalize the experience to others. Sometimes adults mistakenly view the lack of a response as emotional resilience. When children suffer such disorganizing neurobiological trauma, therapeutic change must be in the form of repeated opportunities for new experiences which allow the brain to either break false associations or decrease the overgeneralization of trauma-related associations (Perry, 2006).

For millions of abused and neglected children, their maladaptive and traumatic experiences have profoundly altered their brain development (for review, see Perry, 2008). The traumatic experiences have created a new, but less functional, less flexible state of equilibrium (Perry & Pollard, 1998). Children living in chaos, neglect, abuse, or threat do not have the opportunity to develop the fundamental experiences required to express their full potential for self-regulation, relationships, communication, or thinking. They become poorly socialized and at risk for profound and lasting emotional, behavioral, social, cognitive, and physical health problems (Anda et al., 2006; Perry, 2006; Perry et al., 1995; Perry & Pollard, 1998).

Trauma symptoms common to traumatized children generally feature intrusive recollections; persistent avoidance of associated stimuli or numbing of general responsiveness; and arousal symptoms of hyperarousal, hypervigilance, startle response, sleep difficulties, irritability, anxiety, and physiological hyperactivity. With repeated activation the symptoms will begin to generalize to other stimuli resembling the traumatic memory, eliciting complex, multisystem symptomatology (Perry, Conroy, & Ravitz, 1991). Other symptoms routinely associated with traumatized children are behavioral impulsivity, increased muscle tone, anxiety, a focus on threat-related cues (often no-verbal), affect regulation, language problems, fine and gross motor delays, disorganized attachment, dysphoria, attention difficulties, memory problems, and hyperactivity (Perry et al., 1995). In addition, interfamilial abuse has been increasingly documented as contributory to complex trauma involving chronic affect disregulation, and destructive behavior against self and others, learning disabilities, dissociative problems, somatization, and distortions in concepts about self and others (Hooper et al., 2007; van der Kolk, 1994; van der Kolk, 2001). Studies of global neglect have further contributed to the appalling picture of maltreatment identifying abnormalities in brain size, enlarged ventricles, cortical atrophy, alteration in the corpus callosum, decreased metabolic activity in the orbital frontal gyrus, infralimbic prefrontal cortex, amygdala and head of the hippocampus, lateral temporal cortex, as well as the brainstem (Perry, 2005, 2008).Treatment approaches need to be examined and reexamined in light of the growing knowledge of how the brain learns and how it is affected by environmental influences.

BARRIERS TO INTEGRATION OF
NEUROBIOLOGICAL INFORMATION

Many well-intended intervention efforts have been misinformed about the fundamental principles of brain organization, development, and functioning, and were predestined to fail (Perry, 2006; 2009; Perry & Hambrick, 2008; van der Kolk, 2004, 2006). Both Perry and van der Kolk clearly contend that treatment designs lacking basic neurobiological principles regarding how the brain develops and changes cannot expect to be effective. This problem has been characteristically evident in treatment of maltreated children (Perry & Hambrick, 2008).

Many approaches ignore a significant noncortical, illogical, nonverbal, sensory-motor-oriented component of social and emotional trauma, frequently resulting in chronic, resistant, and persistent symptomatology (Perry, 2006; Perry & Pollard, 1998; Perry & Szalavitz, 2006; van der Kolk, 2006). Even recent noteworthy discussions of preverbal trauma (Green, Crenshaw, & Kolos, 2010) consider only the limbic and cortical brain, not autonomic level trauma. The history of neglecting low brain contributions to trauma symptomatology has been the result of early therapists being unaware of the principles of neurodevelopment and neurotraumatology (van der Kolk, 2006).

A second limiting factor has been the limited availability of therapeutic services that provide sufficient repetition to reorganize long-standing disorganized low brain systems (Perry, 2006). *When years of chaos, trauma, or neglect have robbed a child of essential organizing experiences, the number of therapeutically necessary repetitions required to stimulate the growth and development of missing or deficient abilities (neural organization of the brain) will be high and require a protracted effort.* This has been discouraging to adults and professionals who expected much quicker results to their nurturing and supportive interventions. Professionals, caregivers, and parents must come to realize that the frequency of remedial repetitions required to modify low brain dysfunctional patterns will be very high. Certainly it will be higher than required to organize higher level brain regions (Perry, 2006). Clearly, traditional therapeutic thinking has not always taken into account how difficult it is to transform dysfunctional neural systems fashioned over years. Therapies and therapists by themselves have been able to provide but a small fraction of the reorganizing contribution required for healing global trauma. Maltreated children frequently need intensified regularity and quality of relational interactions. The standard weekly therapy session is not sufficient to development healthy functioning after years of chaos and dysfunctional living. The greater the degree of disorganization noted in the child the more critical the need for massive quantities of healthy interactions. This may well require therapeutic environments that have an adult to child social ratios as low as 1:1, even for children much older than those normally receiving this much attention (Perry, 2006). In many cases, the required number of healthy interactions essential to transform ingrained low brain neural patterns will be so high that many caretakers (parents, teachers, family, etc.) must be actively committed to participating in the effort (Perry & Hambrick, 2008).

Third, traditional therapies have paid limited attention to post-traumatic changes in body experience or what van der Kolk called the sensate dimensions of life (van der Kolk, 2004, 2006). Neuroscience has demonstrated that emotional states arise from conditions experienced within our bodies, such as hormones, internal organs, or muscles tension (van der Kolk, 1994). Therapies have customarily promoted understanding, acceptance, emotional processing, insight, and problem-solving regarding what happened in the patient's life to create such powerful reactions (van der Kolk, 2004). Contrary to this historical treatment perspective, brain science now informs us that the dorsolateral prefrontal cortex which is involved with insight, understanding, and planning for the future, has virtually no connecting pathways to the lower level brain centers that generate and elaborate these powerful trauma reactions (van der Kolk, 2004, 2006). Consequently, common therapies that are psychodynamic or cognitive behavioral in orientation may pay insufficient attention to disturbed autonomic physical sensations and preprogrammed physical action patterns (van der Kolk, 2006). Perry (2006) continued with this line of thought when he stated that talk therapies and therapeutically relational interactions have not proven effective in changing low brain (brainstem or diencephalon) experience. Again the best cognitive-behavioral or insight-oriented or even affect-based therapies fail if the brainstem is poorly regulated. The child's excessive anxiety, hypervigilance, and habitually activated threat response undermine academic, therapeutic, and social-emotional interventions (Perry, 2006).

NEUROBIOLOGICALLY BASED TREATMENT

Perry (2006), van der Kolk (2006), Cook et al. (2005), and others have made it evident that insight, understanding, integration, acceptance, emotional processing, and problem-solving therapy strategies offer limited assistance to children suffering from common autonomically mediated symptoms such as fear and anxiety states of hyperarousal, hypervigilance, sleep disturbances, as well as physiological reactions of increased heart rate, blood pressure, and respiration (Perry & Hambrick, 2008).

Although treatment for neglect and abuse will ultimately need to focus on higher cognitive issues, the more cortically mediated problems should be addressed later after fundamental low brain regulation is established (Cook et al., 2005). Until state regulation or healthy homeostasis is established at the brainstem level, higher brain mediated treatments will be less effective (Perry & Hambrick, 2008). With young maltreated children, this may mean developing healthy state regulation for the first time in their lives. Using the bottom up analogy of brain processing, establishing a sense of safety and self-regulation (lower brain mediated) must supersede insightful reflection, trauma experience integration, relational engagement, or positive affect enhancement as these last elements of treatment are mediated through cortical and limbic areas (Cook et al., 2005). This new conceptual view of trauma treatment requires us to search for therapeutic methods that offer hope for reprogramming autonomic primitive, low brain dysfunctional or disorganized learning. The solution rests with the notion that if adverse experiences altered the developing brain in negative ways, then healthy therapeutic experiences can change the brain in ways that promote healing, recovery, and restoration of healthy functioning (Perry, 2006).

NEUROBIOLOGICALLY INFORMED INTERVENTION

The challenge of finding helpful interventions for low brain dysfunction may begin by looking into the past. Just as useful medical treatments have been derived from ancient remedies, valuable mental health treatments can also be derived from our ancestral emotional healing practices. Throughout our existence on earth, human beings have calmed each other when overwhelmed, distraught, or distressed through sensory experiences such as touch, through patterned, repetitive movements of dance, holding, rocking; and through rhythmic use of music, drumming, song, or chanting. Neurologically, each of these interventions has their origin in low brain regions rendering them nonverbal, sensorial, and movement oriented. Such methods have been used as healing rituals for thousands of years as part of intensely relational experiences with family, loved ones, and friends being an integral part of the process (Perry, 2009; van der Kolk, 2001). The quest for methods to return traumatized children to a state of quiescence or to create such a state requires a willingness to look back at our neurobiological origin, our developmental history, and our ancestral remedial practices.

To date, the few treatment designs that have utilized developmentally appropriate interventions which emulate normal development have been encouraging (Perry, 2006; Perry, 2009; Perry & Hambrick, 2008; van der Kolk, 2006) In fact, such protocols have been demonstrated to be more effective than traditional talk therapy or pharmacological approaches in achieving reductions in core trauma symptoms, and promoting healthy social emotional development (Miranda, Arthur, Mahoney, & Perry, 1998; Miranda, Schilick, Dobson, Hogan, & Perry, 1999; van der Kolk, 2001, 2007; Barfield et al., in preparation). These early treatment designs demonstrate that the specific nature, pattern, timing, and duration of remedial experiences are crucial to successful therapeutic reorganization of low brain functions. Developmentally appropriate intervention means the remedial activity must match the natural or biological organizing processes of the brain region affected. The pattern and timing of the corrective activity must also match the normal process of that brain region. So, if a brain region is typically organized by specific rhythmic, sequential patterns that normally occur with a caregiver at heart rate (e.g., rocking the child at about 60 beats per minute), the same pattern needs to be replicated in the treatment design through some experiential modality (a rocking chair or swinging at the same rate). Finally, the duration of the activity also needs to approximate the normal developmental course. That is, treatment actions that are primarily sensory or motor in nature must be longer in duration, with frequent repetitions, and with a greater relational concentration than is normally common in traditional therapy designs.

Perry (2006) characterized successful neurobiologically informed treatment as pairing the right therapeutic activity from a specific developmental stage with the physiological needs of a maltreated child. The critical concept therapeutically is that brain regions not activated do not change (Perry, 2006). This inadequate appreciation of neurological change agents has greatly influenced the movement toward pharmacology treatment for low brain symptoms of trauma. The shortcoming of pharmacological intervention is that such treatments fail to create new learning, fail to create natural neurologically patterned calm homeostatic states, or in other words self-regulation. This learning can only be accomplished by repeated, patterned experiences, using the sensory modalities specific to the brain region to be affected.

Nontraditional treatments for hyperarousal and associated symptoms resulting from early histories of chaos; physical, emotional, or sexual abuse; neglect; or violence have not enjoyed widespread use in Western culture (van der Kolk, 2006). Nonetheless, most adults and children with trauma-related problems need some form of body-oriented therapy to regain a sense of control or self-regulation over their bodies, or in the case of early maltreatment, to establish healthy patterns for the first time (Cook et al., 2005; van der Kolk, 2009). Fortunately, there have been some notable attempts to develop specific body-oriented treatment techniques and psychodramatic techniques focusing on experiencing, tolerating, and transforming trauma-related sensations (van der Kolk, 2001). Among these techniques, Eye Movement Desensitization and Reprocessing (EMDR), focusing, sensory awareness, Feldenkrais, rolfing, FM Alexander technique, body-mind centering, somatic experiencing, Pesso-Boyden psychotherapy, Rubenfeld synergy, and Hakomi have all been used successfully, at least with adults (van der Kolk, 2001, 2006).

Although there may be useful applications of these adult techniques for children, remediation for low brain disorganization for children realistically relies heavily on play and play activities that emulate normal healthy behavior, developmentally matched to the brain region targeted for change. Play is a primal, complex process that occurs spontaneously when children are given the freedom to follow their innate nature (Brown, 2009). Play is naturally pleasurable and generally thought to be the organizing activity that shapes the child's physical, social, emotional, and cognitive perceptual view of the world (Brown, 2009; Louv, 2008). Play is the intrinsic, neurological process intended to program the child's brain. These properties make play an excellent process to reorganized brain systems that have been negatively affected by maltreatment. However, it is vitally important that the therapist understand that at the brainstem and diencephalon level play are a primary process that is nonverbal. These low brain regions do not comprehend nor respond to spoken language. They both respond to the "language" of the senses and movement. As such, they are very sensory, primarily visual and tactile, but auditory perception of tone, rhythm, and pitch have an influence as well (Schore, 1994). Primary process communication relies on eye contact, face-to-face gaze, facial gestures, touch, physical movement, and rhythm. These communication mediums are central to low brain remedial efforts as they are the modalities recognized by the low brain. As primary process communication begins, the adult must establish an attuned state with the child. That is, the two are in a harmonic emotional state that actually synchronizes their neural activity, heart rates, and hormonal systems all of which are critical to later self-regulation (Stern, 1985). The adult must maintain themselves in a calm state and be the safe island for the child. The intent of this type of interaction is that the child will synchronize with the adult. In this process the child's arousal level is brought under regulatory control by matching the adult's calmer arousal level. Sensory regulation of the child mediated by the adult must come before self-regulation mediated by the child (Perry, personal communication, 11–14–08). Limiting stimuli (light, sound, movement, and people) to decrease arousal and sooth the child are critical to creating a state of regulation.

Brainstem regulation of the child is done almost exclusively through soothing, calming, pacifying sensory activity. The attuned caregiver rapidly begins to discover the child's favored sensory systems and which activities present the sensory stimulation in ways the child finds soothing and quieting. These activities may include elements of gentle touch, massage, hugs, cuddling, skin-to-skin contact, music, rocking, swinging, grooming, breathing exercises, sucking, chewing, warm baths, lullabies, songs, music, textures of all kinds to feel, pudding painting, finger painting, playing with clay, sand or mud, and so on. The list is limited only by one's imagination, but the activity must be experienced by the child as pleasurable and must be carried out in an intensely relational context. The same activity devoid of positive relational qualities will fail to produce the desired neurological change. It must be remembered that this process is not a cookbook of activities; to the contrary it is a richly relational and neurobiological process, entered into by a child and an adult who want to be emotionally connected at a particular moment in time.

Diencephalon activities, which often are comingled with the brainstem activities under the rubric of low brain remediation, consist normally of rhythmic, sequenced motor or exercise activities for both fine and gross motor play, as well as continued sensory play. Specific activities offering regulation for this brain region may include: rocking, swinging, crawling through tubes, blanket mazes, or boxes, piggy back rides, rocking boats, playground equipment, play with balls, hoops, or bean bags, jumping ball, rocking horses, hula hoops, throwing, catching, kicking, swimming, handclapping games, jumping rope, ball bouncing games, hop scotch, tricycles, scooter boards, bikes, walking through mazes or labyrinths, hatha yoga, yoga, tai chi, reiki touch, pressure points, dance, and so on. Again it is not the activity alone that produces the positive change, but done in conjunction with an intensely positive relational climate.

The search for activities that can be expected to stimulate the low brain centers often leads to consideration of non-Western healing traditions. Fortunately such traditions offer some insights regarding physical movement and breathing through the use of yoga, qigong, and tai chi to regulate emotional and physiological states. These activities may be too advanced for small children, but they are practical for grade school and older children and might be used to augment the exercises mentioned earlier. Yoga and other closely related modalities have been used successfully to regulate core arousal systems in the brain and promote comfort with one's own body. It is a useful method to attain a sense of comfort with one's physical sensations and to develop a sense of inner quietness. In this sense, yoga is believed to calm core regulatory mechanisms in the lower brain regions (van der Kolk, 2009). In fact, some studies found yoga superior to Dialectic Behavioral Training (DBT) in decreasing the frequency of intrusions and severity of hyperarousal symptoms (van der Kolk, 2006). Also, hatha yoga has successfully lowered heart rate and improved muscular and vascular concomitants of posttraumatic stress disorder (PTSD) clients. The gains in low brain self-regulation seemed the result of increased awareness of sensory stimuli during formal practice (van der Kolk, 2006). According to van der Kolk (2001), meditation practitioners became progressively more adept at managing stressful reactions. Yoga seemed to help them feel comfortable with their physical sensations and to develop an inner quietness or stillness. Van der Kolk (2001) also reported mindfulness as a fundamental skill that created a sense of mastery over physiological arousal. This mindful or meditative quality promoted the ability to discern between internal sensations and the external events that precipitated them. The goal of therapy, van der Kolk proposed, was to create the capacity to be mindful of current experience and to create symbolic representations of the past traumatic experience with the aim of uncoupling physical sensation from trauma based emotional responses. The uncoupling was accomplished by decreasing the intensity and duration of hyperarousal states.

NEUROSEQUENTIAL MODEL OF THERAPEUTICS

One of the first neurobiological treatment models of child maltreatment was developed by the Child Trauma Academy. This model uses traditional and nontraditional therapy activities directed by core principles of neuroscience (Perry, 2006; Perry & Hambrick, 2008). The Neurosequential Model of Therapeutics (NMT) is not specifically a treatment technique, but rather a developmentally sensitive and neurobiologically informed method of conceptualizing child trauma and designing interventions (Perry, 2006, 2009). The NMT stresses the importance of prescribing remedial interventions that match the child's functional developmental stage (not necessarily the chronological stage) and the brain region mediating the neuropsychiatric condition (Perry & Hambrick, 2008). The three primary objectives are to first assess specific problems and the mediating disorganized brain region; second, identify key strengths that will enhance remediation; and third, determine specific interventions that will meet the needs of the child (Perry, 2006, 2009).

Successful treatment is dependent on applying several core principles of brain development. First is the importance of restoration of the perception of safety and control in the traumatized child (Perry, 2006). Children do not make progress clinically when they are frightened or feel out of control (Walsh, Blaustein, Knight, Spinazzola, & van der Kolk, 2007). Remember, even with excellent child protective services, investigation, placement, and litigation can easily contribute to the child's fearful out of control experiences. Therapists must work to help the child regain some sense of consistency, routine, familiarity, and control in their lives. Only then will treatment interventions have maximal impact. Human beings do not make developmental progress when under threat (Perry, 2006).

Second, treatment services will be most effective when they mirror children's normal developmental path. An assessment of the neurobiological history is conducted to determine the most appropriate sequencing of services (Perry & Hambrick, 2008). Third, therapeutic services must be consistent, predictable, patterned, and highly repetitive. For such interventions to be successful in reorganizing destructive low brain memory templates, the number of repetitions of positive organizing experiences must be very high. This may require repetitions multiple times a week or even daily. Unfortunately, this is often beyond the capability of traditional weekly therapy sessions. Pragmatically, therapeutic services must be carried out in multiple spheres of the child's life. Only by using parents, caregivers, teachers, and others can the requisite number of repetitions be attainable of constructive change (Perry, 2006). Fourth, since multiple deficits often coexist, they must be addressed in a specific order. The concept is a simple one, treatment must follow the natural hierarchy of brain development, beginning at the lowest level of brain disorganization or pathologically functioning. Commonly, the more closely restorative efforts mimic the normal sequence and process of development the greater the effectiveness (Perry, 2006). As mastery is attained, treatment begins to slowly resemble the next developmental stage. Treatment customarily begins at the lowest disorganized brain region (Perry, 2006).

CONCLUSION

The neurobiological perspective offers revolutionary explanatory power regarding the origin and development of trauma related symptoms and their resistance to treatment. The neurobiological perspective also offers a means to understand traumatic hyperarousal, flashbacks, and retriggering as autonomically mediated low brain activity. Further, it offers an unparalleled conceptual framework for designing interventions for maltreated children, with low brain dysfunction (Perry, 2008; van der Kolk, 2001). To fully utilize the neurological impact of psychosocial trauma on the developing brain of a child and to effectively treat the resulting developmentally specific trauma, the helping professionals involved with children should apply basic principles of brain function and development to intervention for children suffering from complex trauma.

REFERENCES

Anda, R. F., Felitti, V. J., Bremner, J. D., Walker, J. D., Whitfield, C., Perry, B. D., & Giles, W. H. (2006). The enduring effects of abuse and related adverse experiences in childhood; a convergence of neurobiology and epidemology. *European Archives of Psychiatry and Clinical Neuroscience, 256*(3), 174–186.

Barfield, S. (2004). *Best practices in early childhood mental health programs for preschool children: A report to Kansas Department of social rehabilitation services: Division of health care policy, state of Kansas.* Topeka, KS: KU School of Social Work.

Brown, S. (2009). *Play: How it shapes the brain, opens the imagination, and invigorates the soul.* New York, NY: Avery.

Cook, A., Spinazzola, J., Ford, J., Lanktree, C., Blaustein, M. B., Cloitre, M., & van der Kolk, B. (2005). Complex trauma in children and adolescents. *Psychiatric Annals, 35*(5), 390–398. Retrieved from www.traumacenter.org

Gaskill, R. (2007). *Neurosequential model of therapeutics: Protocol for core elements of the therapeutic program.* Unpublished manuscript.

Green, E. J., Crenshaw, D. A., & Kolos, A. C. (2010). Counseling children with preverbal trauma. *International Journal of Play Therapy, 19*(2), 95–105.

Hopper, J. W., Freen, P. A., van der Kolk, B. A., & Lanius, R. A. (2007). Neural correlates of reexperiencing avoidance and dissociation in PTSD: Symptoms dimensions and emotion dysregulation in response to script-driven trauma imagery. *Journal of Traumatic Stress, 20*(5), 713–725. Retrieved from www .interscience.wiley.com. doi:10.1002/jts.2028

Hopper, J. W., Spinazzola, J., Simpson, W. B., & van der Kolk, B. A. (2006). Preliminary evidence of parasympathetic influence on basal heart rate in posttraumatic stress disorder. *Journal of Psychsomatic Research, 60,* 83–90.

Jackson, J. H. (1958). Evolution and dissolution of the nervous system. In J. J. Taylor (Ed.), *Selected writings of John Hughlings* (pp. 45–118). London, England: Staples Press.

Lehrer, J. (2009). *How we decide.* Boston, MA: Mariner Books.

Louv, R. (2008). *Last child in the woods: Saving our children from nature-deficit disorder.* Chapel Hill, NC: Algonquin Books.

MacLean, P. D. (1990). *The triune brain in evolution: Role of paleocerebral functions.* New York, NY: Plenum Press.

Miller, N. E. (1969). Learning of visceral and glandular responses. *Science, 163*(3866), 434–445.

Miranda, L. A., Arthur, A., Mahoney, O., & Perry, B. (1998). The art of healing: The healing arts project, early childhood connection. *Journal of Music and Movement-Based Learning, 4*(4), 35–40.

Miranda, L. A., Schilick, S., Dobson, C., Hogan, L., & Perry, B. (1999). *The developmental effects of brief music and movement program at a public preschool: A pilot project* (Abstract), from www.childtrauma.org/ctaServices/neigh_artsasp

Perry, B. (2006). Applying principles of neurodevelopment to clinical work with maltreated and traumatized children. In N. B. Webb (Ed.), *Working with traumatized youth in child welfare.* New York, NY: Guilford Press.

Perry, B. (2008). Child maltreatment: The role of abuse and neglect in developmental pathology. In T. P. Beauchaine & S. P. Henshaw (Eds.), *Textbook of child and adolescent psychopathology* (pp. 93–128). Hoboken, NJ: John Wiley & Sons.

Perry, B. (2009). Examining child maltreatment through a neurodevelopmental lens: clinical application of the Neurosequential Model of Therapeutics. *Journal of Loss and Trauma 14*, 240–255.

Perry, B., Conroy, L., & Ravitz, A. (1991). Persisting psychophysiological effects of traumatic stress: "The memory of states." *Violence Update, 1*(8), 1–11.

Perry, B., & Hambrick, E. (2008). The neurosequential model of therapeutics. *Reclaiming Children and Youth, 17*(3), 38–43.

Perry, B., & Pollard, R. (1997). *Altered brain development following global neglect in early childhood.* Paper presented at the Society for Neuroscience: Proceedings for Annual Meeting, New Orleans.

Perry, B., & Pollard, R. (1998). Homeostasis, stress, trauma, and adaptation: A neurodevelopmental view of childhood trauma. *Child and Adolescent Psychiatric Clinics of North America, 7*(1), 33–51.

Perry, B., Pollard, R., Blakley, T., Baker, W., & Vigilante, D. (1995). Childhood trauma, the neurobiology of adaptation and the "use-dependent" development of the brain: How states become traits. *Infant Mental Health Journal, 16*(4), 20.

Perry, B., & Szalavitz, M. (2006). *The boy who was raised as a dog: And other stories from a psychiatrist's notebook.* New York, NY: Basic Books.

Schore, A. M. (1994). *Affect regulation and the origins of the self.* Hillsdale, NJ: Erlbaum.

Spinazzola, J., Blaustein, M., & van der Kolk, B. A. (2005). Posttraumatic stress disorder treatment outcome research: The study of unrepresented samples? *Journal of Traumatic Stress, 18*(5), 425–436.

Statistics Surrounding Child Sexual Abuse. (2008). Retrieved 7–28–10, from www .darkness2light.org/knowabout/statistics_2.asp

Stern, D. (1985). *The interpersonal world of the infant.* New York, NY: Basic Books.

Summary of Child Maltreatment. (2007). Retrieved from www.acf.hhs.gov/ programs/pubs/cn07/summary.htm

van der Kolk, B. (1994). *The body keeps the score: Memory and the evolving psycho-biology of post traumatic stress.* Trauma Information Pages: articles. Retrieved 7–15–10, from www.trauma-pages.com/vanderk4.htm

van der Kolk, B. (2001). The assessment and treatment of complex PTSD. In R. Yehuda (Ed.), *Traumatic Stress.* Washington, DC: American Psychiatric Press.

van der Kolk, B. (2006). Clinical implications of neuroscience research in PTSD. *Annals of the New York Academy of Science, 1071*(IV), 277–293.

van der Kolk, B. A., Spinazzola, J., Baustein, M. E., Hopper, J. W., Hopper, E. K., Korn, D. L., Simpson, W. B. (2007). A randomized clinical trial of eye movement (EMDR), fluoxetine, and pill placebo in the treatment of posttraumatic stress disorder: Treatment effects and long-term maintenance. *Journal of Clinical Psychiatry, 68*, 0.

Walsh, K., Blaustein, M., Knight, W. G., Sinazzola, J., & van der Kolk, B. A. (2007). Resiliency factors in the relation between childhood sexual abuse and adult-hood sexual assault in college-age women. *Journal of Child Sexual Abuse, 16*(1), 1–17. Retrieved on 7–28–10, from http://jcsa.haworthpress.com

CHAPTER 3

The Long-Term Health Effects of Child Sexual Abuse

KATHLEEN KENDALL-TACKETT

INTRODUCTION

C AN CHILDHOOD SEXUAL abuse impact the health of adult survivors? Unfortunately, the answer is yes. Men or women who have experienced childhood sexual abuse often have poorer health than their nonabused counterparts and these effects last long after the abuse has ended. Without intervention, abuse survivors are significantly more likely to have a number of serious and life-threatening illnesses.

Childhood abuse increased women's risk of cardiovascular disease by ninefold in the National Comorbidity Study (Batten, Aslan, Maciejewski, & Mazure, 2004). Felitti and colleagues (2001) found that men and women who had experienced four or more types of Adverse Childhood Experiences (ACEs) were significantly more likely to have organic diseases, such as ischemic heart disease, cancer, stroke, skeletal fractures, chronic obstructive pulmonary disease, chronic bronchitis, and hepatitis. The types of adverse experiences included childhood maltreatment (physical abuse, sexual abuse, and neglect), parental mental illness, parental substance abuse and parental criminal activity. The effects of ACEs were additive, meaning the more types of ACEs they had experienced, the worse their health.

The effects of childhood abuse are consistent with the research on the health effects of posttraumatic stress disorder (PTSD). For example, data from the Canadian Community Health Survey ($N = 36,984$; Sareen et al., 2007) revealed that even after adjusting for demographic factors and other mental illnesses, participants with PTSD had significantly higher levels of hypertension and heart disease, asthma and chronic obstructive pulmonary disease (COPD), chronic pain syndromes, gastrointestinal illnesses, and cancer. PTSD was also strongly associated with chronic fatigue syndrome and multiple-chemical sensitivity.

CHRONIC PAIN SYNDROMES IN ADULT

Chronic pain is one of the most common symptoms reported by abuse survivors, and it can range from mild to disabling. Unfortunately, it can also be challenging to treat and patients may struggle for years to find answers and get relief from their symptoms.

Past abuse has been related to chronic or recurring headaches, pelvic pain, back pain, and pain syndromes, such as irritable bowel syndrome and fibromyalgia (Kendall-Tackett, Marshall, & Ness, 2003). Sachs-Ericsson, Kendall-Tackett, and Hernandez (2007), using data from the National Comorbidity Study, found that participants with a history of either intimate partner violence or childhood physical or sexual abuse were more likely to report pain when describing their current health symptoms.

Patients with chronic pain often have marked physiological abnormalities in brain structure and function that appear when using technology such as positron emission tomography (PET) scans, computerized tomography (CT) scans, and magnetic resonance imaging (MRIs) of the brain (Bremner, 2005). Two chronic-pain syndromes that have been associated most frequently with past abuse are fibromyalgia and irritable bowel syndrome. Each is described below.

Fibromyalgia syndrome (FMS) is a chronic pain syndrome characterized by widespread musculoskeletal pain, decreased pain threshold, sleep disturbance, and psychological distress (Boisset-Pioro, Esdaile & Fitzcharles, 1995; Crofford, 2007). FMS is diagnosed using American College of Rheumatology (ACR) criteria. FMS includes widespread pain that persists for at least three months, and tenderness in at least 11 of 18 specific tender points (Crofford, 2007).

Boisset-Pioro and colleagues (1995) compared 83 FMS patients with 161 arthritis patients who had no FMS. Fifty-three percent of the FMS patients reported a history of physical or sexual abuse, compared with 42% of non-FMS patients. FMS patients with abuse histories had significantly more symptoms than non-FMS patients. Another study comparing FMS patients with and without a history of abuse found that FMS patients with a history of abuse had more severe symptoms, more pain and greater functional disability than nonabused FMS patients. Sexual abuse appeared to exacerbate the underlying condition (Taylor, Trotter, & Csuka, 1995).

McBeth, MacFarlane, Benjamin, Morris, and Silman (1999) indicated that childhood adversity (child abuse, parental loss, illness of a family member, and parental drug overdose) increased tender point count within a community sample. The odds ratio for child abuse was particularly high ($OR = 6.9$) and child abuse was the best independent predictor of a high tender-point count. Van Houdenhove, Luyten, and Van den Eede (2008) found that 64% of patients in a group for FMS or chronic fatigue syndrome had at least one type of either child or adult trauma. More concerning was that 39% of the group reported abuse during childhood and as adults, indicating a lifelong pattern of abuse.

Irritable bowel syndrome (IBS) is a functional disorder of the lower gastrointestinal tract. In populations of patients in treatment for irritable bowel, abuse survivors can comprise 50% to 70% (Drossman, Leserman, Li, Keefe, Hu, & Toomey, 2000; Leserman et al., 1996). IBS is diagnosed using the Rome criteria. Symptoms include abdominal pain or cramping; altered bowel habits (either diarrhea or constipation), consistency or passage; passage of mucus; and bloating or abdominal distention. The symptoms can be continuous or recurrent, and must be present for at least three months (American Gastroenterological Association, 1997). Symptoms generally present with one of two patterns: diarrhea without abdominal pain and alternating diarrhea and constipation with abdominal pain (Subramani & Janowitz, 1991).

Consistent with findings on other chronic pain syndromes, a relatively high percentage of people with IBS have a history of either physical or sexual abuse. As Leserman and Drossman (2007) note, patients with a history of physical or sexual abuse in childhood, or intimate partner violence as adults, have 1.5 to 2 times the risk of having a functional gastrointestinal disorder.

Walker, Katon, Roy-Byrne, Jemelka, and Russo (1993) compared 28 patients with irritable bowel syndrome (a functional pain syndrome) and 19 patients with inflammatory bowel disease (IBD; an organic illness). Sexual victimization was much more common among the IBS patients than those with IBD. Patients with IBS had higher rates of severe lifetime sexual trauma (32% versus 0%), severe child sexual abuse (11% versus 0%), and any lifetime sexual victimization (54% versus 5%). When patients had co-occurring chronic pelvic pain, they were more distressed and had more functional disability than women who had either complaint alone.

Ali and colleagues (2000) found that women with functional GI illness (such as IBS) were significantly more likely to have been raped than women with organic GI illness (34% versus 10%). Similarly, physical assault was more common in women with functional illness than in women with organic illness (18% versus 10%).

According to some researchers, up to 60% of women in treatment for GI illness had a history of abuse (Drossman, Li, Leserman, Toomey, & Hu, 1996; Leserman et al., 1996). The patients with histories of severe abuse (i.e., rape, life-threatening injuries) had more functional than organic illness. The functional conditions included esophageal pain, dyspepsia (upper abdominal pain), and IBS. The organic illnesses included ulcerative colitis, Crohn's disease, liver disease, and pancreatic/biliary disease. Interestingly, the highest percentages of abuse survivors were among the patients with functional abdominal pain (84%) and liver disease (72%). Liver disease included cirrhosis, and chronic hepatitis B and C. These disorders could be a result of high-risk health behaviors (alcohol abuse, unsafe sex, sharing needles), and could explain why there is a high percentage of abuse survivors in this group.

In another study, researchers followed a group of 174 women who had been referred to a GI clinic for a period of 12 months (Drossman et al., 2000). Half of these patients had been physically or sexually abused, and 14% had experienced severe abuse. Patients who were more severely abused also had poor health status. Patients who were "profoundly pessimistic" about their illnesses had poorer outcomes. Abuse and maladaptive coping were the two most important predictors of health outcome.

HIGHER PATTERNS OF HEALTH-CARE USE

Given these rates of illness, it is not surprising that abuse survivors see doctors more often and have higher patterns of health-care use than their nonabused counterparts. In an HMO sample, Felitti (1991) found that 22% of his sample of child sexual abuse survivors had visited a doctor 10 or more times a year compared with 6% of the nonabused control group. High health-care use was also noted in a study of women who had been battered or raped as adults (Koss, Koss, & Woodruff, 1991).

In addition to office visits, health-care use can include hospitalizations and surgery. Women who have experienced child or domestic abuse are also more likely to have had repeated surgeries; up to twice as often as their nonabused counterparts (Kendall-Tackett, Marshall, & Ness, 2000). Severity of the abuse was the strongest predictor of number of physician visits and total outpatient costs (Kendall-Tackett, 2003; Koss et al., 1991).

WHY CHILD SEXUAL ABUSE MAKES PEOPLE SICK

Researchers have documented that abuse survivors are more prone to physical illness, but we know substantially less about why this occurs. However, researchers have identified five possible pathways by which childhood abuse is likely to influence health in abuse survivors. Adult survivors can be influenced by any or all of these, and the five types influence each other. Indeed, they form a complex matrix of interrelationships, all of which influence health, and include physiological changes, harmful behaviors, cognitive beliefs, social relationships, and emotional health.

PHYSIOLOGICAL CHANGES

Traumatic events change the way the body functions. The body becomes threat sensitized and more vulnerable to stress when faced with subsequent stressors. As described previously, abuse can lower survivors' pain thresholds, making them more vulnerable to chronic pain syndromes. The more severe the abusive experience, the more dramatic the physiologic changes.

Many of the illnesses for which abuse survivors are at increased risk are due to trauma-related changes in the stress response. Severe or overwhelming stress alters and dysregulates the key systems that are designed to protect our health. To understand these findings, it is helpful to review the three systems that respond to a perceived threat. These are described below.

Human bodies have a number of interdependent mechanisms in place designed to preserve our lives when we perceive danger. The human stress response is highly complex. In a simplified form, it can be described as having three components: fight-or-flight, HPA axis, and immune response. Understanding the stress response is key to understanding the link between trauma and health.

The sympathetic nervous system responds first by releasing catecholamines (norepinephrine, epinephrine, and dopamine). This is the fight-or-flight response. The hypothalamic-pituitary-adrenal (HPA) axis responds with a chemical cascade: the hypothalamus releases corticotrophin releasing hormone (CRH), which causes the pituitary to release adrenocorticotropin hormone (ACTH), which causes the adrenal cortex to release cortisol, a glucocorticoid.

A third part of the process is the immune response. One way the immune system responds to threat is by increasing inflammation through the production of proinflammatory cytokines. Cytokines are proteins that regulate immune response. Proinflammatory cytokines increase inflammation and serve the adaptive purpose of helping the body heal wounds and fight infection. A key finding is that both physical and psychological stress can trigger the inflammatory response. In these studies, researchers generally measure markers of inflammation in the plasma, such as proinflammatory cytokines, C-reactive protein, or fibrinogen (Kendall-Tackett, 2010).

Inflammation has an important role to play in the development of disease. Over the past decade, researchers in the field of psychoneuro-immunology (PNI) have discovered that the etiology of common chronic diseases, such as heart disease, diabetes, MS, and Alzheimer's, are due to increased levels of systemic inflammation (Kiecolt-Glaser & Newton, 2007; Pace, Hu, & Miller, 2007; Robles, Glaser, & Kiecolt-Glaser, 2005). These findings have particular relevance to trauma survivors in that the human stress response activates inflammation.

Childhood maltreatment was shown to affect clinically relevant levels of C-reactive protein when measured 20 years later in abuse survivors (Danese, Pariante, Caspi, Taylor, & Poulton, 2007). The participants ($N = 1,037$) were part of the Dunedin Multidisciplinary Health and Development Study, a study of health behavior in a complete birth cohort in Dunedin, New Zealand. Participants were assessed every two to three years throughout childhood, and every five to six years through age 32. The effect of child maltreatment on inflammation was independent of co-occurring life stresses in adulthood, early life risks, or adult health or health behavior. Along these same lines, white blood cell count and fibrinogen were also elevated in those who experienced childhood physical or sexual abuse. Severity of abuse was related, in a dose-response way, to severity of inflammation.

Rape survivors had elevated stress hormones and inflammatory markers in another recent study (Groër, Thomas, Evans, Helton, & Weldon, 2006). In this study, 15 women who had been raped were compared with 16 women who had not. The rape survivors were assessed 24 to 72 hours after their assaults. The sexually assaulted women had higher levels of the stress hormone ACTH, and higher C-reactive protein and proinflammatory cytokines than women in the control group. In addition, the assaulted women had lower B lymphocyte counts and decreased lymphocyte proliferation. The researchers interpreted their findings as indicating that sexual assault activated innate immunity and suppressed some aspects of adaptive immunity. If these long-term alterations persist, they could lead to health problems in rape survivors.

SLEEP DISTURBANCES

Sleep disturbances are also physiological sequelae associated with past abuse. Although sleep disturbances are more likely in people with depression or PTSD, and can be regarded as simply manifestations of these conditions, sleep researchers working with trauma survivors noted that sleep exerts an independent effect on health and should be considered separately (Krakow et al., 2000; Roberts, Shema, Kaplan, & Strawbridge, 2000). In addition, sleep difficulties exacerbate the effects of depression and PTSD, and increase symptomatology (Krakow et al., 2000).

Although a relatively new area of study within abuse research, a number of studies have documented disturbed sleep patterns in women who have been sexually abused. For example, in a European community sample, 68% of sexual abuse survivors reported having sleep difficulties, with 45% having repetitive nightmares (Teegen, 1999). In a French sample, 33% of teens who had been raped indicated that they "slept badly" compared with 16% of the nonassaulted comparison group. Of the assaulted teens, 28% had nightmares (compared with 11%), and 56% woke during the night (compared with 21%; Choquet, Darves-Bornoz, Ledoux, Manfredi, & Hassler, 1997).

Hulme (2000) found that sleep problems among sexual abuse survivors were common in a primary-care sample. Fifty-two percent of sexual abuse survivors reported that they could not sleep at night (compared with 24% of the nonabused group), and 36% reported nightmares (compared with 13%). Intrusive symptoms were also common with 53% of sexual abuse survivors reporting sudden thoughts or images of past events (compared with 18% of the nonabused group).

In a study of sleep disorders in sexual assault survivors, 80% had either sleep-breathing or sleep-movement disorders. Both of these disorders were linked to higher levels of depression and suicidality, and women who had both types of sleep disorders had the most severe symptoms. The authors speculated that fragmented sleep potentiated the symptoms for women after a sexual assault, stretching their fragile coping abilities to the breaking point (Krakow et al., 2000).

Poor sleep quality has a profound effect on health. It compromises immune, metabolic, and neuroendocrine function, chronically activates the HPA axis, and even increases mortality risk (Carmichael & Reis, 2005). In a meta-analysis of 19 studies, Pilcher and Huffcutt (1996) found that sleep deprivation strongly impacts functioning in three broad categories: motor functioning, cognitive functioning, and mood, with the most severe effect being on mood. Indeed, sleep-deprived subjects reported moods that were three standard deviations lower than their non–sleep-deprived counterparts. Interestingly, partial sleep deprivation was more damaging than total sleep deprivation. People with chronically poor sleep also have more car accidents. And among people with chronic conditions, lack of sleep predicted greater functional disability and decreased quality of life.

Not surprisingly, people with poor sleep use more medical services than their non–sleep-deprived counterparts (Stepanski, Rybarczyk, Lopez, & Stevens, 2003).

HARMFUL BEHAVIOR

Childhood abuse also increases the risk of participation in harmful activities that include smoking, eating disorders, substance abuse, and unsafe sexual practices (Kendall-Tackett, 2003). The health impact of all of these behaviors is obvious and well-established. Perhaps the most common harmful behavior among sexual abuse survivors is high-risk sexual activity.

Several recent studies have found that high-risk sexual activity is substantially more common among sexual abuse survivors than their nonabused peers (Hulme, 2000; Kendall-Tackett, 2003; Raj, Silverman, & Amaro, 2000; Springs & Friedrich, 1992). Women who have been sexually abused often engage in consensual sexual activity at an earlier age, have more lifetime sexual partners, and are more likely to participate in high-risk sexual activity including not using condoms or contraceptives (Raj et al., 2000; Stock, Bell, Boyer, & Connell, 1997).

High-risk sexual activity increases the risk for unplanned pregnancies among teens (Raj et al., 2000; Springs & Friedrich, 1992) and adults (Prentice, Lu, Lange, & Halfon, 2002). In a nationally representative U.S. sample of mothers of children under age 3 ($N = 1,220$), women with a history of child sexual abuse were more likely to have both an unwanted pregnancy and late prenatal care (Prentice et al., 2002).

Although sexual abuse increases the risk of teen pregnancy, we cannot assume that all teen mothers have a history of abuse. A recent study of 252 pregnant teens from Montreal found that 79% had no reported history of sexual or physical abuse. However, 21% reported multiple forms of past abuse. Only sexual abuse was related to depression during pregnancy (Romano, Zoccolillo, & Paquette, 2006).

COGNITIVE BELIEFS

Physiological changes and harmful behaviors are obvious causes of health problems in abuse survivors. What may be less obvious is the link between health problems and what people think about themselves and others—their cognitions and beliefs. Cognitions, such as shame, low self-esteem and self-efficacy, all have deleterious effects on health. Hostility is another example of a negative cognition with a well-documented impact on health and it is common among abuse survivors.

For men and women with a hostile world view, life is not benign. As a psychological construct, hostility includes interpersonal mistrust, suspiciousness, cynicism about human nature, and a tendency to interpret the actions of others as aggressive (Smith, 1992). Several recent studies have found high rates of hostility among abuse survivors, a finding that is not surprising given their life experiences. In a sample from primary care, 52% of female sexual abuse survivors indicated that they could not trust others compared with 17% of the nonabused women (Hulme, 2000). Teegen (1999) found in her community sample that approximately half of the sexually abused women described their current views toward life, themselves and others as very negative.

Hostility is a reaction that may have been adaptive at one point in the survivor's life, and served to protect the survivor from further danger. However, as numerous studies in the general population have found, hostility can impair health. In the general population, trait hostility increases physiological arousal because of the way hostile people interpret the world. They are more likely to perceive even neutral events as negative, responding strongly because they perceive interpersonal threat (Kiecolt-Glaser & Newton, 2001).

Hostility has garnered a great deal of attention because of its link to cardiovascular disease, which is the leading cause of death in the United States for both men and women. In their review, Smith and Ruiz (2002) noted that people who are high in trait hostility are more prone to ischemia and constriction of the coronary arteries during mental stress. Trait hostility predicted new coronary events in previously healthy people. And for patients who already have coronary heart disease, hostility sped up the progression of the disease.

More recently, hostility was associated with higher levels of circulating the proinflammatory cytokines in 44 healthy, nonsmoking, premenopausal women. The combination of depression and hostility increased levels of proinflammatory cytokines (Suarez, Lewis, Krishnan, & Young, 2004). There was a dose-response effect: the more severe the depression and hostility, the greater the production of cytokines. A study with men had similar results (Suarez, 2003). The author noted that increased levels of proinflammatory cytokines predicted both future risk of cardiac events and all-cause mortality. He hypothesized that inflammation may mediate the relationship between hostility and these health problems.

Hostility also increases the risk of metabolic syndrome. In a three-year follow-up of 134 white and African American teens, hostility at Time 1 predicted risk factors for metabolic syndrome at Time 2 (Raikkonen, Matthews, & Salomon, 2003). These risk factors were at the 75th percentile for age, gender, and race and included BMI, insulin resistance, ratio of triglycerides to HDL cholesterol, and mean arterial blood pressure.

More recently, Suarez (2006) studied 135 healthy patients (75 men, 60 women), with no symptoms of diabetes. He found that women with higher levels of depression and hostility, and who had a propensity to express anger, had higher levels of fasting insulin, glucose, and insulin resistance. These findings were not true for men and they were independent of other risk factors for metabolic syndrome including BMI, age, fasting triglycerides, exercise regularity, or ethnicity. The author indicated that these findings were significant because prestudy glucose levels were in the nondiabetic range. The author noted that inflammation, particularly elevated IL-6 and C-reactive protein, may mediate the relationship between depression and hostility, and risk of type 2 diabetes and cardiovascular disease, possibly because they increase insulin resistance.

Hostility also has indirect effects on health by impacting the quality of relationships. Hostile persons can undermine relationships through their mistrustful thoughts and antagonistic actions, and are more likely to have negative social relations with others (Smith & Ruiz, 2002). Because of this, trait hostility has a serious impact on marriage and other important relationships. In their review, Kiecolt-Glaser and Newton (2001) noted that hostility assessed early in marriage predicted marital dissatisfaction several years later. And marital dissatisfaction can also have a negative impact on health. Their review revealed that high-stress marriages can slow wound healing, increase the risk of infectious disease, and even neutralize or lessen the effectiveness of vaccines (Kiecolt-Glaser & Newton, 2001). A 13-year longitudinal study of married women found that unsatisfying marriages increased cardiovascular risk over the study period (Gallo, Troxel, Matthews, & Kuller, 2003). Women with poor-quality marriages had higher rates of several markers for cardiovascular disease: low HDL cholesterol, high triglycerides, and higher BMI, blood pressure, depression and anger.

The effects of marital tension seem to be particularly pronounced for women, and as describe in the next section, abuse survivors are at increased risk of having high-strife relationships. In a study of a hospital sample from Sweden, Orth-Gomer and colleagues (2000) followed 292 women for five years after a myocardial infarction (MI). They found that women with high levels of marital strife were nearly three times more likely to have another heart attack or other coronary event as women who were married but not distressed. This relationship held even after adjusting for age, estrogen levels, education, and smoking.

In another recent study, Kiecolt-Glaser and colleagues (2005) found that couples who exhibited high levels of hostility had higher levels of circulating proinflammatory cytokines, and their rate of wound healing was 60% slower than couples low in hostility. In the high-hostility couples, there were fewer cytokines at the wound site, where they were supposed to be, and high levels circulating systemically, where they were more likely to damage vasculature and increase the risk of age-related diseases.

These studies on the health effects of hostility and marital strife in the general population provide insight into some of the mechanisms by which previous abuse can impair adult health. As abuse survivors are at higher risk for both a hostile worldview and high-strife relationships, these factors need to also be addressed when designing interventions in improve their health or prevent health problems.

SOCIAL RELATIONSHIPS

As described earlier, abuse survivors have higher rates of unstable relationships, divorce, and revictimization at the hands of intimate partners. Marital strife, for example, increases the risk of heart disease in women. But positive and supportive relationships buffer stress and even increase longevity. In short, our social relationships can either enhance health or make it substantially worse. Further, abuse survivors often have troubled relationships.

Women who have experienced childhood sexual abuse can have difficult relationships with their partners. In a longitudinal study from Avon, United Kingdom ($N = 8,292$; Roberts, O'Connor, Dunn, Golding, & the ALSPAC Study Team, 2004), women who had been sexually abused were more likely than nonabused women to be single parents, cohabitating in their current relationships, or step-parents. They also reported less satisfaction with their current partners. Although the study authors are not explicit about this, it seems reasonable to hypothesize that women who report low satisfaction in their relationships do not consider these relationships to be good sources of support. And lack of partner support puts them at risk for both depression and health problems.

Hammen and Brennan (2002) sought to explore the relationship between depression and relationship quality in a sample of 812 community women. This is an important issue to consider for abuse survivors because depression is a common sequelae of child sexual abuse (see next section). The women in this study were divided into three groups: formerly depressed, currently depressed, and never depressed. Data were collected from spouses, adolescent children, and independent raters.

Hammen and Brennan's findings demonstrated that interpersonal difficulties were not simply consequences of depressive symptoms. Women who were not currently depressed, but formerly had been, were more impaired on every measure of interpersonal behavior and beliefs than women who were never depressed. The formerly depressed women's marriages were less stable, and they had lower levels of marital satisfaction. There was more spousal coercion and injury. The formerly depressed women had more problems in their relationships with their children, friends, and extended families, and they experienced more stressful life events. Finally, they were more insecure in their beliefs about others. The authors concluded that interpersonal difficulties were a stable component of depression, and that these difficulties were not only difficult to treat, but may make sufferers more vulnerable to future episodes of depression (Hammen & Brennan, 2002).

Lack of support not only increases the risk for depression; it also causes health problems. In a review, Salovey, Rothman, Detweiler, and Steward (2000) noted that social support is related to lower mortality and greater resistance to communicable diseases. Among people with good support, there is a lower prevalence of coronary heart disease, and they recover faster following surgery. When faced with stress, those with few social resources are more vulnerable to illness and mood disorders than are people with good support.

A study of high-risk teens admitted to a psychiatric hospital indicated that social support was an effective buffer in some circumstances. The teens in this study had experienced or witnessed high levels of violence in both their families and communities. Social support shielded these teens from some of the effects of family violence (Muller, Goebel-Fabbri, Diamond, & Dinklage, 2000).

The health effects of social support appear to be especially important for people with lower incomes. Low-income individuals with social support had better cardiovascular health and immune function than low-income people without support. These findings did not occur for those with higher incomes (Vitaliano et al., 2001).

EMOTIONAL HEALTH

Depression, anxiety, and PTSD are among the most common responses to childhood sexual abuse. For many years, researchers assumed that mental health was not related to physical health. We have since learned that that assumption was wrong. Stress, depression, and PTSD all also increase the risk of health problems. Of all the psychological sequelae of past abuse, depression has the most well-documented impact on health.

Depression is a common sequelae of abuse and violence (Campbell & Kendall-Tackett, 2005; Kendall-Tackett, 2003). In the Commonwealth Fund Adolescent Health Survey, physically and sexually abused girls were

5 times more likely to report depressive symptoms (Diaz, Simatov, & Rickert, 2000). In a primary-care sample, 65% of sexually abused women reported feeling blue or depressed compared with 35% of nonabused women (Hulme, 2000). In a study of chronic pain in primary-care patients, women with a history of child or domestic abuse were significantly more likely to be depressed than a matched group of nonabused women (Kendall-Tackett, Marshall, & Ness, 2003).

Unfortunately, depression can lead to poor health in abuse survivors. In the family violence field, we tend to view depression as an outcome—an endpoint we measure in abuse survivors in the wake of traumatic events. However, researchers have now documented that depression also often leads to poor health (Frasure-Smith & Lesperance, 2005).

A number of health problems have been associated with depression including coronary heart disease, myocardial infarction, chronic pain syndromes, premature aging, impaired immune function, impaired wound healing, and even Alzheimer's disease (Kiecolt-Glaser & Glaser, 2002; Kiecolt-Glaser et al., 2005; Simopoulos, 2002; Wilson, Finch, & Cohen, 2002). Of particular interest is the link between depression and cardiovascular disease. Depression is a risk factor for cardiovascular disease (Frasure-Smith & Lesperance, 2005). Patients who become depressed after a myocardial infarction (MI) are two to three times more likely to have another one and are three to four times more likely to die (deJong et al., 2006; Lesperance & Frasure-Smith, 2000). The risk was not only for those suffering from major depression, but for milder forms as well.

Kop and Gottdiener (2005) hypothesized that depression in early adulthood may actually promote vascular injury, and that the immune system may increase further early-stage cardiovascular disease by encouraging lipid and macrophage deposits. For people with preexisting cardiovascular disease, the chronic inflammation associated with depression can reduce the stability of plaque, which can lead to acute cardiac episodes.

Childhood abuse can also increase depression risk during the postpartum period. A study of 200 Canadian women at 8 to 10 weeks postpartum found that women with a history of abuse are more likely to experience both depression and physical health symptoms in the postpartum period (Ansara et al., 2005). A three-year follow-up of 45 Australian mothers with postpartum major depressive disorder found that half had a history of child sexual abuse. The sexually abused women had significantly higher depression and anxiety scores and greater life stresses compared to the nonabused depressed women. Moreover, the sexually abused women had less improvement in their symptoms over time (Buist & Janson, 2001).

In another sample of 53 low-income single mothers, childhood physical or sexual abuse and low self-esteem predicted depressive symptoms, and these symptoms influenced women's reactions to their babies (Lutenbacher, 2002). Everyday stressors, when combined with depression, predicted higher levels of anger in the mothers. But current partner abuse was the best predictor of the mothers' overall abusive parenting attitudes (measured by the Adult-Adolescent Parenting Inventory), and more parent-child role reversal.

CONCLUSIONS

Research over the past decade has dramatically increased our ability to explain why we observe higher rates of disease and disability in abuse survivors. But this picture is far from hopeless. As we recognize the complexity of the forces that are related to the health problems in abuse survivors, we must strive for an approach that addresses all five of these pathways. Health outcomes are unlikely to improve if we continue in our current mind-set of treating mental health and physical health sequelae separately. Survivors of childhood sexual abuse have high rates of depression, anxiety disorders and PTSD. They have higher rates of high-risk behaviors, sleep problems, and hostility than their nonabused counterparts. Only by recognizing and addressing all these underlying factors can we hope to improve the health of adult survivors of CSA. And as men and women understand more about why they are affected, they can address the factors that impair their health—an important part of reclaiming their lives.

REFERENCES

Ali, A., Toner, B. B., Stuckless, N., Gallop, R., Diaman, N. E., Gould, M. I., & Vidins, E. I. (2000). Emotional abuse, self-blame, and self-silencing in women with irritable bowel syndrome. *Psychosomatic Medicine, 62*, 76–82.

American Gastroenterological Association. (1997). American gastroenterological association medical position statement: Irritable bowel syndrome. *Gastroenterology, 112*, 2118–2119.

Ansara, D., Cohen, M. M., Gallop, R., Kung, R., Kung, R., & Schei, B. (2005). Predictors of women's physical health problems after childbirth. *Journal of Psychosomatic Obstetrics & Gynecology, 26*, 115–125.

Batten, S. V., Aslan, M., Maciejewski, P. K., & Mazure, C. M. (2004). Childhood maltreatment as a risk factor for adult cardiovascular disease and depression. *Journal of Clinical Psychiatry, 65*, 249–254.

Boisset-Pioro, M. H., Esdaile, J. M., & Fitzcharles, M. A. (1995). Sexual and physical abuse in women with fibromyalgia syndrome. *Arthritis and Rheumatism, 38*, 235–241.

Bremner, J. D. (2005). The neurobiology of childhood sexual abuse in women with post-traumatic stress disorder. In K. A. Kendall-Tackett (Ed.), *The handbook of women, stress and trauma* (pp. 181–206). New York, NY: Taylor & Francis.

Buist, A., & Janson, H. (2001). Childhood sexual abuse, parenting, and postpartum depression: A 3-year follow-up study. *Child Abuse & Neglect, 25,* 909–921.

Campbell, J. C., & Kendall-Tackett, K. A. (2005). Intimate partner violence: Implications for women's physical and mental health. In K. A. Kendall-Tackett (Ed.), *Handbook of women, stress and trauma* (pp. 123–140). New York, NY: Taylor & Francis.

Carmichael, C. L., & Reis, H. T. (2005). Attachment, sleep quality, and depressed affect. *Health Psychology, 24,* 526–531.

Choquet, M., Darves-Bornoz, J-M., Ledoux, S., Manfredi, R., & Hassler, C. (1997). Self-reported health and behavioral problems among adolescent victims of rape in France: Results of a cross-sectional survey. *Child Abuse & Neglect, 21,* 823–832.

Crofford, L. J. (2007). Violence, stress, and somatic syndromes. *Trauma, Violence, & Abuse, 8,* 299–313.

Danese, A., Pariante, C. M., Caspi, A., Taylor, A., & Poulton, R. (2007). Childhood maltreatment predicts adult inflammation in a life-course study. *Proceedings of the National Academy of Sciences USA, 104*(4), 1319–1324.

deJong, P., Ormel, J., van den Brink, R. H. S., van Melle, J. P., Spijkerman, T. A., Kuijper, A., . . . Schene, A.H. (2006). Symptom dimensions of depression following myocardial infarction and their relationship with somatic health status and cardiovascular prognosis. *American Journal of Psychiatry, 163,* 138–144.

Diaz, A., Simatov, E., & Rickert, V. I. (2000). The independent and combined effects of physical and sexual abuse on health. Results of a national survey. *Journal of Pediatric & Adolescent Gynecology, 13,* 89.

Drossman, D. A., Leserman, J., Li, Z., Keefe, F., Hu, Y. J. B., & Toomey, T. C. (2000). Effects of coping on health outcome among women with gastrointestinal disorders. *Psychosomatic Medicine, 62,* 309–317.

Drossman, D. A., Li, Z., Leserman, J., Toomey, T. C., & Hu, Y. J. B. (1996). Health status by gastrointestinal diagnosis and abuse history. *Gastroenterology, 110,* 999–1007.

Felitti, V. J. (1991). Long-term medical consequences of incest, rape, and molestation. *Southern Medical Journal, 84,* 328–331.

Felitti, V. J., Anda, R. F., Nordenberg, D., Williamson, D. F., Spitz, A. M., Edwards, V., Koss, M. P., & Marks, J. S. (2001). Relationship of childhood abuse and household dysfunction to many of the leading causes of death in adults. In K. Franey, R. Geffner, & R. Falconer (Eds.), *The cost of child maltreatment: Who pays? We all do* (pp. 53–69). San Diego, CA: Family Violence and Sexual Assault Institute.

Frasure-Smith, N., & Lesperance, F. (2005). Reflections on depression as a cardiac risk factor. *Psychosomatic Medicine, 67,* S19–S25.

Gallo, L. C., Troxel, W. M., Matthews, K. A., & Kuller, L. H. (2003). Marital status and quality in middle-aged women: Associations with levels and trajectories of cardiovascular risk factors. *Health Psychology, 22,* 453–463.

Groër, M. W., Thomas, S. P., Evans, G. W., Helton, S., & Weldon, A. (2006). Inflammatory effects and immune system correlates of rape. *Violence and Victims, 21*(6), 796–808.

Hammen, C., & Brennan, P. (2002). Interpersonal dysfunction in depressed women: Impairments independent of depressive symptoms. *Journal of Affective Disorders, 72*, 145–156.

Hulme, P. A. (2000). Symptomatology and health care utilization of women primary care patients who experienced childhood sexual abuse. *Child Abuse & Neglect, 24*, 1471–1484.

Kendall-Tackett, K. A. (2003). *Treating the lifetime health effects of childhood victimization.* Kingston, NJ: Civic Research Institute.

Kendall-Tackett, K. A. (2010). (Ed.). *The psychoneuroimmunology of chronic disease.* Washington, DC: American Psychological Association.

Kendall-Tackett, K. A., Marshall, R., & Ness, K. E. (2000). Victimization, healthcare use, and health maintenance. *Family Violence & Sexual Assault Bulletin, 16*, 18–21.

Kendall-Tackett, K. A., Marshall, R., & Ness, K. E. (2003). Chronic pain syndromes and violence against women. *Women & Therapy, 26*, 45–56.

Kiecolt-Glaser, J. K., Belury, M. A., Porter, K., Beversdoft, D., Lemeshow, S., & Glaser, R. (2007). Depressive symptoms, omega-6: omega-3 fatty acids, and inflammation in older adults. *Psychosomatic Medicine, 69*, 217–224.

Kiecolt-Glaser, J. K., & Glaser, R. (2002). Depression and immune function: Central pathways to morbidity and mortality. *Journal of Psychosomatic Research, 53*, 873–876.

Kiecolt-Glaser, J. K., Loving, T. J., Stowell, J. R., Malarky, W. B., Lemeshow, S., Dickinson, S. L., & Glaser, R. (2005). Hostile marital interactions, proinflammatory cytokine production, and wound healing. *Archives of General Psychiatry, 62*, 1377–1384.

Kiecolt-Glaser, J. K., & Newton, T. L. (2001). Marriage and health: His and hers. *Psychological Bulletin, 127*, 472–503.

Kop, W. J., & Gottdiener, J. S. (2005). The role of immune system parameters in the relationship between depression and coronary artery disease. *Psychosomatic Medicine, 67*, S37–S41.

Koss, M. P., Koss, P. G., & Woodruff, M. S. (1991). Deleterious effects of criminal victimization on women's health and medical utilization. *Archives of Internal Medicine, 151*, 342–347.

Krakow, B., Artar, A., Warner, T. D., Melendez, D., Johnston, L., Hollifield, M., . . . Koss, M. (2000). Sleep disorder, depression, and suicidality in female sexual assault survivors. *Crisis, 21*, 163–170.

Leserman, J., & Drossman, D. (2007). Relationship of abuse history to functional gastrointestinal disorders and symptoms: Some possible mediating mechanisms. *Trauma, Violence, & Abuse, 8*, 331–343.

Leserman, J., Drossman, D. A., Li, Z., Toomey, T. C., Nachman, G., & Glogau, L. (1996). Sexual and physical abuse history in gastroenterology practice: How types of abuse impact health status. *Psychosomatic Medicine, 58*, 4–15.

Lesperance, F., & Frasure-Smith, N. (2000). Depression in patients with cardiac disease: A practical review. *Journal of Psychosomatic Research, 48*, 379–391.

Lutenbacher, M. (2002). Relationships between psychosocial factors and abusive parenting attitudes in low-income single mothers. *Nursing Research, 51,* 158–167.

McBeth, J., MacFarlane, G. J., Benjamin, S., Morris, S., & Silman, A. J. (1999). The association between tender points, psychological distress, and adverse childhood experiences: A community-based sample. *Arthritis and Rheumatism, 42,* 1397–1404.

Muller, R. T., Goebel-Fabbri, A. E., Diamond, T., & Dinklage, D. (2000). Social support and the relationship between family and community violence exposure and psychopathology among high risk adolescents. *Child Abuse & Neglect, 24,* 449–464.

Orth-Gomer, K., Wamala, S. P., Horsten, M., Schenk-Gustafsson, K., Schneiderman, N., & Mittleman, M. A. (2000). Marital stress worsens prognosis in women with coronary heart disease: The Stockholm female coronary risk study. *Journal of the American Medical Association, 284,* 3008–3014.

Pace, T. W., Hu, F., & Miller, A. H. (2007). Cytokine-effects on glucocorticoid receptor function: relevance to glucocorticoid resistance and the pathophysiology and treatment of major depression. *Brain, Behavior and Immunity, 21*(1), 9–19.

Pilcher, J. J., & Huffcutt, A. I. (1996). Effects of sleep deprivation on performance: A meta-analysis. *Sleep, 19,* 318–326.

Prentice, J. C., Lu, M. C., Lange, L., & Halfon, N. (2002). The association between reported childhood sexual abuse and breastfeeding initiation. *Journal of Human Lactation, 18,* 219–226.

Raikkonen, K., Matthews, K. A., & Salomon, K. (2003). Hostility predicts metabolic syndrome risk factors in children and adolescents. *Health Psychology, 22,* 279–286.

Raj, A., Silverman, J. G., & Amaro, H. (2000). The relationship between sexual abuse and sexual risk among high school students: Findings from the 1997 Massachusetts youth risk behavior survey. *Maternal and Child Health Journal, 4,* 125–134.

Roberts, R., O'Connor, T., Dunn, J., Golding, J., & the ALSPAC Study Team. (2004). The effects of child sexual abuse in later family life: Mental health, parenting and adjustment of offspring. *Child Abuse & Neglect, 28,* 525–545.

Roberts, R. E., Shema, S. J., Kaplan, G. A., & Strawbridge, W. J. (2000). Sleep complaints and depression in an aging cohort: A prospective perspective. *American Journal of Psychiatry, 157,* 81–88.

Robles, T. F., Glaser, R., & Kiecolt-Glaser, J. K. (2005). Out of balance: A new look at chronic stress, depression, and immunity. *Current Directions in Psychological Science, 14,* 111–115.

Romano, E., Zoccolillo, M., & Paquette, D. (2006). Histories of child maltreatment and psychiatric disorder in pregnant adolescents. *Journal of the American Academy of Child & Adolescent Psychiatry, 45,* 329–336.

Sachs-Ericsson, N., Kendall-Tackett, K., & Hernandez, A. (2007). Childhood abuse, chronic pain, and depression in the national comorbidity study. *Child Abuse & Neglect, 31,* 531–547.

Salovey, P., Rothman, A. J., Detweiler, J. B., & Steward, W. T. (2000). Emotional states and physical health. *American Psychologist, 55,* 110–121.

Sareen, J., Cox, B. J., Stein, M. B., Afifi, T. O., Fleet, C., & Asmundson, G. J. (2007). Physical and mental comorbidity, disability, and suicidal behavior associated with posttraumatic stress disorder in a large community sample. *Psychosomatic Medicine, 69*(3), 242–248.

Simopoulos, A. P. (2002). Omega-3 fatty acids in inflammation and autoimmune diseases. *Journal of the American College of Nutrition, 21,* 495–505.

Smith, T. W. (1992). Hostility and health: Current status of a psychosomatic hypothesis. *Health Psychology, 11,* 139–150.

Smith, T. W., & Ruiz, J. M. (2002). Psychosocial influences on the development and course of coronary heart disease: Current status and implications for research and practice. *Journal of Consulting and Clinical Psychology, 70,* 548–568.

Springs, F. E., & Friedrich, W. N. (1992). Health risk behaviors and medical sequelae of childhood sexual abuse. *Mayo Clinic Proceedings, 67,* 527–532.

Stepanski, E. J., Rybarczyk, B., Lopez, M., & Stevens, S. (2003). Assessment and treatment of sleep disorders in older adults: A review for rehabilitation psychologists. *Rehabilitation Psychology, 48,* 23–36.

Stock, J. L., Bell, M. A., Boyer, D. K., & Connell, F. A. (1997). Adolescent pregnancy and sexual risk-taking among sexually abused girls. *Family Planning Perspective, 29,* 200–203, 227.

Suarez, E. C. (2003). Joint effect of hostility and severity of depressive symptoms on plasma interleukin-6 concentration. *Psychosomatic Medicine, 65,* 523–527.

Suarez, E. C. (2006). Sex differences in the relation of depressive symptoms, hostility, and anger expression to indices of glucose metabolism in nondiabetic adults. *Health Psychology, 25,* 484–492.

Suarez, E. C., Lewis, J. G., Krishnan, R. R., & Young, K. H. (2004). Enhanced expression of cytokines and chemokines by blood monocytes to in vitro lipopolysaccharide stimulation are associated with hostility and severity of depressive symptoms in healthy women. *Psychoneuroendocrinology, 29,* 1119–1128.

Subramani, K., & Janowitz, H. D. (1991). The irritable bowel syndrome: A continuing dilemma. *Gastroenterology Clinics of North America, 20,* 363–367.

Taylor, M. L., Trotter, D. R., & Csuka, M. E. (1995). The prevalence of sexual abuse in women with fibromyalgia. *Arthritis & Rheumatism, 38,* 229–234.

Teegen, F. (1999). Childhood sexual abuse and long-term sequelae. In A. Maercker, M. Schutzwohl, & Z. Solomon (Eds.), *Posttraumatic stress disorder: A lifespan developmental perspective* (pp. 97–112). Seattle, WA: Hogrefe & Huber.

Van Houdenhove, B., Luyten, P., & Van den Eede, F. (2008). Early-life stress in chronic pain and fatigue syndrome: Prevalence, consequences, and etiopathogenetic pathways. *Family & Intimate Partner Violence Quarterly, 1*(2), 101–114.

Vitaliano, P. P., Scanlan, J. M., Zhang, J., Savage, M., Brummett, B., Barefoot, J., & Siegler, I. C. (2001). Are the salutogenic effects of social supports modified by income? A test of an "added value hypothesis." *Health Psychology, 20,* 155–165.

Walker, E., Katon, W., Roy-Byrne, P., Jemelka, R., & Russo, J. (1993). Histories of sexual victimization in patients with irritable bowel syndrome or inflammatory bowel disease. *American Journal of Psychiatry, 150,* 1502–1506.

Wilson, C. J., Finch, C. E., & Cohen, H. J. (2002). Cytokines and cognition—The case for a head-to-toe inflammatory paradigm. *Journal of the American Geriatrics Society, 50,* 2041–2056.

SECTION II

ASSESSMENT

CHAPTER 4

Navigating the System

The Complexities of the Multidisciplinary Team in Cases of Child Sexual Abuse

PATTI VAN EYS and BONNIE BENEKE

INTRODUCTION

C HILD SEXUAL ABUSE (CSA) is a physical and emotional violation that impacts the individual, family, and society. And it is a crime. A continual challenge facing helping professionals is to find the balance between promoting internal healing in those affected by CSA and helping clients navigate the confusing external world they face on disclosure of this violation. This challenge is made especially complex and profound when the number and variety of professionals involved in CSA cases become a source of confusion and frustration. In order for professionals to maintain a clear vision of their own roles in the drama of CSA, it is critical to understand the roles of each member of the system.

THE EMERGENCE OF MULTIDISCIPLINARY TEAMS

The 1980s brought a dramatic increase in acknowledgment of CSA and a growing awareness that child protective services (CPS), law enforcement, and the criminal justice system were not working together in response efforts. As a result, children were being repeatedly interviewed; there was no mechanism in place for coordination of services. It is now well accepted that the best response to the challenges of CSA investigations is the formation of a multidisciplinary team (MDT) of professionals. Many states include statutory mandates for an MDT approach to CSA investigations (Kolbo & Strong, 1997). The MDT approach brings together professionals and agencies needed to offer comprehensive services for CSA response: law enforcement, child protective services, prosecution, mental health, victim advocacy, and the medical community. Each agency remains responsible for fulfilling its own role while learning to understand others' roles and responsibilities.

Child Advocacy Centers In 1985, former Congressman Robert "Bud" Cramer from Alabama organized an effort to create an improved response to investigations of CSA. In his then role as District Attorney, he wanted a better way to help young victims of sexual abuse. Through Cramer's vision, the National Children's Advocacy Center (NCAC) in Huntsville, Alabama, was established (1985) and earned a national reputation providing training, technical assistance, and ultimately becoming a resource center supporting child abuse professionals.

The NCAC became the model for Children's Advocacy Centers (CACs) and supported other communities in CAC development. CACs are child-focused, facility-based programs in which representatives from many disciplines work together on MDTs to conduct interviews and make team decisions regarding cases of child abuse. CAC models for child abuse intervention are proven and effective, bringing together trained professionals to investigate and provide medical and mental health care as well as support to child victims of abuse, while holding offenders accountable through the court system. CAC locations are child-focused and designed to create a sense of safety and security for child victims and their supportive caregivers.

The primary goal of CACs is to ensure that children disclosing abuse are not further victimized by the system designed to protect them and a second goal is to facilitate and to support the child's healing process. Communities with a CAC experience many benefits: rapid response to reports of child sexual abuse, improved coordination, reduction in the number of child interviews, more efficient medical and mental health referrals, more offender prosecutions, and reduction of child and family stress (Walsh, Jones, & Cross, 2003). To date, there are more than 700 accredited CACs across the country. In 2009, CACs served more than 254,000 child victims of abuse (National Children's Alliance, 2010).

In 1987 the National Children's Alliance (NCA) was formed and created standards and an accreditation process for CACs to ensure quality service provision for abused children. The NCA accreditation process follows 10 standards that ensure effective, efficient, and

consistent delivery of services. Services generally include multidisciplinary response to investigations, forensic interviewing, forensic medical
evaluations, victim advocacy, specialized mental health services, and
community education and outreach.

REPORTING PRACTICES

Another outgrowth of the growing awareness of child sexual abuse
was the further utilization and enforcement of the federal law that
mandated the reporting of knowledge or suspicion of child sexual abuse.
All 50 states have passed a mandatory child abuse and neglect reporting
law in order to qualify for funding under the Child Abuse Prevention
and Treatment Act (CAPTA; January 1996 version). The Act was originally passed in 1974, has been amended several times and was most
recently amended and reauthorized on June 25, 2003, by the Keeping
Children and Families Safe Act of 2003 (P.L.108-36). The following
section details the issue of mandated reporting.

MANDATED REPORTING

Professionals do the bulk of reporting. In 2008 more than half of the reports
(57.9%) were made by professionals (teachers, law enforcement, doctors,
nurses, social services staff). Remaining reports were nonprofessionals
such as friends, neighbors, and relatives. Child sexual abuse accounted
for 9.1% of these reports and of all the reports, 80.1% were maltreated by a
caregiver (Myers, 2011). A report is triggered by suspicion, not certainty,
and is required when a professional has information that would lead a
competent professional to believe maltreatment is likely. Not only is
reporting suspected abuse the law, a new report may bolster previous
reports on a particular suspect, resulting in protective efforts not only for
the alleged victim, but also other children. This additional reason may help
child clients feel better about a therapist's report. Reporting suspected
abuse supersedes confidentiality, but does not fully abrogate it. Only
information required by the reporting law is necessary; other sensitive
clinical information is not reported. Typically, the child's demographics,
contact information, and the nature of the abuse suspicions are required.
The reporter should give as much detail about why abuse is suspected as
possible so that the report will not simply be screened out. Many reports
are not investigated due to the weakness of the report. Thus, when
reporting, the circumstances of how the child disclosed, what the child
reported, and other reasons for suspected abuse (e.g., you see bruises, the
child does not want to go home from the office due to fear, the child played

out a highly sexualized scene in her play therapy session, the caregiver reported behaviors consistent with sexual abuse such as sexual behaviors or sexual knowledge beyond the child's age).

Liability for intentional failure to report is a crime. Each state has its own consequences for intentional failure to report suspected child abuse; for example, Tennessee imposes fines and/or jail time. In addition, if suspected abuse is not reported and the child is further harmed or killed, the professional can be sued for malpractice as precedented in *Landeros v. Flood*, 1976 (Myers, 2011). A number of states include laws specifically giving authorization for lawsuits against professionals who willfully fail to report.

THE SYSTEM PLAYERS: COMMENTS FROM THE FIELD

The segments below were written by professionals currently working within the roles they describe. Following these descriptions is a flow chart depicting the child welfare system process (Figure 4.1).

Child Protective Services (CPS) Comments From Mindy Guy and Mary Levinson-Marinelli, CPS, Nashville, Tennessee

Once a report has been made, it is the function of CPS to investigate allegations of child abuse and to assess the safety of children and the needs of at-risk families in order to link children and families with appropriate services. A CPS investigation begins with a referral from professionals or private citizens. The law protects the identity of the referent to remain confidential.

When a referral is made, CPS supervisory staff determines whether the report necessitates further involvement of CPS. CPS staff relies on CPS policy and a structural decision-making tool in order to make determinations regarding the assignment of a referral. If a report does not meet the criteria for an investigation, the report can be "screened out" by a supervisor. If screened in, the supervisor decides the appropriate response priority. There are two tracks within CPS in Tennessee that address reports of child abuse and neglect. The CPS *Assessment Track* assesses allegations pertaining to minor physical abuse and child neglect. It is the role of the assessment worker to engage the family in order to determine if services are needed. The CPS *Investigative Track* investigates allegations of severe
(continued)

abuse, which include sexual abuse and exploitation, severe physical abuse and child fatalities. In some states, a separate division of CPS may be responsible for referrals alleging child abuse and neglect that pertain to day cares, schools, facilities, and churches, where the alleged perpetrator's employment is affected by the allegations. In Tennessee, the separate division of CPS also addresses allegations of abuse and neglect pertaining to children in state custody.

In cases of severe abuse it is the responsibility of the CPS investigator to collaborate with other members of the Child Protective Investigative Team (CPIT)[1] who must work together when addressing issues of severe abuse. It is the role of the CPS investigator to collaborate with law enforcement in order to obtain evidence regarding the allegation of abuse. Initially, caregiver(s) are interviewed by the CPS investigator and the process of the continuing investigation is explained. A CPS investigator often utilizes the services of the Child Advocacy Center, so that an alleged victim of severe abuse (primarily sexual abuse) can be interviewed by a forensic interviewer. If a child makes a disclosure of sexual abuse, it is the responsibility of the CPS investigator to refer the child for a medical examination. A CPS investigator must also interview possible witnesses or professionals involved with the family. Ideally the CPS investigator and the assigned detective jointly interview the alleged perpetrator, allowing for a more thorough investigation through shared information. Once an investigation has been completed, the case is presented to the entire CPIT. Here, it is determined if an allegation of severe abuse is indicated, and if criminal charges should be pursued.

Through CPS risk assessment, services may be provided to the family so continuity of placement remains intact. If a child is deemed to be at imminent risk of harm, the CPS investigator consults a CPS supervisor and a child welfare attorney, so that appropriate action can be taken. If a child is placed out of the custodial parent's home as a result of being at imminent risk of harm, child placement services become involved through public child welfare.

All members of the CPIT are bound by rules of confidentiality, which prohibit team members from divulging information to anyone outside the team. Therapists can often gain access to records following a completed investigation and are advised to be in close contact

(continued)

---

1. CPIT is the equivalent of MDT in the state of Tennessee.

(*continued*)
with their MDT members. Outside professionals are also expected to keep CPS information confidential. For example, if a CPS investigator contacts an outside therapist, and the discussion includes concerns about the family, that therapist is prohibited from divulging to the family concerns expressed by the investigator because divulging the information could pose risk to the child.

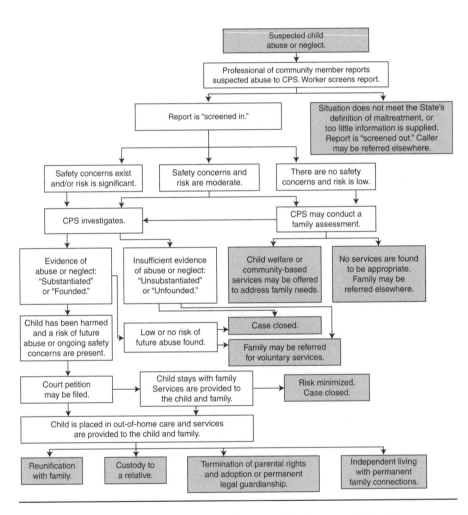

Figure 4.1 Child Welfare Information Gateway 2010   www.childwelfare.gov

Law Enforcement Comments of Captain David Imoff, Metropolitan Nashville Police Department, Sex Crimes Unit

This component of the MDT has a number of duties including:

- Responding to calls in an appropriate manner (that is, one commensurate with urgency of the call), stabilizes the scene, and takes initial statements as appropriate.
- Performs criminal history record checks on alleged offenders.
- Collects and preserves physical evidence.
- Interviews child victims or witnesses consistent with the team's decision/protocol.
- Conducts photo lineups or live lineups to confirm the identifications of perpetrators if necessary.
- Interviews adult witnesses in cooperation with CPS.
- Facilitates the use of technological investigative tools such as monitors telephone conversations.
- Interviews the alleged perpetrators.
- Takes suspect into custody when and if appropriate.
- Presents criminal cases in lawsuits to obtain warrants to grand juries; at preliminary hearings; in criminal court.
- Testifies in juvenile or family court, if necessary, to ensure the child's protection.
- Takes child into protective custody if CPS assesses that the risks require removal. (Pence & Wilson, 1994)

The role of law enforcement in the Child Protective Investigative Team (CPIT)[2] is to investigate all criminal allegations of child sexual abuse. It is important that law enforcement fully conveys their role within the team, that other team members understand what that role is and why it is significant. It is not enough for law enforcement to know what occurred or to believe the victim. Law enforcement must satisfy several requirements to successfully prosecute a case, including initially determining whether a crime did in fact occur, and then establishing where the offense took place in order to determine venue, which establishes jurisdiction. When those two questions
(continued)

---

2. CPIT is the equivalent of MDT in the state of Tennessee.

(continued)

have been answered, law enforcement must determine who committed the offense and obtain enough evidence to sustain a conviction.

The level of proof required to arrest any suspect of any crime is *probable cause*. Probable cause is a set of articulable facts that would lead a reasonable person to believe that the offense was committed, and that the person being arrested is responsible. The level of proof needed to convict someone of a criminal offense is *"beyond a reasonable doubt."* It can lessen frustration of team members, family members and others associated with the system (therapists, social workers, etc.) when they understand the standards of proof that law enforcement must satisfy.

It is incumbent upon law enforcement to have open and honest dialogue with the victim(s) and their families. All parties must know who is involved in the system, understand their respective roles, and know what to expect during the course of an investigation. Often families do not realize the amount of time involved from initial disclosure to final adjudication. This process can take anywhere from one to two years depending on the circumstances of each case. There are complicating factors within the legal system, including the sheer number of cases, the defendant's legal response to inquiries, such as attorneys' requests for discovery and possible challenge of evidence. Such factors cause inevitable delays.

Most victims and their families will not have experienced this level of criminal victimization and they are typically traumatized, confused, angry and hurt from the time of the assault forward. Our hope is to aid victims and their supportive caregivers in their journey through the system, fully describing to bewildered and hurt families "the long road ahead."

Forensic Interviewer Comments From Emily Cecil, MSSW, Training Coordinator, Tennessee Chapter of Children's Advocacy Centers and Trudy Hughes, Executive Director, New Hope-Blount County CAC, Maryville, Tennessee

Forensic interviewers (FI) aid the MDT in the investigative process by providing a developmentally appropriate, legally defensible, neutral, *(continued)* fact-finding interview of the child(ren) involved in an allegation. FIs must consider the various needs of CPS, law enforcement, and prosecution while keeping the child as first priority.

Forensic interviewing is a relatively new profession, evolving from investigative interviewing and empirical research of only the last 25 years and only recently benefiting from universally accepted guidelines (American Professional Society on the Abuse of Children [APSAC], 2002). Forensic interviewing has seen rapid expansion that has prompted a number of new research based protocols.

The NCA standards state that forensic interviews may be provided by law enforcement officers, child protective services personnel, or a specialized forensic interviewer. Documentation of 40 hours of nationally or state-recognized forensic interview training including child development is required as is regular peer review and ongoing training (National Children's Alliance Standards for Accredited Members; revised 2008 and effective January 1, 2010).

Upon referral for a forensic interview, typically from law enforcement or CPS, contact with core members of the MDT is made. After information regarding the child and nature of the allegations are discussed, an interview is scheduled as close to the alleged incident as possible. Immediately before the interview, the forensic interviewers meet with the core members of the MDT to obtain necessary details of the case. While the interview is being conducted, law enforcement, CPS and other approved MDT members watch from a closed-circuit television. The interviewer consults with these professionals before they conclude the interview. If the interview was recorded, law enforcement or child protective services are given the DVD and the FI documents the interview according to local protocols. This information is confidential and should be treated like other protected health information.

Many times mental health professionals feel as though they have important information to communicate before the interview and/or there is important information they want communicated to them after the interview takes place. Filtering information given to the FI and supporting the neutral environment is crucial. Therapists must consider: "What information do I have that will maximize the FI's ability to effectively and accurately communicate with this child?" rather than asking, "What information do I have that will assist the FI in obtaining a disclosure?" Information that assists in effective communication may include facts about the child's mental health, developmental skills, and

(continued)

(*continued*)
ability to communicate. Information that is not useful may include statements from caregivers and other individuals involved as well as conjecture and personal opinions about what may or may not have occurred.

The forensic interview is confidential; many factors determine what and how much information can be released to other professionals and must be considered on a case-by-case basis. Initiating a discussion with your local FI and MDT members is instrumental in developing a plan for information sharing.

The legal proceedings can be frustrating for FIs and other MDT members, as well as to children and their families, due to court backlog and lack of timeliness of prosecution or family court disposition. With time lags in proceedings, the child has often matured and developed over this time lapse and may present very differently as a witness. Further, the child served by a CAC has ideally accomplished some degree of healing and recovery and thus may not present as the same "victim" as at the time of the investigation—again, judge/jury need to view and experience the child as "victim" as a component of their decision-making process. Presence and availability of the videotaped interview serves well when these issues arise. However, many jurisdictions either do not allow videotaping of interviews or the admission of videotapes into evidence. Some states also disallow the testimony of a forensic interviewer. Finally, to combat burnout in this challenging system, self-care and building healthy MDT relationships is important.

Medical Examiner Comments From Suzanne Starling, MD, Professor of Pediatrics, Medical Director, CHKD-Child Abuse Program, Norfolk, Virginia

The medical examination is an essential component of the evaluation of suspected sexual abuse in children. The examination serves several purposes: it provides potential medical evidence, including testing for sexually transmitted infections, allows a medical provider to provide medical evidence in court proceedings, and most importantly, it reassures the child and family regarding the child's genital health. Since genital tissue heals rapidly, is very elastic and resistant
(*continued*)

to injury, and since many acts of abuse to children do not involve activities that would be expected to cause injury, the evidentiary value of the exam is often the least important reason for the examination. Only a very small proportion of children, less than 5%, will have evidence of injury on examination (Heger, Ticson, Velasquez, & Bernier, 2002). Most families, and many investigators and judges, erroneously believe that there will be medical evidence of abuse in every case. Families can be reassured that lack of physical evidence does not preclude the possibility of sexual abuse and does not hamper the investigation and prosecution of child abuse. The most common medical evidence a provider gives in court is to explain the normal exam to the judge or jury. Examinations occur as emergency acute assault examinations or as scheduled exams. Most exams take place several days to weeks or months after the abuse has occurred, and are therefore scheduled into a medical clinic setting. Although parents are often nervous about the examination, studies have found that children typically are not as concerned (Waibel-Duncan, & Sanger, 1999). Sexual abuse evaluations are not at all similar to adult pelvic examinations, a common misconception among adults, and are completely painless to the child. The sexual abuse examination begins with a medical interview of the caregivers. In some centers the child also is interviewed by the medical provider, although in others, the child is interviewed by forensic interview staff or investigators. The child and parent are prepared for the exam by having the procedure explained to them. Many exams are conducted using a colposcope, a magnifying device that resembles a pair of binoculars on a stand. The actual configuration of colposcope varies from center to center; some are on rolling stands and some may be attached to the wall. This equipment does not touch the child, and is used for magnification and photography of the exam. Because most examinations are photographed or videotaped for medical legal purposes and to allow peer review of the exam findings, the use of camera equipment also is explained to the family. In this age of daily media exposure, children rarely have any difficulty understanding the presence and use of the photographic equipment.

During the examination itself, the child usually will be placed in a hospital gown. She will be weighed and measured prior to exam and often will be asked to provide a urine sample. The exam itself consists of a complete head to toe medical exam of the child, including genital exam. In prepubertal children, the exam consists entirely of an

(*continued*)

(*continued*)

external inspection of genitalia; there is no internal examination done in prepubertal children. The exam is not painful to the child. If there is a suspicion of sexually transmitted infections (STIs), then testing is performed, typically by urine testing or external genital swabs. Children with evidence of infection such as gonorrhea or chlamydia are treated with antibiotics. Only in adolescents may the exam also include an internal speculum exam and STI testing.

Emergency sexual assault exams are similar to scheduled exams. If a minor presents for medical care within 72 hours of the abuse, she usually will receive an acute examination. Many of these take place in emergency departments, although the exam sites will vary by location. In addition to the procedures noted above, children undergo forensic evidence collection, often referred to as a "rape kit." This consists of collecting a series of swabs from various body locations in an attempt to identify DNA products. In many cases hair and blood samples are also collected. In adolescents, medications are given to prevent STIs and emergency contraception is offered. Patients with injury noted on exam generally are referred to a scheduled forensic examination for follow-up to ensure healing of the injuries and compliance with medications.

At the conclusion of the evaluation the exam results are explained to the patient and family and they are reassured about the child's health. Even a child or adolescent with injuries can be reassured that the injury will heal completely and only a trained examiner would be able to tell that she had been injured. Most infections, with the exception of viral infections such as HIV and genital warts, can be successfully treated with antibiotics, and the patient can be reassured that the infection will resolve completely. Any ongoing medical issues identified during the exam will be referred to the child's physician for follow-up.

A medical report is generated at the conclusion of the evaluation. This report contains the history of the case as relayed by the care-givers, as well as details of the examination findings. Most medical reports do not contain detailed or new historical information unless a forensic interview is conducted by the medical provider. As with any medical document, nonmedical team members often find the medical terminology difficult to interpret, and a discussion with the examiner usually is necessary to properly frame the examination findings. A copy of the medical examination usually is required by the investigators

(*continued*)

and the courts for the investigation and prosecution of the case. However, because the report contains primarily detailed medical findings with very little new social information or history, its utility to the children's therapists or others involved in the mental health evaluations may be limited.

Prosecutor (District Attorney) Comments From Sharon Reddick, Assistant District Attorney General, Nashville, Tennessee

"Child sexual abuse is a crime both against the child victim and against the peace and dignity of the State."[3] It is the criminal component of this multilayered problem in which the district attorney (DA) is involved. The DA is referred to in a variety of ways: the DA, the prosecutor, the State. All are interchangeable titles used in referring to the attorney employed by the State to represent the State's interests in all criminal prosecutions. As such, the DA is not technically the "victim's lawyer"; however, a crime against an individual child is a crime against "the peace and dignity of the State of Tennessee." Therefore, it is easy and not entirely inaccurate to think of the DA as the lawyer who represents the child victim in criminal court.

The role of the DA in all child sexual abuse cases should begin well before the case gets into court. In best practice, the DA's office is a member of the MDT, collaborating closely with and occasionally providing guidance to police investigators, child protective services investigators, forensic interviewers, and forensic medical examiners in the early stages and throughout any investigation of child sexual abuse allegations. Based on the fruits of the investigation, the DA then makes charging decisions—meaning that he or she compares the facts of the case with the criminal code and decides whether to charge the alleged perpetrator and, if so, with what. It is important to note that the DA is not limited solely to the issue of whether he or she believes the alleged perpetrator is guilty. The DA must also consider whether
(continued)

---

3. Criminal indictments in most states, regardless of the crime charged, include language like this.

(continued)

the case can be proven "beyond a reasonable doubt" in contemplating cases for prosecution and making charging decisions.[4] It is rare for the DA to have any direct contact with the child victim or their family unless and until a decision to prosecute is made.

If the decision to prosecute is made, the DA prepares an indictment, which is then presented to a grand jury. The grand jury can either "True Bill" the indictment (make a finding that the perpetrator should be arrested and the case should go to court), "No True Bill" the indictment, or request further information. Once the grand jury True Bills an indictment, an arrest warrant is issued for the perpetrator and the prosecution commences. In certain circumstances child sexual abuse suspects are arrested on warrants issued by a magistrate at the request of a police officer (usually after consultation with the DA) prior to a grand jury becoming involved. This is typically done when there is some emergent circumstance requiring the suspect to be taken into custody right away. In this situation a preliminary hearing is required after which the DA prepares an indictment for the grand jury to review.

When the perpetrator is arrested the DA or Victim Witness Coordinator (in DA's office) should make contact with the victim through his or her caregivers. From that point forward the DA continues to be responsible for making all decisions related to the prosecution; however, these decisions can and should be made in close consultation with the victim (depending on the age and developmental level) and/or the caregiver. In many states, victims of child sexual abuse, like all victims of crime, are afforded certain rights by the Victims' Rights Amendment[5] (e.g., right to confer with prosecution, right to be informed of all proceedings). How much involvement they have in the decision-making process beyond those fundamental rights will be determined by the individual DA and by the circumstances of each individual case. At a minimum, the DA should consult with the victim and/or the caregiver prior to making offers for settlement, and the victim's wishes should be strongly considered and highly regarded before making plea agreements.

(continued)

---

4. "Beyond a reasonable doubt" is the legal burden of proof that must be met by the State for conviction in all criminal cases.
5. Victims' Rights Amendment Act of 2004.

Depending on the facts and circumstances of the individual case, there could be situations in which the child victim's and/or the caregiver's testimony would be needed prior to trial or settlement. These situations include preliminary hearings, bond hearings, certain evidentiary hearings, and so on. The DA should avoid these situations as much as possible while still maintaining the integrity of the prosecution. When these situations are unavoidable, care is taken to prepare the child witness on what to expect and to minimize anxiety as much as possible. Likewise, when a prosecution results in a jury trial, the DA and victim witness coordinator will meet with the child and prepare the child to testify. This preparation includes visiting the court room, going over what the victim can expect and the questions he or she will be asked, as well as giving the child the opportunity to ask any questions and express any concerns he or she might have about testifying. Many parents and caregivers are anxious about their child having to testify and wish to avoid it at all costs. But children can do it! It is an important role for the caregiver and therapist, as well as the DA and victim witness coordinator, to help the child understand that testifying is not a continuation of his or her victimization but an opportunity to reclaim power.

Therapists and DAs can work together in a number of ways to benefit the child, including:

- The DA can keep the therapist apprised of the prosecution status so that the therapist is aware when children have to meet with the DA and/or go to court and can address these situations in therapy if necessary.
- The therapist can assist the child and the family to realistically process their wishes about the outcome of the prosecution and can assist them in communicating their wishes with the DA.
- When appropriate, the therapist can be present during the child's meetings with the DA and during court appearances to provide support to the child and guidance to the DA on how best to communicate with the child.
- The therapist should be prepared to testify at trial. The DA should communicate with the therapist about the fact that he or she cannot testify for the child but he or she may occasionally be needed and required to testify about certain disclosures the child made in therapy. In these situations the DA should always

(continued)

(continued)

consult with the therapist about the questions to be asked and the specific purpose of the testimony.

- The therapist should be prepared to testify at the perpetrator's sentencing hearing. The therapist is often in the best position to inform the Court of the trauma and emotional toll that the sexual abuse took on the child victim. This information may be considered by the Judge when fixing the perpetrator's sentence.

Family Advocate Role Comments From Jane Orton, LCSW, PIP; Clinical Director, National Children's Advocacy Center, Huntsville, Alabama

Defining the "advocate" role in Child Advocacy Center (CAC) settings is complicated by differing titles across centers (e.g., Family Advocate; Victim Advocate), differing employment status (e.g., CAC employees, DA office employees), and some differences in job description, yet all advocate roles share core values and essential duties.

The Family Advocate (FA) role was created in 1996 to provide support to nonoffending caregivers of child abuse victims. This addition supported the original intent of the MDT approach, that is, to respond to sexual abuse cases in a child-friendly manner, with all system players working together to coordinate efforts so the process would be efficient and supportive of the child, minimizing additional trauma. Traditionally, FAs have provided support and information designed to increase the caregiver's coping abilities so they are better able to help their child cope effectively with abuse-related issues. In effect, the FA supports the abused child indirectly through his or her caregiver. Having a supportive caregiver is paramount to the child's ability to move past the trauma experience in a positive fashion. Friedrich, Einbender, and McCarty (1999) state, "Parental support is critical, outstripping abuse characteristics in predicting, at the least, short-term behavioral reaction to the abuse." Research also shows that nonoffending mothers and fathers experience significant distress following a disclosure of sexual abuse from their children (Elliott & Carnes, 2001).

Family Advocates act as liaisons to other services within the agency. For example, at the National CAC in Huntsville, FAs assist

(continued)

with victim referrals to therapy by making the initial scheduling calls to the victim or caregiver. Moreover, the FA meets with the caregiver for the initial intake meeting for victim therapy services.

Of great importance is the advocate's role to routinely inform families about victim's rights. State and federal laws mandate that all victims of crime be informed regarding their rights as a crime victim, including information about crime victim's compensation. Nonoffending family members who are affected by the crime may also be entitled to services. While advocate functions may be broad, they ultimately lead to supporting child victims through the maze of procedures and services to safety and emotional healing through strengthening and empowering natural and adjunctive support systems.

Public Child Welfare Comments From Elizabeth Black, Tennessee Department of Children's Services, Permanency Unit

The public child welfare system in most jurisdictions is responsible for providing services and protection to maltreated children and their families, including both early intervention and prevention services in the child's home as well as out of home care services for those children and youth not able to safely remain at home.

While the MDT has the primary responsibility for conducting child sex abuse investigations, the public child welfare system has the primary responsibility for ensuring the child's safety, permanency and well-being. Specifically, the child welfare system is responsible for making decisions about whether the child should do the following and are listed in priority order:

- Remain in his or her own home safely.
- Remain safely in his or her own home with the perpetrator out of the home.
- Be removed from the home and placed with close family members or other persons with whom the child has a significant relationship.
- Enter state custody for placement with relatives or in a family setting with unrelated foster parents.

(continued)

(*continued*)

- Enter state custody for placement in a group home or other congregate care facility.

The public child welfare system must carefully balance the need to protect the child from abuse and ensure that reasonable efforts be made to keep the child within his or her own family.[6] A long history of repeat allegations, the child being at a particularly vulnerable age, a willingness of the family to receive services, and confidence in a parent or relative to protect the child are all factors in making this decision. In many jurisdictions, this decision will be made by the child protective services worker along with his or her supervisor.

Based on a judicial finding that the child was subject to abuse or neglect and the child does enter state custody, the public child welfare system will be responsible for making determinations about where the child will be placed and whether the child will be able to return safely to his or her own parents or family members. Once this judicial determination has been made and a child enters state custody, in many jurisdictions, the case will transfer to a custodial or foster care case manager.

Most public child welfare systems use family conferencing as the primary means for making these critical decisions regarding both placement and permanency for and with children and their own families. As appropriate, the child's therapist should be a member of this team. The person responsible for the building, preparing and maintaining of this team is most often the child's custodial or foster care case manager. Action steps should be tailored for each child and family and might include diligent searches, engaging informal supports, and ensuring needed assistance for adults considering permanency options.

(*continued*)

---

6. The 1980 Adoption Assistance and Child Welfare Act (AACWA) initially required these "reasonable efforts" to maintain children in their families by providing services aimed at preventing the unnecessary removal of children from their parents. The 1997 Adoption and Safe Families Act (ASFA) further clarified that these "reasonable efforts" to keep children within their own families or return them as quickly as possible would not be required with respect to the parent of a child if the court determines that the parent subjected the child to aggravated circumstances. These aggravated circumstances are determined by state law and may include sexual abuse.

These teams must make critical decisions within timelines guided by the Adoption and Safe Families Act (ASFA). Permanency hearings must take place no later than twelve (12) months after a child first entered state custody and at least every twelve (12) months thereafter until a child exits state custody. The public child welfare system must, subject to certain exceptions such as the child being placed with a relative, petition for the termination of parental rights after a child has been in state custody for fifteen (15) of the last twenty-two (22) months.

Guardian Ad Litem Comments From Jeanah McClure, JD, Nashville, Tennesse

The term "guardian ad litem" (GAL) literally translates to "a guardian for the lawsuit." Practically speaking, however, a GAL is a representative appointed by the court to protect and represent the interests of someone who is incapable of representing himself or herself; children fall into this category due to their minority status. For children with CSA histories, a GAL is an advocate for a child whose welfare is a matter of concern to the court. A GAL is the only person in the legal system whose sole concern is the best interest of the child. Their main duties include: (1) information gathering for the court; (2) making recommendations to the court regarding services, safety, and permanency for the child; and (3) advocating for speedy decisions for the sake of the child.

Those eligible for GAL appointments differ by jurisdictions; however, in general, they come from a variety of personal and professional backgrounds (some states require that a GAL be an attorney). The common denominator for GALs is that they are responsible adults with solid common sense and they have undergone specialized GAL training. The GAL conducts an independent investigation, which may include record review, viewing the forensic interview, and interviewing those who may have factual information about the child. The GAL for the child should not re-interview the child victim about the allegations of sexual abuse, but should both learn about the child's needs and concerns and explain the judicial process in child's terms, including that a judge will be making decisions about his or

(continued)

(continued)

her situation. The GAL should ask the child what he/she wants the GAL to tell the judge.

The adjudicatory hearing is the forum where decisions are made by the judicial officer about child protection. The burden of proof is clear and convincing evidence. Therapists' input is necessary as their part of the case may help build the evidence to that level in the mind of the trier of fact. The therapist will be cross-examined by defense counsel. The therapist's only obligation is to tell the truth regarding the questions asked. Therapists should not feel so pressured that the responsibility for the correct decision rests on their shoulders. It does not. Each of the witnesses—the CPS worker, the FI, the child's statements or testimony, the parents' testimony—all factor into the decision of the judge. Generally, judges fashion orders that keep children safe.

Following the investigatory phase, the therapist should ask to review the child welfare/CPS materials and the forensic interviews. These materials can help define the issues for the therapist. CPS should release these materials to the therapist if asked. In some jurisdictions, the GAL is a part of the MDT and can facilitate getting the records from child welfare and child protective services to the therapist. Ideally, the system works in such a way that giving these records to the therapist once the investigation is over is routine. In general, the therapist should not hesitate to communicate with the GAL or the child welfare case manager and attorney assigned to the case if there are any issues that need to be addressed in the child's environment.

Court Appointed Special Advocates (CASA) Comments From Lynne Farrar, Executive Director, CASA Works, Inc.

Court Appointed Special Advocates (CASA) are volunteers who are appointed by the Juvenile Judge to advocate for children in the juvenile court system only. While the criminal court determines what happens to the perpetrator, the Juvenile Court oversees and determines what happens for the child. This is often confusing to families.

Following 30 hours of extensive training, CASA volunteers have authority to talk to everyone on behalf of the child (e.g., caregivers, teachers, service providers). CASA volunteers become a full member

(continued)

of the "team" surrounding the child to determine the best course of action to ensure a safe, permanent, loving home. In a system full of case managers, attorneys, and service providers, it is often CASA who weaves between the parties to keep the focus on the needs of the child while respecting the rights of the parents. CASA volunteers submit a written, comprehensive, objective report to the court outlining the history of the child and family, the current situation, and ultimately recommendations in the best interest of the child. CASA volunteers have only one or two cases at a time, so have the luxury of spending ample time getting to know the needs of the children they serve.

In Juvenile Court, the judge determines by adjudication that there is "clear and convincing evidence" that abuse occurred. Then, the focus becomes what is best for the child. The child may be in foster care or the child could remain in the home while the family adheres to a Court Ordered Safety Plan. In either case, child welfare, together with the parents and attorneys, devise a plan for the safety of the child. The court oversees the progress of this plan to determine when and if the child can return home to the family or if parental rights should be terminated so the child can be adopted.

In an overburdened social service system, communication often suffers. Therapists may see the child and/or parents, but do not have the benefit of seeing the whole situation as the case progresses. CASA volunteers can be helpful in letting therapists know the history of the child and family and making sure the therapist knows the plan for reunification. Judges rely on the expertise of the therapist to determine what is best for the child. Likewise, as CASA volunteers keep therapists informed, it is helpful for therapists to let the CASA volunteer and family know the emotional needs of the child and the progress of therapy.

Mental Health Provider Comments From Lori Myers, LCSW, RPT, Clinical Supervisor and Therapist at the Sexual Assault Center, Nashville, Tennessee

The therapist is an educator, support person, trauma specialist, advocate, and coordinator of services. Therapists first educate the child and family on the dynamics of child sexual abuse, while aiding

(continued)

(*continued*)
the caregivers in navigating the multidisciplinary team and the system. It is a delicate process of allowing the child time to heal while working with the caregivers to aid them in navigating the system and learning to parent a traumatized child while concurrently processing their own confusion, hurt and concern for the child.

While working within the system, the therapist must continue to focus on his or her primary role of helping the child heal. The therapist works with the child to educate about trauma, offenders, privacy, safety, risk reduction, and coping strategies and to create a trauma narrative. A crucial piece in the healing process is integrating the child's caregivers in the therapeutic process to provide the child with a support system that will follow him or her past graduation from therapy. This begins to rebuild the family structure and aid the family in regaining peace within their home.

Therapists also bridge communication gaps within the multidisciplinary team, advocating for the best interest of the child and family. While serving as a liaison between providers and working with the child and family to regain trust, peace, and support, the therapist facilitates the family in reclaiming their lives. It is a delicate balancing act to continue to advocate for the child and family while at the same time staying within the role of therapist and not becoming the case manager, DCS worker, prosecutor, or detective.

Therapists may be called to testify in court proceedings. Therapists can be asked to make recommendations, comments, or draw conclusions that are out of the therapist's area of expertise and scope of practice. The therapist frequently is asked to corroborate the forensic interview or testimony of the child. It is not the role of the therapist to investigate or attempt to glean the "truth" or story from the child or family. This is an area where therapists continually need to draw boundaries with the multidisciplinary team.

SYSTEM ISSUES FOR THERAPISTS

Therapists are charged with a great responsibility to aid vulnerable children and families in their healing process resulting from child sexual abuse. This section explores confidentiality issues faced by therapists and provides direction for therapists who are in the position of helping children navigate court involvement or who may themselves be asked to provide expert witness testimony in child sexual abuse cases.

CONFIDENTIALITY ISSUES

Clinicians should always tell children and their caregivers the limits of confidentiality at the beginning of treatment. Framing the duty to report as a need to keep children safe can soften the situation, as can an explanation that the therapist would be breaking the law if she did not report. Clinicians can provide information to the child about what will happen next (e.g., a person whose job it is to keep kids safe will come to talk with you). It can be therapeutic to include a supportive caregiver in the reporting process, whenever the inclusion of the caregiver will not result in further harm. If it is believed that the child will be harmed further due to the report, it is recommended that the child be taken directly from the clinician's office to a safe place while the investigation takes place.

Confidentiality of client information is a key concept across all the major disciplines in health and mental health (e.g., American Medical Association, 2010; American Nurses Association, 2001; American Psychological Association, 2002; National Association of Social Workers, 1999). Additionally, every state has laws that make certain records confidential. The federal Health Information Privacy Protection Act (HIPPA) also governs confidentiality of records. While confidentiality applies ethically to all settings, laws concerning confidentiality in the legal setting are called *privileges*. Most states have physician-patient and psychotherapist-patient privilege laws. Typically, nurse-patient or social worker-patient privilege laws do not exist. However, if these persons are the psychotherapist, then privilege would apply through that law. Privileges clearly apply when professionals testify in court and are asked to produce confidential information. The professional or the attorney for the client should object to the divulging of confidential information, claiming the "privilege" that the client holds. A therapist might state in court, "Your honor, I would rather not answer this question because I believe the information is privileged."

Sometimes it is in the best interest of the client for privileged information to be released in court. The client (if of age) or client's caregiver then should be asked to give written consent for the professional to share the privileged information in court or to release records to the court. In emergencies, however, a professional may have little choice but to release confidential (or privileged) information without prior release from the client. The law does allow release of such information in true emergency situations. Finally, court-ordered medical or psychological evaluations are an exception to confidentiality and to privilege, as all parties know from the outset that the information will be given to the court. It is important, however, to ensure that the child client and caregivers understand this limit on confidentiality prior to doing the evaluation.

COURT TESTIMONY

Members of the MDT often find themselves in the position of being called to court to testify in child sexual abuse cases or in the role of aiding a child in preparation for the child's testimony. Court testimony can be a stressful aspect of the MDT role. The following section discusses some of the issues inherent in court testimony.

The Child's Testimony The child is usually the state's most important witness (Myers, 1998, p. 104), and it is typically in the child's best interest to take part in the hearing that will bring justice to the child. Research tells us that when children are prepared for court testimony in advance, and have emotional support through the process, most testify effectively and with limited trauma (American Academy of Pediatrics, 1999; Goodman et al., 1992; Myers, 2005). Therapists should inquire in their community if there are any court preparation classes available for child victims. Many communities have such classes, usually coordinated through the local CAC and often given by the DA's office.

The Sixth Amendment is clear that the defendant has the right to face-to-face confrontation with prosecution witnesses. This drives the reality that children must usually testify in the physical proximity of the defendant, their abuser. However, the right to face-to-face prosecution is not absolute (Hall & Sales, 2008). In cases where a child might be seriously traumatized, the U.S. Supreme Court ruled that a child may testify outside the presence of the defendant (*Maryland v. Craig*, 1990). Further, while the courtroom is typically open to the public, the judge has some limited authority to close the courtroom if a child will be traumatized by public proceedings (Myers, 2011). Some communities are working toward "in camera" testimonies (e.g., in the judge's chambers) or testimonies over closed-circuit TV in order to minimize trauma to the child (Myers, 1998). The therapist could appeal to a judge regarding these issues.

If therapists are faced with the job of helping to prepare a child for court, therapists can help the child in two important ways. First, they can emphasize telling the truth. Next, they can help the child become comfortable with the process and coach them in ways to take care of themselves in the process. For example, the therapist can explain the court process to the child so that the child is more confident and not caught off guard (the therapist may need to talk with the DA to do this well). The therapist can help the child learn coping skills for anxiety to use during the court experience. The therapist can also work with the child's support network to ensure that there are appropriate support persons with the child at the trial. Finally, the therapist can role-play with the child regarding the courtroom scenario, perhaps having the child sometimes take the role of attorney or judge in order that the child experiences some power and control regarding the system. The therapist will not take the child through his or her own testimony, but instead can make up some "mock trial" for the child to role-play. Such a mock trial might be something like a trial regarding the culpability of the "Big Bad Wolf" in *Little Red Riding Hood*.

Expert Witness Role   Being an effective expert witness regarding CSA involves a number of well-established principles on being an expert witness as well as having specialized knowledge regarding child mal-treatment (Myers, 1998, 2011). Providers can be called to testify as the child's provider, as an expert witness, or as both at the same time. To be considered an expert witness, the court follows a routine process in which the attorney who called the professional as an expert asks qualifying questions to persuade the judge that the professional possesses sufficient knowledge, skill, experience, training, and education to qualify as an expert. The opposing counsel then may question the professional in what is called *voir dire*. The judge ultimately decides if the professional meets the standard. Many therapists meet the standard if they have the educational training and experience specific to the questions of the case. Expert witnesses should prepare to testify by meeting with the attorney who called them in order to go over questions that will be asked. The expert also typically reviews pertinent records, although professionals must keep in mind that any records they review for testimony could be included in the court record and could compromise confidentiality.

There are three main forms of expert testimony including: (1) opinion testimony (most common), in which the expert gives opinion that a child's symptoms, for example, are consistent with child sexual abuse; (2) lecture to the judge or jury in which the expert could, for example, educate the jury on the common occurrence of sexually abused children recanting abuse; and (3) hypothetical questions in which the expert is asked about a hypothetical set of facts that mirror the facts of the case on trial and the expert gives opinion on that hypothetical case. Experts are often asked hypothetical questions on cross-examination and it is advisable for experts to be reasonable but also stick to the original opinion.

Expert witnesses should always maintain a calm, professional de-meanor, refusing to be cajoled, tricked, or bullied into losing composure. Healthy confidence with a good sense of recognizing one's own limitations or the limitations of the literature or field is what the grounded expert witness should strive to maintain. It is always fine to say "I don't know" or to ask for clarification of the lawyer's question.

Many providers who work with children who have been sexually abused are called to testify in court regarding a child's disclosure of sexual abuse under a hearsay exception. Hearsay is defined as *an out of court assertion that is repeated in court to prove the truth of the matter asserted*. Most states have a child hearsay exception for reliable statements by children in child abuse cases. To gain further specific knowledge about witnessing regarding the "proof" of sexual abuse, the reader is referred to Myers's (2011) chapter entitled "Proving Child Maltreatment in Court," pp. 388–396. For issues of child sexual abuse in the context of child custody battles, the reader is referred to the work of Kathleen Colbourn Faller (e.g., 1991).

CONCLUSION

Allegations of child sexual abuse set off a process involving multiple and diverse helping professionals within a complex system that requires sophisticated navigation. When MDT members clarify their roles and communicate effectively among disciplines, the quality of aid to affected families increases. It is hoped that the role clarifications articulated above will help families, mental health practitioners and other helping professionals effectively navigate the systems involved in child sexual abuse cases.

REFERENCES

American Academy of Pedatrics. (1999). Guidelines for the evaluation of sexual abuse of children: Subject review, *Pediatrics, 103*(1), 186–191.

American Medical Association. (2010) *Code of medical ethics: Current opinion with annotations, 2010-2011.* American Medical Association.

American Nurses Association. (2001). *Code of ethics for nurses.* Silver Spring, MD: American Nurses.

American Professional Society on the Abuse of Children. (2002). *Practice guidelines: Investigative interviewing in cases of alleged child abuse.* Elmhurst, IL: Author.

American Psychological Association. (2002). The ethical principles of psychologists and code of conduct. Washington, DC: Author.

Colbourn Faller, K. (1991). Possible explanations for child sexual abuse in divorce. *American Journal Orthopsychiatry, 61*, 86–87.

Elliott, A. N., & Carnes, C. N. (2001). Reactions of nonoffending parents to the sexual abuse of their child: A review of the literature. *Child Maltreatment, 6*(4), 314–331.

Friedrich, W. N., Einbender, A. J., & McCarty, P. (1999). Sexually abused girls and their Rorschach responses. *Psychological Reports, 85*(2), 355–362.

Goodman, G. S., Taub, E. P., Jones, D.P.H., England, P., Port, L. K., Rudy, L., & Prado, L. (1992). Testifying in criminal court. *Monographs of the Society for Research in Child Development, 57* (5, Serial No. 229).

Hall, S. R., & Sales, B. D. (2008). *Courtroom modifications for child witnesses: Law and science in forensic evaluations.* Washington, DC: American Psychological Association.

Heger, A., Ticson, L., Valasquez, O., & Bernier, R. (2002). Children referred for possible sexual abuse: Medical findings in 2384 children. *Child Abuse & Neglect, 26,* 645–659.

Kolbo, J., & Strong, E. (1997). Multidisciplinary team approaches to the investigation and resolution of child abuse and neglect: A national survey. *Child Maltreatment, 2:* 61–72.

Myers, J. E. B. (1998). *Legal issues in child abuse and neglect* (2nd ed.). Thousand Oaks, CA: Sage.

Myers, J. E. B. (2005). *Myers on evidence in child, domestic, and elder abuse cases.* New York, NY: Aspen.

Myers, J. E. B., Ed. (2011). *The APSAC handbook on child maltreatment* (3rd ed.). Los Angeles, CA: Sage.

National Children's Alliance Standards for Accredited Members (Revised 2008 and effective January 1, 2010) www.nationalchildrensalliance.org/index.php?s=76

Pence, D., & Wilson, C. (1994). *Team investigation of child sexual abuse: The uneasy alliance.* Thousand Oaks, CA: Sage.

Waibel-Duncan, M. K., & Sanger, M. (1999). Understanding and reacting to the anogenital exam: implications for patient preparation. *Child Abuse & Neglect, 23,* 281–286.

Walsh, W. A., Jones, L. M., & Cross, T. P. (2003). Children's advocacy centers: One philosophy, many models. *APSAC Advisor, 15*(3), 3–7.

CHAPTER 5

The Forensic Interview
A Challenging Conversation

LINDA CORDISCO STEELE

INTRODUCTION

A S PARENTS WE wish for our children to have safe and happy child-hoods, free from harmful or frightening experiences. Sadly, that goal is not always possible. In 2008 there were 3.3 million reports to Child Protective Services alleging possible maltreatment of 6.0 million children (U.S. Department of Health and Human Services, 2010). Seventy-one percent of those 3.3 million reports were for neglect, the most common form of child maltreatment. Sixteen percent of reports were alleging physical abuse and 9% were for sexual abuse (Greenbaum et al., 2008). In one year more than 7 million children were reported to have witnessed violence against a parent (McDonald, Jouriles, Ramisetty-Mikler, Caetano, & Green, 2006). When there is an allegation of child abuse or when a child is present during a violent or criminal act against another person, it is necessary for that child to be interviewed as a potential witness. A forensic conversation is challenging for a child for many reasons. The conversation is with a stranger and most often in an unfamiliar location. The topic(s) inquired about may be embarrassing or frightening because of the content, and the child may have limited vocabulary to describe their emotional and sensorial experience. The attempt to recall and give words to their experience often evokes uncomfortable internal responses and distressing memories. Finally, forensic conversations demand a level of detail, explanation, and clarification that is unfamiliar to a child and certainly not part of everyday conversations.

The adult is also in an unfamiliar role, as a forensic conversation with a child follows an unusual pattern. Adults are typically in the role of the expert when talking with children, perhaps providing information or testing their knowledge or social responses. Adults frequently speak with a child with whom they share a history, culture, and common language, allowing the adult to fill in gaps in the child's descriptions and explanations. This shared context gives the adults greater confidence in their ability to understand the child's language, interpret nonverbal responses, provide support, and apply their own knowledge and experiences to the sparse descriptions often provided by a child.

WHAT MAKES AN INTERVIEW "FORENSIC"?

A forensic interview is conducted as part of a larger investigative process and is intended to elicit information that is uniquely the child's, which can be used to further law enforcement and child protection investigations. Forensic interviews should be conducted in a developmentally sensitive and legally sound manner, utilizing research and practice-informed techniques. The interviewer should maintain a supportive, but objective and hypotheses-testing stance throughout the interview. Saywitz and Camparo (2009) clarify the role of the forensic interviewer, saying, "The forensic interviewer is considered a fact finder, objectively gathering details of legal relevance and documenting children's statements verbatim, if possible. He or she is supportive but remains neutral to the veracity of the information provided and refrains from a relationship that could unduly influence children's reports" (p. 114).

CHILDREN'S RELUCTANCE

When children are victims of maltreatment or have witnessed harm of another person, are they able and willing to talk about their experience when asked? While this question is open to debate, research and practice support that some children do and some do not (Faller, 2003, 2007; Lamb, Hershkowitz, Orbach, & Esplin, 2008; Olafson & Lederman, 2006). Three primary sources have historically yielded information on children's willingness to talk about their experiences of child sexual abuse: studies reviewing children's behavior in substantiated cases of child sexual abuse, surveys asking adults about childhood experiences of sexual abuse including disclosure status, and information elicited from child sexual offenders about methods of gaining and maintaining children's cooperation and silence. Lyon and Ahern assert that research clearly indicates that a subset of children are reluctant to disclose abuse and are at risk for recantation even when allegations of sexual abuse are true. They emphasize the necessity of interviewers possessing a good understanding of the dynamics of child sexual abuse in order to better adapt interview approaches to the children's needs (Lyon & Ahern, 2011).

Large national surveys conducted with adults who were promised anonymity document that the majority of people abused as children never report during childhood, with some participants disclosing for the first time during the survey (Finkelhor, Hotaling, Lewis, & Smith, 1990; Smith et al., 2000). Additionally, the participants articulated a variety of factors that influenced children's reluctance, including a close relationship with the abuser, fear of not being believed, embarrassment and shame, and concern for the welfare of others (Anderson, Martin, Mullen, Romans, & Herbison, 1993; Fleming, 1997).

Lyon and Ahern (2011) also consider information gleaned from offenders about the interplay of relationship and secrecy in child sex abuse finding that offenders used a combination of positive inducements, threats of loss of love or attention or predictions of disbelief, as well as authority, control, and force to maintain the secrecy. Offenders also described a progression of interaction beginning with trust-building behaviors, desensitization to inappropriate touch and talk, and finally progression to sexual acts as tactics employed.

When considering the research on children's disclosure patterns, London, Bruck, Ceci, and Shuman (2005, 2007) reviewed studies focusing on cases of substantiated child sexual abuse and found there were high rates of disclosure during the forensic interview. However, London's most recent literature review acknowledges that delay, lower disclosure rates, and recantation may occur when a close relationship to the perpetrator and a lack of family support are present (London, Bruck, Wright, & Ceci, 2008). Other studies have documented that the discovery of sexual abuse through means other than an outcry from the child, such as diagnosis of an STD (Chaffin, Selby, & Wherry, 1997; Lawson & Chaffin, 1992) or identification through electronic recordings of abuse (Cederborg, Lamb, & Laurell, 2007), correlates negatively with the child's willingness or ability to acknowledge or describe abuse.

FAMILY AND CASE DYNAMICS

Not all children who participate in a forensic interview have experienced or observed abuse or violence. A credible denial of maltreatment from a child is a welcome outcome for all involved. For children who do have something to tell, many are able to be forthcoming in the interview, providing important details and clarification (London et al., 2007, 2008). However, a number of factors correlate with greater reluctance on the part of some children to disclose abusive experiences or domestic violence. Not surprisingly, because we are talking about children, relationship is critical. Children are often reluctant to reveal maltreatment at the hands of a parent or other loved or respected adult; likewise lack of belief and support by a parent or caregiver can diminish the child's willingness to disclose in the formal interview, as well as increase the risk of recantation. Young age, as well as cognitive or verbal limitations or disabilities are also associated with disclosure reluctance, whether from hesitancy or inability to articulate their experiences (Faller, 2007; Imhoff & Baker-Ward, 1999; Lamb et al., 2008; Malloy, Lyon, & Quas, 2007; Pipe et al., 2007).

The source of referral for the forensic interview may predict the child's willingness to be open with the interviewer. Although many children are interviewed in response to previous statements to an adult alleging abuse, children may be also be referred for a forensic interview following statements from a child or adult witness, medical issues indicative of sexual contact, disclosure during crisis or therapeutic interventions, information discovered through pictures, writings, or electronic transmissions of some kind, or offender confessions (Cederborg et al., 2007; Faller, 2007; Lyon, 2007; Lyon & Ahern, 2010). In these conditions, the child has heretofore not made an "outcry" and may not be prepared to talk about his or her experiences.

The relationship between previous outcry and active disclosure during the forensic interview is clearly documented (London et al., 2005, 2007; Lyon, 2007; Olafson & Lederman, 2006; Pipe et al., 2007). Olafson and Lederman (2006) define disclosure as a "clear verbal statement that at least one abusive act took place; although a disclosure need not be a complete report of everything that happened" (p. 29). Children identified as being in "active disclosure" are children who have made statements alleging abuse to an adult prior to the interview.

A third group of children may be referred for a forensic interview for reasons that are unclear such as frequent contact with a person identified as an abuser of other children, concerning and ambiguous statements about exposure or contact, unusual sexual behaviors in a young child, or statements to another child. Best practice guidelines serve to optimize forensic interview procedures and yield the best quality and quantity of information from children in active disclosure, but may be less effective with children who are more reluctant.

FROM RESEARCH TO PRACTICE

There are two types of research that inform our practice: analogue/ laboratory research and field research. Analogue studies explore the impact of question formats and interview strategies by questioning children about staged mundane activities or following medical procedures with the added benefit of the ability to measure children's accuracy in reporting. Analogue research allows for the control of specific factors such as the child's age, role as an observer or participant, and the possibility of the introduction of misinformation during the questioning process. Field studies, while rarer and more challenging, provide valuable information about how children respond to questioning and interview approaches within the stressful context of a forensic interview. These studies allow us to form an opinion about the child's comfort and cooperation and to measure the amount of information elicited, but lack a mechanism for evaluation of the accuracy of the information.

The most extensively studied interview structure is the NICHD (National Institute of Child Health and Human Development) protocol, which recommends a highly structured interview with a preparatory phase focusing on narrative practice and interview instructions, a series of questions for transitioning to the substantive topic that become increasingly more focused, and rigorous use of open-ended questions with an admonition to avoid focused or option-posing questions until late in the interview (Lamb, Hershokowtz, Orbach, & Esplin, 2008; Lamb, Orbach, Hershkowitz, Esplin, & Horowitz, 2007; Orbach & Lamb, 2007). Although the NICHD researchers have conducted several studies looking at the introduction of gender-neutral drawings after the completion of the substantive portion of the interview, they do not support the use of media during the interview (Aldridge et al., 2004; Brown, Pipe, Lewis, Lamb, & Orbach, 2007; Teoh, Yang, Lamb, & Larrson, 2010). Information gleaned from the NICHD research has influenced the design of interview protocols by highlighting the importance of incorporating strategies designed to increase children's narratives and added to recommendations from previous research and instruction (Bourg et al., 1999; Faller, 2003, 2007; Home Office, 2002; Perona, Bottoms, & Sorenson, 2006; Saywitz, Goodman, & Lyon, 2002, 2010; Yuille, 2002).

Additionally, the NICHD research demonstrated the benefits of eliciting as much information as possible from free-recall memory. Children access free-recall memory when describing an event in their own way and with their own words, and this information is likely to be more accurate. The use of recognition prompts may be necessary, but more direct questions, particularly option-posing questions, are to be delayed as long as possible.

Interviewers limit a child's descriptions by asking closed questions, which result in shorter answers. As closed questions direct the child's attention to issues that are of interest to the interviewer, such questions risk narrowing the child's testimony and may increase the possibility of misunderstanding on the part of either party (Lamb et al., 2008; Saywitz & Camparo, 2009; Saywitz, Lyon & Goodman, 2011).

Forensic questioning formats lie along a continuum with open-ended/free-recall prompts being the preferred method for eliciting information and recognition prompts (multiple-choice, yes/no questions, and leading questions) being the most direct. General and specific "wh" questions, followed by a request to "tell me about that" may be necessary to elicit additional information from a reluctant child. Recognition prompts should be used with care and also followed by the "tell me more" request. Children are most suggestible about elements of their experience that they do not recall or are less sure of. One-word answers or yes/no responses make it difficult to know if the information is coming from the child or from the interviewer (Peterson, Dowden, & Tobin, 1999; Perona, Bottoms, & Sorenson, 2006; Poole & Lamb, 1998).

Interviewing the "Child Who Shows Up"

Children vary widely as to their developmental age, cognitive abilities, cultural and social status, and experience with using language to describe their lives. Lamb and Brown (2006) describe children as learning to communicate through their interactions with adults, saying, "Children depend on their adult conversational partners, both for an understanding of the task and for retrieving and reporting detailed information about their experiences. We can thus view children as apprentices learning how to communicate effectively (p. 216). As previously stated, the forensic conversation is uniquely challenging for a child, requiring him or her to recall, visualize, and recount remembered events without the benefit of input from an adult observer or co-participant. The child's memory and language abilities interact as he or she attempts to recount a remembered event. Although challenging for all children, forensic interviews present greater obstacles for some children than for others. Age, developmental stage, and temperament of the child, family, and cultural influences (Fontes, 2005, 2008; Rogoff, 2003), and the presence of other factors such as disabilities (Davies & Faller, 2007; Greenbaum et al., 2008), poverty, or multiple stressors on the child or family (Finkelhor, 2008) can diminish the child's ability to describe and clarify autobiographical events, much less potentially confusing or frightening experiences (Perona et al., 2006).

It is widely acknowledged that children remember and recount less about events than do adults, with the youngest children recalling the least information (Klemfuss & Ceci, 2009; Orenstein & Haden, 2002).

With limited experience in the world and, consequently, limited language, a young child has greater difficulty providing verbal accounts of molestation, abuse, or violence. Such events are physical and emotional experiences, rather than experiences of words; and young children often lack the vocabulary to describe sensorial impressions, anatomical details, and contextual elements. Even children older than preschoolers may remember and reexperience traumatic incidents, but still struggle to find words to adequately describe such unique and stimulating events. In addition to young age, disabilities, poor cognitive and communicative abilities, and multiple forms of victimization may all be factors that diminish a child's ability to put words to their experience (Imhoff & Baker-Ward, 1999; Malloy et al., 2007; Pipe et al., 2007).

When the interviewer and the child come from different cultural backgrounds (including language, ethnicity, socioeconomic standing, and widely varying patterns of family and attachment) the adult's ability to adjust the conversation to the child and his or her ability to "apprentice" this child in the forensic conversation is doubly challenging (Faller & Fontes, 2007; Fontes, 2005, 2008; Reese & Farrant, 2003; Rogoff, 2003). In summary, forensic interviewers may struggle to "address the important and complicated factors that make some children unwilling to talk about their experiences" (Lamb, Hershkowitz, Orbach, & Esplin, 2008, p. 17).

INTERVIEW STRUCTURE

"Every child is unique, and there is no single correct way to interview children. There is no gold standard that all interviewers must follow" (Myers, 2005, p. 43). Understandably though, this is not a conversation to make up as one goes along. A phased approach is universally recommended which may be labeled as an interview structure, guideline, or protocol. For the sake of expediency, the term *structure* will be used, although it has no more favor than other terminology. Forensic interview structures incorporate many of the same phases, but the phases may be labeled individually or grouped. Phases include introductions, rapport building, narrative practice, guidelines/rules, a strategy for transitioning to the substantive topic, narrative description, follow-up questioning, clarification, and closure. Adaptations to the structure will be needed to address developmental considerations, cultural issues, and investigatory concerns (Faller, 2007; Fontes, 2005, 2008; Imhoff & Baker-Ward, 1999; Saywitz, Lyon, & Goodman, 2011; Saywitz & Camparo, 2009).

Rapport

Rapport is established in a variety of ways. A comfortable environment, warm interviewer demeanor, attentive listening, facilitation skills, and developmentally sensitive questioning all contribute to building rapport with a child. Research provides little direction in setting up a child-friendly interview environment (Russell, 2004), although consensus exists about many considerations. The ideal room should be attractive to a child, safe, private, and not too stimulating with warm pastel colors and comfortable furniture. Posters or artwork in the room should be appealing to a child or teen, but not of a fantasy nature. The room can be equipped for audio or video recording, and the ability for case investigators or other children's advocacy center (CAC) staff to observe is optimal (Bourg et al., 1999; National Children's Alliance, 2010).

Opinions differ about some elements of a child-friendly room with one approach encouraging minimalism in furnishing and equipping the room and the alternative approach recommending the inclusion of simple materials. A small table and chairs and a child-size easel with large paper and markers may be helpful for younger or reluctant children. The goal is not to encourage play, but rather to provide simple, versatile forms of media that may be used to build rapport, assess developmental skills, and to facilitate conversation. All materials should be in good repair (Cordisco Steele, 2005; Faller, 2007; Pipe & Salmon, 2009).

Bottoms, Quas, and Davis (2007) describe the importance of social support saying, "A socially supportive interviewer can enhance children's eyewitness reports by reducing their suggestibility (compliance) and by aiding memory recall after a delay"(p. 151). Interviewer demeanor combined with a child-friendly environment can help to communicate that this is a safe place for children. Physical contact with the child is to be avoided in the forensic interview setting, but a sense of openness and interest can be communicated through behaviors and voice tone (Davis & Bottoms, 2002). Nonverbal behaviors include an open posture, a relaxed and friendly facial expression, demonstrated attention to the child, a relaxed pace with no sense of rush or pressure, and appropriate mirroring of gestures. Verbal behaviors that communicate social support and provide scaffolding for the child's statements include encouragers ("uh huh," "hmmm," "I see"), paraphrasing, summarizing, follow-up questions, and silence. Strong responses such as gasps or "how awful" are to be avoided. Paraphrasing, also known as *reflection* or *active listening*, can be especially useful in communicating to the child that the forensic interviewer is truly listening. For the child who typically gives shorter responses, the combination of paraphrasing the child's statement paired with "tell me more about . . . " provides additional scaffolding (Evans & Roberts, 2009). Summarizing is best described as an extended form of paraphrasing, which ties together a number of the child's statements or may be used as a follow-up with the child who gives long and detailed narratives to ensure that the interviewer is tracking important information. A relaxed atmosphere that incorporates moments of silence throughout the interview allows the child periods of time to think, to formulate responses to questions, and perhaps work through ambivalence about putting experiences into words.

Narrative Practice

A narrative practice phase provides an opportunity for the interviewer and child to establish a different conversational pattern, in which the child is immediately acknowledged as the expert or "holder of the information," the one who does the talking, and the interviewer establishes herself as a good and active listener. The inclusion of narrative practice in the early stage of the interview is shown to increase a child's informative responses to open-ended prompts in the substantive portion of the interview, which can lessen the need to rely on direct or leading prompts (Hershkowitz, 2009; Lamb et al., 2008; Poole & Lamb, 1998; Sternberg et al., 1997). This phase comes more easily to some children than to others.

Children from high narrative families have more experience with engaging in elaborative conversations and may readily respond to this opportunity (Cheyne & Tarulli, 2005; Fivush, Haden, & Reese, 2006; Reese & Farrant, 2003). Other children, lacking experience with expanded conversation, may need paraphrasing and additional prompts to be able to provide narrative descriptions. This second group of children may actually benefit most from narrative practice. An appropriate practice topic can be selected from common child experiences (i.e., a recent holiday, birthday, the first day of school,) solicited from the child's caregiver or introduced by the child during rapport building. Many children initially supply a relatively skeletal description of the target experience. The interviewer should prompt for additional description by selecting a word or phrase from the child's statements and request further elaboration or explanation, thus encouraging the child to provide detailed descriptions. The interviewer is provided an opportunity to establish a baseline of linguistic functioning for each individual child and to develop a working hypothesis about how to best question this child to obtain the optimal quality and quantity of information (Lamb et al., 2008; Saywitz & Camparo, 2009; Saywitz, Lyon, & Goodman, 2011).

GUIDELINES OR RULES FOR THE INTERVIEW

Informing the child about the rules or guidelines for the interview, paired with the opportunity to implement those guidelines, further instructs the child about the different conversational flow or "how we talk about things in this room" (Cordon, Saetermoe, & Goodman, 2005; Faller, 2003, 2007; Saywitz, Lyon, & Goodman, 2011) and clarifies his or her role as a witness. The age of the child dictates the number of guidelines and, perhaps, the specific guidelines that may be most helpful. Preschoolers are seldom able to make use of interview instructions, given their challenges with monitoring their own conversations and memory. Beneficial instructions may include "I was not there and don't know what happened. When I ask you questions, I don't know the answer to those questions," as well as permission to say "I don't know" and "I don't understand that question." A request to "tell the truth" or to "only talk about things that really happened" emphasizes the importance of the conversation and is sometimes paired with a broader conversation and testing procedures for the meaning of "truth" and "lie" or a request for a promise of truthfulness (Lyon & Dorado, 2008; Lyon et al., 2008). Interviewers may ask a child to identify a statement about the color or name of an object in the room as being a truthful statement or being a lie. Alternatively, interviewers may employ a prepackaged approach such as the "Qualifying Children to Take the Oath: Materials for Interviewing Professionals" developed by Thomas Lyon and Karen Saywitz (2000). This testing process is recommended in some protocols and not in others; but ultimately this is a decision made at the local level, influenced by state statutes, and determined by prosecutor or court preference.

Instructions are easy to administer and do not require much time. Younger and more compliant children may benefit from practice to ensure that they understand an instruction.

TRANSITION TO THE SUBSTANTIVE PORTION OF THE INTERVIEW

Any topic raised by the child related to safety concerns or possible maltreatment should be explored. This may include the referral topic and in such cases the interviewer would simply follow the child's lead. However, many children wait for an invitation from the interviewer to address the substantive topic. An open prompt such as "Tell me why you are talking with me today" or "What are you here to talk about?" invites the child to begin the conversation in his or her own words. This type of prompt is most likely to be successful when the child has initiated the investigation through an "outcry" statement and has received a supportive response (Faller, 2007; Lamb et al., 2008; Saywitz, Lyon, & Goodman, 2011). A child demonstrating minimal reluctance may respond to more focused, but still nonleading prompts, such as "It's very important to tell me why you are here to talk to me today" or "It is my job to talk with kids when something may have happened to them. It's very important that you tell me why your mom (dad or whoever accompanies the child) brought you to talk to me."

Once the topic has been broached, the interviewer should invite the child to "start at the beginning and tell me everything" or a variation that is developmentally suited to this child.

In day-to-day practice, however, there are many avenues that bring children to a forensic interview and a child may demonstrate reluctance to transition to the substantive topics for a variety of reasons. Most interview structures provide direction for focusing a child who is nonresponsive to the open prompts. Some interview structures (NICHD Interview Guidelines, Lyon's 10-Step Investigative Interview) recommend a series of increasingly focused prompts concerning statements the child has previously made or circumstances of those statements (Lamb, 2007, 2008; Lyon, 2005). The approach is applicable where the child has made previous statements.

When a child demonstrates reluctance to address the allegation topic, the interviewer should consider an array of possibilities. Perhaps the child has not experienced any maltreatment and actually has nothing to report. A young child may have made concerning statements or exhibited behaviors without any understanding of the serious nature of his or her communication and without certainty on the adult's part that the child actually is reporting abuse. Alternatively, a child may be referred for an interview because of statements from a witness or discovery of evidence of maltreatment and there are no prior statements by the child. Additionally, children who made an "outcry" to a trusted adult may be reluctant to talk to a relative stranger during the formal interview. In such circumstances the interviewer is challenged in designing appropriate focused and nonsuggestive transitions to open discussion about possible maltreatment. Saywitz, Lyon, and Goodman (2011) articulate the dilemma, saying, "Research findings support beginning with very general prompts, but when these do not elicit a disclosure, protocols recommend that alternative strategies for engaging in a conversation about points of potential forensic relevance be conducted in the least leading fashion possible. However, there is little research testing the independent contribution of the various strategies" (p. 345). One approach (CornerHouse: RATAC) instructs the interviewer to introduce an anatomical drawing, request names of body parts, and follow with a series of questions about a variety of appropriate and inappropriate touches (Anderson, et al., 2010; Vieth, 2006; Walters et al., 2003). Other interview structures take a more eclectic approach in an attempt to craft a transition to the particular needs of the child and case. One such strategy recommends that the interviewer engage the child in focused conversations about personal topics such as people, activities, locations, specific periods of time, or topics such as secrets, rules, safety, or worries (American Professional Society on the Abuse of Children [APSAC], 2002; Cordisco Steele, 2005; Faller, 2007). Some children may be assisted by spending more time in the rapport-building phase of the interview, which may be facilitated by an extended, multisession interview format (Carnes, Nelson-Gardell, Wilson, & Orgassa 2001; Hershkowitz, Lamb, Orbach, Sternberg, & Horowitz, 2006; Hershowitz & Terner, 2007; LaRooy, Katz, Pipe, & Lamb, 2010; LaRooy, Lamb, & Pipe, 2009). Interviewers are advised, in all techniques, to avoid questioning approaches that are suggestive, coercive, or manipulative and to demonstrate acceptance of the child's responses. Refusal to accept the child's answers or continued repetition of the same question may influence the child to change his or her response.

GATHERING DETAILS

When a child acknowledges an experience of maltreatment, the interviewer faces the challenge of eliciting detailed information from the child without the use of leading questions. Following directives from research indicating that open prompts elicit the highest quality and quantity of information, interviewers should emphasize questions that tap free-recall memory (Lamb et al., 2007, Lamb et al., 2008; Saywitz, Lyon, & Goodman, 2011). The narrative practice phase of the interview should have given the child some understanding of narrative description of a remembered event and also provided the interviewer a glimpse into the child's narrative style (Lamb & Brown, 2006; Sternberg et al., 1997). Particularly with a child in active disclosure the interviewer should rely on free-recall prompts gaining as much description of the event in the child's words as possible and avoiding the impulse to move quickly to "wh" questions or recognition prompts (Lamb et al., 2007, 2008; Lyon, 2005). A narrative child should not be interrupted to ask for clarification; rather, it is the interviewer's responsibility to attend to elements that require clarification, using cued open prompts to request further explanation. Pacing remains important throughout the interview and the interviewer should allow time for additional thoughts from the child. Option-posing questions, such as multiple choice or yes/no questions, should be used sparingly and only as necessary. When there have been multiple incidents of abuse the child should be encouraged to describe individual incidents. It is helpful to begin with the most memorable incidents, using prompts such as, "Tell me about a time that you remember well," or "a time when something different happened," or "a time when something happened in a different place" or "in a different way." The child can also be asked to tell about the last time and the first time if they are able to recall those times.

Even highly narrative children may omit forensically important details, because of their lack of experience as a witness, because details are painful or frightening to think and talk about, or because the child did not attend to all details of an event (Myers, 2005). It is widely acknowledged that witnesses (children or adults) do not store complete information about well-remembered personal experiences, and from a developmental perspective, the younger the child the less information will be stored. When addressing missing elements in a child's description of an event, interviewers must balance the use of focused prompts, which may help a child to recall additional information, with the risk of encouraging guessing or suggestion of information to the child. We have research that tells us that such prompts are potentially more risky, but nothing that addresses the conditions under which they may be helpful in jogging the child's memory. Peripheral elements of a well-remembered event may be challenging for a child, even when those elements may seem to be of forensic significance. Elements such as number of times, dates of occurrences, or specific singular elements of any kind, while of interest to investigators, may not have been encoded by the child. Details contained within the child's narrative descriptions are usually considered more reliable (Friedman & Lyon, 2007; Lamb et al., 2008; Myers, 2005).

Issues raised earlier about the use of media in the rapport-building phase apply to the substantive portion of the interview with concern that media may encourage fantasy or prove distracting to the child. Additionally there is concern that interviewers can become overly dependent on a particular tool, such as anatomical drawings, rather than implementing research-based techniques that encourage narrative description. However, other interviewers and experts believe that some reluctant children are assisted by access to media, which may serve to facilitate context-reinstatement, diminish embarrassment, and allow additional modes of expression for the child (Faller, 2003, 2007; Pipe & Salmon, 2009; Salmon, Roncolato, & Gleitzman, 2002; Thierry et al., 2005; Wesson & Salmon, 2001). When language fails a child who attempts to explain particular details, allowing the child to use media to demonstrate may prevent the interviewer's tendency to resort to complex and potentially suggestive questions. For example, a child may use free drawing or a doll to clarify confusing statements about positioning or the arrangement of their clothing.

CLOSURE

It is recommended that the interview ends as it began, with the emphasis on the child. At the close of the interview, the interviewer should turn the conversation to positive or neutral topics.

The child's questions or concerns should be addressed to the best of the interviewer's ability. If the child has become distressed during the conversation, the interviewer may spend more time in rapport building and everyday conversation, allowing the child time to become more comfortable again. The child should always be thanked for his or her participation in the interview.

TRAINING AND SUPERVISION OF INTERVIEWERS

Though family members and professionals have been questioning children about possible maltreatment for many years, child forensic interviewing is just coming into its own as a professional role with a body of knowledge and specific skill set. Research about the impact of questioning approaches and forensic strategies is growing at a rapid pace and we are incorporating literature related to developmental, cultural, and family influences on the disclosure process. The empirical knowledge provides direction to interviewers about good practice. Opinions vary as to the professional affiliation and previous knowledge that best prepare a person to conduct forensic interviews and a more systematic investigation of personal and professional qualities of a forensic interviewer needs to be undertaken.

Forensic interviews do not occur in isolation and the practice of forensic interviewers is not solely determined by their skill sets and personal preferences. A forensic interviewer, whether a child interview specialist (CFIS) or a child protective services (CPS) or law enforcement (LE) investigator who interviews child witnesses does so in the course of an investigation and works at the direction and discretion of multiple authorities, including agency guidelines and standards, state procedural and statutory requirements, political influences, and local historical practice. Even the presence of a children's advocacy center and/or a multidisciplinary team does not ensure uniformity in practice. Saywitz and Camparo (2009) write, "MDTs vary widely in configuration, function, composition, training, and attendant legislation. Studies are often unable to control for significant preexisting factors (e.g., demography of catchment areas, characteristics of children served, such as age and type/severity of abuse)" (p. 114).

Conducting a high-quality forensic interview of a child is a complex task, so one would not expect interviewers to be adequately prepared in a one-week training program. Research clearly indicates that only when preliminary training is followed by access to ongoing training, in addition to oversight of the interviewer's practice through individual supervision and/or peer review, can interviewers develop and maintain good interview skills (Aldridge & Cameron, 1999; Lamb et al., 2000, 2002; Warren et al., 1999). However, we lack clear direction as to the best format for delivery of feedback, timing, and frequency of feedback, and mechanisms for developing an infrastructure that can provide the oversight. Review of an interviewer's work is only as beneficial as the quality of that feedback, influenced by the reviewer's knowledge of best practice and their skills in supervision. Vicarious traumatization, often an issue for those working daily with abused children, should also be addressed through supervision and peer review (Conrad & Kellar-Guenther, 2006; Harrison & Westwood, 2000). The needs of interviewers at different skill levels and with a variety of professional backgrounds and day-to-day job tasks have not been well defined. More research is warranted to inform practice parameters around the best format and timing for feedback, the skill level needed for interview mentors, and effective implementation of peer review.

CONCLUSION

In sum, conducting a forensic interview of a child is a complex task that requires knowledge of child development, an appreciation of the needs of criminal and child protection investigations, knowledge of existing research and practice standards, and the implementation of a unique skill set for eliciting information from a child. Additionally, good forensic interviewers must maintain an open-minded, hypotheses-testing approach while providing noncoercive support to a child. This burgeoning field calls for continuous dialogue regarding the most effective ways to integrate emerging information that comes from science and case law into best practice standards in order to provide the most helpful forensic interviews to the children we serve.

REFERENCES

Aldridge, J., & Cameron, S. (1999). Interviewing child witnesses: Questioning techniques and the role of training. *Applied Developmental Science, 3*, 136–147.

Aldridge, J., Lamb, M. E., Sternberg, K. J., Orbach, Y., Esplin P. W., & Bowler L. (2004). Using a human figure drawing to elicit information from alleged victims of child sexual abuse. *Journal of Consulting and Clinical Psychology, 72*, 304–315.

American Professional Society on the Abuse of Children. (2002). Guidelines on investigative interviewing of alleged child abuse. (Available from APSAC National Operations Manager, Daphne Wright & Associates, Management Group, P.O. Box 3, Charleston, SC 29417.)

Anderson, J., Ellefson, J., Lashley, J., Lukas Miller, Al.Olinger, S., Russell, A., Stauffer, J., & Weigman, J. (2010). The CornerHouse Forensic Interview Protocol: RATAC. *The Thomas M. Cooley Journal of Practical & Clinical Law, 12*(2), 103–331.

Anderson, J., Martin, J., Mullen, P., Romans, S., & Herbison, P. (1993). Prevalence of childhood sexual abuse experiences in a community sample of women. *Journal of the American Academy of Child & Adolescent Psychiatry, 32,* 911–919.

Bottoms, B. L., Quas, J. A., & Davis, S. L. (2007). The influence of interviewer-provided social support on children's suggestibility, memory, and disclosures. In M. E. Pipe, M. E. Lamb, Y. Orbach, & A. C. Cederborg (Eds.), *Child sexual abuse: Disclosure, delay, and denial* (pp. 135–158). Mahwah, NJ: Erlbaum.

Bourg, W., Broderick, R., Flagor, R., Kelly, D., Ervin, D., & Butler, J. (1999). *A child interviewer's guidebook.* Thousand Oaks, CA: Sage.

Brown, D. A., Pipe, M. E., Lewis, C., Lamb, M. E., & Orbach, Y. (2007). Supportive or suggestive: Do human figure drawings help 5–7 year old children to report touch? *Journal of Consulting and Clinical Psychology, 75,* 33–42.

Carnes, C., Nelson-Gardell, D., Wilson, C., & Orgassa, U.C. (2001). Extended forensic evaluation when sexual abuse is suspected: A multisite field study. *Child Maltreatment, 6,* 230–243.

Cederborg, A. C., Lamb, M. E., & Laurell, O. (2007). Delay of disclosure, minimization, and denial of abuse when the evidence is unambiguous: A multivictim case. In M. E. Pipe, M. E. Lamb, Y. Orbach, & A. C. Cederborg (Eds.), *Child sexual abuse: Disclosure, delay, and denial* (pp. 159–173). Mahwah, NJ: Erlbaum.

Chaffin, M., Lawson, L., Selby, A., & Wherry, J. N. (1997). False negatives in sexual abuse interviews: Preliminary investigation of a relationship to dissociation. *Journal of Child Sexual Abuse, 6,* 15–29.

Cheyne, J. A., & Tarulli, D. (2005). Dialogue, difference and voice in the zone of proximal development. In Harry Daniels (Ed.), *An introduction to Vygotsky.* New York, NY: Routledge.

Conrad, D., & Kellar-Guenther, Y. (2006). Compassion fatigue, burnout, and compassion satisfaction among Colorado child protection workers. *Child Abuse & Neglect, 30,* 1071–1080.

Cordisco Steele, L. (2005). *National children's advocacy center child forensic interview structure.* Unpublished manuscript. Available from: mwells@nationalcac.org.

Cordon, I. M., Saetermoe, S. L., & Goodman, G. S. (2005). Facilitating children's accurate responses: Conversational rules and interview style. *Applied Cognitive Psychology, 19,* 249–266.

Davies, D., & Faller, K.C. (2007). Interviewing children with special needs. In K. C. Faller (Eds.). *Interviewing children about abuse: Controversies and best practices* (pp. 152–163). New York: Oxford University Press.

Davis, S. L., & Bottoms, B. L. (2002). The effects of social support on the accuracy of children's reports: Implications for the forensic interview. In M. Eisen, J. Quas, & G. S. Goodman (Eds.), *Memory and suggestibility in the forensic interview* (pp. 437–458). Mahwah, NJ: Erlbaum.

Evans, A. D., & Roberts, K. (2009). The effects of different paraphrasing styles on the quality of reports from young child witnesses. *Psychology, Crime, & Law, 15,* 531–546.

Faller, K. C. (2003). *Understanding and assessing child sexual maltreatment* (2nd ed.). Newbury Park, CA: Sage.

Faller, K. C. (2007). *Interviewing children about sexual abuse: Controversies and best practice.* New York, NY: Oxford University Press.

Finkelhor, D. (2008). *Childhood victimization: Violence, crime, and abuse in the lives of young people.* New York, NY: Oxford University Press.

Finkelhor, D., Hotaling, G., Lewis, I., & Smith, C. (1990). Sexual abuse in a national survey of adult men and women: Prevalence, characteristics, and risk factors. *Child Abuse & Neglect, 14,* 19–28.

Fivush, R., Haden, C. A., & Reese, E. (2006). Elaborating on elaborations: Role of maternal reminiscing style in cognitive and socioemotional development. *Child Development, 77,* 1568–1588.

Fleming, J. M. (1997). Prevalence of childhood sexual abuse in a community sample of Australian women. *Medical Journal of Australia, 166,* 65–68.

Fontes, L. A. (2005). *Child abuse and culture: Working with diverse families.* New York, NY: Guilford Press.

Fontes, L. A. (2008). *Interviewing clients across cultures: A practitioner's guide.* New York, NY: Guildford Press.

Friedman, W., & Lyon, T. D. (2007). The development of temporal metamemory. *Child Development, 76,* 1472–1491.

Greenbaum, J., Dubowitz, H., Lutzker, J. R., Johnson, K. D., Orn, K., Kenniston, J., et al. (2008). *Practice guidelines: Challenges in the evaluation of child neglect.* Available at: www.apsac.org

Harrison, R. L., & Westwood. M. J. (2000). Preventing vicarious traumatization of mental health therapists: Identifying protective practices. *Psychotherapy, Theory, Research, Practice, Training, 46,* 203–210.

Hershkowitz, I. (2009). Socioemotional factors in child sexual abuse investigations. *Child Maltreatment, 14,* 172–181.

Hershkowitz, I., Lamb, M. E., Orbach, Y., Sternberg, K. J., & Horowitz, D. (2006). Dynamics of forensic interviews with abuse victims who do not disclose abuse. *Child Abuse & Neglect, 30,* 253–269.

Hershkowitz, I., & Terner, A. (2007). The effects of repeated interviewing on children's forensic statements of sexual abuse. *Applied Cognitive Psychology,* 1131–1143.

Home Office. (2002). *Achieving the best evidence in criminal proceedings: Guidance for vulnerable and intimidated witnesses, including children.* London, England: Her Majesty's Stationery Office.

Imhoff, M. C., & Baker-Ward, L. (1999). Preschoolers' suggestibility: Effects of developmentally appropriate language and interviewer supportiveness. *Journal of Applied Developmental Psychology, 20*(3), 407–429.

Klemfuss, J. Z., & Ceci, S. J. (2009). Normative memory development and the child witness. In K. Kuehnle & M. Connell (Eds.), *The evaluation of child sexual abuse allegations: A comprehensive guide to assessment and testimony* (pp. 153–180). Hoboken, NJ: John Wiley & Sons.

Lamb, M. E., & Brown, D. A. (2006). Conversational apprentices: Helping children become competent informants about their own experiences. *British Psychological Society, 24*, 215–234.

Lamb, M. E., Hershkowitz, I., Orbach, Y., & Esplin, P. W. (2008). *Tell me what happened: Structured investigative interviews of child victims and witnesses.* West Sussex, England: Wiley-Blackwell.

Lamb, M. E., Sternberg, K., Orbach, Y., Hershkowitz, I., Horowitz, D., & Esplin, D. (2000). The effects of intensive training and ongoing supervision on the quality of investigative interviews with child sexual abuse victims. *Applied Developmental Science, 6*, 114–125.

Lamb, M. E., Orbach, Y., Hershkowitz, I., Esplin, P., & Horowitz, D. (2007). A structured forensic interview protocol improves the quality and informativeness of investigative interviews with children: A review of research using the NICHD investigative interview protocol. *Child Abuse & Neglect, 31*, 1201–1231.

LaRooy, D., Katz, C., Malloy, L. C., & Lamb, M. E. (2010). Do we need to rethink guidance on repeated interviews. *Psychology, Public Policy and Law, 16*, 373–392.

LaRooy, C., Lamb, M. E., & Pipe, M. E. (2009.) Repeated interviewing: A critical evaluation of the risks and Potential Benefits. In K. Kuehnle & M. Connell (Eds.), *The evaluation of child sexual abuse allegations: A comprehensive guide to assessment and testimony* (pp. 153–180). Hoboken, NJ: John Wiley & Sons.

Lawson, L., & Chaffin, M. (1992). False negatives in sexual abuse disclosure interviews: Incidence and influence of caretaker's belief in abuse in cases of accidental abuse discovery by diagnosis of STD. *Journal of Interpersonal Violence, 7*, 532–542.

London, K., Bruck, M., Ceci, S. J., & Shuman, D. (2005). Disclosure of child sexual abuse: What does the research tell us about the ways that children tell? *Psychology, Public Policy, and Law, 11*(1), 194–226.

London, K., Bruck, M., Ceci, S. J., & Shuman, D. (2007). Disclosure of child sexual abuse: A review of the contemporary empirical literature. In M. E. Pipe, M.E. Lamb, Y. Orbach, & A. C. Cederborg (Eds.), *Child sexual abuse: Disclosure, delay, and denial.* Mahwah, NJ: Erlbaum.

London, K., Bruck, M., Wright, D., & Ceci, S. (2008) Review of the contemporary literature on how children report sexual abuse to others: Findings, methodological issues, and implication for forensic interviewers. *Memory, Special Issue: New Insights into Trauma and Memory, 16*, 29–47.

Lyon, T. (2007). False denials: Overcoming methodological biases in abuse disclosure research. In M. E. Pipe, M. E. Lamb, Y. Orbach, & A. C. Cederborg (Eds.), *Child sexual abuse: Disclosure, delay, and denial* (pp. 41–62). Mahwah, NJ: Erlbaum.

Lyon, T. D. (2005). *Ten step investigative interview.* Los Angeles, CA: Author. Available at http://beworkspress.com/ThomasLyon/5/

Lyon, T. D., & Ahern, E. C. (2011). Disclosure of child sexual abuse: Implications for interviewing. In J. E. B. Myers (Ed.), *The APSAC handbook on child maltreatment* (3rd ed., pp. 233–252). Los Angeles, CA: Sage.

Lyon, T. D., & Dorado, J. (2008). Truth induction in young maltreated children: The effects of oath-taking and reassurance on true and false disclosures. *Child Abuse and Neglect, 33*, 71–74.

Lyon, T. D., Malloy, L. C., Quas, J.A., & Talwar, V. (2008). Coaching, truth induction and young maltreated children's false allegations and false denials. *Child Development, 70*, 914–929.

Lyon, T. D., & Saywitz, K. (2000). Qualifying children to take the oath: materials for interviewing professions. Unpublished manuscript [Online]. Available: hal-law.usc.edu/users/tlyon/articles/competency.PDF

Malloy, L. C., Lyon, T. D., & Quas, J. A. (2007). Filial dependency and recantation of child sexual abuse allegations. *Journal of the American Academy of Child & Adolescent Psychiatry, 46*, 162–170.

McDonald, R., Jouriles, E. N., Briggs-Gowan, M. J., Rosenfield, D., & Carter, S. S. (2007). Violence toward a family member, angry adult conflict, and child adjustment difficulties: Relations in families with 1- to 3-year-old children. *Journal of Family Psychology, 21*, 176–184.

Myers, J. E. B. (2005). *Myers on evidence in child, domestic, and elder abuse cases* (Vol. 1). New York, NY: Wolters Kluwer.

National Children's Alliance: Standards for Accredited Members. (2010) Available at www.nationalchildrensalliance.org

Olfason, E., & Lederman C. S. (2006). The state of the debate about children's disclosure patterns in child sexual abuse cases. *Juvenile and Family Court Journal, 27*.

Orbach, Y., & Lamb, M. E. (2007). Young children's references to temporal attributes of allegedly experienced events in the course of forensic interviews. *Child Development, 78*, 1100–1120.

Ornstein, P., & Haden, C. (2002). The development of memory: Toward and understanding of children's testimony. In M. Eisen, J. Quas, & G. S. Goodman (Eds.), *Memory and suggestibility in the forensic interview* (pp. 29–62). Mahwah, NJ: Erlbaum.

Perona, A. R., Bottoms, B. L., & Sorenson, E. (2006). *Research-based guidelines for child forensic interviews*. Available at www.haworthpress.com/web/JAMT

Peterson, C., Dowden, C., & Tobin, J. (1999). Interviewing preschoolers: Comparisons of yes/no and wh-questions. *Law and Human Behavior, 23*, 539–555.

Pipe, M. E., Lamb, M. E., Orbach, Y., Sternberg, K. J., Stewart, H. L., & Esplin, P. W. (2007). Factors associated with nondisclosure of suspected abuse during forensic interviews. In M. E. Pipe, M. E. Lamb, Y. Orbach, & A. C. Cederborg (Eds.), *Child sexual abuse: Disclosure, delay, and denial* (pp. 76–96). Mahwah, NJ: Erlbaum.

Pipe, M. E., & Salmon, K. (2009). Dolls, drawing, body diagrams, and other props: Role of props in investigative interviews. In K. Kuehnle & M. Connell (Eds.), *The evaluation of child sexual abuse allegations: A comprehensive guide to assessment and testimony* (pp. 153–180). Hoboken, NJ: John Wiley & Sons.

Poole, D. A., & Lamb, M. E. (1998). *Investigative interviews of children: A guide for helping professionals*. Washington DC: American Psychological Association.

Reese, E., & Farrant, K. (2003). Narrative and self, myth, and memory: Emergence of the cultural self. In R. Fivush & C. A. Haden (Eds.), *Autobiographical memory and the construction of a narrative self: Developmental and cultural perspectives* (pp. 28–48). Mahwah, NJ: Erlbaum.

Rogoff, B. (2003). *The cultural nature of human development*. New York, NY: Oxford University Press.

Russell, A. (2004). Forensic interview room set-up. *Half a nation: The newsletter of the state and national finding words courses*. Arlington, VA: American Prosecutors Research Institute.

Salmon, K., Roncolato, W., & Gleitzman, M. (2002). Children's reports of emotionally laden events: Adapting the interview to the child. *Applied Cognitive Psychology, 17*, 65–79.

Saywitz, K. J., & Camparo, L. B. (2009). Contemporary child forensic interviewing: Evolving consensus and innovation over 25 years. In B. L. Bottoms, C. J. Najdowski, & G. S. Goodman (Eds.), *Children as victims, witnesses, and offenders: Psychological science and the law*. New York, NY: Guilford Press.

Saywitz, K. J., Goodman G. S., & Lyon, T. D. (2002). Interviewing children in and out of court. In J. E. B. Myers, L. Berliner, J. Briere, C. T. Hendrix, C. Jenny, & T. A. Reid (Eds.), *The APSAC handbook on child maltreatment* (2nd ed., pp. 349–377). Los Angeles, CA: Sage.

Saywitz, K. J., Lyon, T. D., & Goodman, G. S. (2011). Interviewing children. In J. E. B. Myers (Ed.), *The APSAC handbook on child maltreatment* (3rd ed., pp. 233–252). Los Angeles, CA: Sage.

Smith, D. W., Letourneau, E. J., Saunders, B. E., Kilpatrick, D. G., Resnick, H. S., & Best, C. L. (2000). Delay in disclosure of childhood rape: Results from a national survey. *Child Abuse & Neglect, 24*, 273–387.

Sternberg, K. J., Lamb, M. E., Hershkowitz, I., Yudilevitch, L., Orbach, Y., Esplin, P., & Hovav, M. (1997). Effects of introductory style on children's abilities to describe experiences of sexual abuse. *Child Abuse & Neglect, 21*, 1133–1146.

Teoh, Y. S., Yang, P. J., Lamb, M. E., & Larrson, A. S. (2010). Do human figure diagrams help alleged victims of sexual abuse provide elaborate and clear accounts of physical contact with alleged perpetrators? *Applied Cognitive Psychology, 24*, 287–300.

Thierry, K., Lamb, M., Orbach, Y., & Pipe, M. E. (2005). Developmental differences in the function and use of anatomical dolls during interviews with alleged sexual abuse victims. *Journal of Consulting and Clinical Psychology, 73*, 1125–1134.

U.S. Department of Health and Human Services. (2010). *Child maltreatment 2007*. Washington DC: U.S. Government Printing Office.

Vieth, V. I. (2006). Unto the third generation: A call to end child abuse in the United States with 120 years. *Journal of Aggression, Maltreatment & Trauma, 12*, 5–54.

Walters, S., Holmes, L., Bauer, G., & Vieth, V. (2003). *Finding words: Half a nation by 2010: Interviewing children and preparing for court*. Alexandria, VA: American Prosecutors Institute.

Warren, A., Woodall, C., Thomas, M., Nunno, M., Keeney, J., Larson, S., & Stadfeld, J. (1999). Assessing the effectiveness of a training program for interviewing child witnesses. *Applied Developmental Science, 3*, 128–135.

Wesson, M., & Salmon, K. (2001). Drawing and showing: Helping children to report emotionally laden events. *Applied Cognitive Psychology, 15*, 301–320.

Yuille, J. (2002). *The step-wise interview: Guidelines for interviewing children.* Available from John C. Yuille. Department of Psychology, University of British Columbia, 2136 W. Ma., Vancouver, BC, Canada V6T IZ4.

CHAPTER 6

Developmentally Sensitive Assessment Methods in Child Sexual Abuse Cases

SANDRA HEWITT

INTRODUCTION

C HILD SEXUAL ABUSE is often determined by how well a child can talk about what has happened. Very young or developmentally disabled children do not have the capacity to fully express their experiences in words—yet they are among the most vulnerable of children. This chapter addresses the importance of assessment with young children, the parameters of a developmentally focused assessment, and what can be done when a child is at risk but the professionals involved are unable to document sexual abuse. These foundational practice issues with very young children are also applicable to older developmentally disabled children whose verbal communication renders them unable to effectively respond to a standard forensic interview.

THE NEED FOR DEVELOPMENTALLY SENSITIVE ASSESSMENT

Physical abuse and neglect allegations in cases involving young children are not measured primarily by language but are dependent on physical findings. Sexual abuse assessment with young children can be more problematic as, even though the abuse may include penetration, the child often heals quickly and without evidence of damage. Even if there is demonstrated physical damage, putting experience into words that would allow prosecution is still difficult for very young children.

Other arguments against assessing very young children focus on the child's inability to respond in words, and contend that if the child cannot talk about it, then nothing can be done about it and they probably will not remember anyway. This faulty reasoning fails to integrate recent research purporting that very early experiences are in fact encoded, if not in language then in procedural memory (memory for actions and sequences of events). As protective adults we must not identify lack of language on the part of the child as a barrier to our ability to protect children; we must find other methods of identifying risk.

At present the assessment for child sexual abuse focuses on the use of forensically defensible interviews, which are carefully crafted and skillfully conducted; however, very young or disabled children often cannot successfully respond to a standardized interview because they lack the language, concepts, and ability to describe their experiences. If language is used as the criterion for documentation of sexual abuse, these children will fail—a developmental discrimination. If, however, it is understood that although young children cannot express their experiences in words, they are still vulnerable to the effects of abuse, then the need for developmentally adapted assessment becomes evident.

There is reliable and convincing research that documents the long-term impact of early adversity on the developing brain (Cicchetti & Curtis, 2005; Ogawa et al., 1997; Sroufe, Egelend, Carlson, & Collins, 2005). Researchers in early child development understand the impact of this data and press for increased attention and protection during these formative years. Sexual abuse issues also need to be part of this focus, but if a child cannot talk about the experience, how can it be documented? An important lesson comes from early childhood research. Attachment, when measured at 12 months of age, relies on the child's behaviors toward his or her caretaker as an expression of his or her relational history with the caregiver. Young children possess an exquisite repertoire of early interactional patterns that reflect their experiences and can be reliably measured. If this is the case, then good assessment for child sexual abuse may benefit from a shift of focus from the child's words to the child's behaviors. Along with this fundamental shift, the second critical adjustment is to understand the goal of assessment to be protection, not prosecution (unless there are physical findings that can determine the perpetrator) because these children cannot put their experience into words that would allow criminal prosecution.

Parameters of Developmentally Focused Assessment Hewitt (1990) argued for a developmentally based protocol that emphasizes children's behaviors (anchored in standardized testing) as well as their statements, and includes a detailed history of their current status and needs. A more detailed discussion of these procedures can be found in *Assessing Allegations of Sexual Abuse in Preschool Children: Understanding Small Voices* (Hewitt, 1990).

STEP 1: INTERVIEW OF PRIMARY CARETAKER(S)

Because these children are unable to relate their own histories, their caretakers must provide information for them. This information should begin with a good history of the child's developmental history and current status—not the abuse allegations. It is only with a foundation of this information that a full understanding of the child is developed, and it is this information that shapes the structure of the child's assessment. Elements of this interview should include two major areas: early history and current status, and a history of the allegations.

PART 1: HISTORY AND CURRENT STATUS

The Child's Developmental History

- Pregnancy, birth, delivery:
  Were there any problems or concerns that would affect the child now?
- Medical problems:
  Have there been any medical problems that may affect the child's current status or the child's reaction to genital touch (for example, repeated exams for urinary infections, multiple enemas)?
- Developmental milestones:
  Are developmental milestones on target? Did the child walk and talk on time or are there delays that can affect his or her ability to participate in an assessment?
- Early caretakers:
  Have caretakers been consistent and appropriate, or is there a history of multiple moves and multiple caretakers? This can affect the child's ability to trust and relate to the interviewer.
- Attachment/separation history:
  What is the nature of the parent's relationship with the child?
  (Note: Children's experiences with their primary caretakers shape their attachments and it is this template the children bring to your interview. If they have not learned to trust or to cooperate with their caretaker, then you may have to spend more time to create a

working relationship with them than with other children who more readily trust adults.)

- Early traumas:
Have there been events or circumstances that have been traumatic for the child; that is, a history of abuse and neglect, witnessing family violence, death of a sibling or parent, multiple caretakers, abrupt separations? All of these may affect the child's current status, and behaviors displayed may be related to traumas other than the alleged abuse.

Current Status

- Caretakers:
Who are the primary caretakers in the child's life and how many are there? Children with multiple moves and multiple caretakers can be at risk for attachment problems. On the other hand, if the parent is dysfunctional, but another caretaker (effective grandparent, good day-care provider) is available the child can still experience secure attachment interactions.
- Routines:
Are there organized and consistent daily routines or does the child live in a chaotic situation? The environment helps shape a child's sense of internal organization as well as his or her attachment— and this shapes the quality of the responses.
- Idiosyncratic names:
Are there people in the child's environment who may be named but their names not understood by the interviewer?
- Genital names:
What names are used for genitals? Using this information can help you ask the child the most understandable questions.

Sexual History:

What exposure has the child had to sexuality?
- Prior abuse:
Is there a history of physical abuse, sexual abuse, neglect, rejection, harsh discipline, exposure to domestic violence or community violence?
- Exposure to sexual activities:
What sexual activity has the child seen: hugging, kissing, foreplay, intercourse, pornography? Children can present as sexualized when they have been exposed to sexual activities but have not been abused themselves; the argument can be made that premature exposure to

adult sexuality can put children at risk as their normal boundaries for sexual interactions are altered.
- Exposure to explicit sexual materials:
Pornography on screen or in print.

Possible Risk Factors

- Chemical abuse:
Is there a history of chemical abuse in the setting? Has the child been exposed to this? At what level?
- Physical abuse:
Has the child been physically abused or have they witnessed physical abuse?
- Boundaries:
  - Sleep: Does the child sleep alone or with the parent? Has he or she been in the parent's bed during intercourse or foreplay?
  - Bathing: Does the child bathe with anyone in the family? Is there supervision?
  - Family nudity: Is the child exposed to nudity, if so who, how often, when, where?
- Mother/father history of sexual abuse:
A history of trauma can make parents either more sensitive to/aware of possible abuse to their child or it can suppress their awareness of abuse.
- Adult attachment history:
A parent's own history of attachment is often replicated with his or her child. Secure attachment is a buffering factor to the effects of abuse, while insecure attachment may heighten a response because the parent-child relationship is less attuned and supportive.
- Social connectedness:
Is the child's family isolated or does it have helpful social support?
  - Custody battle:
Are allegations occurring in the context of contested custody proceedings? This does not automatically nullify concerns, but the examiner should consider different hypotheses regarding why the child might tell at this time and systematically explore these issues.
- Marital sexual history:
What is the role of sexuality between the parents and how might this affect the child?

In sum, this part of the interview screens for several preexisting factors that can affect children's statements and their responses to any abuse.

The assessor needs to address any problems or concerns that would impair the child's ability to express his or her needs or concerns. All of these issues impact the child's current status, for better or worse, and his or her presentation at the time of assessment. These issues also offer information about other possible areas of concern.

PART 2: ABUSE CONCERNS

The second part of the intake interview is about the abuse concerns; it begins with the primary caretaker, but can also be used with other significant caretakers.

History of Concerns

- First incidence of concern:
  - What happened? Where? When?
  - Describe child's behaviors
  - Describe child's statements
  - Are there other details?
  - What was the precipitating stimulus for the disclosure?

Often interviews focus on the most recent event, while earlier behaviors may have preceded the current concern. Gathering an historical perspective of the concerns can strengthen the importance of the current concerns.

- How it was handled by the recipients of the information:
  - Were they angry?
  - Did they shame or blame the child?
  - Did they express or imply fear?
  - Did they fall apart at the disclosure versus a calm acceptance?
  - What questions were asked?
  - What words were used?

What is the impact of this response on the child's reporting? Contamination of the report is considered here; if there was contamination, what was it and how pervasive was it?

- Other incidents of concern, in order of occurrence:
  - Repeat the above questions for the next and each following incident.

Screening for Significant Behaviors

The child's repertoire of behaviors, over time and across situations, is at the core of abuse assessment for this age. Behaviors precede language;

document these carefully to get the larger picture. Behaviors are also less resistant to contamination as they often occur spontaneously and their appearance may be related to the abuse concerns.

Dimensions of Behavioral Assessment

- Sleep problems
- Play quality
- Toileting
- Bathing
- Fears/phobias
- Compulsive behaviors
- Separation problems

Because young children frequently display dysregulation from sexual abuse in their behaviors, documenting changes or unusual variations in old behaviors adds to more understanding of possible abuse. Also consider that behavioral changes could be a result of the dynamics in the family system or of other trauma.

- Objective measures:
  - Child development inventory (or other developmental assessment measure)
  - Child Sexual Behavior Inventory (CSBI) (Friedrich, 1997)
  - Child Behavioral Checklist (CBCL) (Achenbach, 1991)
  - Trauma Symptom Checklist for Young Children (TSCYC) (Briere, 2005)

Anchoring behaviors in objective measures gives the opportunity to compare the targeted child's behaviors with those of his or her peers, and to document the nature, intensity, and atypicality of his or her experience.

- Collateral information:
  - Medical exam data.
  - Day-care reports—and completion of testing if appropriate.
  - Relatives who have done child care.
  - Child protection investigation notes.
  - Police investigation reports.
  - Children's advocacy interviews.

The primary reporter may not always have all of the data; collateral sources can provide additional information to support the allegations.

PART 3: RULE-OUT HYPOTHESIS

- Are there any problems or concerns that would impair the child's ability to express his or her needs or concerns?

Always consider alternate ways the child's behaviors or statements can be explained. Doing this adds credibility to the report, but it also helps ground the findings in objective thinking.

STEP 2: OBSERVATION AND ASSESSMENT OF THE CHILD

OBSERVATION OF THE PARENT AND CHILD IN FREE PLAY

Watch the child and caretaker together as they explore some toys. Quietly sit back and just observe; this is often a window into the relationship. Do they play separately or together? Is the parent intrusive, passive, or nonresponsive? Is this pattern a long-standing one or something related to the current crisis? If it is a new pattern it may reflect a need of the caretaker's at this time of crisis. How the child uses the parent when they encounter problems gives you a good window into the kind of attachment relationship they share.

CREATE A RELATIONSHIP WITH THE CHILD

When the child comes with the caretaker, the caretaker's response to you helps shape how the child responds to you. If the caretaker is comfortable with you, it lets the child know you are someone who is safe. See if the child will relate to you and allow you to join their play. Creating a relationship with a young child is central to any assessment with the child.

INTERVIEW WITH TECHNIQUES MATCHING THE CHILD'S DEVELOPMENTAL STAGE

If the child has little speech or if speech is unintelligible, then you will need a very simple interview, for example, "Do you have eyes? Where are your eyes?" "Do you have a nose, where is your nose?" "Do you have a tummy, where is your tummy?" "Do you have a peepee?" Use the name the parent says the child uses for their private parts—not your own word. "Does somebody hurt or tickle your peepee?" Use somebody and not anybody, as "any" is a harder concept for a child to manage. Adapt the words and body part to the alleged abuse. This very simple but basic interview is a starting point and can be used for small children who lack sufficient language or concepts to narrate their experiences.

One interview format may not fit all children at this age. You may have to adapt a standard interview format to match the child's level of development. Take time to learn where the child is developmentally and how to choose questions that match this level of developmental. Here is where the behavioral repertoire gathered earlier can help clinicians adapt to the child's level of responding. You will need to decide if you can do this questioning with the parent inside or outside of the room. Some parents will sit quietly and allow you to interact with the child, other parents may be distracting for the child.

STEP 3: WRITING FINDINGS

The outline earlier becomes the structure of the report, with notations in the report about the process and procedures used. Any assessment done with children this young rarely goes to criminal court—unless there are clear medical findings, the donor of those findings can be identified, or there is an eyewitness to the abuse. The use of standardized testing, as well as history and observations, will help clarify the child's status and needs. Observations and history with the parent also supplement opinions. Local demands will determine what kind of report the court will accept and how it should be presented. Most family courts welcome professional observations, perspective, and recommendations that help them understand and direct the case out of an adversarial realm into a protective realm.

WHEN RISK EXISTS BUT THERE IS NO DOCUMENTATION

Evaluation must be separate from intervention, but evaluation should include recommendations for appropriate intervention. In cases where sexual abuse concerns exist, prevention education and family support can be helpful avenues for intervention, regardless of documentation of abuse.

PREVENTION EDUCATION

Teach and practice safety rules with the family. It is important to give the child new rules for behaviors and to clarify the ones that are not okay. You can teach the child to say no and have the parent read and discuss a prevention book such as *It's My Body* (Freeman, 1984) or *Your Body Belongs to You* (Spelman & Weidner, 1997). You can lead with this kind of practical guide, but involvement of parents is critical as they will be the ones following the child after treatment. Children cannot prevent sexual abuse, and adult caregivers need to be the protective resource for their child.

FAMILY SUPPORT

Young children are embedded in their families and if the family is not functioning well, it may not meet the child's needs; the child may then experience not only one trauma, but two—the terrifying absence of a reliable caretaker. Stabilizing the family and strengthening the primary caretaker are critical issues for children this age. When caretakers' needs are addressed, then they can focus on the needs and well-being of their children. An assessment of the caretaker's status and the impact of this trauma on him or her, the impact of the allegations on other children in the family, and the impact on the family dynamics is critical for the abused child's healing. Many caretakers will experience their own traumas at the news that their child has been sexually abused. This also means helping nonoffending parents get help for their own secondary trauma.

TREATING POSTTRAUMATIC STRESS RESPONSES

Parents and caretakers are at risk for traumatic stress responses following abuse. Trauma-Focused Cognitive-Behavioral Therapy (TF-CBT) (see Cohen, Mannarino, & Deblinger, 2006) has been shown to be effective in treating the effects of trauma with older children and adults. Other developmentally sensitive treatment models exist that integrate play, expressive arts, cognitive-behavioral interventions, and family systems work into a child's trauma treatment (Gil, 2006, current volume; Goodyear-Brown, 2009, current volume).

REUNIFICATION APPROACHES WITH THE CHILD AND ALLEGED OFFENDER

Transitioning the child back to contact with an alleged offender after allegations are founded or unfounded should not be left to chance. If it has not been done, a risk evaluation for the alleged offender should be done prior to any reunification treatment. The "clarification" process developed by Dr. Libby Ralston at the Dee Norton Low Country Children's Center in South Carolina is used in treatment with families as a precondition for child safety and reunification. In cases with documented abuse, the "abuse clarification" involves the perpetrator of the abuse defining the abuse as wrong, accepting responsibility for the abusive actions, and for any child or family disruption. The offender acknowledges and defines the abusive behaviors, any grooming to gain access to the child, and any threats given to avoid disclosure. This process is documented in Lipovsky, Swenson, Ralston, and Saunders (1998). The nonoffending caregiver is also a part of this process as a protective resource for the child. The clarification conference takes place once the offender is able to complete this process. At the conclusion of the clarification conference the protective caregiver states his or her acceptance of responsibility for protecting the child, and actions that he or she will take and rules that will be enforced to protect the child in the future.

Whether abuse is or is not confirmed, a "protection clarification" process clarifies the responsibility of the adult caregivers to protect the child, to identify any barriers to past protection, and to define specific protective actions that the caregivers will take in the future. The child's role is to share with the therapist any rules the child needs for the family in order to feel safe. When the child is too young to identify such rules, the therapist can define required safety/protective rules/behaviors for the caregiver. The protection clarification involves the adult caregiver verbally articulating their responsibilities as a protective parent; it introduces the new responsibilities, roles, rules, and boundaries for the family, and the caregiver's responsibility to implement, abide by, and enforce these protective actions. This process can occur at any time when the caregiver is willing and able and may be ordered by the family court and/or may be used as a measurable indicator for the court that reunification is appropriate or not appropriate. The caregiver's willingness and ability to provide this protection clarification for the child can serve as a behavioral measure of the ability and willingness to be child-focused. This clarification process addresses the child's reality of the experience and provides the potential for future safety and trust between the child and his or her caregivers.

Another approach, therapeutic management (Hewitt, 1990), includes involving the custodial parent for an initial interview to discuss the case, the child's status and current needs. His or her need for treatment after the trauma of the allegations is assessed and needed referrals are made. Then the protocol is explained and the custodial parent is invited to work with the child to discuss and develop a list of touches that are safe and not safe, as well as any additional prevention education that is needed. Individual work with the alleged offender repeats the above sequence— assessing the current status, discussing the allegations, making a list of appropriate/inappropriate touch to share with the child, and then working with the child to create a joint understanding of the alleged abuse, and new rules for touching as well as prevention education, evaluation of the relationship, and appropriate steps toward increased contact (visits in therapy, supervised visits, unsupervised visits with follow-up).

Some cases are inappropriate for any unsupervised contact. Children's safety centers have been developing across the country. They provide a safe place for an allegedly abusive parent and the child to meet in a room with developmentally appropriate materials for play, while a trained observer records behaviors, and there are special procedures for drop-off and pick-up. Notes from the visits can be shared with the therapist and/or the court to allow the best decisions to be made for the child's contact with the alleged abuser. Cases of alleged sexual abuse with young children often demand monitoring over time and across situations as the child remains vulnerable due to his or her age. There is little research or data regarding reunification after sexual abuse with very young children, or what the long-term effects of child sexual abuse are when the victim is a very young child. Most of the work in the area of reunification is informal clinical practice, which needs future evaluation to ascertain the value of its application in cases of small children.

LEGAL MATTERS

Cases involving very young children do not go to criminal court unless there is physical evidence, an eyewitness or eyewitnesses, or recorded media that can be linked to the perpetrator. Cases go to family court where the issue is *protection*, not prosecution. This offers an opportunity to shift the court focus from adversarial to the needs of the child's well-being. Information provided to the legal system that focuses on the child's status and needs can help judges craft an order that has the child's protection as its focus. The court needs education to understand the needs of these youngest children so they can receive the safety they need. This education can be done by any professional who is familiar with the research and advocating for the needs of their young charges.

ASSESSING DEVELOPMENTALLY DISABLED CHILDREN

Certain developmental achievements such as adequate communication and memory skills are necessary to make a disclosure. Very young children with disabilities, especially in the areas of language and cognition, may not be able to disclose in a way that is recognized as disclosure. Although persons with disabilities make up from 3% to 5% of the population (LaPlante & Carlson, 1996), children with developmental disabilities are at higher risk for maltreatment (e.g., Sobsey & Doe, 1991; Vig & Kaminer, 2002). Sullivan and Knutson (2000) found that children who were mentally challenged had four times the risk of nondisabled peers for all types of maltreatment, including sexual abuse. Lyon and Saywitz (1999) found significant language delays in a population of children 4 to 7 years old with developmental delays who were alleged abuse victims. The need for special interview methods is critical when working with developmentally disabled children (Nathanson, Crank, Saywitz, & Ruegg, in press; Pipe, Lamb, Orbach, & Cederborg, 2007; Saywitz, Snyder, & Nathanson, 1999). Understanding their needs and status is essential in helping to match these needs with the type of inquiry they require. Older developmentally delayed children, who lack the cognitive or verbal skills to respond to a standardized interview, can also profit from the use of the assessment protocol outlined earlier as it can accommodate to their special needs.

Parents Who Ask Leading and Suggestive Questions

Research supports the fact that leading and suggestive questioning can give rise to false allegations (Ceci & Bruck, 1996), as young children are most vulnerable to this type of inquiry. Statements can be coached, but it is still difficult for a young child to show a response that integrates behaviors, emotions, and statements without experiencing the concerns he or she reflects. Utilizing specially trained early childhood teachers can be very helpful here to provide neutral observations and to complete standardized testing. Their information can assist the evaluator in discerning if the child is indeed displaying atypical behaviors or making atypical statements.

Parents Who Dismiss a Child's Statement or Underreport

These cases often do not appear for assessment at the parent's initiation, but they may be referred by sources other than the parent. Parents who seem blind to their child's concerning sexual behaviors are often abuse survivors themselves and the trauma of their own history can prompt them to be hypervigilant or to underreport. Again, the earlier protocol can compare and contrast the parent's perspective with that of other caregivers as well as that of the evaluator. A careful pre-interview assessment that gathers information from several areas can help inform the evaluator of the contrast between the parent's perspective and that of other caregivers as well as whether to direct the child for a shorter standard forensic interview or a longer extended evaluation process.

Preemptive Interviewing and Multiple Interviews

When a very young or developmentally disabled child appears to be at risk for having been abused, he or she is often referred for a standardized interview to see what can be reported. The children can make statements that are confusing or unclear because they may not understand the demands of the situation, or the questions are beyond their developmental level (e.g., "how many" and "when" are among the concepts that young children have not yet mastered). Their failure to interview well can undermine their credibility, but more importantly, the very system that should protect them may disregard their information. The result is often a return to contact with an alleged offender but without a therapeutically managed reunification process. These children cannot advocate for their own needs, and they are the most dependent on external resources for their protection. The use of standardized interviews should be restricted to children with demonstrated competencies and alternate developmentally based assessment procedures used.

In the quest to respond to the needs of the very young or developmentally disabled child, there is the temptation to repeat a standardized interview with the child, anticipating that maybe "just one more try" will produce the needed information. Repeated interviewing of these children most often produces the opposite effect of the protection they need; it can demonstrate their incompetence while failing to expose the skills they do have to express their histories. Continuing to interview the child bears its own risk of getting responses not tied to facts because of the pressure to respond. It can also shape the child to focus on sexual matters (how many people talk with young children about sex?) as well as abuse. The more appropriate approach is to shift the assessment to a protocol that matches the child's developmental stage, that is, one that gathers information, grounds it in normative data, and then argues for protection when the child's words cannot.

As the recognition that the case will not be prosecuted strengthens, this should open up new avenues of intervention. If there is required contact with an alleged offender, then the access should be in a safe, neutral, supervised setting (i.e., children's safety centers) with observers who can indicate the impact on the child via the behaviors. Some children show a warm joyful contact while others can be fearful and withdrawn. The observations of their interactions are often a stronger index of the dyad's history than any of their words. As the child matures they can be taught basic, age appropriate prevention education. The required contact with the alleged offender can involve the alleged offender assisting in teaching healthy boundaries, monitoring inappropriate interactions, and setting limits and boundaries. The person can also be involved in the removal of any censures about telling that may have been given. These cases are not about prosecution, they are about protection, and the building of strong, safe, prevention skills. This developmentally sensitive approach can move a family from a traumatized, victim-focused stance to a well-educated, supported, and protective position.

PARENTS WHO ALLEGE CHILD SEXUAL ABUSE AS A WAY TO GAIN CUSTODY

This issue often emerges in conjunction with a contested custody matter, or when frightened and concerned parents are reacting to what they have seen or heard that might indicate abuse. Parents repeatedly alleging sexual abuse of their child may want an assessment that focuses on aspects of the child's history, which would demonstrate specific abuse-related information. An evaluation that looks at the child across different domains and situations is helpful here. The format detailed earlier can provide information about the way the different caretakers see the child's current status, and ground these observations in normative data. This data, when compared with parent's data, helps to provide a more balanced picture of the child's status and needs. Three cases are presented to highlight the complexity of these cases.

CASE STUDIES

Case 1

The parents were married but with a great deal of animosity and distrust between them. The couple separated when the child was almost two and a half, but father saw the child for limited visits until the mother moved with the child to a distant state. Father went to court and was awarded visitation. Six weeks after the move he met the child in her new state for several time limited visits, across several days. After one of the last visits the child complained to her day-care provider that her bottom hurt. The provider informed the mother and later that evening the mother questioned the child. She videotaped the conversation in which the child said the father put a stick in her vagina. The mother informed the police, the child was interviewed by professionally trained staff using a standard forensic interview, and the child repeated the statement given to the mother. The father was charged with sexual abuse. The court also ordered an evaluation of the child.

This evaluation reviewed the case history and attached documents and noted that the medical examination completed the day after the report found no evidence of physical damage that would be consistent with a stick being inserted in the vagina of the young child (although tissue in this area can heal rapidly) and the child was not upset with the examination. In his interview the father denied any form of

(continued)

(*continued*)
inappropriate touch with the child and wanted a quick resolution to the case so he could resume contact. The mother was interviewed about the child's early developmental history, current status, and the chronology of behavioral and sexual concerns around the abuse allegations. The mother also completed standardized testing—a child development inventory, the Child Behavior Checklist, and the Child Sexual Behavior Inventory. Child development skills were well above average (consistent with the child's presentation), the Child Behavior Checklist was also within normal limits (as would be expected given the passage of time between the alleged event and this evaluation and no contact with the alleged offender), but the Child Sexual Behavior Inventory was significantly elevated for both developmentally related sexual behavior and sexual abuse specific behaviors (these were endorsed at the 99th percentile).

Mother's journal notes written after each of the visits with the father showed no evidence of behavioral or emotional problems with the child after the daily visits, except for the evening of the videotaping, and normal behaviors followed thereafter. The child was observed with the mother. She was cheerful, outgoing, and had excellent speech and language for her age; her play was age-appropriate, if not advanced. She used her mother for help as needed and engaged her in play. At the end of the observation the examiner interacted with both the mother and child, working to create rapport and a comfortable relationship with the child.

When the child was seen alone with the examiner, the child's play was active and reciprocal, again with good language and articulation, and an easy engagement with the examiner. In this context pictures of different facial affect were presented and the child identified the feelings appropriately (happy, sad, mad, scared) with some ability to talk about situations in which she felt these emotions. After the break the child was seen for a systematic survey of touch. The child spoke comfortably about being hugged, kissed, and tickled—all of which she liked. She did not like spankings. When asked about touches on her private parts (the child's words for genitals were used), she was shown a picture of a nude female child's body and asked (pointing to the crotch on the child drawing) if "somebody hurts or tickles *you*, here, where you go potty?" The child repeated that her father put a stick in her bottom—but did so with a cheerful and animated demeanor.

The examiner documented the history, current status, and response of the child—indicating a response to genital touch by the
(*continued*)

father, with the incongruence of statement and affect also noted. A later criminal trial dismissed abuse charges. The case went to family court to address the matter of visitation and father was awarded time with the child, but with supervision by a relative.

Behaviors rather than utterances were the main focus of this case. Because of the strong dislike of the father by the mother her responses may not capture the full scope of these young children's responses, and she may have asked leading or suggestive questions in querying the information. Despite the verbal allegations recorded by the mother, data from other domains (day care, medical examination, standardized testing), including mother's diary about her child before and after the allegations, showed no behavioral disturbances at the time of the alleged penetration. Abuse could not be determined and the child was court-ordered into resumed visits with her father. Follow-up indicated she did well after the visits.

Case 2

Mother Alleges Sexual Abuse of Her Son by the Father

A speech- and language-delayed almost-3-year-old boy began to display signs of behavioral and emotional disruption after visitation with his father in the months after the couple's separation. The child would cling and cry on separation, and refuse to separate from his mother on return. After one visit he spontaneously told his mother, "Peepee Daddy kiss," and grabbed his crotch as he said this. Father denied any inappropriate touching of his son, but mother reported a history of sexualized touching with his younger sister when she was about 11 years old and he was a teenager. This was not reported as abusive.

The mother brought the child for the first evaluation session and he was observed to have one- to two-word sentences, "Car," "Two Trains." With his mother he played freely and often invited her into the play, exhibiting more skill and elaboration than his utterances would indicate. He was alert and aware of his surroundings and repeatedly invited his mother to join him in his play or to assist him as he played. His interactions with the examiner were limited. The father brought the child to the second evaluation session. The father directed the play and the child silently watched or followed his

(continued)

(continued)

offerings, but the child interacted only briefly with his father and then only around the toy cars and later with the dinosaurs. Although father asked multiple questions of his son, the child responded with limited words as well as limited eye contact.

Both parents completed screening measures for developmental status. The mother indicated developmental skills commensurate with the child's age, with the exception of speech and language. The mother endorsed significant levels of sleep disturbance on the Child Behavior Checklist with borderline scores for emotional reactivity and somatic complaints. The Child Sexual Behavior Inventory was not significant for developmentally related sexual behaviors, but sexual abuse–specific items were endorsed at a clinically significant range.

Father reported developmental skills significantly below the child's age on all scales of the Child Development Inventory. He endorsed no items of concern on the scales of the Child Behavior Checklist, but this was in contrast to his verbal report of his son's sleep and behavior problems. The Child Sexual Behavior Inventory was not significant for either normative or sexual abuse–related behaviors, with only two items out of the 36 items endorsed. On the third appointment the child was able to separate from his mother and a brief survey of touch was done. The child was asked, in individual questions, who hugs, kisses, spanks or hits him, and, finally, if somebody touches him on his penis, "Here, where you go potty," pointing to the child's crotch. The child was alert and followed the questions presented. He reported with a "yes" that his mother hugs him, kisses him, and tickles him. When asked if he could "show me where these hugs go," and so forth, he was able to demonstrate where these touches went. He repeated demonstrations for kissing and tickling; he denied his mother touched his peepee. He responded that his father hugged him, his father tickled him, and he spontaneously demonstrated how his father hit him by slapping his bottom when asked if someone hit him. When asked, "Does somebody hurt or tickle you, here, where you go potty?" the child responded "Daddy. Kiss. Peepee." This was delivered with a steady, solemn gaze at the examiner.

Due to the child's difficulties in verbally disclosing his experiences, several adult observations were forwarded to the court. These observations included the mother's endorsement of behavioral dysregulation (which was consistent with her verbal report), the early childhood education teacher's descriptions of the child's sudden fearful and

(continued)

withdrawn behavior, plus the atypical statements of the child, the father's concerning sexual history with his sister, and the son's repeated, clear statement about his father kissing his penis. The court ordered supervised visitation. The supervisor's behavioral logs indicated a strong resistance by the child when his father would change his diapers or try to help him with toileting. As the child grew older he would deliberately shut the door so the father was not in the bathroom, while allowing the supervisor to help him with toileting.

Tension between the father and the supervisor brought the case to court for a hearing. The supervisor's notes were submitted, along with other observations from the child's preschool teacher regarding his fearfulness at toileting, and the earlier evaluation. The court ordered the continuation of the supervised visitation. As the child grew older his vocabulary and expressive language increased, but as this happened, father cancelled visits more frequently until he was having very limited contact—with continued supervision. The father was later under criminal investigation for alleged sexual misconduct in another situation. Findings from this investigation raised significant concerns about the father's behaviors in other domains. Eighteen months after the initial report, the case was reviewed in court and all visits were stopped.

Case 3

A $3\frac{1}{2}$-year-old girl complained of hurting in her genital area and asked her mother if she wanted to play a "tickle tickle" game with her like she did with her father. With further examination by the mother the child also said she played this with her father at bedtime when both she and her father are in their underwear with their pajamas off.

Mother reported this to her pediatrician, he reported to the police, and the child was referred to a children's advocacy center (CAC) for evaluation. The medical evaluation at the CAC found no physical evidence of sexual abuse (not unusual for a young child as the mucosal tissue in the genital area of these children heals rapidly), and the interview did not confirm abuse. The child was referred for individual psychological evaluation.

The evaluation involved individual work with the child but also observation of the child with each parent. The mother brought her daughter to the first appointment and the child was very
(continued)

(continued)

disorganized and unreliable in her comments. She had difficulty sustaining attention and responding to questions. She refused questions about any sexualized activity. She reported enjoying time at her father's and her father's play with her and her brother.

Mother completed two test measures. On the Child Sexual Behavior Inventory, significant elevations in the areas of both developmentally related sexual behaviors and sexual abuse specific behaviors were endorsed. On the Child Behavior Checklist elevated levels of activity and anger were prominent. Observations of free play between the mother and child showed increased motor activity by the child, resistance to the mother's directions, and outbursts of anger. Mother saw these responses as a reaction to the father. During this interview mother also reported her own history of child sexual abuse and voiced fears that her history would be repeated with her daughter. The father brought his daughter to the second appointment. When they entered the room the child joined her father on the couch and sat close to him as they talked together. She also sustained attention as everyone talked. In free play she used her father to help her with difficult puzzles. She was able to focus and attend to the work at hand in his presence. Father's reporting on the Child Sexual Behavior Inventory showed no significant elevations and father's Child Behavior Checklist was also within normal limits. The child's preschool teachers were also interviewed. They reported no atypical sexual behaviors at school. Their Child Behavior Checklist was within normal limits except for concerns about distractibility and some hyperactivity.

Over the next two months the parents separated. The mother reported several more allegations of possible sexual abuse to the police after the child returned from visits: the child made statements about undressing to her underwear at her father's; she began jumping on her mother's pelvic area and tickling her mother's breasts; she insisted her mother lie down while she crawled over her mother's face—making sure her underwear brushed the mother's face and insisting that she get "low enough" as she crawled on her mother. The mother withheld the child from visits. The father denied the allegations, took the case to court, and the court ordered evaluation of both parents. During this period the mother reported additional allegations of sexual abuse by the father.

Once again his unsupervised contact was suspended but he could see the child in a professional office. The child and her father were

(continued)

seen together a few weeks later. Initially the child was somewhat reluctant to interact with or approach her father, and he did not push this. He invited her to do some drawing on a white board and later to play a board game with her on the floor. The child was responsive to her father's requests and completed a drawing of swirls in different colors, and then followed her father's directions for a short game of Candyland. At the end of the hour the father moved to sit on the office sofa as he and the examiner talked about the session. The child played with toys but then came to sit by her father. He engaged her in describing their bedtime routine and the child spoke in an organized and coherent manner, responding appropriately to her father's questions, leaning against him at the end of the hour.

Psychological evaluations of each parent were completed and the court ordered placement of the child and her younger brother with the father and supervised visits with the mother, who was also referred to therapy for her own history of sexual abuse and her current concerns.

CONCLUSION

Sorting out allegations of sexual abuse with young children involved in custody disputes is challenging for any professional. The use of standardized testing, across multiple domains and over time, along with individual assessment and collateral observations, can help provide an objective view of the child from various points of view. It can also help in anchoring professional recommendations for the child's best interest when allegations are alleged but not substantiated during a marital dissolution process. These young children are the most vulnerable and the least able to protect themselves. Developmentally appropriate assessment can help insure they are afforded the protection they need.

REFERENCES

Achenbach, T. M. (1991). Manual for the child behavior checklist/4-18 and 1991 profile. Burlington, VT: University of Vermont, Department of Psychiatry.

Briere, J. (2005). *Trauma symptom checklist for young children.* Lutz, FL: Psychological Assessment Resources.

Ceci, S., & Bruck, M. (1996). In K. Kuehnle (Ed.), *Assessing allegations of child sexual abuse.* Sarasota, FL: Professional Resource Exchange.

Cicchetti, D., & Curtis, J. (2005). An event related potential study of the processing of affective facial expressions in young children who experienced maltreatment during the first year of life. *Development and Psychopathology, 17,* 641–677.

Cohen, J., Mannarino, A., & Deblinger, E. (2006). *Treating trauma and traumatic grief in children and adolescents*. New York, NY: Guilford Press.

Friedrich, W. N. (1997). *Child sexual behavior inventory*. Lutz, FL: Psychological Assessment Resources.

Gil, E. (2006). *Helping abused and traumatized children: Integrating directive and nondirective approaches*. New York, NY: Guilford Press.

Goodyear-Brown, P. (2009). *Play Therapy with Traumatized children: A Prescriptive Approach*. Hoboken, NJ: John Wiley & Sons.

Hewitt, S. K. (1999). *Assessing allegations of sexual abuse in preschool children: Understanding small voices*. Thousand Oaks, CA: Sage.

Ireton, H. (1990). *Child Development Inventory Assessment of Children's Development, Symptoms, and Behavior problems*. San Antonio, TX: Pearson Assessments.

LaPlante, M. M., & Carlson, D. (1996). *Disability in the United States: Prevalence and causes, 1992*. Based on the national health interview survey, disabilities statistical Report (7). Washington, DC: National Institute on Disability and Rehabilitation Research.

Lipovsky, J. A., Swenson, C. C., Ralston, M. E., & Saunders, B. E. (1998). The abuse clarification process in the treatment of intrafamilial child abuse. *Child Abuse & Neglect, 22*, 729–741.

Lyon, T. D., & Saywitz, K. J. (1999). Young maltreated children's competence to take the oath. *Applied Developmental Science, 3*, 16–27.

Nathanson, R., Crank, J. N., Saywitz, K. J., & Ruegg, E. (in press). Enhancing the oral narrative of children with learning disabilities. *Reading and Writing Quarterly*.

Ogawa, J. R., Sroufe, L. A., Weinfield, N. S., Carlson, E. A., & Egeland, B. (1997). Development and the fragment self: Longitudinal study of dissociative symptomatology in a nonclinical sample. *Developmental and Psychopathology, 9*, 855–879.

Pipe, M., Lamb, M., Orbach, Y., & Cederborg, A. (2007). *Child sexual abuse: Disclosure, delay, and denial*. New York, NY: Routledge.

Saywitz, K., Snyder, L., & Nathanson, R. (1999). Facilitating the communicative competence of the child witness. *Applied Developmental Science, 3*(1), 58–68.

Sobsey, D., & Doe, T. (1991). Patterns of sexual abuse and assault. *Journal of Sexuality and Disability, 9*(3), 185–199.

Spelman, C. M., and Weidner, T. (1997). *Your Body Belongs to You*. Park Ridge, IL. Albert Whitman & Company.

Sroufe, L. A., Egeland, B., Carlson, E. A., & Collins, A. (2005). *The development of the person: The Minnesota study of risk and adaptation from birth to adulthood*. New York, NY: Guilford Press.

Sullivan, P. M., & Knutson, J. F. (2000). Maltreatment and disabilities: A population-based epidemiological study. *Child Abuse & Neglect, 24*, 1257–1274.

Vig, S., & Kaminer, R. (2002). Maltreatment and developmental disabilities in children. *Journal of Developmental and Physical Disabilities, 14*(4), 371.

CHAPTER 7

Comprehensive and Therapeutic Assessment of Child Sexual Abuse

A Bridge to Treatment

PATTI VAN EYS and ALANNA TRUSS

INTRODUCTION

B ROADLY SPEAKING, THE evaluation of children who may have experienced sexual abuse serves two main purposes: (1) determining the likelihood and nature of sexual abuse to inform legal decision making, and (2) understanding the child's functioning to inform treatment planning. Forensic assessment focuses on the first goal; clinical assessment on the second. "There are some differences in the method of evaluating children who may have been abused, depending on whether the evaluator is conducting a forensic or a clinical assessment" (American Academy of Child and Adolescent Psychiatry, 1997). There are clear forensic interviewing guidelines that increase the likelihood of obtaining detailed, specific, and accurate information (see Chapter 5). In clinical evaluation, the goal is to understand children's perceptions of their traumatic exposure, rather than obtain forensically sound disclosures, as these perceptions are most important for treatment. It is complicated when systems are not clear on this goal and expect clinical evaluation to serve a forensic purpose. It is imperative to clarify our specific roles and the roles of others within the system as we approach comprehensive clinical assessment of children with known or suspected sexual abuse.

In contrast to clear practice parameters for forensic evaluations of child sexual abuse (CSA), existing literature reveals no clear parameters for conducting clinical evaluations with this population; however, a few common themes emerge. These include the need for (1) both clinical interviews and standardized assessment measures (e.g., King et al., 2003), (2) multi-informant assessment (e.g., Burrows Horton & Cruise, 1997), (3) broadband and abuse specific assessment tools (e.g., Fricker & Smith, 2001), and (4) assessing specific areas such as trauma exposure, posttraumatic stress disorder (PTSD), depression, anxiety, and sexual behavior problems (e.g., Miller & Veltkamp, 1995). Generally missing are discussions of strategies for comprehensive clinical evaluation of CSA and conceptualizing the information gained in order to inform intervention. This void in the literature is striking given that effective therapy relies heavily on good initial and ongoing assessment. It may reflect the common misconception that CSA has a similar impact on most children and most sexually abused children will therefore benefit from the same basic treatment approach. However, the growing literature on CSA reveals multiple and varied impacts, which are dependent on the specific nature of the abuse as well as other relevant factors (e.g., other maltreatment, family dynamics). Many outcomes commonly associated with CSA (e.g., anxiety, depression, somatic complaints, conduct problems) also occur in children without maltreatment histories. A thorough clinical assessment is essential in better understanding these factors and informing intervention.

One excellent resource on comprehensive assessment of CSA is Friedrich's (2002) book. Friedrich argues for a theoretical framework to guide assessment and discusses three domains (parent-child attachment, self-regulation, and self-development), strategies for assessing them, and subsequent treatment planning. He includes appendices rich with assessment tools.

The goal of this chapter is to provide a comprehensive, user-friendly discussion of clinical evaluation of sexually abused children with utility for treatment planning. Effective evaluation with this population requires an understanding of sound assessment principles paired with common sexual abuse specific dynamics and challenges. Our evaluation framework incorporates these ideas as well as knowledge gained in our clinical experience with CSA. Clinical scenarios are used to highlight the complexities and need for flexibility in the assessment process.

ASSESSMENT IN THE CONTEXT OF CHILD SEXUAL ABUSE

Assessment falls on a continuum from ongoing informal assessment conducted by therapists to formal assessment that often includes a multi-informant, multimeasure approach. This chapter is slanted toward formal psychological assessment; however, some strategies included are also useful in intake and routine sessions. Although formal, comprehensive assessment is valuable for treatment planning, assessment also needs to be an individualized, ongoing, routine part of therapy, to evaluate progress, and to continuously tweak treatment goals appropriately.

GENERAL ASSESSMENT

To help children progress from maladaptive symptoms to a place of health, one must assess the "whole child" within each child's unique context (e.g., developmental level, family system, cultural context). Thus, effective assessment of CSA begins with general principles of psychological assessment of children (for review, see Groth-Marnat, 2009; Sattler, 2002, 2008). A useful way to conceptualize comprehensive assessment is through the HOT (**H**istory, **O**bservation, and **T**esting) approach.

History (H)   A complete history of the child and child's system is gained through interviews and record review. General areas to consider include *description of the current problem(s)* (onset, frequency, intensity, previous treatment); *family background* (socio-economic status (SES), culture, family constellation and relationships, family emotional/medical history, changes/stressors, violence); *developmental history* (prenatal including substance exposure, birth and postnatal, developmental milestones, family atmosphere, attachment process, temperament, medical, emotional, and behavioral history, trauma); *parenting practice* (parent-child relationship quality, discipline techniques, child-rearing attitudes, parenting style, caregiver roles, caregiver's childhood); *academic history* (adjustment to school, achievement); *social relatedness* (peers, family members, adults); *deviance* (substance abuse, sexual behavior problems, aggression, legal problems); *strengths* (family, child, caregiver, community). We prioritize gathering records from the following sources: educational, medical, mental health, child welfare, and legal. Because we serve custodial children we are frequently faced with limited history from substitute caregivers. Even with a solid informant, we may confront gaps that may be filled through relevant records as illustrated below.

A 15-year-old boy with a history of sexual abuse and neglect, raised by his aunt from age 5, was failing academically and in legal trouble for aggressive threats.

We obtained early medical records (previously unknown to his aunt) indicating a diagnosis at age 3 of a seizure disorder and signs of a rare genetic syndrome, but no medical follow-up. Our child psychiatrist remarked, "This medical history could explain much of his current behaviors!" Without records, we might have unknowingly attributed more of his symptomatology to his early neglect and abuse and missed the need to refer him to neurology and genetics.

Observation (O)   Consistent with multi-informant assessment, "O" includes clinicians' and others' (e.g., caregivers, teachers, case workers) observations. Clinicians should observe the child's relationship to his caregivers, reactions to other children both familiar (e.g., classmates) and unfamiliar (e.g., children in lobby), and reactions to the examiner and other clinic staff. For example: How does a child react to meeting the examiner? How does he respond to tasks outside his comfort zone? What is noteworthy about the child's ability to express herself, to remember, to attend/focus, and to use appropriate eye contact? How does the antsy child respond to redirection? Does the guarded child finally "warm up" to the examiner? Is the youngster oppositional? Indiscriminately affectionate? Overly submissive? The value of observation is illustrated below.

An 8-year-old girl being interviewed for various "bad things that happen to children" was cooperative on noninterpersonal traumas (e.g., house fire) but became agitated when interpersonal traumas were introduced. With encouragement she attempted to reengage, only to wet her pants when asked further questions about interpersonal abuse. She denied sexual abuse, but became increasingly agitated on sexual abuse specific items, yelling loudly, "No! No!" These observations provided valuable information regarding extreme emotional guardedness.

Testing (T)   Testing helps to clarify or refine emerging clinical impressions following "H" and "O." Sometimes "T" is not necessary because the clinician has obtained enough through interviews, records, and observations. Areas needing further assessment might include, but are not limited to, intellectual and/or academic functioning and specific symptomatology or psychopathology not determined fully through interview. Such information may inform treatment planning as illustrated by the clinical example below.

A 9-year-old boy, sexually victimized at school by a peer, had continuing symptoms (e.g., inattention, sexual gestures and language) despite a year of sex abuse specific therapy and a school safety plan. At referral, his symptoms were fully attributed to sexual abuse reactivity. Assessment revealed a diagnosis of Tourette's Syndrome, which explained his issues with inattention and sexual behaviors, both of which subsided with appropriate pharmacological treatment.

Although the previous example showed how testing clarified an over-looked diagnosis due to misattribution of symptoms to sexual abuse, we more often see children labeled with conditions such as Attention Deficit Hyperactivity Disorder (ADHD) and Bipolar Disorder, when symptoms are best accounted for by trauma-related reactions.

Testing also helps clinicians gain more information from guarded youngsters who may warm up over several hours due to strengthened rapport. The examiner typically begins with tasks that promote success and are not emotionally demanding. For example, the examiner might begin with "Let's list as many feelings as we can think of in one minute." This assesses the child's emotions vocabulary in a fun, brief, less-demanding task. Or, an examiner might begin with structured intellectual tasks that are more familiar (e.g., "school-like") and emotionally neutral.

Types of Assessment Measures Within the "T" Component of the HOT Approach

Both objective and projective measures aid in gaining a comprehensive understanding of sexual abuse issues within a psychological evaluation. Following is a description of these types of measures.

Objective Tests   Objective tests have right and wrong answers (e.g., intelligence tests) or cutoff scores that show clinically significant symptom levels (e.g., behavior symptom checklists). Such tests are standardized and well-normed on samples of children similar to the children being tested, which allows meaningful comparisons.

Projective Tests   Sometimes indirect measures known as "projective tests" help children reveal important information regarding their subjective and idiosyncratic world- and self-views. Projective testing can be construed as a form of extended interview that allows clinicians to create hypotheses regarding the child's inner workings. Still within a structured assessment milieu, the child may warm to the assessment process through techniques such as drawings, storytelling, completing sentences, or other tasks designed to give the child psychological distance from troubling issues. The typically ambiguous stimuli presented in projective testing do not suggest a certain response and most children do not suppose they are revealing anything about themselves, allowing children to "project" their own perceptions and revealing their particular points of view, issues, values, wishes, and struggles relating to self and relationship with others. The child is told that there are no right or wrong answers, often removing performance anxiety.

Projective testing differs from objective testing because it is not as tightly standardized or normed and does not have right and wrong answers. One projective test, the Rorschach Inkblot Test (Rorschach, 1941), provides extensive norms and standardization (Exner, 1995), the validity of which has been heavily debated (e.g., Parker, 1983). Friedrich (2002) argues for inclusion of the Rorschach in assessing CSA, both for discerning psychosis as well as through use of other indices that can shed light on a child's inner world (e.g., coping index, egocentricity index). We find the Rorschach to be useful in cases where: (1) a very guarded child might "warm up" due to the ambiguous nature of the task; (2) there is a question of a thought disorder; (3) idiosyncratic content might surface (sometimes sexual, aggressive, or morbid); and (4) we seek observations of how a child approaches a very ambiguous, unstructured task. The following example shows the utility of the Rorschach in CSA assessment.

Lisa, age 7, with an extensive abuse history, was referred for concerns about possible psychosis and dissociation. The Rorschach indicated a thought disorder and psychosis. Her reality testing was poor, and her responses were largely morbid, mutilatory, and focused on genitalia and excrement (e.g., "a dead bird . . . everything's eaten it"; "a pretty mother ant but they killed it"; "a dead person . . . looks like he's going number two"; "It looks like it's having a baby . . . the red stuff.") At times, she actively dissociated in response to "triggers" from the inkblots. Once treated with antipsychotic medication, Lisa focused more in therapy and her dissociative disorder became more accessible to treatment.

Through projective stories some children reveal their inner worlds while others remain concrete and guarded. We routinely use the Roberts Apperception Test for Children (RAT-C; McArthur & Roberts, 1982), which is both gender- and race-specific and offers scenes that pull for issues such as school attitudes, parent-child relationships, peer relationships, anger control, and nurture. The Thematic Apperception Test (TAT; Murray, 1943) has several cards that we find useful with youth. The Tell-Me-A-Story test (TEMAS; Constantino, Malgady, & Rogler, 1988) is effective with teens, as the drawings are more contemporary and colorful and pull for adolescent transitions. Further, the TEMAS is race/ethnic ambiguous. Some tests provide theoretical guidelines (e.g., TAT) or quasi-standardized, formal scoring systems for projective storytelling (e.g., RAT-C, TEMAS) while others do not (Projective Storytelling—PST). We typically interpret projective stories thematically, looking for themes such as loss, victimization, resilience, aggression, sexuality, discipline, self-worth, externalization of blame, empathy, problem solving, and relationship to authority. We also note whether the child is able to describe the picture beyond the superficial level indicating the possibility of a rich or impoverished inner life, an inhibited or disinhibited style, a high or low cognitive capacity, or some combination. We note whether the story told makes sense given the stimulus picture and if not, we wonder about defensiveness, thought disorder, or oppositionality.

Projective Storytelling (PST; Caruso & Pulcini, 1990) and the Sexual Projective Card Set (SPCS; Behavioral Technology, 1996) are maltreatment specific projective storytelling tools. These include highly suggestive stimuli that are less apt to pull for purer projections than more ambiguous pictures. These tools are not validated or intended for standardized use, but for use as interview and therapy tools to draw out abuse-specific attributions, feelings, and cognitions.

Consider 7-year-old Amanda with documented physical abuse, neglect, and domestic violence, and concerns about sexual abuse. Though denying sexual exposure when asked directly, her projective stories included extreme sexual content including an older male relative being sexual toward a young girl and using common perpetrator tricks. In response to a picture of a man laying on a bed with a small child propped on his chest, Amanda stated, "I know what it is. I can't say it. I can't believe you gave me this one." She then told about "pa" telling the little girl to get on top of him "in the right spot that is right here" (pointed to man's pelvic region). "Pa" reassured the little girl not to be scared, that it was "the right thing to do." He justified his actions stating, "All I am doing is trying to make you feel better and hugging you." When finished, Amanda gave the card to the examiner, saying, "I can't look at this picture anymore. Put it away."

Ten-year-old Kate's story in response to a picture of two adults in verbal confrontation portrayed her anger at her birth mother who had chronically exposed her to unhealthy, chaotic, adult relationships.

Once upon a time there was this lady. She had an argument with her husband because he was cheating on her. She had a 4-month-old baby. He said it wasn't his because he wore his "whitie tighties" so it wasn't his. He found out it was his, and he said, "This can't be! I wore my tightie whities!" His wife said, "I don't know, but you have to pay child support." The whole time this was going on the 3-year-old was watching. There was lots of chaos in the house. The police came. The family had to go to court. Mom had to go to jail. The Dad was beating up on her. The baby had to go into foster care. They all got separated. They never saw each other again. The End.

Some children respond well to storytelling while others seem to prefer drawing projectively. We typically try both modalities and include drawings of a person (Draw-A-Person, DAP; Koppitz, 1968) and of "your family doing something" (Kinetic Family Drawing, KFD; Burns, 1970) to ascertain how children view themselves and significant others in relationship. After having children describe their drawing(s), we ask routine questions tailored to a child's age, gender, and circumstances (see the Appendix to this chapter for a list of possible questions). The KFD can provide perspective on a child's sense of role and identity within a family. The DAP typically reveals a child's attitudes regarding self or idealized self. Children generally engage readily in the DAP and KFD; however, we sometimes note resistance or confusion. One overly compliant 8-year-old boy in foster care due to a history of maternal neglect was asked to "draw your family doing something." This passive child, who had worked hard all morning on assessment tasks, became resistant, insisting, "I don't want to talk about my family; I don't want to draw my family" and "What family do I draw?" When his reluctance was gently processed, along with the instruction, "You can include anyone you choose . . . there is no right or wrong way to do it," he decided to draw just his foster mother and himself holding hands while waiting for the school bus. He included hearts coming from both figures and he wore a jet-pack that could lift them up and take them to his foster mother's favorite place. His KFD reflects a nurturing and safe relationship as well as a strong and growing attachment to his foster mother.

Most children reflect themselves in their DAP; some reflect important others.

An oppositional and disturbed preteen drew "Amy," her deceased birth mother who had exposed her to a life of prostitution, chaotic violence, and neglect before dying two years earlier. While guarded and overtly oppositional on interview, she revealed projectively her unprocessed and complicated grief with continuing deep ambivalence about the relationship with her deceased mother. When asked Amy's "biggest problem," she said, "Doesn't have time to take care of her children" but when asked what is "the best thing about Amy," she responded, "She's the best mother ever." When asked what makes Amy sad, she responded, "When her boyfriend hurts her," and when asked what makes her angry, she responded, "When her boyfriends hurt her children."

To ascertain a child's emotional understanding and experience, or to learn more about a child's feelings related to particular persons or events (e.g., before foster care; during foster care), we lead the child through a Color-Your-Heart (CYH) task (Goodyear-Brown, 2002, 2010). The child color codes a heart with certain emotions, which the examiner may need to guide. We suggest that the four basic emotions (sad, happy, mad, and scared) be used at minimum. The child is directed to "fill in the amount of each feeling that is in your heart today" (or "for your relationship with your mother," or "before the abuse," etc.). The examiner then goes back over the colors with the child, asking her to list the things that make her happy, sad, angry, or scared. These are recorded on the heart by the respective colors.

A final semi-projective measure we include is the Incomplete Sentences (IS) task (e.g., Loevinger & Wessler, 1970). This brief, easy-to-administer task is an effective warm-up to assessment. For example, the stem "I like . . ." might elicit child responses such as "ice cream," "you," or "my foster mom." We look for self-reflection themes across sentences that give clues to the inner workings of the child. We offer the choice for the child to write his own answers or for the examiner to read the sentence stems and the child give verbal answers.

Consider Tianna, a 13-year-old sexually abused girl. Her IS revealed how her sexual abuse had impacted her relationships with males as well as concerns about physical touch (e.g., I am afraid "of boys," Boys "I hate," I don't like "people touching me," and It isn't nice "to touch other people").

HOT APPROACH: ABUSE SPECIFIC ISSUES

Abuse specific information might naturally surface through objective or projective measures, general interviews, or record review; however, for thorough coverage of known or suspected CSA history and sequelae, clinicians are advised to specifically query certain areas if not already covered in the general assessment. These areas are introduced in the sections below and include trauma exposure and symptoms related to Posttraumatic Stress Disorder, Developmental Trauma Disorder, trauma-genic factors of abuse and related cognitive distortions, and safety issues. Embedded within these main sections are other important CSA specific issues for assessment including sexual reactivity/sexual behavior problems, factors surrounding the disclosure of abuse including family stress, loss and/or disruption following disclosure, other forms of abuse in the family (e.g., domestic violence, neglect, sibling abuse, physical, emotional), proximity to offending family member(s), status of nonoffending caregiver (e.g., supportive or not), and involvement with the "system" such as child welfare and court.

Trauma Exposure   Understanding a child's trauma history is an essential part of the clinical evaluation process for CSA as well as more general assessment. Given the impact of trauma exposure, failing to inquire about these experiences can lead to misattributions about the causes of presenting challenges. The literature is clear that more often than not, children who have been sexually abused have also been exposed to additional traumatic events (Cohen, Mannarino, & Deblinger, 2006). Although our society is generally biased toward thinking that sexual abuse has a more negative impact than other forms of abuse (e.g., physical abuse, neglect) and trauma (e.g., house fire, vehicle accident), there is no data to support this. Therefore we need to understand the entirety of a child's trauma history in order to decipher which event(s) are causing current impairment. Sometimes symptomatology can be clearly linked to a particular trauma, whereas other times the traumatic events are interrelated and their impact cannot be teased apart. This understanding is essential in identifying appropriate treatment targets.

Through involvement in a Tennessee Trauma-Focused Cognitive-Behavioral Therapy (TF-CBT) learning collaborative (LC), we learned that most clinicians engage in minimal inquiry about trauma (e.g., Have you been sexually abused? Physically abused?). This approach has limitations: (1) many children do not understand the terms *physical/sexual abuse*; (2) some children may not consider their experiences to be abusive or to be what the clinician is looking for (e.g., child may not think that breast fondling is sexual abuse); (3) physical and sexual abuse represent a narrow sliver of possible traumatic events; (4) bluntly asking these questions can cause discomfort and reduce honest responding. The LC adopted *The Adolescent Trauma History Checklist and Interview* (*Trauma History Interview*, Habib & Labruna, unpublished) designed to address many of these limitations. The *Trauma History Interview* is a fairly exhaustive list of possible traumatic experiences. We normalize this measure by telling children that we use it with all children. Honest responding is facilitated by the yes/no response format and not requiring trauma details. The question order also facilitates honest responding as early items are more common and less personal (e.g., natural disasters, knowing someone who was in a war), which acclimates the child to the flow and response format before being faced with more difficult items (e.g., physical and sexual abuse). After getting a yes/no response to all items, the clinician returns to endorsed items and asks when and for how long the trauma occurred. The child is never asked to provide further details. Finally, the clinician asks which trauma continues to bother him the most (target trauma), which is then used when inquiring about trauma symptoms on the UCLA PTSD Index (see below). Administering this measure as an interview allows for useful behavioral observations (e.g., dysregulation when asked about sexual abuse) as well as opportunities for the clinician to gauge the child's understanding (the authors indicate that the language and presentation is flexible and can be modified to make it appropriate for each child's developmental level). The following two examples illustrate the importance of broad trauma inquiry.

Tony, a 15-year-old boy in foster care, was referred due to debilitating school avoidance. No gradual exposure behavior plan had worked. On the Trauma History Interview, Tony endorsed several traumatic events. On the final item, which asks about any additional traumas, Tony related that at age 6, he was left behind in the family trailer for a week after the family moved. He drank water from the toilet and ate dog food in order to survive. This history of abandonment put his school avoidance and separation anxiety into perspective as he had finally found a caregiver committed to him and he did not want to lose her. Treatment planning became clarified in terms of trauma work around this abandonment.

On the Trauma History Interview, 9-year-old Brian endorsed exposure to physical abuse, domestic violence, and neglect consistent with his documented history. Most importantly, he was able to disclose sexual abuse that he had never felt comfortable sharing. With the therapist's support, Brian was able to share this information with his grandmother, which resulted in an additional CPS referral and investigation.

Posttraumatic Stress Disorder (PTSD)   PTSD, a diagnostic label first coined to describe the debilitating trauma symptoms of Vietnam War veterans, is now more broadly used as an explanation for the cluster of symptoms often seen in response to any trauma, including CSA, experienced as life-threatening and during which the person experienced helplessness as described in the *Diagnostic and Statistical Manual of Mental Disorders*, fourth edition, Text Revision (*DSM-IV-TR*; American Psychiatric Association, 2000). Per *DSM-IV-TR*, symptoms of PTSD cluster into three categories, including *Re-experiencing* (e.g., recurrent and intrusive distressing recollections of the event); *Avoidance* (e.g., inability to recall important aspects of the trauma); and *Increased Arousal* (e.g., irritability). Screening for PTSD symptoms constitutes an important aspect of assessment for children who have had traumatic experiences, and should be completed once the clinician has established the presence of traumatic experience(s) and identified the target trauma(s) (e.g., through history gathering and the *Trauma History Interview*). We recommend several measures for assessing specifically the symptoms of PTSD (see Table 7.1).

The University of California at Los Angeles Posttraumatic Stress Disorder Reaction Index (UCLA PTSD Index; Steinberg, Brymer, Decker, & Pynoos, 2004), endorsed by the National Child Traumatic Stress Network, is the measure adopted by the Tennessee TF-CBT LC. One major benefit of the UCLA PTSD Index is that its questions correspond directly to the PTSD criteria from the *DSM-IV*, which facilitates PTSD diagnosis. This measure is best administered as an interview, for similar reasons as those described for the *Trauma History Interview*. There are both child and caregiver report versions of this measure. Although this measure is useful diagnostically, it does not provide norms that allow for a comparison of the child's symptoms with others. A web training on the administration and scoring of this measure is available at: www.nctsnet .org/nctsn_assets/video/ptsdproducer_files/Default.htm. Two other

Table 7.1

Sample Assessment Measures Specific to Trauma, Dissociation, and Parenting

Assessment Type	Assessment Tool	Administration Format	Age	Norms Available
Trauma Exposure and Symptoms	UCLA PTSD Reaction Index—Child Version (Steinberg, Brymer, Decker, & Pynoos, 2004)	Child report/ interview	7–18	Symptom cutoffs
	UCLA PTSD Reaction Index—Parent Version (Steinberg, Brymer, Decker, & Pynoos, 2004)	Parent report	all	Symptom cutoffs
	Trauma Symptom Checklist for Children (TSCC; Briere, 1996)	Child report	8–16	Yes
	Trauma Symptom Checklist for Young Children (TSCYC; Briere, 2005)	Parent report	3–12	Yes
	Symptom Checklist for Sexually Abused Children (Wolfe, 1998)	Clinician rating	clinician discretion	No
	The Adolescent Trauma History Checklist and Interview. Unpublished measure (Habib & Labruna)	Child or parent report	all	No
Trauma-Related Dysregulation	Child Dissociative Checklist (Putnam, Helmers, & Trickett, 1993)	Parent report	≈2–12	Symptom cutoffs
	Adolescent Dissociative Experiences Scale (A-DES; Armstrong, Putnam, Carlson, Libero, & Smith, 1997)	Child report	≈12–19	No
	Self-Injurious Behavior Checklist (Friedrich, 2002)	Child report	clinician discretion	No
	Self-Injurious Behavior Interview (Friedrich, 2002)	Clinician interview	clinician discretion	No

(continued)

Table 7.1
(continued)

Assessment Type	Assessment Tool	Administration Format	Age	Norms Available
	Child Sexual Behavior Inventory (CSBI; Friedrich, 1997)	Parent report	2–12	Yes
Parenting	Parent-Child Relationship Inventory (PCRI; Gerard, 1994)	Parent report	3–15	Yes
	Parenting Stress Inventory (Abidin, 1995)	Parent report	0–12	Yes

measures that we commonly use to assess trauma symptoms are the Trauma Symptom Checklist for Children (self-report, ages 8–16) and Trauma Symptom Checklist for Young Children (caregiver report, 3–12) (Briere, 1996, 2005). These measures are well-normed, which facilitates an understanding of the child's symptoms relative to the general population. The TSCC was developed for children with sexual abuse histories and includes scales measuring sexual distress and sexual preoccupation. Finally, a useful and informal CSA specific measure for simple and complex PTSD symptoms is Wolfe's (1998) checklist.

Along with these objective measures, projective measures often help clinicians gain more understanding of PTSD symptoms, attributions regarding the trauma, and how "on the surface" the trauma lies. Consider this 12 year old's projective story to a card in which a child has a chair raised above his head as if to smash it on the ground. The story depicts significant trauma related thought intrusion, hyperarousal, and dysregulation.

Once upon a time there was a girl that went crazy. Her name was Jana.[1] She was so mad at the world, thinking about rape, Granny dying, mother incarcerated, that she just couldn't take it. So she ran so far and then saw the chair and started banging it on the ground. "I just can't take no more of this stuff! Just no more at all!" Then she stood there and picked up another chair. "Why me? Why does all of this happen to a 12-year-old?" She kept slamming it. Ran so far . . . the end.

---

1. In actuality, the name given was the name of the child telling the story.

DEVELOPMENTAL TRAUMA DISORDER (DTD)

Although the PTSD diagnosis has been updated over the years to include child specific symptoms, and though it is often useful in cases of very specific, life-threatening traumatic events (e.g., natural disaster, serious car accident, or stranger rape), it has, in the experience of many clinicians, been seen as sometimes falling short to best explain child maltreatment in general, and CSA in particular. Some children who have experienced CSA may not meet full criteria for PTSD but may still struggle with partial PTSD and other symptoms such as depression, shame, and negative attributions of self related to CSA. For other children, PTSD does not seem to capture the full developmental effects of childhood trauma when it occurs within the family context in an early, chronic, and often extreme form. These youngsters present with severe disturbance in their emotion regulation and attachment capacities. They also may demonstrate significant disturbance of learning, memory, and bodily functions, as well as an impaired sense of self-efficacy. This more complicated set of symptoms has been proposed by the National Child Traumatic Stress Task Force (van der Kolk, 2005) to be included in the *Diagnostic and Statistical Manual (DSM-V)* as Developmental Trauma Disorder (DTD). There is no one measure to assess for DTD; however, there are measures that target specific areas incorporated in the proposed diagnosis. We suggest that the *Trauma History Interview* and UCLA be administered, as noted earlier, along with specific evaluation of dissociation, attachment capacity, self-perception, and emotional regulation. See Table 7.1 for suggested measures.

System Trauma as Part of DTD   It is important to assess how much "system trauma" the child has experienced. How many unfamiliar people have questioned the child about personal and difficult matters? How many placement changes has the child experienced? Has the child had important losses of pre-adoptive caregivers, foster families, or group home staff? How have the multiple losses compounded symptoms of CSA and DTD? How has the child's sense of trust in others, and in the system, been challenged? How have the system disruptions impacted the academic progress of the child? All of these issues are important to include in assessing a child with CSA who also has a more complicated history within the system.

TRAUMAGENIC FACTORS AND RELATED COGNITIVE DISTORTIONS

After considering a child's CSA effects in the context of diagnostic and behavioral symptoms, the next step is to consider the psychological messages that have been internalized through the experience of CSA. Finkelhor and Browne (1986) developed a framework conceptualizing four main factors of psychological injury inflicted by sexual abuse including *traumatic sexualization, betrayal, stigmatization,* and *powerlessness.* These factors are best considered as broad categories useful for organizing clinicians' understanding of sexual abuse. Wolfe's (1998) checklist includes sections relevant to each area.

Traumatic Sexualization   Traumatic sexualization is "a process in which a child's sexuality (including both sexual feelings and sexual attitudes) is shaped in a developmentally inappropriate and interpersonally dysfunctional fashion as a result of sexual abuse" (Finkelhor & Browne, 1986, p. 633). Children emerge from traumatic sexualization with inappropriate repertoires of sexual behavior, confusions, and misconceptions about their sexual self-concepts, and unusual emotional associations to sexual activities. This can occur through exchange of affection, gifts, privileges, and attention for sexual favors. It can create distorted importance and meaning to the child's sexual parts or other body parts (i.e., fetishism). Confusion and misconceptions about sexual norms, behaviors, and morals can be transmitted. Traumatic sexualization can occur by creating a fearful connection between abuse circumstances and sexual matters. Consider the following clinical scenario.

Megan, a 17-year-old, had been sexually abused by her stepfather since age 11. Megan's DAP overemphasized the hair. She confessed that her lovely long hair was her treasure and had been a main focus of her stepfather's sexual attention. She had been proclaimed her stepfather's favorite; he bought her gifts and gave her special privileges. Megan equated her sense of self-worth with being able to provide for others sexually and her hair was a particular part of her body that had become sexualized.

A specific manifestation of traumatic sexualization, perhaps best construed as a PTSD "re-experiencing" symptom are sexual behavior problems (SBP). Assessment of SBPs is essential for treatment planning. We recommend assessing SBPs through interview, and when appropriate, through use of the TSCYC, TSCC, and Child Sexual Behavior Inventory (Friedrich, 1997).

Eight-year-old Sarah had been chronically sexually abused in her birth home, as well as exposed to adult sexual behavior from birth to age 3. Her adoptive family of five years had struggled with her SBPs directed toward her three younger siblings and had sent her to two residential centers specializing in SBPs, but to no avail. Upon assessment, Sarah admitted her problem saying, "My head says touch, touch, touch, and my brain says, okay, go ahead and sneak and do it." Consider the following Incomplete Sentence: I just can't "stop." She also stated, "You can do it without someone seeing (implying touching others). Because it's a habit. Did you have that feeling when you were a little girl?"

This preoccupied 8-year-old was struggling mightily against her urges to sexually act out. Assessment results helped frame a recommendation for addressing intense body triggers.

Common distortions of youngsters with traumatic sexualization might include: I can always get what I want through sex; My best asset is my sexiness; I will never have sex again, even when I'm married; I will never date again; I don't feel "right" unless I have sex a lot; I was created a woman so that men could use me for their pleasure; I have a right to sexually hurt little kids because that is what was done to me.

Betrayal   Betrayal "refers to the dynamic by which children discover that someone on whom they were vitally dependent has caused them harm" (Finkelhor & Browne, 1986, p. 634). Betrayal also occurs when someone on whom children were vitally dependent knew about but did not stop the abuse; this particular circumstance is perhaps one of the most difficult dynamics to work with in treatment. To assess this area, clinicians typically begin by asking caregivers questions regarding their general involvement with parenting their children as well as with specific involvement around the CSA, including their level of knowledge and protection, reaction after disclosure, and current reaction to the abuse. Friedrich's (2002) book (Appendix A) and Wolfe's checklist (1998) are helpful for assessing this dynamic. Wolfe includes family support and reactions to disclosure. Finally, Crisci and Lowenstein (1998) provide youth-friendly activities to assess perceived dynamics between the child and nonoffending caregiver(s).

Several factors affect the experience of betrayal. Younger children may not realize they are being manipulated by their trusted "other" until they are old enough to understand relationships. Children who are suspicious from the start of the grooming behavior may feel less betrayed than those for whom what seemed like loving contact is suddenly and shockingly sexual. Youngsters abused by family members or close friends will likely feel more betrayed than youngsters abused by more distant others. Children whose family members react negatively to disclosure, for example by blaming or invalidating, may feel more betrayed. Youngsters with betrayal as a main dynamic may have cognitive distortions such as: *I can't trust anyone; I'll never marry because men can't be trusted; even moms can't be trusted.*

Consider the following clinical scenario regarding betrayal.

Twelve-year-old Donny was left for a weekend with a man his family met at a flea market while his mother and stepfather drove long-haul trucks. Donny told his caregivers about the man sexually abusing him but was not believed. Instead, they left him again with this man who kept him isolated in the woods. Donny was sexually abused for three months multiple times a day before his mother discovered via the Internet that the man was a registered sexual offender. Consider Donny's Incomplete Sentences: Mothers should "believe me when I say Mitch is molesting me"; Fathers should "listen to me—I tried to tell Tom (stepfather)."

Powerlessness   Powerlessness is seen in many children with CSA. This traumagenic factor might emerge on measures of depression, in the telling of projective stories and drawings, on Incomplete Sentences, on personality measures showing lowered self-efficacy, on interview, and on caregiver measures. Children experience powerlessness when someone bigger and in a position of more power has contravened the child's will, desires, and sense of efficacy. Children may find their attempts to halt the abuse ineffective, or may feel too afraid to attempt to stop it. Children's personal body space is invaded against their will, they may be forced or coerced, or simply feel threatened by the authority of the other. Indeed, powerlessness often occurs without perpetrator use of force, simply through the subtle coercion inherent in the disproportionate level of power and the child's dependency or perceived dependency on the abuser. Threats are not necessary; powerlessness can come about when a child feels trapped, if only by the realization of the consequences of disclosure (e.g., my mother will be devastated; my father will go to prison). When a child does disclose and is not believed, his sense of powerlessness increases. Common cognitive distortions for children who feel powerless following CSA are: *The world is not safe; I'm too weak to protect myself; I'll never be able to fend for myself; I'll always need to be with a strong, powerful, protective man to feel okay; Girls are weak; I must be a wimp.* Consider the powerlessness reflected in 12-year-old Jana's projective story in response to a picture of a girl sitting up in bed.

Once upon a time there was a girl named Jana. She was getting raped again. It was 9:00 at night when she went to sleep. The girl named Jana went into the bathroom. Her two cousins were in there. They grabbed her and put her on the ground. They raped her at the same time. She found a knife and stabbed them and ran. They got her again. They raped her again. "Help me! Help me!" Then she tried to hit them. He got off. She ran and ran. She got away and started walking. . . . "Somebody help me!" She was bleeding. Then she woke up . . . with a start . . . she was scared . . . she started thinking for a minute . . . just a dream.

Feelings of powerlessness may also manifest in fantasies of protection and strength as portrayed in the following scenario.

Eight-year-old David described feeling safe in his foster home because of the imagined presence of security cameras. He told a fantastical story about his scheme to be safe at his mother's house, which included his friends guarding the house and

David instructing them through walkie-talkies. David told a similar story about his Grandpa having guns and traps to protect them from his father.

Stigmatization Stigmatization refers to the "negative connotations (e.g., badness, shame, and guilt) that are communicated to the child around the [sexual] experiences and that then become incorporated into the child's self-image" (Finkelhor & Browne, 1986, p. 635). First, the very secrecy of the sexual acts leaves a youngster knowing innately that "this is bad and I can't talk about it." Stigma can be compounded not only by messages from the abuser, but also reinforced by attitudes learned through family and community. A child may have prior knowledge about sexual activities being deviant and/or taboo. Some cultural or religious groups have powerful messages regarding sexual activity (e.g., females who are not virgins are "spoiled goods"). Younger children may be less affected by this factor because they may still be unaware of the prevailing cultural messages around sexuality. The circumstances and way a child is treated after disclosure of CSA greatly impact the level of stigma a child feels. For example, if a child is not believed, is scapegoated after telling, or is blamed for the sexual activity, he will likely experience higher stigma. If a family's circumstances change for the worse, a child may blame herself because she connects the problems with her disclosure. Children often struggle with cognitive distortions around issues of stigma. Some common distortions include: *It was my fault; I didn't say no; Now my family is poor; I never should have told; It felt good—I must secretly have wanted my brother to do it to me—that makes me a pervert; I had an erection when he did it to me—I must be gay; I'm a slut, like my mom says; Everyone will be able to tell I'm not a virgin; My dad's in prison and it's my fault; I am dirty; I am bad.*

Stigmatization can best be measured over time in therapy; however, an assessment can pick up on themes of stigma through measures of depression, projective stories and drawings, Incomplete Sentences, formal personality measures, and interview. Feiring, Taska, and Lewis (1998) offer a set of questions regarding stigma in a study entitled "My Feelings About the Abuse Questionnaire." Friedrich (2002) includes these questions in his Appendix N. The following two scenarios illustrate stigmatization.

Eight-year-old Douglas, a youngster with an extreme history of sexual abuse by his mother and her partners, now in a loving home for three years, presented as severely behaviorally disturbed. He named his DAP "Weirdo" and described him as "having eyes all over his body but he is still blind." This statement matches other data that confirm David's sense of incompetency and "differentness." Further, he projected his feelings of "badness" into his DAP, stating, "Weirdo gets into trouble one to two times a day . . . he's ADHD also . . . but doesn't take medications."

Twelve-year-old Deandre was sexually abused by his older brothers and physically abused by caregivers. Deandres carries self-blame for "breaking his family up" because, at age 7, the school personnel noticed carpet burns on his body (sustained while resisting the abuse) and called child protection to investigate. He stated, "I shouldn't have jumped around so much." His assessment is replete with examples of low self-esteem, significant guilt, and salient self-blame.

A final example of stigmatization is 9-year-old Lola, a rejection-sensitive youngster in foster care with a history of neglect, physical, emotional, and sexual abuse. Consider her letter to her foster mom:

"Lola is stupid and a retard. . . . Everybody hates me and they always will so I might as well kill myself if I will be treated like garbage! I have had enough bad things happen to me but nobody cares. . . . So I shouldn't care about myself. . . . God doesn't care about me or love me . . . that's why I wish I was never born at all because nobody will care or love me . . . I deserve to go to hell." Consider also one of her Incomplete Sentences that depicts stigmatization: *"I am ashamed about tearing up my Bible; how stupid I am! Now God doesn't even love me."*

SAFETY ISSUES

An important part of assessing for CSA involves the child's current sense of safety. If, for example, the child is not sleeping due to fear that the perpetrator will return, or if the child will not leave the house due to fear that she will run into her perpetrator, then such issues must be prioritized in therapy. The clinician must discern between real and perceived danger, safety planning around the former, and teaching coping skills to address the latter. Some areas to assess include: domestic violence, suicidality, self-injury, dangerous behaviors such as running into the street, extreme aggression toward others, extreme out of control behaviors that result in parental force in order to discipline, and sexual behavior problems. If substantial levels of risk are noted, the clinician must engage in immediate education and safety planning with the caregivers. Friedrich (2002, Appendix G) offers a Safety Checklist for use in the caregiver interview when assessing CSA.

Integration of Assessment Findings and Transition to Treatment: Marissa

The following case material integrates all aspects of the comprehensive assessment model detailed in this chapter. This integrated assessment pulls together the components of the HOT model in a comprehensive manner that culminates in treatment considerations.

(continued)

(continued)
HISTORY

Marissa, age 9, had a severe maltreatment history including early, chronic neglect and physical and emotional abuse by her mother, stepfather, and maternal grandparents in addition to sexual abuse by her stepfather and his abuse of her mother. Child welfare investigated 16 reports of maltreatment when Marissa was between the ages of 4 and 6 years old; however, none resulted in Marissa and her younger siblings being removed. She was psychiatrically hospitalized three times for symptoms of "violent rages," general oppositionality, and emotional dysregulation. She disclosed sexual abuse during her third hospitalization and was immediately removed into foster care at age 7½. Her current foster placement had endured for a year and her foster mother was considering adoption, though had reservations. Marissa's foster mother was using a strict behavioral approach to manage Marissa's controlling and oppositional behaviors. She noted significant improvements including less-frequent bedwetting and fewer meltdowns; however, she had concerns that Marissa was not developing a true relationship with her, that she seemed to require "constant reassurance," was frequently attention seeking and aggressive, and was, in her foster mother's words, "wearing me out." Current diagnoses included: ADHD, Mood Disorder NOS, and PTSD. Earlier diagnoses included: Oppositional Defiant Disorder, Intermittent Explosive Disorder, and Bipolar Disorder. Although she had been on many different medications in the past including psychostimulants, antihypertensives, atypical antipsychotics, and mood stabilizers, she was currently only taking a psychostimulant medication for ADHD.

OBSERVATION

Marissa presented as an overly pleasing, anxious girl. Although often avoidant, she also wanted to cooperate and win our favor. She sat primly and focused on the examiners, often complimenting us. When asked to list the things that made her feel "Best" on her Color-My-Heart (CMH), she listed "Ya'll" and "Having fun at Vanderbilt (our clinic)." She apologized for small errors and cleaned up in a strikingly compliant, "put on" manner. She displayed anxiety about the day, wanting to know exactly what the rules were for the assessment and seeking reassurance (e.g., *"Am*
(continued)

I being good?"). Marissa demonstrated anxiety about her caregiver's whereabouts, needing to check the lobby frequently. Finally, she exhibited controlling behaviors (e.g., taking over the writing on the CMH, double checking the examiner's spelling, wanting to choose the order of activities).

Across the long assessment day, Marissa cooperated fully with intellectual and academic testing as well as the Incomplete Sentences task, but when we initiated the *Trauma History Interview* and projective tasks, clearly pulling for emotional content, she became resistant. She tried to subtly stall one activity by taking a long time on the coloring portion prior to the "question" portion. More overtly, she stated, *"I don't want to talk about my past . . . no! no! no!"* She asked to go to the bathroom several times as one way to avoid the tasks at hand, once returning and stating, *"I really didn't have to use the bathroom. It's just that when I talk about my [birth] mom, I start to get really upset. I was in the bathroom calming down."* This observation was invaluable to us later in terms of helping frame treatment recommendations. In providing feedback about her PTSD symptoms we were able to use the bathroom example to help her understand abuse related "triggers" and then to encourage her to take part in trauma-focused treatment to learn to better manage those triggers.

TESTING

While Marissa's caregiver did not highlight significant PTSD symptoms on the TSCYC, instead framing her problems as "she was never disciplined," Marissa had significant endorsements on her self-reported PTSD measures and showed overt PTSD triggering experiences during the interview and projective storytelling.

Marissa endorsed several different types of trauma on the Trauma History Interview and chose sexual abuse by her stepfather as the most salient. Marissa reported significant PTSD symptoms on the UCLA across all three symptom clusters. On her Incomplete Sentences, she answered as follows: *I will always remember "I was in three bad homes—I was in a really hurt home"*; and, *When I was little "I was a little baby and then I had lots of bad houses."*

Marissa's projective stories were particularly telling. She transformed from a compliant, hands-in-the-lap child of restricted affect to an animated, on-her-feet child, yelling and cussing. Note the following stories that highlight her traumatic experience with her sexually and domestically abusing stepfather.

In response to the RAT-C picture depicting a man and woman who appear to be in gentle conversation, she told the following story:

(continued)

(continued)

This is going to be a bad one! There's a dad and a mother (Meg)[2]. He's put his finger on her chin and they are going to kiss. This is John[3] trying to kiss her a long time. The daughter (me) is like, "Oh, get away from my mom, big old pop!" "What did you just say, smart girl?" "You better shut up, Pop! Because I said so." "Want me to throw a hard table at you or just kick you on your belly? You are such a brat." I said, "Shut up, old pop. You're gonna give me and my momma a nervous break." Mom says, "Honey, please don't start this . . . he's just a boy." "He's not a boy he's a big old mean Pop and I'll kick him on his face and jump on his stomach until he dies!" Mother joined me and then me and Mom live happily ever after.

In responses to a PST picture depicting an adult male by the side of the child's bed, perhaps tucking a child into bed at night, she created this story:

This man (John) tucked me in and I said, "Go away, shut up, big old pop." He then shoved me on the table on my mouth. Then I went (kick, kick) and "You better shut up, big old pop!" I say, "Good night, stupid old brat, shut up, pop!" He said, "You are going to go up and help me take my shower in the morning." I said, "Okay, oh, whatever. Good night, brat. Good night, stupid little brat old pop." Then I kicked him and I escaped from my window and when it was the morning . . . John came in and said, "I have to take a bath." I didn't say anything! He said, "what in the b and w and d and f is she doing? She's a brat! And she's really a brat! She is a b and m and I'm going to take my own shower dear, okay?" The mother said "Okay." The End.

These and other stories reflect the conflict and abuse dynamics with her stepfather, her continued strong and negative emotions around her abuse, and her anger and fantasies of revenge. Her stories show her fantasies about how she and her mother might have gained power over him, reflecting her actual feelings of helplessness. Her stories let us see that her mother was not protective, indeed she colluded with the abuser. Other stories made reference to the mother wanting the girl to come into the bed with herself and the father to which the girl protested that she did not want to sleep (again!) with the father because *"He'll get her and bug her"* and *"He'll squish her in a scary way."* Still, Marissa's projected fantasies were that she and her mother get revenge and escape his abuse together and live "happily

(continued)

---

2. She used the name of her birth mother.
3. She used the name of her stepfather.

ever after." She had not worked through the ambivalent feelings she held about her primary caregiver. At the assessment, she exhibited a growing attachment and security to her pre-adoptive mother. On her CMH, she listed for "Best" feeling: *"Loving Mom"* and for "Sad" feeling: *"When Mom is not home."*

Anxiety was a salient assessment finding through behavioral observations, on projective tools, and objective measures (e.g., SCARED[4]). She endorsed significant anxiety symptoms, focusing on fears about separation from her pre-adoptive mother and of being alone at night as well as general worrying and being nervous about her performance, the future, and new situations. She endorsed a number of somatic complaints tied to anxiety. On her CMH she listed as a "Scared" feeling, *"I worry when Mom's late coming home."*

Data suggested that Marissa attempted to cope through avoiding her trauma experiences, restricting her affect and behaviors, and trying desperately to both be "in control" and a "good girl." In witnessing her avoidance around her trauma, we began to realize the great amount of energy she used daily to keep her anxiety and trauma memories under wraps. It is no wonder she had significant meltdowns and oppositional behaviors. Her projective wishes for power and for a protective and loving mother gave us important information for therapy. Her "how can I please my caregiver and others in order to survive" defense had kept Marissa from developing an authentic sense of self and was likely one of the reasons that her foster mother had not managed to feel a sense of attachment connection with Marissa.

LINKS TO TREATMENT PLANNING

Marissa needed to begin a trauma-focused approach to therapy, having previously received only supportive therapy that had not given her the coping tools needed to manage her strong feelings related to her trauma. Her caregiver had not been involved in sessions. She had not worked through issues related to insecure attachment and limited sense of self-efficacy. We recommended Trauma-Focused Cognitive-Behavioral Therapy (TF-CBT), including gradual exposure to her trauma along with the incorporation of solid coping skills. Further, TF-CBT includes essential caregiver involvement. Not only could her pre-adoptive mother support

(continued)

---

4. Screen for Child Anxiety Related Disorders (SCARED).

(continued)

Marissa's coping skills and be witness to her trauma narrative, but she would benefit from learning about how early neglect and abuse had affected Marissa's ability to form relationship, to trust, and to develop a healthy sense of herself. Marissa's caregiver needed to reframe Marissa's "undisciplined and wearing behavior" through the lens of maltreatment and attachment trauma. We also recommended that more focused attachment therapy occur in Marissa's home, including working specifically on the insecure attachment that Marissa felt with her caregiver and her need to experience unconditional love rather than conditional acceptance dependent on the strict behavioral system.

The profile that emerged from gathering pertinent History, Observation, and Testing revealed a child who fit the proposed term, Developmental Trauma Disorder (DTD), discussed above. She experienced early and chronic maltreatment, general familial violence, neglect, and betrayal by primary caregivers that set her up to manifest continuing problems with emotional, somatic, and behavioral dysregulation in the face of trauma cues both internal and external, as well as challenges with attaching to a caregiver. She was operating from a base of control rather than a base of trust. By using the results of the assessment to educate Marissa, her pre-adoptive mother, her child welfare worker, and her therapist, we were able to help all involved create new attributions for Marissa's challenges in order to begin treatment that would be trauma and attachment focused.

CONCLUSION

We hope that this chapter has provided helpful insight into the process and usefulness of comprehensive, individually tailored evaluation for better understanding children and their unique treatment needs. This understanding is essential for appropriately choosing from the array of available treatment options covered in the next section. Regardless of specific treatment model selection, ongoing assessment by clinicians throughout the treatment process is crucial for effective treatment.

REFERENCES

Abidin, R. R. (1995). *Parenting stress index* (3rd ed.). Lutz, FL: Psychological Assessment Resources.

American Academy of Child and Adolescent Psychiatry. (1997). Practice parameters for the forensic evaluation of children and adolescents who may have been physically or sexually abused. *Journal of the American Academy of Child & Adolescent Psychiatry, 36,* 423–442.

American Psychiatric Association. (2000). *Diagnostic and statistical manual* (4th ed., Text rev.). Arlington, VA: American Psychiatric Association.

Armstrong, J. G., Putnam, F. W., Carlson, E. B., Libero, D. Z., & Smith, S. R. (1997). Development and validation of a measure of adolescent dissociation: The adolescent dissociative experiences scale. *Journal of Nervous & Mental Disease, 185,* 491–497.

Behavioral Technology Inc. (1996). *Sexual projective card set.* Salt Lake City, UT: Behavioral Technology.

Briere, J. (1996). *Trauma symptom checklist for children.* Lutz, FL: Psychological Assessment Resources.

Briere, J. (2005). *Trauma symptom checklist for young children.* Lutz, FL: Psychological Assessment Resources.

Burns, R. C. (1970). *Kinetic family drawings (KFD): An introduction to understanding children through kinetic drawings.* New York, NY: Brunner/Mazel.

Caruso, K. R., & Pulcini, R. J. (1990). *Projective storytelling card interactive assessment and treatment system.* Reading, CA: Northwest Psychological.

Cohen, J., Mannarino, A., & Deblinger, E. (2006). *Treating trauma and traumatic grief in children and adolescents.* New York, NY: Guilford Press.

Constantino, G., Malgady, R. C., & Rogler, L. H. (1988). *TEMAS (Tell-me-a-story).* Los Angeles, CA: Western Psychological Services.

Crisci, G., Lay, M., & Lowenstein, L. (1998). *Paper dolls and paper airplanes: Therapeutic exercises for sexually traumatized children.* Indianapolis, IN: KIDSRIGHTS.

Exner, J. E. (1995). *The Rorschach: A comprehensive system: Vol. 3. Assessing children and adolescents.* New York, NY: John Wiley & Sons.

Feiring, C., Taska, L., & Lewis, F. M. (1998). The role of shame and attributional style in chldren's and adolescent's adaptation to sexual abuse. *Child Maltreatment, 3,* 129–142.

Finkelhor, D., & Browne, A. (1986). The traumatic impact of child sexual abuse: A conceptualization. In S. Chess & A. Thomas (Eds). *Annual Progress in Child Psychiatry and Child Development* (pp. 632–648). New York, NY: Brunner/Mazel.

Fricker, A. E., & Smith, D. W. (2001). Trauma specific versus generic measurement of distress and the validity of self-reported symptoms in sexually abused children. *Journal of Child Sexual Abuse, 10,* 51–66.

Friedrich, W. N. (1997). *Child sexual behavior inventory.* Lutz, FL: Psychological Assessment Resources.

Friedrich, W. N. (2002). *Psychological assessment of sexually abused children and their families.* Thousand Oaks, CA: Sage.

Gerard, A. B. (2005). *Parent-child relationship inventory.* Los Angeles, CA: Western Psychological Services.

Goodyear-Brown, P. (2002). Digging for Buried Treasure: 52 Prop-Based Play Therapy Interventions for Treating the Problems of Childhood. Nashville, TN: Author.

Goodyear-Brown, P. (2010). *Play therapy with traumatized children: A Prescriptive Approach*. Hoboken, NJ: John Wiley & Sons.

Groth-Marnat, G. (2009). *Handbook of psychological assessment* (4th ed.). Hoboken, NJ: John Wiley & Sons.

Habib, M., & Labruna, V. The Adolescent Trauma History Checklist and Interview. Unpublished measure.

Horton, C., & Cruise, T. K. (1997). Clinical assessment of child victims and adult survivors of child maltreatment. *Journal of Counseling and Development, 76*, 94–104.

King, N. J., Heyne, D., Tonge, B. J., Mullen, P., Myerson, N., Rollings, S., & Ollendick, T. H. (2003). Sexually abused children suffering from post-traumatic stress disorder: Assessment and treatment strategies. *Cognitive Behaviour Therapy, 32*, 2–12.

Koppitz, E. M. (1968). *Psychological evaluation of children's human figure drawings*. Yorktown Heights, NY: Psychological Corporation.

Loevinger, J., & Wessler, R. (1970). *Measuring ego development: Vol. 1 construction and use of a sentence completion test*. San Francisco, CA: Jossey-Bass.

McArthur, D. S., & Roberts, G. E. (1982). *Roberts apperception test for children*. Los Angeles, CA: Western Psychological Services.

Miller, T. W., & Veltkamp, L. J. (1995). Assessment of sexual abuse and trauma: Clinical measures. *Child Psychiatry and Human Development, 26*, 3–10.

Murray, H. A. (1943). *Thematic apperception test*. Printed in the USA: President and Fellows of Harvard College.

Parker, K. (1983). A meta-analysis of the reliability and validity of the rorschach. *Journal of Personality Assessment, 47*, 227–231

Putnam, F. W., Helmers, K., & Trickett, P. K. (1993). Development, reliability, and validity of a child dissociation scale. *Child Abuse & Neglect, 17*, 731–741.

Rorschach, H. (1941). *Psychodiagnostics*. (Hans Huber Verlag, Trans.). Bern, Switzerland: Bircher. (Original work published 1921)

Sattler, J. M. (2002). *Assessment of children: Behavioral and clinical applications* (4th ed.). San Diego, CA: Sattler.

Sattler, J. M. (2008). *Assessment of children: Cognitive foundations* (5th ed.). San Diego, CA: Sattler.

Steinberg, A. M., Brymer, M. J., Decker, K. B., & Pynoos, R. S. (2004). The university of California at Los Angeles post-traumatic stress disorder reaction index. *Current Psychiatry Reports, 6*, 96–100.

van der Kolk, B. A. (2005). Developmental trauma disorder. *Psychiatric Annals, 35*, 401–408.

Wolfe, V. V. (1998). Child sexual abuse. In E. J. Mash & R. A. Barkley (Eds.), *Treatment of childhood disorders* (2nd ed., pp. 588–597). New York, NY: Guilford Press.

APPENDIX

Draw-A-Person Questions (DAP)

The following questions are suggested as a pool of *possible* questions you might use with children and teens as a follow-up to a DAP task. Clinicians are encouraged, however, to create their own set of questions that are tailored to the child's age, gender, interests, and situation. The task is used to get to know the child's projections that may reflect such matters as self-image, fears, and fantasies. We often begin with a broad, open-ended directive such as, "Now, tell me about your picture" to see what we obtain from a purer projection. Then, we move to some of the more structured prompts below. There is no particular order to follow, but it is best to begin with the first two questions and then proceed.

1. What is the name of your person? (Establish boy or girl if not apparent by drawing or name.)
2. How old is she?
3. What is her favorite color, food, movie, song, actor, activity, and so on.
4. What is the best/worst thing that has happened to her?
5. What does she want to do when she grows up?
6. If she could have three wishes, what would they be?
7. What makes her happy? Sad? Angry? Scared?
8. What secrets does she keep?
9. Who is nice to her? How?
10. Who is mean to her? What happens?
11. Is she afraid of anyone? Who?
12. How has she been hurt in her life?
13. Who is her favorite grown-up?
14. Does she have any dreams? (If yes . . .) Good ones? Bad ones? What are they about?
15. If she could change one thing about herself, what would it be?
16. If she could change one thing about her life, what would it be?
17. If she could change one thing about the world, what would it be?
18. With whom does she live?
19. What does she like about different members of the family?
20. When she gets in trouble, how is she disciplined?
21. What would her mom want to change about her? Her Dad? (Basic caregivers included here.)
22. If she could be any animal, what would she be? Why?
23. If she were stranded on a desert island, what one person would she want to join her? What if she could add two people? Three?
24. How does she sleep at night?

DRAW A FAMILY DOING SOMETHING: KINETIC FAMILY DRAWING (KFD)

For follow-up questions related to a child's KFD the reader is referred to Friedrich's (2002) Appendix E, *Attachment-Related Interview Questions to Use with Children* (p. 287). Friedrich's questions are specific to attachment areas. Following, find a list of possible follow-up questions to use with a KFD more generally. Like the DAP, the following questions are only suggestions. Clinicians are encouraged to initiate their own prompts as they see fit for the child's unique situation. Begin with an open directive such as, "Tell me about your picture," and have the child describe the various members of the family and what they are doing. Reflect the child's responses to see if they will tell you more details without specific prompts and then proceed to the possible prompts following.

1. Who in your family is having the best time in your picture? Why?
2. Who is having the hardest time? Why?
3. Who is the funniest person in your family? The huggiest? The loudest? The most quiet? The one who yells the most? The saddest?, and so on.
4. Who in the family is the best cook? The best "fixer of things"?
5. What would your mother say she really likes about you? Your father? (Use all basic caregivers.)
6. Who do you like to play with in your family? What do you play?
7. Who would you most like to "hang out" with in your family?
8. If you fell down (or had a bike wreck, etc.) and got hurt when you were with your family, what would happen?
9. If you got sick, what would your family do?
10. If something bad happened at school, who in the family would be easiest to talk to about it?
11. Who in the family fights the most?
12. Who is the favorite child in the family? Who is the child who gets in trouble the most?
13. What one thing would you change about your family?
14. What one thing do you think your family would like to change about you?
15. If your family had a fairy godmother and could have one wish, what would it be?

EVIDENCE-BASED TREATMENTS AND OTHER EFFECTIVE APPROACHES

CHAPTER 8

Determining Best Practice for Treating Sexually Victimized Children

BENJAMIN E. SAUNDERS

The race is not always to the swift, nor the battle to the strong, but that's the way to bet.

—Damon Runyon

DETERMINING "BEST PRACTICE" in any endeavor, including psychotherapy with child and adolescent victims of sexual assault, is necessarily a moving target for three reasons. First, the phenomenon may change over time. In the past, the term *child sexual abuse* signified a relatively narrow set of experiences. It typically was taken to mean abuse by a family member (father-child or perhaps sibling sexual assault) or sexual assault of young children by adult strangers with a primary sexual interest in children, that is, pedophiles. Today, child sexual abuse (CSA) may indicate a wide range of sexual victimization experiences encountered by children and adolescents, such as being the subject of pornographic pictures distributed on the Internet, sexual assault by a peer or dating partner, children being made to observe adults engaging in sexual activity or watch pornography, drug- or alcohol-facilitated rape, exploitation through prostitution, or a long list of other sexually related victimization experiences. Our definitional perspective about the breadth of sexual victimization in childhood and adolescence has expanded over time and this change affects ideas about what might be considered best therapy practice with a much wider range of victims.

A second reason is that standards used by the field to determine best clinical practice also change over time. The suitability of various psychological therapies for CSA victims was judged differently years ago than it is today. Specifically, the weight given to scientific evidence for treatment efficacy in making determinations about best practice has increased substantially. Two decades ago, few methodologically sound, clinical treatment research studies that could be used to guide practice had been conducted with child or adolescent victims of sexual abuse (Finkelhor & Berliner, 1995; Kolko, 1987; Saunders & Williams, 1996). Today, simply having an innovative and intriguing idea for a new treatment, a persuasive theoretical argument presented by a well-respected leader in the field, and some anecdotal reports of treatment success with interesting cases are no longer sufficient criteria for an intervention to be judged a best practice. Now, a threshold level of empirical evidence for treatment efficacy is required. Exactly what the threshold is may be debated, but some positive findings from empirical tests of treatment effects are required. So, the rules of the best practice game tend to change over time.

Finally, and most importantly, new knowledge is constantly being acquired through increasingly sophisticated scientific research and from frontline practice experience, sometimes at a dizzying pace. New knowledge frequently means that previously well-accepted ideas about common interventions need to be revised or even abandoned altogether, as do judgments about what therapies constitute best practice. Treatments found to be only minimally effective, ineffective, or even harmful need to be revised or discarded altogether. Interventions that remain untested or inadequately tested increasingly are viewed with skepticism as other treatments are more thoroughly tested and found to be efficacious. And, totally new interventions may need to be developed and tested in response to new knowledge. The quantity and pace of these changes frequently are difficult for the field to digest, and incorporating them into everyday practice rarely goes smoothly. Historically in the mental health field, empirical evidence for efficacy has not been a major consideration in psychotherapeutic treatment selection. However, this perspective is changing and clinicians now are called on to respond to new knowledge by changing their longstanding practice approach, which sometimes is met with resistance. Because of these reasons, any description of specific best practices is necessarily time-bound, tied to the accepted scientific knowledge and practice lore of the day, and likely to change in the future.

Given the dynamic nature of the field, determining current best practice means practitioners need to regularly reevaluate the clinical principles, assumptions, conventional practice wisdom and research findings that guide the way they conduct their practice with CSA victims. New information concerning the definitions and the epidemiology of CSA; the impact of sexual victimization experiences on child functioning; the biological, psychological, and social mechanisms that underlie the development of abuse-related problems by victims; and improved approaches to assessment and treatment of victims and their families will challenge current assumptions and lead to changes in norms for best clinical practice. This chapter examines several questions and issues where new knowledge or new conceptualizations are affecting judgments about best practice treatment of CSA victims. The implications for best practice with CSA victims are discussed. Some of the conclusions made may seem provocative, which is intended.

TREATING "SEXUAL ABUSE"

It is not uncommon for children who have been sexually victimized to be referred for "sexual abuse treatment" as if all sexual abuse incidents and all child reactions to sexual assault are homogeneous. This sort of phraseology implies that being a sexual abuse victim is the sole defining characteristic of a child, the cause of all of his or her problems, and a singular approach to treatment is sufficient. It also implies that sexual abuse itself is something to be treated.

Unlike other forms of child maltreatment, children often are automatically referred to mental health treatment after a report of sexual abuse. In a longitudinal study of 201 children living in families reported to authorities for allegations of intrafamilial sexual abuse, physical abuse, or domestic violence, children in families reported for sexual abuse were twice as likely to be referred to mental health treatment and received three times more sessions of counseling compared to children reported for other forms of family violence even after assessed mental health problems were controlled (Saunders, Williams, & Rheingold, 2003; Saunders, Williams, Smith, & Hanson, 2005). These findings suggest that compared to other child victims, sexual abuse victims are much more likely to be referred to treatment because of what happened to them rather than due to any emotional difficulties they may have. Professionals tend to react more swiftly to CSA reports than other types of maltreatment in getting child victims mental health services even though the mental health needs of CSA victims may be similar to those of children suffering other types of victimization. Sexual abuse seems to spark a professional reaction at all levels that is more intense compared to other types of maltreatment.

Sexual abuse is a historical event in the lives of some children that unfortunately cannot be changed. Best practice treatment does not target the event. Rather it seeks to reduce abuse-related emotional and behavioral difficulties and prevent the emergence of new abuse-related problems. As noted above, sexual abuse incidents are highly diverse and the problems that may result from being sexually abused vary substantially in quality and intensity from victim to victim. Some victims may be resilient and suffer few problems, whereas others have extraordinarily complex difficulties. Few, if any, cognitive, emotional, or behavioral problems are exclusive to being sexually abused. Therefore, having a history of sexual abuse with no other assessment information should not dictate a particular treatment approach and the notion of *treating sexual abuse* is a misnomer the field should discard. Best practice is for treatment to be responsive to the individual psychological needs of each victim and not be based primarily on the nature of the emergent abuse report.

DO ALL SEXUALLY ABUSED CHILDREN NEED TREATMENT?

A large and robust scientific research literature documents that experiencing sexual assault in childhood increases victims' risk for the development of an assortment of emotional, behavioral, and social problems, sometimes dramatically (Berliner, 2011; Kendler et al., 2000; Kilpatrick et al., 2003; Nelson et al., 2002; Putnam, 2003; Saunders et al., 1999). There is little doubt that compared to nonvictims, victims of sexual assault in childhood or adolescence are much more likely to develop serious mental health disorders such as posttraumatic stress disorder, major depression, problematic substance use, behavior disorders, delinquency, and many other problems.

However, when interpreting the CSA impact literature for the purposes of best practice treatment planning, it is critical to remember what is meant by *increased risk*. A risk factor is a characteristic that is associated with a greater likelihood of a particular outcome occurring. Not everyone with a risk characteristic will develop the associated outcome, and not everyone with the outcome will have the risk factor. Also, a risk factor is not necessarily a cause of the outcome. It is simply a probabilistic relationship. The presence of the characteristic only raises the actuarial probability that the outcome will occur, not insure it. The degree the risk factor raises the probability can be small, medium, or large. For example, sexual assault in childhood has been found to be a strong risk factor for some outcomes such as anxiety disorders and substance abuse, increasing the odds of having them by factors ranging from 3 to 8 times depending on the specific disorder (Chaffin, Silovsky, & Vaughn, 2005;

Kilpatrick, Saunders, & Smith, 2003; Saunders et al., 1999). However, it is a moderate risk factor for depression, increasing the odds about 2 times (Kendler et al., 2000; Saunders et al., 1999).

More interesting, it turns out that specific victim characteristics (e.g., gender, age) and sexual assault incident characteristics (e.g., sexual penetration, perceived life threat during the assault) have been found to better explain the risk for mental health problems associated with child sexual assault (Acierno et al., 2001; Hanson, Borntrager, Self-Brown, Kilpatrick, Saunders, Resnick, & Amstadter, 2008; Kilpatrick et al., 2003; McCauley et al., 2009). If victims and the sexual assaults they suffer have more of these characteristics, the risk for various mental health problems considerably increases compared to situations where they are not present. Consequently, some CSA cases may carry only a small or moderate increase in risk while others present an extremely high risk for the development of mental health problems. So the well-accepted (and technically accurate) principle that CSA is a risk factor for many problems has become more complicated as increasingly sophisticated research has been conducted. It is not just a history of some form of CSA, but a range of more specific characteristics that are important to understanding the risk for victims. This information affects how to do best practice because it needs to be incorporated into assessment and treatment planning to better tailor intervention to an individual victim.

These findings concerning risk force us to recognize and acknowledge that though the increased risk is sometimes striking, for no disorder or problem is the prevalence rate for the wide range of CSA victims 100%. For example, in a national probability sample of adult women, Saunders et al. (1999) found that nearly one-third of the CSA victims had a lifetime history of PTSD, a prevalence rate 3 times greater than for nonvictims of CSA. But, this finding also means that more than two-thirds of female CSA victims had *not* met full PTSD diagnostic criteria. The general pattern of these findings is similar to other research studies with community samples. In repeated studies, commonly 40% of victims report no or minor mental health problems (Finkelhor & Berliner, 1995; Putnam, 2003). Therefore, somewhat surprisingly, research has found that some children can experience very serious traumatic events such as sexual abuse, and not necessarily develop serious mental health problems (Fitzgerald, Danielson, Saunders, & Kilpatrick, 2007). Sexual abuse clearly raises the likelihood for developing serious mental health problems, and a large portion of CSA victims will develop serious and long-lasting problems. However, some will not. For whatever reasons, these children are resilient to the potentially severe traumatic impact of sexual abuse.

Recognizing the reality of resilience has implications for conducting best practice and raises the tricky question: Should sexually abused children who exhibit no or subclinical symptoms receive mental health treatment? Such a question clearly challenges common practice where the large majority of CSA victims are routinely referred for treatment because of the nature of the abuse they experienced regardless of their problem profile. For some, this question may seem ridiculous on its face because of this longstanding practice. However, if the answer is, "Of course they need treatment," the next question is, for what? What problems will be corrected through treatment? A final question is: If one believes resilient and naturally recovering children should be engaged in mental health treatment, should they receive the same type of treatment as children with very serious abuse-related problems?

Another facet that must be considered when answering these questions is the potential side effects of engaging a child in mental health treatment when it may not be needed. Any treatment, including psychological therapies, can have unintended, harmful consequences. All treatments have an outcome matrix. Some clients get better, some get worse, and some stay the same. Even the best evidence-based therapies are not always helpful to everyone. And, some patients, hopefully a small minority, may actually deteriorate in treatment. Berliner and Saunders (1996) found that depending on the outcome assessed, anywhere from 2% to 14% of CSA victims worsened over time even when receiving best practice treatment. This deterioration rate was smaller than that of treatment as usual and one cannot conclude that the treatment caused the worsening. However, the finding illustrates the point that when making treatment decisions we must consider that even the best treatments potentially can have detrimental effects on a small portion of patients.

Other treatment "side effect" issues to consider include the stigma still attached to seeing a therapist; the child's time lost from school, play, friends, and other positive activities; a parent's time away from work, other children, or other activities; the hidden financial cost of attending therapy, such as lost wages and travel costs; and the cost of paying for therapy. Although best practice therapy can be highly effective with a large proportion of clients, we must remember that it is not a totally benign process. Engaging in therapy has personal and instrumental costs for every client. Therapy does not always result in clinical improvement and for some, may have unintended negative consequences. From a best practice standpoint, the question remains: Do all victims of sexual abuse need professional mental health treatment? The evidence-based answer seems to be, no.

Of course, this conclusion raises several other difficult questions. How do we determine which sexually abused children need which of the effective treatments available and which do not? How do we go about making this decision? Is the current state of the research reliable enough to guide such a critical decision? Do we have the proper clinical assessment tools to make it? Though further research will improve our precision, the answer likely is a qualified yes. Limited trauma treatment resources mean that treating children who very likely do not need it deprives a child who does. Evidence-based triage is necessary. A thorough, evidence-based assessment of the child's family and psychosocial history, full trauma history, past and current functioning, abuse-related problems, and family and social network coupled with a knowledge of the risk and mediating factors associated with CSA and common mental health problems are necessary to make informed treatment decisions for individual children.

POLYVICTIMIZATION

Another complicating factor in determining best practice with sexually abused children and adolescents is the fact that many, perhaps most, are not victims of sexual abuse alone. A growing body of research has found that it is common for children to have been the victims of and/or witness to several types of interpersonal violence on multiple occasions (Brady & Caraway, 2002; Finkelhor, Ormrod, & Turner, 2007; Finkelhor, Ormrod, & Turner, 2009; Finkelhor, Turner, Ormrod, & Hamby, 2009; Saunders, 2003). These and other studies demonstrate that for a large portion of sexually abused children, sexual abuse is not the only type of victimization or traumatic event they have experienced. These findings lead to the question: Why do we call them *sexual abuse victims* when they have experienced many forms of victimization, exposure to violence, and other potentially traumatic events?

The usual focus of professional attention and intervention for most children is the incident spawning the emergent report to authorities. Children tend to be identified and labeled by the nature of the report currently being investigated, regardless of their full traumatic event history. Therefore, even though a child may have a long history of other forms of abuse, violence, and other potentially traumatic life events, if the current report is about sexual abuse, he or she likely will be labeled a *sexual abuse victim*. The tendency is to attribute whatever problems the child may have at the time to the sexual abuse and services are determined by the label rather than the child's full history or actual clinical presentation (Saunders et al., 2003). However, it is not uncommon for some multiply victimized children to identify experiences other than the reported sexual abuse as the worst or most distressing trauma for them. Consequently, viewing the child exclusively as a sexual abuse victim and under-attending to the other traumas they may have experienced will lead to improper assessment, case formulation, and treatment. Best practice should recognize the high prevalence of polyvictimization and the implications of complex victimization histories for treatment planning and mental health services. Specifically, with multiply victimized children, therapists should not assume that sexual abuse is the most serious or distressing trauma in a child's life and automatically attribute presenting problems to sexual abuse.

COMORBIDITY

Similar to polyvictimization, many research studies have found that sexually abused children frequently have comorbid mental health problems. In the National Survey of Adolescents, 71% of girls with PTSD also met diagnostic criteria for major depression and 24% also had substance abuse or dependence disorders. Similar comorbidity results were found for boys. Most interesting, a history of sexual assault was more likely to predict a comorbid presentation (two or more disorders) than a single disorder presentation (Kilpatrick et al., 2003). In the Navy Family Study, nearly half of the children with major depression also had PTSD, approximately 40% of those with problematic alcohol or drug use had PTSD and more than 50% of those with drug and alcohol problems had depression (Saunders et al., 2005). In both of these studies, children and adolescents with a history of two or more victimization types were far more likely to exhibit comorbid disorders than those who had experienced only a single type. These and other studies lead to the conclusion that having multiple, serious mental health problems appears to be a very common presentation for sexually abused children and adolescents and that sexually abused children with histories of other forms of victimization, violence, and trauma are more likely to have comorbid disorders. The high prevalence of comorbid problems has significant implications for how to determine best practice for these victims.

UNDERLYING PRINCIPLES

The issues and the research described above form an empirical topographical background for considering best practice with sexually abused children. These findings lead to the following 19 guidelines that underlie best practice treatment decisions with cases of child sexual abuse.

1. Child sexual abuse is a historical event in a child's life, not a disorder to be treated.
2. The term *child sexual abuse* encompasses a highly diverse set of sexual victimization experiences that carry varying levels of risk for different mental health problems.
3. Child sexual abuse victims may exhibit problems that vary widely in their nature and intensity from victim to victim.
4. A history of child sexual abuse increases the risk of the victim developing certain serious mental health problems.
5. The increase in risk can be low, moderate or large depending on the abuse situation and the mental health outcome.
6. Specific victim, sexual assault incident, and family and community response characteristics are associated with a greater likelihood of various mental health disorders.
7. A large proportion of sexually abused children also have experienced other types of serious victimizations, violence, and traumatic life events.
8. Older sexually abused children are more likely to have a history of polyvictimization.
9. Sexually abused children often have comorbid mental health problems.
10. Children who have experienced multiple types of victimization, violence, and trauma are more likely to have comorbid mental health problems.
11. Because of the prevalence of polyvictimization, children should not be labeled by the emergent report of sexual abuse.
12. Because of the prevalence of polyvictimization and the other possible etiological factors, mental health problems should not automatically be attributed to sexual abuse.
13. Case formulation and subsequent treatment should incorporate the child's complete history and presentation and not focus exclusively on sexual abuse.
14. Most sexually abused children need effective, evidence-based mental health services to treat and/or prevent the development of serious mental health problems.
15. Not all sexually abused children need mental health treatment.
16. Some sexually abuse children are highly resilient and will not develop clinically meaningful mental health problems.

17. Some children will initially develop problems related to sexual abuse, but will recover in a timely manner using their own coping abilities and support from family and friends.
18. Some children do not improve and a small proportion will get worse even when best practice treatment is used.
19. The personal, familial, social, and financial costs need to be considered, as well as the potential clinical benefits and risks when recommending mental health treatment for sexually abused children.

These underlying guidelines grow out of the state of the current research and clinical literature. As noted earlier, they may well need to change as new knowledge is acquired or other changes occur in the field.

ASSESSMENT

Doing best practice treatment is dependent on conducting a thorough, evidence-based assessment to inform case formulation and guide treatment planning. Ongoing assessment during therapy is needed to assess treatment effects and inform adjustments to intervention as needed. Most clinicians who work with children commonly conduct some sort of evaluation of a child's psychosocial history, current functioning, and the quality of parent-child interaction to determine a problem list and diagnosis to be approached in treatment. However, the issues described earlier imply that best practice assessment with sexually abused children requires additional assessment components.

COMPREHENSIVE TRAUMA HISTORY

Because sexually abused children often have complicated histories of potentially traumatic and stressful life events, conducting a comprehensive assessment of their trauma history is critical. A clinical assessment of a child's trauma history should not be confused with forensic interviewing. The purpose of this assessment is not to gather evidence for legal purposes. Rather, the goal is to understand the full range of difficult life events the child may have experienced. The trauma history should screen for common types of victimization such as physical abuse by caregivers, physical assault by peers, other sexual assaults, and witnessing serious violence in the home, at school, and in the community. Special situations may require screening for incidents specific to them. For example, new immigrant children may have experienced or witnessed serious violence in their homeland or during transport. In addition to interpersonal violence, children may have been exposed to other types of potentially traumatic events, such as dog attacks, motor vehicle accidents, residence fires, natural or man-made disasters, or the traumatic death of a loved one. Therefore, careful screening for a wide range of experiences should be conducted.

When screening for past traumas, proper introductions that normalize the events to be asked about and dispel common stereotypes about the events will result in more accurate screening results. Single "gate" questions should be avoided and multiple screening questions should be used to screen for each trauma type when possible. Screening questions should be behaviorally specific, and subjective summary terms that require the child to self-define them should be avoided. For example, asking children a single question such as, "Have you ever been physically abused?" requires them to define physical abuse for themselves, which may result in inaccurate responses since the child's definition may not match that of the therapist. Children should be asked several behaviorally specific questions that cover a reasonable range of common behaviors representing the type of victimization being screened. For example, children may be asked questions such as, "Has your parent ever hit you with a belt so hard it left a bruise or a mark?" and "Has a parent ever hit you in the face with a fist?" to screen for a history of physical abuse. Such questions are less open to subjective interpretation or confusion by the child and more accurate information will be obtained. Standardized screening measures with validated questions are invaluable in getting accurate trauma history information.

In addition to asking if a child has experienced a type of victimization, specific incident characteristics known to be associated with increased risk for mental health problems should be assessed as well. For example, some critical sexual assault incident characteristics that should be assessed include whether sexual penetration of the vagina, anus, or mouth by a penis, finger, tongue, or object occurred during any sexual assault incident; whether it was a single incident or a series of assaults by the same offender; the level of fear activation the child felt during the assaults; whether the child believed she would be seriously injured or even killed during the assault; and whether the child experienced physical pain or injury as a result of the assault. Each of these characteristics (among others) has been found to increase risk for mental health difficulties if they are present. Specific incident characteristics to be assessed will be different for different forms of victimization and should be developed depending on the current research demonstrating risk.

ASSESSMENT OF COMMON PROBLEMS

Children, caregivers, and referring professionals usually have specific concerns when they bring a child to treatment, and these issues should be a clear focus of assessment. However, since sexually abused children frequently have comorbid problems, assessing for a range of common outcomes, even when they are not part of the initial complaints by those involved, is critical to understanding the child's presentation fully. At minimum, all sexually abused children should be assessed for symptoms of PTSD, depression, and behavior difficulties because these are the most common problems associated with sexual abuse. Older children should be assessed for problems with drug or alcohol use and delinquent behavior. Assessment of other problems can be conducted as indicated by the situation.

Use of Standardized Measures   Best practice in mental health assessment for sexually abused children includes the use of reliable and valid standardized measures for both initial and ongoing assessment. There is a large number of well-validated self-report, parent-report, and teacher-report measures and interview schedules for all of the constructs commonly assessed in child sexual abuse cases. Some are instruments that are used in general child mental health assessment. Several standardized measures have been developed specifically for use with sexually abused children and adolescents. Standardized measures are available that assess a child's trauma history and common problems, and reviews of many of these measures are readily available (Acierno, 2000; Chadwick Center, 2010; Hawkins & Radcliffe, 2006; National Child Traumatic Stress Network, 2010). Given the wide range of valid, no- or low-cost, easy-to-use measures now available, therapists concerned with doing best practice should include them as part of their evaluations and ongoing assessment of treatment progress.

CASE FORMULATION

A comprehensive assessment will provide valid information about two questions: (1) What, if any, clinically significant problems does the child have that would benefit from treatment; and (2) Based upon the child's history, including trauma history, what problems is the child at serious risk for developing? The answer to the first question should be relatively straightforward to answer in most cases based on the assessment information.   The most difficult challenge in problem assessment is when the child uses avoidance coping methods that mask serious symptoms.

Sexually abused children frequently avoid talking about their history, the sexual abuse, other traumas, and problems they may have in order to cope with reexperiencing symptoms and anxiety-provoking reminders. In these situations, the child may present with no or few problems. The challenge for the therapist is to determine if the child is, in fact, coping well, or if the child is simply avoiding reminders and memories in order to control intrusive and other symptoms. Making this distinction usually can be accomplished by seeing how the child reacts when the abuse or other trauma is brought up in assessment. If the child is willing to talk freely about other topics, even sometimes difficult topics unrelated to the abuse or other traumas, but then shuts down, is silent, or anxiously denies any problems, then avoidance is usually the answer. If the child is able to approach the abuse and past traumas, discuss them at least in part, and is able to express appropriate emotion, then he may be using adaptive coping methods. With experience, therapists can learn to titrate soft reminders of the abuse and other traumatic events during the assessment process to test for avoidance vs. adaptive coping.

Sexually abused children frequently have comorbid problems, so triage of what problems to approach first is often necessary. The primary triage is usually between externalizing and internalizing problems. Generally, if the child has both internalizing and externalizing problems, gauging the seriousness of the behavior is necessary. If the behavior is putting the child in serious danger (e.g., problematic substance use, serious delinquency, suicide attempt, risky sexual behaviors), seriously threatens their continued participation in school or a foster care placement, or is of such magnitude that frustrated caregivers demand that something be done immediately, then the problematic behavior should be targeted first. Serious disruptive and sexualized behaviors are usually the most troubling for caregivers and other adults such as teachers and caseworkers, and these problems may need to be approached first in order to win the confidence and continued participation of caregivers. If the problematic behavior is less serious and can be tolerated by the adults around the child, then a treatment for the internalizing problems that is known also to improve behavior problems may be used.

The most common presentation for sexually abused children with internalizing symptoms is a combination of depression and PTSD symptoms. PTSD is frequently comorbid with depression, though depression is more often seen without PTSD. These problems are usually treated in tandem using the same treatment approach. Most evidence-based treatments for children with PTSD also have positive effects on depression and there is seldom a need to triage these problems.

Treatment of sexual abuse victims is not only about their current problems. It also should have prevention of future abuse-related problems as a secondary goal of treatment. For example, a 7-year-old sexual abuse victim is unlikely to have drug and alcohol problems. However, that child is at increased risk for those problems developing in adolescence and at least part of treatment should be focused on what can be done now to prevent those problems in the future. Therefore, developing a longitudinal risk profile is part of case formulation. The risk literature can be applied to the assessment results to develop a risk profile for the child. Treatment components can then be incorporated that approach these issues, usually later in the treatment course.

Case formulation is based on assessment results. A set of current problems is developed and triaged. Threatening externalizing problems may have to be managed first. Less serious behavior problems can be treated with internalizing symptoms. Generally internalizing symptoms can be treated simultaneously depending on the mix and the therapy chosen, and triage is not necessary. Prevention of possible future problems is an important secondary goal of treatment.

INTERVENTION APPROACHES

There is no shortage of treatment approaches that claim to be of help to victims of child sexual abuse. Saunders, Berliner, and Hanson (2004) reviewed 25 treatment approaches commonly used with cases of child physical or sexual abuse. The California Evidence-Based Clearinghouse for Child Welfare (Chadwick Center, 2010) lists 30 programs claiming to be useful with cases of child sexual abuse and 11 different programs for "Trauma Treatment." A quick Internet search for treatment approaches for child sexual abuse victims results in a long list of interventions claiming to be helpful. Clearly, many treatments, interventions, and programs are available and nearly all claim to be effective with victims of child sexual abuse with PTSD, depression, behavior problems, and trauma-related problems. Given this large array of available therapies all claiming to be helpful, how does a busy frontline practitioner sort out the good from the poor or even harmful interventions and decide which treatment to use with a particular client with particular disorders and problems?

COMMON ERRORS

In making decisions about the best treatment approach to use, practitioners should avoid making the following common logical errors in judging the effectiveness of a treatment.

Reliance Solely *on Case Anecdotes and Remembered Cases* Practice experience is often the most important and at the same time potentially misleading basis practitioners can use to make treatment decisions. Nothing can help a therapist understand the emotional effects of sexual abuse like hearing a young child describe the fear and anxiety she felt while being sexually abused, or how she reexperiences those feelings each day and tries her best to avoid them. Greater experience doing treatment helps therapists hone their clinical skills, better understand their personal strengths and weaknesses, and learn how to use their personal attributes more effectively in therapy. Like most people, therapists often over-attend to great successes and dismal failures. Cases where a difficult child made tremendous progress, and those where therapy just did not help, always stand out. Also, therapists frequently hear from colleagues about cases that seemed to respond well to a particular approach and those that did not. These clinical experiences provide valuable information that needs to be incorporated into future practice.

The difficulty comes when only these extraordinary cases form the basis for future treatment selection. Individual cases may have many unknown or unrecognized reasons why they did well or poorly. If therapists rely only on their own remembered clinical successes and failures and the selected anecdotal reports of colleagues to make treatment decisions, they may not understand the response of the full range of cases and they are less likely to learn about new effective treatments.

Failure to Appreciate Resilience and Natural Recovery As discussed earlier, a portion of sexual abuse victims are resilient and do not develop serious problems, and others recover over time without professional treatment (Broman-Fulks et al., 2007; Hanson et al., 2001; Hyman & Williams, 2001; Lynskey & Fergusson, 1997; Saunders et al., 1999). What these findings mean is that some sexual abuse victims that become involved in treatment improve simply because of their own resilience and the natural course of recovery rather than due to any therapeutic effects of interventions delivered by professional therapists. These clients likely will be viewed as treatment successes, even though the treatment may have made little or no contribution to their improvement.

Confusing Client Satisfaction With Clinical Improvement Many organizations collect client satisfaction information as part of their program evaluation or quality assurance efforts. Clinics and therapists may be acknowledged or even rewarded for having high client satisfaction ratings. Client satisfaction is clinically important in that if clients prematurely drop out of treatment because they are dissatisfied with the organization, the therapist, or the therapy being delivered, treatment cannot be completed and symptoms may persist unnecessarily. Positive expectations and commitment to therapy greatly enhance the therapeutic alliance and client satisfaction facilitates each. However, client satisfaction and clinical improvement are different constructs. High client satisfaction does not necessarily signify treatment effectiveness. Clients can like their therapists, appreciate the organization, and be satisfied with the treatment approach being used, and still not get better. Conversely, some clinically effective treatment procedures may result in transitory client dissatisfaction. For example, sexual abuse victims frequently are in treatment for symptoms of PTSD. Effective PTSD treatments usually include some form of exposure therapy as part of the treatment protocol. These procedures are designed to help the client confront reexperiencing symptoms, challenge dysfunctional avoidance coping methods, and reduce hyperarousal symptoms through the habituation process (Foa, Hembree, & Rothbaum, 2007). Exposure procedures can be anxiety-provoking for clients and lead to some level of temporary dissatisfaction with treatment and even anger toward the therapist until the therapeutic benefit is realized. So, there may be times when clients are dissatisfied with treatment but they are getting better. Therefore, clinicians should not confuse client satisfaction and clinical improvement.

Misattribution of the Cause of Change   Some CSA victims in treatment will have other experiences and help apart from professional mental health treatment that enables them to recover. Some child victims receive high levels of caring, support, and good advice from close family members, friends, and other adults. Victims may become involved in new activities or establish new, positive social relationships that are helpful for them (Zoellner & Maercker, 2006). They may be taking medications that help reduce symptoms. Most important, the abuse has stopped, the offender is usually gone, and they may feel safer as a result. Protective and therapeutic factors such as these help prevent the development of serious problems after sexual abuse and greatly facilitate victim recovery. If these victims are in treatment, practitioners may attribute client improvement primarily to the therapy approach being used when in fact the outside support, activities, or other interventions may be far more important to recovery. Similarly, a treatment may be deemed ineffective when the lack of improvement is due to factors outside the therapy such as new stressful events or family disruption.

These and other common errors can lead to false conclusions, positive or negative, about the efficacy of treatment approaches. Descriptions of treatments that identify CSA victims as appropriate clients universally seem to claim effectiveness. However the basis for these claims is not always clear. Many times declarations by the developers, testimonials by patients, and anecdotal reports of success by proponents may be the sole support for the claims. Unfortunately, effectiveness studies of the impact of usual treatment in child mental health services do not encourage us to accept these unsupported claims. For example, Weisz, Donenberg, Weiss, and Han (1995) conducted a meta-analysis of nine effectiveness studies of usual child mental health services delivered in the community. Treatment effect sizes ranged from −.40 to +.29, and the mean effect size was .01. The authors concluded that in general, the typical child mental health services delivered had **no discernable impact** on the usual course of presenting problems. Therefore, given the common logical errors described above and the general findings about treatment as usual, anecdotal reports of success do not form a sufficient basis for declaring a treatment useful in the twenty-first century.

EVIDENCE SUPPORTED INTERVENTIONS ARE AVAILABLE

Given the constantly changing definitional and knowledge landscape and the pitfalls of the common errors in clinical decision making described above, how can practitioners working with victims of child sexual abuse make good choices about which treatments to use with which clients? This is the role of clinical science, to provide scientifically sound and trustworthy information that can be used in making these decisions. The errors described earlier and many other threats to drawing valid conclusions about the efficacy of treatment are controlled in the clinical science process, and the actual utility of the intervention is revealed. Repeated, well-designed and rigorously conducted randomized clinical trials (RCT) produce a solid base of scientific data concerning the efficacy of a treatment approach with the intended clients for the intended problems. After testing through the clinical science process, some interventions may be found to produce clinically significant improvement, while others are found to be less efficacious or possibly even harmful to clients. Practitioners can use this objective, scientific information in their treatment decision making.

The most basic form of applying science to practice is the concept of Evidence-Based Practice (EBP). The Institute of Medicine (IOM; 2001) defined EBP as being composed of three elements: (1) using the very best scientific evidence, (2) using the very best clinical experience, and (3) applying this scientific and practice knowledge in a manner consistent with the patient's values. The American Psychological Association issued a statement defining evidence-based practice in psychology that had similar components (American Psychological Association, 2005). Both the IOM and the APA list scientific evidence as the first criterion in clinical decision making.

As noted earlier, the weight given to scientific evidence of efficacy in clinical decision making for victims of CSA is increasing, and in some clinical settings has become a necessary condition for adoption. Increased use of scientific evidence raises the question: How much evidence is required to conclude that a treatment is clearly efficacious and thus evidence-based?

An Evidence Supported Intervention (ESI) is one that has reached a specified threshold of empirical research support for its efficacy. That is, a sufficient number of scientifically sound clinical trials have been conducted to conclude that the treatment, when delivered with fidelity, is likely to result in a clinically meaningful improvement on the target problems it was designed to treat with the patient populations for which it was developed. Authorities vary in the criteria and thresholds they use in ranking the evidence supporting an intervention (Chadwick Center, 2010; Saunders et al., 2004; Substance Abuse and Mental Health Services Administration, 2010). Most require at least two methodologically sound RCTs that find clinically meaningful treatment effects for the intervention to be considered efficacious. The presence of more empirical evidence, such as multiple RCTs by different research groups, sustaining a treatment effect over a follow-up period, greater methodological rigor, positive findings with different client populations, larger effect sizes, positive findings in community service settings and positive findings from systematic reviews (Cook, Mulrow, & Haynes, 1997) increase confidence in the treatment. With treatment models where many RCTs exist and some studies have found positive results while others have not, the direction of the clear bulk of the evidence is used to make a judgment regarding efficacy.

The good news for the CSA field is that a considerable number of treatments have been developed, empirically tested, and found to be effective for many of the major problems experienced by victims of CSA. Saunders and colleagues (2004) found that 16 of the 25 treatments they examined had at least some empirical support for their efficacy with abuse victims. Silverman and colleagues reviewed 21 child trauma treatments with empirical support for efficacy (Silverman et al., 2008). The National Registry of Evidence-based Programs and Practices (NREPP: SAMHSA, 2010) lists 12 treatments that have been found to be effective with children who have experienced violence or trauma. The California Evidence-Based Clearinghouse for Child Welfare (Chadwick Center, 2010) lists eight programs that have been tested specifically with child sexual abuse victims that are categorized as either Supported or Well-Supported by research evidence for efficacy. Several of these treatment approaches and programs have a substantial body of research supporting their efficacy. These Evidence Supported Interventions are effective in reducing common problems experienced by CSA victims, such as PTSD, depression, and behavior difficulties. Therefore, while gaps still remain, effective, evidence-based treatment approaches are available for most of the serious problems commonly experienced by child victims of sexual abuse. The challenge is for therapists to use them with their CSA clients.

WHY USE ESIs?

A paraphrase of the quote from Damon Runyon that leads this chapter is probably the best reason for using evidence supported interventions. Though no treatment approach, including the most well-supported ESIs, results in improvement in every client, empirical research suggests that ESIs offer the best chance for recovery for CSA victims with clinically significant problems. There is a growing consensus in the child abuse field that the central factor in making decisions about best clinical practice should be scientific evidence of efficacy (Chadwick Center, 2004; Chaffin & Friedrich, 2004). Therefore, ESIs that target the clinically important problems a CSA victim has should be the first-line, default choice of treatment approaches.

In fact, the quantity and quality of treatment outcome research for some treatment approaches are now at levels where not using them when called for raises an ethical question. If an empirically tested, well-supported, effective treatment exists for the major problems a client has, can a therapist ethically not use that treatment and use an untested approach instead? What are the limits of clinical judgment in relationship to overwhelming scientific evidence and when does it bump against therapists' ethical obligation to help their clients? These are important questions that therapists now must wrestle with given the large body of scientific research available today that was not available just two decades ago. Today therapists dealing with abused and traumatized children likely have several obligations that therapists in the past were less concerned with because of the paucity of applicable research. Today, mental health practitioners have a duty to: (1) be familiar with available mental health interventions and their supporting literatures, both clinical and research; (2) be trained, knowledgeable, and skilled in the use of scientifically proven mental health interventions; and (3) use proven and effective treatments with appropriate clients in their daily work.

Table 8.1
Internet Resources for Locating Information About Evidence Supported Interventions
for Child Sexual Abuse

National Registry of Evidence-Based Programs and Practices	http://www.nrepp.samhsa.gov
California Evidence-Based Clearinghouse for Child Welfare	http://www.cebc4cw.org
National Child Traumatic Stress Network	http://nctsn.org/nccts/nav.do?pid=ctr_top_trmnt
National Center for PTSD	http://www.ptsd.va.gov
Cochrane Collaboration	http://www.cochrane.org
Campbell Collaboration	http://www.campbellcollaboration.org
Child Physical and Sexual Abuse: Guidelines for Treatment	http://academicdepartments.musc.edu/ncvc/resources_prof/reports_prof.htm

FINDING RELEVANT ESIs

Given the size of the existing treatment literature for CSA victims and the pace of new, clinical discoveries, it is unrealistic to expect busy community therapists to be able to keep up with primary source research studies. Luckily, there are several reliable and useful resources available online that review the literature and provide updated, concise information about ESIs. Some rank the empirical support for the treatments and programs reviewed according to specific criteria so that therapists can easily see which are well-supported and which are not. On most sites, therapists can do quick and simple searches to locate candidate treatments that might be applicable to their clients. Table 8.1 presents several of the most important resources available that describe treatment programs.

TREATMENT SELECTION

Treatment selection should be guided by the principles of evidence-based practice, results of the assessment, and the case formulation process. The case formulation process will result in description of the most prominent problems to be approached in a triaged order if necessary. The tools listed above can be used to develop a pool of candidate treatment approaches with adequate support for their treatment efficacy. In general, the treatment should be selected that: (1) most closely targets the matrix of problems revealed by the assessment, (2) has been used successfully with the population that most closely resembles the child and family in terms of age, gender, racial/ethnic identification, culture, and so on, (3) is the most efficient in anticipated treatment duration and cost, (4) has the strongest support for effectiveness, and (5) the therapist is skilled in delivering. The approach that most closely matches these criteria should be the default treatment for this child.

The final criteria spawns the question, what if there is a clear match between the child's problems and a highly efficacious treatment, but the therapist is not trained in it or cannot deliver it adequately? The answer to this question is dependent on the other resources that are available to the child. If other qualified therapists in the community are trained in the appropriate treatment, the therapist should refer the family to the trained therapist. If a trained therapist is not available, the therapist may look for a second choice evidence supported intervention that can be delivered. Alternatively, if the therapist is experienced and has been trained in other approaches that have some techniques in common with the preferred treatment, he may seek consultation and supervision from a trained therapist and attempt to deliver the preferred treatment.

Best practice dictates that whatever treatment approach is selected, ongoing assessment of the target problems should be conducted to monitor treatment effects. Even the most well-supported ESIs are not effective with every patient. Regular assessment will monitor problem change. If problems are persistent well into treatment, the therapist may consider alternative treatment approaches. If problems decrease to the desired levels, treatment can be ended appropriately. Without ongoing assessment, therapists are essentially flying blind in treatment.

AN IMPORTANT TREATMENT

At this point in time, the most well-supported treatment for the most common problems experienced by sexually abused children is Trauma-Focused Cognitive-Behavioral Therapy (TF-CBT; Cohen, Mannarino, & Deblinger, 2006). TF-CBT is a components-based, relatively brief treatment that that has been found to be effective with sexually abused children with significant symptoms of PTSD, depression, and moderate behavior problems. As the name implies, it uses cognitive-behavioral procedures to treat these problems. Supportive parents or caregivers are involved in all treatment procedures and the development of effective parenting skills is a key element of the treatment. Children and parents learn information about the trauma, basic stress-management skills, affective processing, and cognitive coping and processing skills first. The child constructs a trauma narrative as a gradual exposure procedure and applies the skills learned to manage the associated fear and anxiety.

The treatment may include *in vivo* exposure if necessary, and ends with conjoint parent-child and enhancing future safety components. TF-CBT has been found to be effective in eight randomized controlled trials, and a Cochrane systematic review supports the efficacy of CBT with sexually abused children (Macdonald, Higgins, & Ramchandani, 2006). TF-CBT has been found to be effective with children as young as 3 years old. In addition to the treatment manual, free online training in TF-CBT is available from **TF-CBT** *Web* (www.musc.edu/tfcbt) and free automated consultation is available from **TF-CBT** *Consult* (www.musc .edu/tfcbtconsult). Because of its strong empirical support, ease of administration, wide applicability, and readily available training, TF-CBT should be considered the first-choice treatment for sexually abused children with clinically significant symptoms of PTSD, abuse-related depression, or moderate behavior problems.

CONCLUSION

Therapists working with CSA victims have the benefit of a large body of research describing the scope and impact of CSA and tested treatments that did not exist 20 years ago. The challenge for therapists seeking to do best practice is how to incorporate the growing scientific information that is available into their therapy. This chapter has reviewed some of this research and how it might be applied to practice. A set of underlying principles based upon research was offered as a framework for guiding best practice. Principles for assessment, case formulation, and treatment selection were also offered.

REFERENCES

Acierno, R. (2000). *Screening measures for domestic violence, sexual assault, and physical assault.* Charleston, SC: National Violence Against Women Prevention Research Center, Medical University of South Carolina. (www.musc.edu/ vawprevention/research/screening.shtml)

Acierno, R., Gray, M., Best, C., Resnick, H., Kilpatrick, D., Saunders, B., & Brady, K. (2001). Rape and physical violence: Comparison of assault characteristics in older and younger adults in the National Women's Study. *Journal of Traumatic Stress, 14*(4), 685–695.

American Psychological Association. (2005). American Psychological Association Policy Statement on Evidence-Based Practice in Psychology. Washington, DC: Author. Retrieved 7/17/2010 from www.apa.org/practice/guidelines/ evidence-based.pdf

Berliner, L. (2011). Child sexual abuse: Definitions, prevalence, and consequences. In J.E.B. Myers (Ed.), *The APSAC handbook on child maltreatment* (3rd ed.). Los Angeles, CA: Sage.

Berliner, L., & Saunders, B. E. (1996). Treating fear and anxiety in sexually abused children: Results of a controlled two-year follow-up study. *Child Maltreatment, 1*(4), 294–309.

Brady, K. L., & Caraway, S. J. (2002). Home away from home: Factors associated with current functioning in children living in a residential treatment setting. *Child Abuse & Neglect, 26*, 1149–1163.

Broman-Fulks, J. J., Ruggiero, K. J., Hanson, R. F., Smith, D. W., Resnick, H. S., Kilpatrick, D. G., & Saunders, B. E. (2007). Sexual assault disclosure in relation to adolescent mental health: Results from the national survey of adolescents. *Journal of Clinical Child & Adolescent Psychology, 36*, 260–266.

Chadwick Center for Children and Families. (2004). *Closing the quality chasm in child abuse treatment: Identifying and disseminating best practices.* San Diego, CA: Author. Retrieved 3/16/2011 from http://www.chadwickcenter.org/Documents/Kaufman%20Report/ChildHosp-NCTAbrochure.pdf

Chadwick Center for Children and Families. (2010). *California evidence-based clearinghouse for child welfare* (www.cebc4cw.org/). San Diego, CA: Author. Retrieved 7/27/10 from www.cebc4cw.org/search/maltreatment-type and www.cebc4cw.org/search/topical-area/7

Chaffin, M., & Friedrich, B. (2004). Evidence-based treatments in child abuse and neglect. *Children and Youth Services Review, 26*, 1097–1113.

Chaffin, M., Silovsky, J. F., & Vaughn, C. (2005). Temporal concordance of anxiety disorder and child sexual abuse: Implications for direct versus artifactual effects of sexual abuse. *Journal of Clinical Child & Adolescent Psychology, 34*(2), 210–222.

Cohen, J. A., Mannarino, A. P., & Deblinger, E. (2006). *Treating trauma and traumatic grief in children and adolescents.* New York, NY: Guilford Press.

Cook, D. J., Mulrow, C. D., & Haynes, R. B. (1997). Systematic reviews: Synthesis of best evidence for clinical decisions. *Annals of Internal Medicine, 126*, 376–380.

Finkelhor, D., & Berliner, L. (1995). Research on the treatment of sexually abused children: A review and recommendations. *Journal of the American Academy of Child & Adolescent Psychiatry, 34*, 1408–1423.

Finkelhor, D., Ormrod, R. K., & Turner, H. A. (2007). Poly-victimization: A neglected component in child victimization. *Child Abuse & Neglect, 31*, 7–26.

Finkelhor, D., Ormrod, R. K., & Turner, H. A. (2009). Lifetime assessment of poly-victimization in a national sample of children and youth. *Child Abuse & Neglect, 33*, 403–411.

Finkelhor, D., Turner, H., Ormrod, R., & Hamby, S. L. (2009). Violence, abuse, and crime exposure in a national sample of children and youth. *Pediatrics, 124*, 1411–1423.

Fitzgerald, M., Danielson, C. K., Saunders, B. E., & Kilpatrick, D. G. (2007). Youth victimization: Implications for prevention, intervention & public policy. *The Prevention Researcher, 14*(1), 3–7.

Foa, E. B., Hembree, E. M., & Rothbaum, B. O. (2007). *Prolonged exposure therapy for PTSD: Emotional processing of traumatic experiences*. Oxford, United Kingdom: Oxford University Press.

Hanson, R. F., Borntrager, C. F., Self-Brown, S., Kilpatrick, D. G., Saunders, B. E., Resnick, H. S., & Amstadter, A. B. (2008). Relations among gender, violence exposure, and mental health: The National Survey of Adolescents. *American Journal of Orthopsychiatry, 78*(3), 313–321.

Hanson, R. F., Saunders, B. E., Kilpatrick, D. G., Resnick, H., Crouch, J. A., & Duncan, R. (2001). Impact of childhood rape and aggravated assault on adult mental health. *American Journal of Orthopsychiatry, 71*(1), 108–1119.

Hawkins, S. S., & Radcliffe, J. (2006). Current measures of PTSD for children and adolescents. *Journal of Pediatric Psychology, 31*(4), 420–430.

Hyman, B., & Williams, L. (2001). Resilience among women survivors of child sexual abuse. *Affilia, 16*, 198–219.

Institute of Medicine. (2001). *Crossing the quality chasm: A new health system for the 21st century*. Washington, DC: National Academy Press.

Kendler, K. S., Bulik, C. M., Silberg, J., Hettema, J. M., Myers, J., & Prescott, C. A. (2000). Childhood sexual abuse and adult psychiatric and substance use disorders in women. *Archives of General Psychiatry, 57*, 953–959.

Kilpatrick, D. G., Ruggiero, K. J., Acierno, R. E., Saunders, B. E., Resnick, H. S., & Best, C. L. (2003). Violence and risk of PTSD, major depression, substance abuse/dependence, and comorbidity: Results from the national survey of adolescents. *Journal of Consulting and Clinical Psychology, 71*(4), 692–700.

Kilpatrick, D. G., Saunders, B. E., & Smith D. W. (2003). *Research in brief: Youth victimization: prevalence and implications (NCJ 194972)*. Washington, DC: National Institute of Justice, U.S. Department of Justice.

Kolko, D. J. (1987). Treatment of child sexual abuse: Programs, progress, and prospects. *Journal of Family Violence, 2*(4), 303–318.

Lynskey, M. T., & Fergusson, D. M. (1997). Factors protecting against the development of adjustment difficulties in young adults exposed to childhood sexual abuse. *Child Abuse & Neglect, 21*, 1177–1190.

Macdonald, G. M., Higgins, J. P. T., & Ramchandani, P. (2006). Cognitive-behavioural interventions for children who have been sexually abused. *Cochrane Database of Systematic Reviews*, Issue 4. Art. No.: CD001930. doi: 10.1002/14651858.CD001930.pub2

McCauley, J. L., Conoscenti, L. M., Ruggiero, K. J., Resnick, H. S., Saunders, B. E., & Kilpatrick, D. G. (2009). Prevalence and correlates of drug/alcohol-facilitated and incapacitated sexual assault in a nationally representative sample of adolescent girls. *Journal of Clinical Child & Adolescent Psychology, 38*(2), 295–300.

National Child Traumatic Stress Network. (2010). *Measures review database*. Los Angeles, CA and Durham, NC: Author. Retrieved 10/12/10 http://nctsn.org/nccts/nav.do?pid=ctr_tool_searchMeasures

National Crime Victims Research and Treatment Center. (2007). *Clinical assessment interview for children & adolescents*. Charleston, SC: Author.

National Crime Victims Research and Treatment Center. (2007). *Event history interview for children & adolescents.* Charleston, SC: Author.

Nelson, E. C., Heath, A. C., Madden, P. A., Cooper, M. L., Dinwiddie, S. H., Bucholz, K. K., . . . Martin, N. G. (2002). Association between self-reported childhood sexual abuse and adverse psychological outcomes: Results from a twin study. *Archives of General Psychiatry, 59,* 139–145.

Putnam, F. W. (2003). Ten-year research update review: Child sexual abuse. *Journal of the American Academy of Child & Adolescent Psychiatry, 42*(3), 269–278.

Saunders, B. E. (2003). Understanding children exposed to violence: Toward an integration of overlapping fields. *Journal of Interpersonal Violence, 18*(4), 356–376.

Saunders, B. E., & Williams, L. M. (1996). Introduction to special section. *Child Maltreatment, 1*(4), 293.

Saunders, B. E., Berliner, L., & Hanson, R. F. (Eds.). (2004). *Child physical and sexual abuse: Guidelines for treatment* (Revised Report: April 26, 2004). Charleston, SC: National Crime Victims Research and Treatment Center, Medical University of South Carolina at http://academicdepartments.musc.edu/ncvc/resources_prof/OVC_guidelines04-26-04.pdf

Saunders, B. E., Kilpatrick, D. G., Hanson, R. F., Resnick, H. S., & Walker, M. E. (1999). Prevalence, case characteristics, and long-term psychological correlates of child rape among women: A national survey. *Child Maltreatment, 4*(3), 187–200.

Saunders, B. E., Williams, L. M., & Rheingold, A. (2003). *Predictors of child mental health services for families reported for violence.* Presentation at the VII European Conference on Traumatic Stress, Berlin, Germany.

Saunders, B. E., Williams, L. M., Smith, D. W., & Hanson, R. F. (2005). *The Navy's future: Issues related to children living in families reported to the family advocacy program, Final report of the Navy family study.* Charleston, SC: National Crime Victims Research and Treatment Center, Medical University of South Carolina.

Silverman W. K., Ortiz, C. D., Viswesvaran C., Burns, B. J., Kolko, D. J., Putnam, F. W., Amaya-Jackson, L. (2008). Evidence-based psychosocial treatments for children and adolescents exposed to traumatic events. *Journal of Clinical Child & Adolescent Psychology, 37,* 156–183.

Substance Abuse and Mental Health Services Administration (SAMHSA). (2010). *National registry of evidence-based programs and practices.* Washington, DC: U.S. Department of Health and Human Services. www.nrepp.samhsa.gov/

Weiss, J.R., Donenberg, G.R., Weiss, B., & Han, S.S. (1995). Bridging the gap between laboratory and clinic in child and adolescent psychotherapy. *Journal of Consulting and Clinical Psychology, 63,* 688–701.

Zoellner, T., & Maercker, A. (2006). Posttraumatic growth in clinical psychology: A critical review and introduction of a two component model. *Clinical Psychology Review, 26*(5), 626–653.

CHAPTER 9

Trauma-Focused Cognitive-Behavioral Therapy

MONICA M. FITZGERALD and JUDITH COHEN

INTRODUCTION

MORE THAN 65% of children experience at least one traumatic event before adulthood with half of these having multiple traumatic experiences (Copeland, Keeler, Angold, & Costello, 2007). A significant proportion of these children develop posttraumatic stress disorder (PTSD) and other comorbid problems such as depression, anxiety disorders, substance use, and externalizing behavior problems (Copeland et al., 2007). If untreated, these problems place children at risk for serious mental and physical health problems in adulthood and associated increased economic costs (Felitti et al., 1998). Fortunately effective evidence-based psychosocial treatments are now available to minimize these negative trauma-related outcomes (American Academy of Child and Adolescent Psychiatry, AACAP, 2010).

Trauma-Focused Cognitive-Behavioral Therapy (TF-CBT) (Cohen, Mannarino, & Deblinger, 2006; www.musc.edu/tfcbt) is currently the most rigorously tested, efficacious treatment for children and adolescents impacted by childhood PTSD and co-occurring mental health and behavioral problems and their caregivers and is the most widely disseminated trauma-specific intervention in the field (Silverman et al., 2008). TF-CBT is effective for children suffering from exposure to a wide array of traumatic experiences, including child abuse, domestic violence, community violence, terrorism, childhood traumatic grief, natural disasters, HIV/AIDS-related traumas, and multiple traumas. To date, nine randomized controlled trials (RCT) of TF-CBT have been published (for a summary, see Table 9.1 and refer to Weisz & Kazdin, 2010). In addition to these RCTs, TF-CBT has been tested in quasi-experimental trials (CATS Consortium 2010; Jaycox et al., 2010; Weiner, Schneider, & Lyons, 2009) and open, noncontrolled trials (e.g., Deblinger, McLeer, & Henry, 1990), two focusing specifically on childhood traumatic grief (Cohen, Mannarino, & Knudsen, 2004; Cohen, Mannarino, & Staron, 2006).

As seen in Table 9.1, the majority of TF-CBT trials have included children who had experienced sexual abuse and who suffered from clinically significant PTSD symptoms or sexually inappropriate behaviors. A large multisite investigation of TF-CBT (Cohen et al., 2004) also provided evidence that TF-CBT is efficacious with multiply traumatized youth. In this trial, more than 90% of participants referred for treatment for sexual abuse had experienced at least one other traumatic event (an average of 3.7 different types) (Cohen et al., 2004). The majority of TF-CBT trials have involved contact sexual abuse and a caregiver participating in treatment. A recent community study also documented the effectiveness of TF-CBT in improving children's PTSD and anxiety symptoms when provided by community therapists in a community domestic violence center. Importantly, many of these children had ongoing contact with the domestic violence perpetrator and thus were living in ongoing danger (Cohen et al., 2011). Children participating in TF-CBT RCTs typically had clinically significant PTSD symptoms. Most studies had some exclusionary criteria for children and caregivers (e.g., acute psychosis, active suicidal ideation, serious substance abuse, and/or severe developmental/cognitive delays).

These trials demonstrate that by the end of a relatively short treatment course (8 to 16 sessions), TF-CBT is superior to comparison treatments in resolving a range of trauma-related mental health outcomes and adaptive functioning, including children's PTSD symptoms and diagnosis, depression, anxiety, externalizing behavior problems, social competence, sexually reactive behavior problems, shame, and abuse- or trauma-related cognitions (Cohen et al., 2004; Cohen & Mannarino, 1996, 1998a; Deblinger, Lippmann, & Steer, 1996; Cohen et al., 2011). TF-CBT is also effective in improving caregiver distress and parenting skills, which have been found to mediate child outcomes (Cohen & Mannarino, 1998a). Of particular note, TF-CBT has been shown to be more effective in improving a wide variety of mental health problems than active comparison treatments which included nondirective, supportive therapies and child-centered therapies (CCTs), a

Table 9.1

Summary of Completed TF-CBT Randomized Controlled Trials

Study	Target Population $N -$ Ss Starting Study or Treatment	Number/ Length of Sessions	Treatment/Control, $N =$ Ss in Data Analyses	Major Findings
Cohen & Mannarino, 1996	Sexually abused U.S. preschool children, 3–6-year-olds $N = 86$	12, 1.5 hrs	*TF-CBT* 39 TF-CBT 28 Nondirective Supportive Therapy (NST)	TF-CBT superior to NST in improving PTSD, internalizing, and sexual behavior symptoms
Deblinger, Lippmann, & Steer, 1996	Sexually abused U.S. children, 7–13-year-olds $N = 100$	12, 1.5 hrs	*TF-CBT* 24 TF-CBT child only 22 TF-CBT parent only 22 TF-CBT parent + child 22 Community Control	TF-CBT provided to child (combined groups) significantly superior to control for improving PTSD symptoms; TF-CBT provided to parents (combined groups) significantly superior to control for improving child depression, behavior problems, and parenting skills
Cohen & Mannarino, 1998	Sexually abused U.S. children, 8–14-year-olds (PTSD symptoms not required for entry) $N = 82$	12, 1.5 hrs	*TF-CBT* 30 TF-CBT 19 Nondirective Support Therapy (NST)	TF-CBT superior to NST in improving depression and social competence at posttreatment and in improving PTSD and dissociation at 12-month f/u among treatment completers
King et al., 2000	Sexually abused Australian children, 5–17-year-olds $N = 36$	20, 100 minutes	*TF-CBT* 12 TF-CBT child only 12 TF-CBT parent and child 12 Waitlist Control	TF-CBT condition superior to WL in improving PTSD symptoms and sexual abuse-related distress; inclusion of parent only minimally improved child outcomes

(continued)

201

Table 9.1
(Continued)

Study	Target Population N – Ss Starting Study or Treatment	Number/Length of Sessions	Treatment/Control, N = Ss in Data Analyses	Major Findings
Deblinger, Stauffer, & Steer, 2001	Sexually abused U.S. children, 2–8-year-olds $N = 44$	11, 1.75 hrs	21 TF-CBT Group 23 Supportive Therapy Group 11 children's groups; 11 parents' groups (run simultaneously)	TF-CBT condition superior in improving PTSD symptoms, emotional/behavioral problems, and sexualized behavior in children; TF-CBT produced larger effect sizes for mothers' symptoms and greater gains in children's safety knowledge and skills for coping with potentially abusive situations
Cohen, Deblinger, Mannarino, & Steer, 2004	Sexually abused multiply traumatized U.S. children, 8–14-year-olds $N = 229$ Average of 2.7 additional traumatic events	12, 1.5 hrs	*TF-CBT* 89 TF-CBT 91 Child-Centered Therapy (CCT)	TF-CBT significantly superior in improving PTSD, depressive, behavior, and shame symptoms in children and a number of parenting problems in participating parents
Cohen, Mannarino, Perel, & Staron, 2007	Sexually abused U.S. children, 10–17-year-old female children and their primary caregivers $N = 24$ Average of 2 additional traumatic events		12 TF-CBT + sertraline 12 TF-CBT + placebo	No difference between groups; decreased PTSD symptoms and overall emotional/behavioral problems in children; decreased depressive symptoms in parents. Improved parental support and emotional reactivity

Study	Population	Sessions	Conditions	Results
Jaycox et al., 2010	U.S. children exposed to Hurricane Katrina $N = 125$	10, 1 hr	CBITs in schools TF-CBT in MH clinic	Access to CBITS superior to TF-CBT. Response to TF-CBT modestly better
Deblinger, Mannarino, Cohen, Runyon, & Steer, 2011	Sexually abused U.S. children, 4–11-year-olds $N = 210$	8 or 16, 90 min	All TF-CBT: 8 sessions, no TN*; 8 sessions, with TN*; 16 sessions, no TN*; 16 sessions, with TN*	TF-CBT significantly improved children's PTSD, personal safety, and parenting skills across conditions. 8 sessions W TN was superior for improving abuse-related fear, anxiety, and parental abuse-related distress; 16 sessions No TN was superior in improving effective parenting practices and reducing children's externalizing behavior problems
Cohen, Mannarino & Iyengar, 2011	7–14-year-old children $N = 124$	8, 90 min	64 TF-CBT 60 Child-centered Therapy (CCT)	TF-CBT superior to CCT in improving IPV-related PTSD and anxiety

*TN = Trauma Narrative

203

waitlist control (King et al., 2000), and a community control condition (Deblinger et al., 1996; Cohen et al., 2011). Further, TF-CBT appeared to be particularly more effective than CCT for children *with* multiple traumas and higher levels of depression comorbid with PTSD symptoms (Deblinger, Mannarino, Cohen, & Steer, 2006). TF-CBT was also found to be superior to active comparison treatments in significantly reducing children's self-reported shame and improving trust and the sense that their reports of abuse were believed by caregivers. Further, TF-CBT also had a greater impact on caregivers' self-reported depression symptoms, emotional distress related to the child's abuse, parenting practices, and parental support than CCTs (Cohen, Deblinger, Mannarino, & Steer, 2004). TF-CBT treatment gains in children's shame symptoms remained significant at the one-year follow-up (Deblinger et al., 2006). These findings are particularly relevant for children who have experienced sexual abuse who are prone to developing distorted or unhelpful cognitions and attributions about oneself (e.g., shame, self-blame, low self-worth), other people (impaired interpersonal trust), the world, and/or social contract, which is related to greater PTSD, depression, externalizing behaviors, dissociation, and relationship difficulties (Deblinger & Runyon, 2005; Feiring, Cleland, & Simon, 2010), as well as poorer treatment response (Cohen & Mannarino, 1998b, 2000). For more detailed information about the empirical research on TF-CBT, see Cohen, Berliner, and Mannarino (2010).

TF-CBT: MODEL DESCRIPTION

TF-CBT is a structured components-based treatment for children ages 3 to 18 years with primary trauma symptoms including *affective* difficulties (e.g., fear, worry, depression, anger, and mood instability), *behavioral* difficulties (e.g., avoidance of trauma reminders, reduced or problematic social interactions, modeling of violent behavior and/or sexualized behaviors, and substance use), *biological* difficulties (e.g., physical manifestations of trauma), *cognitive* symptoms (e.g., distorted, unhealthy cognitions about self, others, world, such as self-blame, low self-worth, shame), *social* difficulties (e.g., impaired attachments, affiliating with deviant peers, problematic family interactions), or *school* difficulties (e.g., trouble concentrating or learning, poor grades, decreased attendance, or school-related trauma reminders). TF-CBT incorporates elements of cognitive-behavioral, attachment, family, humanistic, and psychodynamic principles as well as research findings about the psychophysiology of childhood trauma. TF-CBT is a family-focused approach: parents and children are included equally in this model and several conjoint child-parent sessions are included. This treatment is typically implemented within 12 to 20 sessions.

The primary goals and themes of TF-CBT are to (1) help the child and parent gain life skills to manage stress and regulate emotional, behavioral, and cognitive states effectively; (2) include nonoffending parents or other caretaking adults in treatment whenever possible in order to improve parental understanding of the child's trauma experiences and responses and the parent's optimal response to these; (3) achieve mastery over trauma-related triggers, memories, thoughts, feelings, and traumatic avoidance through the use of gradual exposure throughout the entire course of treatment; (4) help children and families make meaning and contextualize the traumatic experiences through cognitive and affective processing (focusing on the present and future versus living in the past); and (5) enhance safety and optimize future developmental outcomes. Other important considerations are the centrality of the therapeutic relationship and the importance of culture, which are addressed elsewhere (Cohen et al., 2006). Consistent with these overarching themes, the TF-CBT model has nine core treatment components, described by the acronym PRACTICE. The PRACTICE components include initial skills-based components (P-R-A-C) followed by more trauma-specific components (T-I-C-E), with Gradual Exposure (GE) integrated into all treatment components. The core components are introduced according to a sequence that progressively builds on skills and concepts presented earlier.

TF-CBT components are provided individually to child and parent; each progresses in parallel with conjoint sessions occurring near the end of TF-CBT treatment. TF-CBT therapists determine the pace of treatment and progress from one component to the next based on the unique needs of each child and family and clinical circumstances. Weekly practice of skills outside of session in real-world settings is incorporated throughout TF-CBT and tools such as fidelity checklists help to ensure effective delivery of the model.

Fidelity to the TF-CBT model involves (1) providing all of the PRAC-TICE components unless there is a clinical indication to not provide one (e.g., in vivo exposure would not be provided if the child had no generalized avoidance); (2) providing all of the components in the PRACTICE order unless there is sound clinical justification to *alter* the sequence (e.g., Enhancing Safety Skills would be delivered first if there was an immediate safety concern); (3) including Gradual Exposure (GE) in all treatment components to help children and caregivers gradually achieve mastery over trauma-related fear and avoidance. GE involves incrementally increasing the intensity and/or duration with which children and caregivers learn to cope with traumatic reminders within a safe, controlled, therapeutic context; and (4) providing TF-CBT within the appropriate time frame (8 to 25 sessions) and with the appropriate proportionality (approximately ⅓ of sessions devoted to PRAC skills; ⅓ to Trauma narration and processing; and ⅓ to ICE components. For children requiring many sessions for re-regulation of affect and behavior, this proportion may be altered to ½ of sessions for PRAC skills and ½ of sessions for TICE components).

TF-CBT MODEL COMPONENTS

The PRACTICE components are the core of the TF-CBT model. More detailed descriptions are available elsewhere (i.e., Cohen et al., 2006; www .musc.edu/tfcbt; www.musc.edu/tfcbtconsult). Parents are included in every component. Although **Assessment** is not part of the formal PRAC-TICE skills, it is a critical aspect of TF-CBT. Routinely assessing children for exposure to traumatic events, posttraumatic stress symptoms, and other common co-occurring trauma sequelae (e.g., depressive or anxiety symptoms, externalizing behavior symptoms) is essential to guide initial treatment planning and to track children's symptoms and response to treatment. Commonly used measures to assess trauma exposure and symptoms in TF-CBT implementation include the UCLA Posttraumatic Stress Disorder Reaction Index (UCLA PTSD RI; Steinberg, Brymer, Decker, & Pynoos, 2004) or the Child PTSD Symptom Scale (Foa, Johnson, Feeny, & Treadwell, 2001).

Psychoeducation begins at the initial assessment and continues throughout the treatment process. Families often feel alone, fearful, confused, guilty, and unsure of how the trauma will affect their child and family. The therapist normalizes the child's and parent's responses to the traumatic event and clarifies misconceptions about the trauma, with the aim of supportively communicating to the child and caregiver several key themes, including (a) they are not alone in their experience of trauma or the only one who feels this way; (b) they are not weird, strange, or crazy to feel this way or think these things, given their experience; and (c) there is hope, and children recover with therapy (i.e., TF-CBT works). Therapists also provide information about common emotional, behavioral, and physiological reactions following abuse and trauma. Specific information about the child's diagnosis is also provided, if appropriate. Importantly, from the very start, TF-CBT therapists begin to identify children's trauma reminders ("triggers"); educate children and parents about the role of these reminders in eliciting trauma-related emotions, behaviors, physical problems, or other difficulties; and that TF-CBT will develop positive coping strategies for these. GE is incorporated into psychoeducation by using the names of trauma experiences (e.g., "sexual abuse," "domestic violence," "death") and educating parents and children about trauma triggers and their connection to children's trauma symptoms. Consistent with the GE approach, the therapist often first provides information about trauma from a more general perspective to introduce relevant topics and then gradually focuses in on the child's reactions to his or her personal experience of the trauma. The therapist chooses creative therapy activities (card games, board games, brochures/handouts) that match the child's interests to provide psychoeducation and to answer common questions about the trauma. The specific kind of information provided to the child and caregiver varies according the type of abuse or traumatic events that were experienced and is matched to the child's developmental level. When children have experienced more than one type of traumatic event, such as sexual abuse *and* domestic violence, the therapist will gradually provide information about all types of trauma, but introduces only one type of trauma first (sometimes the child chooses), in order to not overwhelm the child or parent and make the content digestible. For children who have experienced multiple or complex traumas, therapists must understand the underlying theme of the child's trauma experience; this should be a focus of GE rather than only focusing on a series of trauma types. For example, a child was removed from her mother at 3 years old due to repeated neglect, physical abuse, and substance abuse, and then placed with her great grandmother only to witness this caregiver die of a stroke when the child was 5 years old. She was then placed and subsequently removed from a series of foster homes due to sexual and physical abuse and neglect. She identified her worst trauma as "grandma died" but the therapist did GE around "grownups haven't been there to take care of you," incorporating individual examples of this as therapy progressed.

Parenting skills. The parenting component provides caregivers with effective strategies to optimally understand and support their child following trauma. Therapists help caregivers to recognize and address their children's trauma-related problems *as well* as their personal response to the child's trauma experience and its impact on parenting and maintenance of child trauma reactions. The caregiver's ability to address personal traumatic reactions and become a primary source of support and security facilitates the child's treatment response. For example, a mother who was abused by her boyfriend became fearful and mistrustful of the world after this boyfriend sexually abused her 7-year-old daughter. Mother began closing the blinds when arriving home, checking the locks frequently, and allowing her daughters to sleep in her bed with the lights turned on at night. In turn, her daughters developed intense nighttime fears, generalized anxiety, and aggressive, controlling behaviors at home and school. In therapy the mother explained that she felt so guilty about the domestic violence and sexual abuse her children experienced that she stopped disciplining them and they have now become "problem kids" due to their anxiety and aggression. Her own fears, helplessness, and lack of felt safety have sent strong messages to her children about danger in their home and the world. The therapist first clarified connections between the mother's fears and compulsive "safety" behaviors and her daughters' increased anxiety. The therapist then worked with mother to tailor a family safety plan to reduce fear at home and to establish external safeguards (e.g., obtaining legal advocacy, preventing unwanted perpetrator contact). Mother then felt more in control and confident presenting the family safety plan to her daughters. She was able to gradually reintroduce rules and consequences in her home, including a reward plan for the children learning to sleep alone in the dark.

In the parenting component, therapists teach caregivers safe and effective ways to manage child behavioral problems, such as disruptive, aggressive, or noncompliant behavior or fears, sleep problems, and inappropriate sexual behaviors. Providing parents with parenting skills is important because child abuse and trauma often result in behavior problems, and parents of abused children often lack effective parenting strategies and/or feel guilty about disciplining their children who have experienced trauma. The parent management skills taught in TF-CBT overlap with those taught in other evidence-based parenting programs (Eyberg, Nelson, & Boggs, 2008) and focus on increasing positive parent-child encounters and teaching reinforcement of positive child behaviors. These skills may include praise, compliment exchange, selective attention and active ignoring, rewards, contingency management plans, giving effective instructions, and use of logical and appropriate consequences for misbehavior (e.g., time out, withdrawal of privileges). Therapists actively teach, coach, and reinforce parent's use of parenting skills. GE is incorporated into the parenting component by helping parents understand the connection between the child's behavior problems and the child's traumatic experiences.

Relaxation skills provide children and parents individualized skills to manage physiological arousal and symptoms of fear and anxiety that are often associated with traumatic responses and PTSD. Teaching the body to physiologically relax reduces the child's perceptions of fear and anxiety and encourages a sense of empowerment and mastery over symptoms. These skills can also be helpful to distract children/caregivers from upsetting and traumatic thoughts and refocus on pleasurable activities and self-soothing.

Therapists typically begin with identifying skills the child already uses for coping with stress, releasing tension, self-soothing, and relaxing their body. Clinicians aim to build upon the healthy, positive coping skills in the child's repertoire and reduce and replace any maladaptive, harmful coping behaviors (e.g., aggression, running away, substance use). Clinicians explain the difference between normal fear and anxiety responses and traumatic stress reactions. Therapists provide specific methods of stress management skills such as controlled diaphragmatic breathing, progressive muscle relaxation, quick tension and relaxation (e.g., Raggedy Ann/Tin Soldier), and pleasant imagery. Relaxation strategies also include listening to calming music, creating calming words/mantras, relaxation songs, prayer, yoga, physical exercise, dance, meditation, visualization, and arts. The methods of teaching and practicing these skills in session are tailored to the developmental level and interests of the child (use of props, stuffed animals, bubbles, books, CDs/iPod). Children often teach their caregivers the skill so that their caregivers can help them practice using relaxation strategies outside of session (first within nonstressful situations, and then in response to trauma triggers). Caregivers become more attuned to their child's stress states and help the child differentiate when they are truly in danger versus when they are having a trauma trigger (and feeling unsafe), and provide prompts to use relaxation skills.

For example, a 14-year-old boy who was sexually abused in a bathroom at school often experienced sexual abuse reminders when in the boy's locker room during gym class, even though the perpetrator had been removed from the school and there was no objective reason for him to be fearful in this setting. The clinician used sports examples to help him learn to identify his physiological fear responses (increased heart rate, gastrointestinal pain, headaches), and then he developed a relaxation plan that involved listening to his iPod while he changed clothing in a bathroom stall, or quietly rapping a favorite tune, so that he could distract himself and tolerate the physiological arousal and anxiety he experienced on gym days. Helping the child to use learned stress management skills to cope with trauma-related distress when faced with trauma triggers or reminders between sessions illustrates how GE is incorporated into this component.

Affective modulation helps children learn the skills necessary to accurately identify, express, and regulate positive and negative emotions and to help children and caregivers understand healthy versus unhealthy or maladaptive forms of emotional expression. First, the therapist helps the child and caregiver understand and learn the basic skills of emotional regulation, and then these skills are applied to emotions associated with the abuse and trauma. Individual affective modulation strategies are developed according to the needs, developmental level, and interests of each child and often include seeking social support, self-soothing, positive self-talk, distraction and thought stopping, positive imagery, problem solving, and interrupting inappropriate behavior (e.g., hitting) as a way of expressing negative emotion (fear, irritability, frustration). Caregivers are also taught how to model these skills (labeling feelings and effective coping) and reinforce the child's use of healthy affective regulation skills. GE is implemented in this component by helping children identify and practice strategies for coping with negative affective states associated with trauma reminders.

A variety of creative techniques are employed in TF-CBT to encourage feeling identification and expression, including the use of emotion games (bingo, charades, cards), photographs of faces, books, and drawing. An 8-year-old boy who was sexually abused by his 19-year-old stepbrother only talked about feeling "mad all the time" when he entered therapy and had difficulty identifying other emotional states. His mother also displayed hostility and limited positive affect in session and often expressed feelings of revenge and anger toward her current husband for *his* older son's abusive behavior. Affect modulation work with both child and caregiver in parallel sessions helped to expand the child's emotional vocabulary to include positive feeling states as well as other negative feeling states of disgust, sadness, irritability, and frustration (described as "the ickies"), and longing for his brother who he was "mad at but also missed." In parent sessions, the mother became aware of the impact of her negative emotional expression on her son and thus minimized his exposure to her angry/hostile expressions about the perpetrator and trauma impact and increased her display of positive emotions. The mother learned to encourage her son's use of affective regulation strategies when he became affectively dysregulated between treatment sessions and/or experienced trauma triggers. Example trauma triggers were varied such as seeing or hearing about other big brothers, hearing car tires skid (his brother used to skid his car into the driveway), seeing camping gear or hearing about friends' camping trips, which reminded him of the abuse occurring in a tent during family camping trips, and smelling beer or cigarettes because his brother smoked and smelled of alcohol often during the abuse. The mother praised and rewarded the boy each week for using the coping skills on his list (i.e., going to his special "chill-out" zone, shooting baskets, riding bikes, drawing cartoons or painting, playing game-boy) and did not discourage his expression of positive emotions about his older brother. For example, when the boy would see other brothers interacting, he was praised for asking his father or peers to shoot baskets and distract himself and/or finding his sketch book to write and draw about his feelings of loss and anger.

Cognitive coping helps children and caregivers understand the connections among thoughts, feelings, and behaviors and provides techniques for identifying and changing inaccurate, distorted, or unhelpful thoughts that are causing negative feelings and behaviors. Clinicians teach about the interrelationship among thoughts, feelings, behaviors, and healthy cognitive coping by using examples from daily life (nontrauma-related) such as school, bus, sports, work scenarios in which thoughts may not be accurate or helpful and helping children and caregivers recognize that how you think about events influences how you feel and behave. Techniques include using the "cognitive triangle," cartoons, thinking bubbles, scenarios and books illustrating examples of thinking styles, cued videos, and acting out scenarios with puppets and dolls that generate discussion about the feelings in different scenarios (see Cohen et al., 2006; www.musc.edu/tfcbt). All techniques are adapted to the age and developmental skills of the child.

Children and parents learn to examine their own patterns of negative thinking ("Am I falling into a thinking trap?" "Is my thought accurate? Is it helpful, does it make me feel better?") and to change dysfunctional thoughts about everyday events, which often extends to thinking about the traumatic events that the child experienced. When children spontaneously discuss trauma-related thoughts and accompanying distress (e.g., "I shouldn't have told, now we are all apart," "I didn't fight back"), clinicians ask clarifying questions, review psychoeducation, ask children what others have told them or discussed already about the topic, and help children identify affective regulation and coping skills to reduce distress related to these thoughts. However, therapists do not focus on challenging these thoughts through cognitive restructuring with children until after the trauma narrative is created and cognitive and emotional processing occurs. Caregivers also benefit from gaining personalized coping skills and are introduced to more formalized cognitive restructuring to address their patterns of distorted or unhelpful thoughts related to their child's trauma.

Trauma narrative and cognitive processing. The trauma narrative (TN) is created by helping the child develop a narrative (often, but not always in the form of a written book) about his or her traumatic experiences. The goal of the TN is to encourage children to directly describe their personal trauma experiences and organize their narratives in some preserved format that the therapist and child can review during subsequent sessions to process maladaptive cognitions in future components and share the narrative with the caregiver. Over several sessions, the clinician helps the child to describe the details of what happened before, during, and after the traumatic experiences, and helps the child include increasing details, thoughts, feelings, and physiological reactions in the narrative. Developing the TN involves gradual exposure, which allows the child to experience the negative feelings (fear, panic, shame, sadness, disgust) and physiological reactions associated with the trauma in small doses in a safe, controlled environment. The goal is for the therapist to help the child describe traumatic memories and the difficult feelings associated with the trauma until these are no longer so frightening or painful that the child must avoid them. Through this process the TN provides an opportunity for "making the unspeakable speakable," which provides mastery of these feared memories and diminishes the power and control of these memories. The TN offers an opportunity for children to discuss the meaning the trauma has in their past, present, and future and contextualize it into their life. Thus another goal of the trauma narration and processing component is for children to gain a better understanding of the impact that their trauma experiences have had on their lives, and through this process, to alter this impact in the present and future.

Clinicians may use a variety of therapeutic devices and structured activities to complete the TN, depending on the age, developmental abilities, and interests of the child. These may include writing a book, drawing a set of pictures, or using other creative arts (writing poems or songs, acting it out, making a PowerPoint presentation) to describe the traumatic event(s) and the child's reactions. Narratives are often organized according to the temporal sequence of the child's life, but do not include all of the child's adverse experiences. Chapters often focus on the strengths/personality of the child, what life was like before the traumatic events started, including my relationship with the person/people who perpetrated the trauma(s), the first or different types of traumatic event(s) experienced, "the worst time" or "hot spots" (i.e., trauma reminders or triggers), and a final chapter addressing how the child has changed, what has been learned/accomplished, advice for other children who have experienced trauma, and their hopeful future. As such, the TN is not only about traumatic events, but also designed to help the child put the traumatic events in the larger context of their life. An example of a child's trauma narrative is provided below in the case description.

The back and forth supportive interchange, and discussion between the child and therapist about the child's traumatic experiences and current thoughts/feelings related to the trauma is an essential part of the TN in helping the child process and organize the experience and tolerate negative feelings associated with the trauma. If GE has been properly integrated into earlier components, developing the narrative should not be a sudden "leap" in exposure, but only a gradual, incremental increase from previous sessions. It is sometimes helpful to use analogies when reviewing the rationale for TN, such as cleaning out a wound or removing a splinter (it really stings at first, but is essential for reducing distress, preventing infection, and allowing healing to occur, so that children can get on with their fun life activities). Some children may be interested in reading a children's book about the type of trauma they experienced and how other kids feel about it and recover. The clinician offers praise for any progress (small and big) mastering avoidance, confronting scary memories, and paces the exposure process accordingly. Fun rewards are built in for being brave, such as playing games or special time on the computer after the TN work is accomplished in session.

A highly avoidant boy who experienced sexual abuse and domestic violence refused to start the TN and provided rationales for not engaging in this task. After many failed attempts, the therapist encouraged the boy to start his TN focusing on this sentiment, and the boy entitled his book "All the reasons why I do *not* want to talk about the abuse!" and began describing all of the ways it was "scary, stupid, yucky, and bad," thus engaging in GE. In each TN session, the boy needed persistent prompting and reminders to use his coping skills to manage distress, and he often negotiated with the therapist regarding what he had to accomplish to play "throw the stuffed animals." Ultimately, he was able to produce a fully detailed narrative about the different events he experienced, and indicated at the end of therapy that talking about the abuse was the worst and best part of therapy.

Another component of GE involves rereading their trauma narratives in subsequent sessions and including more details about what happened, as well as how they were feeling, what they were thinking, and their body sensations at the time the traumatic experiences occurred. This allows therapists to identify dysfunctional cognitions that children would not necessarily share during direct questioning. **Cognitive processing** of the narrative includes addressing these inaccurate and unhelpful cognitions and replacing them with more optimal thoughts, which can be added to the narrative. In the case example of the 7-year-old girl, the therapist used information gained in the TN to identify unhelpful thought patterns revealed in her TN related to themes of anger and self-blame that continued to distress the young girl ("I didn't say no or stop. I am mad at him for tricking me. I am mad at myself"). To address these types of thoughts, the clinician uses a variety of cognitive restructuring strategies (Socratic Questioning, Responsibility Pie, Best Friend Role Play, or thought experiments) to process and challenge these beliefs to gain a more balanced, healthy perspective.

As the child develops the TN in individual child sessions, the clinician typically shares it with the caregivers (with the child's permission) during parallel parent sessions. The goals include helping the parents gain understanding and empathy of their child's experience, become desensitized themselves to the details, thoughts, and feelings, and to prepare to support the child during the conjoint parent-child sessions when the child shares the narrative with the parent. Children who have experienced sexual abuse or other trauma(s) may consequently develop generalized fears that interfere with their ability to function. Children may avoid people, places, or objects that in and of themselves are inherently innocuous but now serve as trauma reminders (cues/triggers) of the traumatic event. Trauma triggers may include smells, sights, and sounds (such as cologne, clothing, and hair of perpetrator). In the child's mind these cues are dangerous given they are associated with the traumatic event. For example, children who have been sexually abused at night often develop fears of the dark, of their room, and/or of sleeping alone, and will become highly distressed if they encounter these situations. Another example of generalized avoidance of trauma reminders is an adolescent's school refusal due to being assaulted in the school gym.

In vivo ("living") mastery is a form of GE that involves gradually facing trauma cues and reminders in person in real settings in which the fear stimulus initially occurred to overcome avoidance and to regain optimal functioning. This is different from imaginal exposure where the child remembers, thinks about, and talks about a feared object or activity, but it is not really there. Before implementing in vivo interventions, it is first necessary to confirm that the feared stimulus (e.g., darkness, sleeping in room alone) is truly innocuous and safe (i.e., has the perpetrator been removed from the home, the school is safe and has precautions in place). Typically, the clinician develops an in vivo exposure plan with the child and caregiver by first gaining as much information about the feared situation/object as possible, collaboratively setting up a hierarchy (listing least feared to most feared according to the child) and assisting with pacing the exposure (e.g., set up a way for the child to let you and caregiver know their level of distress throughout the process), and building in praise, encouragement, and other rewards for successes. Once the exposure plan is developed, the child is gradually and repeatedly placed in closer and closer contact with a feared object/situation in real life until the children can tolerate gradually increasing duration and intensity of exposure. The child uses the PRAC skills mastered earlier in treatment to process and tolerate fear. The therapist collaborates closely with others needed to support the in vivo exposure plan (e.g., teachers, school, or caregiver) to ensure that they provide praise/rewards when the child is successful with each step of the plan, that they reinforce coping, and do not inadvertently promote avoidance. When successfully implemented, in vivo procedures help children reduce their fears by mastering trauma reminders so that they are able to function optimally across various settings and meet developmental milestones.

Conjoint child-parent sessions involve meeting together with child and caregiver for the therapeutic activities. When children have completed trauma narratives and processing, and are ready to share their narratives with caregivers, the therapist uses clinical judgment to evaluate the child's and the caregiver's readiness to participate in conjoint sessions. At this point in treatment, caregivers ideally have participated in parallel parent sessions focused on preparing them to encourage, hear, and praise their children for talking openly about their traumatic experiences. GE involves the child sharing the trauma narrative directly with the parent, the therapist referring directly to the types of trauma the child experienced when preparing the child, and directive psychoeducation about trauma and other safety topics (developing a plan for safety and/or coping with reminders in the future). When caregivers and their children come together to share the narrative, the therapist serves as a coach and provides any redirection, prompts, or scaffolding, if needed.

Enhancing safety and development focuses on providing safety skills to help the child and family to maintain safety in the present and future, optimize the child's normal development, and regain a sense of security. GE is implemented in this component through talking about prevention of future traumatic events, and the content covered varies depending on the child's trauma exposure history and current safety needs. Safety planning is addressed earlier in TF-CBT if there are acute safety concerns. For example, a sexually abused child who exhibits high levels of sexualized behaviors at intake will benefit immediately from psychoeducation about healthy sexuality, individualized safety skill training (learning the sexual behavior rules), provided in collaboration with the parent, reduction of sexually stimulating activities, and safety monitoring to reduce these inappropriate behaviors. Parents and therapists carefully consider the child's developmental level and the child's current living situation in practicing body safety skills and/or developing a safety plan. For example, many children are still living with ongoing threats to their safety and it is critical that safety planning take into consideration how children, parents, and others in the community can contribute to the child's optimal sense and reality of safety. The therapist is careful not to communicate that the child could or should have done something differently in the past that might have prevented their previous victimization. GE is implemented in this component through talking about and practicing safety skills, developing plans for coping with trauma reminders, and preventing future traumatic events. Clinicians use varied materials (brochures, books, videos) and techniques (behavioral rehearsal/role-play, no-go-tell for young children) to teach knowledge and skills related to relevant topics (e.g., bullying, assertiveness).

Determining When TF-CBT Is Complete TF-CBT is considered complete when all components have been provided and when the information gained through assessment (self-report measures, child/caregiver report, and observation) indicates adequate reduction of trauma-related symptoms and optimal adaptive functioning. Typically, this occurs within 8 to 20 sessions. However, children who have experienced sexual abuse and other trauma may have other problems and family stresses, such as impending divorce, illness, and ongoing legal involvement that require additional interventions or ongoing providing of TF-CBT components to consolidate these skills. Assessment may also elucidate additional treatment goals that go beyond the scope of the TF-CBT model and require a different, evidence-based intervention. When children and their families do end treatment, their accomplishments and successes are celebrated, often with a graduation ceremony or party planned by the child.

CASE EXAMPLE OF TF-CBT

The following case example of a 7-year-old Caucasian girl named Sara elucidates the use of TF-CBT with a child experiencing sexual abuse in the context of ongoing neglect and attachment disruption. Identifying information and case details are altered to ensure client confidentiality.

Case Examples

HISTORY AND PRESENTING PROBLEMS

When entering therapy, Sara lived with her father, stepmother, and two younger step-siblings in a large metropolitan area and periodically visited with her biological mother. She was originally referred by a local child protection center for a psychological assessment at a university-based outpatient, trauma-focused mental health treatment center to determine eligibility for TF-CBT. Sara's parents had originally sought evaluation and treatment for Sara's escalating sexualized behaviors at school and home following a two-month summer visit with mother that culminated in mother absconding with her. In the year before this incident, the child welfare department had removed Sara from mother's care due to neglect and placed her in her father's protective custody, granting Sara's mother periodic visitation. Before gaining custody, Sara's father had limited contact with Sara on the weekends and, although generally concerned about her well-being due to the mother's instability, he was unaware of the

(continued)

full extent of Sara's trauma history and neglect exposure. On intake, the parents identified Sara's primary presenting concerns as sexualized behaviors (i.e., masturbating at home and at school in front of others, placing stuffed animal heads between her legs, sexualized dancing, and inappropriate sexual verbalizations and interest), *emotional distance*, and tendency to lie about the trivial and significant (e.g., having a blemish on her body and making false allegations of her stepmother hitting her at home).

ASSESSMENT OVERVIEW GUIDING TF-CBT

A comprehensive psychological evaluation was conducted across two sessions to collect information about Sara's trauma exposure and emotional and behavioral functioning, family strengths, and treatment needs. Information was gathered through semi-structured clinical interviews with all family members, observation of parent-child interactions, and a battery of child and parent self-report measures. The battery included a trauma screener to determine the full range of potentially traumatic events to which Sara had been exposed and measures of posttraumatic stress and trauma-related symptoms (i.e., the UCLA-PTSD Reaction Index; Steinberg et al. 2004; and Trauma Symptom Checklist for Young Children [TSCYC; Briere, 2005), as well as measures of depressive symptoms (i.e., the Child Depression Inventory, CDI; Kovacs, 1992), general child behavior (i.e., Child Behavior Checklist, CBCL; Achenbach, 1991), sexualized behaviors, such as boundary problems, exhibitionism, self-stimulation, sexual anxiety, sexual interest, sexual intrusiveness, and sexual knowledge (Child Sexual Behavior Inventory, CSBI; Friedrich, 1997), and parent functioning (e.g., Beck Depression Inventory-II; Beck, Steer, & Brown, 1996; Parenting Stress Inventory-Short Form, PSI-SF; Abidin, 1995).

In brief, the assessment information indicated a significant history of trauma exposure for Sara, including neglect characterized by maternal substance abuse, lack of monitoring, and regular exposure to sexually explicit adult behaviors and alcohol abuse by adults in the home occurring from birth to age 6 when Sara primarily lived with her mother. In her early childhood, Sara's father left the home and was in the Navy. Sara experienced significant family instability (frequent moves, many adults in home) and early parentification, as she often had responsibility for caring for herself and other adults and was charged with making adult decisions. In addition to

(continued)

(*continued*)

consistently being exposed to adult sexual activity, Sara allegedly experienced sexual abuse by a babysitter's teenage grandson when she was 4 years old. The abuse allegation was originally disclosed by a child who attended Sara's day care who identified Sara as one of the offender's victims, but Sara never disclosed the sexual abuse to her parents or previous health professionals.

Per the assessment information on the UCLA PTSD RI and TSCYC, Sara was clinically elevated on posttraumatic stress symptoms, such as intrusive thoughts; trauma reenactment in her play (e.g., simulating sexual intercourse with her dolls, masturbation, and sexual talk and gestures); hyperarousal and hypervigilance; avoidance of trauma-related memories, thoughts, and distress; and restricted affect and dissociative behaviors (i.e., seeming spaced out, preoccupied, or interpersonally unresponsive). Sara met full *DSM-IV* diagnostic criteria for posttraumatic stress disorder (309.81). She also exhibited high levels of general anxiety, depression, somatic problems, and symptoms of sexual concerns on the TSCYC, moderate depressive symptoms on the CDI, clinically elevated sexual behaviors on the CSBI, and clinical levels of internalizing and externalizing problems on the CBCL. With regard to family functioning, her parents reported mild depressive symptoms, and they were experiencing significant levels of parenting stress related to Sara's behavior problems and trauma reactions and ongoing family stressors such as periodic contact with the biological mother on visits while the father's parental rights and custody were being challenged. Further, both parents were feeling disconnected emotionally from Sara given Sara's emotional withdrawal and tendency to "shut down" and difficulty communicating her feelings and needs. Further, the parents were distressed by her sexualized behaviors and often reacted with intense, frustrated responses.

TF-CBT TREATMENT COURSE

TF-CBT was determined to be the most appropriate treatment for Sara given her significant trauma-related symptoms and her current stable and safe placement in a supportive home environment. Her parents were eager to gain help with Sara's behaviors and participate in treatment, although they expressed dissatisfaction with the previous mental health treatment they sought for Sara soon after gaining custody. They explained that the four months of previous therapy

(*continued*)

resulted in minimal progress and they were unsure of the therapy procedures given as they were not enlisted to participate in her treatment. The overview of TF-CBT and rationale for treatment was provided with a summary of assessment findings in the feedback session with the family members individually and conjointly, and TF-CBT treatment goals were set collaboratively.

Sara and her family received twenty-four, 60- to 90-minute sessions of TF-CBT delivered weekly over the course of 7½ months. Sara and both of her parents actively participated in a full course of therapy and responded well to treatment interventions overall. Treatment length was somewhat longer than usual due to several case-specific circumstances, including scheduling challenges due to parent work conflicts, complex legal involvement related to court-ordered maternal visitation and custody conflicts, erratic/ inconsistent maternal behavior on visits, a new abuse disclosure made by Sara in treatment, which required reporting, and intensive safety skills training and parental coaching in behavior management strategies to adequately address sexualized behaviors and general behavior problems.

The initial stage of treatment primarily focused on providing **psychoeducation** about trauma reactions and **parenting skills** to the parents who were extremely distressed by Sara's sexualized behaviors, lying, and withdrawn, nonresponsive behaviors. The **enhancing safety** component of treatment was integrated at this time into treatment given that Sara needed to learn appropriate, safe body boundaries to increase her and others' safety and replace inappropriate sexualized behaviors with healthy, prosocial behaviors. The therapist gained parental approval and involvement to use a psychoeducational book about body safety skills to teach Sara the basic knowledge (identifying anatomical body parts, reinforcing concepts that her body was her own, healthy sexuality, okay and not okay touches) and privacy rules (not showing others her private parts or asking others to show her their private parts, touching her private parts, or talking about her friend's private parts). Sara's parents were critical in this process because they had not yet provided information about healthy sexuality to Sara or clear instruction about body rules in a calm manner. Further, the parents never initiated conversation about the alleged sexual abuse experience at day care and instead avoided topics related to sexuality other than reprimanding Sara when she displayed inappropriate sexualized

(continued)

(continued)

behaviors. The parents were prepped to join sessions to review the safety skills, body safety rules at home and school, and were taught alternative ways to respond when Sara engaged in a sexual behavior, such as reinforcing appropriate safe touch and body rules, monitoring her closely, decreasing exposure to stimulating or sexual content (e.g., strict TV monitoring, all family members wearing clothes at home), and avoiding intense reactions of shock, disapproval, and shaming when she displayed a sexual behavior. Further, the parents had planned distraction techniques when Sara would masturbate (begin an art project, go outside to play, help in a cooking project). There were still periodic occurrences of Sara lying for no apparent reason, but the parents were surprised to notice such a marked decrease in all sexual behaviors (less sexual talk, fewer gestures at school, less reenactment and sexual play with dolls, less masturbation) in response to these interventions. The parents also benefited from discussing their fears about what they believed sexual behaviors and trauma experiences meant for Sara's future, such as loss of innocence, having life-long problems, and early sexual activity and risky behavior as a teenager. These cognitive distortions and unhelpful thoughts were addressed/reviewed throughout treatment.

As a part of **the parenting skills** component, the parents were taught child-directed play skills (description, reflection, imitation, praise, selective attention, and affection) to increase warmth and positivity in the parent-child relationship given that they complained of lack of "attachment" and feeling distant from Sara. The family incorporated 5-minute focused play times to practice these skills at home and also began regularly having "sharing times" at home when Sara was given 5 minutes of undivided attention by each parent to share her feelings and thoughts about her daily activities, and her parents would practice supportive communication skills (active listening, reflection, praise, emotion coaching). The lying behaviors were targeted by selectively attending and praising honest behaviors, ignoring minor, inconsequential lies, and providing time-limited logical consequences (privilege removal) when Sara was dishonest. Sara showed an immediate positive response to her parents using play skills and engaging in sharing times, and her range of affect began to increase and her parents felt more positive and bonded in their relationship.

The therapist provided psychoeducation about neglect to Sara, normalizing Sara's feelings of confusion, anxiety, and discomfort

(continued)

related to experiencing so many family moves, new adults in the home, unpredictable behaviors by her mother, who was abusing substances, caring for other adults who were drunk and "passed out," and fending for herself with regard to eating meals and finding a safe quiet place to rest. Sara engaged very well in learning fun, calming **relaxation strategies** such as blowing bubbles and taking deep belly breaths, doing yoga poses "to help me relax," and creative games focusing on building her emotional vocabulary. Building emotion identification and emotion expression skills in the **affective expression** component of TF-CBT was stressed throughout all of treatment given Sara's restricted affect and difficulty expressing feelings with her family. Sara engaged well with the therapist in creative activities such as taking digital photos of herself and the therapist displaying different emotions and talking about bodily sensations accompanying emotions and the causes and consequences of emotions. Sara made feeling cards and was proud to share with her parents how she could identify what she and others were feeling as well as herself and the therapist. Sara once commented that she "never does this stuff" referring to "talking about feelings" with her parents. The therapist spent time with the parents in parallel parent sessions discussing the importance of their roles in labeling emotions expressed in the family and reinforcing Sara's identification of feeling states outside of sessions. Through gradual exposure, the therapist first helped Sara identify basic feelings and non-trauma-related events (e.g., Sara drew pictures about "When I am with my family . . . I am happy!," "When I am by myself, I am sad . . . I don't like to be alone"). Over the course of four sessions, Sara had significantly expanded her emotional vocabulary from three to nine feelings, and she began distinguishing feeling intensity using "kind of" and "really" when discussing her emotions. She wanted to draw and color her own personal Feelings Thermometer (0–10) to describe feeling intensity, and she made accompanying faces to identify the feeling she was focusing on, with "scared" being the face colored all red. Sara described missing her mother and feeling confused by not seeing her regularly.

During this time in therapy the parents became distressed by the court-mandated visits over holidays for Sara and her mother, and frustrated by the lack of communication by the mother about whether she would show up. In parallel parent sessions, they benefited from discussing their wide range of emotions (fear of visits having a
(continued)

(continued)

negative impact on Sara's emotional well-being, anger toward the court and the mother, fear of retribution if they attempted to stop visits) and identifying relaxation and coping skills. Further, the therapist helped the parents use supportive communication skills to discuss Sara's feelings and reactions related to her visits (even feelings that were difficult to accept such as love, longing, disappointment), so that they would be seen as viable emotional resources for their daughter and be better able to ensure her safety.

During part of a session focusing on emotion identification, the therapist integrated psychoeducation about child sexual abuse and commented on how children who have been sexually abused sometimes feel. Sara spontaneously disclosed that she and her friend had been touched "in that way" by an older boy when she was at her babysitter's a long time ago, and clarified that the boy touched her private parts. Sara's affect did not change when she discussed the abuse. Given that this was the first formal disclosure of abuse in more than three years, Sara's parents were shocked and needed support in parallel sessions to discuss their reactions given that they had always "believed" the prior allegation but never knew for certain and had hoped it had not happened. The therapist reported the disclosure to authorities, and the family was aware of all steps in this process. The parents were stunned by the significant increase in Sara's openness and expression following the disclosure session, and reported that Sara initiated a 30-minute discussion with her parents about her abuse experiences and life with her mother when she arrived home from therapy. The therapist continued teaching Sara about child sexual abuse using a psychoeducational game in the next sessions. At first Sara felt anxious saying the words "sexual abuse" and exhibited some avoidance, off-task behavior, and agitation during the psychoeducation activities, once exclaiming, "You are not letting me just play!" However, Sara was fairly easy to redirect and engage in time-limited games, she responded well to praise, and liked to focus on rewards. Sara quickly became comfortable with the material (learning facts about child sexual abuse) and wanted to share what she had learned with her parents in conjoint sessions. Although Sara's relationship with her parents was improving, Sara periodically would show increased behavior problems and on one occasion lied about being hit by her stepmother. This accusation was unfounded but needed to be directly addressed in sessions. Sara encountered difficulty identifying

(continued)

her feelings and thoughts related to such an event, and the therapist used the **cognitive coping** component activities to help her discuss the interrelationship between thoughts, feelings, and behaviors and identify coping skills when she was feeling distressed.

One part of Sara's coping plan involved enhancing safety. Sara identified ways she could help herself feel safe as well as ways that *other adults could help* to keep her safe, including "1. Do not leave me alone; 2. Do not make me watch the kids (siblings) by myself; 3. Ask me to use my feeling cards; 4. Help me tell the truth." Sara and her family discussed ways to feel safe and cope on periodic visits with her mother. They made a family album for her to take to her mother's house to comfort her when she was missing her parents and also had safety steps and ways to contact an adult if she needed help or felt unsafe.

To begin work on the **trauma narrative (TN)**, the therapist read a book called "Jesse's Story" with Sara, which offers a description of a young girl's child sexual abuse experience. Sara exhibited some anxiety while listening to the book but agreed to make her own story. In the TN sessions, the therapist served as the "reporter" while Sara recounted the details of the events that comprised her book. Sara colored pictures to accompany each chapter's content, as well as set up figurines to show certain sexual abuse behaviors or to emphasize points. Her TN book had the following chapters: (1) *Special Things About Me and My Family*: I am a good climber, I jump rope backwards, I am smart, I like giraffes, ice cream, trees, and swimming. My family watches movies and goes to the park together. (2) *What I have Learned in Therapy:* I learned all about child sexual abuse through playing games, I learned about feelings-sad, happy, scared, mad, embarrassed. I learned to calm myself down, like using bubbles to take DEEP belly breaths! (3) *This is the Story about the Bad Thing that Happened to Me. . . . I decided to call it Sexually Abused*: One day the boy tricked me. While we were outside he told me and my friend that he wanted to hold our hands, but instead he touched my private parts . . . my vagina. He tricked me. I didn't say STOP! (4) *How I Felt and What I was Thinking*: I thought the boy was nice, so I didn't say NO. . . . He's mean, he was being fake. He tricked me . . . . I want him punished! I am mad at him and I am mad at me. I felt gross and thought it was scary. What would have happened if I didn't have undies on? Ewww, disgusting. (5) *What Happened Next (when I told)*: I went inside and told that the boy touched my privates and she made the boy go downstairs and locked the door. The [babysitter] told my mom.

(*continued*)

(continued)

She looked like she was mad, but mom didn't yell or cry. (6) *Being Safe, Coming to Therapy*: Now I am safe with my dad and step-mom. My family and I came here to talk about my feelings . . . (7) *My Fabulous Future!*

The back and forth, supportive interchange and discussion between the child and therapist about the child's traumatic experiences and current thoughts/feelings related to the trauma is an essential part of the TN in helping the child process and organize the experience and tolerate negative feelings associated with the trauma. When Sara described her sexual abuse experience, at first her affect was somewhat flat and did not match content, but when asked to elaborate about her feelings related to her mother (to facilitate details in the TN), Sara's affect would markedly change and she would display genuine affect and increased anxiety. At that time, Sara's mother had not been consistently showing up for periodic supervised visits, and this was an ongoing stressor. When recounting the sexual abuse experiences at day care (which occurred three years earlier at age 4), Sara described feelings of missing her mother while at day care and also not understanding *why* she had to go. In the **cognitive processing** of the TN, Sara benefited from talking more about her mixed feelings about her mother (e.g., missing, frustration, disappointment, uncertainty, anxiety, and responsibility for providing her mother with emotional support). Sara's feelings of regret for not saying *no* and frustration that she let the perpetrator trick her were the "hot spots" the therapist used cognitive processing techniques to challenge. Psychoeducation about offender operandi and feelings normalization helped Sara understand that young children often feel scared when offenders act nice and then hurt them, and they do not know what to do or how to act. As Sara developed a more healthy perspective, she made comments such as "He was big . . . he should have known better. . . . I was just like a baby and didn't even know what to do—how would I? I was so little and scared!" Sara's parents reviewed drafts of Sara's book to prepare for Sara sharing her trauma narrative and gradually also challenged their distorted thoughts about how the abuse had changed their daughter.

Near the end of treatment, Sara added a *Things to Come* final section of her book that explained that her family and her "may decide to continue working on talking about my feelings," and listed specific topics that she would like to discuss, many of which related to her unresolved relationship with her mother. During the sharing of the TN in the

(continued)

(*continued*)

conjoint session, Sara's parents showed a very positive, supportive response praising her for her courage and ability to openly list the topics she still felt confused or upset by. The dramatic increase in supportive family communication around emotionally arousing topics was a clear sign of treatment response and skill generalization, given that family reunification issues were ongoing and needed to be discussed in an ongoing manner. In parallel parent sessions, the therapist emphasized the importance of the parents continuing "talking time" and special play time to encourage open communication, especially given Sara's history of being avoidant and internalizing her distress.

Before treatment was completed, the therapist reinforced the **enhancing safety** skills incorporated throughout all of treatment and reviewed safety plans and coping plans to deal with future trauma reminders. The therapist and all family members agreed that treatment was over, given that symptom improvements were shown in all primary areas of child and family functioning, per child and parent report measures and parent-child observation, with the exception of increased sadness and behavior problems surrounding Sara's mother's scheduled visits, and parental distress related to the ongoing custody battle and legal involvement. More specifically, the parents reported no problematic sexual behaviors, beyond manageable behaviors when Sara periodically encountered trauma triggers (e.g., accidental exposure to adult sexual material on television when visiting a friend's house) and a significant reduction in Sara's posttraumatic stress symptoms such that she no longer met diagnostic criteria for PTSD. The father and stepmother remarked that Sara now played "normally" (no sexual content) with her toys, shared more about what she was thinking and how she was feeling, lied minimally about trivial matters, and seemed to "just get along better" with family members and friends. Per their report, she was doing well at school and had few class disruptions, and overall seemed to cope when "things go wrong." Sara commented on feeling good about sharing her feelings with her counselor and parents and only desired that, "I want my mom to be a good mom . . . and show me more attention." Thus, upon treatment completion, Sara still needed support, reassurance, and skills reinforcement from her family to cope with ongoing negative feelings such as disappointment related to her relationship with her mother. The family mutually ended treatment and agreed to seek support from a counselor in the future if they had questions or concerns about Sara's adjustment and well-being.

SUMMARY

TF-CBT is an evidence-based mental health intervention for children ages 3 to 17 that addresses child and family emotional, behavioral, and adaptive functioning after trauma. The core target of TF-CBT is to help children overcome traumatic avoidance, shame, sadness, fear, and other trauma-specific problems. TF-CBT is a manualized yet flexible components-based model; its components are summarized by the acronym PRACTICE. It has been successfully implemented by community practitioners in the United States and in a number of international settings. More information about TF-CBT is available at www.musc.edu/tfcbt and in the treatment manual (Cohen et al., 2006).

REFERENCES

Abidin, R. R. (1995). *Parenting stress index, third edition: Professional manual.* Odessa, FL: Psychological Assessment Resources.

Achenbach, T. (1991). *Manual for the child behavior checklist/4-18 and 1991 profile.* Burlington: University of Vermont Department of Psychiatry.

American Academy of Child and Adolescent Psychiatry. (2010). Practice parameter for the assessment and treatment of children and adolescent with post-traumatic stress disorder. *Journal of American Academy of Child & Adolescent Psychiatry, 49,* 414–430.

Beck, A. T., Steer, R. A., & Brown, G. K. (1996). *Manual for the Beck depression inventory-II.* San Antonio, TX: Psychological Corporation.

Briere, J. (2005). *Trauma symptom checklist for young children: Professional manual.* Florida: Psychological Assessment Resources.

Briere, J. (2005). *Trauma symptom checklist for young children: Professional manual.* Odessa, FL: Psychological Assessment Resources.

CATS Consortium (2010). Implementation of CBT for youth affected by the World Trade Center disaster: Matching need to treatment intensity and reducing trauma symptoms. *Journal of Traumatic Stress, 23,* 699–707.

Cohen, J., & Mannarino, A. (1998a). Factors that mediate treatment outcome of sexually abused preschool children: Six- and 12-month follow-up. *Journal of the American Academy of Child & Adolescent Psychiatry, 37*(1), 44–51.

Cohen, J. A., Berliner, L., & Mannarino, A. (2010). Trauma-focused CBT for children with co-occurring trauma and behavior problems. *Child Abuse & Neglect, 34,* 215–224.

Cohen, J. A., Deblinger, E., Mannarino, A. P., & Steer, R. (2004). A multisite, randomized controlled trial for children with sexual abuse-related PTSD symptoms. *Journal of the American Academy of Child & Adolescent Psychiatry, 43,* 393–402.

Cohen, J. A., & Mannarino, A. P. (1996). A treatment outcome study for sexually abused preschool children: Initial findings. *Journal of the American Academy of Child & Adolescent Psychiatry, 35,* 42–50.

Cohen, J., & Mannarino, A. (1998b). Interventions for sexually abused children: Initial treatment outcome findings. *Child Maltreatment, 3*(1), 17–26.

Cohen, J., & Mannarino, A. (2000). Predictors of treatment outcome in sexually abused children. *Child Abuse & Neglect, 24*(7), 983–994.

Cohen, J. A., Mannarino, A. P., & Deblinger, E. (2006). *Treating trauma and traumatic grief in children and adolescents.* New York, NY: Guilford Press.

Cohen, J. A., Mannarino, A. P., & Iyengar, S. (2011). Community treatment of PTSD for children exposed to intimate partner violence: A randomized controlled trial. *Archives of Pediatrics & Adolescent Medicine, 165,* 16–21.

Cohen, J. A., Mannarino, A. P., & Knudsen, K. (2004). Treating childhood traumatic grief: A pilot study. *Journal of the American Academy of Child & Adolescent Psychiatry, 43,* 1225–1233.

Cohen, J. A., Mannarino, A. P., & Staron, V. R. (2006). A pilot study of modified cognitive-behavioral therapy for childhood traumatic grief (CBT-CTG). *Journal of the American Academy of Child & Adolescent Psychiatry, 45,* 1465–1473.

Copeland, W. E., Keeler, G., Angold, A., & Costello, J. (2007). Traumatic events and posttraumatic stress in childhood. *Archives of General Psychiatry, 64,* 577–584.

Deblinger, E., McLeer, S., & Henry, D. (1990). Cognitive behavioral treatment for sexually abused children suffering post-traumatic stress: Preliminary findings. *Journal of the American Academy of Child & Adolescent Psychiatry, 29*(5), 747–752.

Deblinger, E., Lippmann, J., & Steer, R. (1996). Sexually abused children suffering posttraumatic stress symptoms: Initial treatment outcome findings. *Child Maltreatment, 1,* 310–321.

Deblinger, E., Mannarino, A. P., Cohen, J. A., Runyon, M. K., & Steer, R. (2011). Trauma-focused cognitive behavioral therapy for children: Impact of the trauma narrative and treatment length. *Depression and Anxiety, 28,* 67–75.

Deblinger, E., Mannarino, A. P., Cohen, J. A., & Steer, R.A. (2006). A follow-up study of a multi-site, randomized controlled trial for children with sexual abuse-related PTSD symptoms: Examining predictors of treatment response. *Journal of the American Academy of Child & Adolescent Psychiatry, 45,* 1474–1484.

Deblinger, E., & Runyon, M. (2005). Understanding and treating feelings of shame in children who have experienced maltreatment. *Child Maltreatment, 10*(4), 364–376.

Eyberg, S. M., Nelson, M. M., & Boggs, S. R. (2008). Evidence-based psychosocial treatments for children and adolescents with disruptive behavior. *Journal of Clinical Child & Adolescent Psychology, 37,* 215–237.

Feiring, C., Cleland, C., & Simon, V. (2010). Abuse-specific self-schemas and self-functioning: A prospective study of sexually abused youth. *Journal of Clinical Child & Adolescent Psychology, 39*(1), 35–50.

Felitti, V. J., Anda, R. F., Nordenberg, D., Williamson, D. F., Spitz, A. M., Edwards, V. . . . Marks, J. S. (1998). Relationship of childhood abuse and household dysfunction to many of the leading causes of death in adults— The adverse childhood experiences (ACE) study. *American Journal of Preventive Medicine, 14*(4), 245–258.

Foa, E. B., Johnson, K., Feeny, N. C., & Treadwell, K. R. T. (2001). The child PTSD symptom scale (CPSS): Preliminary psychometrics of a measure for children with PTSD. *Journal of Clinical Child Psychology, 30,* 376–384.

Friedrich, W. N. (1997). *Child sexual behavior inventory: Professional manual.* Odessa, FL: Psychological Assessment Resources.

Jaycox, L. H., Cohen, J. A., Mannarino, A. P., Walker, D. W., Langley, A. K., Gegenheimer, K. L., . . . Schonlau, M. (2010). Children's mental health care following Hurricane Katrina: A field trial of trauma-focused psychotherapies. *Journal of Traumatic Stress,* Vol. 23(2), 223–231.

King, N. J., Tonge, B. J., Mullen, P., Myerson, N., Heyne, D., Rollings, S. . . . Ollendick, T. H. (2000). Treating sexually abused children with posttraumatic stress symptoms: A randomized clinical trial. *Journal of the American Academy of Child & Adolescent Psychiatry, 39,* 1347–1355.

Kovacs, M. (1992). *The child depression inventory.* North Tonawanda, NY: Multi-Health Systems.

Silverman, W. K., Ortiz, C. D., Visweswaran, C., Burns, B. J., Kolko, D. J., Putnam, F. W., & Amaya-Jackson, L. (2008). Evidence-based psychosocial treatments for children and adolescents exposed to traumatic events. *Journal of Clinical Child & Adolescent Psychology, 37*(1), 156–183.

Steinberg, A. M., Brymer, M. J., Decker, K. B., & Pynoos, R. S. (2004). The University of California at Los Angeles post-traumatic stress disorder reaction index. *Current Psychiatry Reports, 6,* 96–100.

Weiner, D., Schneider, A., & Lyons, J. (2009). Evidence-based treatments for trauma among culturally diverse foster care youth: Treatment retention and outcomes. *Children and Youth Services Review, 31*(11), 1199–1205. DOI: 10.1016/j.childyouth.2009.08.013

Weisz, J. R., & Kazdin, A. E. (Eds.). (2010). *Evidence based psychotherapies for children and adolescents* (2nd ed.). New York, NY: Guilford Press.

CHAPTER 10

Eye Movement Desensitization and Reprocessing (EMDR) Psychotherapy With Children Who Have Experienced Sexual Abuse and Trauma

ROBBIE ADLER-TAPIA, CAROLYN SETTLE, and FRANCINE SHAPIRO

"I T'S LIKE YOU stuck a vacuum hose in my ear and sucked out all the crap." Such was the response of a 10-year-old boy while participating in trauma reprocessing with EMDR. He had been sexually abused by his mother's boyfriend over the course of four years. He had refused to acknowledge let alone discuss the shame of what had happened to him prior to participating in EMDR.

INTRODUCTION

Sexual abuse and trauma can have a long-term and pervasive impact in the lives of children of all ages (Felitti et al., 1998). Children experience sexual abuse and trauma in many ways and perpetration of children takes many forms. A child may be sexually abused by a parent or other family member, a friend, an acquaintance, or a stranger. Children can also experience sexual trauma by being exposed to inappropriate and explicit adult sexual behaviors in the media. The abuse may have also resulted in the child experiencing physical trauma and medical injuries due to an assault.

Abuse may have occurred once in a single setting or more than once in multiple settings from multiple perpetrators. However, it is not possible to predict the impact of the sexual abuse and trauma on the individual based on a formula that weighs each of these variables. Symptom manifestation uniquely varies and must be assessed for each child. Because of the impact and complexity of child sexual abuse, psychotherapy is often beneficial to prevent the long-term sequalae of abuse.

WHAT IS EMDR?

Eye Movement Desensitization and Reprocessing (EMDR) is a comprehensive and integrative eight-phase psychotherapy treatment approach (Shapiro, 1989, 1995, 2001) that is guided by the Adaptive Information Processing model. According to this model, a wide range of pathology is caused by unprocessed memories of trauma and other disturbing events. Consequently, the goal of EMDR is to assist the client in reprocessing relevant memories in order to both alleviate symptoms and foster personal growth. EMDR is recognized worldwide as a frontline treatment for trauma (American Psychiatric Association, 2000; Bisson & Andrew, 2007). Currently there are approximately eight randomized controlled trials demonstrating the efficacy of EMDR in the treatment of traumatized children (for a review, see Adler-Tapia & Settle, 2009). The research also provides evidence that EMDR is an efficacious treatment for children who have experienced trauma from child sexual abuse. In a randomized controlled trial comparing EMDR psychotherapy with Cognitive Behavioral Therapy (CBT) in the treatment of girls who had been sexually abused, the researchers concluded that both treatments produced significant improvement on the child and parent measures, with no difference in outcome between treatments (Jaberghaderi, Greenwald, Rubin, Dolatabadim, & Zand, 2002). In this study, EMDR therapy was described as more efficient, using fewer sessions (EMDR mean of 6.1 sessions versus a CBT mean of 11.6 sessions), and EMDR required no homework as is required in the CBT treatment protocol. Another randomized controlled trial identified traumatized adolescents and young women, ages 16 to 25, who were victims of child abuse (Scheck, Schaeffer, & Gillette, 1998). Sixty women between the ages of 16 and 25 were randomly assigned to two sessions of either EMDR or an active listening (AL) control. Despite treatment brevity, the results were highly significant in the EMDR condition. The two sessions of EMDR both reduced psychological distress and brought patient scores to within one standard deviation of nonpatient or successfully treated norm groups on all measures. In both studies of EMDR with children who experienced sexual abuse, EMDR is indicated as an efficacious treatment for this population.

ADAPTIVE INFORMATION PROCESSING THEORY

Adaptive Information Processing (AIP) theory posits that symptoms arise from memories that include thoughts, beliefs, emotions, body sensations, and sensory experiences that were encoded, stored, and retained from the time of the disturbing event. Part of the difficulty arises when these memory associations appear to be retained without having been reprocessed to a more adaptive resolution. Regardless of the time since the distressing event, the information has not been assimilated, accommodated, and reprocessed through to the individual's current orientation and continues to interfere with daily functioning. For instance, negative beliefs that an individual might hold such as, "I'm not good enough," or "I can't trust anyone" are viewed as evidence of the disturbing events that carry these perspectives. Consequently, in EMDR therapy the information processing system and associated memory networks are the focus of treatment. With the EMDR psychotherapy treatment procedures, clinicians are guiding the client to access experiences that have been encoded and retained, retrieve the encoded information, and through the innate information processing system reprocess the information to more adaptive resolution. As an integrative psychotherapy informed by AIP theory, EMDR is compatible with elements of other psychotherapy interventions. When working with child clients, EMDR may incorporate play therapy and other efficacious treatment tools for working with children. AIP offers a theoretical understanding of the therapeutic relationship, and case conceptualization that includes identifying appropriate memories, both positive and negative, to be targeted and reprocessed through the complete eight-phase integrative EMDR psychotherapy approach. Therefore, even though some elements of the goals and objectives of the phases of EMDR may be evident in other treatment modalities, it is the aggregate of the theory, case conceptualization, and accurate implementation of the protocols and procedures of this integrative psychotherapy that truly defines EMDR.

AIP in Psychotherapy With Children   Because children have typically not developed the cognitive concepts, language, and historical life experiences of adolescents and adults, therapists need to adjust the language and the implementation of EMDR when providing psychotherapy for child clients. This can be accomplished by conceptualizing the implementation of the eight phases of EMDR through a developmental lens and then enacting the psychotherapy by integrating child clinical tools such as play therapy and art therapy. For example, play therapy offers children a medium to express feelings that can be used in EMDR when children do not have the verbal skills to express themselves.

When conceptualizing EMDR psychotherapy with children who have experienced sexual abuse, it is imperative for the therapist to consider how the child has experienced and retained the memory of the event. This is what needs to be accessed and reprocessed with EMDR. It is important to ask the child what bothers them and to reprocess what is most disturbing for the child. Even though input from parents and caregivers can provide additional clues to the child's history and symptoms, when the caregiver was not present at the time of the abuse, obviously the caregiver's own narrative of the event is most likely not as accurate as what the child demonstrates in therapy.

Finally, child psychotherapy offers a unique opportunity to develop resources, emotional regulation, and coping skills for children. Children often encode memories based on sensory motor experiences, so they may not have a coherent narrative to describe to the therapist. However, integrating child therapy techniques can facilitate the implementation of the procedural steps of EMDR therapy with child clients.

The Eight Phases of EMDR in Psychotherapy With Children

Since Shapiro created EMDR therapy, there has been expansion of its use with child and adolescent clients who have experienced a wide range of traumatization (Adler-Tapia & Settle, 2008; Greenwald, 1999; Lovett, 1999; Tinker & Wilson, 1999). This section briefly describes the goals, objectives, and terms used in each phase of EMDR with specific focus on using EMDR with children. This chapter includes suggestions for how EMDR can be adapted and modified for use with children.

With EMDR there is no need to create a coherent narrative or to gather facts about the disturbing event. Instead the focus of psychotherapy is on the symptoms the child presents and describes. For example, a parent might report that a child is not sleeping, acting out, having difficulty with friends, and so on, while the child might explain this as, "other kids just don't like me." Children typically do not consider the etiology for the symptoms, but instead report the issues or stressors that are currently bothering them with no explanation for causality. With AIP, the therapist views the etiology for the child's symptoms as the memory networks of previous disturbing events, understanding that what the child reports may be expressed in metaphor, may not appear in a coherent narrative, and may not necessarily make sense to the therapist. For example, a 2-year-old may not be able to tell her father that she is scared and sad because her mother has not returned. The 2-year-old might express her distress by demonstrating behavioral issues such as having temper tantrums and by dysregulation such as sleep and feeding disturbances. To address these symptoms in EMDR, the therapist might have the 2-year-old play in the sand tray and ask the child to create a picture of what makes her sad or what feels scary. It is the child's formulation and expression of the distress that is the focus of the psychotherapy.

Also, the therapist may need to assist the child in developing self-soothing and calming resources before proceeding to reprocess the past. It is common for children to avoid addressing things that bother them so it is the therapist's responsibility to help the child understand that what is bothering them can improve. For example, using the metaphor of removing a splinter is commonly understood by children. The therapist can explain to the child, "If you get a splinter, do you keep it in your finger or take it out? And when you take it out does it hurt a little bit before it feels better? What does your mom or dad (or caretaker) do to help it feel better after you take out the splinter?" With this type of explanation, children have a metaphor to understand how reprocessing the past may hurt, but eventually the child will heal.

CLIENT HISTORY AND TREATMENT PLANNING

As part of the standard practice of conducting an intake that includes exploring the client's history and creating a treatment plan, clinicians listen for the negative beliefs and symptoms that arise from how the trauma was encoded and retained in the client's memory networks. When creating a treatment plan, the therapist considers experiences in the child's life that are contributing to symptom manifestation and organizes those experiences in a three-prong approach focused on reprocessing the etiological memories to healthy resolution. Experiences are organized as the past events, current triggers, and future concerns. This past-present-future organization of the treatment plan guides the therapeutic process. With this three-prong approach, AIP theory postulates that it is the memory of past events that are setting the stage for current symptom manifestation. Current experiences can trigger those etiological memory networks influencing the child's reaction to the present event triggering symptoms that interfere with the child's daily functioning. Finally, in this three-prong approach, EMDR explores how the child wants to feel about the future when symptoms have resolved. This future work includes planning and practicing for future events with the goal of therapy concluding with in vivo successes.

Forensic Issues in EMDR With Child Sexual Abuse Clients   It is important to consider that with some cases it is not forensically suitable to work with past events when there is an ongoing investigation. The therapist might need to amend the implementation of EMDR because of ongoing criminal and civil investigations, especially when working with law enforcement, child welfare, and family court issues. It is important to explain the EMDR procedures and potential outcomes (e.g., reduced vividness of memory image, decrease or elimination of disturbing affect) to the child's caregivers, case managers, attorneys, and law enforcement, and to have written informed consent. Handling forensic cases will be illustrated in the case studies included in this chapter.

When child sexual abuse cases are forensically complicated, it is possible for the therapist to work with the child's symptoms without specifically targeting events that may be the focus of the investigation. Again, it is important for the therapist to consult with the parties in the case. In this manner, psychotherapy with EMDR is especially helpful because the therapist does not provide any interpretation of the child's statements nor does the therapist offer any information for the child to consider when reprocessing symptoms and/or traumatic events. This is explained in the three cases that follow.

Treatment Planning With Children Once the forensic issues have been assessed and parties consulted who would have input regarding informed consent for treatment (attorneys, law enforcement, child welfare personnel), the therapist then needs to create a treatment plan.

It is important to create the treatment plan from the child's perspective with input from caregivers. For adult clients, the three-prong approach may explore the etiological events that are clustered around the negative belief about themselves (i.e., the negative cognition). For children, it is important for the therapist to ask, "When you think about that thing that happened to you, what's your bad thought about you, now?" The child can verbally respond to this inquiry from the therapist or the therapist can integrate play therapy, sand tray, and other skills and tools for working with children. After completing the goals of this first phase of EMDR, the therapist moves to the Preparation Phase.

PREPARATION PHASE

During this phase in EMDR the therapist is educating the client about psychotherapy and trauma, teaching the mechanics of EMDR, and developing resources to continue with trauma reprocessing in phases 3 to 7 of the EMDR-phased treatment model. The mechanics of EMDR include teaching bilateral stimulation (BLS), Safe/Calm Place, Stop Signal, and a metaphor to describe how the client needs to be able to have dual attention in which the client experiences the safety of the present in the therapist's office while also accessing the memory networks most likely associated with current symptoms. The therapist is teaching the child to have access to the past event while also experiencing the safety of the therapist's office. The goal of EMDR is to access the traumatic and/or distressing life event thought to be underlying the presenting symptoms to reprocess the past event to adaptive resolution thereby resolving the presenting symptoms.

Bilateral stimulation (BLS) is alternating stimulation of attention elicited by having the client visually follow the therapist's fingers to create eye movement across the midline of the brain and back. BLS can also be created with alternating sensory input through auditory and/or tactile stimulation such as drumming, clapping, tapping, or marching as examples of types of bilateral stimulation that are especially effective with children

The Safe/Calm Place protocol for EMDR guides the child through identifying a place that the child can use for self-soothing, which then incorporates bilateral stimulation into the protocol to strengthen and reinforce the effect of the Safe/Calm Place. Children can draw, create a collage, paint, or create imaginary safe/calm places that can be used for self-soothing and calming during EMDR sessions and between sessions if needed.

ASSESSMENT PHASE

This phase is aimed at accessing and stimulating the associative memory networks through a series of questions that include: choosing a target memory or incident, identifying the image that represents the worst part of the memory with the remaining cognitive, emotional, and sensory data. These are eventually linked together to capture the child's experience of the event. Two baseline measures are also used to assess the progression of reprocessing. The validity of the positive cognition (VoC) is measured on a scale of 1 to 7 where 1 is completely false and 7 completely true. A VoC of 7 is the goal when installing the positive cognition during the Installation Phase of EMDR. The "Subjective Units of Disturbance Scale" (SUDS) is measured on a scale of 0 (no disturbance) to 10 (the most disturbing). A SUDS of 0 is the goal for the Desensitization Phase of EMDR.

Incorporating play therapy, sand tray, and art therapy into the procedural steps of the Assessment Phase allows the therapist to access how the child has experienced the traumatic and distressing life events. EMDR does not require that the child create a coherent narrative or gain insight into the etiology of the child's symptoms in order for the child to communicate and reprocess the disturbing and traumatically stored experiences to adaptive resolution.

With the assistance of the therapist, the child is asked to create an image of the picture that represents the worst part about what happened. This can be done verbally, with art, sand tray, play therapy, and other expressive skills. The therapist then asks the child again to identify the negative cognition (NC) or the "bad thought about you" when the child thinks about what happened. The therapist then explores what the child would rather believe instead or asks, "What is the good thought about you that you want to believe now?" The therapist then elicits a measurement of the VoC, the emotion, SUDS, and body sensation about the event or target that is the focus of this reprocessing session. Once the therapist has elicited these elements of the memory to access and activate the memory network, the therapist continues with the next phase of the EMDR trauma reprocessing.

DESENSITIZATION PHASE

This phase of EMDR begins when the bilateral stimulation is added to the information elicited during the Assessment Phase. The client is asked to hold together the image that represents the worst part of the target event, the negative cognition, the emotions, and body sensations, while the therapist implements the BLS. The child is asked to "just notice" what he or she is feeling, seeing, and remembering or to be "mindful." The therapist may have taught the child mindfulness during the Preparation phase, however, children often need to be reminded. So the therapist might say to the child, "Just notice your body from your head to your toes, your legs, your tummy, and just pay attention to it and tell me what you notice." The child can draw a picture or the therapist can demonstrate with gestures and ask the child to point to any place they notice anything in their body. If the therapist has to remind the child about just noticing body sensations, the therapist may have to repeat the directions of "bring up that thing that happened and those words (NC), and notice your body," and then the therapist begins sets of BLS. Periodically the therapist will stop the BLS and ask the child to report what is emerging during the sets of BLS. Children may respond verbally, draw pictures, continue to work in the sand tray, or find an expressive technique to provide a quick check in with the therapist. This continues until it appears that the distressing material is reprocessed and the disturbance no longer exists. Desensitization Phase is complete when the child assesses the disturbance level at a 0 on the SUDS. Children can express their SUDS by showing the distance between their hands, or reporting "how much" or "how big" the disturbance feels to them. To the surprise of many therapists, children often reprocess quickly and are ready to go play. When the child reports no more disturbance associated with the memory, the therapist proceeds to the next phase.

INSTALLATION PHASE

This phase of EMDR therapy is designed to assess and strengthen the positive cognition (PC). This phase is completed when the client reports the VoC as a 7. The therapist will ask the child to hold together the target event and the positive cognition (PC) and rate how true the PC feels now. For children, explaining the VoC as a bridge with 7 steps from the negative cognition to the positive cognition assists children in understanding the concept. Once the original VoC is measured, the therapist then uses BLS to increase the VoC until the VoC reaches a 7. When the positive cognition is "installed," the therapist then proceeds to the 6th phase of EMDR.

Body Scan

This phase of EMDR therapy is designed to address any residual affective experiences identified by scanning the body. This phase is complete when the client reports experiencing a clear body scan. For children, games and drawings can be used to teach the child about body sensations and how somatic complaints are often the result of distress and discomfort. The therapist may demonstrate how the child can scan his or her body with the hand-held magnifying glass to note where there are any feelings in the child's body. Or the child may be asked to notice any body sensations by drawing a silhouette of the child's body and marking where the child notices anything in his or her body. If the child identifies body sensations, the therapist asks the child to just notice what's happening in the body and continues sets of BLS until the body feels comfortable and there is a clear body scan. Completing a target includes reaching a SUDS of 0, a VoC of 7, and a clear body scan (CBS). Children very quickly learn this process and then begin to spontaneously identify other things that bother them that they wish to reprocess with EMDR.

Closure Phase

This phase of EMDR therapy is designed to stabilize the client at the end of sessions. For children, it is important to end each therapy session with plans for coping with triggers and distressing symptoms between sessions. One specific technique that works well with children is to teach children to imagine placing all of the distressing symptoms that might arise between sessions into containers. In the session the therapist can have the child draw or build a container to hold any symptoms that feel overwhelming to the child to be addressed in the next session. Children especially enjoy drawing scary or uncomfortable thoughts or feelings and locking those in a box for later reprocessing.

Reevaluation Phase

This phase includes assessing the work from previous sessions, reprocessing any additional targets with continued evaluation of the treatment plan, ongoing symptom assessment, and discharge planning for graduation from psychotherapy. Because children process quickly, therapists may incorrectly suspect that the child is avoiding or denying any concerns because the child does not want to participate in therapy. Nevertheless, it is important for the therapist to consider the impact of demand characteristics in which the child responds in a manner to please the therapist. Children may learn how to answer the therapists questions such as telling the therapist that the SUDS is 0 when the child is avoiding the intense emotions and memories associated with the event. Therefore, it is ultimately the symptoms reported by the child, caregivers, teachers, case managers, and other adults in the child's life that are the primary tools to reevaluate progress in treatment. The assessment of symptoms and review of treatment plan goals are the final step in case conceptualization with EMDR.

VARIABILITY IN CASES: THE RANGE IN HISTORIES FOR CHILDREN WHO ARE SEXUALLY ABUSED AND TRAUMATIZED

For the purpose of elucidating the variability in case scenarios for children who have experienced sexual abuse and trauma, this section describes three cases that encapsulate what children endure. All of these cases are the combination of several actual cases where specific identifying variables have been omitted. Each case suggests potential case conceptualization through the eight phases of the EMDR comprehensive psychotherapy treatment approach and expands the standard procedures to the complexities of working with children who have been sexually abused. These cases have been chosen to illustrate the range of cases that therapists might encounter when working with children who have been sexually abused with an emphasis on the implementation of particular areas of EMDR. With more complex cases, the therapist may need to spend more time working on the first two phases to prepare the child for the trauma processing phases of the therapy (phases 3 to 7). In other cases, the therapist may be able to quickly move to trauma processing because the child has adequate internal and external resources with which to cope with the traumatic events.

The following three cases illustrate the variability in working with children who have experienced sexual abuse and case conceptualization with the eight phases of EMDR.

Case Studies

EVAN

Evan's case represents using the eight phases of EMDR therapy without the complications of the legal or child welfare system.

(continued)

Client History and Treatment Planning Phase

At age 6, Evan was sexually abused by an older child on the playground at school and yet Evan wanted the friendship to continue; therefore, he participated in the sexual behavior and did not report to anyone what was occurring. This is not to suggest that Evan had any responsibility for what happened, but for therapists to consider that some children continue to participate in sexual activities with other children out of loyalty, fear of getting in trouble, and curiosity. As hard as this might be for adults to accept and understand, children may have been educated about inappropriate touching and yet still not report these behaviors to adults.

During the Client History and Treatment Planning Phase, it is important to explore the child's symptom presentation and how the therapist assesses the ways in which this child is manifesting the aftereffects of the exposure to trauma. Evan's symptoms included avoidance of any places where he might encounter the perpetrator, anger, and a fear of "getting in trouble." Evan's symptoms could have been assessed as oppositional-defiant disorder (ODD) if the sexual abuse by the other child had not been identified; indeed, some mental health providers might still assess Evan as evidencing symptoms of ODD even knowing about his history of sexual abuse. In therapy, Evan's symptoms were attributed to acute stress disorder (ASD) because he entered therapy five days after the teacher found Evan and the older child underneath the sliding board on the playground at school. On intake it was evident that Evan had stability and a support network available to him with adults available to intervene to keep him safe.

Preparation Phase

Evan began reprocessing his trauma in the second session of EMDR after learning the mechanics of EMDR, practicing a Safe/Calm/Comfortable Place, and learning the Butterfly Hug (a type of bilateral stimulation that clients often use for self-soothing) (Jarero, Artigas, & Hartung, 2006).

Assessment to Closure Phases

With Evan's case, trauma reprocessing through the EMDR eight phases moved quickly. Evan sat on the floor in the therapist's office and addressed his negative belief about himself as "I'm bad." Evan reported that he felt this negative belief in his "broken heart" at a very high disturbance. Reprocessing continued for 15 minutes until Evan
(continued)

(*continued*)

started giggling. Evan reprocessed the SUDS to a 2, but got stuck when his conscience interfered. He held himself partially responsible for what happened. Evan attributed his hesitancy to "being embarrassed" because his body responded, he was curious, and he did not say "No" to his friend. The therapist concluded that Evan needed to identify and reprocess his blocking beliefs. Evan needed additional information to understand that physiologically his body would respond to stimulation even if he did not want to participate in the sexual behavior. Once Evan accepted this information, he reprocessed his SUDS to a 0, installed the positive cognition of "I'm okay" and cleared his body of the "bad and yucky feelings." Evan did not have to report the memories that he experienced as shameful and embarrassing.

Reevaluation Phase

In a follow-up session, Evan reported that he was feeling good and his heart was "whole" now. Evan scored his first soccer goal and then hit a homerun in baseball. He did well in school and even learned how to say no when other children suggested that he participate in activities that made him uncomfortable. This skill was not only important for Evan to master with regard to any inappropriate sexual advances from other children, but was also important in other areas of his life as he began to report that he felt more confident saying no when he thought other children were "making bad choices." Initially, the therapist suggested that Evan and his family read the book *Those Are My Private Parts* (Hansen, 2007), and as Evan prepared for graduation from therapy, he discussed how he had helped a disabled cousin learn how to say no to other children.

Closure Phase

Evan's parents intervened and protected him and sought EMDR for Evan both individually and as a family. Evan's parents simultaneously sought their own therapy, read about how to help Evan, and participated in a parents' group for children who had been sexually assaulted. Evan is currently thriving in his home, school, and community where his father reports that he tells other children about being safe.

Now compare Evan's situation to the next case of Iliana. Evan's case is much "easier" to conceptualize and write a treatment plan through the eight phases of EMDR therapy. Evan's case was not

(*continued*)

complicated by legal and/or forensic involvement, even though it is important for therapists to always consider the possibility that any case can become a forensic case. It is possible for any case to become complicated by criminal investigations, civil lawsuits, and custody disputes that arise after treatment has begun. For this reason, it is helpful for the therapist to begin treatment conceptualizing the case including a forensic process.

Iliana

All eight phases of the EMDR can generally be used in criminal court cases with the agreement of the legal team. However, Illiana's case illustrates how the therapist may need to initially focus on the Preparation and Assessment Phases to stabilize the client in more complex forensic situations where the child has not been able to make a statement and there is an open and active criminal investigation.

Client History and Treatment Planning

Iliana was a 6-year-old girl stolen in the middle of the night from her home as she slept and found the next morning half naked in a stranger's backyard. What happened to her? What did she remember versus what could she recall? In this child's life, she was accustomed to falling asleep and then being carried to her bed in her home where she did not have a regular sleeping assignment in a specific room or bed. Family members reported that if Iliana fell asleep, it was common for caregivers to pick her up and carry her somewhere to sleep for the night. Once Iliana was asleep, she would not awake even if someone moved her. Her memory network accustomed her to being carried by an adult after she had fallen asleep. The forensic evidence suggested that Iliana was carried to an unknown place and assaulted. Iliana's play suggested that she had become somewhat aware that something "scary" was happening to her when someone began sexually assaulting her. Iliana's drawings and play indicated that she began to have physical and sensory memory fragments from the time she woke up in a car in the dark. She could not make sense of what was happening to her at the time because she had no schema or previous experiences with which to process the event. Like many young children, the evidence of the assault was apparent because of the physiological damage to Iliana's body, but Iliana was not able to explain what had happened. When she was referred for psychotherapy, she was healing from body injuries that caused her pain in sitting, urinating, and walking, all of which she could not understand.

(continued)

(continued)

Iliana was also being relentlessly questioned by family members who were vicariously traumatized. Family members searched for clues about who had perpetrated such an atrocity on a loved one in an attempt to gain relief from their own responsibility and feelings of culpability. The parents were in a bitter custody battle and, with Iliana's assault, the volatility in the child's family increased significantly. There was no one available to calm Iliana because the adults in her life could not move beyond their own trauma. She was also administered a regimen of medication that included injections to attempt to prevent the child from developing a sexually transmitted disease. The traumatic abduction and rape were the beginning of a series of horrendous events in this child's life. In this case, the dynamics are extensive and overlapping. Where does one start in case conceptualization for psychotherapy? Stabilization of the child and her support system is obviously a crucial starting place while also maneuvering the medical and legal hurdles in her care.

In this extremely complicated scenario, the therapist formulated the treatment plan during the Client History and Treatment Planning Phase of EMDR while simultaneously interacting with a treatment team that included legal and medical professionals. Implementing and executing the goals of the treatment plan are integrated into the Preparation Phase of EMDR. In order to differentiate case conceptualization from treatment planning, it is helpful to consider that case conceptualization consists of considering the big picture, especially in complicated cases where children are sexually abused. Case conceptualization is a fluid and dynamic process that unfolds from beginning to end of psychotherapy while the Treatment Plan is the piece of case conceptualization that identifies the specifics of how psychotherapy gets implemented.

Preparation Phase

For Iliana, case conceptualization through the Preparation Phase of EMDR incorporated stabilizing her emotionally and physically, assisting her with the ongoing and intrusive forensic and medical issues, and listening for potential targets to reprocess with EMDR. The therapist was always listening for symptoms from Iliana and her caregivers while observing the needs of this child and her family. The therapist provided support and guidance for Iliana's family during this process as they dealt with their own feelings, trauma, and questions about the system. Finally, the therapist provided consultation to law enforcement

(continued)

and medical care providers on how to work with Iliana as these other professionals fulfilled their respective responsibilities.

For the therapist, the dance between Iliana's needs and forensic demands were evident in both the treatment plan and case conceptualization. In addition to stabilizing Iliana, reprocessing her current symptoms and triggers were the focus of treatment. Her symptoms included nightmares, a fear of men in hats, physiological trauma that made it painful to urinate and defecate, and her terror of receiving twice weekly injections to prevent infections and sexually transmitted diseases. With Iliana's hypervigilance about personal safety, the therapist taught her relaxation skills, deep breathing, and fun imagery while allowing Iliana to work with the therapy dogs. Therapy also included integrating sand tray work to provide an expressive opportunity for Iliana to explore her experiences and feelings.

Because Iliana's psychotherapy took place in an advocacy center where she was medically examined after the police found her, the environment was initially threatening to Iliana. The first step in the therapeutic process was to focus on desensitizing the environment. If a child is seen at an advocacy center, a child welfare office, or any environment where the child might associate negative experiences, the therapist needs to be cognizant of the possible contamination of the therapeutic environment. At the advocacy center, incorporating the therapy dog into Iliana's treatment created a positive association with psychotherapy.

Iliana's case was forensically complicated because she was a victim in an ongoing investigation and a potential witness; therefore, EMDR was indicated for her treatment. EMDR provided the opportunity to document her history, create a treatment plan, and develop coping skills without contaminating Iliana's recall of her traumatic event.

Assessment Phase

Although the questions of the Assessment Phase access the memory and initiate reprocessing of the encoded memory networks, in this case, no BLS was done to initiate the accelerated trauma reprocessing of the Desensitization, Installation, and Body Scan Phases. Like many young victims, Iliana was so traumatized she was not able to participate in a forensic interview; therefore, the therapist asked the questions in the procedural steps of the EMDR Assessment Phase in order to assist her in accessing the information while the police taped the sessions to retrieve the information. The questions allowed the information to emerge spontaneously, and this uncontaminated information was provided to law enforcement in order to further the investigation.

(continued)

(*continued*)

With the ever-present police investigation and Iliana's fear that the "bad guy" was out there somewhere, identifying a target to access with Iliana was limited and calculated. Initially she was asked to focus on the portion of her memory that included the "nice lady" who found her and called the police. Iliana created a sand tray representation of the bad thought, "I'm hurt," and the good thought, "I'm okay." For Iliana, this horrendous experience incorporated two strangers, a man who hurt her and a lady who helped her. Iliana was able to quickly focus on all the people who were helping her and that only one "bad man hurt her." All the police at the advocacy center rallied around her and were obviously touched by this child's plight; however, Iliana was initially intimidated by the police uniforms because of her culture where she learned that the police were to be feared. Through the Assessment Phase questions, she reprocessed her fear of police to a resolution where "police are people who are nice and have a job to help you." As she created multiple sand trays, Iliana reprocessed her anxiety about cars as she lined up toy cars in the sand tray, and later raced the cars through the sand tray until cars no longer "make me have bad thoughts." Because of the forensic issues it was decided to forego further EMDR processing at this time.

After several months, Iliana began to create windows in the sand tray and to draw pictures of a scary man in a window. After the victim advocate walked the grounds of Iliana's home, he reported that Iliana's home had no locks on the windows that were easily opened. With this missing resource to address Iliana's ongoing anxiety, the therapist introduced a window that the little girl in the sandbox could lock to keep out the bad guys and asked Iliana, "I wonder if locks on the windows inside Iliana's home would help her?" Without speaking Iliana began to smile and draw pictures with rainbows in the windows. Given this information, the police officers collected funds and contacted a local hardware store to install locks on all the windows in Iliana's home. Her sleep improved and nightmares occurred less frequently.

While in the extended Assessment Phase, the therapist provided opportunities for Iliana to identify traumatic events along with Iliana's good and bad thoughts about her experiences and the emotions and body sensations associated with the events Iliana identified as "things that are bothering me." Because the perpetrator of Iliana's trauma was not apprehended and the case was an open police investigation, the treatment team decided that during this episode of care the therapist

(*continued*)

should not continue with the trauma reprocessing phases of EMDR, but rather therapy should focus on her symptoms and documenting what she discussed in therapy without ever asking her any questions about the past. Even so, Iliana's symptoms improved, her laughter returned, and she danced through the advocacy center.

Closure and Reevaluation

For Iliana, returning to school and her dance class became a priority as she was no longer interested in what happened on that bad day. Her perpetrator has not been apprehended, but Iliana believes he has "moved away so he won't get in trouble." After the initial shock of the event, Iliana's parents attended mediation and begrudgingly cooperated to care for Iliana. Iliana's progression through the Assessment Phase of EMDR evidenced symptom improvement; however, with the open criminal investigation, Iliana's parents decided not to continue therapy. The therapist recommended to the family that to fully complete the trauma reprocessing, they would need to take Iliana to an EMDR therapist when the treatment team was in support of addressing the past events including the assault. The therapist also cautioned the family that symptoms could continue or new symptoms could arise until such time as the memory network was fully reprocessed.

Iliana's case is an example of a deplorable assault of a child, yet Iliana has a family to care for her and an extensive support system that had historically and consistently met her basic needs until this event occurred. In spite of this horrific event, Iliana's prognosis is optimistic. Unfortunately, many children are victims of sexual abuse specifically because the child's home environment is neglectful and unsafe; therefore, the child is not only harmed in his or her own home, but also experiences a complete upheaval of what is familiar when the child is placed in the child welfare system.

EDGAR

Edgar's case demonstrates how you can use EMDR therapy effectively even with the difficulties of collaborating with the child welfare system and the juvenile court. Unlike Iliana's case, no criminal investigation was occurring in Edgar's case.

Client History and Treatment Planning

Edgar was being sexually abused by his mother's boyfriend. Edgar's mother was not stable—she actively used drugs and displayed a concurrent mental health issue. For Edgar, his basic needs were never

(continued)

(continued)

met—even in utero. He was a substance-exposed newborn. Born with cocaine in his system, Edgar had to be detoxed for several days in the local hospital neonatal intensive care unit. While Edgar was in the hospital his mother rarely visited. The hospital then called the child welfare system; however, the assessment from the child welfare worker was that Edgar's mother provided a minimally adequate home for the baby. It is surprising that Edgar even survived. He was most likely present during his mother's sexual interactions with her boyfriend and other males and Edgar may have been included in the mother's interactions and molested by the mother's paramours. After his mother's boyfriend left, 3-year-old Edgar still did not have his needs met, but the sexual abuse stopped temporarily until his mother allowed her next paramour into the home. Finally, this 8-year-old boy realized that he could use his sexuality to get his other needs met. He became a street child and supported himself through prostitution. He then used drugs to cope with the hopelessness of escaping this life and finding a different path in his future. Finally, he was arrested, incarcerated in a juvenile facility, and then perpetrated on by older youth. For the first time, Edgar entered therapy at age 13, hopeless after being severely and chronically traumatized. Where to start? With children in Edgar's situation it is necessary to consider each session as a single episode of care with the possibility that this will be the only session. This is the ongoing struggle in case conceptualization with children who have no stability.

Preparation Phase

Developing therapeutic rapport and client stabilization are part of treatment planning with EMDR. Then the therapist can explore opportunities to teach resources and seed for trauma reprocessing to be addressed in Phases 3 to 7 of the EMDR therapy. In seeding for future therapy with Edgar, the therapist explored what he needed to be able to reprocess his traumatic past, assess and reprocess present triggers, and consider a positive future. With clients in unstable environments—especially children—case conceptualization with EMDR suggests that the therapist may consider what portion of each treatment goal can be achieved in any one session. It is possible for therapists to begin working through aspects of EMDR therapy without completing the entire treatment plan. The therapist needs to contemplate what can reasonably be accomplished with this child during this episode of care. Because a therapist might not have the opportunity to complete the entire eight-phase therapy with the

(continued)

child, the therapist can still implement some of the procedures during the time that the therapist is working with the child. For example, if a child is in a residential treatment center (RTC), the therapist may only have contact with the child for a limited period of time; therefore, in case conceptualization the therapist may decide that time only allows for the development of resources and no trauma processing during this episode of care.

Edgar was not able to identify a place or a time in his life where he ever felt safe or comfortable; therefore, developing an imaginary safe place by creating a collage with magazine images created a picture that Edgar had available for affective management and to help calm himself if he encountered overwhelming feelings. Edgar left therapy with the original copy of his safe place in case he did not return, but the therapist kept a copy in Edgar's file in case he came back. Edgar did return for services for seven weeks. In that time, the therapist developed resources with him including Edgar's fantasy with several television characters who possessed the skills that Edgar wished to acquire. Each session the therapist asked Edgar to report at least one positive experience in which he felt like he had dealt with a difficult situation in a new and positive way. For example, one other young man in the home where Edgar was placed was particularly annoying to him. Many incidents occurred in which Edgar did not make progress and earn privileges because he would engage in physical altercations with the other teen. Initially Edgar reported that he no longer engaged physically, but only verbally. This was a big step for Edgar, who felt that he always needed to let other residents know he could and would protect himself by fighting. This mastery experience was installed with short slow sets of BLS to create a scaffolding of success experiences that Edgar could draw upon to feel good about himself. Then Edgar began to report that his nemesis was actually "just another messed up kid like me who can't hurt me." The staff in Edgar's home reported that Edgar had gone 10 days without a physical altercation with anyone, and Edgar beamed. With his safe place and multiple behavioral successes, Edgar was willing to process a "scary memory" that he did not want to discuss.

Assessment Phase

With his two resources, Edgar decided to identify the image that represented a memory that haunted him. Edgar made a list of 10 "awful memories" by symbols only, because he reported that he was too ashamed to talk about what he remembered. Edgar thought of the image that represented the worst part of the memory he chose to

(continued)

(*continued*)

reprocess without ever telling the therapist the memory. Edgar reported that his negative cognition was "I'm disgusting" and his positive cognition was "I'm okay." Edgar initially reported that the level of disturbance was a 10 out of 10 and that he felt "icky feelings" in a part of his body he did not want to identify to the therapist.

Desensitization Phase

Edgar reprocessed this target as he often held his breath, closed his eyes tightly, and put his hand to his throat as if he was going to throw up. The therapist repeatedly checked with Edgar who was committed to "finishing this thing." After approximately 20 minutes Edgar laughed and had the therapist stop the BLS when he stated, "Wow that was intense!" This time Edgar reported that the disturbance was gone and he not only believed he was "okay, but a darn strong person!"

Installation Phase

This phase was quick as Edgar had spontaneously identified an even stronger positive cognition than the one he initially identified in the Assessment phase. Edgar confirmed the positive cognition of "I'm not only okay, but a darn strong person" that was installed with BLS to a VoC of 7.

Body Scan Phase

Edgar struggled the longest to rid himself of the disgusting feelings in his body. Edgar needed information to understand that even though his body responded from the sexual assaults, this did not indicate he had a choice. Once Edgar learned about his body, he accepted that his body had not betrayed him in all of the horrible encounters he endured. Edgar wept for the first time and then relaxed.

Edgar was able to complete several of the targets he had identified for EMDR reprocessing without even discussing what he found most challenging. In spite of Edgar's history, he made sufficient progress to be released from the juvenile corrections program and move to a group home. Edgar continued to be successful even though he was not provided additional EMDR services because of lack of funding.

CONCLUSION

Reading accounts of children's traumatic experiences is disturbing and yet these cases capture the epitome of what occurs to children on a daily basis. Until we can prevent children from experiencing such atrocities, a multi-agency team of professionals is needed to protect and treat children. One part of this comprehensive service plan is trauma treatment with EMDR.

As demonstrated by these forensic cases (i.e., a civil case, an open criminal investigation, and a child welfare case), the therapist is cautioned to work closely with all the members of the team while also recognizing that case conceptualization, which follows through the eight phases of the EMDR therapy, can assist in reprocessing to full adaptive resolution the trauma experienced by the child. Even though EMDR is very effective with this population, episodes of care through the eight phases of EMDR are dictated by the legal system until such time as the child can participate in completing all eight phases of the EMDR therapy conceptualized through the Adaptive Information Processing theory.

How would AIP Theory explain Iliana, Edgar, and Evan's symptoms? In these stories of sexual abuse of children, EMDR tapped the associative memory networks of the abuse that each child had endured. For children like Iliana, Edgar, and Evan, psychotherapy has historically focused on teaching coping skills and excavating the traumatic events. With many therapies, the child is directed to create a coherent narrative of each traumatic event, address any cognitive distortions associated with the events, and then learn to cope. With EMDR, the opportunity to access the residual memory networks of abuse and then reprocess those networks through to adaptive resolution is the ultimate goal of case conceptualization. Children not only learn to cope, but heal from traumatic life events, offering the child the opportunity to return to the potential with which they were born and experience a healthy future trajectory.

EMDR treatment integrates play therapy, family systems therapy, and other types of psychotherapy commonly used with children into a psychosocial developmental framework. Therapists learn to integrate clinical skills into a comprehensive eight-phase model. When treating children with sexual abuse and trauma, the therapist is provided an integrative approach with which to conceptualize treatment that includes goals and objectives that can be understood by children and their caregivers, as well as by child welfare, law enforcement, and medical professionals.

Even though variability exists in the types of sexual abuse and trauma that children experience, EMDR therapy provides a template for organizing treatment without impeding the medical and forensic process. EMDR does not provide any information to the child that would potentially taint the child's testimony or recall of the event. EMDR provides the opportunity for the client to fully reprocess any disturbance of a traumatic event without having to discuss details or create a coherent narrative. EMDR assists the client in achieving resolution of symptoms because this form of psychotherapy has targeted how the child has retained the memory of the event, not how the adult has reported the event. With research to support EMDR as evidence-based practice, the use of EMDR in the treatment of children with sexual abuse and trauma provides children with the opportunity for healing while sustaining the work product to be admissible and solid in court.

REFERENCES

Adler-Tapia, R. L., & Settle, C. S. (2008). *EMDR and the art of psychotherapy with children.* New York, NY: Springer.

Adler-Tapia, R. L., & Settle, C. S. (2009). Establishing EMDR with children as evidence based practice: A review of the literature. *Journal of EMDR Practice and Research, 3*(4), 232–247.

American Psychiatric Association. (2000). *Diagnostic and statistical manual of mental disorders* (4th ed., Text rev.). Washington, DC: Author.

Bisson, J., & Andrew, M. (2007). Psychological treatment of post-traumatic stress disorder (PTSD). Cochrane database of systematic reviews 2007, Issue 3. Art. No.: CD003388. DOI: 10.1002/14651858.CD003388.pub3 Accessed 09/06/10 at http://onlinelibrary.wiley.com/o/cochrane/clsysrev/articles/CD003388/frame .html

Felitti, V. J., Anda, R. F., Nordernberg, D., Williamson, D. F., Spitz, A. M., Edwards, V., & Koss, M. P. (1998). Relationship of childhood abuse to many of the leading causes of death in adults: The adverse childhood experiences (ACE) study. *American Journal of Preventive Medicine, 14*(4), 245–258.

Greenwald, R. (1999). *Eye movement desensitization and reproessing (EMDR) in child and adolescent psychotherapy.* Northvale, NJ: Jason Aronson Press.

Hansen, D. (2007). *Those are my private parts.* Redondo Beach, CA: Empowerment.

Jaberghaderi, N., Greenwald, R., Rubin, A., Dolatabadim, S., & Zand, S. O. (2002). A comparison of CBT and EMDR for sexually abused Iranian girls. *Clinical Psychology and Psychotherapy, 11,* 358–368.

Jarero, I., Artigas, L., & Hartung, J. (2006). EMDR integrative group treatment protocol: A post-disaster trauma intervention for children and adults. *Traumatology, 12,* 121–129.

Lovett, J. (1999). *Small wonders: Healing childhood trauma with EMDR.* New York, NY: The Free Press.

Scheck, M., Schaeffer, J. A., & Gillette, C. (1998). Brief psychological intervention with traumatized young women: The efficacy of eye movement desensitization and reprocessing. *Journal of Traumatic Stress, 11,* 25–44.

Shapiro, F. (1989). Eye movement desensitization: A new treatment for post-traumatic stress disorder. *Journal of Behavior Therapy and Experimental Psychiatry, 20,* 211–217.

Shapiro, F. (1995). *Eye movement desensitization and reprocessing: Basic principles, protocols, and procedures.* New York, NY: Guilford Press.

Shapiro, F. (2001). *Eye movement desensitization and reprocessing: Basic principles, protocols, and procedures* (2nd ed.). New York, NY: Guilford Press.

Tinker, R. H., & Wilson, S. A. (1999). *Through the eyes of a child: EMDR with children.* New York, NY: Norton.

CHAPTER 11

Trauma-Focused Integrated Play Therapy (TF-IPT)

ELIANA GIL

INTRODUCTION

THIS TREATMENT MODEL, trauma-focused integrated play therapy (TF-IPT), is the crystallization of my clinical experience over nearly four decades and is highly influenced by the work of several gifted clinicians and researchers. It was utilized and refined in various settings by many of my colleagues, primarily in sexual abuse treatment centers. The decision to manualize it occurred when we applied for and received a funding opportunity to conduct research (randomized, comparison study using our TF-IPT model) with a population of young sexually abused children in Fairfax, Virginia, in 2008. My position was then Director of Clinical Services at Childhelp. The research project was funded by the National Children's Alliance, and it encountered many challenges that could not be overcome: The sample size was too small to draw many conclusions; however, preliminary results, currently being prepared for publication, indicate the potential for this model to be helpful to abused children and their families (Achilles & Gil, in press).

The trauma-focused integrated play therapy (TF-IPT) model was highly influenced by the work of Judith Herman, in particular her treatment phasing (Herman, 1992, 1997). In fact, this model of therapy with children was based on Herman's model of working with adult survivors of complex trauma and includes her three stages: Safety, Rememberance and Mourning, and Reconnection. We have renamed these phases somewhat, and they are called (1) *Establishment of Safety and Relationship Building,* (2) *Trauma-Processing,* and (3) *Social Reconnection.* Gaining optimal engagement from children in general is challenging—abused and traumatized children present yet additional challenges and special concerns. Because this model's developer is a registered play therapist and registered art therapist as well as a mental health professional with expertise in the treatment of childhood trauma and family therapy, an integrated approach (which values and incorporates expressive therapies in a more substantive way) is the cornerstone of the model.

RATIONALE FOR AN INTEGRATED APPROACH

As Lazarus (2006) has stated, "No single approach has all the answers, but each orientation offers some worthwhile methods and notions" (p. 17). In addition, more and more data support the notion that 30% to 53% of possible change due to therapy occurs as a result of the therapeutic relationship and clients/patients feeling warmth toward their therapists and sensing that they are understood by them. Duncan, Sparks, and Miller (2006) assert that "The amount of change attributable to the (therapy) alliance is about 7 times that of specific model or technique" (p. 226).

Thus in the last few decades a distinct field of integrative therapies has been articulated and continues to gain credibility (Gold & Stricker, 2001; Messer, 1992; Stricker & Gold, 1996). Integrative theory proposes an inclusionary methodology that serves as the foundation for TF-IPT. Because this model integrates more than two distinct theories and fields of study, it can best be understood as an assimilated psychodynamic psychotherapy integration (Stricker & Gold, 1996), which Stricker (2010) describes this way: "Assimilative integration retains allegiance to a single theoretical school but then introduces techniques drawn from other schools, integrated in as seamless a way as possible" (p. 16). The underlying theoretical model of TF-IPT is the conceptualization of trauma and its impact as originally described by Eth and Pynoos (1985), van der Kolk (1987), and Herman (1992, 1997).

This model has been adapted and expanded as new information became available. Particular attention has been paid to those more recent theories, approaches, and techniques that incorporate the mind-body connection (Levine, 1997; Ogden, Minton, & Pain, 2006; van der Kolk, McFarlane, & Weisaeth, 1996), attention to the development and interpersonal nature of the brain (Baddock, 2008; Siegel, 1999; Ziegler, 2002), and a focus on selecting therapeutic responses that target parts of the brain that have been over- or understimulated by traumatic stress (Crenshaw, 2009; Perry, 2009; Perry, Pollard, Blakley, Baker, & Vigilante, 1995; Perry & Szalavitz, 2007). For purposes of this chapter, I utilize the trauma model as a primary theoretical orientation and cognitive-behavioral, expressive, and attachment-based therapies as integrated approaches to advance and achieve therapeutic goals.

THE USE OF TF-CBT PRINCIPLES IN TF-IPT

To date, the most highly recommended evidence-based treatment for sexually abused children is trauma-focused cognitive-behavioral therapy, and most professionals who specialize in working with abused children are now familiar with and trained regarding this model. The original research studies that validate Trauma-Focused Cognitive-Behavioral Therapy (TF-CBT) were conducted between 1996 (Deblinger, Steer, & Lippman) and 1999 (Deblinger, Steer, & Lippman). The model's primary reference is the book *Treating Trauma and Traumatic Grief in Children and Adolescents* (Cohen, Mannarino, & Deblinger, 2006). In addition, web training became available more than a decade ago that provides 10 hours of continuing education credit, at no cost, regarding TF-CBT (www.musc.edu/tfcbt).

TF-CBT is a structured treatment that relies on cognitive-behavioral theories and applications to do a variety of things: Assist the child in cognitive processing and reprocessing of the trauma, encourage the child to develop and share a trauma narrative, and enhance coping strategies through the provision of psychoeducation to both children and their parents. The parent's considerable potential to assist the child is tapped by buffering the parent's ability to manage their children's behavior problems, by helping them provide adequate and safe discipline, and by enhancing their shared communication. The TF-CBT therapist tends to be directive, goal-oriented, creative, and structured. They describe themselves as relationship-based, and flexible in their use of play and art strategies. At the same time, they recommend against having too many (toy) distractions in the room. Although the original model was tested in a 12-week timeframe, TF-CBT is usually best provided in longer time frames. Several TF-CBT principles have been incorporated into this model, particularly the focus on the engagement and involvement of parents, the provision of psychoeducation to parents and children, explanations of the CBT triangle, cognitive review and processing, and the need for children to develop adaptive coping strategies.

THE INTEGRATION OF EXPRESSIVE THERAPY PRACTICES IN TF-IPT

The expressive therapies have long been considered useful in a variety of settings. Art therapy, puppet therapy, music therapy, dance, movement, and drama therapies have all been utilized with varied populations and for healing purposes. Expressive therapies are described as "The use of art, music, dance/movement, drama, poetry/creative writing, play, and sandtray within the context of psychotherapy, counseling, rehabilitation, or health care" (Malchiodi, 2005, p. 2).

Because these therapies do not rely exclusively on verbal communication, they can offer more ample invitations to those who have compromised language skills (young children, developmentally delayed children, children recently adopted from foreign countries, as examples), and those children and teens, and adults who for whatever reason feel unable or unwilling to engage verbally. Children who have been traumatized may respond differentially, either repeating narratives of their trauma indiscriminately and in agitated fashion, or shutting down, becoming verbally constricted, and choosing instead various levels of silence. Many traumatized children (kidnapped, tortured, witnesses to crimes, sexually abused, as examples) become terrified and immobilized by the traumas they endure, and *not telling* may be the only semblance of control they can exercise. Still others maintain fear-based silence for long periods of time convinced that the person who hurt them will somehow know that they have told. Bloom (2005) asserts that "from what we are learning about the psychobiology of exposure to violence, the victim experiences and remembers the trauma in nonverbal, visual, auditory, kinesthetic, visceral, and affective modalities, but is not able to 'think' about it or process the experience in any way" (p. xvi). Nader and Pynoos (1991) note that both play and art tap into primary process thinking and so allow the child to process the event without the censorship or inhibitions of secondary process thinking. Rubin (2006) states:

> Today, through neuroscience (Solomon & Siegel, 2003), we can better understand why the arts are so therapeutic—that in order to master trauma, it is necessary first to access the nonverbal right hemisphere (through images, sounds, and movements); and then to enable it to communicate with the left, in order to gain cognitive and affective mastery. Thanks to the disciplines of the expressive arts therapies, in the hands of experienced clinicians, patients of all ages can play and create their way to mental health. (p. 12)

The invitation to either speak or do other things can create feelings of safety that can allow for more productive outcomes. In my experience, power struggles with children about their verbalization of what happened to them are fruitless and often elicit more hesitancy or even false compliance. The introduction of expressive therapies can be a welcome relief and set the necessary groundwork for future work. Although reviewing all the expressive therapies is out of the scope of this chapter, I refer readers to other literature on this subject (Hinz, 2009; Klorer, 2000; McNiff, 2009; Malchiodi, 2005). However, because TF-IPT relies on play, art, and sand therapies, I will include a brief summary of those expressive therapies.

Play Therapy   Play therapy is described by the Association for Play Therapy Board of Directors as *the systematic use of a theoretical model to establish an interpersonal process wherein trained play therapists use the therapeutic powers of play to help clients prevent or resolve psychosocial difficulties and achieve optimal growth and development.* The rich history regarding the development of play therapy has been well-documented, especially by Schaefer and O'Connor (1983), and O'Connor and Schaefer (1994). Play therapy has been found to be a useful therapy for a range of childhood problems, and in spite of the fact that most of the literature on play therapy discusses case examples, illustrations of play therapy as clinical intervention, and the broad application of play therapy theory and technique, more and more research is being conducted (Bratton, Ray, & Rhine, 2005). Several authors have promoted the use of play in the resolution of childhood trauma and have integrated play-based strategies in their work with children and families (Carey, 2006; Gil, 2006, 2010; Goodyear-Brown, 2010; Kelly & Odenwalt, 2006). It is important to note that children can utilize a unique type of play called *posttraumatic play*, which appears to be an internally driven gradual exposure technique (Gil, 2010; Goodyear-Brown, 2010). The trauma-focused integrated play therapy model utilizes nondirective play therapy, in part, to allow children to access this important type of play.

Art Therapy   Art therapy, according to Rubin (2005) is difficult to define "because it is a hybrid, the child of both psychology and art" (p. 221), yet she cites the original definition proposed in 1961 by Elinor Ulman, which states, "Anything that is to be called art therapy must genuinely partake of both art and therapy" (p. 221). Children's art has normal developmental features and the literature on normal stages of children's drawing is extensive (Gardner, 1980). Thus children's art can be utilized both in assessment and treatment. Malchiodi has documented the use of art with children (1998); those who have witnessed violence (Malchiodi, 1997) and trauma survivors (Malchiodi, 2008). Clearly, art therapy can help clinicians advance therapeutic goals, particularly when working with trauma, which in and of itself, may benefit from externalization and projection opportunities (Gil, 2003).

Sand Therapy   Sand therapy can be defined as "an expressive and projective mode of psychotherapy involving the unfolding and processing of intra- and inter-personal issues through the use of specific sandtray materials as a nonverbal medium of communication, led by the client and facilitated by a trained therapist" (Homeyer & Sweeney, 1998, p. 6). There are several volumes that seek to provide clinicians with an overview of the different types of theories and applications of sand therapy with diverse populations (Carey, 1999; Lowenfeld, 1979; Mitchell, & Friedman, 1994; Turner, 2005).

Children and adults alike are usually intrigued by the invitation to touch, sift, sculpt, and play with fine, white sand, in a rectangular container painted blue on the bottom and sides. This treatment allows for externalized creations of internal "worlds" of affect, cognitions, perceptions, picture memories, and compartmentalized aspects of difficult life experiences. This therapy allows for mental and physical assimilation, access to symbol language and metaphor, and the possibility of both chronicling events (creating narrative scenarios), and utilizing a type of guided imagery that can promote insight and change. Sand therapy is becoming more and more common within the context of psychotherapy and is gaining wider acceptance, particularly as the neuroscience promotes the use of many of the expressive therapies for addressing traumatic impact (Baddock, 2008).

Attachment-Based Principles in TF-IPT   As more and more clinical work has been done with abused and traumatized children and their families, it has become very clear that their treatment must be conducted within the social and family context in which the abuse occurs. This is necessary both because the uncompromised, clear, empathic, and consistent support, nurturance, and guidance from parents has been found critical to children's improved outcomes, and because the family context and specifically, caretaking patterns of response, can either advance or sabotage clinical improvements in the child. In particular, in many cases of childhood trauma, the incidents of abuse may coexist with a context of impaired parent-child relationships, family conflicts, family stressors and vulnerabilities, as well as family strengths.

The TF-IPT model includes parent's participation in two ways: By providing them with supportive psychoeducation and coaching as needed, and by informing them of the clinical process and designing specific ways that the child's therapy process can be supported by parents and caretakers. However, funding and staffing limitations did not allow us to provide the full array of services that we believe is critical to therapeutic success and that includes focused enhancement of the parent-child relationship, in order to reinforce, model, teach, and strengthen the appropriate caretaking patterns to influence positive attachment. The TF-IPT model recognizes the importance of incorporating these valuable services and ongoing efforts seek to incorporate a more structured approach regarding parent-child relationships.

Trauma-Focused Integrated Play Therapy

Trauma-focused integrated play therapy provides children and their families with a structured, goal-oriented process designed to promote therapeutic relationships, address traumatic material in a variety of ways, capacitate the parents to provide support and guidance, and facilitate a reintegration of the child (with new insights and skills) into his or her social environment and caretaking system. When this model was tested in a research project, we conducted the program in 12 sessions, which often lasted longer than three months given patterns of missed appointments, new crisis situations, legal procedures that caused emotional upheaval, or other issues that needed attention before resuming the curriculum. Realistically, this model is best suited to a six- to nine-month period of time (typical with our clinical population). We found that the following activities greatly enhanced the potential for successful treatment participation: (1) structured format and time-limited "lessons," no longer than 20 minutes; (2) parallel psychoeducation to children and their parents; (3) repetition and review for children and their parents or caretakers; (4) practice in and out of clinical setting (at-home reviews); (5) a structured beginning and ending using Affective Scaling; and (6) the inclusion of a brief mindfulness breathing exercise.

TREATMENT PHASES

This model is phase-oriented: The first phase sets the therapy context, allows the therapeutic relationship to build, encourages a period of exploration by the child client, and most importantly, creates opportunities for the child to access reparative resources and activities. The second phase addresses traumatic material directly with the intent of creating a trauma narrative and restoring control and mastery. The third phase of treatment is to encourage positive social interactions, identify coping strategies, refine new skills, and affiliate with others.

Phase 1: Establishment of Safety and Relationship Building

Of the three distinct phases of treatment in this model, we consider this first phase to be the most relevant to success in the establishment of safety and laying down the foundation of relational connection. Simply put, during this phase of treatment, the clinician serves two roles: Within session, the clinician familiarizes the child with the setting, the structure, and offers a nondirective play therapy stance in order to create an atmosphere of permissiveness for the child. Throughout this time, the clinician begins to make an assessment of the child's overall functioning. Outside the session, the clinician serves as a persuasive advocate exploring the type and level of safety in the child's ecosystem. This may include conversations with school personnel, after-school day-care providers, foster parents, and other caretaking professionals. Understanding the resources that are immediately available to the child and building a strong alliance between and among the treatment team solidifies and maximizes clinical efforts.

During this initial phase of treatment, the clinician carefully constructs a clinical environment in which the child perceives choices, can develop trust slowly, and few clinical demands or expectations are made. Children referred for services have often experienced some frenzied responses that can include multiple interviews by law enforcement or social services, medical exams, discussions with attorneys (guardian ad litem appointed to represent children), CASA workers (Court Appointed Special Advocates), among other well-meaning helpers following required protocols designed to protect children in a legally substantiated way. All this can leave children weary and confused. A permissive environment that is child-centered and nondirective can feel like a relief and restore a child's sense of personal control.

In this first phase of treatment, children are shown around, asked their ideas about why they have come to treatment (and if inaccurate, they are given the accurate context of why they are in therapy), and simply allowed to choose what they want to do, what they want to play with, and how long they wish to spend with any single activity. The clinician provides reflective and empathic communication, follows the child's lead, and provides unconditional acceptance. The clinical quest is to allow children to explore, to find comfort in their play, and eventually, to encourage and welcome children's use of symbolic play to manifest concerns or confusions, worries and joys.

Judith Herman (1997) made a statement that became a guiding principle of my work and greatly influences the pacing I believe critical to therapy progress: "Though the single most common therapeutic error is avoidance of the traumatic material, probably the second most common error is premature or precipitate engagement in exploratory work, without sufficient attention to the tasks of establishing safety and securing a therapeutic alliance" (p. 172). The establishment of safety through relationship, predictability, and empathic care is clearly a prerequisite for moving ahead to the second phase of treatment.

The following directive play-based activities are usually utilized in the first phase of treatment:

> *Build a World in the Sand*: Children are asked to use as few or as many miniatures as they want, bring them to the sand box, and "build a world in the sand."
>
> *Color Your Feelings*: Children are asked to make a "list of the feelings they have most of the time," and then pick a color that best shows that feeling.
>
> Using this "affective color code" that they make, they are given ginger-bread silhouettes and asked to show the type and amount of feelings they have when they are with one person or another or in one situation or another.
>
> *Individual Play Genogram*: Clinicians help children make their family genogram and then ask them to find miniatures that "best show their thoughts and feelings about each person in their family, including themselves."
>
> *Environment Project*: Children pick a small animal (of any type) and they are provided with a cardboard oval plate and asked to "build an environment" for the animal they chose. Once the first (projective) environment is made, children are asked to build "a safe environment" for their animal.

PHASE 2: TRAUMA PROCESSING

When conducting research with TF-IPT, we structured the first phase of therapy to take five sessions, which were designed to be primarily nondirective, including nondirective play therapy time, and sometimes requested children's participation in play-based activities, considered low key and user-friendly. During the second phase of treatment (four or five sessions in length), clinicians guide children through a more directive exploration of their abuse, in essence creating a narrative of what occurred, how they felt and thought about it, and differentiating between the past and the present. In doing this work, the overriding goal is for children to clarify their thinking, express their feelings through words, actions, or symbolic play, and achieve a certain sense of mastery over the thinking and telling of something that might have been intolerable earlier. A benefit that occurs is that children are matching a difficult thought, memory, sensation, or feeling (as they take control of the trauma memory by organizing it and acknowledging it) with an experience of safety. As one of my child clients confided, "Now when I talk about it, it feels really far away and I don't feel so scared anymore."

The original TF-CBT model encouraged children to make a verbal narration that could be shared with his or her parent. Our TF-IPT model holds no such standard regarding verbal expression and in fact, we believe the child's symbolic expression to be equally valid. That is not to say that we do not process the narrative in whatever form it is provided; however, we do not require a child to talk to us in order to gauge progress.

The play-based activities that we utilize in this phase of treatment are:

Yes/No/Maybe Game: Children read statements about child abuse and then they must choose cards to assert their agreement/disagreement or question about the statements.

CBT Triangle: We use a cartoon character called Thinkafeelado, developed by Brian Narelle. This character will eventually have story books that show him explaining the relationship between what is felt, thought, and done.

Cartoon Narrative: Children are given comic-book type rectangles and invited to make simple drawings that indicate the sequence of behavior when they were victimized. Clinicians place bubbles on top of heads and children fill in thoughts. In addition, bubbles are made for "heart" and "feet" and children fill in what they feel and what they do or want to do.

Reconstructive Tasks: Children are given props and encouraged to "show" what happened to them, what they thought and felt, what they did or want to do.

Color Your Life: This art activity asks children to use colors to show positive or negative life experiences to date.

Sand Therapy: Children are asked to use a sand box, divide it in two parts, and show (with miniatures) what it was like before and after they told.

PHASE 3: SOCIAL RECONNECTION

After the trauma has been explored and processed, the last phase of our treatment model (two or three sessions) focuses on the child's restoration to age-appropriate social contact, identification of important resources in a variety of settings, and helping the child balance his or her view of the abuse. In other words, this is a time for helping the child view the abuse in perspective. The exploration of the trauma emphasizes and clarifies a number of issues including the responsibility for the abuse being with the abuser; restoration of trust so that children do not expect to be victimized in the future; identification of helpers who are available to listen to and respond to children's concerns and worries. Our hope is that lingering doubts that can cause shame or fear or guilt have been resolved and that children have the best possible understanding of the abuse that they can have given their age and cognitive abilities. Clearly, a 12-year-old's understanding will differ greatly from a 4-year-old child but the hope is that within their own particular range of understanding, a more positive and realistic view of the abuse has emerged. One 6-year-old girl told me, "I love my dad but what he did was wrong. He made a mistake. Dads know not to do that!" There was no attribution of responsibility in any of these statements, and that is what we are looking to achieve.

The play-based activities used in Phase 3 include:

Flowers in Vase: Children are given art supplies to make a flower and place the name of a support person or coping strategy on each petal. They are then given a vase and take their flower home.

Mindfulness Exercise Regarding Hope: Children are given a glass and water and asked to fill it halfway. Clinicians then guide discussion of how the glass is viewed and how seeing things half-full (versus half-empty) is more hopeful.

It is important to note that many of these play-based activities are chosen by children throughout their treatment and may be used more than once. When children choose these activities, they are given some time to complete and process them before moving on to scheduled activities. Sometimes children participate more fully in specific activities and not others. These choices are simply noted. When children want to play in the play therapy office most of the time and/or resist efforts to do the specific play-based activities, we may negotiate using half the time for free-play and half the time for the specified activity.

At the outset of treatment, clinicians review with parents the entire TF-IPT manual prior to children beginning treatment. They are aware that the middle phase of treatment may be difficult for children. They are invited to participate at the end of each session or each phase, based on clinical decisions specific to the case. Parents may be in concurrent individual, marital, and family therapy or they may be participating in conjoint parent-child sessions. These clinical decisions (outside the research structure) are left with the clinician. In addition, clinical recommendations about group therapy for children after completing the TF-IPT model will be considered depending on child or family needs.

Several assessment instruments are given to parents and children (if age appropriate) for completion at the outset and end of treatment. These instruments include the Trauma Symptom Checklist for Children (Briere, 1996), the Child Behavior CheckList (Achenbach & Rescorla, 2001), and the Child Sexual Behavior Inventory (Friedrich, 1997).

Clinical Case Example

Antonio was seen when he was 8 years of age by a male intern working under my supervision and utilizing nondirective play therapy. Mother had requested services one year after participating in our program with her daughter, 5. Her daughter had been in treatment at our program for over one year and had made great progress and was free of the behavioral problems, which had led up to, and followed, her disclosure.

Mother confided that she could not shake the feeling that the same adult male relative who sexually abused her daughter might have also abused her son. She asked Antonio directly whether he was abused and he denied it vehemently. So much so in fact, that his response made mother even more suspicious. Mother also talked about her son's tendency toward perfectionism, low-frustration level, and consistent volatility. In fact, Antonio's anger truly concerned his mother, particularly because he had become less and less responsive to parental discipline and recently, he had become aggressive with his sister, something mother found intolerable.

Mother filled out standard psychological instruments and Antonio's externalized behaviors were evident. Since this child had not disclosed sexual abuse, clinical efforts focused on relationship building, which produced positive outcomes. After about four months of meeting with his therapist, Antonio hinted to his therapist that the relative that abused his sister had abused him; however, at this time he was not interested or willing to talk about the abuse in any detail *or* do any work related to these incidents. Instead, he told his mother that he wanted to take a break from therapy (his sister had done the same at one point in her treatment). We supported him in this choice and emphasized that if and when he was interested in exploring the abuse, we would like to work with him. After a few months respite, he asked his mother to return to see his therapist.

(continued)

By the time he returned to treatment, our research project was underway and he was randomly selected to receive the TF-CBT model. He had not participated in abuse-specific treatment in the past, so he qualified to participate in the study. His therapist had been trained in TF-CBT and found it quite interesting and easy to provide. His relationship with Antonio was so strong that when he told him about this shift in the work they would do, Antonio was receptive, although at times required the lessons to be conducted with more familiar play activities.

Antonio remained resistant to in-depth verbal discussions regarding his abuse. He was characteristically and relentlessly avoidant, changing the subject, shrugging his shoulders, and saying he didn't know. He made the most minimal attempt at a narrative and the cursory descriptions he offered were noncommittal and superficial. However, his participation set the foundation for the work he did once the TF-CBT model was completed.

Antonio's therapist believed that Antonio's very angry behaviors signaled underlying unresolved issues. At times, Antonio hinted that he thought about the abusive relative from time to time, that he was really angry that he was still living next door, and that he resented the fact that some of his family (especially his grandfather) still seemed to defend the abuser rather than take a stand the way his parents had done (they had decided "never to speak to him again," after he had obtained a plea bargain and avoided jail by being on probation for two years). Antonio also seemed to long for a better relationship with his very busy father, and this issue apparently seemed to be troubling to Antonio.

Antonio's therapist talked things over with him and encouraged Antonio to spend a little more time working on his past abuse because he felt that it was affecting him more than Antonio acknowledged. The clinical discussion included mention of different issues that boys have when they have been abused, and Antonio's clinician noticed how Antonio seemed shocked that there were a few books written about abuse of boys. "I didn't think it happened to lots of boys, I thought most kids who came here were girls." Antonio was so surprised, in fact, about the prevalence of abuse of boys that his therapist opted to show him a videotape segment from a tape called *Breaking the Silence*. This videotape has a segment in which a boy, about 10 or 11 years old, talks about his victimization. Antonio watched with wide open eyes and "seeing" another victim truly seemed to have a positive impact on his willingness to share some of his reactions to his trauma.

(continued)

(continued)

TF-IPT began in earnest after Antonio appeared more interested to learn about other boys and how they reacted to the abuse. However, at the same time, Antonio stopped short of volunteering information, giving anything other than monosyllabic answers, and reverting to familiar shrugging. Antonio's therapist explained the structure of their new meetings that would seem a little different than the TF-CBT model. Specifically, the structure of TF-IPT included having Antonio fill out Affective Scaling Worksheets at the beginning and end of therapy, and teaching Antonio a brief mindfulness exercise. Antonio seemed to be receptive as his therapist introduced some play-based activities. Early on, Antonio was invited to make a drawing of anything at all (free drawing). He asked if he could use the paints, and his therapist made those available to him. He was very meticulous about filling the large piece of paper with paints and lining up several colors side by side. He seemed to relax making this painting and told his therapist as much. He was less excited about doing a self-portrait but still gave it a good effort and seemed to start and stop several times, apparently having qualms about making representational art. He told his therapist in frustration, "I can't draw," and took many of his attempts and scrunched them into balls. His perfectionism truly revealed itself and it seemed that he was unable to quiet his inner critic. He volunteered that his dad was just like him and always said, "If you're not going to do it right, just don't even do it." Eventually, he abandoned efforts to make either a self-portrait or a kinetic family drawing.

When he participated with another art activity called "Color Your Feelings," Antonio was able to reveal a bit more about his abuse. When asked to make a list of feelings he has most of the time, he opted to put them in a bottle with anger at the very top. "This is kind of like it is, I'm mad most of the time," he said candidly. His therapist commented, "Well, I think that's the feeling you show most of the time but I think that there might be lots of these other feelings that you just don't show as much." He then labeled the other feelings in his bottle and used different colors to show them. This seemed a rather large movement for Antonio who heretofore had been loathe to indicate any kind of emotions. As he left he said to his clinician, "I like drawing now, maybe next time I can draw some more."

His therapist prepared another activity for Antonio, wanting to ride the momentum from the previous session. He brought in a mask and following up on the dichotomy between what is shown on the

(continued)

exterior and what is felt internally, he asked Antonio to paint the first mask showing "the way you show yourself to the outside world, to your friends and family." Antonio complied and it took him two full sessions to complete his art project (see Figure 11.1).

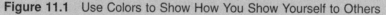

Figure 11.1 Use Colors to Show How You Show Yourself to Others

This mask was painted in very distinctive little squares, a very red mouth, a red streak going vertically over his left eye (looking like a scar), and some green squares painted over his eyes. Very thick black lines were added to emphasize the eyebrows and the lips. He filled in all the little squares on the face with a blue marker (which obviously provided him with a greater sense of control than using wet paints). He said very little about this painting other than: "People can't really see me, maybe they're confused by me." In looking at the mask, initial impressions include the red scar across his eye, perhaps indicating his sense of being injured. The placement of the scar is also interesting because it is near his line of vision, it is very visible to the naked eye, and, given the context of the rest of the mask, it really stands out. The redness in the mouth is consistent with his familiarity and comfort with the expression of anger, and the very small squares may indicate his own sense that he keeps his feelings, thoughts, and experiences

(continued)

(continued)
quite compartmentalized and guarded. The process he used coloring in all the squares showed a great desire to manifest self-control and structure. Given this art activity, it is quite easy to see why it has taken so long for Antonio to feel comfortable enough to begin to share his deeper feelings. The establishment of a strong and supportive relationship, one devoid of judgment, appears to have been the necessary first step in this treatment process, clearly guided by Antonio.

The second mask that Antonio drew was highly revealing and it became clear that art would be his treatment of choice. He had found liberation in externalizing images, words, and colors to convey the extent of trauma impact. Thus Figure 11.2 is Antonio's foundation for the work yet to come.

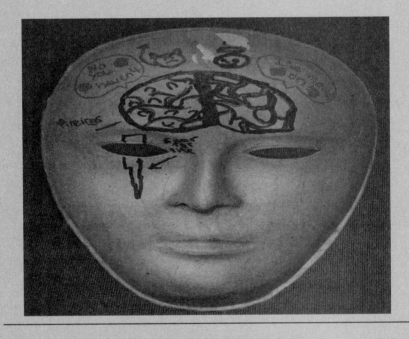

Figure 11.2 Show What You Really Feel on the Inside

This mask appears less structured, and unique to this one is the lack of marks on the bottom half of the mask, giving almost the appearance of "room to grow." The forehead provides us with a clear portrait of the conflict that Antonio has been experiencing internally.

(continued)

His brain clearly has two disparate feelings: One half says (in a bubble), "I've moved on!" with a picture of an angel nearby. The other says, "No you haven't," with a picture of a devil. On the side of the brain that has the devil, he adds what he calls "fire rings," perhaps suggesting his propensity for anger. A black scar (not colored red inside but just outlined) covers his right eye, the side where the devil brain and fire rings reside, and he adds the words "scar for life," indicating just how deeply Antonio experiences his victimization. For a child who began therapy talking about how therapy was "a waste of time, nothing had happened to him, he didn't want to come," things had truly shifted.

Antonio told his therapist that he really liked to come to therapy now, showing a sense of mastery and pride over his ideas and how he had been working. When Antonio's therapist went on vacation, he left his sketch pad and told him that if he wanted to keep working on all those feelings that he had listed in the bottle, he was welcome to draw more about it. Antonio took that suggestion to heart and brought back some more art work. See Figures 11.3, 11.4, 11.5, and 11.6.

It's very interesting to note that each of these pictures is drawn *with* Antonio's abuser. This was not specifically requested so it is interesting to note that Antonio views his feelings as directly related to the abuse and the abuser. In the first drawing (Figure 11.3, "Hurt"), Antonio depicts himself with tears coming from his eyes and no mouth (inability to speak, ask for help, get help for himself) and he has a band-aid on his shoulder. The placement of the band-aid is interesting in that it corresponds with where boys might flex their muscles to indicate strength. This could signal Antonio's concern about his masculinity and inability to defend himself. The abuser has what appears to be sharp nails coming out of his arm, the arm he's pointing at Antonio while laughing, "ha, ha, ha." These are both simple line drawings and yet they convey ample affective expression.

Figure 11.4 aptly indicates fear. He looks to be shaking, folding his arms in front of his body, standing still, teeth shattering, and yet looking to his right, where the abuser's head lurks over his own, with sharp teeth and wide eyes. There is a stillness to this picture (in spite of the small lines that indicate shaking) that show how helpless and disempowered Antonio felt in the presence of this adult male. Figure 11.5, titled "Confusion," is a powerful image of feeling befuddled, with wide circles for eyes, a small round mouth shaded in,

(*continued*)

(continued)

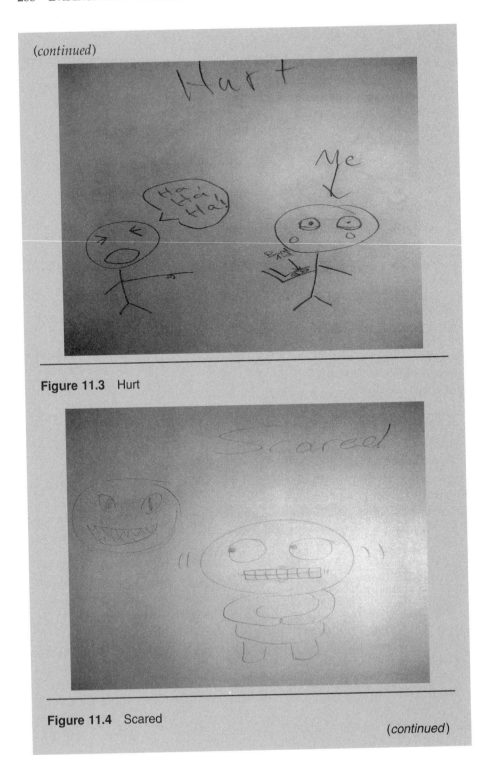

Figure 11.3   Hurt

Figure 11.4   Scared

(continued)

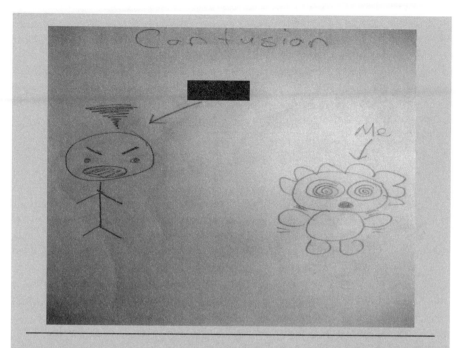

Figure 11.5 Confused

and hair, which appears to be standing on edge. His arms again have small lines indicating movement. This movement appears consistent with arms that might be flailing around. The abuser has a threatening mouth (round circle with sharp lines inside), furrowed brows, and some lines in the shape of a tornado on top of the abuser's head.

Finally, Figure 11.6 shows a very small figure, which looks like an infant who is crying and has his eyes shut. This figure, more than any other, shows the experience of helplessness and disempowerment. In this picture, the abuser again appears angry and powerful as it towers over the smaller, sad figure.

Antonio managed to chronicle his trauma narrative, not so much in facts and details, but by providing an "emotional narrative" that clearly illustrates the impact of the trauma on this young boy. It is nearly two years after the fact and Antonio finally relieves himself of the singular isolation of secrecy. He also makes himself vulnerable to his therapist and himself and he faces the pervasive sense of helplessness he experienced by being able, at the same time, to disavow the abuser's power over him at this time. He remembers details of his trauma (and reactions) while he also feels safe and secure, within the context of a

(continued)

(continued)

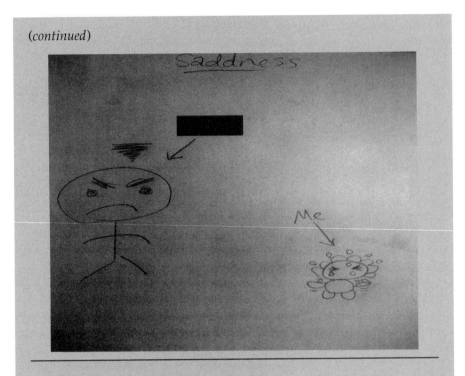

Figure 11.6 Sad

positive relationship that he trusts, and a relationship in which he feels heard and validated.

Antonio added one last picture (see Figure 11.7), once again indicating how well he had compartmentalized his traumatic sexual experience and signaling some of the ways he had tried to cope.

Initially, he was focused on his ability to get physically strong and fight off unwanted attention from his abuser. You see at the top of the figure that his abuser peeks out from behind the bushes, clearly relentlessly stalking Antonio and pressuring him so much that Antonio begins to fortify himself with exercise in order to protect himself. However, those efforts don't work.

In the next frame, Antonio's abuser is closer and looks mean and focused. In this picture, Antonio is crying and praying, "Get me out of here." He looks completely helpless and showing himself in this way to his clinician was a strong indication of his trust in the relationship. Antonio is able to show himself completely stripped from the bravado that characterized his early presentation in

(continued)

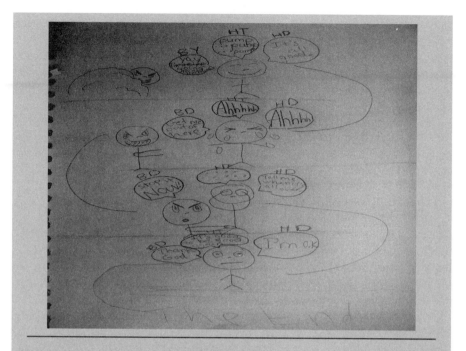

Figure 11.7 The Process of Healing

therapy. The next frame goes even further: Antonio reveals his abuser's power over him. The abuser tells him to "stop" crying, and Antonio covers his eyes and says, "Tell me when it's over," completely surrendering to his adult abuser and later feeling very guilty and ashamed that he didn't fight him off.

Finally, the last frame at the bottom says, "It's good to be good again," "Thank God," and "I'm okay." His facial expression, however, belies these words. He does not have a smile (rather a straight line for a mouth), his eyes look very open, even startled, and his arms point downward. At this juncture, Antonio feels much better than before: He has shared his secret, he has depicted his experience in a very powerful way, and he has begun to expose himself to the very emotions and thoughts that produced the anger that he acts out against his family and against peers.

This artwork allowed a bird's-eye view of how Antonio perceived his experience, and it signaled several areas that could use psycho-education. Antonio's clinician used the bubbles that Antonio drew on his faces to return and have him fill in even more

(continued)

(*continued*)

ideas. At this point, Antonio's clinician returned to the books that Antonio had noticed earlier in the treatment but that he was not able to read at that time. Antonio also asked to watch the videotape again (of the boy victimized by a neighbor), and he made a sand tray spontaneously that showed the "past, present, and future" about the abuse. He chose a little warrior for himself but in his sand scenario of the past, his little warrior was face down in the sand. He stood up a little warrior in the middle section representing the present, and in the future, he upgraded his little warrior to a very strong, adult warrior who was intimidating to others.

Antonio's clinician asked him to choose a few more miniatures to show how he might feel in the future. He told Antonio that while he understood his desire to show himself as a warrior that no one could hurt and that would likely be viewed as threatening to others, he wondered what else, in addition to this aggressive figure, he could choose. This caused Antonio to dig deep and add a few more miniatures to what he had already created. He put a boy and his dog for the past, adding that he was a "good kid who liked to run and play outside and took good care of his dog." He added a boy with his dog and a teacher and books and soccer balls for the present, indicating that he was a good student and a good athlete. He talked about how his parents always came to watch him play ball and they cheered for him a lot.

Finally, for the future, he put older male and female figures on either side of him and he also added a man in a black suit with a briefcase saying that he would be a lawyer when he grew up and he would prosecute bad guys and work for justice. He also put in another dog next to the lawyer, this time an attack dog, claiming, "Even lawyers need a loyal guard dog!"

After this phase of therapy, Antonio moved into the third phase of treatment, which focused on his peer relationships, his aggressive stance (now relabeled as *compensatory for feelings of helplessness*), and his desire to have a best friend. At this juncture, Antonio's therapist was working with another youngster, the same age and background, who likewise had developed hostility in response to his experience of abuse. The possibility of doing "pair therapy" (Selman & Schultz, 1990) was presented to both sets of parents, and after reassurances about confidentiality (and the fact that the kids lived in different counties and did not attend the same schools), they agreed to allow their children to participate. This relationship-focused therapy proved to be perfect for

(*continued*)

Antonio and Alex who had both developed compensatory anger in order to protect themselves. During the first few sessions, their apparent enjoyment of each other was evident. Antonio shared with his therapist, "I feel like I've been knowing him a long time."

The final issue to be addressed in Antonio's therapy was some of the family dynamics that seemed to create problems at home. In particular, Antonio seemed to feel lonely and disconnected from his busy father, who spent a lot of his time on the road with work and who seemed to have a pattern of trying to encourage Antonio in what Antonio perceived as a critical manner. Antonio's father was a hard-working man who was often fatigued and wanted peace and quiet in his home. He loved his son deeply and wanted the best for him but often found himself inpatient with Antonio's distractibility.

Antonio seemed to miss his father and was frustrated that he didn't get to see him much and that dad missed so many of his sports events. In addition, Antonio was keeping a secret from his father, a secret that he suspected would elicit his ire. "My dad is going to be really mad that I didn't punch him (the abuser) out," he confided to his therapist. Antonio was convinced that his father would be very disappointed, perhaps angry at him, for failing to protect himself.

Meanwhile, Antonio's mother was also frustrated both with her husband's absence from the home and the way he seemed to expect her to take care of all home-related issues by herself. When Antonio's therapist proposed family sessions with both parents, mother immediately stated that her husband would not come to therapy under any circumstances and that she was done "fighting a losing battle." Antonio's therapist called father directly and found him surprisingly receptive when father heard that Antonio needed his father and that his presence would be very helpful to his son.

Family therapy with Antonio and his family went well. Antonio had told his therapist that he wanted to tell his dad about what had happened (mother had been encouraged to help her son talk to his father but had found it an impossible task). He wanted to "get it over with," and he was afraid that if he kept this secret much longer it would just get bigger and bigger in his mind. It seemed that Antonio hoped for his father's support and forgiveness, all the while terrified that he would encounter his disapproval, disappointment, and anger.

(continued)

(*continued*)

Antonio chose to share his drawings with his parents. The meeting was very successful for Antonio. He sat between his parents as he showed them the pictures; he was able to show them everything he wanted, and his parents responded in a loving, supportive, and appropriate way. If father was angry or disappointed in his son, he showed no hint of it. He mostly seemed empathic and encouraging, saying some of the things he had been coached to say, and adding many of his own deeply felt observations. He said to his son, "You are very brave to talk about this and I'm so sorry that this man was so crazy as to do this to a little boy. He should have known better and I am quite mad with him, which I am going to tell him directly!" Antonio gave a broad smile. Mother was likewise moved to tears and happy to see her husband's reactions. Later she confided, "I think that's the first time that he really understood what that man did to the kids!" In fact, it was likely that this was the first time Antonio's father allowed himself to feel the painful emotions associated with his children being hurt by a family relative. Later the parents talked about how each of them felt guilt for not having been able to spare their children from this hurtful experience.

This case illustrates the pivotal role of establishing a therapy relationship and allowing children to pace and to express themselves in a variety of ways. It also demonstrates the benefit of nondirective play therapy in order to allow children to explore and to locate reparative mechanisms of their choice. Finally, the integrative nature of this work is demonstrated by the fact that this therapy is trauma-focused primarily, later integrating expressive therapy, pair therapy, family therapy, and principles of systems theory, child development, and cognitive-behavioral approaches.

CONCLUSION

TF-IPT is driven by trauma theory and integrates a variety of theories and approaches designed to facilitate the processing of trauma, to encourage relationship-building, to make full use of the expressive therapies that elicit children's more full engagement and participation, and broaden the possibilities of varied forms of healing. In particular, TF-IPT values expressive therapies both because they provide children with ample, natural reparative mechanisms and ways of processing their injuries and because nondirective play therapy, in particular, places few demands on children and allows them to dictate the pacing of their work. It is clear by now that no one model will work for every person in every situation, and we must remain open to maximizing our clinical potential to be viewed as helpful, trustworthy, and supportive by our clients. The building of a therapy relationship appears not only desirable but pivotal to positive treatment outcome. What we do to inform and to promote our goals is less important than who we are and how invested we can become in connecting with our clients.

Finally, as our field is currently exploding with new treatment models, certification processes, and encouragement to become more evidence-based in the services we provide, it is a time of great excitement, creativity, study, and accountability. The clinical field is quite young, clinicians are eager to do their best, and an integration of science and practice, research-informed clinical work, and increased clinical research is desirable and necessary. Hopefully, greater consensus can be reached about the complexity of childhood trauma and the articulation of how to provide meaningful services in cases of childhood trauma so that negative effects are ameliorated through responsible, individualized, client-centered treatment.

REFERENCES

Achenbach, T. M., & Rescorla, L. A. (2001). *Manual for the ASEBA school-age forms & profiles*. Burlington: University of Vermont, Research Center for Children, Youth, and Families.

Achilles, G., & Gil, E. (in press). *A randomized controlled pilot study comparing trauma-focused cognitive behavioral therapy to trauma-focused integrated play therapy*. Childhelp Children's Center of Virginia, Fairfax, VA. emgil@earthlink.net

Baddock, B. (2008). *Being a brain-wise therapist: A practical guide to interpersonal neurobiology*. New York, NY: Norton.

Beezley, P., Martin, H. P., & Kempe, R. (1976). Psychotherapy. In H. P. Martin (Ed.), *The abused Child: A multidisciplinary approach to developmental issues and treatment* (pp. 201–214). Cambridge, MA: Ballinger Press.

Bloom, S. (2005). Foreword. In A. M. Weber & C. Haen (Eds.), *Clinical applications of drama therapy in child and adolescent therapy* (pp. xv-xviii). New York, NY: Brunner-Routledge.

Bratton, S. C., Ray, D., & Rhine, T. (2005). The efficacy of play therapy with children: A meta-analytic review of treatment outcomes. *Professional Psychology: Research and Practice, 36, 4,* 376–390.

Briere, J. (1996). *Trauma symptom checklist for children professional manual*. Lutz, FL: Psychological Assessment Resources.

Carey, L. J. (1999). *Sandplay therapy with children and families*. Northvale, NJ: Aronson.

Carey, L. (2006). (Ed.). *Expressive and creative arts methods for trauma survivors.* Philadelphia, PA: Kingsley.

Cohen, J. A., Mannarino, A. P., & Deblinger, E. (2006). *Treating trauma and traumatic grief in children and adolescents.* New York, NY: Guilford Press.

Crenshaw, D. (2006). Neuroscience and trauma treatment: Implications for creative arts therapists. In L. Carey (Ed.), *Expressive and creative arts methods for trauma survivors* (pp. 21–38). Philadelphia, PA: Kingsley.

Deblinger, E., Steer, R., & Lippman, J. (1996). Sexually abused children suffering posttraumatic stress symptoms: Initial treatment outcome findings. *Child Maltreatment 1,* 310–321.

Deblinger, E., Steer, R., & Lippman, J. (1999). Two-year follow-up study of cognitive behavioral therapy for sexually abused children suffering posttraumatic stress symptoms. *Child Abuse & Neglect, 23,* 1371–1378.

Duncan, B. L., Sparks, J. A., & Miller, S. D. (2006). Client, not theory, directed: Integrating approaches one client at a time. In G. Stricker and J. Gold (Eds.), *A casebook of psychotherapy integration* (pp. 225–240). Washington, DC: American Psychological Association.

Eth, S., & Pynoos, R. (1985). Developmental perspective on psychic trauma in childhood. In C. R. Figley (Ed.), *Trauma and its wake, Volume 1: The study and treatment of post-traumatic stress disorder* (pp. 36–52). Bristol, PA: Brunner/Mazel.

Friedrich, W. N. (1997). *Child sexual behavior inventory professional manual.* Lutz, FL: Psychological Assessment Resources.

Gardner, H. (1980). *Artful scribbles: The significance of children's drawings.* New York, NY: Basic Books.

Gil, E. (2003). Art and play therapy with sexually abused children. In C. A. Malchiodi (Ed.), *Handbook of art therapy* (pp. 152–166). New York, NY: Guilford Press.

Gil, E. (2006). *Helping abused and traumatized children: Integrating directive and nondirective approaches.* New York, NY: Guilford Press.

Gil, E. (Ed.). (2010). *Helping children heal interpersonal trauma: The power of play.* New York, NY: Guilford Press.

Gold, J., & Stricker, G. (2001). Relational psychoanalysis as a foundation for assimilative integration. *Journal of Psychotherapy Integration, 11,* 47–63.

Goodyear-Brown, P. (2010). *Play therapy with traumatized children: A prescriptive approach.* New York, NY: John Wiley & Sons.

Herman, J. (1992, 1997). *Trauma and recovery: The aftermath of violence—from domestic abuse to political terror.* New York, NY: Basic Books.

Hinz, L. D. (2009). *Expressive therapies continuum: A framework for using arts in therapy.* New York, NY: Routledge.

Homeyer, L. E., & Sweeney, D. S. (1998, 5th printing). *Sandtray: A practical manual.* Royal Oak, MI: Self-Esteem Shop.

Kelly, M. M., & Odenwalt, H. C. (2006). Treatment of sexually abused children. In C. E. Schaefer & H. G. Kaduson (Eds.), *Contemporary play therapy: Theory, research, and practice* (pp. 186–211). New York, NY: Guilford Press.

Klorer, P. G. (2000). *Expressive therapy with troubled children.* New York, NY: Aronson.

Lazarus, A. A. (2006). Multimodal therapy: A seven-point integration. In G. Stricker & J. Gold (Eds.), *A casebook of psychotherapy integration* (pp. 17–28). Washington, DC: American Psychological Association.

Levine, P. (1997). *Waking the tiger: Healing trauma.* Berkeley, CA: North Atlantic.

Lowenfeld, M. (1979). *The world technique.* London, England: Allen & Unwin.

Malchiodi, C. A. (Ed.). (2008). *Creative interventions for working with traumatized children.* New York, NY: Guilford Press.

Malchiodi, C. (2005). *Expressive therapies.* New York, NY: Guilford Press.

Malchiodi, C. A. (1997). *Breaking the silence: Art therapy with children from violent Homes* (2nd ed.). New York, NY: Brunner-Routledge.

Malchiodi, C. A. (1998). *Understanding children's drawings.* New York, NY: Guilford Press.

McNiff, S. (2009). *Integrating the arts in therapy: History, theory, and practice.* Springfield, IL: Thomas.

Messer, S. (1992). A critical examination of belief structures in integrative and eclectic psychotherapy. In J. C. Norcross & M. R. Goldfried (Eds.), *Handbook of psychotherapy integration* (pp. 130–168). New York, NY: Basic Books.

Mitchell, R. R., & Friedman, H. S. (1994). *Sandplay: Past, present, and future.* London, England: Routledge.

Nader, K., & Pynoos, R. S. (1991). Play and drawing techniques as tools for interviewing traumatized children. In C. E. Schaefer, K. Gitlin, & A. Sandgrund (Eds.), *Play diagnosis and assessment* (pp. 375–389). New York, NY: John Wiley & Sons.

O'Connor, K. J., & Schaefer, C. E. (1994). *Handbook of play therapy, Vol.2, Advances and innovations.* New York, NY: John Wiley & Sons.

Ogden, P., Minton, K., & Pain, C. (2006). *Trauma & the body: A sensorimotor approach to psychotherapy.* New York, NY: Norton.

Perry, B. D. (2009). Examining child maltreatment through a neurodevelopmental lens: Clinical applications of the neurosequential model of therapeutics. *Journal of Loss & Trauma, 14,* 240–255.

Perry, B. D., Pollard, R. A., Blakley, T. L., Baker, W. L., & Vigilante, D. (1995). Childhood trauma, the neurobiology of adaptation, and "use-dependent" development of the brain: How "states" become "traits." *Infant Mental Health Journal, 16,4,* 271–291.

Perry, B., & Szalavitz, M. (2007). *The boy who was raised as a dog: And other stories from a child psychiatrist's notebook: What children can teach us about loss, love, & healing.* New York, NY: Basic Books.

Rubin, J. A. (2005). *Artful therapy.* New York, NY: John Wiley & Sons.

Rubin, J. A. (2006). Introduction. In L. Carey (Ed.), *Expressive and creative arts methods for trauma survivors* (pp. 9–13). Philadelphia, PA: Kingsley.

Schaefer, C. E., & O'Connor, K. J. (1983). *Handbook of play therapy.* New York, NY: John Wiley & Sons.

Selman, R. L., & Schultz, L. H. (1990). *Making a friend in youth: Developmental theory and pair therapy.* Chicago, IL: University of Chicago Press.

Siegel, D. (1999). *The developing mind: How relationships and the brain interact to shape who we are.* New York, NY: Guilford Press.

Solomon, M. F., & Siegel, D. J. (2003). (Eds.). *Healing trauma: Attachment, mind, body, and brain*. New York, NY: Norton.

Stricker, G. (2010). *Psychotherapy integration: Theories of psychotherapy series*. Washington, DC: American Psychological Association.

Stricker, G., & Gold, J. (1996). An assimilative model for psychodynamically oriented integrative psychotherapy. *Clinical Psychology: Science and Practice, 3,* 47–58.

Stricker, G., & Gold, J. (1996). An assimilative approach to integrative psychodynamic psychotherapy. In F. W. Kaslow & J. Lebow (Eds.), *Comprehensive handbook of psychotherapy: Vol. 4. Integrative/Eclectic* (pp. 295–316). New York, NY: John Wiley & Sons.

Turner, B. A. (2005). *The handbook of sandplay therapy*. Cloverdale, CA: Tenemos Press.

Ulman, E. (1961). Art therapy: Problems of Definition. *Bulletin of Art Therapy, 1*(2), 10–20.

van der Kolk, B. (1987). *Psychological trauma*. Washington, DC: American Psychiatric Publications, www.appi.org

van der Kolk, B. (2005). Developmental trauma disorder: Toward a rational diagnosis for children with complex trauma histories. *Psychiatric Annals, 35*(5), 401–408.

van der Kolk, B., McFarlane, A. C., & Weisath, L. (Eds.). (1996). *Traumatic stress: The effects of overwhelming experiences on mind, body, & society*. New York, NY: Guilford Press.

Ziegler, D. (2002). *Traumatic experience and the brain: A handbook for understanding and treating those traumatized as children*. Jasper, OR: Acacia.

CHAPTER 12

Parent-Child Interaction Therapy for Sexually Abused Children

ANTHONY J. URQUIZA and DAWN BLACKER

INTRODUCTION

DURING THE PAST decade, Parent-Child Interaction Therapy (PCIT) has garnered increasing attention from clinicians (Eyberg, 2004; McNeil & Hembree-Kigin, 2010) as an effective intervention—helping families with children who have severe behavioral problems. Much of this attention has been the result of riding the crest of a general movement toward evidence-based practices (Weisz & Gray, 2007). That is, PCIT has been recognized as an evidence-based practice (Chadwick Center for Children and Families, 2004; Saunders, Berliner, & Hansen, 2004), it has a clear and well-articulated theoretical foundation and protocol (McNeil & Hembree-Kigin, 2010), and there are models to support dissemination and implementation (Urquiza et al., 2007). Another important reason for this increase in attention is that PCIT is highly effective in reducing child behavioral problems, improving parenting skills, and enhancing the quality of parent-child relationships (Zisser & Eyberg, 2010). So, it should not be a surprise that PCIT has gained substantial interest from clinicians and clinical administrators alike, because of its value in addressing a serious and common child outpatient mental health problem—disruptive behavior. Initially developed for families who had oppositional defiant families, there has been an effort to broaden the application to many additional types of families and child problems. The focus of this chapter is

279

to highlight the value of PCIT with children and families in which sexual abuse has occurred.

WHAT IS PARENT-CHILD INTERACTION THERAPY?

PCIT is an intervention founded on behavioral, developmental, and social learning principles. It has been primarily designed for children between 2 and 8 years of age who have some type of externalizing disorders (Eyberg & Robinson, 1983; McNeil & Hembree-Kigin, 2010). The underlying model of change is similar to that of a parent-training program; that is, modifying the way parents interact with their children diminishes child behavior problems, which in turn promotes more positive parenting (Borrego & Urquiza, 1998). However, PCIT is unique in that it incorporates both parent and child within the treatment session, and uses live and individualized therapist coaching to change aspects of the interaction that cause dysfunction in the parent-child relationship (which are identified as the source of the child's disruptive behavioral problems).

PCIT is conducted in two phases. See Table 12.1 for an outline of the overall course of treatment. The first phase focuses on enhancing the parent-child relationship (often described as Child-Directed Interaction, or CDI), and the second phase focuses on improving child compliance (often described as Parent-Directed Interaction, or PDI). Both phases of treatment begin with a didactic training, followed by a therapist coaching parents while they play with their children. Traditionally, the coaching is conducted from an observation room via a "bug-in-the-ear" receiver (i.e., a small electronic receiver that looks like a hearing aide, which receives a low frequency FM signal, transmitted from an adjacent observation room) that the parent wears. The therapist-coach talks to the parent through the bug-in-the-ear device in real-live time while the parent is interacting (i.e., playing with age-appropriate toys) with the child. Although the therapist-coach is very active in talking to the parent, there is little to no direct communication between the therapist-coach and the child. Parents are taught and required to practice specific skills of communication and behavior management with their children.

In Table 12.2, the specific skills that parents and/or caregivers are taught in PCIT are listed in detail.

As presented earlier, in CDI (typically 7–10 sessions; see Table 12.2 for an outline of the CDI portion of PCIT), the primary goal is to create or strengthen a positive and mutually rewarding relationship between parents and their children by modifying the way parents interact with their children. Parents are taught to follow their children's lead in play by describing their activities and reflecting their appropriate verbalizations. They are also taught to praise their children's positive behavior, telling

Table 12.1
Overview of the Course of Treatment for PCIT

1. Intake and Pretreatment Assessment (1–2 sessions)
   - Standardized assessment measures:
     - Eyberg Child Behavior Inventory (Eyberg & Pincus, 1999)
     - Child Behavior Checklist (Achenbach & Ruffle, 2000)
     - Parenting Stress Inventory (Abidin, 1995)
2. Child-Directed Interaction/Relationship Enhancement (7–10 sessions)
   - Child-Directed Interaction didactic–PRIDE skills:
     - **P**raise
     - **R**eflection
     - **I**mitation
     - **D**escription
     - **E**nthusiasm
   - Avoid critical statements
   - Avoid commands
   - Avoid questions
   - Avoid "No–Don't–Stop–Quit–Not"
3. Mid-treatment assessment (1 session)
   Same as pretreatment assessment.
4. Parent-Directed Interaction/Strategies for Compliance (7–10 sessions)
   - Parent-Directed Interaction didactic–BE DIRECT skills:
     - **B**e specific with commands
     - **E**very command positive stated
     - **D**evelopmentally appropriate
     - **I**ndividual commands
     - **R**espectful and polite
     - **E**ssential commands only
     - **C**hoices when appropriate
     - **T**one of voice neutral
   - Giving effective commands
   - Responding to compliance/noncompliance
   - Practicing consistency, problem-solving, reasoning skills
5. Posttreatment assessment (1 session)
   Same as pretreatment assessment.

them specifically what is laudable about their actions, products, or attributes. By the end of CDI, parents generally have shifted from rarely attending to their child's positive behavior to frequently and consistently praising appropriate child behavior. For example (C = Child statement; P = Parent statement; T = Therapist/Coach statement):

C: (10 minutes into a treatment session, Bobby, a 4-year-old distractible and overactive child, is sitting on his chair coloring with markers)

Table 12.2
Child-Directed Interaction (Relationship Enhancement) and Parent-Directed
Interaction (Strategies for Compliance)

PRIDE

Child-Directed Interaction (Relationship Enhancement) concepts:

Praise   Providing a labeled/unlabeled praise for the child's desired behavior will increase the frequency of that behavior.

Reflection   Repeating or paraphrasing your child's statement demonstrates that you are listening/understanding what they say.

Imitation   Playing with the same toys as your child shows that you care about what they are doing and find it interesting, too.

Description   Telling your child what they are doing tells them that you are interested and paying attention to what they are doing.

Enthusiasm   Conveys excitement and warmth in your child's activity–showing that you care about them.

BE DIRECT

Parent-Directed Interaction (Strategies for Compliance) concepts:

Be specific with commands   Providing clear and specific commands increases your child's understanding that he or she will know what you want them to do.

Every command positively stated   Tell your child what you *want* them to do, not what you want them to stop doing.

Developmentally appropriate   Make sure the command you are delivering is something that your child is able to do.

Individual commands   Give one command at a time; multiple commands can be confusing and unclear.

Respectful and polite   Using Please and Thank you encourages your child to also use these words.

Essential commands only   Give commands *only* when needed; too many commands can cause problems.

Choices when appropriate   Giving choices promotes independent and problem-solving skills in your child.

Tone of voice neutral   Keeping your voice calm, at a normal speaking volume, and relaxed demonstrates you are in control.

T: (Statement directed to the parent) Tell Bobby, "You're doing a great job sitting on your chair!" And, at the same time give him a pat on the back.

P: (Statement directed to Bobby) Bobby, I like that you are sitting so nicely on your chair. (Parent also complies by giving Bobby a pat on the back)

T: (Statement directed to the parent) That was a great praise—Bobby is more likely to sit in his chair when you praise him like that; and I am sure that he feels better when you give him some physical affection.

Also, by using more appropriate statements (i.e., the parent praising the child for desired behavior), parents shift from using more controlling or coercive methods of managing their child's behavior, which may inadvertently lead to reinforcement of inappropriate child behavior, to using more positive communication tactics. Through a series of interactions (therapist-coach prompts provided to the parent), the parent is able to get the child to engage in play with the parent, reflect the child's speech (i.e., reinforcing appropriate child verbalizations), and describe the play in a way that conveys their noncontrolling interest in the child's activity. During this time, parents learn to shape their child's behavior by using "selective attention." By using this strategy, parents signal their disapproval of their children's inappropriate behavior by strategically withdrawing their attention. When children behave appropriately again, they are rewarded with their parents' attention and praise. Mastering selective attention teaches parents patience (it is difficult to ignore annoying behaviors), self-control, and that maintaining a positive context for play may not require high levels of parental discipline.

In the second phase, PDI (typically 7–10 sessions following CDI; see Table 12.2 for an outline of the PDI portion of PCIT), the primary goal is to teach effective parenting skills for use in managing children's behavior. In PDI, therapists maintain the focus of parents' attention to their children's positive behaviors while training them to give clear, direct commands. Once parents master giving effective commands, they learn to provide praise for compliance, and strategies for dealing with noncompliance. Parents are taught to deliver a specific and structured sequence of commands that would result in child compliance. If a child refuses to comply with the parental command, then parents are "coached" in how to address this defiance (i.e., they are provided instructions and practice a specific time-out sequence). (See McNeil & Hembree-Kigin, 2010, for a full description of the PCIT program.) By the end of PDI, the process of giving commands and gaining compliance is predictable and safe for both the parents and the child (Eyberg, 1988).

Is PCIT an Effective Intervention?

There have been numerous studies demonstrating the efficacy of PCIT in reducing child behavior problems (e.g., Eisenstadt et al., 1993; Eyberg et al., 2001; Eyberg, 1988; Eyberg & Robinson, 1982) and maintaining these positive effects up to six years after treatment (Hood & Eyberg, 2003). Treatment effects also have been shown to generalize to school settings (Funderburk et al., 1998; McNeil, Eyberg, Eisenstadt, Newcomb, & Funderburk, 1991) and to untreated siblings (Brestan, Eyberg, Boggs, &

Algina, 1997; Eyberg & Robinson, 1982). In addition, PCIT also has been shown to be effective for foster parents (Timmer et al., 2006; Timmer, Urquiza, & Zebell, 2006). Given the documented effectiveness of PCIT in helping nonmaltreating parents manage their behavior-problem children, recent research has supported similar benefits with high-risk families, including abusive parents (Chaffin et al., 2004; Timmer, Urquiza, Zebell, & McGrath, 2005), families involved in domestic violence (Timmer, Ware, Zebell, & Urquiza, 2010), and kin-caregivers of maltreated children with a history of maltreatment (Timmer, Urquiza, & Zebell, 2006). In addition, there has been research examining PCIT with different cultural and language groups, including Spanish-speaking families (Matos, Torres, Santiago, Jurado, & Rodriguez, 2006; McCabe, Yeh, Garland, Lau, & Chavez, 2005), Native American families (Subia-Bigfoot & Funderburk, 2006), and Chinese families (Leung, Tsang, & Heung, 2007). Finally, recent research has indicated that PCIT appears to decrease trauma symptoms in young children (Timmer, Urquiza, & Zebell, 2007; Urquiza & Timmer, 2008). Although the focus of PCIT treatment gains lies primarily in decreasing child behavioral problems and improving parenting skills, the value of enhancing the quality of parent-child relationships suggests a much larger range of applications.

WHY IS PCIT IMPORTANT FOR SEXUALLY ABUSED CHILDREN?

One important question that may arise when examining the application of PCIT to sexually abused children is, "In what ways would a behaviorally oriented, evidence-based, parenting program benefit a child who has a history of being sexually abused?" The following sections describe several facets of PCIT that can be beneficial for certain types of children and families who have experienced sexual victimization—especially families in which the children exhibit some type of behavioral disruption.

Child Sexual Abuse Victims Have Behavioral Problems   It is important to examine the entire range of factors present at the time of a child victim's entry to mental health services. It is well understood that child sexual abuse victims have a range of common and disturbing responses to their victimization (see Chapter 1). That is, common referral problems for child sexual abuse victims include symptoms associated with trauma (e.g., nightmares, dissociation), depression (e.g., sadness, decreased concentration), cognitive distortions (e.g., worthlessness, shame), and sexually reactive behavior. Less commonly recognized referral problems for which some sexually victimized children seek treatment include exhibiting disruptive, defiant, and oppositional behavior in response to their sexual victimization. Although it can reasonably be argued that any type of victimization can lead to anger and defiance—the range of responses that lead to a specific child being labeled as defiant/oppositional can be complicated to determine. For example, we know that some victims of child sexual abuse experience concurrent physically aggressive events, such as exposure to domestic violence or child physical abuse (Jouriles & Norwood, 1995). There is a wealth of literature describing the experience of violence (i.e., being abused) and exposure to violence (i.e., exposure to domestic violence) as a significant predictor of aggressive, noncompliant, defiant behavior in children (e.g., Milner, 2000). This pattern of disruptive child behavior appears to derive from a combination of parents' frequent modeling of aggressive and hostile behavior, and the child's own angry emotional responses and resulting oppositional behavior tied to being raised in such coercive and hostile environments.

It is also important to include the absence of positive, warm, and nurturing parenting (something also found within violent families) as a contributor to children's disruptive behavior problems (Fantuzzo et al., 1991). Some victims of child sexual abuse live in families with chaotic lifestyles in which consistent and positive parent-child relationships are infrequent or nearly nonexistent. This may also lead to some victims of child sexual abuse exhibiting behavioral problems not directly related to their sexual victimization, but related to the overall chaotic and dysfunctional lifestyle in which they were raised. More simply stated, although children who are sexually abused can come from diverse backgrounds, it should be understood that *some* child sexual abuse victims live in families in which they have concurrent problems that will lead to their presentation of defiance and aggression *not directly* related to symptoms associated with their sexual victimization. In fact, there is some indication that child sexual abuse victims are likely to be overrepresented in families with other types of mental health, substance abuse, and/or violence-related problems (Capaldi, Kim, & Pears, 2009). Of course, the population of children who have disruptive behavioral problems resulting from inconsistent and poor parenting is exactly the reason that PCIT was developed, and is the group for which PCIT is most effective. It should therefore not be a surprise that PCIT is a valuable intervention for children with disruptive behavioral problems who are also victims of child sexual abuse.

Child Sexual Abuse Victims Have Trauma Symptoms One of the more consistent findings with young children who have experienced sexual victimization is the presence of one or more traditional trauma-related symptom(s) or symptom cluster(s) including nightmares, hypervigilence, anxiety, behavioral disturbance (anger outbursts, noncompliance, and aggression), and affective dysregulation (temper tantrums, crying, whining). It is important to note a distinction between younger and older children and their responses to trauma; younger children appear to be more responsive to the stability (or lack of stability) of parental functioning, and older children less likely to be adversely impacted by parent instability. In particular, younger children (i.e., toddlers, preschool-age) are highly responsive to parent cues of affective stability and distress related to childhood sexual victimization, often because their means of coping is still co-regulated by the parent, whereas older children (i.e., school-age, adolescents) tend to rely more on their own coping skills and cognitions, may be more independent from distress experienced by a parent figure, and may develop other sources of support (e.g., peers, extended kin). Because of this, approaches to treatment with younger children are likely to be more effective if the intervention includes both the parent and child (Runyon, Deblinger, Ryan, & Thakkar-Kolar, 2004).

Recently, research has shown young traumatized children to have a significant reduction in trauma symptoms as a result of their involvement in PCIT (Mannarino, Lieberman, Urquiza, & Cohen, 2010). This finding—that a behavioral, intensive parenting program would result in a reduction of trauma symptoms—may be initially puzzling to some. However, on closer inspection, there are several reasons why young traumatized children—including children traumatized as a result of their sexual victimization—would benefit from PCIT. These include:

- *Management of disruptive behavior.* As stated earlier, some sexually abused children come from chaotic and dysfunctional families, and therefore are consistently exposed to poor and inconsistent parenting, which leads them to exhibit defiant, oppositional, and aggressive behavior, which then qualifies them as an appropriate match for PCIT. There are also indications that support the notion that externalizing behavior problems are a direct result of exposure to a traumatic event (Valentino, Berkowitz, & Stover, 2010). For some children, their traumatic response is exhibited through defiant and disruptive behaviors. It should therefore not be a surprise that helping parents manage their child's disruptive behavior in a positive, consistent, and firm manner—which is an objective of PCIT—should result in a decrease in trauma symptoms.
- *Improved child relationship security and stability with their primary caregiver.* In addition to the management of challenging child behavior, PCIT also provides for a more positive and supportive parent-child

relationship. One of the avenues to recovery from sexual victimization involves eliciting support from important caregivers. That is, supportive parenting is associated with positive child outcomes in many domains (Greenberg, 1999; Kim et al., 2003)—especially when a child is required to deal with some type of adverse experience. Therefore, it is essential to sustain a positive parent-child relationship and parental support in order to optimize the child's ability to deal with any adverse or abusive experience, including child sexual abuse. The combination of parental stress associated with child sexual abuse and problematic child symptoms can erode a parent's ability to be supportive, warm, and understanding. One benefit of PCIT is that it provides a mechanism to strengthen the parent-child relationship through coaching of positive affiliative behaviors (e.g., praising, physical affection). Throughout PCIT, there is an emphasis on assisting parents to recognize and verbally deliver positive statements to their child (concurrently, there is an emphasis to fail to acknowledge minor negative and inappropriate behaviors) in an effort to help parents maintain a warm and supportive relationship with their child. It is important to remember that the early foundation of PCIT derives from Eyberg's (2004) effort to create an intervention that emulated two early pioneers in play therapy— Axline (1947) and Guerney (1964). In her description of the origin of PCIT, Eyberg (2004) explained that she supported the play therapy goals and techniques proposed by the Axline and Guerney's therapeutic approaches, which promoted warmth and acceptance. Eyberg believed that developing an intervention that promoted the healthiest parenting style, authoritative parenting (Baumrind, 1966, 1967), which included the combination of nurturing interaction, clear communication, and firm limit-setting, was the best approach (Eyberg, 2004).

- *Parents as therapists: Supporting parent-child communication.* Although there are many perspectives on what exactly constitutes psychotherapy, there is a rich literature describing parents functioning in a supportive, therapeutic-like role with their child (see Guerney, 2000; L. Guerney & B. Guerney, 1987; Hutton, 2004). The central aspects of this type of filial therapy relationship include (1) a positive relationship between a child and parent, (2) focus on development of appropriate and safe expression/communication, and (3) the use of the medium of play as a central theme (Urquiza, Zebell, & Blacker, 2009). Within PCIT, parents are provided direct instruction about how to engage their child in positive and collaborative play (especially in the first component of PCIT). As a result, there is typically a more warm, supportive, and affectionate relationship developed between the parent and child. Often, this includes positive verbal statements and physical affection exhibited by both the parent and the child. Similarly, the focus on safe and effective communication is a central tenet to PCIT. Parents are directed to communicate issues of safety, concern for the child's well-being, and positive regard for all appropriate and nonaggressive/hostile interactions. Because involvement in play activities is generally perceived by both parent and child as positive and enjoyable, sharing such activities within a PCIT session contributes to the overall positive experience that both parent and child convey toward each other while strengthening the communication between the dyad. This allows the parent to be more responsive to a child who has been victimized.

- *Management of the sexually abused child's affect.* It is well recognized that traumatized young children have difficulty managing their feelings relative to emotionally difficult situations. At the same time young children have underdeveloped coping skills and a limited understanding of the traumatic experience they have endured. In addition to developing a more positive and secure parent-child relationship, PCIT can also directly address many of the feelings that a child experiences. Consistent throughout common PCIT protocol is the identification of the child's thoughts, feelings, and behaviors. Should a child experience some type of unpleasant affect, especially an affect related to feelings of anger, frustration, embarrassment, and shame, which are often felt by sexually abused children, parents are coached to recognize and describe these feelings to the child. As children have the experience of the feeling paired with the label presented by parents, they begin to understand the meaning of the distressing affect, which is one of the first steps to being able to discuss and manage these feelings. As children continue to understand these feelings, then parents can assist them in learning to engage in some strategies to manage these feelings (e.g., deep breathing, counting, progressive relaxation).

Danielle—A Case Example

Danielle was a 5-year-old Caucasian girl referred to PCIT by her child protective services social worker. She was referred to mental health services due to cruelty to small animals, oppositional behavior, and aggressiveness. In addition to a history of aggression toward adults, she was physically aggressive toward her infant brother

(continued)

(e.g., purposefully dropping brother, attempting to smother brother with a pillow). Prior to placement with child protective services, Danielle had been living with her biological parents (and her infant brother and 8-year-old sister). Both parents had substance abuse and mental health problems, although at the time Danielle was placed in protective custody her parents were no longer living together and she was removed from her mother's care. Court records indicate that Danielle's mother allowed several men to sexually victimize her so that the mother could acquire illegal drugs from these men. At intake for mental health services, Danielle was given *DSM-IV-TR* diagnoses of oppositional defiant disorder and posttraumatic stress disorder. Additionally, an evaluation of her intellectual ability indicated that she was of "low average" intellectual functioning. Because Danielle was a dependent, she was brought to the outpatient mental health clinic by her foster mother. She eventually participated in PCIT with her foster mother. Administration of two standardized parent-report assessment measures indicated that Danielle was in the clinically significant range on scales of aggressiveness, defiance, and disruptive behavior—consistent with her foster mother's verbal report. Because the initial portion of PCIT sessions emphasizes positive parent-child interactions and eliminating negative interactions, parents are informed, then coached, to provide a *Praise* for desired behavior, to *Describe* any appropriate behavior the child exhibits, to *Reflect* back to the child any desired and appropriate statements, and to avoid delivering *Questions, Commands,* and *Critical Statements.* At the beginning of each treatment session, parent and child are asked to play with each other, and the parent is directed (without coaching) to utilize the PRIDE skills (See Table 12.1) while concurrently avoiding Questions/Commands/Critical statements. The therapist-coach observes and "codes" (i.e., maintains a frequency count) the parent and child playing, while coding each parent statement. By carefully tracking each coded interaction, the therapist can assess client progress and shift the focus of treatment to emphasize a particular skill (e.g., if parent praises are low, then they are encouraged/prompted to deliver additional praises). Consistent with most parents who are tasked with parenting very difficult children, the foster mother's delivery of praises was relatively lower than other codes at the beginning of treatment (see Figure 12.1). Because of the severity and chronic nature of Danielle's defiant and oppositional behavior, Danielle's foster mother had initial difficulty ignoring Danielle's

(continued)

(continued)

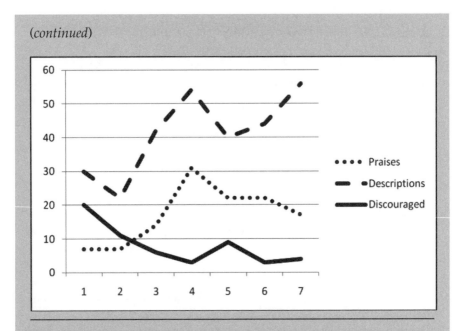

Figure 12.1   PCIT Treatment Sessions 1–7, Dyadic Parent-Child Interaction Coding System
Note: For clarity, Labeled and Unlabeled Praises are combined; Reflections and Descriptions are combined; and Questions/Commands/Critical Statements are combined as "Discouraged." Also, because Danielle's younger brother joined treatment sessions in the second half of PCIT, only data from the first half of PCIT (with Danielle and her foster mother) are included.

minor inappropriate behavior (e.g., whining, complaining, minor temper tantrums) and delivering consistent praises. During the second session, the foster mother reported that Danielle was observed "spanking" her younger brother. After the third session, the foster mother began reporting that Danielle's negative behavior at home lessened slightly (this was concurrently observed in the treatment session). By the fifth treatment session, the foster mother reported significant improvements in Danielle's behavior, and expressed that Danielle seemed to be generally happier. At the sixth session, the foster mother described an incident in which Danielle was watching a television program about a mother who gave her child up for adoption and stated, "I am sad, because if it was my child,

(continued)

I would fight for them." The foster mother explained that Danielle was crying while she made this statement—and it provided an opportunity for Danielle and the foster mother to have a discussion about adoption and being safe. Danielle continued to improve in PCIT sessions, while the foster mother reported that there continued to be positive behavior changes within the home. At approximately the tenth week of treatment, Danielle's 8-year-old sister was also placed in the foster home (with Danielle and her younger brother). This resulted in two difficult weeks, with Danielle increasing her defiant and oppositional behavior, destroying toys, and having multiple temper tantrums. The therapist engaged in discussions with the foster mother, explaining that the addition of the older sister represented a change that was difficult for Danielle to manage, then encouraged the foster mother to maintain the PRIDE skills at home, while encouraging Danielle to express her feelings verbally. After two weeks, Danielle's behavior once again lessened and her prior happier demeanor returned. At the 17th treatment session, it was jointly decided by the parent and therapist to end PCIT because Danielle's behavior had improved and remained stable (see Figure 12.1). After a reassessment of Danielle's case, the foster mother reported no elevated scores on the two previously administered behavioral measures. She reported greater confidence in managing Danielle's behavior and much less stress in the role of parenting. Additionally, the only concern expressed by the foster mother was that Danielle had nightmares and hypervigilence. As such, Danielle received a referral for trauma-focused therapy upon completion of PCIT. Finally, after completion of treatment the therapist was contacted by the foster mother and informed that the foster mother and her husband had decided to seek adoption of Danielle.

The *Dyadic Parent-Child Interaction Coding System – III* (*DPICS-III*; Eyberg, Nelson, Duke, & Boggs, 2005) was designed to assess the quality of parent-child social interactions through observations of dyads in a clinic setting. Frequency counts for parental and child behaviors are recorded during 5-minute standard situations at the beginning of each treatment session. Although the *DPICS-III* has the potential to code many different types of behavior, only three sets of codes were recorded for this case (Praises; Descriptions and Reflections; and Questions/Commands/Critical Statements).

CONCLUSION

In summary, PCIT is an effective and well-researched intervention not commonly recognized as an intervention for children who are victims of child sexual abuse. However, it is important to understand that child sexual abuse victims have both family characteristics (e.g., poor parenting, experience of child physical abuse, exposure to domestic violence, parental mental health or substance abuse problems) and symptoms directly associated with their sexual victimization (trauma symptoms, affective dysregulation, behavioral disturbance) that fall within the domain of appropriate presenting problems for PCIT. A closer examination of the origins of PCIT, the theoretical frameworks thought to underlie the changes in parent-child relationships, and recent research highlighting the value of PCIT for traumatized children bring to light the value of PCIT as one of the most effective tools available today for improving parenting skills, decreasing child behavioral problems, and enhancing the quality (i.e., warmth and acceptance) of parent-child relationships, all of which are important in treating young traumatized and sexually abused children with behavioral problems. These three elements combine to make PCIT a very appropriate intervention for some—but not all—sexually abused children. Some limitations should be noted. First, it is recommended that PCIT is not appropriate for parents who have a history of sexual offending. Specifically, efforts to strengthen the sexually offending parent and sexually victimized child relationship is not generally supported and should be undertaken with great caution. The notion of providing a mental health intervention that increases the amount of control an offending parent has over a child is, at best, very problematic, but more likely inappropriate. Also, PCIT is not an appropriate intervention for sexually abused children who *do not* have behavioral problems. There may be benefits from administering the CDI portion of PCIT to a parent-child dyad in which the child exhibits no behavioral problems (i.e., strengthening the quality of the relationship between the parent and child), but this should be perceived as the exception rather than a common course of treatment for sexually abused children. Instead, child sexual abuse victims who have no disruptive behavioral problems are more likely to benefit from other evidence-based interventions such as trauma-focused cognitive-behavioral therapy (Cohen & Mannarino, 2008) or Combined Parent-Child Cognitive-Behavioral Therapy (Runyon, Deblinger, & Schroeder, 2009). Finally, sexually abused children who receive PCIT may benefit from additional mental health services after the completion of PCIT sessions. As was reported with Danielle, some mental health symptoms (e.g., nightmares) may be best addressed through a nonbehavioral approach.

However, addressing such symptoms is likely to be much easier when the problems of aggression, defiance, and oppositionality are resolved. It may be that PCIT is an intervention that has many positive attributes, but the most significant lies in its ability to generate a positive, supportive, nurturing, and warm parent-child relationship, which is the foundation of both a healthy family and positive child outcomes.

REFERENCES

Abinin, R. R. (1995). *Parenting stress index (PSI)*. (3rd ed.). Odessa: FL. Psychological Assessment Resources.

Achenbach, T. M., & Ruffle, T. M. (2000). The Child Behavior Checklist and related forms for assessing behavioral/emotional problems and competencies. *Pediatrics in Review, 21*, 265–271.

Axline, V. (1947, 1989). *Play therapy*. London: Ballantine Books.

Baumrind, D. (1966). Effects of authoritative parental control on child behavior. *Child Development, 37*(4), 887–907.

Baumrind, D. (1967). Child care practices anteceding three patterns of preschool behavior. *Genetic Psychology Monographs, 75*(1), 43–88.

Borrego, J., & Urquiza, A. J. (1998). Importance of therapist use of social reinforcement with parents as a model for parent-child relationships: An example with parent-child interaction therapy. *Child & Family Behavior Therapy, 20*(4), 27–54.

Brestan, E., Eyberg, S., Boggs, S., & Algina, J. (1997). Parent-child interaction therapy: Parents; perceptions of untreated siblings. *Child & Family Behavior Therapy, 3*, 13–28.

Capaldi, D. M., Kim, H. K., & Pears, K. C. (2009). The association between partner violence and child maltreatment: A common conceptual framework. In D. J. Whitaker & J. R. Lutzker (Eds.), *Preventing partner violence: Research and evidence-based intervention strategies* (pp. 93–111). Washington, DC: American Psychological Association.

Chadwick Center for Children and Families. (2004). *Closing the quality chasm in child abuse treatment: Identifying and disseminating best practices*. San Diego, CA: Author.

Chaffin, M., Silovsky, J., Funderburk, B., Valle, L., Brestan, E., Balachova, T., Jackson, S., Lensgraf, J., & Bonner, B. (2004). Parent-child interaction therapy with physically abusive parents. Efficacy for reducing future abuse reports. *Journal of Consulting and Clinical Psychology, 72*, 491–499.

Cohen, J. A., & Mannarino, A. P. (2008). Trauma-focused cognitive behavioral therapy for children and parents. *Child and Adolescent Mental Health, 13*(4), 158–162.

Eisenstadt, T. H., Eyberg, S.M., McNeil, C. B., Newcomb, K., & Funderburk, B. (1993). Parent-child interaction therapy with behavior problem children: Relative effectiveness of two stages and overall treatment outcome. *Journal of Clinical Child Psychology, 22*(1), 42–51.

Eyberg, S. M. (1988). PCIT: Integration of traditional and behavioral concerns. *Child & Family Behavior Therapy, 10*, 33–46.

Eyberg, S. M. (2004) The PCIT story-part one: The conceptual foundation of PCIT. *The Parent-Child Interaction Therapy Newsletter, 1*(1), 1–2.

Eyberg, S. M., Funderburk, B., Hembree-Kigin, T., McNeil, C., Querido, J., & Hood, K. (2001). Parent-child interaction therapy with behavior problem children: One and two year maintenance of treatment effects in the family. *Child & Family Behavior Therapy, 23,* 1–20.

Evyerg, S. M., Nelson, M. M., Duke, M., & Boggs, S. R.(2005). *Manual for the dyadic parent-child interaction coding system* (3rd ed.). Available online at www.PCIT .org.

Eyberg, S., & Pincus, D. (1999). *Eyberg child behavior inventory and Sutter-Eyberg student behavior inventory-Revised. Professional Manual.* Odessa, FL: Psychological Assessment Resources.

Eyberg, S., & Robinson, E. A. (1982). Parent-child interaction training: Effects on family functioning. *Journal of Clinical Child Psychology, 11*(2), 130–137.

Eyberg, S., & Robinson, E. A. (1983). Conduct problem behavior: Standardization of a behavioral rating scale with adolescents. *Journal of Clinical Child Psychology, 12,* 347–354.

Fantuzzo, J. W., DePaola, L. M., Lambert, L., Martino, T., Anderson, T., & Sutton, B. (1991). Effects of interparental violence on the psychological adjustment and competencies of young children. *Journal of Consulting and Clinical Psychology, 59*(2), 258–265.

Funderburk, B., Eyberg, S., Newcomb, K., McNeil, C., Hembree-Kigin, T., & Capage, L. (1998). Parent-child interaction therapy with behavior problem children: Maintenance of treatment effects in the school setting. *Child & Family Behavior Therapy, 20,* 17–38.

Greenberg, M. T. (1999). Attachment and psychopathology in childhood. In J. Cassidy & P. R. Shaver (Eds.), *Handbook of attachment: Theory, research, and clinical applications* (pp. 469–496). New York, NY: Guilford Press.

Guerney, L. (2000). Filial therapy into the 21st century. *International Journal of Play Therapy, 9*(2), 1–17.

Guerney, L., & Guerney, B. (1987). Integrating child and family therapy. *Psychotherapy, 24,* 609–614.

Guerney, B., Jr. (1964). Filial therapy: Description and rationale. *Journal of Consulting Psychology, 28*(4), 304–310.

Hood, K., & Eyberg, S. (2003). Outcomes of parent-child interaction therapy: Mothers' reports of maintenance three to six years after treatment. *Journal of Clinical Child & Adolescent Psychology, 32,* 412–429.

Hutton, D. (2004). Filial therapy: Shifting the balance. *Clinical Child Psychology and Psychiatry, 9*(2), 1359–1045.

Jouriles, E. N., & Norwood, W. D. (1995). Physical aggression toward boys and girls in families characterized by the battering of women. *Journal of Family Psychology, 9,* 69–78.

Kim, I. J., Ge, X., Brody, G. H., Conger, R., Gibbons, F. X., & Simons, R. I. (2003). Parenting behaviors and the occurrence and co-occurrence of depressive symptoms and conduct problems among African American children. *Depression, Marriage, & Families, 17,* 571–583.

Leung, C., Tsang, S., & Heung, K. (2007, January). *Evaluation of the effectiveness of parent-child interaction therapy (PCIT) in treating families with children with behavior problems in Hong Kong.* Presented at the 7th Annual National PCIT Conference. Oklahoma City, OK.

Mannarino, A., Lieberman, A., Urquiza, A., & Cohen, J. (2010, August). *Evidence-based treatments for traumatized children.* 118th Annual Convention of the American Psychological Association, San Diego, CA.

Matos, M., Torres, R., Santiago, R., Jurado, M., & Rodriguez, I. (2006). Adaptation of parent-child interaction therapy for Puerto Rican families: A preliminary study. *Family Process, 45,* 205–222.

McCabe, K. M., Yeh, M., Garland, A. F., Lau, A. S., & Chavez, G. (2005). The GANA program: A tailoring approach to adapting parent-child interaction therapy for Mexican Americans. *Education and Treatment of Children, 28,* 111–129.

McNeil, C. B., Eyberg, S., Eisenstadt, T. H., Newcomb, K., & Funderbunk, B. (1991). Parent-child interaction therapy with behavior problem children: Generalization of treatment effects to the school setting. *Journal of Clinical Child Psychology, 20*(2), 140–151.

McNeil, C. B., & Hembree-Kigin, T. (2010). *Parent-child interaction therapy* (2nd ed.). New York, NY: Plenum.

Milner, J. S. (2000). Social information processing and child physical abuse: Theory and research. In D. J. Hansen (Ed.), *Nebraska symposium on motivation Vol. 46: Motivation and child maltreatment* (pp. 39–84). Lincoln, NE: University of Nebraska Press.

Runyon, M. K., Deblinger, E., Ryan, E. E., & Thakkar-Kolar, R. (2004). An overview of child physical abuse: Developing an integrated parent-child cognitive-behavioral treatment approach. *Trauma, Violence, & Abuse, 5*(1), 65–85.

Runyon, M. K., Deblinger, E., & Schroeder, C. M. (2009). Pilot evaluation of outcomes of combined parent-child cognitive-behavioral group therapy for families at-risk for child physical abuse. *Cognitive Behavioral Practice, 16,* 101–118.

Saunders, B. E., Berliner, L., & Hanson, R. F. (Eds.). (2004). Child physical and sexual abuse: Guidelines for treatment (Revised Report: April 26, 2004). Charleston, SC: National Crime Victims Research and Treatment Center.

Subia-Bigfoot, D., & Funderburk, B. (2006). *Parent child interaction therapy (PCIT) for Native children.* Presented at the 6th Annual National PCIT Conference. Gainesville, FL.

Timmer, S. G., Urquiza, A. J., Herschell, A., McGrath, J., Zebell, N., Porter, A., & Vargas, E. (2006). Parent-child interaction therapy: Application of an empirically supported treatment to maltreated children in foster care. *Child Welfare, 85*(6), 919–940.

Timmer, S. G., Urquiza, A. J., & Zebell, N. (2006). Challenging foster caregiver-maltreated child relationships: The effectiveness of parent child interaction therapy. *Child and Youth Services Review,* (28), 1–19.

Timmer, S., Urquiza, A. J., Zebell, N., & McGrath, J. (2005). Parent-child interaction therapy: Application to physically abusive and high-risk parent-child dyads. *Child Abuse & Neglect, 29*(7), 825–842.

Timmer, S., Urquiza, A. J., & Zebell, N. (2007, November) *Parent-child interaction therapy: Trauma treatment for young children.* Presentation at the 23rd Annual Meeting of the International Society on Traumatic Stress Studies (ISTSS). Baltimore, MD.

Timmer, S. G., Ware, L., Zebell, N., & Urquiza, A. (2010). The effectiveness of Parent-Child Interaction Therapy for victims of interparental violence. *Violence and Victims, 25*(4), 486–503.

Urquiza, A. J., Porter, A., Timmer, S. G., Klisanac, L., Zebell, N., & McGrath, J. (2007, September). Dissemination of parent-child interaction therapy: What are the outcomes? Paper presented at the 7th Annual PCIT conference. Oklahoma City, OK.

Urquiza, A. J., & Timmer, S. G. (2008, February). *Trauma symptom reduction with delivery of Parent-child interaction therapy services.* 22nd Annual San Diego International Conference on Child and Family maltreatment. San Diego, CA.

Urquiza, A. J., Zebell, N. M., & Blacker, D. (2009). Innovation and integration: Parent-child interaction therapy as play therapy. In A. D. Drewes (Ed.), *Blending play therapy with cognitive behavioral therapy: Evidence-based and other effective treatments and techniques* (pp. 199–218). New York, NY: John Wiley & Sons.

Valentino, K., Berkowitz, S., & Stover, C. S. (2010). Parenting behaviors and posttraumatic symptoms in relation to children's symptomatology following a traumatic event. *Journal of Traumatic Stress, 23*(3), 403–407.

Weisz, J. R., & Gray, J. S. (2007). Evidence-based psychotherapy for children and adolescents: Data from the present and a model for the future. *ACAMH Occasional Papers No. 27. Evidence-based Psychotherapies in CAMHS,* 7–22.

Zisser, A., & Eyberg, S. M. (2010). Treating oppositional behavior in children using parent-child interaction therapy. In A. E. Kazdin & J. R. Weisz (Eds.), *Evidence-based psychotherapies for children and adolescents* (2nd ed). New York, NY: Guilford Press.

CHAPTER 13

Flexibly Sequential Play Therapy (FSPT) With Sexually Victimized Children

PARIS GOODYEAR-BROWN

INTRODUCTION

FLEXIBLY SEQUENTIAL PLAY therapy (FSPT) is a developmentally sensitive, components-based model for treating children and adolescents with posttraumatic symptomatology. In the past 20 years, consensus has grown regarding both the kinds of treatment goals that are appropriate for traumatized children and the general order in which these goals should be pursued. Goals are sequenced in an order that allows for careful stabilization, safety building, augmentation of positive coping, and soothing the physiology with our most vulnerable clients while allowing for more focused treatment and more rapid resolution of existing symptoms when a child presents with multiple resiliencies.

Many of the goals embedded within this model mirror those delineated in Trauma-Focused Cognitive-Behavioral Therapy (TF-CBT) (Deblinger, Cohen, & Mannarino, 2006; Fitzgerald & Cohen, this volume), the most efficacious and thoroughly tested treatment for traumatized children (Silverman et al., 2008). The integration of and heavy reliance on developmentally sensitive mediums, including play and other forms of expression (art, sand tray) in the pursuit of each treatment goal and in the pervasive work of gradual exposure, is fundamental to the FSPT model. Sometimes this integration takes the form of directive, prop-based interventions that target specific therapeutic content related to coping, emotional literacy, soothing the physiology, addressing the thought life, and trauma narrative work. At other times, the medium of play and the metaphoric manipulation that can occur in the child's natural language takes the place of a strictly linguistic process. The mediums of play, art, and sand are particularly effective in encouraging children to confront their trauma specific anxiety, as the positive feelings engendered by engaging in these expressive therapies counter the toxicity of the trauma content (Gil, 2010; Goodyear-Brown, 2010). For example, choosing a miniature to represent the perpetrator and then allowing the child an opportunity to be in charge of its manipulation or containment can serve as an initial approach to extremely anxiety-provoking memories. The goals of the (FSPT) model are mapped in sequence below (see Figure 13.1). Another seminal concept within FSPT is that both directive and nondirective interventions can be useful at different points in treatment (Gil, 2006; Goodyear-Brown, 2010; Schaefer, 2001; Shelby & Felix, 2005). In some cases a child may use the fully equipped playroom almost reflexively to move toward the trauma content. More often, however, avoidance symptoms necessitate the gentle invitations made through prop-based directive interventions.

PROPS IN TREATMENT

Prop-based intervention (PBI) is a core element of the FSPT model. The younger the child, the greater the importance of integrating PBIs as they provide a scaffolding on which the therapeutic learning can be hung. Three constructs inform the decision to integrate props into all components of this trauma treatment model. First, a prop serves as an anchor for whatever therapeutic learning is being conveyed. Children have a natural bent toward physical engagement, so the use of props decreases resistance while allowing for therapeutic content, particularly as it relates to psychoeducation and skills training, to be more easily digested. If, for example, colorful buttons are used to help clients expand their emotional literacy around anger, the buttons that are sent home with the clients can serve as a visual reminder of the therapeutic content that was communicated. Second, new understandings about how people learn have influenced the prominence of props in this model. People are wired for learning in a variety of ways. Some are auditory learners, some are visual learners, and some are kinesthetic learners. Developmental theorists agree that children are first kinesthetic learners. They learn by doing. They may also be secondarily wired for visual or auditory learning. The use of props in therapy allows for children to manipulate appealing, developmentally appropriate objects while also being auditorially and visually stimulated,

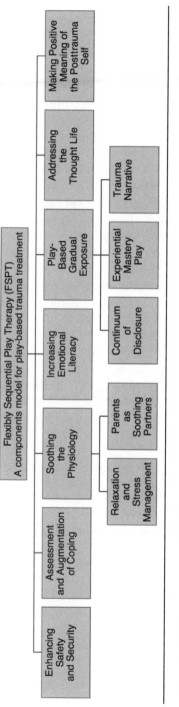

Figure 13.1 Components of FSPT

299

effectively accessing all three modes of learning. Third, and sometimes most importantly, is the value of the prop as a transitional object from the safety of the therapeutic space and the safety of the person of the therapist to the child's other life arenas. Some of our child clients cannot claim the same level of perceived safety in any other environment as that experienced in the therapeutic relationship. Maximizing this relationship and translating its benefits outside of the playroom can offset the tenuous emotional safety that clients may experience in other environments. An example of the use of a prop to serve these three purposes follows.

A subset of child sexual abuse survivors face intense nighttime anxieties. In FSPT, the umbrella treatment goal of soothing the physiology is practically communicated through a variety of PBIs, one of which teaches a deep-breathing procedure with the use of a pinwheel as an external focal point. The pinwheel anchors the initial psychoeducation and aids in skill rehearsal during the session. After these clients have been taught the breathing procedures, they are given a glow-in-the-dark pinwheel and asked to practice their deep breathing each evening by making the glow in the dark pinwheel spin in their darkened rooms. The prop serves as a reminder of the in-office skill practice and aids in skill retention at home, grounding the therapeutic learning. Additionally, the physical act of taking repeated deep breaths counters the anxiety that often arises as sexually abused children prepare for bed. The physiological relaxation is supported by the luminescent glow in the darkness as the glow-in-the-dark pinwheel becomes an external focal point and a connection between the safety of the playroom/play therapist and this nighttime environment.

COMPONENTS OF TREATMENT

The components of the FSPT model will be discussed individually in the following sections. Keep in mind that the length of time spent pursuing each treatment goal will vary based on individual case dynamics. Moreover, when a child client arrives at the point in treatment when play-based trauma narrative work begins or a play-based gradual exposure program is created, it is not unusual for the clinician to return briefly to earlier treatment components to enhance specific coping strategies or establish deeper levels of safety as these more difficult parts of treatment are approached.

ENHANCING A SENSE OF SAFETY AND SECURITY

Clinicians are unable to ensure the safety of clients in their myriad environments. However, we are charged with helping our clients experience a sense of safety within the four walls of our offices. The experience of safety in the playroom is often augmented by a child's active, kinesthetic involvement with the space. We can promote experiences of safety within the unique environment of the playroom. Although our intentional words, "You are safe in here," can offer verbal reassurances, the perceived level of safety can be most deeply felt as the child actively constructs the safety within the playroom. Not all children need this physical involvement, but the playroom lends itself to this use for all who do. An example follows.

Joey, an 8-year-old boy, was sexually abused by his uncle during a family reunion at the beach one year prior to his referral for treatment. Joey, on entering the playroom, explored the environment for several minutes and then chose a black-and-green miniature monster. The monster's two heads—one at the top of his body and the other attached to the end of his arm—were each dominated by a mouth full of fangs. Joey stated, "He's a bad man," and then, as he examined the toy more closely, "He's got two kinds of badness." Joey then chose two large army figures and said, "This is my dad and this is Buddy (dad's best friend)." He put all three figures in the sand tray and then chose a miniature sofa and attached one of the heads of the two-headed monster to the sofa with a pair of miniature handcuffs and placed each of his protectors (dad and dad's best friend) on either side of the chained monster. Then he said, "He's chained up now." We explored what it felt like to have the two-headed monster tied up. Joey said, "He can't hurt anybody now." We took a picture of the arrangement of miniatures and helped Joey re-create the picture in his head so that he could visualize the containment of this symbol when he was feeling anxious in other environments.

A figurine of a two-headed monster chosen to represent an uncle who sexually abused a child client is infinitely more approachable than the perpetrator himself. The child's choice of a two-headed monster hints at the perceived duality with which survivors wrestle when grappling with dimensions of the perpetrator's behavior. The majority of child sexual abuse crimes are committed by adults who are familiar to the child (Finkelhor, Ormrod, & Turner, 2009; Finkelhor, Ormrod, Turner, & Hamby, 2005; Putnam, 2003). This statistic increases the likelihood that sexually abused children will have some experiences of the perpetrator's behavior in benign or even enjoyable settings. Children may have difficulty reconciling these aspects of a perpetrator's public persona with the abusive acts they have experienced. The more dichotomous the child's thinking, the more difficult this reconciliation may be. The containment of these perpetrator symbols in play is one of the ways that young children begin to establish a sense of safety within the playroom. Within the four walls of the playroom, children come up with idiosyncratic solutions for handling a perceived threat. If the miniature weapons are perceived as threatening, the child may hide all the weapons. In other cases, the solution a child might implement takes the form of insisting that everyone whisper during the session "so that the bad guys won't know what we are planning." Sometimes bigger, stronger helping figures are enlisted in the play. Sometimes the therapist is asked to actively join the child in making the playroom safe. This might involve killing all the bad guys, spraying monster spray in the room, helping the child to boss back a perpetrator symbol, or grapple with a specific three dimensional representation of a cognitive distortion, or any number of other processes. In essence, the invitation that play offers children to become kinesthetically involved expands the range of therapeutic possibility.

A range of more specific interventions can be used that reinforce existing safe places for the client or guide the client in creating new safety images. Sand trays, art, and other play mediums can be used to create external safety images that can be internalized. A child's sensory impressions of the safe place can be enhanced throgh a series of focused questions, such as, "What can you hear, smell, taste, etc.?"

ASSESSING THE CHILD'S CURRENT COPING REPERTOIRE AND
AUGMENTING POSITIVE COPING

Prior to introducing trauma reminders or unpacking the trauma-specific content, it is wise to assess the child's current coping repertoire and to augment the child's positive coping strategies (Deblinger et al., 2006; Felix, Bond, & Shelby, 2006; Kimball, Nelson, & Politano, 1993; Shelby & Berk, 2009). Some children may have natural resiliencies that positively mitigate their responses to the abuse (Bogar & Hulse-Killacky, 2006), while others may have coping impairments that manifest in an array of developmental arenas (Perry, Pollard, Blakely, Baker, & Vigilante, 1995). During coping assessment with children, care must be taken to create an atmosphere in which the child can share both adaptive and maladaptive coping strategies, without prejudging any of them in a way that might curtail the child's honest disclosure. In other words, interventions that allow children to give an exhaustive list of their coping strategies are most helpful (Shelby, Bond, Hall, & Hsu, 2004). Once current coping has been assessed, the therapist can use a variety of playful strategies to educate the client about aspects of positive coping and to augment adaptive coping strategies (Goodyear-Brown, 2010).

SOOTHING THE PHYSIOLOGY

Many children who have experienced sexual abuse have also experienced other forms of victimization (Brady & Caraway, 2002; Copeland et al., 2007; Felitti et al., 1998; Finkelhor, Ormrod, & Turner, 2007, 2009). The severity of clinical symptomatology is often correlated to the level of threat experienced and the invasiveness of the sexual abuse (i.e., the level of violence involved, penetration versus nonpenetration [Boney-McCoy & Finklehor, 1996; Gidycz & Koss, 1989]). Many children who have been sexually abused have developed a pattern of hypervigilance as a response to the trauma. They are constantly aware of the nuances of the world around them and live in a state of hyperarousal, continually scanning the environment for hints of potential danger. Any therapeutic activity that offers an experience of relaxation and allows children an opportunity to decrease their level of physiological arousal can be beneficial.

The suggestion to relax may have particularly dangerous associations for a sexual abuse survivor. Perpetrators, intent on soothing an understandably escalated victim, may murmur encouragements to "loosen up" or "take it easy" while inflicting harm on their victims. Clinicians should choose their words carefully when assisting a client in managing stress reactions so as to avoid triggering the client's learned wariness. For these children, the relaxing of one's guard is often accompanied by a sense of impending threat. When the dire consequences that a sexually traumatized child expects do not accompany the relaxation, the conditioned association between relaxation and danger can be weakened. The brain that has been trained to equate heightened states of physiological arousal with a sense of normalcy may need titrated doses of exposure to the experience of relaxing in order to shape its tolerance for relaxation. The doses may also need to be short in duration but administered frequently, daily in some cases (Gaskill & Perry, this volume). Nonoffending caregivers can often be recruited to help give children these daily experiences of relaxation and nurture. Therapists can help parents and children to develop a list of soothing rituals such as hair brushing, nail painting, being pushed in a swing set, reading a special book together nightly, and any number of other soothing activities. The FSPT model also offers a variety of prop-based playful activities that encourage relaxation (Goodyear-Brown, 2010).

Parents as Partners

Parents play many roles in the lives of recovering trauma victims. Symptomatic children may need parents to be co-regulators of affect, keepers of their stories, reinforcers of the truth, meaning makers, and celebrators of the children's victories. The co-regulation role that a parent may play in the life of a sexually abused child cannot be overestimated. The younger the child, the more important it is to have parents involved in treatment (Runyon, Deblinger, Ryan, & Thakkar-Kolar, 2004). Children who present for treatment with dysregulation resulting from high levels of anxiety need parents to provide intentionally soothing experiences. Sexually abused children may also exhibit externalizing behavior problems. Parents who perceive these behaviors as simply defiant will discipline the behaviors accordingly. However, parents may sometimes miss the underlying dysregulation issues and inadvertently choose the path of correction when they might choose instead to soothe or co-regulate the child with equally powerful results. It is important that the psychoeducation offered to parents when their children are in trauma treatment includes both streams of information: one related to behavior management strategies and consistent discipline, and the other related to attuned responsiveness and soothing strategies. Initially developed as part of an attachment protocol, a set of strategies that aid parents in de-escalating their children and more effectively managing the anxiety reactions that are often part of a posttraumatic response are presented to parents in FSPT. These skills are codified in the acronym SOOTHE and include: Soft tone of voice and face, Organize, Offer, Touch/Physical Proximity, Hear the underlying anxiety, and let go (Goodyear-Brown, 2009, 2010).

Parent-child interaction therapy (PCIT) (Eyberg, 2004; McNeil & Hembree-Kigin, 2010) is a dyadic treatment approach that allows parents to practice discrete skill sets that may benefit children who have been sexually abused. The positive relationship-enhancement skills taught in this model maximize the potential for the parent to offer effective support during trauma processing. The behavior management skills can equip parents to provide more consistent discipline and reduce the number of externalizing behaviors (Zisser & Eyberg, 2010). As problematic child behaviors decrease, positive parenting increases (Borrego & Urquiza, 1998), and the parent becomes a more easily accessed support figure for the child.

One of the potential consequences of child sexual abuse, particularly when a child has been sexually abused by one parent and unprotected by the other, is the removal of children from their biological homes. Foster and adoptive parents require education on both attachment and trauma dynamics as they relate to the recovery process for these clients. Moreover, children may hope to develop a shared narrative, a story of their past that is shared with the current caregiver. Filial therapy (Guerney, 2000; VanFleet, Ryan, & Smith, 2005) and child-parent relationship therapy (CPRT) (Bratton, Landreth, Kellam, & Blackard, 2006; Landreth & Bratton, 2006; Chapter 14, this volume) are dyadic treatment methods that encourage the parent and child to play together in ways that allow for the communication of the child's story. Inclusion of the parents in trauma narrative clarification and/or rehearsal may also be an important part of the treatment and will be discussed later in this chapter.

EMOTIONAL LITERACY

The emotional vocabulary of children who have been sexually abused, particularly if the abuse has been part of a chronic pattern of polyvictimization, is often impoverished. Children often come to treatment using the term "bad" to describe their primary feeling state. Since exploration of the feelings engendered by different aspects of the abuse may be part of the trauma narrative process, it is wise to target the expansion of emotional vocabulary prior to beginning this narrative work. The term *emotional literacy* includes a child's emotional vocabulary, how well he can articulate feeling states in general, how well he can understand his own emotional reactions, communicate these feelings appropriately, and accurately assess the feeling states of others. Training in this area includes the child's associations between feelings, somatic states, and specific situations; discussion and games that allow for exploration of the nuance of various emotions, and the use of bibliotherapy materials to teach about emotions; and role-plays that help children practice appropriate feelings communications. A variety of specific interventions that target this goal of increasing a client's emotional literacy are more fully articulated elsewhere (Goodyear-Brown, 2002, 2005, 2010).

THE CONTINUUM OF DISCLOSURE

In the context of the FSPT model, disclosure can refer to a child's first articulation of abuse, but more commonly will refer to the child's ongoing gradual exposure process: the process through which the child allows us a glimpse into his story, deals with the anxiety that this exposure to the trauma content brings, and then communicates a little bit more of his story. In either context, the use of play materials allows for children to communicate their story in their primary language. Play comes naturally to children (Schaefer & Drewes, 2009) and the pleasure that is engendered by play mitigates the anxiety related to approaching the trauma content, while leeching the toxicity out of the trauma content through counterconditioning.

Children will often test the therapist by providing a glimpse of the trauma content in the playroom. The therapist's ability to act as a container strong enough and safe enough to handle the trauma content without being overwhelmed will inform a child's decision to give the therapist another glimpse. If the therapist can communicate "I see what you're showing me and you can show me more," the child will come nearer and nearer to the trauma content, often bridging the gap from play behavior to verbal narrative. For example, a 4-year-old boy, during his third session, takes the tail off of a dinosaur and repeatedly shoves a play microphone into the remaining open hole while making guttural sounds. This is the child's first atypical use of the toys and his first communication of abuse. The play is itself an exposure to the anxiety raised by the trauma. The therapist's ability to be a container for the material will invite the child to share more.

Research supports the common clinical assumption that patterns of nondisclosure and recantation exist (Lamb, Hershkowitz, Orbach, & Esplin, 2008; Lyon & Ahern, 2011). The role of the forensic interviewer is to carefully structure language in such a way as to give children every opportunity to disclose without leading the child. The forensic interview may or may not result in an articulated set of details. Once this process has been completed, children often enter a therapeutic relationship. After rapport has been established, children often begin to give us snapshots of the trauma, and as we provide containment and consistently communicate, "I see what you are showing me and you can show me more," we build safety and invite further spontaneous disclosures. While these snapshots of the child's perceptions of the trauma may or may not hold up under the scrutiny of the court, they often help children begin to gather the pieces (thoughts, feelings, sensory impressions) of their traumatic experiences much like a metal detector gathers shrapnel. Indeed, many playful parallels can be made between this prop and stored traumatic memories.

EXPERIENTIAL MASTERY PLAY—A FORM OF GRADUAL EXPOSURE

Children who have been sexually abused often enter treatment feeling disempowered. In order to regain a sense of mastery in relation to their environment, they will often choose figures to represent the perpetrator and other figures to represent self-objects. Children who have experienced abuse often have difficulty allowing themselves to be nurtured. However, if they choose a self-object, the therapist can nurture this object and children can receive the nurture vicariously until they are ready to receive it themselves. Moreover, the miniaturization, through the play materials, of people or dynamics that previously seemed overwhelmingly powerful allows children to feel a sense of mastery and control that previously alluded them. As they experience a sense of competence and master the play-based version of their trauma material, they are empowered to expand their story to become coherent narratives.

TRAUMA NARRATIVE

One of the most important aspects of TF-CBT is the telling of the story of what happened. An integral part of the FSPT model is the allowance it makes for children to tell their story in a variety of ways, many of which may be nonverbal. Although the linguistic imprint may not be easy to access, trauma does leave indelible marks on our most vulnerable charges. If the abuse was experienced prelinguistically, a linguistic imprint may not even exist, making nonverbal reenactment a viable means of narrative expression. A fundamental tenant of the FSPT model is that the narrative may be approached and augmented through a variety of developmentally sensitive, nonlinguistic means.

The dyadic dance that often occurs between children and the content that they perceive as toxic is one that the therapist can support through the use of the playroom. When a sexually abused child presents with post-traumatic stress disorder (PTSD) symptoms that fall within the intrusive or avoidance symptom clusters, exposure to the anxiety-producing content becomes an essential treatment goal. For better or worse, these children must face the parts of the trauma that cause them the most anxiety. Offering children high-interest, age-appropriate tools to represent important aspects of the trauma can empower them to approach the anxiety-producing content. In some cases, child sexual abuse (CSA) survivors may naturally titrate the doses of exposure to the anxiety producing content through the play. A child may talk about her sense of being tainted from the abuse while she is actively washing a female baby doll. One can argue that the act of cleansing the baby doll mitigates the anxiety related to approaching her feelings of dirtiness, allowing her to talk about them briefly. A subset of children will stay in the metaphor they have created to represent the abuse throughout the whole of the trauma narrative phase and experience symptom resolution without bringing the trauma out of metaphor and into reality (Gil, 2006; Goodyear-Brown, 2010).

This makes sense as one considers that the words used to verbalize a trauma may not tap the emotions or sensory impressions of the trauma. The building of a coherent, integrated narrative may best be accomplished for children through art, sand, puppet plays, or other metaphoric expressions. The neurochemical release that often occurs when a child is experiencing a trauma impedes the brain's ability to integrate the sensory aspects of the trauma with the linear, linguistic, logical narrative of the trauma. Children can emerge on the far side of a traumatic event with the ability to talk about what happened without ever experiencing a connection between the verbal narrative and the somatic or affective content related to the event. The FSPT model also offers a set of specific play-based interventions that target a variety of sense memories that may need to be integrated into the trauma narrative (Goodyear-Brown, 2010) in order to give it coherence.

ADDRESSING THE THOUGHT LIFE

This area of work includes identifying cognitive distortions, teaching thought-stopping procedures, challenging cognitive distortions, crafting more helpful cognitions, and rehearsing them and then using them regularly while receiving positive reinforcement for doing the hard work involved in all of these processes. The placement of this goal toward the end of treatment, in the sequential flow of the FSPT model, may give a false impression that this arena is an afterthought. In fact, it is placed after trauma narrative work because of its pivotal importance. Although superficial cognitive distortions and false attributions surrounding why the trauma happened may be identified early in treatment (such as, "It's my fault"), and certainly cognitive coping work can be done early in treatment, children are not likely to reveal their idiosyncratic distortions until they are detailing their trauma narratives. For example, a 10-year-old creates a sand tray, choosing a miniature with a short skirt to represent herself. As the tray is processed, it becomes clear that she believes that her choice to wear the short skirt caused the perpetrator to choose her. This distortion can be challenged, but is not likely to become explicit until the child is wrestling with it in three dimensions.

MAKING POSITIVE MEANING OF THE POSTTRAUMA SELF

It is never the goal of trauma treatment to help the child forget the "bad thing" that happened, but rather to be able to integrate it into a life story that acknowledges suffering and embraces the resilience, hard work, and new knowledge that characterize a child's healing journey. Children who have completed a course of FSPT are often better equipped, in terms of psychoeducation and trauma-specific skills training, than children who have not faced such difficulties. An intentional termination process that allows for a celebration of the client's work and results in a meaningful good-bye with the therapist is important. A range of PBIs that give practical, playful structure to the work of termination exist and can be strategically chosen to support this process (Goodyear-Brown, 2005, 2010, 2010b).

Case Example

Caleb, a 9-year-old boy, was brought to treatment after he developed obsessive-compulsive symptoms related to his sexual abuse. During the initial interview, mom described the series of events that led up to his referral for treatment. Over a period of several years, Rick, a 12-year-old neighborhood kid, developed a friendship with Caleb. Rick's mom, a single mother who worked full time, often left his older sister in charge during the after-school hours. Caleb's mom offered to help out with supervision, and Rick consequently spent more and more time at Caleb's house. On one occasion he spent several nights in a row with them. Caleb's mom would make a palette on the floor in the room that Caleb shared with his sibling. Several months ago, Rick's after-school arrangements changed so that the two boys did not see each other with regularity anymore, and when mom would offer to have Rick spend the night, Caleb showed little interest.

Several weeks prior to mom seeking treatment, Caleb woke up in the middle of the night complaining of an upset stomach. After he vomited, he said, "I want my whole family to go to heaven." Mom reassured him that God loved each of them and would take care of them and then tucked him back into bed. The next day he still seemed upset, and when mom questioned him, he confessed to being worried that mom and dad might die. Caleb's appetite decreased drastically and after several days of not eating, mom again asked Caleb what was wrong, and he said, "Rick had sex with me." Caleb stated that Rick would often crawl into bed with him in the night and ask to "do things." Mom told Caleb how happy she was that he told her. Over the following weeks, Caleb began to disclose more and more details of the abusive incidents to mom. At first mom thought that this was a good sign, but then Caleb began to repeat himself. He would search her out in the house and say, "Did I tell you about him putting his finger in my bottom?" Mom would reassure him that he'd already

(continued)

(*continued*)
told her that part, but he would be compelled to tell her again . . . and again . . . and again. Caleb's family valued their faith and religious practice deeply. Mom recognized, however, that Caleb had morphed the religious parctice of confession into a compulsion. Mom was exhausted. Caleb wasn't eating, his sleep was repeatedly interrupted, and he was continually harassed by anxious thoughts.

During our initial session, I let Caleb know what I knew about the reasons that he was coming to see me. I invited him to explore the playroom. He spent some time examining the various miniatures on the sand-tray shelves and eventually chose the large wire tornado and placed it in the sand. We talked about what it might be like to be a tornado and Caleb said, "All mixed up all the time—like me." Caleb was giving physical form to his internal chaos.

I let him know that I knew about his repetitive thoughts. He jumped on the opening and said, "Yeah . . . if I haven't confessed it out loud, it might not be forgiven." I said, "Sounds like you want to be forgiven for each thing that happened . . . like somehow you are to blame." He replied, "Well yeah, I didn't stop him." FSPT prioritizes the enhancement of safety and security when treating traumatized children, but the specific intervention strategies used to enhance the safety may vary depending on the unique needs and presenting problems of the client. In this case, in order to feel safe, Caleb needed normalization of his feelings, psychoeducation about perpetrator/victim dynamics, and a containment strategy to help with the overwhelming thoughts/memories/images of the sexual acts, which were constantly being replayed. Part of building a sense of safety and security for this client involved psychoeducation about how younger children can be coerced into engaging in inappropriate behaviors by older children simply because of a perceived difference in size, strength, or power, threats that may have been made, or rewards that may have been promised. As I provided him with this menu of normalizing patterns, he brightened and said, "Yeah, he's a lot taller . . . and he's pretty strong, too." I suggested that he choose a miniature to represent himself and one to represent Rick. He chose a nondescript little boy for himself and a burly chested male action figure wearing camoflauge pants, no shirt, and a long leather coat to be Rick.

As he handled the action figure, he said, "When I ride the bus home, I'm always lookin' out the window. I'm kinda scared to play outside, in case he comes down." I suggested that we bring mom
(*continued*)

in and make a safety plan together so that he could play outside in his yard. I also offered, "And in here, you get to decide what happens to this guy (pointing to the burly chested action figure)." Caleb said, "He should go to jail!" and immediately put him into the large jail that I keep in the office. He then chose several wild animal figurines and placed them in front of the jail as watch guards, so that the perpetrator symbol would "be too scared to break out." Having a variety of containment devices in one's playroom can aid in this process.

Caleb seemed driven to tell me as much about what happened as he could. This is a departure from the pattern of most children, who are reticent to tell their stories and usually do not share much at the beginning of treatment. He talked about feeling guilty all the time and like he "had to tell it all again." In addition to his metaphorical containment of the danger through the perpetrator symbol, this client needed a practical containment device where he could store the obsessive thoughts. Caleb worried that "maybe he hadn't told that part" and kept rehearsing the details of the sexual abuse, seemingly unable to free himself from the ropes of guilt. I offered him a variety of actual container boxes of various shapes and sizes, and he spent the rest of the session decorating one with images of safety. He glued two popsicle sticks to the top in the shape of a cross and said that God would help him keep the thoughts in there. Mom came into the room for the last part of the session and we wrote down on brightly colored sticky notes the specific sexual acts that he had already talked about with mom. Each of these was put in the box. I encouraged Caleb to leave the descriptions in the box until next time he came to see me.

Caleb brought his box back to the next session. He had decorated it some more and had added a couple of new descriptions over the week. He reported that "most of the time" if he began to worry about whether he'd actually talked about a specific sexual act, he would look through the sticky notes and be reassured that he had. During this second session we focused on his coping repertoire. He agreed that he had been coping with the anxiety stirred up by the sexual abuse by obsessively repeating the details. He had understood from his church experiences that confession is the way to get rid of guilt, so every time he would feel anxious or guilty, he would repeat the details. He agreed that rehearsing the details took up too much of

(continued)

(*continued*)
his brain space and kept him from enjoying life. Using the CopeCake handouts (Goodyear-Brown, 2010b), I taught Caleb the four ingredients of positive coping strategies. Coping strategies should: (1) Be good for you, (2) Be good for others, (3) Be easy to do, and (4) Make you feel better. Caleb agreed that the repetitions of verbal details did not make him feel better, so didn't really pass the test as a good coping strategy. Using the Coping Umbrella (Goodyear-Brown, 2002, 2010), the client generated a list of age-appropriate coping strategies that included "shooting hoops" and "playing with my dog" among other adaptive coping strategies. While we talked, Caleb moved a slinky back and forth between his hands. At the end of the session, he said, "This makes me feel better, too," referring to the kinesthetic activity of manipulating the Slinky. He and mom picked one up on their way home.

In the next session, we read the book *Brave Bart*, a bibliotherapy resource that introduces the idea that trauma can cause dysregulation in our bodies. After we read the book, I asked Caleb if his body had been giving him signals that it was upset. Caleb said, "Yeah . . . I get this oozy feeling sometimes when I think about the touching stuff." I invited him to draw a picture of the oozy feeling, and he drew a little boy with a frightened face. Then he colored a big green glob in his belly and said, "That's the oozy feeling." I taught him how to take deep, diaphragmatic breaths in playful ways. First, mother was invited into the room, and I modeled how to breathe by lying down, putting a ball on my belly, and intentionally making it roll off by taking a deep enough breath. We all took turns practicing. Then we practiced blowing big bubbles and used progressive muscle tension and relaxation exercises (PMR), pairing the PMR with a child-friendly, playful stimulus (Goodyear-Brown, 2010) to expand Caleb's skill base related to relaxation. I invited him to create a soothing image in the sand tray. I then explored the image with him, augmenting his experience of soothing by helping him pinpoint the sounds, smells, and tastes that he might experience in his safe place. After the safe place expansion, I asked Caleb to identify a color that he associated with happiness, warmth, and a sense of being calm. I then guided him through a visualization in which he first pictured the green glob in his belly, keeping in mind the oozy feeling, and then imagined a bucket of the warm, rich, happy color pouring into him, starting at his head and filling up his
(*continued*)

body, pushing out the green glob. Mom listened to the visualization and it was agreed that she would lead him through a version of this same exercise at bedtime if the "oozy feeling" resurfaced. Much of the sexual activity occurred in this client's bed, so his physiology was primed for hyperarousal symptoms to occur at bedtime. I offered him a glow-in-the-dark pinwheel as another external focal point for practicing the deep breathing. His therapeutic homework was to make the pinwheel spin for 2 to 3 minutes at bedtime each night. The nightly physiological exercise of deep breathing began to counter the shallow breathing that often accompanied his bedtime hyperarousal, while providing a reminder of the safety of the playroom and therapist.

The second dimension of the Soothing the Physiology component of FSPT enhances the role of parent as partner in the co-regulation process. However, this mom needed very little extra equipping. She and her son shared a secure attachment relationship; as soon as she was made aware of the abuse that was occurring, she moved appropriately into a protective role with him, was helping to build as coherent a narrative as she could, and was emotionally available to him. They seemed to enjoy each other's company, and he did not present a challenge in the discipline arena. So, whereas many families, particularly when dealing with foster and adoptive caregivers and children with multiple caregiver disruptions, need a significant amount of systematized dyadic intervention, I simply enlisted the already supportive bond between Caleb and his mom, drawing her into the interventions described above. Additionally, I shared with her the SOOTHE strategies. This set of strategies codifies a range of de-escalating, structuring, and nurturing responses that can be intentionally implemented with anxious children. Originally designed as part of a protocol for treating children with multiple caregiver disruptions who present with externalizing behavior problems, the strategies themselves are applicable to the many forms that a child's dysregulation might take including pervasive anxiety. Caleb's mom was a nurturing, attuned parent, but she wasn't used to dealing with a child swamped by anxiety, and she reported feeling better equipped to deal with his anxious moments after receiving some training in the SOOTHE strategies.

Once a sense of safety had been established, at least within the four walls of the playroom, coping had been augmented, and Caleb's anxious hyperarousal symptoms were alleviated, we moved to

(*continued*)

(*continued*)

emotional literacy work. I invited the client to complete a Color-Your-Heart (Goodyear-Brown, 2002, 2010). In this activity, the client is asked to pair four basic feelings (happy, sad, mad, and scared) with colors and then to choose a fifth feeling, which is usually indicative of a feeling with which the client is actively wrestling. The client chose "nervous" as his fifth feeling and colored in a significant amount of his heart with this color. When he was finished, there was a still a considerable amount of space left uncolored in the heart. I commented on the empty space and offered additional colors. I went over a menu of feelings and feeling faces with the client, giving examples of feelings and situations in which they might occur and asked what colors/feelings he might want to add to his heart. After exposure to the feelings menu, he chose guilty and ashamed and filled in the rest of the heart to reflect these feeling states. We started playing an emotional literacy game and made Rice Cake Feeling Faces (Goodyear-Brown, 2002) with mom during our next session while normalizing the myriad emotions a child might feel after these kinds of experiences.

As soon as the client's self-regulation skills seemed sufficiently augmented, we began preparing for exposure/response prevention work, which required the identification of the harassing thoughts, the development of a mechanism to stop them, and the replacement of these thoughts with more helpful cognitions or with boss back talk (Goodyear-Brown, 2010b). Some of the client's most repetitive thoughts were "I'm dirty," "I'm bad," "Someone might touch me again," and "I'm a homosexual." I read Caleb *Daniel the Dragon Slayer*, from *The Worry Wars* (Goodyear-Brown, 2010b), and we began to use the metaphor of feeding the dragon to describe the process by which avoidance of the things that make us anxious only encourages those things to grow. For Caleb, whenever he began to feel anxious, he would mitigate that anxiety by obsessively repeating (usually to someone else) one of the traumatic events he experienced. Within the metaphor, when he began to think "I'm bad" and to feel the anxiety related to that, the dragon would say, "You better confess again, just in case!" Prior to treatment, Caleb had asked to go see his priest on multiple occasions to confess these experiences again and again, feeling as if he could never get "right enough."

Part of the flexibility of the FSPT model is that, although the goals are set out in sequential order, it is possible to be working on several

(*continued*)

goals at once, or to work on the component that is most needful during any particular session. Caleb's safety needs required containment of the trauma material at the start of treatment. Because we did this piece early in treatment, many details of the trauma narrative had already been discussed and recorded by the time we reached the phase of treatment where this work might more typically begin. However, there were a total of 8 to 10 separate episodes during which the client was coerced into sexual activity with Rick. These discrete events had not been placed in any kind of sequential order, or integrated with sensory content in order to create a coherent narrative. If a child is able to engage in some therapeutic work related to sequencing the traumatic events, the therapist, client, and parent can often join together, take a meta-analytic look at the pattern of abuse, and draw some new conclusions or glean some new understandings of the traumatic events. With children, sensory dimensions of trauma may more easily be accessed through play, sand, and the visual arts. Moreover, the trauma content itself may be so overwhelming that children are initially able to approach it only through symbols and metaphor, making the expressive arts the perfect vehicle for this kind of exploration.

Over the course of the next couple of sessions, we took each sticky note out of the box, talked about it more fully, and placed it on a timeline that began when Caleb first met Rick and extended through the present. At several points along the way, I invited Caleb to draw a picture, create a sand tray, mold a symbol in clay, and so on, to explore the sensory impressions related to the trauma and to aid in integration of trauma content across the two hemispheres of the brain. For example, Caleb was particularly troubled by one episode in which Rick had stuck his finger in Caleb's bottom after he had put it in his own bottom. Caleb had multiple levels of anxiety over this event, including, in his words, the overall "wrongness" of it, but extending to the physical discomfort involved and concerns about "yucky germs" being shared. This last concern was not acknowledged or verbalized until after the client had created his bedroom in the sand and was replaying this scene. Caleb had a secret fear that he had caught a disease during that experience. Once this worry was vocalized, Caleb's mother and I agreed to provide more psychoeducation regarding how STDs are contracted and to schedule a trip to his pediatrician so that he could hear that he had a clean bill of health. This obsessive thought had been present since the abuse

(continued)

(continued)

occurred, but it was not until we engaged in a play-based trauma narrative process that the cognitive distortion surfaced in a way that could be accessed and resolved. It is for this reason that the goal of addressing the thought life is sequentially placed as one of the last components of the FSPT model—not because the thought life is unimportant, but because it is so important. The idiosyncratic irrational beliefs that might be informing trauma symptomatology for a young person may not be fully understood until the trauma narrative process is complete. Often, the thought life work begins early in treatment. In this case, we began to combat the idea that Caleb was somehow to blame for his abuse in session 1, but couldn't pinpoint the most personal beliefs linked to the abuse until rapport had been built and the traumatic events had been approached through a variety of portals.

One week during this phase of treatment, Caleb got out of bed after being put to bed for the night and said that he felt like his "head was going to explode with all the bad things I've done." Caleb came to his next session and insisted that he would always be dirty. I encouraged the client to draw pictures of what would help him feel clean. He drew a picture of Jesus with a fire hose spraying all the dirt off of him. We explored this drawing and eventually made it three-dimensional with play materials. Caleb filled the play fire extinguisher with water and doused his self-object over and over again with water.

Caleb was continuing to fight his worry dragon and reported feeling more and more powerful in relation to the anxiety as he resisted repeating the details and used his boss back talk. Caleb worked the exposure/response prevention hierarchy that we outlined early in treatment, and was given a small reward chosen from a list that he and mom had generated together each time he fought the dragon. He reported a reduction in feelings of guilt and shame, no longer felt driven to confess over and over again what had happened, and he had reestablished healthy eating and sleeping patterns. I asked if his mother would write a letter celebrating the hard work that he had done in treatment. He, in turn, created an award drawing for her, to thank her for supporting him through his recovery process. In the final phase of treatment, we used puppets to role play troubling touch scenarios that might come up in the future. Caleb reported feeling equipped to stand up for himself in future situations in which he might feel uncomfortable and said during his last session, "Who knows . . . maybe what I've learned can help somebody else!"

CONCLUSION

FSPT is a components-based model of trauma treatment that has at its core a reliance on the processes of play and other prop-based forms of expression that help increase the felt safety of clients, aid in the communication of trauma-specific psychoeducation, facilitate skill building, mitigate the toxicity of the trauma content and allow for counter-conditioning to occur while creating a more coherent narrative. When the therapist gives directive prompts that require the child to be exposed to anxiety-related, traumagenic memories, the play and art materials serve as co-regulators of affect in the sessions. The treatment goals that guide FSPT are informed by current best practice guidelines for the treatment of child sexual abuse and employ clinically sound, prop-based interventions in the pursuit of these goals while valuing the metaphoric communication that often happens in the playroom with young children. Play-based gradual exposure work allows children to self-titrate their doses of exposure to the anxiety-producing material as symptoms are extinguished, thus allowing them to achieve a sense of mastery over their traumatic past and integrate it into a positive sense of self as they continue to grow.

REFERENCES

Berliner, L. (2011). Child sexual abuse: Definitions, prevalence, and consequences. In J.E.B. Myers (Ed.), *The APSAC handbook on child maltreatment* (3rd ed.). Los Angeles, CA: Sage.

Bogar, C. B., & Hulse-Killacky, D. (2006). Resiliency determinants and resiliency processes among female adult survivors of childhood sexual abuse. *Journal of Counseling Development, 84*, 318–327.

Boney-McCoy, S., & Finkelhor, D. (1996). Is youth victimization related to trauma and depression after controlling for prior symptoms and family relationships? A longitudinal study. *Journal of Consulting & Clinical Psychology, 64*, 1406–1416.

Borrego, J., & Urquiza, A. J. (1998). Importance of therapist use of social reinforcement with parents as a model for parent-child relationships: An example with parent-child interaction therapy. *Child & Family Behavior Therapy, 20*(4), 27–54.

Brady, K. L., & Caraway, S. J. (2002). Home away from home: Factors associated with current functioning in children living in a residential treatment setting. *Child Abuse & Neglect, 26*, 1149–1163.

Bratton, S., Landreth, G., Kellam, T., & Blackard, S. (2006). *Child parent relationship therapy (CPRT) treatment manual: A 10 session filial therapy model for training parents.* New York, NY: Taylor & Francis.

Cohen, J. A., Mannarino, A. P., & Deblinger, E. (2006). *Treating trauma and traumatic grief in children and adolescents.* New York, NY: Guilford Press.

Copeland, W. E., Keeler, G., Angold, A., Costello, E. J. (2007). Traumatic events and posttraumatic stress in childhood. *Arch Gen Psychiatry, 64*(5), 577–584.

Eyberg, S. (2004) The PCIT story—part one: The conceptual foundation of PCIT. *The Parent-Child Interaction Therapy Newsletter, 1*(1), 1–2.

Felitti, V. J., Anda, R. F., Nordenberg, D., Williamson, D. F., Spitz, A. M., Edwards, V., . . . Marks, J. S. (1998). Relationship of childhood abuse and household dysfunction to many of the leading causes of death in adults: The adverse childhood experiences (ACE) study. *American Journal of Preventative Medicine, 14*, 245–258.

Felix, E., Bond, D., & Shelby, J. (2006). Coping with disaster: Psychosocial interventions for children in international disaster relief. In C. Schaefer & H. Kaduson (Eds.), *Contemporary play therapy: Theory, research, and practice* (pp. 307–329). New York, NY: Guilford Press.

Finkelhor, D., Ormrod, R. K., Turner, H. A., & Hamby, S. L. (2005). The victimization of children and youth: A comprehensive, national survey. *Child Maltreatment, 10*, 5–25.

Finkelhor, D., Ormrod, R. K., & Turner, H. A. (2007). Poly-victimization: A neglected component in child victimization. *Child Abuse & Neglect, 31*, 7–26.

Finkelhor, D., Ormrod, R. K., & Turner, H. A. (2009). Lifetime assessment of poly-victimization in a national sample of children and youth. *Child Abuse & Neglect, 33*, 403–411.

Gidycz, C. A., & Koss, M. P. (1989). The impact of adolescent sexual victimization: Standardized measures of anxiety, depression, and behavioral deviancy. *Violence and Victims, 4*(2), 139–149.

Gil, E. (2006). *Helping abused and traumatized children: Integrating directive and nondirective approaches.* New York, NY: Guilford Press

Gil, E. (Ed.). (2010). *Helping children heal interpersonal trauma: The power of play.* New York, NY: Guilford Press.

Goodyear-Brown, P. (2002). *Digging for buried treasure: 52 prop-based play therapy interventions for treating the problems of childhood.* Nashville, TN: Author.

Goodyear-Brown, P. (2005). *Digging for buried treasure 2: 52 more prop–based play therapy interventions for treating the problems of childhood.* Nashville, TN: Author.

Goodyear-Brown, P. (2009). Play therapy with anxious preschoolers. In C. Schaefer (Ed), *Play therapy for preschool children.* Washington, DC: American Psychological Association.

Goodyear-Brown, P. (2010). *Play therapy with traumatized children: A prescriptive approach.* Hoboken, NJ: John Wiley & Sons.

Goodyear-Brown, P. (2010b). *The worry wars.* Nashville, TN: Author.

Guerney, L. (2000). Filial therapy into the 21st century. *International Journal of Play Therapy, 9*(2), 1–17.

Lamb, M. E., Hershkowitz, I., Orback, Y., & Esplin, P. W. (2008). *Tell me what happened: Structured investigative interviews with child victims and witnesses.* London, England: John Wiley & Sons.

Landreth, G. L., & Bratton, S. C. (2006). *Child parent relationship therapy: A 10-session filial therapy model.* New York, NY: Routledge.

Lyon, T.D., & Ahern, E.C. (2011). Disclosure of child sexual abuse. In J. E. B. Myers (Ed.), *The APSAC handbook on child maltreatment* (3rd ed., pp. 233–252). Newbury Park, CA: Sage.

Kimball, W., Nelson, W. M., & Politano, P. M. (1993). The role of developmental variables in cognitive-behavioral interventions with children. In A. J. Finch, W. M. Nelson, & E. S. Ott (Eds.), *Cognitive-behavioral procedures with children and adolescents: A practical guide* (pp. 25–66). Needham Heights, MA: Allyn & Bacon.

McNeil, C. B., & Hembree-Kigin, T. (2010). *Parent-child interaction therapy* (2nd ed.). New York, NY: Plenum.

Perry, B., Pollard, R., Blakely, T., Baker, W., & Vigilante, D. (1995). Childhood trauma, the neurobiological adaptation and "use-dependent" development of the brain: How "states become traits." *Infant Mental Health Journal, 16*(4), 271–291.

Schaefer, C. E. (2001). Prescriptive play therapy. *International Journal of Play Therapy, 19*(1), 57–73.

Schaefer, C. E., & Drewes, A. A. (2009). The therapeutic powers of play and play therapy. In A. A. Drewes (Ed.), *Blending play therapy with cognitive behavioral therapy* (pp. 3–15). Hoboken, NJ: John Wiley & Sons.

Shelby, J. S., & Berk, M. S. (2009). Play therapy, pedagogy and CBT: An argument for interdisciplinary synthesis. In A. A. Drewes (Ed.), *Blending play therapy with cognitive behavioral therapy: Evidence-based and other effective treatments and techniques* (pp. 17–40). Hoboken, NJ: John Wiley & Sons.

Shelby, J. S., & Felix, E. D. (2005). Posttraumatic play therapy: The need for an integrated model of directive and nondirective approaches. In L. A. Reddy, T. M. Files-Hall, & C. E. Schaefer (Eds.), *Empirically based play interventions for children* (pp. 79–103). Washington, DC: American Psychological Association.

Shelby, J. S., Bond, D., Hall, S., & Hsu, C. (2004). *Enhancing coping among young tsunami survivors*. Los Angeles, CA: Authors.

Sheppard, C. (2001). *Brave Bart: A story for traumatized and grieving children*. Grosse Pointe Woods, MI: National Institute for Trauma and Loss in Children.

Putnam, F. W. (2003). Ten-year research update review: Child sexual abuse. *Journal of the American Academy of Child & Adolescent Psychiatry, 42*(3), 269–278.

Runyon, M. K., Deblinger, E., Ryan, E. E., Thakkar-Kolar, R. (2004). An overview of child physical abuse: Developing an integrated parent-child cognitive-behavioral treatment approach. *Trauma, Violence, & Abuse, 5*(1), 65–85.

VanFleet, R., Ryan, S. D., & Smith, S. (2005). Filial therapy: A critical review. In L. Reddy, T. Files-Hall, & C. E. Schaefer (Eds.), *Empirically-based play interventions* (pp. 241–264). Washington, DC: American Psychological Association.

Zisser, A., & Eyberg, S. M. (2010). Treating oppositional behavior in children using parent-child interaction therapy. In A. E. Kazdin & J. R. Weisz (Eds.), *Evidence-based psychotherapies for children and adolescents* (2nd ed., pp. 179–193). New York, NY: Guilford Press.

CHAPTER 14

Child-Parent Relationship Therapy With Nonoffending Parents of Sexually Abused Children

SUE C. BRATTON, PEGGY L. CEBALLOS, GARRY L. LANDRETH, and
MARY B. COSTAS

INTRODUCTION

C HILDHOOD SEXUAL ABUSE (CSA) affects far too many children in our society, diminishing their capacity to enjoy a normal childhood. Statistics from the 2008 National Child Abuse and Neglect Data System (NCANDS) showed that about 9.1% of an estimated 772,000 child abuse cases investigated by child protection services (CPS) involved sexual abuse (U.S. Department of Human Health and Services, 2010). Although the immediate and long-term effects of CSA vary greatly with nearly 30% of child abuse survivors initially showing no clinical symptoms (Kendall-Tackett, Meyer-Williams, & Finkelhor, 1993), a vast body of research has linked childhood sexual abuse to a host of adverse consequences across the lifespan (Molnar, Buka, & Kessler, 2001; Rafanello, 2010). Early treatment is imperative to minimize the impact on children's development. The younger the child at the onset of abuse, the greater potential of adverse effects (Perry & Szalavitz, 2006); hence, the significant need to identify mental health interventions shown to be effective with the youngest of survivors.

The effects of CSA on child survivors have been well-documented; conversely, the effect on caregivers' well-being has received scant attention in the literature (Elliott & Carnes, 2001; West, 2010). Winton (1990) proposed that the nonoffending parent also needs support to cope with a myriad of symptoms, including anger, guilt, depression, and feeling powerless (McCourt & Peel, 1998). Providing treatment that reduces parental stress and empowers parents to help their child is particularly important in light of research that links the well-being of sexually abused children to the quality of the parent-child relationship (Costas & Landreth, 1999; Kouyoumdjian, Perry, & Hansen, 2005).

The importance of a secure parent-child relationship on children's socioemotional development has been well-documented (Albright & Tamis-LeMonde, 2002; Ryan & Bratton, 2008; Siegel & Hartzell, 2003; Thompson, 2002). For children who have experienced a traumatic event, the caregiver-child attachment holds even greater importance. Experts in childhood trauma concur that involving caregivers in treatment is an essential element of the healing process (Perry & Szalavitz, 2006; Schore, 2003). Children look to their parents to help them regulate emotions and cope with stressful situations (Hyman, Gold, & Cott, 2003; Landreth & Bratton, 2006; Siegel & Hartzell, 2003). For children who have experienced sexual abuse, maternal response has been shown to be particularly important. Research suggests that children's psychological adjustment and well-being following the event is more dependent on maternal response than the characteristics of the abuse itself (Coohey & O' Leary, 2008; Tremblay, Herbert, & Piche, 1999). Interventions that strengthen the mother-child bond, while also providing emotional support for caregivers, seem particularly relevant to this population's needs.

Child-Parent Relationship Therapy (CPRT; Landreth & Bratton, 2006) is a play therapy–based intervention that combines parental support and education to foster a healthier parent-child relationship. The relationship is viewed as the vehicle for effecting change in the child and in the parent. Parents learn to understand and respond to their children's needs, and children learn that they can count on their parents to reliably and consistently meet their needs for love, acceptance, and safety. The alignment between the treatment focus and goals for CPRT and the needs of this population warrant consideration of CPRT as part of the overall treatment plan for CSA. This chapter briefly describes the CPRT model and its suitability with nonoffending parents and their children. A case illustration provides a glimpse of CPRT in practice and is followed by recommendations for CPRT's use with this population.

CHILD-PARENT RELATIONSHIP THERAPY

CPRT (Landreth & Bratton, 2006) is an empirically supported, manualized treatment model that focuses on strengthening the parent-child bond in order to help parents better understand and respond to their child's social, emotional, and behavioral needs. Based on the filial therapy model developed by Bernard and Louise Guerney in the 1960s, caregivers are taught child-centered play therapy (CCPT) principles and skills to use with their own children during supervised play sessions (Guerney, 1964). CPRT is predicated on (1) the belief that a secure parent-child relationship is the essential and curative factor for children's well-being, and (2) confidence in parents' ability to learn and apply the necessary attitudes and skills to become therapeutic agents in their children's lives. Central to the success of CPRT is the requirement that treatment providers are first trained in CCPT principles and skills, and then trained and supervised in the 10-session CPRT treatment protocol (Bratton, Landreth, Kellam, & Blackard, 2006) to ensure treatment fidelity. Readers are directed to Landreth and Bratton (2006) for an in-depth understanding of the model, and referred to the manualized CPRT protocol (Bratton et al., 2006) for training content and process. The treatment manual contains the protocol and therapist's guide, as well as parent notebook, handouts, and additional resources.

Using a small group format of 6 to 8 parents, the CPRT model calls for a careful balance of supportive and didactic experiences designed to maximize parents' success in learning and applying the CPRT skills. Groups typically meet once per week for two hours, although CPRT has been successfully used in more intensive formats. Initial treatment goals include creating an atmosphere of safety, acceptance, and encouragement, while helping parents begin to normalize their experience through sharing with group members. Sessions 1 to 3 concentrate on demonstration and role-play of basic CCPT skills including following the child's lead, reflection of feelings, and reflecting verbal and nonverbal content of child's play. The primary focus in sessions 4 to 10 is skill refinement through supervision of weekly parent-child play sessions, along with the added skills of limit setting, choice-giving, encouragement, and esteem-building responses.

EVIDENCE BASE FOR CPRT WITH NONOFFENDING CAREGIVERS

The CPRT model has been investigated in 34 outcome studies and has demonstrated moderate to large treatment effects on a variety of presenting issues (Bratton, Landreth, & Lin, 2010). Although according to standards set forth by the American Psychological Association, CPRT falls short of being considered a "well-established" treatment, it meets the criteria for a "promising" treatment for several populations and disorders, including children who have experienced sexual abuse (Baggerly & Bratton, 2010). An outcome of particular note in regard to treating nonoffending parents is CPRT's beneficial effect on parental stress. Of 15 controlled outcome studies that measured stress reduction, 12 studies found a statistically significant reduction and the remaining 3 showed a nonsignificant, yet notable reduction in stress in the parent-child relationship. Additional positive outcomes consistently supported by research include: (1) decrease in children's externalizing problems, internalizing problems, and broad-spectrum behavior problems, and (2) increase in parental empathy and acceptance (Bratton, Landreth, & Lin, 2010). Two studies have investigated the effects of CPRT with nonoffending parents of sexually abused children. Both studies offer support for CPRT's utility with this population and provide an impetus for further research.

Costas and Landreth (1999) used stratified random assignment to assign 31 parents of sexually abused children to CPRT or a no-treatment wait list control, of which 26 completed the study (CPRT, $n = 14$; control, $n = 12$). Between group differences over time revealed that parents receiving CPRT training demonstrated: (1) statistically significant gains in their empathic interactions with their children as rated by independent raters blind to the study, (2) statistically significant increase in parents' acceptance of their children, and (3) statistically significant reduction in parent-child relationship stress. Although not statistically significant, parents reported a marked improvement from pretesting to posttesting on their child's anxiety, emotional adjustment, self-concept, and overall behavior problems.

West (2010) used a mixed-methods research design to conduct an in-depth examination of the experience of eight nonoffending parents of sexually abused children who participated in CPRT. Following the recommendation of Costas and Landreth (1999) to consider extending number of sessions, CPRT was extended to 11 weeks to allow more time for processing parents' feelings concerning the abuse. Quantitative data showed an overall mean improvement from pretest to posttest on parental empathy, and an overall mean decrease on parental stress and child behavior problems. Qualitative data was obtained from coding of semi-structured interviews to determine patterns and themes in the parents' comments. Analysis of qualitative data revealed nine themes, similar in content to anecdotal parent comments noted by Costas and Landreth. The theme most supported by parents' comments was the perception of an enhanced parent-child relationship, followed by parents' report of changes within themselves and parents' report of changes within their child.

RATIONALE FOR CPRT FOR SEXUALLY ABUSED CHILDREN AND THEIR PARENTS

Because perpetrators of sexual abuse have violated children's sense of safety, boundaries, and trust, sexually abused children often experience difficulties forming healthy relationships (Massat & Lundy, 1998). Perhaps most devastating is the potential adverse effect on the parent-child relationship, given that the parent-child bond is one predictor of children's psychological adjustment following abuse (Tremblay, Herbert, & Piche, 1999). CPRT's primary aim is to enhance the quality of the parent-child relationship. CPRT research with nonoffending parents supports this claim. "Feeling closer to my child" was parents' most cited comment during posttreatment interviews (Costas & Landreth, 1999; West, 2010).

BENEFITS FOR PARENTS

Nonoffending parents experience a high level of distress related to their children's abuse (Easton, Wickham, & West, 2002; Elliot & Carnes, 2001). Parents report feelings of anger and guilt, lack of parental confidence, fear for their children's long-term well-being, and a sense of powerlessness (Easton et al., 2002). Interventions that provide emotional support and empower parents to help their child have been emphasized as a crucial element in the overall treatment of CSA (Coohey & O'Leary, 2008; Kouyoumdjian et al., 2005). CPRT's small group format is purposefully structured to provide parents with emotional support as they share their family's difficult experience, which has often been held in secrecy. Sharing feelings of guilt, shame, anger, and powerlessness within a safe, supportive environment can decrease feelings of isolation and help parents experience that "they are not alone." This type of sharing also allows parents to normalize their current experiences as well as their children's reactions to the situation.

Research findings support CPRT's benefit for nonoffending parents, including reduction in parental stress and increases in parental empathy and acceptance of their child (Costas & Landreth, 1999; West, 2010). Further, parents reported increased confidence in their parenting and their ability to help their child, greater ability to understand their children's needs and feelings, increased acceptance of their child, and more patience with their children. Parents also reported feeling less guilt, less alone in their experience, and a sense of relief that they could share their secret with other parents who had similar experiences.

BENEFITS FOR CHILDREN

According to Gil (2006) sexually abused children struggle to make sense of the abuse and experience confusing thoughts and feelings. A vast body of research has linked CSA to a host of adverse effects on children, including low self-esteem, guilt, depression, anger, fearfulness, sense of helplessness, inability to trust others, somatic complaints, regressive behaviors, sleep disturbances, eating disorders, and inappropriate sexualized behaviors (Gil, 2010; Paine & Hansen, 2002; Rafanello, 2010). Children must be provided a safe and developmentally responsive means to express their feelings in order to avoid the manifestation of more severe emotional, social, and behavioral problems (Gil, 2006).

Through the strengthening of a consistent, empathic, and safe relationship with the nonoffending parent, the child is able to restore a sense of trust in adults. In CPRT, parents learn to provide this kind of healing relationship for their child. Through the weekly parent-child play sessions, parents give their children the opportunity to express feelings, thoughts, and their troubling experiences, while experiencing acceptance and empathy from the parent (Costas & Landreth, 1999). Creating a venue in which children can share their experience with parents and parents can respond appropriately to their child's disclosure enhances open communication in the dyad and facilitates the child's development of a tolerable and coherent narrative of the experience. In addition, when children are allowed to play freely within a safe and supportive environment, they can gain a sense of control and mastery over events they feel little control over, thereby reducing feelings of helplessness and fear, and increasing a sense of personal empowerment and self-esteem. With a goal of fostering the child's self-regulation and self-control, parents also learn how to respond to and place limits on sexualized behaviors and other inappropriate externalized behaviors in a manner that is respectful of the child's feelings while at the same time setting firm boundaries. CPRT teaches parents skills that not only help them become sensitive to their children's needs, but also help them consistently respond in ways that facilitate their children's healing and psychological well-being, with the potential to continue to do so long after treatment ends (Landreth & Bratton, 2006).

Case Illustration

BACKGROUND INFORMATION

At time of intake for CPRT, Mrs. A was a 28-year-old Caucasian mother whose 5½-year-old daughter, Laura, was believed to have been sexually abused. Based on Laura's sexualized behavior with a boy in her preschool class, school officials reported suspected abuse

(continued)

to Child Protective Services (CPS) when Laura was 5 years old. Although the medical exam and initial forensic interview were inconclusive, CPS concluded that, at a minimum, Laura had experienced sexual abuse characterized by oral sex. CPS suspected but was unable to confirm that Laura's stepfather, who had been in her life since she was 2 years old, was the perpetrator. Mr. A denied the abuse. Mrs. A allowed him to continue to live with them until a court order was issued 3 months later, stating that he could not have contact with Laura. At the time of the report, Mrs. A and her husband were working full time and owned their home in a middle-class neighborhood. After Mrs. A's husband moved out, their relations had become strained and he had gradually discontinued financial support. Mrs. A reported that due to financial problems, she and Laura had recently moved to a one bedroom apartment.

Based on Laura's reported sexual acting-out behavior at her preschool and her increasing level of aggression and defiance at home, CPS referred Laura for play therapy at an agency specializing in CSA. After 6 months of therapy, during which Mrs. A participated in regular parent consultations, Laura's therapist referred Mrs. A for CPRT at the same agency. She believed that although Laura had been making progress, her strained relationship with her mother was a barrier to her optimal growth. In particular, Mrs. A's limited ability to provide emotional support and comfort appeared to be a major source of distress for Laura. Other factors that pointed to CPRT being a good fit for Mrs. A's needs included: (1) her expressed sense of being powerless to help her child; (2) feelings of guilt that she had not initially believed Laura; and (3) a lack of social support (Mrs. A had no contact with family members, and had no friends other than at work).

INITIAL ASSESSMENT FOLLOWING REFERRAL

Assessment typically focuses on the readiness of both mother and child to participate in this model of treatment. The CPRT therapist met with Mrs. A to gather family history and current concerns. Mrs. A displayed a high level of emotional distress and conflicting feelings about her daughter's abuse and her own life circumstances. She clearly felt guilty for not protecting her daughter, and expressed fear that her daughter would be "scarred for life." While she presented as vulnerable emotionally, Mrs. A seemed to genuinely want to better understand Laura's feelings and needs and learn ways that she could help her heal from the abuse.

(continued)

(continued)

A 20-minute family play observation is completed to help assess the parent-child dynamics. During the observation, Mrs. A seemed to have a high need to control the situation, while Laura vacillated between seeking to please her mother and expressing aggression toward her. As the observation progressed, Laura's aggression, and her mother's attempts to control her, increased in a reciprocal manner resulting in numerous power struggles. At one point, Mrs. A was obviously distraught. Laura responded by ceasing to throw toys and, looking equally distraught, said, "Mommy, please don't be mad." As a result of the assessment and the recommendation of Laura's therapist, it was determined that Mrs. A would begin group CPRT with five other mothers whose children had experienced sexual abuse.

PRE-CPRT SESSION

In order to give this population of parents additional time to tell their children's abuse story and process their experience and related feelings, parents met the week prior to Training Session 1 to get acquainted and share why they were participating in the group. An additional goal was to form an alliance with parents and begin building a sense of safety in the group. Although Mrs. A was able to describe her problems with Laura, particularly "the dreaded bedtime power struggles," she was noticeably quieter than the other mothers in regard to sharing her own experience and feelings about the abuse. However, she seemed interested as the others shared about their difficult journey toward healing. At the end of the session, CPRT Parent Notebooks (Bratton et al., 2006) were dispersed and an overview of the 10 sessions was provided.

SESSION 1–3: LEARNING CPRT PRINCIPLES AND SKILLS

Establishing an atmosphere of safety, acceptance, and encouragement is the top priority in sessions 1 to 3, especially for this population of parents who need plenty of opportunity to share and normalize their experiences. However, the CPRT model requires that the therapist be mindful of balancing parents' need for support with teaching the foundational CCPT attitudes and skills in order to ensure that parents are prepared to begin their play sessions with their child after week 3. Beginning skills include following the child's lead, reflection of feelings, and reflection of verbal and nonverbal content of child's play. More importantly, parents are taught that

(continued)

during the weekly 30-minute special playtime with their child, they are to focus their full attention and convey a genuine interest in and acceptance of their child by communicating these healing messages: (1) I am here, (2) I hear you, (3) I understand, and (4) I care (Landreth & Bratton, 2006). This attitude and expression of acceptance on the parents' part is at the core of developing a closer and more secure parent-child bond and facilitating healing within the child. For sexually abused children, experiencing an enhanced relationship with their parent in which they are accepted and prized is especially important in their healing process and can help children feel supported as they work through their abuse experience. An important training dimension of CPRT, especially during the early sessions, is demonstration and role-play of skills.

During Session 1, Mrs. A continued to share little in the group, but she seemed less anxious than the previous week. Her nonverbals indicated that she was able to connect with the other parents' experiences and feelings. Mrs. A participated more during didactic activities. She seemed to need the structure provided by the therapist in order to feel safe to speak up.

Session 2 began with parents sharing their homework assignment to notice and reflect four different feelings expressed by their child over the past week. Although Mrs. A had participated in the feeling practice exercise the week before, she reported that Laura did not express any feeling other than "happy," and was able to describe several incidents and how she responded. Mrs. A's difficulty in acknowledging her daughter's more negative feelings continued to be problematic. As other parents described times when their children had expressed anger and sadness, she listened but seemed more closed off. Later, when it was time to role-play CCPT skills, Mrs. A seemed stiff and uncomfortable, particularly when it was her turn to role-play the child. The therapist noted that her initial concerns that Mrs. A might need extra support to fully benefit from CPRT seemed valid. She planned to talk with Mrs. A next week to arrange for her to conduct her play sessions at the clinic under her supervision.

Mrs. A arrived early to Session 3, as did another mother whose abuse story was similar in that, initially, neither had believed that their husband could have abused their child. For the first time, Mrs. A was able to verbally acknowledge her guilt. The other mother affirmed her feelings, letting Mrs. A know that she, too, had felt ashamed and afraid that she had damaged her relationship with her

(continued)

(*continued*)

child, but that she had worked hard to repair the relationship and forgive herself. By this point other parents had arrived to the group and shared similar stories. This interchange appeared to be a pivotal point for Mrs. A. She now seemed more open to showing her vulnerability and feelings in the group. The therapist commented that she seemed more relaxed, like a "burden had been lifted from her shoulders." Mrs. A replied with tears in her eyes, "It's a relief to be able to tell how ashamed I am that I didn't believe her . . . to find out that I'm not the only one makes me feel like maybe I'm not such a horrible mother." This experience appeared beneficial to Mrs. A, but it also seemed to bring up feelings that she had likely repressed. She seemed preoccupied during most of Session 3, and again, struggled during role-play of skills, particularly in the role of the child. Session 3 review and role-play of CCPT skills is critical, because parents conduct their first play session with their child during the week between Session 3 and 4. Two parents were scheduled to be the "focus" of supervision for next week, meaning they agreed to come to the clinic during the week and video-record their play sessions to be shown in Session 4 (*two different parents are scheduled for each of the remaining weeks*). The therapist pulled Mrs. A aside after the session was over, and let her know that she was aware that tonight's session had been difficult. After processing her myriad feelings, it was agreed that for the next several weeks, Mrs. A would conduct her play sessions with Laura at the clinic, with the therapist available for support and feedback. This arrangement allowed the therapist to review CCPT skills with Mrs. A one-on-one.

Mrs. A brought Laura in for the play session as scheduled. The therapist was able to spend 10 minutes reviewing a few basics, primarily focusing on two skills: (1) allowing Laura to lead the interaction by choosing to play with any of the toys in the playroom, and (2) showing focused attention and keen interest in Laura and her play. Because Mrs. A was anxious about Laura "doing something that was not okay," the therapist quickly reviewed how to handle situations in which Mrs. A might be concerned for Laura's safety or feel personally uncomfortable. Mrs. A expressed concern that Laura might throw the toys and break something. After reassuring Mrs. A that other children threw toys in the playroom and that Laura was unlikely to break anything of value, the therapist role-played an example of how Mrs. A could respond (using a calm, matter-of-fact

(*continued*)

voice): "Laura, the toys are not for throwing, but you can play with them in most any other way." If Laura continued to throw the toys, Mrs. A was instructed to repeat the statement calmly, and if she sensed that Laura was angry, to reflect her feeling along with the limit. Further, if Laura continued to break the limit, to respond by restating the limit, adding, "If you continue to throw the toys, Laura, we will have to leave the play room." Her therapist assured Mrs. A that she would be learning additional limit-setting strategies over the next few weeks. The therapist had scheduled the play session in a room with a two-way mirror. Mrs. A seemed to feel less anxious knowing that the therapist would be there if she needed her. Although Mrs. A's rate of response was less than desired, she was able to follow Laura's lead and appeared genuinely interested. She continued to have difficulty reflecting feelings, but because Laura was enjoying her time with her mother, she expressed very little aggression, and none directed at her mother. The one time that she pounded the punching bag several times, Mrs. A seemed to have difficulty with the activity, but remained relatively calm. Following the play session, the therapist was able to offer brief encouragement by emphasizing the CCPT skills that Mrs. A had demonstrated (e.g., allowing Laura to lead her play, her focused attention and interest, and what appeared as greater acceptance of Laura's angry feelings). Mrs. A expressed surprise that Laura had not "misbehaved" like last time. The therapist was able to help Mrs. A see the connection between Laura's enjoyment of having her mother's full attention and her reduced need to act out. Although the therapist attempted to briefly explore Mrs. A's reaction when Laura was punching the bop bag, Mrs. A was resistant, saying that it had not bothered her. Because Mrs. A expressed concern that she was not as good at the CCPT skills as the other mothers, it was agreed that she would wait until Session 6 to show her video, and that the therapist would continue to meet with her at the clinic for her weekly play session with Laura.

SESSIONS 4–10: GROUP PROCESS OF SUPERVISED PLAY SESSIONS

Skill refinement through supervision and processing of parent-child play sessions is the major activity in sessions 4 through 10. Each session begins with all parents sharing their experiences during the special playtimes with their children, with the majority of time spent viewing videos and giving feedback to the two parents of focus for

(continued)

(continued)

that week. The use of video supervision has several advantages: (1) holds parents accountable, (2) facilitates greater insight as parents view themselves, (3) provides more opportunities for vicarious learning, (4) allows parents to see the impact of the play session on their children, and (5) permits the therapist to reinforce skills as they are demonstrated and make suggestions for alternative responses and actions when needed. Perhaps more important, viewing play sessions within the group format permits the therapist to offer parents support and encouragement in a more concrete and meaningful manner, while also providing opportunities to build group cohesion as parents are able to share and support each other's struggles. In sessions 4 through 8, foundational skills continue to be emphasized, along with the added skills of limit setting, choice-giving, encouragement, and self-esteem–building responses. To ensure success during this practice phase, parents are restricted to practicing the CCPT skills only during the 30-minute play sessions, thus avoiding feelings of failure that inevitably arise when parents try to apply their new skills too quickly to problems that arise on a daily basis. In the final two sessions, parents are helped to generalize and apply their new skills to everyday interactions with their children.

In Session 4, Mrs. A seemed relieved as she heard other parents express their nervousness during their first play session, especially when she saw that they struggled to use the new skills. Although she gave only minimal feedback about her session, she seemed to gain strength from seeing others supported in their struggles. During her weekly play session with Laura, Mrs. A demonstrated progress in reflecting Laura's verbal and nonverbal play content. She appeared slightly more relaxed, but feelings continued to be a source of difficulty.

CPRT Session 5 was particularly difficult for Mrs. A. During informal sharing, one mother shared her fear that her own experience of sexual abuse as a child was keeping her from responding to her child's abuse story in a healthy manner. Because that parent had worked on this issue in her own therapy, she was able to show a high level of insight. Mrs. A was noticeably quiet during and after this interaction. The therapist was aware of a change in Mrs. A's affect, but sensed that she needed more time before she would be ready to openly process her feelings.

(continued)

Mrs. A kept her appointment to conduct her third play session with Laura prior to CPRT Session 6. The therapist spent 10 minutes going over reflection of feelings, especially the importance of reflecting Laura's feelings of anger or sadness. The therapist explained that Laura needed to know that it is okay for her to feel mad about the abuse, or sad that she does not get to see her friends from the old neighborhood, or confused about how she feels about her father; maybe mad at him for what he did, but also remembering the fun things that they did together and missing him. Laura needed to know that her mom accepted her even when she felt really angry. Mrs. A appeared thoughtful and replied, "I never thought of it that way . . . I thought it was best for her to not dwell on the negative stuff."

During her play session with Laura, Mrs. A showed continued progress in mastering the CCPT skills. For the first time, Mrs. A was able to reflect some of Laura's feelings. Laura's play was noticeably more focused. About 15 minutes into the session, Laura started to play with the doll house. She placed the baby doll all alone in the bedroom and the mother figure in the living room, and said that the baby was crying. Mrs. A made several appropriate responses, including "She feels sad." As Laura's play became increasingly intense, Mrs. A's body language conveyed acceptance and a genuine interest in Laura and her play. Although her response rate continued to be slower than what is desired, she was able to respond to Laura's feelings several times throughout the play sequence. The therapist knew that this play session had been important for both mother and child, and reflected that to Mrs. A afterward. Mrs. A was obviously impacted by her experience with Laura. She knew that Laura's play had been meaningful, although she could not explain why. What she said next was profound, "I could feel her [Laura's] sadness . . . how alone she felt." The therapist was able to spend a few more minutes with Mrs. A reflecting on what seemed like a significant moment with her daughter.

Session 6 began with Mrs. A expressing her nervousness about showing her video. Group members offered encouragement, remarking on their own struggles and mistakes. Mrs. A had her video set to the beginning of Laura's doll house play, saying that she knew Laura's play was important, but did not know how to respond. Group members, too, could see that Laura's play was meaningful and commented on Mrs. A's ability to be fully with Laura throughout her play, even though she was silent. As the therapist processed the

(continued)

(*continued*)

experience and the other mothers offered support, Mrs. A again shared that, "I could really feel her [Laura's] sadness . . . how alone she felt." At that point she began to cry, saying that she knew "how that baby was feeling," because she now realized that was how she felt as a child. She chose not to share details, but disclosed to the group that she had been sexually abused as a child. She explained that she had never told anyone else. The therapist was careful to respect her privacy, but at the same time provide acceptance and validation for Mrs. A's feelings and the courage it took for her to share her experience. While helping Mrs. A learn to respond to Laura's playing out of her abuse experience would be essential to Laura's integration of her experience into a coherent narrative—one that she could share with her mother—now was not the time. First, Mrs. A would need help to work through her own abuse story. Following the group session, Mrs. A stayed to ask about finding her own therapist. Because Laura enjoyed playing in the childcare area when her mom and the therapist talked, and to avoid overwhelming Mrs. A by having to come to the clinic three days per week, it was arranged for Mrs. A to see her own counselor after her weekly play sessions with Laura. Given Mrs. A's disclosure, and the likelihood that the next several weeks would be difficult, the therapist decided to continue to monitor the weekly play sessions.

Over the remaining CPRT sessions, Mrs. A came to realize that she had been afraid of Laura's feelings because they mirrored her own repressed feelings that she did not believe were valid or acceptable. She was aware of the reciprocal effect between her self-acceptance and her ability to accept her daughter's feelings and needs, as well as the effect on Laura's behavior. In Session 10, as parents described changes in themselves and in their children, Mrs. A was the first to share, "Laura knows that I'm here for her when she needs me. . . . I'm so proud to be able to say that. . . . Since starting our play sessions, she has opened up and was able to tell me things that she was afraid to tell me before. . . . It has helped me feel like I can help my daughter recover from the abuse . . . that she will grow up healthy and normal." In describing changes in Laura, Mrs. A reported that her aggression and sexually acting-out had decreased significantly, as had their power struggles. She was especially grateful that she had learned how to respond to Laura's sexualized behaviors in a way that communicated acceptance while

(*continued*)

limiting the behavior. She stated that the limit setting and choice-giving strategies had been very helpful, but that learning to acknowledge and accept her daughter's feelings had made the "real difference." Finally, she remarked on how much closer she felt to Laura. With tears in her eyes, she described the new night time ritual that Laura called "cuddle time," saying it was hard to tell who enjoyed it most. This was in stark contrast to the bedtime power struggles that Mrs. A had shared with group members in their first session together.

No doubt, Mrs. A's individual counseling was a factor in the growth and insight that she showed, yet the support she received from group members seemed to be a significant force in her growing acceptance of her feelings regarding her abuse experience. The skills she learned and was able to apply in play sessions with Laura also seemed important to Mrs. A's growing confidence in her ability to understand and respond to Laura's needs. When asked what she believed had made the biggest difference, Mrs. A had a ready answer, "My relationship with Laura . . . she now knows that she can tell me anything . . . that I love her no matter what."

The above case illustration provides a glimpse into the content and process of CPRT, showing how a strengthened parent-child bond served as the vehicle for change within parent and child. This case example focused primarily on how change was facilitated within the parent through the group process and parent-child play sessions. It has been our experience in working with this population, that in most cases, the change within the parent is the most critical factor in the child's growth. In addition, discussion of adjunct services and other systemic involvement, such as teacher consultations, that are thought to be important elements in cases involving child sexual abuse were omitted due to space limitations.

CONSIDERATIONS FOR CPRT AS A TREATMENT FOR CSA

Child abuse is a multifaceted problem and its impact on the child and the family depends on numerous variables. Thus, mental health professionals should use clinical judgment and carefully consider the extent of the trauma on both child and parent prior to determining if CPRT is appropriate. The following suggestions are offered for consideration when making decisions regarding providing CPRT to this population.

There are cases when individual play therapy for the child and/or individual therapy for the nonoffending parent is necessary prior to, or in conjunction with, CPRT. As illustrated in the case example, clinical judgment may dictate that parent-child play sessions be held at the clinician's office under supervision, rather than at home. Parents often need additional support to cope with strong feelings about their child's abuse that can arise when the child re-enacts elements of the abuse during play sessions, especially when the parent has his or her own sexual abuse history. Although it is expected for this group of caregivers to present with a high level of emotional distress, when the level of distress prevents the parent from being able to focus on the child's needs, CPRT, alone, would not be clinically indicated. Clinicians should also carefully consider the extent of the child's trauma. In cases of repeated abuse or complex trauma, a child typically requires the type of therapeutic environment that only a trained mental health professional can offer. In these cases, children often need to express painful experiences that may be overwhelming to their parents. We argue, however, that at some point in the child's recovery, involving parents in the manner that CPRT prescribes is helpful to their healing process.

Based on our experience with this population, we suggest that the CPRT model be extended by at least one additional session for the purpose of providing parents time to share their often complicated experiences and feelings surrounding the abuse. For similar reasons, West (2010) suggested extending training to 15 sessions. Expanding the number of sessions would also allow clinicians flexibility to address concerns unique to this population, including the effects of sexual abuse, understanding court procedures, and preventative measures that can be taken to ensure children's safety.

CONCLUSION

Early childhood sexual abuse can have a significant adverse effect on children's development (Perry & Szalavitz, 2006), especially when the abuse has been pervasive and resulted in disruptions in a secure parent-child relationship. Although the immediate and long term effects of CSA vary greatly, a vast body of research has linked childhood sexual abuse to devastating consequences across the lifespan (Rafanello, 2010; Tourigny, Hébert, Daigneault, & Simoneau, 2005). The importance of a healthy parent-child relationship to mediate the effects of abuse has been well-documented (Coohey & O'Leary, 2008; Kouyoumdjian, Perry, & Hansen, 2005; Perry & Szalavitz, 2006). CPRT is a play-based intervention that is responsive to the needs of parents and children. Its focus on the significance of the parent-child relationship in children's recovery, and its use of play to foster a secure and predictable caregiving experience for the child, makes CPRT a good fit for this population. Because non-offending parents are often plagued by feelings of guilt, anger, power-lessness, and helplessness, the emotional support offered to parents during CPRT group meetings can serve as a healing force that facilitates their emotional well-being. Further, as parents begin to better under-stand and respond to their children's needs through successful applica-tion of child-centered skills, they are empowered and develop confidence in their ability to be helpful in their children's recovery. Preliminary outcome research supports CPRT's beneficial effects on parents and children (Costas & Landreth, 1999; West, 2010). CPRT, when delivered by a competent and specially-trained mental health professional, offers much promise for alleviating unnecessary suffering for child survivors of sexual abuse and their parents.

REFERENCES

Albright, M. B., & Tamis-LeMonde, C. S. (2002). Maternal depressive symptoms in relation to dimensions of parenting in low-income mothers. *Applied Developmental Science, 6*(1), 24–34.

Baggerly, J., & Bratton, S. (2010). Toward a firm foundation in play therapy research. *International Journal of Play Therapy: Special Issue on Research, 19*(1), 26–38.

Bratton, S., Landreth, G., Kellum, T., & Blackard, S. (2006). *Child parent relationship therapy (CPRT) treatment manual: A ten session filial therapy model for training parents.* New York, NY: Routledge.

Bratton, S., Landreth, G., & Lin, Y. (2010). What the research shows about filial therapy. In J. Baggerly, D. Ray, & S. Bratton (Eds.), *Effective play therapy: Evidence-based filial and child-centered research studies and guidelines.* New York, NY: John Wiley & Sons.

Coohey, C., & O'Leary, P. (2008). Mothers' protection of their children after discovering they have been sexually abused: An information-processing perspective. *Child Abuse & Neglect, 32,* 245–259.

Costas, M. B., & Landreth, G. L. (1999). Filial therapy with nonoffending parents of children who have been sexually abused. *International Journal of Play Therapy, 8*(1), 43–66.

Elliott, A. N., & Carnes, C. N. (2001). Reactions of non-offending parents to the sexual abuse of their child: A review of the literature. *Child Maltreatment, 6*(4), 314–331.

Easton Wickham, R., & West, J. (2002) *Therapeutic work with sexually abused children.* London, England: Sage.

Gil, E. (2006). *Helping abused and traumatized children: Integrating directive and nondirective approaches.* New York, NY: Guilford Press.

Gil, E. (2010). *Working with children to heal interpersonal trauma: The power of play.* New York, NY: Guilford Press.

Guerney, B. G. (1964). Filial therapy: Description and rationale. *Journal of Counseling Psychology, 28*(4), 304–310.

Hyman, S. M., Gold, S. N., & Cott, M. A. (2003). Forms of social support that moderate PTSD in childhood sexual abuse survivors. *Journal of Family Violence, 18*(5), 295–300.

Kendall-Tackett, K. A., Meyer-Williams, L., & Finkelhor, D. (1993). Impact of sexual abuse on children: A review and synthesis of recent empirical studies. *Psychological Bulletin, 113*(1), 164–180.

Kouyoumdjian, H., Perry, A., & Hansen, D. (2005). The role of adult expectations on the recovery of sexually abused children. *Aggression and Violent Behavior, 10*, 475–489.

Landreth, G. L., & Bratton, S. C. (2006). *Child parent relationship therapy: A 10-session filial therapy model.* New York, NY: Routledge.

Massat, C. R., & Lundy, M. (1998). "Reporting costs" to nonoffending parents in cases of intrafamilial child sexual abuse. *Child Welfare, 77*(4), 371–388.

McCourt, J., & Peel, J. C. F. (1998). The effects of child sexual abuse on the protecting parent(s): Identifying a counseling response for secondary victims. *Counselling Psychology Quarterly, 11*(3), 283–300.

Molnar, B. E., Buka, S. L., & Kessler, R. C. (2001). Child sexual abuse and subsequent psychopathology: Results from the national comorbidity survey. *American Journal of Public Health, 91*(5), 753–760.

Paine, M., & Hansen, D. (2002). Factors influencing children to self-disclose sexual abuse. *Clinical Psychology Review, 22*, 271–295.

Perry, B. D., & Szalavitz, M. (2006). *The boy who was raised as a dog and other stories from a child psychiatrist's notebook: What traumatized children can teach us about loss, love, and healing.* New York, NY: Basic Books.

Rafanello, D. (2010, January/February). Child sexual abuse prevention and reporting: It is everyone's responsibility. *Child Sexual Abuse Exchange*, 50–53.

Ryan, V., & Bratton, S. (2008). Child-centered/non-directive play therapy with very young children. In C. Schaefer, P. Kelly-Zion, & J. McCormick (Eds.), *Play therapy with very young children* (pp. 25–66). New York, NY: Rowman & Littlefield.

Schore, A. (2003). *Affect dysregulation and disorders of the self.* New York, NY: Norton.

Siegel, D. J., & Hartzell, M. (2003). *Parenting from the inside out.* New York, NY: Penguin.

Thompson, R. (2002). *The roots of school readiness in social and emotional development* (Rep. No. 1). Kansas City, MO: Ewin Marion Kauffman Foundation.

Tourigny, M., Hébert, M., Daigneault, I., & Simoneau, A. C. (2005). Efficacy of a group therapy for sexually abused adolescent girls. *Journal of Child Sexual Abuse, 14*(4), 71–93.

Tremblay, C., Herbert, M., & Piche, C. (1999). Coping strategies and social support as mediators of consequences in child sexual abuse victims. *Child Abuse & Neglect, 23*, 929–945.

U.S. Department of Health and Human Services, Administration for Children and Families, Administration on Children, Youth and Families, Children's Bureau. (2010). Child Maltreatment 008. Available from www.acf.hhs.gov/programs/cb/stats research/index.htm#can

West, B. (2010). *Child parent relationship therapy (CPRT) with parents of children who have been sexually abused: A mixed methods investigation.* Unpublished doctoral dissertation, University of North Texas, Denton, Texas.

Winton, M. A. (1990). An evaluation of a support group for parents who have a sexually abused child. *Child Abuse & Neglect, 14,* 397–405.

CHAPTER 15

Trauma Informed Art Therapy and Sexual Abuse in Children

CATHY MALCHIODI

N INE-YEAR-OLD MARLENE CREATED a series of drawings and paintings for me, depicting the following story during several art therapy sessions:

A bumblebee with a large stinger chases a cat around her house. The bee eventually catches up with her and stings her while she screams loudly, but no one comes to help. The bee comes back and stings her again and again on other days. Finally, one day she runs away and hides at her friend's house down the street. Police come and take the bee away in their car and a nice lady takes the cat to a hospital to visit a doctor. The cat is put in a room and given some toys to play with. The cat feels safe, but the cat worries that her mother will be angry with her for going with the nice lady. The cat also worries that something is wrong with her and feels sick to her stomach. She wonders if the doctor and her mother will find out that the bee stung her. Later, the cat goes with the nice lady to a home where there are other cats and a man and a lady who give them dinner, read them stories at night, and play with them. The cat feels a little bit better, but she still feels sick once in awhile. She wonders if she will die. She also has really bad, scary dreams and sometimes forgets where she is. Her teacher gets mad at her when she does not stay awake in school. The end.

Like many children who are sexually abused, Marlene uses art expression to create visual symbols and metaphors to describe what happened to her. In her story and drawings, the girl (the cat) was forced to have repeated intercourse with her stepfather; after repeated abuse, she ran away to a neighbor's home and fortunately the neighbor called the police and protective services when the child disclosed what happened. A social worker took the child to have medical and forensic examinations with a doctor who confirmed the sexual abuse and recommended that child protective services intervene. Child protective services determined that the child should remain in foster care for the short term until the home situation was resolved and safety could be established. The girl responded positively to her foster care parents, but continued to have many trauma reactions including intrusive memories (nightmares), somatic complaints, and dissociative episodes that interfered with her attention span.

Not all children who are sexually abused use art to communicate symbolically or to tell complete stories of their maltreatment through their art expressions. Experiences of sexual abuse and subsequent trauma reactions are different, depending on psychosocial, developmental, cultural, behavioral, and cognitive factors described throughout this book. In reality, there is a continuum of response to sexual abuse, ranging from relatively few trauma reactions to profound disruption in attachment, behavior, cognition, and interpersonal functioning. Responses to creative interventions by children who have been sexually abused reflect this continuum as well as their own idiosyncratic preferences for self-expression and use of art materials.

Fortunately, many children can use the creative process of art making to convey their experiences and how their trauma reactions manifest; all children can benefit from art's inherent qualities to help regulate affect and reduce arousal when it is correctly applied as an intervention. This chapter provides a basic rationale and guidelines for the application of trauma informed art therapy in individual work with sexually abused children with a particular emphasis on those who have experienced multiple incidents. A neurodevelopmental approach and current best practices in trauma intervention are used to illustrate the importance of art expression in addressing the complexities of child sexual abuse.

ART THERAPY AND SEXUAL ABUSE

Art therapy is a form of expressive therapy that combines psychotherapeutic theories and techniques with an understanding of the psychological aspects of the creative process or art making (Malchiodi, 2006). The purpose of art therapy is much the same as other expressive modalities—to improve or maintain mental health and emotional well-being. In contrast to other expressive therapies that use performing arts (music, movement, or drama) or play activities in treatment, art therapy capitalizes on drawing, painting, sculpture, photography, and other forms of visual art expression. Art making is seen as an opportunity to express oneself imaginatively, authentically, and spontaneously, and as an experience that, over time, can lead to personal fulfillment, emotional reparation, and transformation. Practitioners of art therapy also agree that the creative process, in and of itself, can be a health-enhancing and growth-producing experience (Malchiodi, 2006).

Art therapy, like play therapy and sand therapy, originated as a psychoanalytic approach to helping individuals externalize and repair emotional problems through traditional visual media in the form of drawings, paintings, and clay sculpture; these approaches are widely accepted as developmentally appropriate in the treatment of children, particularly those who have experienced abuse or violence (Gil, 2006; Malchiodi, 2008). Because of its roots in psychoanalysis, the field of art therapy originally embraced a psychodynamic approach to intervention with sexually abused children. Cohen and Phelps (1985), Drachnik (1994), Levinson (1986), Oster and Gould (2004), and others mainly defined art therapy as a way of explaining the meaning of children's art expressions and that the art expressions of children who were sexually abused are inherently different than nonabused children. In this sense, art expression served as a form of assessment and visual communication that complemented verbal psychotherapy.

More recently, emerging information on the impact of trauma and the brain has dramatically increased the understanding of how art therapy facilitates children's recovery from trauma, in addition to serving as a form of communication or adjunctive treatment. Drawings and other forms of art expression are not only a means of disclosure of abuse, but also support sensory processing, stress reduction, and eventual trauma integration. For this reason, the contemporary application of art therapy with abused children includes neurodevelopmental, somatic, and cognitive-behavioral approaches, among others (Malchiodi, 2008). For example, Gil (2006), a play therapist and art therapist, provides a perspective that includes neurobiology principles and an emphasis on helping abused children learn and manage self-regulation while integrating family members into overall treatment. Pifalo (2007) combines trauma-focused cognitive behavioral therapy (CBT) approaches with art therapy to address the effects of sexual abuse in children. In her work with severely abused children, Klorer (2003, 2008) sees art therapy as a neurodevelopmentally appropriate way to help children conceptualize and express experiences, often without verbal disclosure of actual events. In brief, most contemporary art therapists concur that because of the visual nature of traumatic memories and how they are stored in the brain, art therapy may offer an effective means to support the processing and integration of trauma and eventual reparation and recovery in children (Malchiodi, 2000, 2003, 2009).

TRAUMA INFORMED ART THERAPY

In my practice as an art therapist and mental health counselor, most children I see have been chronically abused and often physically mal-treated and neglected. As a result, these children generally have a variety of severe trauma reactions (hyperarousal, avoidance, dissociation, and intrusive memories), learning and psychosocial challenges, and attach-ment difficulties (Cook, Blaustein, Spinazzola, & van der Kolk, 2003). In many cases, psychodynamic and CBT strategies alone cannot address the reactions of children whose cognitive, developmental, and interpersonal skills are compromised by multiple traumatic experiences of sexual abuse, physical abuse, and neglect.

Art therapy, like other creative and expressive arts therapies, has a unique role as an intervention with traumatized children, including those who have been sexually abused. The International Society for Traumatic Stress Studies (ISTSS) (Foa, Keane, Friedman, & Cohen, 2009) summarizes the role of the creative art therapies, including art therapy, in the treatment of posttraumatic stress disorder (PTSD). The ISTSS summary underscores the growing interest in the relationship between the creative arts therapies and the brain, including how the brain processes traumatic events and the possibilities for reparation through art, music, movement, play, and drama interventions.

Trauma informed art therapy (Malchiodi, 2010) integrates neurode-velopmental knowledge (Perry, 2006; Steele & Rader, 2002) and the sensory qualities of art making in trauma intervention. According to the Substance Abuse and Mental Health Services Administration (SAMHSA, 2010), trauma informed interventions specifically address the consequences of trauma in the individual and recognize the interrelation between trauma and symptoms of trauma. A comprehensive view of neurological, biologi-cal, psychological, and social effects of trauma and violence ultimately informs intervention (Jennings, 2004). In sum, a trauma informed approach must take into consideration how the mind and body respond to traumatic events; recognizes that symptoms are adaptive coping strategies rather than pathology; includes cultural sensitivity and empowerment; and helps to move individuals from being not only survivors, but ultimately "thrivers" through skill building and resilience enhancement (Malchiodi, 2010).

Because young survivors of sexual abuse may also be without the means to place memories in historical context through language, art therapy combined with neurobiological, somatic, and cognitive-behavioral approaches can assist children in bridging sensory memories and narrative. Trauma informed art therapy is based on the idea that art expression is helpful in reconnecting implicit (sensory) and explicit (declarative) memories of trauma and in the treatment of PTSD (Malchiodi, 2003). In particular, it is an approach that assists children's capacity to self-regulate affect and modulate the body's reactions to traumatic experiences in the earliest stages to set the stage for eventual trauma integration and recovery.

Trauma informed art therapy capitalizes on four specific areas with traumatized children. These areas include: (1) arousal reduction and affect regulation; (2) externalization; (3) sensory processing; and (4) attachment (Malchiodi, 2008). The proceeding section discusses these areas in detail, including sample interventions to illuminate the major principles of trauma informed art therapy with children who have been sexually abused.

AROUSAL REDUCTION AND AFFECT REGULATION

Trauma informed practice begins with helping children reduce uncomfortable reactions, self-soothe, learn to modulate stress, and feel safe. For children who have experienced chronic sexual abuse and have trauma reactions that include uncontrolled hyperarousal, repeated fear responses, anxiety, and attention difficulties, this can be a lengthy process, but necessary to begin during early sessions. An initial focus on arousal reduction and affect regulation does not mean that traumatic events and memories are not addressed, but instead underscores the need for gradual exposure to upsetting material while providing children with ways to adaptively cope and feel in control. In order for children to progressively confront traumatic material, it is important that they learn methods and activities to reduce distress and become an empowered, active participant in their own recovery.

Fortunately, art materials when combined with sensitive directives can help children to learn relaxation skills and provide needed self-soothing experiences.

Lambert (2010) identified a network in the brain that modulates anxiety and is based on a simple premise—that repetitive work with one's hands to produce a rewarding outcome has a positive effect on emotions. This accumbens-striatal-cortical circuit in the brain is activated by hands-on, physical work of a soothing nature. In a practical sense, this bit of neuroscience informs us that simply helping children determine what kinds of reward-driven, repetitive activities they enjoy offers the possibility for reduction of distressful emotions.

For example, early in treatment I introduced Marlene to several simple breathing exercises for relaxation and showed her several arts and crafts activities that involved easily mastered, repetitive skills. As it turned out, she indicated that she enjoyed making clay and paper beads and stringing them to create necklaces and bracelets with my occasional help. For Marlene, stringing beads while we talked about difficult topics helped to reduce trauma reactions, particularly her anxiety; it later became a self-soothing activity she could use between sessions while in foster care when she became worried or afraid. During one session when her worries became the focus of the session, I introduced "how to make a worry doll," showing her how to use yarn to wrap simple wire armatures and make small dolls to hold onto her worries for her. The metaphor of "holding onto worries" was effective for Marlene, but the repetitive act of wrapping colored yarns added to her level of relaxation and self-mastery skills.

Addressing the need for safety and security is also important to a trauma informed approach. In art therapy, this translates to helping abused children experience safety through the senses as well as practical hands-on learning. Marlene particularly enjoyed taking care of a small toy animal I gave her during one of our sessions. As part of the activity, I explained to Marlene that her toy animal (a furry kitten to match her cat metaphor) needed a place to live where it felt happy, loved, and safe and asked her if we could make such a place for the kitten out of the materials we had in the art and play room. After some discussion about what the kitten might need to feel happy and secure, Marlene decided to create a home for it using a shoe box, fabric scraps, feathers, and other soft materials; in subsequent sessions, she added toys, crayons, and other small objects so the kitten could "play and draw pictures."

Like many abused children, Marlene positively responded to the task because of the tactile and soothing nature of the prop (a furry toy). As her art therapist, I was able to use the activity to help her explore ways that she could feel safe, including identifying good and bad touch through her toy cat and a safety plan for the kitten if someone tried to hurt it. In the case of Marlene, the activity not only provided an opportunity to care for something else as she would like to be cared for herself, it also gave us a way to talk about real-life situations that she might face when she needed to find safety or escape harm.

EXTERNALIZATION

Most forms of therapy engage individuals in processes designed to help externalize memories, thoughts, feelings, and experiences. In its basic sense, art therapy encourages externalization through drawing, painting, collage, clay, and other art media (Malchiodi, 2003, 2006). When children express themselves through art, they create a tangible product that is essentially a container for sensory, kinesthetic, or perceived experiences.

In contrast to other experiential therapies, such as sand therapy or play therapy, art therapy usually results in something that is concrete and permanent that remains intact after the session has ended.

Many helping professionals, including art therapists themselves, refer to art therapy as a "non-verbal therapy" (Malchiodi, 2006). Although the act of art making may be defined as nonverbal, there is evidence that a strong connection exists in the brain between language and art expression. Drawing, for example, facilitates children's verbal narratives of emotionally laden events; children who draw while talking about events relate more than twice as many details as children who simply talk about their experiences (Gross & Haynes, 1998; Lev-Weisel, 2007; University of Haifa, 2010). In brief, art expression can increase memory retrieval while helping children to simultaneously organize and communicate narratives more easily than if only asked to use words to convey a memory of an event.

Externalization of trauma memories is important for sexually abused children because they may be without the symbolic representations and the language necessary to place the trauma into a historical context (van der Kolk, 1994). Many trauma experts believe that in cases of repeated sexual abuse, language to describe the trauma becomes inaccessible because of "speechless terror" that overtakes the traumatized brain. At the same time, most models for the treatment of stress reactions suggest that children traumatized by abuse need the opportunity to disclose their experiences in order to eventually integrate traumatic memory (Malchiodi, 2000; Steele, 2007).

When words are not possible or available, art may be one of few ways for some children to communicate what has happened. For Marlene, her first disclosure of distressful sexual abuse was through drawing; like many abused children, she used metaphor and symbols to convey her stories. Even though she understood that she was seeing me for art therapy because of sexual abuse, I honored her metaphors and symbols, allowing the "cat" to provide distance and to become the voice for her stories of physical and emotional trauma. Marlene was able to use drawing and storytelling from the perspective of the "cat" to externalize her experiences until she became comfortable enough to tell me the details of how she was maltreated by her stepfather. Marlene could use drawing readily, but other children may not feel comfortable using art expression or may even find it difficult to use art as communication because of the neurodevelopmental impact of chronic sexual abuse. The latter may externalize their experiences through art expressions that reflect developmental delays or may benefit from using art materials or play activities in other ways, including reducing arousal reactions as described earlier. A trauma-informed approach takes this into consideration, respecting that the need for avoidance of uncomfortable implicit memories of trauma may be necessary until attachment and trust have been established.

Although art can help traumatized children externalize stories, most professionals who use art as part of intervention concur that directing children to depict traumatic events is not always necessary and can be counterproductive in some cases. Marlene's drawings were spontaneous and she easily engaged in art expression and storytelling about her creations. Even when children are comfortable using drawing, painting, or clay to depict stories about traumatic events, it is equally important to engage them in making images that provide opportunities to experience times that the trauma was not happening. With Marlene, it was helpful to have her create a series of drawings about times when the "cat was not being hurt by the bee" in order to redirect her to positive, enjoyable moments for a part of each session. Because art is a sensory activity that taps emotional areas of the brain, helping children explore nontraumatic times via creative expression helps to shift attention and allow children to practice some "good feelings" through a hands-on, sensory level, too.

The content of art expressions invariably brings up one perennial question about children's art products: Can the art expressions of these children reveal anything about their maltreatment? In brief, the answer is, "It's complicated." A number of symbols and characteristics continue to be noted by practitioners of art therapy, but most studies have been inconclusive in identifying specific images or styles found in all art expressions of children who have experienced sexual abuse (Malchiodi, 1998, 2000). This is not surprising because of the continuum of abuse and children's responses to abuse are based on temperament, type of incidents, culture, and environment, among other factors. In brief, although all art externalizes something about its creator, it does not manifest itself in a consistent manner in children and adolescents who have been abused, and their creative responses are largely individual (Malchiodi, 1998).

Although content and style of sexually abused children is idiosyncratic, developmental characteristics in artistic expression during childhood do provide some support for the identification of posttraumatic stress reactions in abused children's human figure drawings (HFDs) (Malchiodi, 2009). In a study of HFDs by children who had been exposed to a traumatic event such as sexual abuse and who were identified as experiencing posttraumatic stress reactions as measured on a standard and accepted instrument and a control group determined to be without posttraumatic stress, significant differences were found in the two group's drawings. The HFDs of the children with posttraumatic stress reactions showed developmental delays in content when compared to the control group. This finding is not particularly surprising in light of the wide consensus that severe trauma and stress reactions can interfere with development over time, including cognition and physical development (Silva, 2004).

SENSORY PROCESSING

By nature, art is a sensory experience. It not only has visual qualities, but also involves tactile, kinesthetic, olfactory, and auditory senses. Because highly charged emotional experiences such as trauma are encoded by the limbic system as a form of sensory reality, most professionals agree that expression and processing of sensory memories is necessary to successful intervention (Rothschild, 2000). Steele (2007) observes that trauma intervention involves finding ways to access implicit memories because language may not be available; if memories cannot be communicated linguistically, sensory-based interventions allow these experiences to be expressed. While art expression was once believed to be merely cathartic, in a trauma-informed approach its sensory qualities and the experiential or "action-oriented" nature of the creative process (Weiner, 1999) are central to trauma recovery. The sensory nature of art making is helpful to children like Marlene because creative expression, along with the therapist's direction, encourages child clients to imagine, rehearse, and reframe events in an active, hands-on manner.

Because art materials stimulate the senses, it is important to be knowledgeable about just how art making stimulates implicit memories. For some children, materials that are not so easily controlled—such as paints with large brushes—can quickly turn into chaos; a spilled paint jar in the art therapy room may provoke sudden fear or anxiety similar to spilling a milk container at home that results in violence or punishment from a parent. Clay may be self-soothing for one child whereas another child may find it difficult to touch because it has sensory reminders of uncomfortable events. For example, using wet clay or paints provoked hyperactivity and anxiety in Marlene; in particular, she voiced concern about "getting messy" and "not being neat," expressing worries about spoiling the art table and getting punished if the clay or paint stained her clothes. Other children may have idiosyncratic responses to materials based on past experiences with art, cultural influences, or personality; for example, some children depict sexual themes more readily in clay or may begin to sexually act out in response to using it. These reactions are individual, but do underscore that when using a variety of art media with children, therapists should be sensitive and observant of how child clients react to materials.

Finally, the sensory qualities of art expression are particularly useful with sexually abused children in combination with somatic approaches. Somatic experiencing is a method of focusing on the body's or physiological memory of the trauma rather than taking an insight-oriented or cognitive approach (Rothschild, 2000; van der Kolk, 1994). Asking children to use colors and shapes to indicate on a body outline where trauma reactions are felt in the body is an effective art-based somatic technique (Malchiodi, 1997, 2008). Because sexually abused children often use dissociation as an adaptive coping skill in response to abuse and lose track of how fears and worries impact their bodies, it is important to address this in a child-friendly way during treatment. I like to start with helping children locate good sensations, including those that help to calm and relax before eventually moving to where any "worries" (implicit trauma memories) or other negative feelings are felt in the body. This approach helped Marlene who was able to identify how and where she felt trauma reactions "in colors, shapes, or images" on the body outline and especially when intrusive memories occurred. I also encouraged her to explore in drawing and other materials "how your body would feel if it were relaxed and calm." These activities capitalize on using sensory integration to help children learn to recognize how their bodies react to trauma, but also allow them to practice feelings to replace or at least diminish distress.

ATTACHMENT

Siegel (1999) explains attachment as "an inborn system in the brain that evolves in ways that influence and organize motivational, emotional, and memory processes with respect to significant caregiving figures" (p. 67). With regard to trauma's interference with attachment, Perry (2006) observes, "Experience can become biology" (p. 1); this statement reflects the all too often outcome for sexually abused children whose attachments have been disrupted, have developed abnormally, or have never developed. However, when chronic abuse interrupts healthy relationship patterns early in life, Perry and Siegel also inform us that attachment can be developed though appropriate interventions that recapitulate normal relationships in childhood.

In a stable family, children generally have multiple opportunities to engage in creative experimentation through art and play, accompanied by praise, guidance, and support from adults. Unconditional appreciation from significant others and caregivers is a part of developing attachment to others, healthy relationships, and a positive sense of self. Simply put, introducing art making within a positive, supportive relationship with the therapist helps traumatized children recover the "creative life" (Cattanach, 2008) and re-create conditions for learning attachment, trust, and self-efficacy.

Although all forms of psychotherapy and counseling are relational in nature, the practice of relational therapy emphasizes that emotional well-being depends on having a satisfying, mutual relationship with others.

Art therapy is uniquely relational because of the application of creative activities within the therapist-child dynamic. For Marlene, building a relationship with me through art activities was particularly important because of her profound mistrust of adults and early disruptions in her relationships with her mother and biological father. In fact, her years as a toddler and preschooler were unstable in terms of living conditions, and she and her mother resided in multiple households and homeless shelters; extended family contact was also limited and her mother had several brief relationships with men after her father left them when Marlene was 18 months old.

Although there are many ways to recapitulate normal attachment-building experiences of childhood between therapist and child, an important goal in Marlene's case involved art therapy sessions that included her mother, Elena. In preparation for Marlene to return home to live with her mother, we scheduled several sessions at which child and mother were present for parent-child art therapy. To some extent, the purpose of these sessions involved giving each a chance to use art to express their perceptions and experiences; the major portion was devoted to modeling to Elena how to enjoy art and play activities with her child and help her learn ways to increase attachment through engaging in sensory activities together. Marlene also had the opportunity to show Elena some of the self-soothing projects we worked on in earlier sessions, including making worry dolls together and collaborating, designing, and fabricating a new "safe place" for Marlene's toy kitten. As Riley (2001) notes, the nonverbal dimensions of these types of joint activities tap into early relational states before words are dominant; the goal is to strengthen parent-child bonds through teaching the brain to establish new, more productive skills and relationships.

A BRIEF WORD ON ART THERAPY AND CULTURE

Trauma informed art therapy includes attention to culture when designing interventions for sexually abused children. It is often said that art expression is a nonthreatening activity for children and one that is readily accepted as pleasurable. In reality, this is not always true, and children's unique worldviews must be considered when applying art as an intervention. Cultural issues in the application of art therapy to trauma intervention have not been sufficiently explored and defined, but there are some well-recognized considerations in work with children.

First, the sensory experience of art making described earlier in this chapter often stimulates children to behave in ways that mirror experiences, values, and beliefs developed outside the art therapy room. For example, Marlene's fears of "making a mess" quickly became apparent when offered clay or paint; Marlene's cultural and family background instilled strong rules about behavior and pride for keeping her clothes neat and clean. When selecting soothing art activities for Marlene, I first interviewed her about her previous experiences with art, including handiwork such as sewing or crafts and preferences for materials. There can be a great deal of self-soothing to be reexperienced in well-known crafts that bring forth memories of success, cultural pride, or self-esteem. Depending on learning or role models that have dictated how one creates or makes art, some children may prefer to copy or trace images or follow specific directions for projects.

In terms of art supplies, the culturally sensitive professional who uses art as intervention should try to have materials on hand that support and nurture creative expression with children from various cultures. For example, there are multicultural clays, felt markers, and crayons that reflect a variety of skin tones. In collecting photo images for a collage, it is important to assemble a wide range of pictures of various ethnicities, families, lifestyles, and beliefs. Craft materials such fabric, yarns, beads, and other objects can be invaluable in stimulating those children whose creative expression may have involved jewelry making or traditional needle arts (Malchiodi, 2005).

CONCLUSION

This chapter has provided a very brief overview of the role of trauma informed art therapy in work with sexually abused children like Marlene. Many of these children require long-term intervention if abuse has been chronic and complicated by neglect, separations, and other events. Fortunately, emerging information on how trauma impacts the brain has helped to clarify why action-oriented methods like art therapy are helpful as part of an overall program of intervention. As more information unfolds on how sensory activities like art affect trauma recovery, therapists will undoubtedly be able to more effectively help these children move from merely surviving terrible events to thriving posttrauma.

REFERENCES

Cattanach, A. (2008). Working creatively with children and their families after trauma: The storied life. In C. Malchiodi (Ed.), *Creative interventions with traumatized children* (pp. 211–223). New York, NY: Guilford Press.

Cohen, F., & Phelps, R. (1985). Incest markers in children's artwork. *The Arts in Psychotherapy, 12,* 265–283.

Cook, A., Blaustein, M., Spinazzola, J., & van der Kolk, B. (2003). *Complex trauma in children and adolescents.* National Child Traumatic Stress Network: Complex Trauma Task Force.

Drachnik, C. (1994). The tongue as a graphic symbol of sexual abuse. *Art Therapy: Journal of the American Art Therapy Association, 11*(1), 58–61.

Foa, E., Keane, T., Friedman, M., & Cohen, J. (2009). *Effective treatment for PTSD: Practice guidelines from the International Society for Trauma Stress Studies.* New York, NY: Guilford Press.

Gil, E. (2006). *Helping abused and traumatized children: Integrating directive and nondirective approaches.* New York, NY: Guilford Press.

Gross, J., & Haynes, H. (1998). Drawing facilitates children's verbal reports of emotionally laden events. *Journal of Experimental Psychology, 4,* 7–13.

Jennings, A. (2004). *Models for developing trauma informed behavioral health systems and trauma specific services.* Alexandria, VA: National Association of State Mental Health Program Directors.

Klorer, P. (2003). Sexually abused children: Group approaches. In C. A. Malchiodi (Ed.), *Handbook of art therapy* (pp. 339–350). New York, NY: Guilford Press.

Klorer, P. (2008). Expressive therapy for severe maltreatment and attachment disorders: A neuroscience framework. In C. Malchiodi (Ed.), *Creative interventions with traumatized children* (pp. 43–61). New York, NY: Guilford Press.

Lambert, K. (2010). *Lifting depression: A neuroscientist's hands-on approach to activating your brain's healing power.* New York, NY: Basic Books.

Levinson, P. (1986). Identification of child abuse in art and play products. *Art Therapy: Journal of the American Art Therapy Association, 3*(2), 61–66.

Lev-Wiesel, R., & Liraz, R. (2007). Drawings vs. narratives: Drawing as a tool to encourage verbalization in children whose fathers are drug abusers. *Clinical Child Psychology and Psychiatry, 12*(1), 65–75.

Malchiodi, C. (1997). *Breaking the silence: Art therapy with children from violent homes.* New York, NY: Brunner/Mazel.

Malchiodi, C. (1998). *Understanding children's drawings.* New York, NY: Guilford Press.

Malchiodi, C. (2000). Using art in trauma recovery with children. *Trauma and Loss: Research and Interventions, 1*(1), 7–12.

Malchiodi, C. (2003). *Handbook of art therapy.* New York, NY: Guilford Press.

Malchiodi, C. (2005). The impact of culture on art therapy with children. In E. Gil & A. Drewes (Eds.), *Cultural issues in play therapy* (pp. 96–111). New York, NY: Guilford Press.

Malchiodi, C. (2006). *Art therapy sourcebook* (2nd ed.). New York, NY: McGraw-Hill.

Malchiodi, C. (2008). *Creative interventions with traumatized children.* New York, NY: Guilford Press.

Malchiodi, C. (2009). *The effect of posttraumatic stress disorder on children's human figure drawings.* Ph.D. dissertation, Northcentral University, United States—Arizona. Retrieved September 11, 2010, from *Dissertations & Theses: A&I.* (Publication No. AAT3368184).

Malchiodi, C. (2010, September 12). Trauma informed art therapy. *Trauma and Children*. Retrieved September 13, 2010, from http://tlcinstitute.wordpress .com/2010/09/13/trauma-informed-art-therapy/

Oster, G. D., & P. G. Crone (2004). *Using drawings in assessment and therapy: A guide for mental health professionals*. New York, NY: Brunner-Routledge.

Perry, B. (2006). Death and loss: Helping children manage their grief. *Early Childhood Today*, 15(4), 1–3.

Pifalo, T. (2007). Jogging the cogs: Trauma-focused art therapy and cognitive behavioral therapy with sexually abused children. *Art Therapy: Journal of the American Art Therapy Association*, 24(4), 170–175.

Riley, S. (2001). *Group process made visible: Group art therapy*. Philadelphia, PA: Brunner-Routledge.

Rothschild, B. (2000). *The body remembers*. New York, NY: Norton.

Siegel, D. J. (1999). *The developing mind: Toward a neurobiology of interpersonal experience*. New York, NY: Guilford Press.

Silva, R. (2004). *Posttraumatic stress disorders in children and adolescents*. New York, NY: Norton.

Steele, W. (2007). When cognitive interventions fail with children of trauma: Memory, learning, and trauma interventions. Retrieved September 12, 2010, from www.starrtraining.org/research

Steele, W., & Rader, M. (2002). *Structured sensory intervention for traumatized children, adolescents and parents: Strategies to alleviate trauma (SITCAP)*. Lewiston, NY: Edwin Mellon Press.

Substance Abuse and Mental Health Services Administration (2010). Trauma informed care. Retrieved September 12, 2010, from http://mentalhealth .samhsa.gov/nctic/trauma.asp

University of Haifa. (2009, March 11). Drawing enhances verbalization in children of drug-addicts. *ScienceDaily*. Retrieved September 11, 2010, from www .sciencedaily.com/releases/2009/03/090311180718.htm

van der Kolk, B. (1994). *The body keeps the score*. Cambridge, MA: Harvard Medical School.

Weiner, D. (1999). *Beyond talk therapy: Using movement and expressive techniques in clinical practice*. Washington, DC: American Psychological Association.

CHAPTER 16

Group Therapy With Sexually Abused Children

LIANA LOWENSTEIN and RACHEL COOK FREEMAN

INTRODUCTION

G ROUP THERAPY IS one of the most widely used treatment modalities for child sexual abuse. This chapter provides a rationale for the use of groups to treat sexually abused children and their non-offending caregivers, and presents an overview of group structure and composition. A sample curriculum for a treatment group for female survivors of sexual abuse ages 7 to 12 is outlined, and a case study highlights group process issues.

RATIONALE FOR GROUP THERAPY

Sexually abused children can experience a myriad of feelings and symptoms including guilt, shame, fear, depression, anxiety, sleep problems, low self-esteem, and posttraumatic stress disorder (Chadwick Center for Children and Families, 2004; Finkelhor, 1986; Gil, 1991). If left untreated, these symptoms can result in long-term negative effects for the child (Duffany & Pano, 2009). Moreover, survivors of sexual abuse often feel estranged, isolated, and alienated (Foa, Keane, Friedman, & Cohen, 2009).

Individual and family therapy can be very helpful for sexually abused children, but there are unique advantages of group therapy. Universality—the discovery that one's own experience has been shared with others—is an important curative factor in group treatment as it counters elements of secrecy, isolation, and the sense of being different (Briere, 1991; Grotsky, Camerer, & Damiano, 2000; Mandell & Damon, 1989; Yalom, 2005). Vicarious learning, the learning that results from observation of fellow group members, also occurs in group therapy (Yalom, 2005). Additionally, the group setting can encourage greater risk-taking and catharsis. Children who are initially cautious to explore and express certain issues may open up as they see other peers engage in activities. The group becomes an ideal modality because it enhances interpersonal skills (Connors, Schamess, & Strieder, 1997; Grotsky et al., 2000).

GROUP COMPOSITION AND STRUCTURE

When working with sexually abused children, the most effective groups are those that are same sex and made up of children who are no more than two years apart in age (Grotsky et al., 2000; Jensen, 2004; Mandell & Damon, 1989). Most group therapy models offer closed groups, with members of a group comprising a single cohort, rather than fluid group membership (Schnurr et al., 2003).

The ideal number of participants for a successful group is six to eight (Grotsky et al., 2000; Mandell & Damon, 1989; Rivas & Toseland, 2005). Weekly 90-minute group sessions are most typical and effective with sexually abused children (Grotsky et al., 2000; Mandell & Damon, 1989). Co-therapists are recommended for leading these groups for safety reasons and to ensure that each child's individual needs are met. If two therapists are leading the group, they have a better ability to focus on each individual child, respond to issues that arise in the group, and observe behaviors, reactions, and responses of each child. Because inappropriate physical interactions and boundary issues often occur among members within sexual abuse groups, having co-therapists provides additional protection and accountability for the therapists if such issues were to arise.

CONCURRENT NONOFFENDING CAREGIVER GROUP

It is best practice to conduct a concurrent nonoffending caregiver group while children are involved in their own sexual abuse group (Cohen & Mannarino, 2000; Deblinger, Stauffer, & Steer, 2001; Grotsky et al., 2000; Harvey & Taylor, 2010; Mandell & Damon, 1989; Smith & Kelly, 2008). The nonoffending caregiver group should address child development, parenting, abuse dynamics, safety issues, and ways of strengthening the parent-child relationship. Involving the child's primary caregivers empowers the caregivers and enhances their ability to parent their children effectively.

It is recommended to integrate a joint caregiver-child activity (discussed later in this chapter) into the last 30 minutes of every session to enable caregivers to practice skills learned in the group, and to receive input and support from the therapists.

ASSESSMENT AND SCREENING

Prior to involvement in group treatment, a comprehensive assessment should be conducted on each child and family. This assessment should combine psychometric testing with individual and family clinical interviews (the reader is referred to the chapters on assessment in this volume for further information). Appropriate pregroup assessment and screening allows the therapists to build trust and rapport with and assess each individual group member. Additionally, the pregroup sessions provide the therapists the opportunity to explain the group therapy process and benefits to the children and caregivers to decrease fears and reservations.

INTERVENTIONS

The interventions described below are appropriate for children aged 7 to 12. Some of the interventions can be modified for younger or older age groups. Note that sharing details of the sexual abuse (creating a trauma narrative) is not a part of the group treatment curriculum, as it is recommended that this module be addressed in individual therapy.

Each session follows a similar format: (1) icebreaker activity (10 minutes); (2) selection of Rule Cards (5 minutes); (3) themed activities and group discussion (45 minutes); (4) joint caregiver-child activity, Feel Better Bag, *My Body* song, snack, and clean-up (30 minutes).

Session 1: Getting Acquainted and Establishing Safety

The first group session focuses on familiarizing members with the group purpose and format, alleviating anxiety, getting acquainted, defining rules, building cohesion, establishing trust and safety, beginning to talk about sexual abuse, and forming a sense of group identity. The group leaders begin with a brief verbal introduction that reiterates salient issues such as the purpose and format of the group, confidentiality, and so on. Group members can then decorate their name tags.

Group rules and boundaries can be established and enforced through the use of Rule Cards (Lowenstein, 2002). Each rule is written onto a separate sheet of cardboard. There should be the same number of rule cards as there are group members. The rule cards are placed in a bag. At the beginning of each session, each group member draws one rule card from the bag. For the duration of the session, if a group member breaks a rule, the person holding the rule card holds it up as a reminder of the group rule. Sample rule cards include: listen when someone is talking; talk nicely to each other; no talking without the talking stick; be respectful of property; keep confidences (do not tell each other's stories outside the group); it is okay to pass; and keep one arm's length away from each other.

Icebreakers   Once the group rules are established the members can be engaged in an icebreaker activity. An effective icebreaker is fun, developmentally appropriate, involves all group members, and helps participants to become acquainted. The Balloon Bounce Game (adapted from Lowenstein, 2006) is one suggested activity. To prepare the activity, getting acquainted questions are written onto balloons, such as: (1) What do you like to do for fun? (2) What's one of your favorite movies? (3) What's your favorite color? One balloon is distributed to each member. The balloons are thrown into the air and participants must try to keep them in the air without them touching the ground until the leader yells, "Stop!" Then everyone lets the balloons fall to the ground. One member is chosen to pick up a balloon and answer the question written on it. The balloons are thrown back into the air, and the game continues until each member has had a turn.

An icebreaker activity is introduced at the beginning of each subsequent session. For suggested icebreaker techniques, see Cavert (1999) and Rohnke and Butler (1995).

The scavenger hunt activity (Lowenstein, 2006) is appropriate for the first session as it is engaging, it builds cohesion, and it promotes open communication about feelings and sexual abuse. The leaders develop a list of 10 to 15 scavenger hunt items for group members to create or collect. For example:

- Definition of sexual abuse.
- Outline of a hand.
- Five feelings children might have when they have been sexually abused.
- Two people with the same shoe size.
- Words of advice to help children who feel the abuse was their fault.
- Group of children holding hands and singing a song aloud.

The group is divided into two teams. The teams are given 10 minutes to collect or create as many items on the scavenger hunt list as they can.

The team that collects or creates the most items from the list wins. Bonus points can be awarded for creativity and positive participant behavior. A group leader should be assigned to each team to assist with reading and writing and to facilitate appropriate group interaction. At the end, the therapists can highlight positive interactions observed during the activity, comment on teamwork, and validate the feelings that were identified with respect to the sexual abuse.

Coping Teaching healthy coping strategies is an important goal in sexual abuse treatment. The Feel Better Bag (Lowenstein, 2006) is used as a tool to facilitate healthy coping. This bag is given to each child at the end of the first session to take home. During the joint caregiver-child segment of each session, the children and caregivers are taught a coping strategy and are provided with a prop that serves as a reminder of the strategy. The children take the prop home to place in their Feel Better Bag and are instructed to use the prop to help them practice the coping strategy. Caregivers are taught the strategy as well so they can coach their children to practice at home. For example, group members can be asked to draw a picture of a happy memory and to place the picture in their Feel Better Bag. They can then look at the picture each night at bedtime as a way to elicit and focus on positive feelings. The *My Body* song (Alsop, 1983) is taught to the group in the first session, and is sung at the end of each subsequent session. Children and adults alike benefit from the song's empowering message.

SESSION 2: LEARNING AND TALKING ABOUT SEXUAL ABUSE

The second session provides psychoeducation and facilitates open communication regarding sexual abuse. The Sexual Abuse Game (Crisci, Lay, & Lowenstein, 1996) provides a means by which talk is integrated into an engaging game. A spinner and question cards are required for the game (see Crisci et al., 1998). Group members take turns spinning the wheel and answering a question that corresponds to the category on the wheel (Learning, Feeling, Telling). Below are sample question cards:

Learning
1. What does sexual abuse mean? Have each person in the group give an example of sexual abuse.
2. Why do you think children often keep sexual abuse a secret?
3. True or false: Children who are sexually abused are usually messed up forever.

Feeling

1. Fill in the blank: Since I told about the sexual abuse I have been feeling . . .
2. What are some of the reasons why children sometimes blame themselves for the sexual abuse?
3. True or false: Some children feel two ways toward the abuser (for example, they love the abuser but also feel angry toward the abuser).

Telling

1. Who did you first tell about the sexual abuse, and what happened when you told?
2. If you could say one thing to the person who abused you, what would you say?
3. What has helped you the most since people found out about the sexual abuse?

Group members respond well to the game format because it is a familiar play activity. Moreover, the game elicits material for meaningful therapeutic interchange.

SESSION 3: IDENTIFYING AND EXPRESSING FEELINGS

Many children lack the emotional, cognitive, and verbal abilities to communicate their feelings directly. Children may also suppress their feelings, or restrict their feelings vocabulary to "happy," "sad," and "mad." In such cases, children need permission to express themselves openly, and enhance their feelings vocabulary so they have a means of identifying a range of feeling states.

When children are limited in their ability to talk about their feelings, it can help to combine discussion with engaging play-based activities. *Ali's Story* (Crisci et al., 1996, p. 82) makes use of the power of therapeutic storytelling and art. The leader reads aloud the story "Ali and Her Mixed-Up Feeling Balloon." Each child is then provided with a "My Feeling Balloon" worksheet. Children color the balloon by using a separate crayon to represent each feeling. Children can use more of one color to illustrate feelings that are more intense.

The story can be used to help children explore and discuss aspects related to their sexual victimization. Children can identify with Ali, and they can share in her experiences vicariously. Children's sense of isolation about the sexual abuse may be reduced as they realize that other children, even if they are only fictional characters, have been through similar circumstances.

The balloon is used as a metaphor to allow children to conceptualize how their mixed-up emotions can intensify to the point of feeling that they might explode if the feelings are not dealt with.

SESSION 4: COPING WITH TRIGGERS

Triggers are stimuli that result in a sensory-based reliving of some aspect of the sexual abuse experience. It is important to help children understand, identify, and cope with sensory triggers.

Prior to the group, the leader prepares four plastic bags, for example:

1. Feel bag: Cotton ball, sandpaper, orange rind.
2. Smell bag: Onion, perfume, baby powder.
3. Taste bag: Lemon, salted crackers, candy.
4. Sound bag: Bell, drum, whistle.

The group is engaged in a discussion about the five senses (sight, smell, taste, touch, hearing). The leader then introduces the bags by saying, "When we touch or smell or taste or hear something, our body reacts." The children close their eyes and the items in the bags are passed around the group for the children to touch, smell, taste, and listen to. Children can describe the body reactions and sensations as they handle the items. Children will enjoy the suspense as the mystery items are passed around.

The therapist highlights how the body reacts to sensory triggers, and the children are encouraged to provide their own examples of things they see, smell, taste, touch, or hear and tell how their body reacts. Examples of common triggers related to sexual abuse are then provided. For example, if the abuser smoked, then when the victim sees a pack of cigarettes or smells cigarette smoke this may remind him or her of the sexual abuse, and this can lead to anxious feelings and reactions. Children are then asked to think back to the sexual abuse, and to write or draw the things that remind them of the sexual abuse and to describe their reactions to these triggers. Lastly, group members are provided with grounding strategies to cope with sensory triggers. For example:

Visual: Visualize your safe place or look at comforting pictures.
Auditory: Listen to soothing music, say a mantra out loud (i.e., "It's not real, it's just a flashback, I'm safe now").
Olfactory: Comforting smells (e.g., Scratch 'N Sniff sticker, perfume).
Taste: Chew gum.
Tactile: Caress a comforting object (e.g., stuffed animal or gem stone).

Group members can practice utilizing the above strategies. For instance, if a group member identified men with brown beards as a sensory trigger, then he or she can look at a magazine picture depicting a man with a brown beard while visualizing a safe place to neutralize this trigger.

Session 5: Addressing Self-Blame

Reducing self-blame for the sexual abuse is an essential treatment component. *Gertie and Gordie: The Guilt Free Kids* (Crisci et al., 1996, p. 249) presents various scenarios related to issues of responsibility, and creates a format (via a comic book) for children to challenge and reframe guilty feelings. On each page of the comic book, a child expresses a reason for why he or she feels guilty about the sexual abuse. The other child depicted on the page must come up with a statement to counter the first child's guilty feelings. For example, child number one says, "I feel guilty because I did not stop the abuse." Child number two might then say, "It is hard to stop the abuse when you feel scared or confused." The comic book format is a medium familiar to children and provides emotional distance and humor to an otherwise difficult treatment theme.

Session 6: Understanding Offender Enticement Strategies

Establishing a cognitive framework that allows the child to understand the concepts of trickery, coercion, and manipulation provides the groundwork for the emotional shifts necessary in assigning responsibility to the offender. The concept of offender enticement strategies is illustrated through a puppet show performed by the group leaders (see script and discussion questions in Crisci et al., 1996, p. 302). Two puppets are used (one to represent the abuser, such as a wolf, and one to represent the victim, such as a rabbit). The discussion following the puppet show highlights how offenders manipulate children into going along with the sexual abuse.

The second part of the activity is called "The Abuser's Bag of Tricks." Each group member is provided with a paper bag and several strips of paper. Children begin by writing "The Abuser's Bag of Tricks" on the front of their paper bag. Next, children write on the slips of paper different things their abuser said or did to get them to go along with the sexual abuse. The slips of paper are then placed in the paper bag. This activity helps clients understand that offenders utilize various enticement strategies to gain children's cooperation. Once children understand that offenders purposely manipulate and groom their victims, they are better able to perceive the offender as responsible for the sexual abuse.

SESSION 7: HEALTHY SEXUALITY AND SAFETY

Sexual abuse prematurely introduces children to sexual activity. It disrupts and interferes with the normative process of sexual development. The "Heads or Tails" Game is designed to provide psychoeducation around sexual issues, and ultimately, to help children feel comfortable with their sexuality. To create the game, prepare a set of question cards for the "Heads" category. These are trivia questions that pertain to sexuality, relationships, boundaries, and personal safety. For example:

- True or false: A french kiss is two people kissing while speaking French.
- Name three things that happen to a girl's or boy's body during puberty.
- True or false: It is normal and okay for the abuse to feel good, and for the child to even have an erection or an orgasm during the sexual abuse.
- What should you do if you start to think about the sexual abuse while you are with a boyfriend or a girlfriend?
- If a boy is molested by a male offender, does that mean that boy will be gay?
- What would you do if your boyfriend/girlfriend wanted to have sexual intercourse but you did not feel ready?
- What should you do if someone online wants to meet you in person?

Additional sex trivia questions can be found in Crisci, Lay, and Lowenstein (1996). Also prepare a list of action cards for the "Tails" category. The purpose of the action cards is to channel the children's energy into a positive outlet. Examples of action cards include:

- Hop to the other end of the room and back on one foot.
- Show what happy looks like with your face and body.
- Give the person to your left a high-five.
- Do 10 jumping jacks.
- Give yourself a hug.
- Stomp your feet 10 times then freeze your body for 10 seconds.
- Show what proud looks like with your face and body. (p. 91)

Additional action cards can be found in Lowenstein (2006). The Heads or Tails game is introduced as follows:

> Take turns flipping a coin. If the coin lands on *Heads*, answer a question from the *Heads* list. These questions are about sexuality and relationships. If the

answer is correct (or appropriate), earn 2 points. If the coin lands on *Tails*, everyone in the group follows the instructions from the *Tails* list, then everyone earns one point. Play until all the questions have been answered. At the end of the game, pick a prize from the prize box (if you earned 1–5 points, pick one prize; if you earned 6 or more points, pick two prizes).

Questions can be used to elicit further group discussion. The game format provides a less threatening modality to help children learn and talk about sex-related issues.

SESSION 8: APPROPRIATE BOUNDARIES

Many children who have been sexually abused have difficulty maintaining appropriate boundaries. Moreover, they often lack assertiveness skills, which can put them at risk for further victimization. Kidzspace (Crisci et al., 1996) aims to help children develop appropriate physical boundaries with others, and to learn and practice assertiveness skills. Each group member creates a "safe space of their own" using large sheets of paper and craft materials (e.g., fabric, glitter, string). When designing their space, they are asked to consider what would make it happy and safe and who would and would not be permitted to enter. Signs designating rules for their space can be added, for example, ask before you enter, no name calling, keep one arm's length away, only safe touching allowed, and so on. Group members can then give guided tours of their Kidzspace Creations. Then they can role-play assertive responses to rule violations, such as if someone enters their space without permission. Through this activity, children learn to define their boundaries and strengthen assertiveness skills. It is an empowering intervention and one that lends itself well to the group setting.

SESSION 9: SELF-ESTEEM

Many children who have experienced sexual abuse believe that the abuse defines their life and who they are. They often feel damaged, guilty, hopeless, or helpless. The Write on Board (adapted from Waddell, 2010) puts the abuse experience into context, and helps clients focus on their positive attributes, their support systems, and their positive life experiences. Each group member is provided with a large sheet of paper and several colored markers. The leaders then guide the group members through the following steps:

1. Think of things you like to do that make you feel happy. Write the words on the sheet of paper in various positions (straight, diagonal, etc.).

2. Name some things you can do well. Add the words to the sheet of paper.
3. Identify some important positive life events you have experienced, and write them on the sheet of paper.
4. Think of some places where you like to go where you feel safe. Write these places on the sheet of paper.
5. List some people in your life who love and care about you, and whom you trust. Add these names to the sheet of paper.
6. (Each group member is provided with a small, round, self-adhesive dot sticker.) Stick this little dot in one corner of the sheet of paper. This dot represents the sexual abuse. The sexual abuse happened, and you cannot make it go away. But it is only a little part of your life, compared to all the wonderful things in your life, such as:
   ◦ The things you enjoy doing that make you feel happy.
   ◦ The things you do well that make you feel proud.
   ◦ The positive life events that give you happy memories.
   ◦ The places you like to go that make you feel safe.
   ◦ The people in your life who love you and whom you can trust.

Group members then discuss how they feel as they look at their paper, and the leaders emphasize all the positives in their lives.

SESSION 10: TERMINATION

Termination is a time to process feelings about ending treatment and to celebrate therapeutic achievements. The Last Session Card Game (adapted from Lowenstein, 2010b) was created with these goals in mind. To prepare the game, the following 10 questions are written onto index cards:

1. Tell about a skill you learned in therapy that you can use to deal with problems that arise in the future.
2. Change seats with someone in the group who helped you.
3. What is a positive change you have made during your time in this group?
4. What was least helpful and what was most helpful in this group?
5. Name someone outside of this group who can help you when you have a problem or a worry.
6. What was your favorite activity that you did in this group?
7. Fill in the blank: My proudest moment in this group was when I
   _____.
8. How do you feel about ending this group?

9. What advice would you give the group leaders in working with children who have been sexually abused?
10. Group members often teach group leaders valuable lessons. Ask your group leader to tell something you have taught him or her.

The game is explained as follows: "Take turns picking the top card from the deck of cards. If you get a card with an **even number**, pick a card from the question card pile and **answer the question**. If you get a card with an **odd number**, pick a card from the question card pile and **ask someone in the group to answer the question**. If you pick a Jack, Queen, or King, you get to pick something from the goodie bag. At the end of the game, everyone who played gets to pick something from the goodie bag."

The therapist can observe the game play, highlighting positive changes he or she has seen during the course of the group. Other suggested activities to incorporate into a last group session include My Wish for You (Flinner, 2010); Pat on the Back (Goodyear-Brown, 2005); Lifesavers (Noziska, 2008); and What I Learned Layered Gift (Lowenstein, 2008).

Joint Caregiver-Child Activities

It is beyond the scope of this chapter to describe the activities implemented in the joint caregiver-child segment of the sessions, however, the following are some suggested activities: Toss the Ball (Post Sprunk, 2010); Sweet Dream Box (Snead, 2008); Messages in Art (Gill, 2010); Safety Shield (Gallo-Lopez, 2000); Twizzler Test (Goodyear-Brown, 2002); and Healing Animals (Lowenstein, 2010).

Case Example

THE GROUP

A 10-week group for girls between 8 and 10 years of age who had experienced sexual abuse was facilitated at a sexual assault treatment center. Eight children and their nonoffending caregivers were screened and six were assessed as being appropriate for this group. The children's group met weekly for 90 minutes and was facilitated by two female therapists. A group for the girls' nonoffending caregivers was held concurrently and was led by two therapists, one male and one female.

Individual and family treatment was provided in addition to the group therapy. The six members of the group presented here were

(continued)

Kelly, Lisa, Brooke, Jasmine, Nicole, and Monica. Each child was experiencing trauma-related symptoms and behavioral responses resulting from sexual victimization, such as nightmares, anxiety, excessive fearfulness, poor body image, feelings of guilt and shame, lack of interpersonal boundaries, and social isolation.

PREGROUP SESSION

Prior to the first group session, the group therapists met with each child and her caregiver. During this session, the group leaders reviewed the goals, expectations, and benefits of the group. This pregroup session allowed the therapists to begin to develop rapport with each group member and provided an opportunity to further assess group appropriateness. Additionally, this session helped to reduce feelings of anxiety the children and caregivers might have experienced in relation to starting group therapy.

THE GROUP PROCESS

Note: Although this case study highlights only the children's group, the model described in this chapter integrates joint caregiver-child activities in the last 30 minutes of each group session.

The first group session was focused on establishing safety and building trust and rapport among the members and the group leaders. As the group therapists welcomed the children to the group and began talking about the purpose of the group, the girls created name plates with poster board, markers, and stickers. The group members were initially very quiet as they began decorating their nameplates. In an attempt to facilitate interaction and to engage the girls, leaders made observations about nameplates, such as "It looks like Jasmine and Brooke both love pink" and "Monica has found some really cool stickers. . . . Monica, can you show the other girls those great stickers?"

After the nameplates were created, the group leaders gave a brief introduction to the group and indicated that each girl was participating in the group because she had been sexually abused. This helped the group members to understand that they share a common reason for inclusion in the group. Each member then introduced herself by showing her nameplate and sharing one fun fact about herself. Jasmine and Brooke presented as soft-spoken and nervous whereas Lisa, Kelly, Nicole, and Monica were much more relaxed and animated as they introduced themselves.

(continued)

(*continued*)

The group leaders then led the girls through the creation of group rules using the Rule Cards activity. Next, the group participated in the Balloon Bounce Game. This was a fun way for all of the girls to become actively engaged in the group and to begin getting to know each other better. The girls were each given a balloon that had a Getting Acquainted question written on it. When the leaders asked the girls to stand up and get ready to start bouncing their balloons, most of the girls excitedly started playing with their balloons, tossing them around the room, and some girls even tossed their balloon back and forth to each other. Jasmine stood back and was slower to actively participate. To address this shy member, one of the group leaders asked the girls to stand in a circle so that no one was outside of the group. The group leader continued by praising the girls for the courage it took to come to the group tonight and reassured them that although some of them may be feeling scared, shy, confused, or unsure, those feelings are all very normal and hopefully this activity would help them feel more comfortable. As the girls answered the Getting Acquainted questions, the leaders made connections among the group members by asking questions such as, "Who else likes to play computer games? Is math anyone else's favorite subject?" Through questions such as these, the group leaders helped the girls form relationships, find similarities with each other, and begin establishing trust and rapport.

To begin establishing a closing self-care ritual, the group leaders gave each group member a brown paper bag to decorate. This bag would be their Feel Better Bag (and would be added to over the life of the group). During the caregiver-child segment of the session, each client was given a small container of bubbles. The caregivers and children then blew bubbles together, practicing taking a deep inhale, and then exhaling very slowly into the bubble wand to produce a large bubble, as opposed to several small bubbles that are produced from short, shallow breaths. This activity helped teach the clients the strategy of deep breathing, and sending them home with the bubbles provided them the opportunity to practice this relaxation skill. The leaders modeled positive behaviors for the caregivers such as encouragement, targeted praise, and warmth.

The children and their caregivers were taught the *My Body* song. This would become a favorite part of the group as evidenced by the enthusiasm with which the members would sing the song in later sessions.

(*continued*)

As the group met for its second session, they were moving out of the initial stage of group development and into the transition stage. This stage is characterized by ambivalence, loss of control, anxiety and defensiveness (Corey, 2008). An icebreaker activity called Commonalities (Rohnke and Butler, 1995) was utilized to put the children at ease and to strengthen group cohesion. Next, the group played the Sexual Abuse Game. During the activity, there were several instances when group members expressed common experiences as evidenced by responses such as "Me too" and "That's exactly how I felt." The game was used as a springboard for further discussion. For example, Brooke drew the question "True or false: Some children feel two ways toward the abuser." Brooke answered that this statement was true but she did not elaborate. One of the group leaders asked Brooke to identify two feelings she thought kids might have toward their abuser. Brooke stated that she thought a lot of kids might feel mad at their abuser but might also love him. The therapist followed Brooke's statement by asking the group members to share their feelings toward their abuser. Lisa said that her abuser was her father and she still loves him and misses him. Monica then stated that her abuser was also her father and she hates him and wishes he were dead. The group therapist interjected by saying, "Whatever you are feeling toward the abuser is normal and okay." The game provided psychoeducation to the girls, initiated open communication about sexual abuse, and provided normalization and validation to the members.

By the third group session, group roles had emerged and the girls were entering the conflict phase of group development. Lisa demonstrated leadership qualities, often volunteering to go first and initiating discussion. Monica was at times viewed as the troublemaker because of her occasional aggressive responses and interruptions. Jasmine was the quiet member who had difficulty self-disclosing and taking risks. Nicole had become the scapegoat, often being ostracized or teased for the way she talked or acted. Kelly was the energetic member, often needing redirection. Brooke was a people-pleaser, constantly looking for affirmation and worrying that she wasn't saying the right thing. The group leaders addressed members' roles by modeling appropriate communication and social skills, redirecting when necessary, and teaching and practicing assertiveness skills.

After an engaging icebreaker during this third group meeting, *Ali's Story* was read and discussed, and each group member created a Feeling Balloon. The activity increased the children's feelings vocabulary and

(continued)

(*continued*)

ignited open discussion of feelings. Kelly, for example, colored over half of her Feeling Balloon black (for scared), and she revealed that she is afraid that the abuser (her stepfather) is going to "hurt" her again. She further stated that her mother allows her stepfather to come over at times, which is a violation of the court order. Kelly's disclosure led to a group discussion of what the children could do if they feel unsafe. The issue was further explored through the Safety Shield activity during the caregiver-child segment of the session. Further, the therapist discussed the issue individually with Kelly's mother after the group and in the parent's group in the next session, and a safety plan was put into place.

By the fourth group session, the girls had established a cohesive and trusting group. They appeared to feel safe enough in the group to share more openly. In sessions 4 and 5, the group members identified sensory triggers and discussed feelings of guilt related to the sexual abuse. The children were able to give and receive support and reduce their feelings of guilt and shame. The group leaders continued to model appropriate behaviors and reinforce common themes that provided validation and universality for the girls.

Session 6 was devoted to the Abuser's Bag of Tricks. This activity helped the girls understand and identify offender grooming and enticements strategies, and thus aided them in placing appropriate blame on the abuser. During this activity, the girls were asked to write statements on slips of paper of things that the abuser said or did to trick, manipulate, or entice them into going along with the sexual abuse. These statements were placed in their paper bag labeled the *Abuser's Bag of Tricks*. The bags were then passed around, and each member took a turn reading statements that were written on the strips of paper. This was another activity that elicited responses from the girls such as, "That happened to me too" and "My abuser also said that." This activity evoked intense emotions from some of the group members whose abusers were once loved and trusted family members. Brooke, Jasmine, and Kelly talked about missing the abuser. Other group members expressed anger at being tricked by their abuser. Still others expressed ambivalent feelings toward the abuser, particularly Nicole, who indicated that the abuser manipulated her but was at times loving and nurturing. As this conversation continued, Brooke became very emotional and began crying. The leaders reflected Brooke's emotion by stating, "Brooke, it looks like

(*continued*)

this conversation about abusers is very upsetting to you." Lisa asked Brooke if she wanted a hug. The leaders praised Lisa for asking permission to give Brooke a hug before doing so. Monica began to fidget and appeared uncomfortable with the intensity of emotions Brooke expressed. The leaders tracked Monica's feelings and behaviors by stating, "Monica, it appears that you are fidgeting with the bag and you have an upset expression on your face. What are you thinking and feeling right now?" Monica replied, "It just hurts so bad." The other members agreed with Monica's statement and began offering each other words of support. In previous sessions, Monica would have responded to this type of interaction with an aggressive reaction. The change in Monica's behaviors as well as the interactions and deep connections of the other members showed that this group was successfully moving through the working phase of group development.

The Heads or Tails Game was introduced in the seventh session. This activity provided a nonthreatening, age-appropriate way to discuss healthy sexuality. The group members initially felt awkward talking about sexual issues, as evidenced by their nervous laughter and silly behavior. The action cards helped to channel the children's anxiety into a positive outlet. Some of the question cards elicited deeper discussion. During one such question, Kelly asked if there was something wrong with her because sometimes the abuse felt good. The leaders responded by offering additional education regarding the physiological response to sexual touch. After this normalization was offered, other girls in the group responded that they too were confused by the way their bodies responded to the sexual abuse. This type of sharing and learning continued throughout the game.

In the eighth session, the group leaders initiated discussion on the upcoming termination. Adequately preparing group members for termination provides a corrective experience for children who have abandonment issues and facilitates a positive ending to the group experience. After this brief discussion, the group participated in the Kidzspace activity, focusing on appropriate boundaries. The girls created their own safe space on a large sheet of paper using a variety of craft materials. Then each group member gave a tour of her safe space. Lisa shared that she put a big Stop Sign in the middle of her safe space that symbolized no unsafe touches. Brooke explained that she cut out pictures of mothers and daughters from magazines and glued them to her safe space because her mom is her safe person.

(*continued*)

(*continued*)

Kelly said that she loves dogs and teddy bears so she put lots of them in her safe place. Jasmine included a sign that said, "Knock before entering," which she felt would keep her safer. Nicole drew a group of girls holding hands around the border of her safe space. She said this would always remind her of their group and how it made her feel better. When it was Monica's turn to share, she stated that she didn't want to talk about her safe space. Ever since the conversation about termination, Monica had withdrawn. The group leaders respected Monica's needs and feelings and encouraged her to share her creation when she was ready. After the tours, the group engaged in role-plays, practicing what they would do and say if someone invaded their personal boundaries.

At the beginning of the ninth session, group leaders revisited the discussion of the group's upcoming graduation/termination. This time, Monica openly shared that she didn't want group to end and that she felt sad and angry about it. The group leaders thanked and praised Monica for appropriately sharing her feelings. "Does anyone else feel this way?" they asked. The girls all shook their heads in agreement. This gave the leaders an opportunity to further explore feelings regarding termination. Additionally, the leaders referred to the Feel Better Bag and how this would be helpful to them once group had ended.

The group then moved into the Write on Board activity to address self-esteem. The group members were asked to write on a large sheet of paper the things that make them feel happy, their proud moments, positive memories, and safe people and places. The members were then each given a small red dot sticker and asked to put the dot anywhere on the paper. They were told that this dot represented the sexual abuse they experienced. The group discussed that the dot would never go away, just like the sexual abuse would never go away. However, the sexual abuse was just one thing that happened to them amid all the other positive, happy things that were listed on their paper. The leaders asked how it felt to see so many positive things about themselves on one sheet of paper. Most group members stated that it felt good and that they enjoyed this activity. Jasmine, however, stated that it was still hard for her to believe all of these good things about herself. The group leaders validated Jasmine's feelings and used this as an opportunity to further instill a positive sense of self by asking the girls to share one positive thing about each

(*continued*)

other that they have learned or experienced over the course of the group. This way, not only were the girls being asked to think of positives about themselves, they were also hearing others say positive things to them.

In the final session, the members played the Last Session Card Game. During this game, the group members discussed the things they liked about the group, things they wish had been done differently, what they were most proud of, things they learned during the group, positive coping skills they can use outside of the group, and supportive individuals they can turn to for help outside of the group. The girls shared how they felt better about themselves, their nightmares had gone away, their irrational fears had subsided, and they no longer felt shameful, stigmatized, or isolated. Throughout this card game, the group therapists interjected compliments to highlight the girls' accomplishments.

Each group member had demonstrated positive growth. Early in the life of the group, for example, Jasmine was quiet and slow to participate. By this final session, Jasmine was participating actively. Monica had become more comfortable sharing deep feelings and had also developed empathy for the other girls in the group. Group therapy provided the children a safe environment in which they could gain acceptance, validation, and support from peers, while also successfully reducing overt symptoms and meeting treatment goals.

CONCLUSION

The authors recommend a multimodal treatment approach to treating sexually abused children, which involves individual, group, and family therapy. This chapter has focused on the group component of this comprehensive approach. Suggestions for group composition and structure have been presented along with a curriculum for a 10-week group treatment program for sexually abused girls. The accompanying case example illustrated the curative factors of group treatment and some of the facilitative responses that group leaders can utilize to further enhance the therapeutic experience of group members.

REFERENCES

Alsop, P. (1983). *Songs on sex and sexuality.* Minneapolis, MN: Moose School.

Briere, J. (1991, Spring). Adult survivors: Treatment for the long-term effects of child abuse. *American Professional Society on the Abuse of Children (APSAC) Advisor,* pp. 3–4.

Cavert, C. (1999). *Games (& other stuff) for group.* Oklahoma City, OK: Wood & Barnes.

Chadwick Center for Children and Families. (2004). *Closing the quality chasm in child abuse treatment: Identifying and disseminating best practices.* San Diego, CA.

Cohen, J. A., & Mannarino, A. P. (2000). Predictors of treatment outcome in sexually abused children. *Journal of Child Abuse & Neglect, 24*(7), 983–994.

Connors, K., Schamess, G., & Strieder, F. (1997). Children's treatment groups: General principles and their application to group treatment with cumulatively traumatized children. In J. Brandell (Ed.), *Theory and practice in clinical social work* (pp. 288–314). New York, NY: Free Press.

Corey, G. (2008). *Theory and practice of group counseling* (7th ed.). Belmont, CA: Brooks/Cole.

Crisci, G., Lay, M., and Lowenstein, L. (1996). *Paper dolls and paper airplanes: Therapeutic exercises for sexually traumatized children.* Indianapolis, IN: Kidsrights Press.

Deblinger, E., Stauffer, L. B., & Steer, R.A. (2001). Comparative efficacies of support and cognitive behavioral group therapies for young children who have been sexually abused and their nonoffending mothers. *Journal of Child Maltreatment, 6*(4), 332–343.

Duffany, A., & Pano, P. T. (2009). Outcome evaluation of a group treatment of sexually abused and reactive children. *Research on Social Work Practice, 19*(3), 291–303.

Finkelhor, D. (1986). *Sourcebook on child sexual abuse.* Beverly Hills, CA: Sage.

Flinner, A. (2010). My wish for you. In L. Lowenstein (Ed.), *Assessment and treatment activities for children, adolescents, and families volume two: Practitioners share their most effective techniques* (pp. 150–151). Toronto, ON: Champion Press.

Foa, E. B., Keane, T. M., Friedman, M. J., & Cohen, J. A. (2009). *Effective treatments of PTSD: Practical guidelines from the international society for traumatic stress studies.* New York, NY: Guilford Press.

Gallo-Lopez, L. (2000). A creative play therapy approach to the group treatment of young sexually abused children. In H. Kaduson & C. Schaefer (Eds.), *Short-term play therapy for children* (pp. 269–295). New York, NY: Guilford Press.

Gil, E. (1991). *The healing power of play: Working with abused children.* New York, NY: Guilford Press.

Gill, L. (2010). Messages in art. In L. Lowenstein (Ed.), *Creative family therapy techniques: Play, art, and expressive activities to engage children in family sessions* (pp. 196–197). Toronto, ON: Champion Press.

Goodyear-Brown, P. (2002). *Digging for buried treasure: 52 prop-based play therapy techniques.* Nashville, TN: Author.

Goodyear-Brown, P. (2005). *Digging for buried treasure 2: 52 more prop-based play therapy techniques.* Nashville, TN: Author.

Grotsky, L., Camerer, C., & Damiano, L. (2000). *Group work with sexually abused children: A practitioner's guide.* Thousand Oaks, CA: Sage.

Harvey, S. T., & Taylor, J. E. (2010). A meta-analysis of the effects of psychotherapy with sexually abused children and adolescents. *Clinical Psychology Review, 30*(5), 517–535.

Jensen, M. (2004). *Sexual abuse group treatment: A heroine's journey.* Victoria, BC, Canada: Trafford.

Lowenstein, L. (2002). *More creative interventions for troubled children and youth.* Toronto, ON: Champion Press.

Lowenstein, L. (2006). *Creative interventions for bereaved children.* Toronto, ON: Champion Press.

Lowenstein, L. (2008). (Ed.), *Assessment and treatment activities for children, adolescents, and families: Practitioners share their most effective techniques.* Toronto, ON: Champion Press.

Lowenstein, L. (2010b). (Ed.). *Creative family therapy techniques: Play, art, and expressive activities to engage children in family sessions.* Toronto, ON: Champion Press.

Mandell, J. G., & Damon, L. (1989). *Group treatment for sexually abused children.* New York, NY: Guilford Press.

Noziska, S. K. (2008). *Techniques, techniques, techniques: Play-based activities for children, adolescents, and families.* West Conshohocken, PA: Infinity.

Post Sprunk, T. (2010). Toss the ball. In L. Lowenstein (Ed.), *Creative family therapy techniques: Play, art, and expressive activities to engage children in family sessions* (pp. 250–251). Toronto, ON: Champion Press.

Rivas, R. F., & Toseland, R. W. (2005). *An introduction to group work practice.* Boston, MA: Pearson.

Rohnke, K., & Butler, S. (1995). *Quicksilver.* Dubuque, IA: Kendall/Hunt.

Schnurr, P. P., Friedman, M. J., Foy, D. W., Shea, M. T., Hsieh, F. Y., Lavori, P. W. . . . & Bernardy, N. C. (2003). Randomized trial of trauma-focused group therapy for posttraumatic stress disorder. *Archives of General Psychiatry, 60,* 481–488.

Smith, A. P., & Kelly, A. B. (2008). An exploratory study of group therapy for sexually abused adolescents and non-offending guardians. *Journal of Child Sexual Abuse, 17*(2), 101–116.

Snead, C. (2008). Sweet dream box. In L. Lowenstein (Ed.), *Assessment and treatment activities for children, adolescents, and families: Practitioners share their most effective techniques* (pp. 142–143). Toronto, ON: Champion Press.

Waddell, S. (2010). Write on board. In L. Lowenstein (Ed.), *Assessment and treatment activities for children, adolescents, and families volume two: Practitioners share their most effective techniques* (pp. 142–143). Toronto, ON: Champion Press.

Yalom, I. D. (2005). *The theory and practice of group psychotherapy* (5th ed.). New York, NY: Basic Books.

CHAPTER 17

Effectively Incorporating Bibliotherapy Into Treatment for Child Sexual Abuse

DEANNE GINNS-GRUENBERG and ARYE ZACKS

INTRODUCTION

A S A YOUNG girl, my mother would read nursery rhymes to my sisters and me before sending us to bed. One of her favorites was *Humpty Dumpty*. With her velvety-smooth voice, my mother would read the words off the page. My little sister would sit on her lap, looking at the pictures, while my older sister and I would mouth the words along with my mother.

> Humpty Dumpty Sat on a Wall,
> Humpty Dumpty Had a Great Fall
> All the Kings Horses and All the Kings Men
> Couldn't Put Humpty together Again
> But a kindly old doctor
> With Patience and Glue
> Made Humpty Dumpty
> as good as new.

More than 20 years went by before I discovered the truth: In the original nursery rhyme, there was no kindly old doctor, and Humpty Dumpty was never put back together again. There has been a tremendous change in children's literature over the past 100 years. Whereas stories were once told to frighten children into behaving at the risk of some terrible calamity, today's stories are told to soothe and reassure children. For some, books are an escape into another world. For others, books offer a new life perspective, and for others still, an opportunity for self-exploration. Stories can have an impact on our lives, as we identify with the characters, discuss or reflect on the choices they made, and wonder how those characters would respond to our personal circumstances.

Bibliotherapy allows us, as helping professionals, to take advantage of the story's magic, and help our clients heal and survive the traumas they have experienced. These books help in a number of ways. Some clients benefit by modeling the behavior of a character; others draw their inspiration from the illustrations in the book. Ultimately, the last stage of a successful bibliotherapy process is self-exploration followed by the ability to apply the solution to one's own life.

WHAT IS BIBLIOTHERAPY?

At its most basic level, bibliotherapy is the practice of using literature to help individuals or groups reach their therapeutic goals (Pardeck, 1998). In other words, the clinician chooses either fictional or nonfictional "problem focused" books with believable characters who have dealt with similar problems and successfully resolved them. In the case of children who have been sexually abused, the story serves as a creative tool to help clients experience emotional ties to the character, absorb various coping strategies modeled, receive a message of hope or healing, and ultimately apply the meanings they draw from the stories to their own lives. Alice Bryan (1939) lists six objectives to bibliotherapy, several of which apply to survivors of sexual abuse. These stories exist to: show the reader that she is not alone; offer multiple solutions; help the reader understand human motivation; help the reader recognize the benefits of the experience; provide facts; and encourage the reader to approach a situation realistically. In addition, as children read or listen to a story, they dissect the story on two levels. At the conscious level they focus on the content of the narrative, while on the unconscious level they search for parallels between the experience in the story and their own personal experience. When treating children and adolescents who have been sexually abused, the thematic content of bibliotherapy materials may include any of the following: depiction of trauma and healing, metaphoric descriptions of trauma symptomatology and the normalization of these responses, disclosure dynamics, emotional literacy and affect regulation, stress management, positive coping, appropriate physical boundaries and body safety, information regarding anatomical and physical processes related to gender and sexuality, information aimed at identifying and changing negative thought patterns, self-esteem, and the ultimate journey toward healing.

Bibliotherapy typically takes place within a session, although it may occur in between sessions as well. Some clinicians prescribe books with therapeutically thematic content to be read by caregivers at home to augment the work being done in sessions. Results may not be immediately visible, as it can take some time for the client to apply the lessons of the book to his or her own experience. The bibliotherapy prompts may act as seeds, requiring cultivation by the therapist or other caregivers to grow. Catharsis during a session frequently happens as a story is reenacted through puppetry, sand tray, drawings, dramatization, music, or conversations. Skill-building occurs as the child practices the skills modeled in the story. Additional play-based interventions that target various skill-building dimensions can be used after the reading of a story (Ashby, Kottman, & DeGraaf, 2008; Goodyear-Brown, 2002, 2005, 2010; Kaduson & Schaefer, 1997, 2001; Kenney-Nosizka, 2008; Lowenstein, 2002, 2008, 2010; McGee & Holmes, 2008; Steele, 2009).

HISTORY

The practice of using the written word to help people deal with problems has been used since ancient times. Both the Alexandria library in ancient Egypt and the Thebes library in ancient Greece alluded to the healing power of the written word. The practice came to America in the early 1800s, advocated by Dr. Benjamin Rush. Formally named *bibliotherapy* by Rev. Samuel McChord Crothers in a 1916 *Atlantic Monthly* article, the practice was primarily used to help soldiers recover mentally from injuries that they received in World War I (Jack & Ronan, 2008). Throughout the early to mid-20th century, bibliotherapy was practiced by librarians rather than mental health professionals. Almost all of the early literature on the subject is from librarians, although there were exceptions. The treatment first appeared in *Dorland's Illustrated Medical Dictionary* in 1941.

In 1939, Alice Bryan published a paper titled "Can There Be a Science of Bibliotherapy?" She believed in the anecdotal evidence that bibliotherapy was an effective intervention, but in order to be considered a science and win over the mental health community, Bryan believed that the field required an "accumulation of a body of experimental data" from which to draw scientific conclusions (Jack & Ronan, 2008). Bryan believed that researchers would one day find the data to prove that bibliotherapy belonged among the accepted scientifically proven interventions for treating individuals.

RESEARCH

Investigation on the effectiveness of bibliotherapy with a group of aggressive boys demonstrated decreased aggression in the students who participated compared to no change in the control group of children (Shechtman, 1999). A study on the "I Feel Better Now!" program (a sensory-based intervention program that includes bibliotherapy) conducted by the National Institute for Trauma and Loss showed a statistically significant reduction of posttraumatic stress disorder (PTSD) symptoms (Steele, Kuban, & Raider, 2009). One impediment to bibliotherapeutic research is that it is not a therapy. This makes standardization and evaluation difficult to implement.

However, there has been a wealth of anecdotal evidence that bibliotherapy is an effective intervention for children and adults, for problems that are both large and small. Today, bibliotherapy is widely used by clinicians from a variety of theoretical orientations. The proliferation of excellent children's books in recent years has made the acquisition and incorporation of bibliotherapy materials, including those that deal with themes of child sexual abuse, easier than ever before.

RATIONALE FOR BIBLIOTHERAPY IN SEXUAL ABUSE TREATMENT

Bibliotherapy is particularly well suited to clients who have been sexually abused. Sexual abuse is a crime perpetrated on children that thrives on secrecy, isolation, and shame. Its victims can be fearful to disclose what happened to them, and may think that they are different from everyone else around them. A subset of these children may believe that everyone knows what happened to them. Sexual abuse victims can feel responsible for the abuse, and blame themselves. Many children do not realize that they are being sexually abused. There are numerous barriers to disclosing the event, and the guilt or shame many abuse survivors feel can be particularly powerful for sexual abuse victims.

One major change in children's sexual-abuse literature is the abundance of books that involve a perpetrator that the victim knows. Prior to 2001, almost all children's books dealing with sexual abuse stressed "stranger danger," while ignoring the danger in the room down the hall. Over the past 10 years we have seen an increase in books dealing with sexual abuse where the perpetrator is known to the victim.

Bibliotherapy provides this population with a chance to understand what happened to them, through the voices in the story and the follow-up activities. Of potentially more importance, though, is the use of metaphor in bibliotherapy, which provides sexual abuse victims with a shield.

Fictional characters give victims the emotional distance to allow them to discuss the character's problems without feeling threatened. Animal characters are engaging, provide an additional layer of separation and safety, and have the added benefit of frequently being gender and race neutral. Children learn resiliency from the characters in the story, and find a way to understand their own complex emotions through the eyes of the story's characters.

Victims feel a stronger emotional connection to the story when it is related to their lives. Through this connection, they realize that others have gone through similar experiences, faced similar problems, and have been successful at overcoming their situations. Sexual abuse victims are frequently placed in foster homes or residential care. Some bibliotherapy resources are aimed at helping victims who have been removed from their homes (i.e., placed in foster/residential care) deal with the changing circumstances of their lives.

Sexual abuse victims feel unsafe and powerless. The books selected by the therapist contribute to restoring their sense of safety and power, so that they will be able to move from victimhood to survivorship. Many of these stories provide hope and a bridge toward the future, even when the story ends with unresolved issues facing the main characters. The stories offer children the distance they need, as they can discuss the challenges the character faces rather than their own challenges.

First Meeting Information

Recognizing the value in modifying stories to fit the particular client led me to create a one-page "First Meeting Information Form." Although I change questions on the form according to developmental level, environment, presenting problem, and so on, each form includes "Name one person you can tell a worry." This is helpful in identifying who the child might turn to for support. A response of "Nobody" or a blank response will be important to explore in treatment. Also elicited is information regarding the child's name preference (nickname), favorite foods, favorite TV programs, favorite type of music, favorite movie, favorite superhero, favorite activity, and least favorite thing to do. I find that children feel important filling out the form. Since the form is completed in the waiting room, it offers me the opportunity to observe the interaction between caregiver and child, observe whether the child is encouraged to complete the survey by himself or whether the adult takes charge. The story takes on a greater meaning or importance when we can substitute the client's heroes, activities, or ways to celebrate at the end of the story.

Book Selection Considerations

Books should be chosen with intentionality and with a view to when the book should be used along with the child's treatment continuum. Malchiodi and Ginns-Gruenberg (2008) offer several guidelines in selecting literature to use with this population. They recommend the following: Clinicians should have an array of books in order to depict different family constellations and cultures. It is vital to keep the child's developmental level in mind. Whenever possible, it is important to use a book with illustrations with which the client can identify. Books should have believable characters and match situations and gender. Books that address the impact of abuse on loved ones, and books that are contemporary are also important considerations. Additionally, books that engage the imagination and senses are especially helpful when working with this population.

Presentation of Children's Literature to the "Older Child/Adolescent"

Introducing a children's book to an adolescent or older child can be a challenge to the clinician. Older children are especially resistant to books that they perceive as being meant for younger children. The clinician is challenged to present the book in a way that the older child will benefit from it without feeling that the therapist is treating him as a "little kid." There are several strategies I use to get the older child to read a particular book.

In some cases, I tell my client that I have a younger client who is dealing with a similar problem. I tell the teen that her input would be valuable as to the appropriateness of a book for the younger child, as she is closer in age to the client than I am. At other times (again sharing with the teen that I am considering using it with a younger client) I request their assistance in determining what parts might be too wordy or what parts might be above their heads. In addition to getting the adolescent to read the book, it has the ancillary benefit of building the teen's self-esteem. When appropriate, I have suggested that the teen read the story to younger siblings or neighbors. This has proved to be a great springboard for conversation when the teen attends the next session. Sometimes I explain that even though this book looks like it is for younger children, several teens have commented on how helpful it has been to them, and that they wish they had had a book like this when they were younger. Approaching the issue from another angle, I tell my clients that there are not enough books dealing with this topic for their age range. I invite them to rewrite the story in a way that speaks to peers. Some teens write to younger children on any number of issues covered in the story, such as how they have been affected by the story, how they might have handled certain situations if they were the character, or how things might be different for that character in the future.

RECOMMENDED BOOKS BY TOPIC

This section is meant to be an easy reference for clinicans and is therefore divided into a variety of treatment arenas. Specific bibliotherapy recommendations are given that augment other activities employed in the recovery process. (See Table 17.1.)

Table 17.1
Bibliotherapy for Sexually Abused Children: Cross-Reference of
Topics Covered in This Chapter

Key	
P = Psychoeducation	**PRV** = Prevention
D = Disclosure	**SG** = Shame/Guilt
PSEB = Physical/Sexual/ Emotional Boundaries	**SE** = Self-Esteem
	A = Anger
F = Feelings	**SR** = Stress Reduction
IAS = Intrusive Arousal Symptoms	

Title and Author	Topics Cross-Referenced
Alex and the Amazing Dr. Frankenslime, by Margot Desannoy	PSEB, F, SG, A
A Terrible Thing Happened, by Margaret M. Holmes & Sasha J. Mudlaff	P, D, F, IAS, SG, A
A Child's First Book of Play Therapy, by Marc A. Nemiroff, Jane Annunziata, & Margaret Scott	P, D, F, IAS, SG, A
Annabelle's Secret, by Amy Barth	
Brave Bart, by C. Sheppard	P, D, F, IAS, SG
Cut, by Patricia McCormick	P, F, A
Don't Rant and Rave on Wednesdays, by Adolph Moser	P, F, SE, A
Double Dip Feelings, by Barbara S. Cain & Anne Patterson	P, F, SE
Finding Sunshine After the Storm, by Sharon A. McGee & Curtis Holmes	P, D, PSEB, F, IAS, SG, SE, A, SR
Gabby the Gecko, by Paris Goodyear-Brown	P, D, PSEB, F, IAS, PRV, SG, SE, A
The Girl Who Learned How to Control Her Dreams, by Nancy Davis	P, IAS
Hey, Little Ant, by Philip M. Hoose & Hannah Hoose	P, F, SE
How Can You Tell How People Feel?, by Kristine Humer	P, F
How Long Does It Hurt?, by Cynthia L. Mather, Kristina E. Debye, Judy Wood, & Eliana Gil	P, D, PSEB, F, IAS, SG, SE, A, SR

(*continued*)

Table 17.1

(*continued*)

Key

I Like Me, by Nancy Carlson	P, F, SE
I Love You Rituals, by Becky A. Bailey	P, F, SE, SR
I Told My Secret: A Book for Kids Who Were Abused, by Eliana Gil	P, D, F, IAS, SG, SE, A
If I Tell, by S. Marcy-Webster	P, D, PSEB, F, IAS, SG, SE, A
The Indian and the Dragon, by Nancy Davis	P, D, F, IAS, SG
I Wish I Were a Butterfly, by James Howe	P, F, SE
The Me Nobody Knows: Guide for Teen Survivors, by Barbara Bean & Shari Bennett	P, D, PSEB, F, IAS, SG, SE, A, SR
Ned's Secret: A Story About Child Sexual Abuse, by T. Stephenson	P, D, F, SG
Not in Room 204, by Shannon Riggs	P, D, F, SG
One's Own Self, by Dori Jalazo	P, PSEB, F, A
Paper Bag Princess, by Robert N. Munsch & Michael Martchenko	P, F, SE, A
Peaceful Piggy Meditation, by Kerry Lee MacLean	P, F, SE, SR
Personal Space Camp, by Julia Cook	P, PSEB, F
Please Explain Anxiety to Me!, by Laurie Zelinger & Jordan Zelinger	P, F, IAS, SR
Please Tell, by Jesse (Jessie Ottenweller-Hazelden)	P, D, F, IAS, SG
Relax, by Catherine O'Neill & Toni Goffe	P, F, SG, SR
Right Touch: A Read-Aloud Story to Help Prevent Child Abuse, by Sandy Kleven	P, D, PSEB, F, PRV, SE
Sarah's Waterfall: A Healing Story About Sexual Abuse, by Ellery Akers	P, PSEB, F, IAS, SG, SE, A
Scribbleville, by Peter Holwitz	P, SE
Shades of People, by Shelley Rotner & Sheila M. Kelly	P, F, SE
Some Parts Are Not for Sharing, by Julie K. Federico	P, D, PSEB, F, PRV
Someone in My Family Has Molested Children, by Eliana Gil	P, D, PSEB, F, IAS, SG, SR
The Summer My Father Was Ten, by Pat Brisson	P, F, SG
Tiger, Tiger Is It True?: Four Questions to Make You Smile Again, by Byron Katie & Hans Wilhelm	P, F, SE, A
The Trouble With Secrets, by Karen Johnsen	P, D, PSEB, IAS, PRV
Uncle Willy's Tickles: A Child's Right to Say No, by Marice Aboff	P, D, PSEB, PRV
A Very Touching Book, by Jan Hindman	P, D, PSEB, PRV
Welcome to Therapy, by Cheryl Putt	P, D, F
What Am I Feeling?, by John M. Gottman	P, F, SE
What if Someone I Know Is Gay?, by Eric Marcus	P, F
When Fuzzy Was Afraid of Losing His Mother, by Inger M. Maier	P, F, IAS, SR
When I Was Little Like You, by Jane Porett	P, D, F
Worry Wars: An Anxiety Workbook for Kids and Their Helpful Adults, by Paris Goodyear-Brown	P, D, PSEB, F, IAS, SG, SE, SR
Your Body Belongs to You, by Cornelia Maude Spelman	P, D, PSEB

A PSYCHOEDUCATIONAL APPROACH

A psychoeducational approach should be employed throughout treatment. Therapy is often an overwhelming and anxiety-producing concept for those entering the therapeutic process. Parents frequently believe that they are being blamed for not protecting their child, especially in situations where the caregiver has had negative experiences in the past with "the system." For parents, books about abuse normalize reactions of those dealing with the situation. It is helpful to assess (in a nonthreatening manner) the reading level of the parent. However, even highly educated parents appreciate some books for their simplistic answers. For those affected by the abuse, booklets such as *I Told My Secret* (Gil, 1986) or *Someone in My Family Has Molested Children* (Gil, 1994) provide answers to questions they might be afraid to ask. Common questions asked about the courts, living situations, therapy, and the professionals involved in treatment are provided. *When Your Child's Been Molested* (Brohl & Potter, 2004) and *Helping Your Child Recover from Sexual Abuse* (Adams & Fay, 1992) are books that provide insight and more detailed information in a nonthreatening format.

Being mindful that parental support is the single best predictor of positive outcome in child sexual abuse treatment (Cohen, Deblinger, & Mannarino, 2006), it is imperative that the parent become invested in the process. It is important that caregivers see the therapist as empathic and genuine. To facilitate the parental buy-in, I tend to use books at my initial meeting with the parent(s) (and sometimes even before then). *I Love You Rituals* (Bailey, 2000) emphasizes the importance of sensory interventions, teaching the value of touch, tone of voice, and playfulness to create a bond between parent and child. The combination of a didactic approach combined with bibliotherapy and other media helps them recognize that the roller coaster of emotions they are experiencing is common.

A child who has been sexually abused often has difficulty with emotional, behavioral, and physiological regulation. They do not make the important connection between past experience and current behavior. It is helpful for children to understand that coping skills that helped them survive in the past are now a detriment. Through literature and follow-up interventions, victimized youth and their caregivers learn about the trauma response, individual triggers, and the connection between the abuse in the past and its effect on present experiences.

Brave Bart: A Story for Traumatized and Grieving Children (Sheppard, 2001) is an important story. Kids identify with the intrusive arousal and avoidant symptoms experienced by a traumatized cat. They "join" Bart in learning (from a gentle "therapist cat") how trigger responses are connected to behaviors and feelings. Bart explains to kids what happens in therapy along with helpful coping skills to deal with these reactions. Most important, Bart learns that he is a survivor and that he is brave. In *A Terrible Thing Happened* (Holmes, 2000), Sherman Raccoon tries to avoid dealing with a traumatic event that he saw, and he begins to behave aggressively. He explains how art and activities he did with his counselor helped him learn that he was not to blame and how he was helped to surmount the challenges.

There are a number of interventions offered by experts in the field that educate children in a creative manner to make meaning of what has occurred, to identify, understand, and regulate emotions. These strategies complement and reinforce the messages from the stories. Simple books like *Welcome to Therapy* (Putt, 2006) or *A Child's First Book of Play Therapy* (Nemiroff & Annunziata, 1990) are helpful tools that parents can use to explain therapy to a child, decreasing both their anxiety and the anxiety of the child by creating a familiarity with the unknown. Upon reading the words "Some come when someone hurts them" in *Welcome to Therapy* (Putt, 2006), a colorful and culturally sensitive book, a young client spontaneously offered, "Somebody hurt *my* privates." While disclosures of this nature are rare, story books like this one are a first step in helping to restore a sense of safety to the child.

BOOKS THAT TEACH ABOUT BOUNDARIES

Victimized children often demonstrate significant deficits in the development of boundaries. These deficits include physical, emotional, and sexual boundaries, and occur in both abuse victims and in abuse-reactive children. Children with sexual behavior problems have typically experienced either no boundaries or loose boundaries modeled by family members (Gil & Johnson, 1993). They have been exposed to caregivers who sleep, bathe, and dress in front of them, or expose them to pornographic material. There are a number of excellent books that help children understand the importance of creating physical, emotional, and sexual boundaries and provide ideas for implementation in a nonthreatening format.

A Book for Kids About Private Parts, Touching, Touching Problems and Other Stuff (Gil & Shaw, 2010) explains the continuum of touching from normative to problematic and includes information regarding prevention as well as guidelines for children who may have problem sexual behaviors. This book is a standout for its positive attitude and language, for being matter-of-fact and straightforward, and for being developmentally appropriate and culturally sensitive. It is one of the few books that creates a positive attitude about sexuality, while reinforcing a child's right to privacy.

I believe caretakers, parents, and others will find this book accessible and plain-speaking. I have used it with some kids already and they really seem to "get" the information. Another excellent book that helps children (and their grown-ups) to understand physical anatomy, sexual behavior rules, and appropriate boundaries in a humorous and nonthreatening format is *A Very Touching Book* (Hindman, 1983). Touching is separated into three separate categories—good, bad, and secret—and includes great examples of each. Hindman's description of "secret touching" helps children determine whether or not the "contact" is appropriate and encourages children to tell about undesired sexual contact. *The Right Touch* (Kleven, 1998) clarifies that personal contact and affection are very different from secret, deceptive, or forced touching. *Please Knock!* (Dolgan, 2006) uses poetry as a springboard for discussion about personal body safety.

The concept of respect for one's own personal space and that of others is brilliantly shared by Louis, the loveable narrator in *Personal Space Camp* (Cook, 2007). Children and their helpers are inspired to implement some of the ideas from the story, including hula hoops and bubbles, to reinforce establishing safe boundaries. Older kids will find *Boundaries: A Guide for Teens* (Peter & Dowd, 2004) helpful in understanding physical, emotional, and sexual respect in relationships. Peers share examples of how personal boundaries have been valued or violated in relationships. The journal format helps the reader examine their relationships with others and offers strategies for maintaining healthy boundaries. The issue of boundaries is also addressed in *How Long Does It Hurt?* (Mather & Debye, 2004) and *Me Nobody Knows* (Bean & Bennett, 1993).

BOOKS THAT FACILITATE DISCLOSURE

There are a number of obstacles that impede disclosure, including fear and manipulation by the perpetrator, disbelief of the parent upon initial disclosure, fear of the impact the disclosure may have on the family, and self-blame. When the victim meets with the therapist before disclosure, it is frequently due to changes in behavior by the victim, without a cause being assigned to the changes. If there is already concern that a child may have been sexually abused, particularly when that child has made concerning statements, or in any case where other systems are already involved, a full forensic interview process should be completed prior to the introduction on bibliotherapy content that may mirror the child's experience. If children do not talk about their experiences in the course of such an interview, they may come to treatment with as yet unrevealed traumatic experiences. The introduction of certain bibliotherapy materials allow the child to potentially identify with characters who experienced parallel situations and can act as a springboard for discussion.

Children who have been sexually abused often break their silence after reading books like *Feeling Safe* (Grace & Gould, 2008) and *Gabby the Gecko* (Goodyear-Brown, 2003). Gabby is a friendly, animated character until she is silenced by a wicked wizard. This metaphor is also depicted in *Feeling Safe* in the narrator's drawing of a young child with a lock over her mouth. In both stories, the characters let children know they are not alone in their feelings about the abuse, and witness how both characters experienced healing. "Megaphones to Make a Point"—a technique described in *Digging For Buried Treasure 2* (Goodyear-Brown, 2005)—empowers children to "speak out."

In *If I Tell* (Marcy-Webster, 2007) a young adolescent chronicles the abuse she and her cousin experienced at the hand of an uncle. She describes the conflicted feelings she had about the abuse and disclosing, and offers a realistic, hopeful ending, including the impact the disclosure had on the family. *Me Nobody Knows: A Guide for Teen Survivors* (Bean & Bennett, 1993) is an excellent book for facilitating disclosure in adolescents. It is one of the few books with a diverse teen group photo on the cover that includes teen males. Teens find the interactive format helpful in the healing process. *How Long Does it Hurt? A Guide to Recovering from Incest and Sexual Abuse for Teenagers, Their Friends and Their Families* (Mather, Debye, et al., 2004) may also facilitate disclosure. It provides helpful advice to sexually abused adolescents and those affected by the abuse.

It is important to consider other issues, such as domestic violence, substance abuse, and gender issues, which often coexist with the abuse. I have found it beneficial at the outset of therapy to have several books addressing different issues in plain sight of my clients, such as *What if Someone I know is Gay* (Marcus, 2007), *Cut* (McCormick, 2002), and *Big Book Unplugged: A Young Person's Guide to AA* (Rosengren, 2003).

BOOKS THAT TEACH EMOTIONAL LITERACY

Children who have been victimized often cope by turning off, or avoiding, their true feelings. Some are confused by the intensity of their feelings, which are expressed in socially unacceptable behaviors. Many children who have been sexually abused have experienced deficits in the attachment relationship with their parent(s) and are frequently unable to identify, understand, regulate, and communicate their feelings. There are a number of books that can help these children understand their feelings and expand their vocabulary of emotions. These books open doors and facilitate emotional understanding, as children learn to distinguish, manage, and communicate their feelings. Most importantly, they show children and their parents that there is no such thing as right or wrong feelings.

A psychoeducational approach to introducing parents to emotional literacy is creatively explained in *What Am I Feeling?* (Gottman, 2004). This book teaches parents how to help their child to understand and to express their emotions. In *How Can You Tell How People Feel?* (Humer, 2007) children learn to distinguish between different feelings, while *Double Dip Feelings* (Cain, 2001) teaches young children the concept of experiencing two different feelings at the same time. *Shades of People* (Rotner & Kelly, 2010) and *Lots of Feelings* (Rotner, 2003) use photographs of children and families in a variety of settings who convey many emotions. Books like these help children identify and express emotions and learn about empathy, tolerance, and diversity. *How Are You Peeling?* (Elffers, 2004) is helpful for older children. Expressive faces of fruits and vegetables facilitate understanding of emotions in a fun manner.

It is often the interventions that follow the stories (sometimes suggested by the client and other times by the therapist) that are most bibliotherapeutic. Therapists might invite the child to draw a picture, find pictures in magazines, or create collages that represent a character's feelings or their own feelings on different days. Therapists can also recommend other activities that encourage the identification of thoughts, behaviors, and body sensations associated with a feeling.

BOOKS THAT ADDRESS ANGER

It is important for the therapist to keep in mind that anger is often the protective shield for many emotions, including anxiety, sadness, humiliation, shame, guilt, frustration, fear, jealousy, and hurt. There are numerous books on the healthy release of anger. *Sometimes I'm Bombaloo* (Vail, 2005) is excellent for young children and their caregivers. Children identify with the intensity of the character's anger and accompanying fear that takes place in the story. Children and their caregivers benefit from how Bombaloo's feelings are expressed after the "anger storm."

The animal characters in *Moody Cow Meditates* (MacLean, 2009) are engaging for boys and girls. (It is my experience that boys avoid reading books when girls are pictured on the cover. It seems to make no difference to girls.) Kids relate to Peter the Cow whose day goes from bad to worse as he loses his temper, makes poor choices, gets in trouble, and is teased by the cows in the neighborhood. Readers connect with his resistance ("It won't work") to an intervention recommended by Grandpa. His grandfather succeeds in teaching Moody Cow (Peter) a healthy way to process his anger creatively—"using a meditation mind jar." Following the story, clients make their own moody mind jar (the recipe is at the end of the book). The emotions expressed at this time are cathartic for many children. Resistant clients have requested to take the mind jar home to use between sessions.

Don't Rant and Rave on Wednesdays (Moser, 1994) depicts common but inappropriate anger behaviors. Humorous dialogue coupled with fun cartoon illustrations teaches kids ways to express anger productively. Readers also get an introduction to what may be hiding beneath the anger.

Older children can be more challenging, especially because they bristle at reading books that they consider babyish. Books like *Harry Potter* and movies like *Star Wars* can help when working with an older child. In *Star Wars*, Annakin Skywalker is confronted with intense feelings of fear and anger, the results of which have disastrous consequences. Therapists can help clients contrast Annakin's expressions of anger with those that Harry Potter experiences. Harry Potter works through his anger, primarily by turning to his support network.

Richard Kagan, author of *Rebuilding Attachments* (Kagan, 2004), has shared "Harry Potter and Star Wars" interventions he and clients have created. In *Rebuilding Attachments* (Kagan, 2004) he captures the metaphors and the lessons. He wrote:

Youths who like science fiction can find core principles of trauma therapy in the original Star Wars movies . . . in which the orphaned hero Luke is guided by his mentor, Obi-Wan, to calm, center himself, develop his skills and elicit his powers to help others. Obi-Wan's messages can be used to invoke courage and strength and to help youths see themselves as heroes who can utilize positive energy and guidance to succeed. Obi-Wan's intonation of "Luke" before he destroys the Death star elicits an image of being a hero and not alone. "Use the Force" reminds youths of the positive energy around them. "Stretch out your feelings" is an antidote for the constriction of trauma and opens up perception and solutions. Luke's mentors teach him to give up his assumptions, experience how hatred leads to the "Dark Side," respect his fears, master his angry impulses, and learn to trust again. (pp. 168–169)

BOOKS THAT ADDRESS SHAME, GUILT, AND COGNITIVE DISTORTIONS

Children who have been sexually abused often internalize false cognitions of humiliation and guilt. They believe the abuse was their fault and that they should have been able to stop it from continuing. Sadly this is confirmed when family members deny the abuse could have occurred or agree that the child is at fault. These victims are unlikely to verbalize their feelings of self-hate. The protagonists in stories like *The Indian and the*

Dragon (Davis, 1996) or *The Monster in My House* (Davis, 1996) eventually find healthier resolutions for their feelings of self blame.

Sometimes shame or guilt is a helpful emotion that can illuminate the consequences of problematic behavior. This is the case when a child has perpetrated another child. These individuals may benefit from books like *The Summer My Father Was Ten* (Brisson, 1999). The story focuses on a boy who initially does not take responsibility after causing emotional pain to another. The protagonist eventually apologizes and continues to makes amends throughout his life.

Books like these can help clients explore their own feelings of self-blame and maladaptive coping skills. Moreover, some young people feel encouraged to try strategies that have worked for the protagonist.

Helping clients create positive statements to "turn around" their maladaptive thoughts is a challenge for many therapists. Creative interventions such as Twisted Thinking (Kenney-Noziska, 2008) and Guilt Trip/Guilt Erasers (Crisci, Lay, & Lowenstein, 1998) identify common negative distortions of sexually abused children followed by positive reframes.

Books That Address Self-Esteem

Abused victims tend to have a fragmented view of self. Sexually abused children frequently comment that they feel like "used goods." They feel dirty and out of place. Helping victimized children to recognize their strengths is an important therapeutic goal. However, helping children recognize their strengths takes patience and time. Therapists must recognize that a single story is not transformational. It may be the repetition of thematic content over the course of reading several books related to a given topic that results in a child's paradigmatic shift.

The colorful illustrations and simple text in *I Like Me* (Carlson, 1990) are a great place to start building a young child's self-esteem. The stylish pig with the round tummy models perseverance and is a great role model for kids. *I Wish I Were a Butterfly* (Howe, 1994) is another book that teaches children to find their strengths, as a self-hating cricket discovers his own strengths, and that sometimes, even a butterfly would like to be a cricket. In *Tiger, Tiger, Is It True* (Katie, 2009), very young children are introduced to the connection between thoughts and feelings. Additionally, the concept of stopping negative thoughts and replacing them with healthier, positive self statements is shared.

Older girls will find a strong female role model in *Paper Bag Princess* (Munsch, 1992). Princess Elizabeth (who lives in a castle and wears beautiful clothes) is betrothed to Prince Ronald. She goes to the ends of the earth to rescue her prince from the dragon. Instead of being grateful, the prince comments on what a mess she is, sends her home, and tells her to return when she is dressed like a "real princess." ("Your hair is all tangled and you are wearing a dirty old paper bag.") However, this female protagonist is a confident, feisty, intelligent girl who lets her prince know he is a jerk. Teens are inspired to identify their strengths through discussion and expressive techniques (with a little help from the clinician) like "Mirror, mirror on the wall, what great things about me do I recall?" an activity in *Finding Sunshine after the Storm: A Workbook for Children Healing from Sexual Abuse* (McGhee & Holmes, 2008). *One's Own Self* (Jalazo, 2003) is a beautifully illustrated book that speaks to healing by taking a journey to find and love one's self, amidst a world of others. A strong message about the importance of being available to oneself, recognizing no one is perfect, and discovering one's beautiful soul is inspirational for all ages.

BOOKS THAT ADDRESS STRESS REDUCTION AND RELAXATION

Children who have been sexually abused are often on high alert. Stories that offer imagery, deep breathing, meditation, and muscle relaxation help children self regulate and decrease their anxiety. In *Peaceful Piggy Meditation* (MacLean, 2004) children identify with the personified piggies who feel like they "can't slow down even when you're sitting down." They are motivated to practice breathing and relaxation techniques modeled by the adorable piggies. In *The Worry Wars* (Goodyear-Brown, 2010b), engaging metaphorical stories (the protagonists of which per-sonify the anxiety cycle) set the stage for a host of activities to help children identify, understand, and overcome their own worries. Using reproducible "weapons" they are inspired to "boss back" their own fears and practice the coping strategies used by the heroic characters to win the battle. Children also experience mastery as they put into practice strategies they've learned in *What to Do When You Worry Too Much* (Huebner, 2006). The child-friendly language complemented by colorful illustrations in *Please Explain Anxiety to Me* (Zelinger, 2010) helps children understand the brain-body connection underlying anxiety, and gives ideas on changing their anxiety response. Calming imagery followed by activities and questions for discussion make *Ready, Set, Relax* (Allen & Klein, 1996) a valuable resource for clinicians. Many of the scripts with background music are on the CD *Ready, Set, Release* (Allen & Klein, 1996). Adolescents learn self-soothing techniques from calming scripts in *RELAX.Calm: Using Music, Relaxation, and Imagery to Help Teens Overcome Stress and Anxiety* (Allen & Klein, 2011). Clinicians will appreciate the suggestions for discussion that follow each script.

Case Example

Nuts and Bolts

Carla, a 12-year-old girl, was adopted from an orphanage in Romania. She suffered from a recurring nightmare about ghosts, monsters, and villains attacking her. In reality, she had been sexually abused on multiple occasions at the orphanage. Moreover, rats and mice ran underneath her bed where she believed they would attack her. These haunting memories came back to her in nightmares. Upon awakening, she would bolt into her adoptive parents' room, completely petrified, and scream repeatedly while clinging to them.

I selected *The Girl Who Learned How to Control Her Dreams* (Davis, 1996) to help her cope with her nightmares, as the story paralleled the nightmare Carla was experiencing. The story is about a girl who dreams about scary sharks, monsters, and people hurting other people. A superhero appears in her dreams and teaches the girl she has the power to get rid of monsters both kinesthetically (disintegrating the monster with her wand) and verbally ("People are not for hurting! Go away Now!"). The character in the story understands that her superhero is always on call to come into her dreams and assist her should the monsters ever return. The story ends with the character having better dreams, no longer needing to be in mom's bed, feeling empowered, and realizing she can stand up for herself. This was the beginning of Carla's healing process from the sexual abuse that she endured in the orphanage.

STEPS TAKEN IN THIS BIBLIOTHERAPY SESSION

Telling or reading the story (preselected): I gave her a koosh ball (tactile) to hold while I told her the story. She was intrigued by the idea that we could get rid of her nightmare.

The rehearsal: Following the story line, Carla and I practiced what she wanted to tell the monsters. The release of emotion intensified as she repeatedly yelled, "Stop right now!" "You can't hurt me anymore!" "Poof! Be gone!"

Drawing the traumatic event: Following the story (in which we changed the superhero and the celebration to fit my client's needs), Carla drew a picture of her nightmare. I encouraged her to include

(continued)

(*continued*)

as much detail as possible so we could determine the best way to get rid of the nightmare (or in her case change it to a more palatable story). Once she completed the drawing, she provided a detailed description and in response to my curiosity about different aspects of her drawing, she added more details. It was important to her that I understood each part.

The "follow-up" activity: Carla crafted and decorated a wand from construction paper, making sure to make the "point" at the top to physically eliminate the villain. (This step can be done using a variety of art media.)

Changing the nightmare (experiential master play): Carla needed help to feel powerful over the evil that loomed. Using humor and creativity, she was able to "shrink" and "conquer" the monsters in her nightmare. Her nightmare was "contained" on that small piece of paper. As she engaged in an activity aimed at experiential mastery (Gil, 2010; Goodyear-Brown, 2010), the trauma experience became more manageable.

APPLICATION (INTEGRATING THE CHANGES SHE'D MADE)

It is critical to reinforce work done in session with caregiver-supported homework. Carla's parents were instrumental in creating a ritual for her to share the "revised" dream before she went to bed every night. Carla's mother called to confirm the success that Carla was experiencing, claiming that Carla had not awakened from a nightmare since that session.

During our time together, Carla delighted in bibliotherapy. Many stories were read over and over again, both in therapy sessions and at home. Carla loved to hear the story of *Brave Bart* (Sheppard, 1998), described earlier in this chapter. After hearing the story, Carla began to create her "narrative" in the sand, used puppetry to describe her story, and role-played various characters in the book. It was the follow-up activities that made the difference in her healing process. During one session she showed me a self-soothing "relaxation ritual" she had created from stories we'd read together. She combined imagery from *Pillar of Strength*, a "calming script" in *Ready, Set, Relax* (Allen & Klein, 1996), and text from *Take a Deep Breath: Little Lessons from Flowers for a Happier World* (Stoutland, 2002).

CONCLUSION

Over the past 30 years, I have delighted in recommending bibliotherapy resources for a host of presenting issues. In both my role as a therapist and as co-owner of a therapeutic bookstore (the Self Esteem Shop), I have been amazed at the increased volume of books dealing with sexual abuse, and the high quality of those books. In my practice I have found that therapeutic books have been invaluable additions to my therapeutic toolbox, and increased the effectiveness of my practice. Clinicians who work with sexual abuse survivors are encouraged to look for ways to integrate some degree of bibliotherapy into their work with this vulnerable population.

REFERENCES

Adams, C., & Fay, J. (1992). *Helping your child recover from sexual abuse*. Seattle: University of Washington Press.

Allen, J., & Klein, R. (1996). *Ready, set, relax*. Watertown, WI: Inner Coaching.

Allen, J., & Klein, R. (1996). *Ready, set, release CD*. Watertown, WI: Inner Coaching.

Allen, J., & Klein, R. (2011). *RELAX.Calm: Helping teens manage stress with relaxation and guided imagery*. Watertown, WI: Inner Coaching.

Ashby, J., Kottman, T., & DeGraaf, D. (2008). *Active interventions for kids and teens: Adding adventure and fun to counseling!* Washington DC: American Counseling Association.

Bailey, B. (2000). *I love you rituals*. New York, NY: HarperCollins.

Bean, B., & Bennett, S. (1993). *Me nobody knows: A guide for teen survivors*. San Francisco, CA: Jossey-Bass.

Brisson, P. (1999). *Summer my father was ten*. Honesdale, PA: Boyd Mills Press.

Brohl, K., & Potter, C. (2004). *When your child has been molested: A parent's guide to healing and recovery*. San Francisco, CA: Jossey-Bass.

Bryan, A. (1939). Can there be a science of bibliotherapy? *Library Journal 64*, 7–12.

Cain, B. (2001). *Double dip feelings: Stories that help children understand emotions*. Washington, DC: American Psychological Association.

Carlson, N. (1990). *I like me*. New York, NY: Penguin.

Cohen, J., Deblinger, E., & Mannarino, A. (2006). *Treating trauma and traumatic grief in children and adolescents*. New York, NY: Guilford Press.

Cook, J. (2007). *Personal space camp: Teaching children the concepts of personal space*. Chattanooga, TN: National Center for Youth Issues.

Crisci, G., Lay, M., & Lowenstein, L. (1998). *Paper dolls and airplanes: Therapeutic exercises for sexually traumatized children*. Indianapolis, IN: Kidsrights.

Davis, N. (1996). The girl who learned to control her dreams. In N. Davis, *Therapeutic stories that teach and heal* (pp. 297–300). Oxon Hill, MD: Nancy Davis.

Davis, N. (1996). The Indian and the dragon. In N. Davis, *Therapeutic stories that teach and heal* (pp. 265–30269). Oxon Hill, MD: Nancy Davis.

Davis, N. (1996). The monster in the house. In N. Davis, *Therapeutic stories that teach and heal* (pp. 259–263). Oxon Hill, MD: Nancy Davis.

Dolgan, E. (2006). *Please knock!* Denver, CO: EOZ Press.

Effers, J. (2004). *How are you peeling? Foods with moods.* New York, NY: Scholastic.

Gil, E. (1986). *I told my secret: A book for kids who were abused.* Fairfax, VA: Launch Press.

Gil, E., & Johnson, T. (1993). *Sexualized children: Assessment and treatment of sexualized children and children who molest.* Fairfax, VA: Launch Press.

Gil, E. (1994). *Someone in my family has molested children.* Fairfax, VA: Launch Press.

Gil, E., & Shaw, J. (2010). *A book for kids about touching, touching problems, and other stuff.* Arlington, VA: Gil Center for Healing and Play.

Gil, E. (2010). *Working with children to heal interpersonal trauma: The power of play.* New York, NY: Guilford Press.

Goodyear-Brown, P. (2002). *Digging for buried treasure: 52 prop-based play therapy interventions for treating the problems of childhood.* Nashville, TN: Author.

Goodyear-Brown, P. (2003). *Gabby the gecko.* Nashville, TN: Author.

Goodyear-Brown, P. (2005). *Digging for buried treasure 2: 52 more prop-based play therapy interventions for treating the problems of childhood.* Nashville, TN: Author.

Goodyear-Brown, P. (2010). *Play Therapy with Traumatized Children: A Prescriptive Approach.* Hoboken, NJ: John Wiley & Sons.

Goodyear-Brown, P. (2010b). *Worry wars: An anxiety workbook for kids and their helpful adults.* TN: Paris Goodyear-Brown.

Gottman, J. (2004). *What am I feeling?* Seattle, WA: Parenting Press.

Grace, A., & Gould, M. (2008). *Feeling safe.* New Castle, PA: Shenango Media.

Hindman, J. (1983). *A very touching book: For little people and for big people.* LaGrande, OR: AlexAndria.

Holmes, M. (2000). *A terrible thing happened.* Washington, DC: Magination Press.

Howe, J. (1994). *I wish I were a butterfly.* New York, NY: Houghton Mifflin.

Huebner, D. (2006). *What to do when you worry too much: A kid's guide to overcoming anxiety.* Washington, DC: American Psychological Association.

Humer, K. (2007). *How can you tell how people feel?* New York, NY: Barron's Educational Series.

Jack, S., & Ronan, K. (2008). Bibliotherapy: Practice and research. *School Psychology International Sage Publications, 29*(2), 161–182.

Jalazo, D. (2003). *Owning one's self.* Greensboro, NC: Dori Jalazo.

Kaduson, H., & Schaefer, C. (1997). *101 favorite play therapy techniques.* Lanham, MD: Rowman & Littlefield.

Kaduson, H., & Schaefer, C. (2001). *101 more favorite play therapy techniques.* Lanham, MD: Rowman & Littlefield.

Kagan, R. (2004). *Rebuilding attachments with traumatized children: Healing losses, violence, abuse and neglect.* New York, NY: Routledge.

Katie, B., & Wilhelm, H. (2009). *Tiger, tiger is it true? Four questions to make you smile again.* Carlsbad, CA: Hay House.

Kenney-Noziska, S. (2008). *Techniques, techniques, techniques.* West Conshohocken, PA: Infinity.

Kleven, S. (1998). *The right touch: A read-aloud story to help prevent child sexual abuse.* Kirkland, WA: Illumination Arts.

Lowenstein, L. (2002). *More creative interventions for troubled children and youth.* Toronto, ON: Champion Press.

Lowenstein, L. (2008). *Assessment and treatment activities for children, adolescents, and families.* Toronto, ON: Champion Press.

Lowenstein, L. (2010). *Assessment and treatment activities for children, adolescents, and families volume two: Practioners share their most effective techniques.* Toronto, ON: Champion Press.

MacLean, K. (2004). *Peaceful piggy meditation.* Park Ridge, IL: Albert Whitman.

MacLean, K. (2009). *Moody cow meditates.* Somerville, MA: Wisdom.

Malchiodi, C., & Ginns-Gruenberg, D. (2008). Trauma, loss, and bibliotherapy. In C. Malchiodi (Ed.), *Creative interventions with traumatized children* (pp. 171–173). New York, NY: Guilford Press.

Marcus, E. (2007). *What if someone I know is gay?: Answers to questions about what it means to be gay and lesbian.* New York, NY: Simon & Schuster.

Marcy-Webster, S. (2007). *If I tell.* Indianapolis, IN: Kidsrights.

Mather, C., & Debye, K. (2004). *How long does it hurt? A guide to recovering from incest and sexual abuse for teenagers, their friends and their families.* San Francisco, CA: Jossey-Bass.

McCormick, C. (2002). *Cut.* New York, NY: Scholastic.

McGee, S., & Holmes, C. (2008). *Finding sunshine after the storm: A workbook for children healing from sexual abuse.* Oakland, CA: New Harbinger.

Moser, A. (1994). *Don't rant and rave on Wednesdays: Children's anger control book.* Kansas City KS: Landmark House.

Munsch, R. (1992). *Paper bag princess.* Toronto, Ontario: Canada: Annick Press.

Nemiroff, M., & Annunziata, J. (1990). *A child's first book about play therapy.* Washington, DC: American Psychological Association.

Pardeck, J. (1998). *Using books in clinical social work practice: A guide to bibliotherapy.* New York, NY: Haworth Press.

Peter, V., & Dowd, T. (2004). *Boundaries: A guide for teens.* Omaha, NE: Boys Town Press.

Putt, C. (2006). *Welcome to therapy.* Bloomington, IN: Authorhouse.

Rosengren, J. (2003). *Big book unplugged: A young person's guide to alcoholics anonymous.* Center City, MN: Hazelden.

Rotner, S. (2003). *Lots of feelings.* Minneapolis, MN: Lerner.

Rotner, S., & Kelly, S. (2010). *Shades of people.* New York, NY: Holiday House.

Rudman, M. (1995). *Children's literature: An issues approach.* White Plains, NY: Longman.

Shechtman, Z. (1999). Bibliotherapy: An indirect approach to treatment of childhood aggression. *Child Psychiatry & Human Development, 30*(1), 39–53.

Sheppard, C. (1998). *Brave Bart: A story for traumatized and grieving children.* Grosse Pointe Woods, MI: National Institute for Trauma and Loss in Children.

Steele, W., Kuban, C., & Raider, M. (2009). Connections, continuity, dignity, opportunities model: Follow-up of children who completed the *I Feel Better Now!* trauma intervention program. *School Social Work Journal, 33*(2), 98–111.

Steele, W. (2009). *Trauma intervention program.* Grosse Pointe, MI: National Institute for Trauma and Loss.

Stoutland, A. (2002). *Take a deep breath: Little lessons from flowers for a happier world.* Okemos, MI: Inch by Inch.

Vail, R. (2005). *Sometimes I'm bombaloo.* New York, NY: Scholastic.

Zelinger, L. (2010). *Please explain anxiety to me!* Ann Arbor, MI: Loving Healing Press.

SECTION IV

SPECIAL ISSUES

CHAPTER 18

Clinical Considerations When Children Have Problematic Sexual Behavior

JANE F. SILOVSKY, LISA M. SWISHER, JIMMY WIDDIFIELD JR., and LORENA BURRIS

C LINICIANS WHO TREAT children who have been sexual abused are likely to encounter sexual behavior problems (SBP) as an identified concern. Rates of SBP are higher in clinically referred children who have been sexually abused than children without abuse histories (Friedrich et al., 2001). Preschool children who have been sexually abused are at particular risk, with about a third demonstrating some SBP. SBP is less frequently an issue for school-age children who have been sexually abused (with only about 6% demonstrating SBP; Kendall-Tackett, Finkelhor, & Williams, 1993). Further complicating the clinical picture, many children with SBP have no known history of sexual abuse, although sexual abuse may be suspected or assumed (Bonner, Walker, & Berliner, 1999; Silovsky & Niec, 2002). This chapter is designed to address many of the clinical questions that arise regarding SBP in children ages 12 and younger, such as (a) how to determine if a sexual behavior is problematic, (b) what factors are important to assess for treatment planning, (c) what empirically supported treatment options are available, (d) how does sexual abuse history affect treatment planning, and (e) what factors need to be considered for safety planning, residential placement, and sibling reunifications decisions? Chapter 2 in Section 1 provides background information about typical sexual development and problematic sexual behavior (in addition, fact sheets on sexual development and SBP are available at www.ncsby.org).

The current chapter is designed to provide an introduction to SBP and origins of the behavior. Characteristics of efficacious treatments are described, addressing working with parents, group- and family-based treatments, developmental considerations, and culturally congruent practices. Guidelines for safety planning for the home, school, and community are included, with information on sibling reunification when separation has occurred. The chapter ends with two case examples. Children served may be in the care of multiple and varied caregivers. For this chapter the terms *parent* and *caregiver* are used interchangeably for the sake of simplicity.

PROBLEMATIC SEXUAL BEHAVIOR OF CHILDREN: DEFINITION, ORIGINS, AND CONCEPTUALIZATION

Sexual behavior problems (SBP) are child-initiated behaviors that involve sexual body parts (e.g., genitals, breasts, and buttocks) and are developmentally inappropriate or potentially harmful to self or others (Bonner, 1999; Silovsky & Bonner, 2003a). SBP may involve behaviors that are entirely self-focused (e.g., excessive masturbation) or behaviors that involve other children, ranging from showing or looking at private parts, to fondling, to penetration. Sexual behaviors vary in the degree of mutuality or coercion as well as the potential for harm (Chaffin et al., 2008). Interpersonal and even aggressive SBP have been found in children 12 and under, even as young as 3 years of age (Bonner, Walker, & Berliner, 1999; Friedrich & Lueke, 1988; Gray, Pithers, Busconi, & Houchens, 1999; Johnson, 1988; Silovsky & Niec, 2002).

Although these behaviors may mimic adult sexual behaviors, clinicians are strongly cautioned against conceptualizing children's behavior within frameworks for adult or adolescent sexual offending behaviors, or even adult intimacy. Origins, motives for initiating and continuing SBP, and responsiveness to interventions of children with SBP are quite distinct from adult sex offenders. Children do not have pedophilias. Rather, the origins and maintenance of childhood SBP appear to be due to a combination of individual, familial, social, and developmental factors (Elkovitch, Latzman, Hansen, & Flood, 2009; Friedrich, 2007; Friedrich et al., 2001; Friedrich, Davies, Fehrer, & Wright, 2003). Contributing factors include child maltreatment, coercive or neglectful parenting practices, exposure to sexually explicit media, living in a highly sexualized environment, exposure to family violence as well as individual factors and heredity (Chaffin et al., 2008; Friedrich et al., 2003; Langstrom, Grann, & Lichtenstein, 2002; Merrick, Litrownik, Everson, & Cox, 2008). Children with SBP are quite diverse and no distinct SBP profile for children exists; that is, there is no clear pattern of demographic, psychological, or social factors that distinguish children with SBP from other groups of children (Chaffin, Letourneau, & Silovsky, 2002). SBP do not represent a medical/psychological syndrome or even a specific diagnosis, but rather a set of behaviors considered unacceptable by society and that cause impairment in functioning (Chaffin et al., 2008).

A useful conceptualization is to remember that children with SBP are first and foremost children. Life circumstances combined with individual factors lead to the child learning wrong rules about personal safety and sexual behaviors. For example, a young child may have been sexually abused and may repeat those behaviors with other children in his life. These behaviors may represent reexperiencing symptoms of posttraumatic stress disorder (PTSD) for this young child.

Another example is a child with learning or attention problems who grew up in a home where conflict is the norm. Over time, she became increasingly irritable, argumentative, impulsive, and quick to fight or break other rules, including rules that invade the physical boundaries of others. She may repeat sexual behaviors she has seen on television or even witnessed in her home. SBP in this case is not an isolated behavior disturbance, but rather one part of an overall pattern of disruptive behavior problems. However, SBP may also be at times an isolated problem. A child who was otherwise functioning well at home and school became curious about sexual behaviors he learned about from a movie. He tried out these sexual behaviors with neighborhood friends. Once discovered, he expressed not understanding that these behaviors were not appropriate to do with other children. These examples illustrate how SBP may be a single-focused problem, part of a trauma-related reaction, a symptom of a disruptive behavior disorder or other clinical concerning condition, or a combination of these.

Given this diversity, individualized assessments and treatment decisions are recommended. Detailed assessment guidelines and recommendations are beyond the scope of this chapter, and readers are encouraged to examine the Association of Treatment of Sexual Abusers (ATSA) Taskforce report on Children with Sexual Behavior Problems (www .atsa.org; Chaffin et al., 2008) as well as other publications on the topic (Friedrich, 2002). For this chapter, assessment will focus on safety planning and ways treatment planning may be affected by presence, absence, or uncertain status of sexual abuse history of the child with SBP.

When becoming aware of sexual behaviors in a child client, one of the clinician's first tasks is to assess the types, frequency, duration, severity, history, responsivity to adult intervention, and the social and cultural context of the sexual behaviors. There are common co-occurring clinical concerns for children with SBP to assess: (a) trauma-related symptoms for children who have experienced a trauma, (b) other internalizing symptoms, (c) disruptive behavior disorder symptoms (e.g., attention-deficit hyperactivity disorder, oppositional defiant disorder), (d) social skills deficits, and (e) learning problems. Important developmental and cultural considerations are discussed below. Further, an initial task is to develop a support team for the child and family to facilitate safety planning (Gray, 2010). Gather relevant information regarding supports for the family to provide the children supervision and guidance they need to learn and apply healthy rules about interpersonal behaviors. These include the parents/caregivers' ability to provide supervision and barriers to close supervision and nurturance (such as depression, substance abuse, trauma history, and competing demands), ongoing protective factors and adverse conditions, and external natural support systems (such as extended family members, neighbors, friends, schools, child care, coaches, faith community members). Additional information about safety planning is provided later in the chapter. This assessment information is useful as the clinician addresses important initial questions, such as (a) are the behaviors demonstrated out of the norm, unusual, otherwise problematic, (b) are all the children who were involved in the behavior safe and supported, (c) what actions are needed to create a safety team, (d) what treatment modules best fit the treatment needs of the children, and (e) how to integrate developmental and cultural considerations in treatment planning.

Reporting requirements vary across states, and clinicians are encouraged to be well aware of their reporting requirements and to have a collaborative relationship with their local child protective services systems. If sexual abuse or any type of maltreatment is suspected, an investigation by the appropriate authorities (such as child welfare, law enforcement) needs to be conducted expediently and prior to the clinical assessment of the child. At times, particularly with young children, results of investigations of suspected sexual abuse are inconclusive. These cases are of most serious concern for the child's welfare and for the success of intervention efforts when there is the possibility of *ongoing* sexual abuse (Chaffin et al., 2008, emphasis in original text). In these cases, interventions focused on educating children about sexual abuse, identifying who children might tell if they were being abused, having significant adults support this message, and building support systems around the child may be recommended (Hewitt, 1999).

TREATMENT FOR PROBLEMATIC SEXUAL BEHAVIOR

A small number of rigorously designed studies suggest that SBP in children is responsive to short-term outpatient treatment that actively involves the parents (or other caregivers), and the treatment effects are sustained over time, up to 10 years (e.g., Carpentier, Silovsky, & Chaffin, 2006). Children with SBP have been successfully treated with SBP-specific treatment developed for school-age and preschool-age children (Bonner et al., 1999; Carpentier et al., 2006; Pithers, Gray, Busconi, & Houchens, 1998; Silovsky, Niec, Bard, & Hecht, 2007), as well as with Trauma-Focused Cognitive-Behavioral Therapy (TF-CBT), which is a treatment for the effects of trauma (specifically, child sexual abuse) and includes SBP-specific components (Cohen & Mannarino, 1996, 1997; Cohen, Mannarino, & Deblinger, 2006; Deblinger, Stauffer, & Steer, 2001; Stauffer & Deblinger, 1996). These treatments have been found to be more effective than the passage of time, dynamic play therapy, and nondirective supportive treatment.

A recent meta-analysis examined studies in which SBP has been the primary target of treatment or a secondary target in treatments for the effects of child sexual abuse (St. Amand, Bard, & Silovsky, 2008). Eleven studies were identified as evaluating 18 treatments of SBP as a primary or secondary target. The overall degree of change over the course of treatment was estimated at a 0.46 standard deviation decline in SBP. The meta-analysis was designed to examine the treatments at the level of practice elements (including treatment modules), and not just the overall effect. When practice elements and sample characteristics were examined individually, four parent practice elements (i.e., behavior parent training, rules about sexual behavior, sex education, and abuse prevention skills), one child practice-element (i.e., self-control skills), family involvement, and preschool age group had a significant impact on the effect size variability across treatments. When multiple covariates were examined simultaneously, behavior parent training and preschool age-group were the strongest predictors.

In contrast, the current typical clinical approach of treatment programs for SBP (found in the Safer Society 2002 and 2009 surveys) include practice elements originally designed for adolescent or adult sexual offenders: child components of relapse prevention, assault cycle, and arousal reconditioning (Burton & Smith-Darden, 2001; McGrath, Cumming, Burchard, Zeoli, & Ellerby, 2010). Two of the tested treatments in the meta-analyses included practice elements originally designed for adolescents and adults. The elements did not improve the SBP outcome; in fact, there was a negative impact on the measure of general behavior problems.

The results emphasize that parents or other caregivers are the primary agent of change for SBP in children. Behavior parent training was most strongly associated with reduced SBP. The treatments examined in the meta-analysis that utilized behavior parent training also included modules for the parents on rules about sexual behavior, sex education, and abuse prevention skills. Current practices of treating children with SBP as the primary problem in individual therapy or in inpatient or residential care facilities without significant caregiver involvement during treatment or aftercare are brought into question by these results.

Both SBP-focused and trauma-focused interventions (such as TF-CBT; see Chapter 9) reduced SBP. Important clinical questions arise regarding how to determine what approach is appropriate for individual children who present with both SBP and a trauma history. If the child is exhibiting other significant trauma related symptoms, such as those seen in PTSD, TF-CBT may be the treatment of choice. In contrast, for children without significant internalizing symptoms (e.g., anxiety, depression) or maladaptive attributions associated with the trauma, an SBP focused approach may be a better fit. This may be particularly true in cases where the traumas were distal and not associated with the onset of SBP (Chaffin et al., 2008).

Given the results of the meta-analysis, this section will focus on the components of treatment found most strongly related to SBP reduction: behavior parent training, rules about sexual behavior and boundaries, sex education, and abuse prevention skills (St. Amand et al., 2008). It is important to note that no treatment tested uses these modules exclusively, with treatments addressing the common co-occurring concerns of internalizing symptoms, general behavior problems, social skill deficits, and poor coping skills. To address the multifaceted nature of sexual behavior problems, treatment modules often include affective modulation, anxiety management and coping skills, impulse control and problem-solving strategies, social skills, and empathy development. Many of these modules found in SBP focused treatments overlap with treatment components of TF-CBT.

The components of behavior parent training include relationship-building skills (e.g., praise, communication skills, and positive interaction skills) and developmentally appropriate behavior management strategies (e.g., rules, rewards, behavior charts, time-out, and consequences). The goal is to reduce children's behavior problems by providing consistent environments that support and reinforce adaptive behavior, teach appropriate behavior, and provide developmentally appropriate consequences to behavior problems. Evidence-based behavior parent training models such as parent-child interaction therapy

(Brestan & Eyberg, 1998), The Incredible Years (Webster-Stratton, 2005), Barkley's Defiant Child protocol (Barkley & Benton, 1998), or the Triple-P program (Sanders, Conn, & Markie-Dadds, 2003), integrated with SBP specific treatment components, might be considered when SBP are part of a broad, overall pattern of early childhood disruptive behavior problems (Chaffin et al., 2008).

Teaching families rules about sexual behavior and boundaries directly addresses expectations for the child's behavior and respect for privacy and modesty. This approach helps parents identify how to prevent sexual behavior problems in children by identifying clear rules regarding appropriate behavior and how to teach and maintain appropriate sexual behavior in the home. Rules regarding sexual behavior can be taught in the context of family safety rules (Silovsky, 2009). Often these rules are in simple, straightforward language such as "it is not okay for children to look at or touch others' private parts." Rules can also address not touching private parts in public or engaging in sexual behavior (e.g., kissing, standing close to others) that makes others feel uncomfortable. For children with SBP who also have sexual abuse histories, clinicians are alerted to distinguish who "broke" the sexual behavior rules to reduce possibility of self-blame for past abuse experiences. Caregivers learn how to implement close visual supervision of children and how to monitor the child's environment for inappropriate exposure to sexualized content (presently found commonly in a range of media, such as television, movies, music videos, music lyrics, video games, magazines, internet, and communications via cell phones).

Close visual supervision of children sounds easier than it is in practice, particularly considering single parents with multiple children. Realistic approaches, utilizing technology supports (e.g., "baby" monitors), and problem solving is critical for open communication and planning. Lastly, teaching families such rules provides children with developmentally appropriate expectations regarding respect for self and others, privacy, and modesty. Sexual behavior rules, privacy rules, and clear boundaries promote appropriate and safe ways to show affection. Children learn what appropriate personal space is and how to assert appropriate physical boundaries when around others.

Often children with sexual behavior problems have some misunderstandings and would benefit from developmentally appropriate sex education. School-age children can benefit from learning the biological names and functions of private parts and related body parts (e.g., penis, testicles, vulva, vagina, uterus, anus, buttocks, rectum, bladder, and breasts). Teaching preschool children the names of fewer private parts, such as penis, vagina, buttocks, in the context of learning about nonsexual body parts (e.g., elbow, navel, foot) reinforces that these are all body parts. This information serves to address curiosity and alleviate confusion, and promotes the use of appropriate labels that contribute to better abuse prevention. Conception and puberty are often addressed with school-age children as well, at a level commensurate with the child's age and developmental level. It is recommended that sex education with older children be provided in the context of broader information on relationship choices, friendships, and intimacy decisions. Because of the need for ongoing open communication, an important goal is to help children identify appropriate adults with whom they can talk about their questions regarding sexual matters, intimacy, relationships, and related factors as well as when and where it is appropriate to discuss such matters.

Abuse-prevention skills training for children with sexual behavior problems promotes generalization of knowledge with the purpose of teaching children how to stay safe in situations in which someone attempts to engage in inappropriate sexual behavior. As children learn rules for appropriate sexual behavior, they enhance their understanding that it is not appropriate for others to break the rules with them. Potential exceptions of when a caregiver or medical professional needs to help the child with daily hygiene (e.g., bathing) or to address health concerns can be discussed with children. Basic abuse prevention skills training for children should include learning to be assertive, knowing how to exit a situation in which someone is attempting to engage in inappropriate behavior, identifying adults to whom they can go and tell about the incident, and continuing to tell adults until they are protected. For caregivers, the abuse prevention module of treatment teaches how to ensure safety in the child's many ecologies and establishes the caregiver as a safe person for the child. Children *cannot* be expected to protect themselves from abuse. Providing the parents with education regarding risk and protective factors and their responsibility in monitoring who is taking care of their children is emphasized. Empathy development and acknowledging breaking a sexual behavior rule is a unique treatment goal for school-age children with SBP. Parents (and at times professionals involved in the case) may express great concern that the child with sexual behavior problems has not expressed significant remorse for their behaviors and fear the child is a "psychopath" or "in denial." However, typically developing children's decision making is based on seeking pleasure and avoiding pain. Children tend to view the impact of their behavior in terms of how they were affected and not others. Older school-age children can begin to enhance their understanding and learning of how their behavior affects others and take responsibility for their sexual behavior. Further, children learn that they are not "bad" or flawed in some way because of their sexual behavior, but that they made a poor choice and they can learn to make better choices.

Teaching these concepts through an exercise of writing an apology letter helps the child to organize what they learned in therapy regarding their sexual behavior and, ultimately, demonstrate developmentally appropriate remorse for their behavior. This letter is typically not shared with the person with whom the sexual behavior occurred, though consideration to do so may be warranted for sibling victims if the children are living apart and the permanency plan is reunification. The apology letter exercise enhances moral development within the child by helping him or her recognize how his or her behaviors affected others. Given children's developmental levels, the degree to which they demonstrate remorse and empathy for their sexual behavior problems varies greatly. Therapists should spend time with caregivers to help cultivate an understanding of this developmental aspect of the child and reinforce that a lack of empathy or remorse does not indicate long-term adverse implications for the child. Further, shame is to be avoided as it stigmatizes the youth who can become withdrawn and fail to make progress due to lack of self-efficacy. One way to address this issue is having the parent provide a letter of support for the child during the apology letter exercise.

Additional treatment modules that can be considered as part of the overall treatment plan for these children include affective modulation, anxiety management, coping skills, impulse control, and social skills. These modules are treatment components that are also common with TF-CBT and are described in detail in Chapter 9.

ENGAGING CAREGIVER INVOLVEMENT IN TREATMENT

Parental involvement in treatment for SBP is critical. Parents of children with SBP report high parental stress, and there are considerable environmental influences (e.g., family sexuality) on SBP (Bonner et al., 1999a; Friedrich, et al., 1992, 2001; Pithers et al., 1998; Silovsky & Niec, 2002). Effective treatments for children with sexual behavior problems include direct caregiver involvement in treatment. Sexual behavior problems occur in the child's social ecology. To successfully treat a child's sexual behavior problems, several environmental factors need to be addressed to provide the supervision and guidance to reduce the likelihood of further SBP, support privacy, modesty, and safety, and engage the children in prosocial interactions with peers.

Because children with SBP are often in temporary placements (such as foster homes) or in multiple placements (such as parents with joint custody), a question arises regarding which parent or caregiver should be involved in treatment. It is recommended that the caregiver(s) who provide the primary supervision and care for the child be actively involved in treatment. In some cases, the child has been removed from the home and placed in foster care, but the plan is reunification with the parents in the near future. Ideally, both sets of parents (that is, foster parents and biological parents) are involved in treatment services and the biological parents can view the foster parents as extended support. At times, however, there is significant tension or other circumstances that indicate that caregivers should be seen for services separately. Involving all the caregivers in treatment helps to ensure that the child's current and permanent caregivers are aware of the supervision requirements, are taught behavior management skills including how to address inappropriate sexual behavior, and learn effective communication strategies particularly around sex education.

Despite the importance of parental involvement in treatment, clinicians commonly experience challenges in engaging regular participation of caregivers in treatment. Some caregivers may be reluctant to be actively involved in treatment due to how they perceive the child and/or services (e.g., believing their child is the one who needs to be "fixed," believing their child is a "pedophile" who cannot be helped, or viewing their child as inherently evil and beyond help). Others may have limited motivation to change their parenting behavior, perceiving there is nothing wrong with how they parent and thus no need to change. Motivational interviewing and similar strategies have been found to facilitate adherence and outcome of behavior parent training (Chaffin et al., 2009, 2010; Nock & Kazdin, 2005). Initially spending time listening and reflecting the parents' concerns and perceptions so that they feel understood are important first steps. Requesting permission to provide advice and education as well as utilizing strategies to elicit change then follows. Pros and cons of continuing their current parenting practices as well as learning new strategies can be discussed, starting with the pros of the status quo and cons of changing, and then spending more time on the cons of the current activities and pros of learning more "tools for their parenting tool box." Parents can come to acknowledge that the parenting strategies that worked well for other children are not a good fit for this child when the behavior problems continue to occur. Self-motivation statements can be elicited (e.g., "What steps can you take to help change your child's behavior?" Nock & Kazdin, 2005, p. 874).

Other barriers that may affect a caregiver's ability to fully engage in treatment are a lack of understanding about expectations regarding their involvement in their child's treatment (e.g., assuming that they can drop their child off at therapy to be "fixed") and the erroneous belief that the therapist/agency is an extension of "the system" (i.e., juvenile justice, child welfare) with whom they may have not had positive experiences. Solutions to these barriers include establishing the expectation of caregiver involvement at the first contact with the family and continuing to communicate this expectation with the family during additional contacts. This will allow the therapist to address any further concerns from the caregivers about their involvement before treatment begins. Providing education about effective interventions for children with SBP and engaging in a dialogue with caregivers about their key role in helping to change their child's behavior are generally effective. Finally, clarifying roles of the therapists and other involved agencies, including what information will be shared and with whom, are also helpful strategies. The supportive relationship established with the therapist and the positive outcomes experienced often begin to naturally reinforce and effectively engage most caregivers. Group therapy can be particularly useful for these purposes, as it reduces the stigma and sense of isolation for the parents and provides messages about how different parenting strategies can be effective.

Finally, the caregiver's own trauma history may make it difficult for the caregiver to engage in therapy. Parents are understandably reluctant to disclose personal trauma history early in treatment. They may reveal their personal history over time, particularly when sexual behavior and the abuse history of others are addressed. When this occurs, direct inquiry regarding the caregiver's history of trauma can be conducted in a thoughtful manner to assess their trauma symptoms as well as how they are coping with the treatment topics that are addressed. When trauma symptoms are present and affecting the caregiver's ability to fully participate in treatment, they can be connected to individual services. For example, one caregiver participant became increasingly upset during the caregiver's group and started to become tearful when the group was discussing relatively benign topics. When therapists met with the participant after group, she reported that she was sexually abused as a child by an adolescent family member. She began to describe detailed memories that she was having about the abuse when the topics about child sexual behavior and sexuality were raised during group discussions. This participant was referred to therapy to address her trauma symptoms. Sometimes, the caregiver may need to complete their own treatment before they can participate in their child's treatment and other support systems need to be identified; while some caregivers are able to participate in their own treatment and their child's treatment concurrently.

Other types of concerns that caregivers have about attending treatment are related to external factors, such as lack of child care for their other children, job conflicts, and transportation issues. Therapists can use this opportunity to provide empathy and problem solve with the caregivers. Often, reminding parents that treatment is usually brief (approximately 4 months) can reassure caregivers. Offering letters to employers, stating that the parent has a required appointment without giving specifics of the nature of the appointment, can sometimes alleviate work-related concerns.

GROUP VERSUS FAMILY TREATMENT OF PROBLEMATIC SEXUAL BEHAVIORS

Treatment for SBP in children can be provided in group or family therapy, both of which include children and caregivers in services. The decision on which format to use depends on a variety of individual, family, community, and agency level factors. This section addresses potential benefits and barriers to group and family therapies when planning for treatment of children with SBP.

Group therapy, by nature, can destigmatize treatment. Within the context of children with SBP a group therapy can facilitate directly addressing the sexual behavior as well. Children and parents learn that other families experience similar problems and that there is support for their family. SBP are most commonly interpersonal behavior problems. A group format allows for frequent practice of appropriate behaviors with peers supported by therapists. Children receive feedback on their behaviors from those with the most influence—peers. Caregivers, too, are held accountable in their group for their management of their child's behaviors, sexual and otherwise. Group therapy also allows for families to practice skills with others in the group, which contributes to the environment of social support and learning from one another. Given the sensitive topics addressed and social environment in which group therapy takes place, families with caregivers, children, or both that present with significant reexperiencing symptoms of PTSD may better be served in family therapy.

Community and agency factors affect the feasibility of group therapy. Group therapy provides services to more families in communities in which there is a strong need. This is especially important given the specialty nature of treating children with sexual behavior problems. In order for agencies to be capable of delivering group therapy, there needs to be room and staff available to facilitate group. Conducting group therapy with children who have behavior problems requires sufficient therapist-to-child ratios with therapists well-skilled at engaging children and implementing behavior management strategies. The disadvantage of group therapy is most salient in rural communities in which a group format may present challenges with confidentiality and relationships between community members.

Family therapy for children with sexual behavior problems provides individualized treatment. This format should be considered when there are complex concurrent issues for the child or family, or when crisis intervention is necessary. Logistical or personal reasons may interfere with group therapy options. In instances of families in which parents are divorced, or at times when there is a conflictual relationship between foster and biological parents, separate family therapy is preferred, so as to not interfere with the supportive focus of group therapy.

DEVELOPMENTAL CONSIDERATIONS

Children's cognitive, social, moral, and language development progresses tremendously across the age span of 3 to 12 years, impacting treatment planning and service delivery. Child development is a sequential process that begins at birth and continues through adolescence to adulthood. The path of this process is determined by a child's genetic blueprint and social and cultural environments (Schroeder & Gordon, 2002). Children vary in the rate of development in areas such as physical abilities, cognitive abilities, emotional expression, and social skills. According to Piaget (1932, 1936), cognitive and social development typically occur in a progressive series of stages, with mastery of different tasks and abilities taking place during specific periods of time common for the majority of children. Children of similar ages may develop at a faster or slower rate depending on environmental and genetic factors. Consequently, the type of interventions utilized with children will be influenced by their ages and rates of development.

Approximate age ranges (e.g., 4 to 6, 7 to 9, 10 to 12 years old) for children are designated for the normal time periods in which children develop abilities. Young children (4 to 6 years old) have not yet developed the same cognitive abilities and social skills as school-age children, adolescents, and adults. This developmental immaturity is demonstrated in their lack of impulse control, shorter attention spans, and minimal self-understanding. Preschool children's cognitive abilities give them an understanding of simple rules, but not an understanding of more complex information. For example, preschool children can understand the rule of no talking to strangers, but are often unable to express all possible consequences of this behavior.

Consideration of children's ages and stages of development also impacts the structure and format of sessions. For example, the treatment of sexual behavior problems for preschool and school-age children is quite different. Preschool children (4 to 6 years old) require structure, routine, and repetition of rules in each session due to the limits of their cognitive ability. School-age children (7 to 12 years old) also need structure and routine, but activities involve more cognitive reasoning abilities, particularly near the end of this age range.

Other factors that influence child development are the social and cultural environments in which the child lives. For instance, a nurturing parent-child relationship can support the child's development broadly. On the other hand, exposure to multiple harmful events such as sexual abuse or violence may interfere with a child's development of age-appropriate cognitive abilities, emotional expression, and social skills. In their social and cultural environments, children learn values and morals from the actions and words of their parents or caregivers (National Information Center for Children and Youth with Disabilities [NICHCY], 1992). Young children understand right and wrong behavior and the rewards and punishment of their behavior, especially regarding the rules. For older children, they understand that rules are relative and can be changed if all agree (Crain, 1985) and begin to understand the impact on others of breaking the rules.

Some children may present with developmental disabilities that can affect their sexual development, learning styles, and supports needed. For example, a child who is intellectually challenged may need information presented in basic, concrete language, given in smaller amounts, and supplemented with visual examples (NICHCY, 1992). Caregivers are generally the primary source for information regarding their child's sexual development, which can be more variable when their child has a developmental disability or chronic medical condition (Gordon & Schroeder, 1995; Siddiqi, Van Dyke, Donohoue, & McBrien, 1999; Woodward, 2004). As with typically developing children, youth with developmental disabilities need sex education and information about appropriate ways to express physical affection, with whom, and under what circumstances. They also benefit from opportunities to discuss values and attitudes about sexuality, develop interpersonal skills, and learn about responsibility and making decisions regarding sexual relationships (NICHCY, 1992).

Given the increased risk of sexual abuse for children and youth with developmental disabilities, sexual abuse prevention components (i.e., personal safety skills) are critical. Caregivers and professionals are encouraged to provide guidance and education based on individual learning styles and disability-specific challenges, consider the use of visual supports (e.g., pictures, dolls), repeated information over time, and have the youth demonstrate or practice the information learned (e.g., role-play) (Duncan, Dixon, & Carlson, 2003; Woodward, 2004). Curriculum on sex education for children and youth with disabilities are available (Kupper, 1995) as well as other useful information from the Florida Developmental Disabilities Council (www.fddc.org; Baxley & Zendell, 2005) and the University of South Carolina Center for Disability Resource Library (uscm.med.sc.edu/CDR/sexeducation.htm).

CULTURAL CONSIDERATIONS

Consideration of the child and family's cultural values, beliefs, and customs are of primary importance in the provision of any mental health and social services. The sensitive nature and at times taboo rules around the topics of sexual behavior and children heightens the importance of cultural congruence in service delivery addressing child SBP. Multiple aspects of culture such as religion, spirituality, social class, historical experiences, customs, race, and ethnicity can impact receptivity and response to treatment for children with sexual behavior problems. Professionals are advised to become familiar with the family and integrate cultural beliefs, customs, and primary language into the treatment of children with sexual behavior problems and their families. Families may more readily engage in treatment when the communication used is consistent with their communication styles, verbal and nonverbal behavior, level of comprehension, and culture-specific knowledge (Fouad & Arredondo, 2007; Workgroup on Adapting Latino Services, 2008). In addition, the primary language and English proficiency among family members from diverse cultures may vary, the reading level of treatment material may need to modified, and other forms of communication (audiovisual aids, translated material, bilingual staff, and translators) may be needed for individuals and families that are bilingual or have limited English proficiency (Workgroup on Adapting Latino Services, 2008).

There may be significant variation among children in their cultural and social context, family attitudes, and educational practices that can impact children's knowledge of sexuality and sexual behavior (Friedrich, Sandfort, Oostveen, & Cohen-Kettenis, 2000; Gordon, Schoeder, & Abrams, 1990; Volbert, 2000). Children's public and private sexual behavior and attitudes about modesty, intimacy, and relationships are impacted by cultural values and beliefs of their families and communities. For example, higher frequencies of sexual behaviors in children were found in social environments in which nudity is acceptable, privacy is not reinforced, and exposure to sexualized material is more common than social environments in which modesty and privacy are reinforced (e.g., Friedrich et al., 2000; Thigpen, Pinkston, & Mayefsky, 2003). Furthermore, parents' attitudes toward children's sexuality have been found to impact children's sexual knowledge and behavior (Gordon et al., 1990). When providing sex education to children, it is helpful to plan with the parents or caregivers what information is appropriate and address any concerns or questions, especially when there may be conflicting attitudes based on parents' religious, cultural, or social values and beliefs. Cultural practices such as the person designated to teach male or female children about sexuality and sexual behavior may be a customary role. For example, a traditional practice in some American Indian tribes is for aunts to teach their nieces about sexual matters. Fathers are forbidden to speak to their daughters about sexual matters as this is considered taboo. The therapist can be thoughtful in developing a plan with the parents for sex education that is respectful of the cultural values and provide the children with information about sexuality and sexual behavior from their family's cultural and social perspective. The therapist can encourage children to access the culturally identified supportive influence for sexual matters throughout childhood.

Explaining sexuality and sexual behavior in a manner consistent with the culture and families' approach is recommended. Educational strategies for teaching children about sexual matters may include storytelling, ceremonies, and ritual for American Indian, Alaska Native, Native Hawaiian, and African American families. Additionally, parents may have strongly held cultural or religious beliefs about the appropriateness of children touching their own private parts that may directly affect their receptiveness to treatment for their children. If handled in a culturally sensitive manner and with respect of the values of families, there will likely be improved retention of families in treatment and thus better outcome.

SAFETY PLANNING, LEVELS OF CARE, AND PLACEMENT AND REUNIFICATION DECISIONS

Helping professionals who work with children with sexual behavior problems often face tough decisions regarding level of care, placement into residential treatment settings, and if and when reunification is an appropriate course of action. These issues as well as the dynamics involved in safety planning are discussed in this section.

SAFETY PLANNING

The safety of all children should be considered when assessing a child with SBP. Multiple factors may be considered when assessing whether the sexual behavior involved potential for harm to others including (a) the age/developmental differences of the children involved, (b) use of force, intimidation, or coercion, (c) presence of emotional distress in the child(ren) involved, (d) interference with the child(ren)'s social development; and (e) physical injury or harm (Araji, 1997; Chaffin et al., 2008; Hall, Mathews, & Pearce, 1998; Johnson, 2002). Potential ongoing risks to children in the home must be examined. For example, the child with SBP is sleeping in the same bed with siblings or the siblings are bathing together. However, there may be potential risk to other children who do not live in the home with the identified child. For example, the child attends day care with poor supervision of children or the child with SBP visits a grandparent who has other children in the home, but is unaware of necessary supervision requirements. Families benefit from the development of a natural support team, with initial help identified as early as possible in treatment and the goal of growing the support network over time. The overarching goal is for all children to be safe. Therefore, identifying and addressing potential risks and supports as soon as possible are a priority. Most children with SBP can continue to live in their home or a foster home with other children without further problematic sexual behavior, provided there is appropriate caregiver supervision, safety planning, and effective outpatient treatment.

SCHOOL SUPPORTS

A common concern is whether a child with SBP can attend school without risking other children's safety. Most children with SBP attend school and participate in typical school academic and extracurricular activities without jeopardizing other children's safety (Swisher, Silovsky, Stewart, & Pierce, 2008). In those more rare cases when children demonstrate serious, aggressive sexual behaviors that have not responded to outpatient interventions and supervision, a more restrictive school environment is typically required until their behavior improves (Horton, 1996; Silovsky & Bonner, 2003b). School personnel are often important members of the support team for children and families. The manner in which school personnel are approached and the information provided can dramatically impact the level of support versus concerning reactions that occur. Who and what is addressed with others should be determined on a case-by-case basis after discussion between the therapist, family, and other systems (e.g., probation, child welfare) when involved (Chaffin et al., 2008).

Notifying school personnel about the child's SBP is not always necessary. This is particularly the case when the child's sexual behavior has been restricted to the home setting, the child and family are actively involved in treatment for SBP, the behavior is of low frequency, and the behavior is not ongoing (Chaffin et al., 2008). In cases where the sexual behavior has occurred in school/extracurricular settings, the child is assessed to be at high risk, or the serious sexual behavior continues, notifying the supervisory personnel would be appropriate. Discussions with school personnel should include correcting any misperceptions of the child and/or situation as well as specific realistic supervision strategies and other supports to prevent further SBP (e.g., child should use the bathroom alone, aide to keep child within eyesight during recess). Child and family privacy will need to be protected in this process, such that details of the child's background, such as a trauma history, are not revealed unnecessarily. Alerting other children or children's parents is typically not needed and may instead result in stigmatizing the child (Chaffin et al., 2008).

Levels of Care and Residential Placement Decisions

The majority of children with SBP are successfully treated with relatively short-term treatment on an outpatient basis. It is almost always preferable to treat children with SBP on an outpatient basis in the community in which they live. However, there are circumstances that may warrant the removal of a child with SBP from the home and community. Removal of a child with SBP from the home should be considered when one or more of the following four circumstances are present (Chaffin et al., 2008):

1. The child and caregiver are participating in an outpatient intervention and the child with SBP continues to engage in aggressive or severe sexual behavior with other children.
2. Reasonable efforts have been made to develop a safety plan with the caregiver and/or to assist the caregiver in providing a stable environment and the caregivers are unable or unwilling to provide a healthy, stable environment or are not providing appropriate supervision or are not following the safety plan and the child continues to engage in aggressive or severe sexual behavior with other children.
3. The other child(ren) in the home experience significant distress by the child with SBP's presence and/or the other child(ren) in the

home would feel significantly relieved with the removal of the child with SBP.

4. Risks or behavior are so severe or potentially harmful to self (e.g., the child is actively suicidal) or others (e.g., the child reports planned intention to harm someone sexually or otherwise) that less restrictive placements are not feasible.

In cases in which out-of-home placement is recommended, less restrictive placements (e.g., foster care, placement with a relative) should be considered if children are safe with such a community placement (e.g., not if example 4 above is present). The new caregivers should be provided with information about the child's needs and problems, including SBP and how to supervise the child prior to their placement (Chaffin et al., 2008). Once the child with SBP has shown improvement and/or the caregiver has demonstrated the ability to provide a safe and stable environment with appropriate supervision, then reunification with their caregiver(s) can be considered, and is discussed more thoroughly below.

When compared to inpatient/residential treatment, the advantages of outpatient treatment include maintenance of social relationships, academic supports, and typical activities, the caregivers' ability to more readily participate in the child's treatment and the reduced costs. Outpatient treatment also allows the child and caregiver to directly apply the skills taught in treatment with practice in the home and community. That said, there are circumstances that warrant residential or inpatient treatment, due to threat of harm to self or others.

Although residential/inpatient treatment may be indicated for some children, there are risks to consider. Caregiver involvement (a crucial component in treating children with SBP) in residential/inpatient treatment is difficult to obtain. Residential/inpatient treatment exposes the child to other children with severe behavior problems or mental health disorders, is expensive, and it potentially places the child at risk for victimization by other residents or staff (Chaffin et al., 2008). If placing a child in residential/inpatient treatment is necessary, then there must be a plan for transitioning the child back into the community (e.g., caregiver's home). The transition plan should also include support and education regarding supervision and behavior parent training for caregivers, in order to reduce the likelihood of further problematic sexual behavior in the child.

REUNIFICATION WITH SIBLINGS AND TRANSITION TO HOME

When a child with SBP has been removed from the home, a number of factors should be considered when making the decision to reunify with his or her siblings and/or other children in the home. Active involvement of the children and parents/caregivers in treatment for SBP, and their demonstrated understanding, support, and consistent application of the supervision and safety plan is a prerequisite. A pattern of prosocial behavior in which the child with a history of SBP is following rules, including sexual behavior rules, at home, school, and in the community is an indication that the child can consistently demonstrate self-control and decision-making skills. Collaboration with the therapists for the siblings (if applicable) can facilitate the timing of visitations and reunification, taking into account the siblings' level of distress, trauma symptoms, and desire to be with their brother/sister (Chaffin & Bonner, 1998).

At times siblings are demonstrating readiness for visitation with each other, but reunification with the siblings and/or parents is not yet possible, sometimes for logistical reasons. Consideration of visitation to facilitate positive interactions and sibling relationship development is recommended. When reunification is deemed appropriate, it is recommended that children be reunified gradually. Often it is helpful to provide family treatment, enabling the therapist to address family reintegration, develop and institute support and safety plans, and address emotional reactions to reunification, as well as new or ongoing behavior problems. Family sessions conducted by the therapist to review the safety plan and its application in the home are recommended prior to reunification. Depending on the age of the other children in the home, information about safety, sexual behavior rules/private part rules, and privacy rules are shared. Caregivers should address privacy rules with all family members. At a minimum, family privacy rules should require that all family members be clothed in public areas of the house, that only one child may use the bathroom at a time, that family members should knock on closed doors and wait for permission before entering, and that a violation of these rules should be reported to a caregiver immediately.

It is important to also focus on what the siblings can and should do together. Too often the siblings are not sure how they can interact with each other, and in some extreme situations do not know how to interact in nonsexual ways with each other. Family therapy can emphasize age-appropriate activities and interaction strategies, directly practicing these in session when unfamiliar to the youth.

Typically, reunification begins with brief planned visits. These visits allow the therapist to assess the family's ability and/or willingness to abide by the safety plan. Visits are best planned in advance and involve typical family activities (e.g., eating dinner together, playing board games together). When visits have consistently gone well contact often increases in frequency and duration moving from day-long visits to overnight visits, to weekend visits, and lastly to returning home as progress by the family indicates. The therapist should continue to monitor the family's progress during each stage of reunification, addressing concerns as they arise, making modifications to the safety plan as necessary, and providing positive feedback about what has helped visits go well. (For additional information regarding reunification, including an example of a safety plan, see Swisher et al., 2008.)

Case Examples

The case examples below are presented to highlight differences in case conceptualization and treatment planning dependent on the presentation of symptoms. Key decisions to consider when reading these examples should include what treatment format would be most appropriate and what treatment topics should be emphasized.

- Arianna, a 9-year-old girl, was referred due to reports that she was touching the genitals of her 3-year-old sister with her hands and mouth during baths together and asking her sister to do the same with her. When Arianna was 7 she was sexually abused by her 16-year-old cousin. The abuse involved fondling and oral-genital contact, and occurred about six times over the course of a year. No force or coercion was reported in either the sexual abuse she experienced or the sexual behavior she demonstrated. Her mother reported that Arianna and her cousin had a close relationship and that Arianna didn't understand that what happened to her was inappropriate. The assessment did not reveal significant trauma-related symptoms. No nightmares or other symptoms of significant anxiety or depression were reported. Arianna has poor interpersonal boundaries with others, though mostly men, and she frequently attempts to touch other's private parts with her hands when in close proximity. She has been in trouble at school many times for attempting to touch peers' private parts in the bathroom and during recess. Arianna did report some distress about not having friends and having peer-rejection experiences related to her SBP. Arianna's parents were never married and her father is uninvolved in her life. Her mother is single and expressed

(continued)

(*continued*)

considerable stress related to understanding and managing Arianna's sexual behavior. She had already changed her supervision of her daughters and no longer bathes them together. Further, she was receptive to the safety plan.

Group therapy for children with SBP was recommended for Arianna and her mother. This format and focus was a good fit for the family for a number of reasons. During group therapy Arianna was able to not only learn rules about sexual behavior, boundaries, how to respect the physical space of peers and adults, how to greet others appropriately but also was able to practice these skills each week with other children and adults in the program. The group therapy also addressed affect regulation, coping skills, and impulse control strategies. Further, Arianna's mother not only obtained accurate information about sexual development, prevention of SBP, and parenting strategies to support Arianna's progress, but also social support from the other family members in attendance. A few supplemental family sessions were conducted to help support her sister's basic understanding of rules about privacy and safety and facilitate appropriate activities for the sisters.

- Conner is a 12-year-old boy who was referred for putting his penis into the mouths of his 10-year-old male neighborhood friends on two occasions. He told the friends not to tell anyone or they would all get in trouble. During the intake assessment Conner's mother indicated that Conner is failing most classes at school and is truant once or twice a month. Further, Conner frequently argues with his mother and refuses to do chores at home. When Conner gets angry, he damages his own personal belongings and those of others. The mother is certain that Conner is going to be a "child molester" and will end up in prison for his overall behavior. He does not have a maltreatment history. Conner is adamant that his neighbor initiated the behavior and that he did nothing wrong. His mother is single and works full-time to support her family.

Initial work with Conner and his mother was around developing a support and safety plan. Time was spent with Conner's mother to address her concerns, to identify sources of support, and to institute an initial safety plan. The National Center on Sexual

(*continued*)

Behavior of Youth (NCSBY) fact sheets were used to help dispel some of her misperceptions. A neighbor and a couple members of her faith community were identified as potential sources of support to help supervise and guide Conner. A supervision plan was developed with this support team to help support the mom, particularly during the time after school when she was still at work. The safety plan, including sexual behavior rules, was reviewed with the family and a support team, and Conner responded to this plan with improved behavior and no further SBP.

In addition, a psychoeducational evaluation was conducted. Conner had been labeled a behavior problem in the school, and no prior testing had been administered. The current evaluation indicated that Conner has a reading disability and slow processing speed. Support for the family to work with the school to develop an Individualized Education Plan to address his learning and behavior needs was provided.

Conner and his mother began group treatment for children with SBP. Initially Conner was negative about group participation, but after just a few sessions he became engaged and active in the sessions. Having peers who were further along in treatment provided a positive influence for Conner. Further, the structure and behavior modification used during session (e.g., reinforcing following the rules and positive participation) facilitated adaptive behavior. Behavioral parent training was of particular benefit to his mother given that Conner was demonstrating a significant range of behavior problems. Support from other parents provided ideas for creative implementation of parenting strategies and provided role models for the balance of nurturing parent-child relationship while still instilling clear rules and consequences as needed.

CONCLUSION

Problematic sexual behaviors that are present in children are typically responsive to short-term outpatient therapy. These children with SBP may or may not have a history of sexual abuse. When children have their own history of sexual abuse, the impact of that abuse experience, including PTSD and other trauma effects, guide the treatment planning. Behavior parent training with rules about sexual behavior, abuse prevention, and sex education are core SBP treatment components. Further, developing and sustaining the support team for the child and family are an important focus. At times children are moved from the home or otherwise separated from their siblings initially. Consideration of progress in treatment and planning for beginning visitations and reunification should occur as early as possible respecting the well-being and safety of all children involved. This work requires coordinated services with other professionals involved as well as the informal support system.

REFERENCES

Araji, S. K. (1997). *Sexually aggressive children: Coming to understand them.* Thousand Oaks, CA: Sage.

Barkley, R., & Benton, C. (1998). *Your defiant child: Eight steps to better behavior.* New York, NY: Guilford Press.

Baxley, D. L., & Zendell, A. L. (2005). *Sexuality across a lifespan: Sexuality education for children and adolescents with developmental disabilities.* An instructional guide for parents/caregivers of individuals with developmental disabilities. Florida Developmental Disabilities Council, Tallahassee, www.fddc.org

Bonner, B. L. (1999). When does sexual play suggest a problem? In H. Dubowitz & D. Depanfilis (Eds.), *Handbook of child protection practice* (pp. 209–214). Thousand Oaks, CA: Sage.

Bonner, B. L., Walker, C. E., & Berliner, L. (1999). *Children with sexual behavior problems: Assessment and treatment* (Final Report, Grant No. 90-CA-1469). Washington, DC: Administration of Children, Youth, and Families, DHHS.

Brestan, E. V., & Eyberg, S. M. (1998). Effective psychosocial treatments of conduct-disordered children and adolescents: 29 years, 82 studies, and 5,272 kids. *Journal of Clinical Child Psychology, 27,* 180–189.

Burton, D. L., & Smith-Darden, J. (2001). *North American survey of sexual abuser treatment and models: Summary data 2000.* Brandon, VT: Safer Society Foundation.

Carpentier, M., Silovsky, J. F., & Chaffin, M. (2006). Randomized trial of treatment for children with sexual behavior problems: Ten year follow-up. *Journal of Consulting and Clinical Psychology, 74,* 482–488.

Chaffin, M. (2008). Our minds are made up—don't confuse us with the facts: Commentary on policies concerning children with sexual behavior problems and juvenile sex offenders. *Child Maltreatment, 13*(2), 110–121.

Chaffin, M., Berliner, L., Block, R., Johnson, T. C., Friedrich, W., Louis, D., . . . Silovsky, J. F. (2008). Report of the ATSA task force on children with sexual behavior problems. *Child Maltreatment, 13*(2), 199–218.

Chaffin, M., & Bonner, B. (2002). *Removal and reunification of children and adolescents with sexual behavior problems.* Unpublished Training Curriculum. National Center on the Sexual Behavior of Youth.

Chaffin, M., & Bonner, B. (1998). "Don't shoot, we're your children"; Have we gone too far in our response to adolescent sexual abusers and children with sexual behavior problems? *Child Maltreatment, 3,* 314–316.

Chaffin, M., Funderburk, B., Bard, D., Valle, L. A., & Gurwitch, R. (2010). A combined motivation and parent-child interaction therapy package reduces child welfare recidivism in a randomized dismantling field trial. *Journal of Consulting and Clinical Psychology*, Advance online publication. DOI: 10.1037/a0021227.

Chaffin, M., Letourneau, E., & Silovsky, J. F. (2002). Adults, adolescents and children who sexually abuse children: A developmental perspective. In J. Myers, L. Berliner, Briere, C. T. Hendrix, C. Jenny, & T. A. Reid (Eds.), *The APSAC handbook on child maltreatment* (pp. 205–232). Thousand Oaks, CA: Sage.

Chaffin, M., Valle, L., Funderburk, B., Gurwitch, R., Silovsky, J. F., Bard, D., McCoy, C., & Kees, M. (2009). A Motivational Intervention Can Improve Retention in PCIT for Low-Motivation Child Welfare Clients. *Child Maltreatment, 14*, 356–368.

Cohen, J. A., & Mannarino, A. P. (1996). A treatment outcome study for sexually abused preschool children: Initial findings. *Journal of the American Academy of Child & Adolescent Psychiatry, 35*, 42–50.

Cohen, J. A., & Mannarino, A. P. (1997). A treatment study for sexually abused preschool children: Outcome during one-year follow-up. *Journal of the American Academy of Child and Adolescent Psychiatry, 36*, 1228–1235.

Cohen, J. A., Mannarino, A. P., & Deblinger, E. (2006). *Treating trauma and traumatic grief in children and adolescents*. New York, NY: Guilford Press.

Crain, W. C. (1985). *Theories of development: Concepts and applications* (2nd ed.). Englewood Cliffs, NJ: Prentice-Hall.

Deblinger, E., Stauffer, L. B., & Steer, R. (2001). Comparative efficacies of supportive and cognitive-behavioral group therapies for young children who have been sexually abused and their non-offending mothers. *Child Maltreatment, 6*, 332–343.

Duncan, P., Dixon, R., & Carlson, J. (2003). Childhood and adolescent sexuality. *Pediatric Clinics of North America, 50*, 765–780.

Elkovitch, N., Latzman, R., Hansen, D. J., & Flood, M. F. (2009). Understanding child sexual behavior problems: A developmental psychopathology framework. *Clinical Psychology Review, 29*, 586–598.

Fouad, N. A., & Arredondo, P. (2007). *Becoming culturally oriented. Practical advice for psychologists and educators*. Washington, DC: American Psychological Association.

Friedrich, W. N. (1988). Behavior problems in sexually abused children: An adaptational perspective. In G. E. Wyatt & G. J. Powell (Eds.), *Lasting effects of child sexual abuse* (pp. 171–191). Newbury Park, CA: Sage.

Friedrich, W. N. (2002). *Psychological assessment of sexually abused children and their families*. Thousand Oaks, CA: Sage.

Friedrich, W. N. (2007). *Children with sexual behavior problems: Family-based, attachment-focused therapy*. New York, NY: Norton.

Friedrich, W. N., Davies, W., Fehrer, E., & Wright, J. (2003). Sexual behavior problems in preteen children: Developmental, ecological, and behavioral correlates. *Annals of the New York Academy of Sciences, 989*, 95–104.

Friedrich, W. N., Fisher, J., Dittner, C., Acton, R., Berliner, L., Butler, J., Damon, L., Davies, W. H., Gray, A., . . . Wright, J. (2001). Child sexual behavior inventory: Normative, psychiatric, and sexual abuse comparisons. *Child Maltreatment, 6,* 37–49.

Friedrich, W. N., Grambsch, P., Damon, L., Hewitt, S. K., Koverola, C., Lang, R. A., Wolfe, V., . . . Broughton, D. (1992). Child Sexual Behavior Inventory: Normative and clinical comparisons. *Psychological Assessment, 4*(3), 303–311.

Friedrich, W. N., & Lueke, W.J. (1988). Young school-age sexually aggressive children. *Professional Psychology—Research & Practice, 19,* 155–164.

Friedrich, W. N., Sandfort, T. G., Oostveen, J., & Cohen-Kettenis, P. T. (2000). Cultural differences in sexual behavior: 2-6 year old Dutch and American Children. *Journal of Psychology & Human Sexuality, 12,* 117–129.

Gordon, B. N., & Schroeder, C. (1995). *Sexuality: A developmental approach to problems.* New York, NY: Plenum.

Gordon, B. N., Schroeder, C., & Abrams, M. (1990). Children's knowledge of sexuality: A comparison of sexually abused and nonabused children. *American Journal of Orthopsychiatry, 60*(2), 250–257.

Gray, A. (2010, March). Personal communication.

Gray, A., Pithers, W. D., Busconi, A., & Houchens, P. (1999). Developmental and etiological characteristics of children with sexual behavior problems: Treatment implications. *Child Abuse & Neglect, 23*(6), 601–621.

Hall, D. K., Mathews, F., & Pearce, J. (1998). Factors associated with sexual behavior problems in young sexually abused children. *Child Abuse & Neglect, 22,* 1045–1063.

Hewitt, S. K. (1999). *Assessing allegation of sexual abuse in preschool children: Understanding small voices. Interpersonal violence: The practice series.* Thousand Oaks, CA: Sage.

Horton, C. B. (1996). Children who molest other children: The school psychologist's response to the sexually aggressive child. *School Psychology Review, 25,* 540–557.

Johnson, T. C. (1988). Child perpetrators—children who molest other children: Preliminary findings. *Child Abuse & Neglect, 12,* 219–229.

Johnson, T. C. (2002). Some considerations about sexual abuse and children with sexual behavior problems. *Journal of Trauma and Dissociation, 3*(4), 83–105.

Kendall-Tackett, K., Williams, L. M., & Finkelhor, D. (1993). Impact of sexual abuse on children: A review and synthesis of recent empirical studies. *Psychological Bulletin, 113,* 164–180.

Kupper, L. (1995). Comprehensive sexuality education for children and youth with disabilities. *SIECUS Report, 23,* 3–8.

Langstrom, N., Grann, M., & Lichtenstein, P. (2002). Genetic and environmental influences on problematic masturbatory behavior in children: A study of same-sex twins. *Archives of Sexual Behavior, 31,* 343–350.

McGrath, R., Cumming, G., Burchard, B., Zeoli, S., & Ellerby, L. (2010). *Current practices and emerging trends in sexual abuser management: The Safer Society 2009 North American Survey.* Brandon, VT: Safer Society Press.

Merrick, M., Litrownik, A., Everson, M., & Cox, C. (2008). Beyond sexual abuse: The impact of other maltreatment experiences on sexualized behaviors. *Child Maltreatment, 13*, 122–132.

National Information Center for Children and Youth with Disabilities (NICHCY; 1992). Sexuality education for children and youth with disabilities *News Digest, 1*(3), 2–18. Washington, DC.

Nock, M. K., & Kazdin, A. E. (2005). Randomized controlled trial of a brief intervention for increasing participation in parent management training. *Journal of Consulting and Clinical Psychology, 73*(5), 872–879.

Piaget, J. (1932). *The moral judgment of the child* (M. Gabain, Trans.). New York, NY: Free Press, 1965.

Piaget, J. (1936). *The origins of intelligence in children* (M. Cook, Trans.). New York, NY: International Universities Press, 1974.

Pithers, W. D., Gray, A., Busconi, A., & Houchens, P. (1998). Children with sexual behavior problems: Identification of five distinct child types and related treatment considerations. *Child Maltreatment, 3*(4), 384–406.

St. Amand, A., Bard, D., & Silovsky, J. F. (2008). Meta-analysis of treatment for child sexual behavior problems: Practice elements and outcomes. *Child Maltreatment, 13*(2), 145–166.

Sanders, M. R., Cann, W., & Markie-Dadds, C. (2003). The Triple P-positive parenting programme: A universal population-level approach to the prevention of child abuse. *Child Abuse Review, 12*, 155–171.

Schroeder, C. S., & Gordon, B. N. (2002). *Assessment and treatment of childhood problems: A clinician's guide*. New York, NY: Guildford Press.

Siddiqi, S., Van Dyke, D. C., Donohoue, P., & McBrien, D. M. (1999). Premature sexual development in individuals with neurodevelopmental disabilities. *Developmental Medicine & Child Neurology, 41*, 392–395.

Silovsky, J.F. (2009). Taking Action: Support for Families of Children with Sexual Behavior Problems. Vermont: Safer Society Press.

Silovsky, J. F., & Bonner, B. L. (2003a). Sexual behavior problems. In T. H. Ollendick & C. S. Schroeder (Eds.), *Encyclopedia of clinical child and pediatric psychology* (pp. 589–591). New York, NY: Kluwer Press.

Silovsky, J. F., & Bonner, B. L. (2003b). *Children with sexual behavior problems: Common misconceptions vs. current findings*. NCSBY Fact Sheet. Office of Juvenile Justice and Delinquency Prevention.

Silovsky, J. F., & Niec, L. (2002). Characteristics of young children with sexual behavior problems: A pilot study. *Child Maltreatment, 7*, 187–197.

Silovsky, J. F., Niec, L., Bard, D., & Hecht, D. (2007). Treatment for preschool children with interpersonal sexual behavior problems: A pilot study. *Journal of Clinical Child & Adolescent Psychology, 36*, 378–391.

Silovsky, J. F. (2009). *Taking Action: Support for Families of Children with Sexual Behavior Problems*. Brandon, VT: Safer Society Press.

Stauffer, L. B., & Deblinger, E. (1996). Cognitive behavioral groups for nonoffending mothers and their young sexually abused children: A preliminary treatment outcome study. *Child Maltreatment, 1*, 65–76.

Swisher, L., Silovsky, J. F., Stewart, J., & Pierce, K. (2008). Children with Sexual Behavior Problems. *Juvenile and Family Court Journal, 59*, 49–69.

Thigpen, J. W., Pinkston, E. M., & Mayefsky, J. (2003). Normative sexual behavior of African American children: Preliminary finding. In J. Bancroft (Ed.), *Sexual development in childhood* (pp. 241–254). Bloomington: Indiana University Press.

Volbert, R. (2000). Sexual knowledge of preschool children. *Journal of Psychology & Human Sexuality, 12*, 5–26.

Webster-Stratton, C. (2005). The incredible years: A training series for the prevention and treatment of conduct problems in young children. In E. D. Hibbs & P. S. Jensen (Eds.), *Psychosocial treatments for child and adolescent disorders: Empirically based strategies for clinical practice* (2nd ed., pp. 507–555). Washington, DC: American Psychological Association.

Woodward, L. J. (2004). Sexuality and disability. *Clinics in Family Practice, 6*, 941–954.

Workgroup on Adapting Latino Services. (2008). *Adaptation guidelines for serving Latino children and families affected by trauma* (1st ed.). San Diego, CA: Chadwick Center for Children and Families.

CHAPTER 19

Intervention Application for Self-Injury Following Childhood Sexual Abuse

KEEGAN R. TANGEMAN and JANINE SHELBY

Debbie was drunk again. As she stumbled down the hallway in front of me on the way to my office, I saw it. As I closed my office door, I smelled it on her breath. As she tried to maintain her sobriety poker face, I heard it in her slurred speech. After attempting a few different greetings, she gave up and started swearing, tears rolling down her face. Before I could get a word out, she slumped out of her chair and onto the floor. She closed her eyes and lost consciousness. As I waited for the ambulance, I noticed the tender pink cuts on her forearms, which belied her efforts to appear invulnerable.

INTRODUCTION

THE MYRIAD OF symptoms among chronically trauma-exposed children and adolescents may lead to a complicated diagnostic picture. The diagnosis of posttraumatic stress disorder (PTSD), which is useful for identifying a constellation of symptoms for some trauma survivors, has been questioned in terms of its accuracy in describing the posttraumatic sequelae of young, chronically exposed sexual abuse survivors. Sexual abuse, combined with chronic exposure to domestic violence, community violence, as well as physical abuse and neglect lay the foundation for complex trauma symptoms that go beyond the nosology currently available for trauma-related diagnoses. So, although they may fit under the broad rubric of "trauma survivor," these youth may present with symptoms and symptom clusters that are quite different from those who survive single-incident forms of trauma.

Treatment interventions for young complex trauma survivors have been less researched than therapies for survivors with more typical trauma-related clinical presentations. This dearth of empirical support leaves clinicians lacking guidance as to how to treat the population that, ironically, may show the most severe impairments. In this chapter, we focus on several aspects of clinical care for young complex trauma survivors. We provide a brief review of several efforts to conceptualize severe and prolonged trauma exposure. Then, we discuss the biological and socioemotional impact of such experiences, as well as diagnostic issues, before turning to specific treatment recommendations and interventions. To illustrate these concepts, our discussion of complex trauma is interwoven with a case example.

TRAUMA EXPOSURE TYPE AND PREVALENCE

In the past decade, there has been increased recognition that children who suffer from a combination of early, multiple, and highly traumatic events may experience a similar amalgam of symptoms. These symptoms were referred to as Type II traumas and were delineated from Type I traumas by Lenore Terr (1991). In her conceptualization, Type II traumas involve multiple, ongoing, and chronic traumatic events wherein multiple varieties of trauma may be experienced or witnessed over an extended time period (i.e., ongoing abuse, domestic violence), whereas Type I traumas involve acute, single episode and unanticipated traumatic events (i.e., unexpected natural disasters, terrorist attacks, a single physical assault). Soon after this delineation, research began showing distinct trauma symptom sequelae for these two types of trauma exposure (Famularo, Fenton, Kinscherff, & Augustyn, 1996; Fletcher, 1996).

In addition to evidence for the presence of distinct symptom clusters, the phenomenon may be more prevalent than traditionally suspected. Type II trauma exposure, or *polyvictimization*, has more recently been found to be prevalent (i.e., approximately 1 in 7 to 1 in 10 children; Finkelhor, Ormrod, & Turner, 2007). Specific to childhood sexual assault, abuse by parent figures has been shown to constitute between 6% to 16% of all cases in general population surveys (Finkelhor, 1994; Saunders, Kilpatrick, Hanson, Resnick, & Walker, 1999). Furthermore, approximately a third of all such cases involve abuse by an extended family member (Berliner & Elliott, 2002). Furthermore, as many as 75% of children in clinical samples (Conte & Schuerman, 1987; Elliott & Briere,

1994; Ruggiero, McLeer, & Dixon, 2000) and half of the children in nonclinical samples (Saunders et al., 1999) were the victims of multiple sexual abuse episodes. The term *complex trauma* has emerged in the field, in an effort to describe the constellation of symptoms among those who experience chronic, Type II exposure, or polyvictimization. Complex trauma is said to result from exposure to severe stressors that (1) are repetitive or prolonged, (2) involve harm or abandonment by caregivers/ other responsible adults, and (3) occur at developmentally vulnerable times in the victim's life (Ford & Courtois, 2009).

> Debbie had been sexually abused by an uncle for several years during her middle childhood. Once or twice each week, he entered her bedroom at night, slipped into her bed, and fondled her. She implied that the fondling progressed to other forms of abuse, but she did not want to reveal what else she had endured. Debbie remembered feeling terrified, then numb. After the first two years, she summoned up the courage to tell her mother. Her mother was appalled . . . at Debbie's audacity. "How dare you bring this shame to our family!" Debbie remembers her mother screaming. Debbie knew better than to go to her father. Her father had an explosive temper and a penchant for drinking. At night, when he returned home from his construction job and had a few drinks, Debbie could hear her parents arguing in their bedroom. Sometimes the yelling would get really bad, but the worst part of the arguments was when they suddenly stopped. Then, Debbie knew something had put an end to the argument. So, nothing else was said about the abuse. Debbie's uncle continued to visit. Debbie continued to live as a silent prisoner of abuse in her own home.

DIAGNOSING COMPLEX TRAUMA

Due to the wide array of symptoms and behaviors evidenced by those children and adolescents exposed to complex trauma, diagnoses for these individuals have varied. In a study of 364 abused children, a diagnosis of PTSD was given with less frequency than diagnoses of separation anxiety disorder, oppositional defiant disorder, and specific phobias (Ackerman, Newton, McPherson, Jones, & Dykman, 1998). As these physically and sexually abused children enter adolescence, diagnoses tend to become more severe. Substance abuse disorders, in addition to borderline and antisocial personality disorders (van der Kolk, 2003), become diagnostic *catch-all* labels for adolescents who are having increasing difficulties with aggression and impulse control (Steiner, Garcia, & Matthews, 1997), dissociative and attentional problems (Teicher et al., 2003), and interpersonal relationships (Lyons-Ruth, Dutra, Schuder, & Bianchi, 2006). Thus, some have hypothesized that multiple, alternative diagnoses may be used because the diagnosis of PTSD inadequately captures the complex presentations of chronically, extensively traumatized youth (Cook et al., 2005). Compounding the typical complex trauma symptom amalgam is the fact that many children exposed to pervasive trauma present with developmental delays in cognitive, motor, language, and socialization skills (Culp, Heide, & Richardson, 1987). Some experts have noted that, in the current diagnostic formulation of these symptoms, some diagnoses identify this group of survivors, but only during a particular phase of development (Briere & Hodges, 2008). For example, the vaguely defined "Reactive Attachment Disorder" diagnosis, which is typically diagnosed in young children, may describe the same children who will later be diagnosed with borderline personality disorder.

Efforts to generate a diagnosis for complex trauma have included several new diagnostic formulations, including complex posttraumatic stress disorder (Herman, 1992) or Disorders of Extreme Stress Not Otherwise Specified (DESNOS; van der Kolk, Roth, Pelcovitz, Sunday, & Spinazzola, 2005), and developmental trauma disorder (van der Kolk, 2005). Despite the disparate attempts to label the core phenomenon, commonalities emerge from these diagnostic formulations, including the following symptoms: (a) affect dysregulation; (b) disruptions in relationships or attachment; and (c) disruptions in identity; as well as possible (d) dissociation; (e) dangerousness to self (e.g., self-injurious behavior, suicide attempts); and (f) repetition of harm in interpersonal relationships (e.g., forming relationships with others who engage in violent acts toward them).

Debbie was referred to our clinic after her third suicide attempt. She had overdosed on Tylenol—a serious enough attempt to warrant a 5-day stay in an inpatient unit. During the intake, Debbie revealed that she had been cutting herself for several years. At the age of 17, Debbie had an extensive collection of scars on her arms and legs and continued cutting when she became overwhelmed, which was frequently. Debbie described difficulties in relationships and forming a solid sexual identity. She reported vague but persistent depressive and somatic symptoms and when we came to the trauma
(continued)

history section of the intake, Debbie chuckled. "You name it," she said, "I've had them all." Family substance abuse, domestic violence, physical and sexual abuse were all endorsed. She did not meet criteria for any specific *DSM-IV-TR* diagnosis. In place of a single diagnosis that might have described Debbie's symptom clusters, she was diagnosed with Anxiety Disorder Not Otherwise Specified, Mood Disorder Not Otherwise Specified, and Borderline Personality Disorder traits.

THE IMPACT OF COMPLEX TRAUMA ON DEVELOPMENT

There has been increasing focus on the impact of trauma that occurs during critical developmental periods, in which both psychobiological and socioemotional development may be compromised (Ford & Courtois, 2009). Below, both the biological and the socioemotional literature will be briefly reviewed.

PSYCHOBIOLOGICAL IMPACT

When trauma exposure occurs during key developmental periods (e.g., toddlerhood, preadolescence, early adolescence), a shift occurs from what Ford and Courtois term the *learning brain* to the *survival brain* (2009). While both the learning brain and the survival brain are the same brain with the same capacity, their orientations are entirely different. The learning brain is geared toward exploration and is guided by a balance between novelty and familiarity, while the survival brain is constantly scanning environments and seeking out potential threats so that it can mobilize the body's fight or flight response (Ford & Courtois, 2009). As a result of constant hypervigilance, combined with the effects of betrayal trauma, the child's developing brain uses valuable resources to survive, wasting opportunities for crucial developmental milestones in cognitive, emotional, and social functioning abilities.

There are two significant areas in which the complex trauma-exposed survival brain is affected: dysregulated emotion and information processing (Ford & Courtois, 2009). This emotional dysregulation and compromised information processing traps the child in a survival-brain mode—one that is unable to break the continual cycle of perceived threat and hopelessness, and resulting extreme states of emotional emptiness or distress. As traumatic exposure occurs in childhood and survival brain dominates, impairments in functioning become apparent. For example, in toddlerhood, stress reactivity, attentional difficulties, as well as irritability and oppositionality may be present (Manly, Kim, Rogosch, & Cicchetti, 2001). In preadolescence, children are likely to demonstrate depression, anxiety, or social withdrawal while also evidencing externalizing behaviors diagnostic of oppositional defiant disorder or conduct disorder (Cook et al., 2005). As the traumatized child grows older, impairments in functioning grow more severe. Adolescents attempting to manage a "posttraumatic survival brain" are likely to evidence serious problems in several domains, with resulting incarceration, pregnancy, self-harm, or suicidality common (Ford, Hartman, Hawke, & Chapman, 2008).

Biological impairments, caused by the stunting impact of developmentally adverse trauma exposure impair children's organization and processing of incoming stimuli (Teicher, Andersen, Polcari, Anderson, & Navalta, 2002). The subsequent emotional dysregulation denies the adolescent the ability to self-soothe or modulate emotions; this inability forces the child to cope by use of either dissociation or behavioral acting out. This lack of behavioral regulation has serious implications for the safety of the adolescent and those around him or her. Aggression, sexualized behaviors, and self-injurious behavior have been hypothesized to serve as compulsive avoidance to trauma reminders, attempts to gain control, attempts to escape overwhelming emotion, or attempts to achieve acceptance (Cook et al., 2005). Some of these behaviors have been explained in the literature as a form of *revictimization*; those children who were severely maltreated have an elevated risk of being assaulted later in life (Classen, Palesh, & Aggarwal, 2005). These dangerous behaviors, attempted as a poor form of coping, ironically serve as risk factors for further victimization.

SOCIOEMOTIONAL IMPACT

Complex trauma exposure is likely to occur as a result of victimization by someone known to, and possibly trusted by, the victim. Thus, the ability to generate basic interpersonal trust is often violated among these survivors. As a result, socioemotional development is impacted (Ford & Courtois, 2009). Also known as second injury (Symonds, 1975), betrayal trauma (DePrince & Freyd, 2007) occurs when there is a lack of response or protection from caregivers to the child. This can also take the form of victim-blaming, which exacerbates the child's symptoms. The child is left to manage the difficult sequelae of trauma exposure alone, often being obligated to interact with the perpetrator on a daily basis.

Those children and adolescents exposed to complex trauma, especially in combination with betrayal trauma, have been shown to evidence injuries to their attachment relationships. In these unfortunate instances, approximately 80% of sexually abused children develop insecure attachment patterns (Friedrich, 2002). When attachment is severely disrupted by childhood sexual abuse, risk of psychosocial impairment occurs along three pathways: increased susceptibility to stress, inability to regulate emotions independently, and impaired ability to seek help (Cook et al., 2005). These children demonstrate a disorganized/dissociative attachment style (Lyons-Ruth et al., 2006), a style that is problematic, as it is hypothesized that dissociation prevents the integration of the trauma and may leave the child to maintain an apparent functioning personality, but one that is largely incapacitated psychosocially (Steele & van der Hart, 2009). These findings are especially concerning, given that children are much more likely to use dissociation to cope when exposed to such overwhelming traumatic experiences (Putnam, 2003).

> By the time Debbie started high school, her uncle had stopped abusing her. Although the molestation no longer occurred, she continued to suffer from the aftermath of those experiences. Debbie tried using alcohol in middle school and liked it. She drank heavily at parties and at friends' homes. She developed a pattern of self-destructive behaviors in which she drank, cut her arms or legs, and then lost consciousness. Her friends teased her initially, but eventually stopped inviting her over—Debbie was too much of a liability. Debbie had few effective methods of alleviating her distress following her frequent flashbacks, which were usually triggered by her family's ongoing conflict and arguments. She got drunk because it was a great distraction. When she was intoxicated, her reduced inhibition escalated her difficulty coping with her distress. Cutting was her method of managing this distress. When the drinking and cutting no longer seemed effective to alleviate her suffering, she tried to kill herself.

TREATMENT

Adolescents with complex trauma histories presenting to treatment are typically brought in because of concerns related to their dangerous or risk-taking behaviors. Interestingly, it is the externalizing behaviors (e.g., aggression or self-injury) as opposed to internalizing behaviors (e.g., anxiety or depression) that tend to capture the attention of adults. When a comprehensive intake is completed and it is determined that these behaviors are related to complex trauma history, the clinician's first dilemma occurs. How does a therapist focus on such emotionally charged topics as childhood sexual abuse without causing a level of distress that might push the adolescent to engage in self-injurious behavior? With deficits in attachment, biology, affect regulation, dissociation, behavioral control, cognition, and self-concept, where does one begin?

Although there have been no updated practice parameters since 1998 for adolescents exposed to trauma, several treatments have emerged to address the specific amalgam/cluster/constellation of symptoms common among complex trauma survivors (DBT, Linehan, 1993; ITCT-A, Briere & Lanktree, 2008; SPARCS, DeRosa & Pelcovitz, 2009; STAIR-PE, Cloitre, Koenen, Cohen, & Han, 2002; TARGET, Ford & Russo, 2006; TST, Saxe, Ellis, & Kaplow, 2007). These treatments bear close resemblance to each other in terms of their collective focus on safety, stabilization, and affect regulation. Furthermore, the treatments share similar phasing in that they initially emphasize safety and stabilization, seek to enhance coping skills early during the treatment, and focus on developing affect regulation skills before engaging in trauma narratives. In fact, some of the treatments do not include posttraumatic retellings at all. Given the influence of DBT in the treatment literature, some of the interventions described borrow heavily from DBT concepts and treatment interventions. However, the purpose of the case vignette is to describe selected interventions that map onto the more general components of complex PTSD treatments rather than to advocate for the use of any particular treatment protocol.

DIALECTICAL BEHAVIOR THERAPY

At its core, DBT is guided by behavior theory, the biosocial theory of borderline personality disorder (BPD) and the theory of dialectics (Wagner, Rizvi, & Harned, 2007). The heavy emphasis on behavior theory conceptualizes self-harm as behaviors driven by a combination of skills, cued responding, reinforcement, or cognitive factors and utilizes behavioral interventions in treatment (Wagner et al., 2007). These behavioral interventions are presented to patients in separate skills modules, and are taught in a group format (Linehan, 1993). While a thorough description of DBT's biosocial theory is beyond the scope of this chapter, it is important to note that the biosocial theory asserts that BPD and the self-harm often associated with the diagnosis develops from a combination of biologically based predisposition to emotion dysregulation and a severely invalidating environment (Linehan, 1993). Lastly, the theory of dialectics posits that reality is comprised of opposing forces, always changing, and that seemingly opposing views can exist simultaneously (Wagner et al., 2007).

Due to the commonality of emotion regulation deficits found within differing presentations of psychopathology, DBT has also been found to be helpful in treating trauma (Wagner et al., 2007), eating disorders (Wisniewski, Safer, & Chen, 2007), and oppositional defiant disorder (Nelson-Gray et al., 2006).

SPECIAL CONSIDERATIONS FOR CLINICAL PRACTICE

Clinicians should observe caution when conducting a trauma-focused intervention that involves the youth engaging in a narrative of traumatic events. Adolescents with complex trauma histories who engage in self-injurious behaviors may not have the coping resources to integrate their traumatic experiences. This is an important point to underscore—those adolescents using self-injury as a means to cope with extreme emotion rely on a negative reinforcement paradigm. More specifically, when there is a perceived threat that results in cognitive and/or emotion dysregulation, the self-injury serves the purpose of eliminating that dysregulation. As such, before engaging in trauma narratives, clinicians must first help the patient and patient's family establish perceptions of personal and environmental safety, and develop regulatory skills. Accordingly, emphasis is placed on safety and self-regulation as the first and primary components of treatment for these adolescents. Without these core components of treatment, it is likely that any discussion of trauma-related content may trigger perceived threat in the adolescent, thus placing them at an increased risk for self-harm.

SAFETY

Safety can be conceptualized as falling into two categories: physical and psychological, with an emphasis on all parties appropriately involved in the adolescent's treatment.

Physical Safety The first focus should examine the degree to which the adolescent's physical environment is safe. A thorough understanding of the adolescent's environment would include inquiry into several areas: Is the home free of dangers (e.g., broken appliances, broken windows, broken doors)? Is the home secure (i.e., doors and windows lock, there is a system to ensure that unwanted people can be kept out)? Does the adolescent have personal space (e.g., a place to sleep, a place to keep their own belongings)?

In addition to the adolescent's physical environment, the adolescent's physical safety itself is of utmost importance. Tremendous emphasis should be placed on ensuring that means for self-injury are not readily available to the adolescent. Recent studies examining adolescent suicidality have found removal of lethal means to be a significant determining factor in ensuring the adolescent's safety (Asarnow, Berk, & Baraff, 2009).

The therapist should work with the adolescent and his or her caregiver to collect all lethal means and keep these locked, only to be used by the adolescent with sufficient monitoring.

Psychological Safety   The adolescent's perceived psychological safety is an important factor in trauma treatment. A foundation of safety needs to be established in both therapeutic and family relationships. Due to the disrupted attachment styles found in children and adolescents with complex trauma exposure, great care should be taken to ensure that the therapist provides an appropriate perception of safety in the therapeutic relationship. While the therapist takes an active role in developing a positive, safe relationship and therapeutic environment, the adolescent is primed to locate any perception of danger or threat in the environment. If the adolescent becomes emotionally triggered in this context, the adolescent's mistrust is reinforced.

Family involvement is necessary within the safety component of treatment. Not only is parent dysfunction typically a key factor in child and adolescent psychiatric problems and often necessary to address for child/adolescent improvement, parental involvement and emotional functioning has been found to influence children's trauma symptoms and their ability to resolve them (Cohen, Mannarino, Berliner, & Deblinger, 2000). In the emphasis of perceived safety within the family or caregiver relationships, the therapist must attend to the family's response to the adolescent. Primary elements of parent involvement or response in the context of safety include the caregiver's belief and validation of the adolescent's experience, tolerating the adolescent's affect, and managing the caregiver's own emotional response (Cook et al., 2005). It is strongly encouraged to attend to these parent factors before proceeding with treatment. Without assurance that these elements of caregiver response are appropriately attended to, it is likely that the adolescent will not establish a perceived sense of safety, and it is likely that the youth will not progress in treatment. The therapist should employ a variety of treatment modalities (e.g., collateral parent sessions, psychoeducation, identification of safety requirements in vignettes, role-play) to assure that the caregiver can provide assurance of safety to the adolescent.

Safety Planning   After caregiver involvement is elicited, the therapist should work closely with both the adolescent and the caregiver to develop a safety plan for the adolescent's dangerous behaviors. In the creation of a comprehensive safety plan, the therapist will conduct a specific and detailed analysis of triggers for the adolescent's self-injurious behaviors, the self-injurious behaviors themselves, and appropriate responses. Those antecedents to self-injury identified will be addressed in both individual and family therapy (e.g., removal of lethal means, minimizing conflict, and teaching problem-solving skills) (Miller, Rathus, & Linehan, 2007). The safety plan itself should include a means for the adolescent to self-monitor his or her emotions (e.g., an emotional thermometer, emotions scaling and rating systems), with clearly demarcated steps for eliciting assistance *prior to the self-injury*; these steps should progress from least intrusive (e.g., employ coping skills) to most intrusive (e.g., call 911), with the adolescent being instructed to move to the next step, should the situation not be resolved with previous steps (Berk, Henriques, Warman, Brown, & Beck, 2004). The safety plan is to be reviewed with all appropriately participating family members, and should be monitored and regularly evaluated in therapy.

It should be noted that safety planning for adolescent self-injurious behaviors includes a wide variety of behaviors. Because those adolescents with complex trauma histories are often dysregulated and more likely to be re-victimized, special attention should be paid to all relevant forms of self-injurious behavior. These include, but are not limited to, substance abuse, risky sexual behaviors including prostitution, high-risk sensation-seeking behaviors, and gang involvement, in addition to self-injury through cutting, burning, or banging. In the case of ongoing abuse or violence, the therapist is encouraged to help the adolescent develop an additional safety plan that includes a detailed strategy for escaping the dangerous environment and finding an appropriate safe place to stay.

Self-Regulation

Adolescents with complex trauma histories often have poor regulatory abilities across several domains, including affect, behavior, physiology,

It took a long time for Debbie's mother to allow herself to recognize Debbie's suffering and believe her disclosure of abuse. For many years it had been easier to ignore these truths, and remain frustrated with Debbie's dangerous behaviors. Three suicide attempts later, Debbie's mother was finally ready to listen. Their improved communication began with a frank discussion of safety in Debbie's home. As a victim of domestic violence, Debbie's mother was finally forced to acknowledge the impact her husband's grip of violence had on the family. When she did acknowledge her own victimization, the walls of denial came down. She listened to Debbie, and then helped arrange a secret "code" that both Debbie and her therapist could use to communicate concerns about life-threatening behaviors. This information was always kept secret from Debbie's father—if he learned of Debbie's self-injury or other risky behaviors, he would severely punish her. Debbie was uncertain at first. After a few weeks of her mother's support in maintaining a physically and psychologically safe environment for her, she began talking a little more.

cognition, interpersonal relatedness, and self-attribution (Cook et al., 2005). Once the foundation of safety—within the adolescent's physical environment, family and/or caregiver relationships, and therapeutic relationships—has been established, skill building in the area of self-regulation is implemented. Recent models have targeted affect regulation and interpersonal disturbances in adolescents with trauma histories (STAIR-PE; Cloitre et al., 2002) and have emphasized emotion regulation in the context of treatments for suicide and self-injury (DBT; Linehan, 1993). In DBT, individuals are taught modules of skills for coping with and regulating emotional dysregulation; these skills modules represent a collection of techniques borrowed from behavioral therapy, cognitive-behavioral therapies, and eastern Buddhist philosophy (Linehan, 1993). For adolescents exposed to complex trauma, self-regulation treatment should first address emotion distraction techniques as a means of learning to cope with adverse emotions that precipitate dysregulation and self-injury (Linehan, 1993). Trying to teach emotional self-regulation to an adolescent without the means to even effectively distract from the emotional pain is a bit like putting the cart before the horse.

Distraction   Of interest to clinicians addressing the self-regulation component of complex trauma treatment is Linehan's "distress tolerance" skill module. Adolescents should be taught temporary coping skills to use in order to distract themselves from emotional distress; such skills include the ability to engage in alternative, pleasurable activities previously identified by the adolescent (Linehan, 1993). The therapist should work with the adolescent to identify safe, positive activities that the adolescent can participate in when feeling emotionally dysregulated. Over time, by encouraging the adolescent to participate in these specific activities during both times of distress as well as when euthymic, potential risk for a triggered emotional reaction is diminished.

Self-Soothing   Relaxation-based techniques including diaphragmatic breathing and progressive muscle relaxation are commonly found in the literature as a means of reducing both psychological and physiological symptoms of anxiety. Another key self-regulation intervention is encouraging the adolescent to engage in sensory-based activities designed to soothe emotional distress (Linehan, 1993). The therapist and the adolescent are encouraged to create a self-soothing kit—one that contains items that appeal to the adolescent's five senses (Linehan, 1993; see also Berk et al., 2004, for a description of a "hope box" that can be used with suicidal individuals). It is expected that when the adolescents become dysregulated, they can go to their kits and employ sensory-based distraction techniques to alleviate their emotional distress.

Grounding   Chronic trauma exposure may lead children and adolescents to rely on dissociation as a means of coping with overwhelming psychological and emotional distress. This cognitive dysregulation inhibits integration of traumatic experiences by preventing emotional awareness and can put adolescents at further risk of victimization. Due to the likelihood of increased emotional distress within the therapeutic session, the therapist should be aware of antecedents to dissociation and work with the adolescent to prevent it. Implementation of subjective units of distress (SUDs) will facilitate the patient's communication of overwhelming stress in the session.

Techniques such as grounding, in which the therapist directs the child to orient him/herself to the room through a variety of sensory reminders, are helpful to keep the adolescent present. It is important to note that when implementing grounding techniques, the therapist should reassure the adolescent of safety. Points to emphasize include the adolescent's current presence in a safe environment, the differentiation between past memories and current situations, and the adolescent's control.

Debbie was skeptical when I told her that she should sketch more, a hobby she had let slip out of her leisure repertoire. When she questioned the importance of sketching when she was distressed, I asked her if it was so engaging to her that she often forgot what was going on around her. As she nodded, she understood. Debbie's mother agreed to purchase Debbie headphones and an MP3 player so that Debbie could listen to soothing music when she became dysregulated. She spent time in my office creating a playlist that she would later add to her player—a playlist she uses specifically for the purpose of muting her escalating emotions.

Debbie was always good at identifying things she could have done instead of drinking. She had never really thought about what else she could do that would also make her feel better. Debbie admits that she still drinks but fortunately, she reports, it occurs less and less frequently. She enjoys being able to "let herself" participate in other distraction activities. Her mother is less worried. Both admit that this is only the beginning of Debbie's treatment but that, with the enhanced sense of safety she and her family have created, she can now begin her long road toward recovery, integration, and positive growth.

CONCLUSION

Children and adolescents exposed to complex trauma present with a myriad of symptoms. This symptom presentation is further complicated by the interpersonal nature of trauma exposure that includes physical or sexual abuse by a friend, family member, or loved one. The impact of complex trauma exposure has numerous implications for cognitive, socioemotional, and emotion regulation development. Confrontation with trauma reminders or distressing emotions is difficult for many trauma survivors; however, when complex trauma exposed adolescents face these situations they may have particularly inadequate coping repertoires and emotion-regulation skills to manage their distress. Consequently, self-injury serves as an effective, albeit dangerous, form of negative reinforcement to alleviate their distress in the short term. Treating these adolescents requires a skills-based approach in which techniques for emotion distraction and self-regulation are taught in the context of a safe, therapeutic relationship. Without these important skills, these adolescents remain vulnerable to continued self-injury or suicidal ideation. Rushing to "resolve" the trauma without addressing requisite emotion regulation skills may actually push these adolescents to the self-destructive behavior the clinician is trying to eliminate. Conversely, by instilling safe environments and conceptualizing self-harm as ineffective means of coping with an unbearable trauma history, clinicians have a tremendous opportunity to impart life-long emotion regulation and coping skills to a psychologically impoverished subset of adolescents in great need of these resources.

REFERENCES

Ackerman, P. T., Newton, J. E., McPherson, W. B., Jones, J. G., & Dykman, R. A. (1998). Prevalence of posttraumatic stress disorder and other psychiatric diagnoses in three groups of abused children. *Child Abuse & Neglect, 22*(8), 759–774.

Asarnow, J., Berk, M., & Baraff, L. (2009). Family intervention for suicide prevention: A specialized emergency department intervention for suicidal youths. *Professional Psychology: Research and Practice, 40*(2), 118–125. DOI: 10.1037/a0012599

Berk, M., Henriques, G., Warman, D., Brown, G., & Beck, A. (2004). A cognitive therapy intervention for suicide attempters: An overview of the treatment and case examples. *Cognitive and Behavioral Practice, 11*(3), 265–277. DOI: 10.1016/S1077-7229(04)80041-5

Berliner, L., & Elliott, D. (2002). Sexual abuse of children. In J. Myers, L. Berliner, J. Briere, C. Hendrix, C. Jenny, & T. Reid (Eds.), *The APSAC handbook on child maltreatment* (2nd ed., pp. 55–78). Thousand Oaks, CA: Sage.

Briere, J., & Hodges, M. (2008, November). Do we need a child complex trauma diagnosis, or a way to diagnose ongoing attachment symptoms beyond age 5? In K. Nader & K. Gletcher (Chair), *Complex trauma in children and adolescents: Conceptualization and assessment.* Symposium conducted at the meeting of the International Society for Traumatic Stress Studies, Chicago, IL.

Briere, J., & Lanktree, C. (2008). Integrative treatment of complex trauma for adolescents (ITCT-A): A guide for the treatment of multiply-traumatized youth. Retrieved from www.johnbriere.com/articles.htm

Classen, C., Palesh, O., & Aggarwal, R. (2005). Sexual revictimization: A review of the empirical literature. *Trauma, Violence, & Abuse, 6*(2), 103–129. DOI: 10.1177/1524838005275087

Cloitre, M., Koenen, K., Cohen, L., & Han, H. (2002). Skills training in affective and interpersonal regulation followed by exposure: A phase-based treatment for PTSD related to childhood abuse. *Journal of Consulting and Clinical Psychology, 70*(5), 1067–1074. DOI: 10.1037/0022-006X.70.5.1067

Cohen, J., Mannarino, A., Berliner, L., & Deblinger, E. (2000). Trauma-focused cognitive behavioral therapy for children and adolescents: An empirical update. *Journal of Interpersonal Violence, 15*(11), 1202–1223. DOI: 10.1177/088626000015011007

Conte, J., & Schuerman, J. (1987). Factors associated with an increased impact of child sexual abuse. *Child Abuse & Neglect, 11*(2), 201–211. DOI: 10.1016/0145-2134(87)90059-7

Cook, A., Spinazzola, J., Ford, J., Lanktree, C., Blaustein, M., Cloitre, M., . . . van der Kolk, B. (2005). Complex trauma in children and adolescents. *Psychiatric Annals, 35*, 390–398.

Culp, R.E., Heide, J., & Richardson, M. T. (1987). Maltreated children's developmental scores: Treatment versus nontreatment. *Child Abuse & Neglect, 11*(1), 29–34.

DePrince, A. P., & Freyd, J. J. (2007). Trauma-induced dissociation. In M. J. Friendman, T. M. Keane, & P. A. Resick (Eds.), *Handbook of PTSD: Science and practice* (pp. 135–150). New York, NY: Guilford Press.

DeRosa, R., & Pelcovitz, D. (2009). Group treatment for chronically traumatized adolescents: Igniting SPARCS of change. *Treating traumatized children: Risk, resilience and recovery* (pp. 225–239). New York, NY: Routledge/Taylor & Francis.

Elliott, D., & Briere, J. (1994). Forensic sexual abuse evaluations of older children: Disclosures and symptomatology. *Behavioral Sciences & the Law, 12*(3), 261–277. DOI: 10.1002/bsl.2370120306

Famularo, R., Fenton, T., Kinscherff, R., & Augustyn, M. (1996). Psychiatric comorbidity in childhood posttraumatic stress disorder. *Child Abuse & Neglect, 20*(10), 953–961. DOI: 10.1016/0145-2134(96)00084-1

Finkelhor, D. (1994). Current information on the scope and nature of child sexual abuse. *Future of Children, 4*(2), 31–53. DOI: 10.2307/1602522

Finkelhor, D., Ormrod, R., & Turner, H. (2007). Poly-victimization: A neglected component in child victimization. *Child Abuse & Neglect, 31*, 7–26.

Fletcher, K. (1996). Childhood posttraumatic stress disorder. In E. Mash & R. Barkley (Eds.), *Child psychopathology* (pp. 242–276). New York, NY: Guilford Press.

Ford, J., & Courtois, C. (2009). Defining and understanding complex trauma and complex traumatic stress disorders. In J. Ford & C. Courtois (Eds.), *Treating complex trauma disorders* (pp. 13–30). New York, NY: Guilford Press.

Ford, J., & Russo, E. (2006). Trauma-focused, present-centered emotional self-regulation approach to integrated treatment for posttraumatic stress and addiction: Trauma adaptive recovery group education and therapy (TARGET). *American Journal of Psychotherapy, 60*(4), 335–355.

Ford, J. D., Hartman, J. K., Hawke, J., & Chapman, J. (2008). Traumatic victimization, posttraumatic stress disorder, suicidal ideation, and substance abuse risk among juvenile justice-involved youths. *Journal of Child & Adolescent Trauma, 1*, 75–92.

Friedrich, W. (2002). An integrated model of psychotherapy for abused children. In J. Myers, L. Berliner, J. Briere, C. Hendrix, C. Jenny, & T. Reid (Eds.), *The APSAC handbook on child maltreatment* (2nd ed., pp. 55–78). Thousand Oaks, CA: Sage.

Herman, J. (1992). Complex PTSD: A syndrome in survivors of prolonged and repeated trauma. *Journal of Traumatic Stress, 5*(3), 377–391. DOI: 10.1002/jts.2490050305

Linehan, M. (1993). *Cognitive-behavioral treatment of borderline personality disorder.* New York, NY: Guilford Press.

Lyons-Ruth, K., Dutra, L., Schuder, M., & Bianchi, I. (2006). From infant attachment disorganization to adult dissociation: Relational adaptations or traumatic experiences? *Psychiatric Clinics of North America, 29,* 63–86.

Manly, J., Kim, J., Rogosch, F., & Cicchetti, D. (2001). Dimensions of child maltreatment and children's adjustment: Contributions of developmental timing and subtype. *Development and Psychopathology, 13*(4), 759–782.

Miller, A., Rathus, J., & Linehan, M. (2007). *Dialectical behavior therapy with suicidal adolescents.* New York, NY: Guilford Press.

Nelson-Gray, R., Keane, S., Hurst, R., Mitchell, J., Warburton, J., Chok, J., & Cobb, A. (2006). A modified DBT skills training program for oppositional defiant adolescents: Promising preliminary findings. *Behaviour Research and Therapy, 44*(12), 1811–1820. DOI: 10.1016/j.brat.2006.01.004

Putnam, F. (2003). Ten year research update review: Child sexual abuse. *Journal of the American Academy of Child & Adolescent Psychiatry, 42,* 269–278.

Ruggiero, K., McLeer, S., & Dixon, J. (2000). Sexual abuse characteristics associated with survivor psychopathology. *Child Abuse & Neglect, 24*(7), 951–964. DOI: 10.1016/S0145-2134(00)00144-7

Saunders, B., Kilpatrick, D., Hanson, R., Resnick, H., & Walker, M. (1999). Prevalence, case characteristics, and long-term psychological correlates of child rape among women: A national survey. *Child Maltreatment, 4*(3), 187–200. DOI: 10.1177/1077559599004003001

Saxe, G., Ellis, B., & Kaplow, J. (2007). *Collaborative treatment of traumatized children and teens: The trauma systems therapy approach.* New York, NY: Guilford Press.

Steele, K., & van der Hart, O. (2009). Treating dissociation. In J. Ford & C. Courtois (Eds.), *Treating complex trauma disorders* (pp. 145–165). New York, NY: Guilford Press.

Steiner, H., Garcia, I. G., & Matthews, Z. (1997) Posttraumatic stress disorder in incarcerated juvenile delinquents. *Journal of American Academy of Child & Adolescent Psychiatry, 36*(2), 357–365.

Symonds, M. (1975). Victims of violence: Psychological effects and after-effects. *American Journal of Psychoanalysis, 35,* 19–26.

Teicher, M., Andersen, S., Polcari, A., Anderson, C., & Navalta, C. (2002). Developmental neurobiology of childhood stress and trauma. *Psychiatric Clinics of North America, 25*(2), 397–426. DOI: 10.1016/S0193-953X(01)00003-X

Teicher, M., Andersen, S., Polcari, A., Anderson, C., Navalta, C., & Kim, D. (2003). The neurobiological consequences of early stress and childhood maltreatment. *Neuroscience & Biobehavioral Reviews, 27*(1-2), 33–44.

Terr, L. (1991). Childhood traumas. *American Journal of Psychiatry, 148,* 10–20.

van der Kolk, B. (2003). The neurobiology of childhood trauma and abuse. *Child and Adolescent Psychiatric Clinics of North America, 12*(2), 293–317. DOI: 10.1016/S1056-4993(03)00003-8 van der Kolk, B. A. (2005). Developmental trauma disorder. *Psychiatric Annals, 35,* 401–408.

van der Kolk, B. A., Roth, S., Pelcovitz, D., Sunday, S., & Spinazzola, J. (2005). Disorders of extreme stress: The empirical foundation of a complex adaptation to trauma. *Journal of Traumatic Stress, 18,* 389–399.

Wagner, A., Rizvi, S., & Harned, M. (2007). Applications of dialectical behavior therapy to the treatment of complex trauma-related problems: When one case formulation does not fit all. *Journal of Traumatic Stress, 20*(4), 391–400. DOI: 10.1002/jts.20268

Wisniewski, L., Safer, D., & Chen, E. (2007). Dialectical behavior therapy and eating disorders. In L. Dimeff & K. Koerner (Eds.), *Dialectical behavior therapy in clinical practice: Applications across disorders and settings* (pp. 174–221). New York, NY: Guilford Press.

CHAPTER 20

Treatment Considerations With Sexually Traumatized Adolescents

SHARON A. McGEE and C. CURTIS HOLMES

I'd rather eat glass than sit here and talk to you.

THIS EMOTIONAL STATEMENT was boldly expressed at the beginning of a session by a 15-year-old girl who had been sexually abused by a sibling. She had no intentions of ever disclosing the abuse and her disclosure was accidental as are those of many children who have been sexually abused (Bradley & Wood, 1996; Nagel, Putnam, Noll, & Trickett, 1997; Paine & Hansen, 2002; Sgroi, 1988). Consequently, finding herself in a therapist's office where she expected she would have to discuss everything in graphic detail was light years beyond what she was prepared for.

Similarly, an 18-year-old male victim with an air of defiance proclaimed in his initial session that he did not believe his therapist was intelligent enough to help him. When sessions begin this way it can be challenging to know how to proceed. It helps to conceptualize these teens' articulations as attempts to verbally protect themselves, creating what they hope will be an impenetrable barrier, a very common practice for teens (Gries, Goh, & Cavanaugh, 1996; Ullman, 2003).

One such client was Anna,[1] a 15-year-old who was sexually abused over an extended period of time by her mother's boyfriend. Anna painstakingly made the decision to disclose her abuse and the results

---

1. Clients mentioned are a compilation of clients whose names and details have been slightly altered to protect confidentiality.

were disastrous. Almost everyone—including her mother—doubted her. The reaction of the significant adults in her world made Anna consider recanting (Gil, 1996; Hindman, 1989; Malloy, Lyon, & Quas, 2007; Summitt, 1983). Eventually her mother accepted the truth and did believe and support her daughter, seeking help from numerous therapists to no avail. Through each encounter with various therapists Anna refused to speak at all. She would not even state her name. Each therapist tried to help but when Anna would not speak, most labeled her *resistant* and discontinued treatment. When she entered treatment with a new therapist, knowing about her previous experiences before her first session was a key piece of the treatment puzzle.

For six sessions Anna sat with her arms folded, glaring across the room, still refusing to speak. Part of the silence was trauma-related and part was a defense, an effort to make each therapist discontinue treatment so she would not have to deal with her abuse (Mather & Debye, 1994). She was met emotionally where she was and allowed to stay secure in her silence, but her sessions were used to educate and inform (Cohen, Deblinger, & Mannarino, 2004; Donker, Griffiths, Cuijpers, & Christensen, 2009). Though Anna did not speak, the therapist did, talking about trauma, abuse, coping skills, fear, and anything relevant to the recovery process. Toward the end of the sixth session her silence was broken.

"What do I have to do to get you to just shut up?" Anna asked.

"If you will talk, then I won't," I replied, and in that moment we began the conversation of recovery.

BEFORE WE BEGIN

As we explore the effective treatment of sexually abused adolescents, a question emerges. Should male or female therapists treat male or female victims? It is our belief that the therapist's gender is not the most significant issue in successful treatment. What is significant is whether the therapist has experience and specialized training in the areas of trauma therapy, particularly sexual abuse trauma, experience in working with the adolescent population, and the willingness to meet teens where they are emotionally (Bruckner & Johnson, 1987; Hall & Lloyd, 1993; Mather & Debye, 1994). Making assumptions based primarily on therapist gender can inhibit the opportunity for the therapeutic relationship to be healing, not only in relation to the trauma, but for any gender bias that might have developed as a result of the abuse. In our experience therapist gender preferences are less significant with teens than with adults. However, during the intake process, usually at the time of the initial phone call to set up an appointment, it is important to assess whether the therapist's gender is a relevant factor based on the client's preferences. If a preference is stated, efforts should be made to meet the teen's request.

WHAT DO WE MEAN BY ADOLESCENT?

Generally, adolescence is defined as a transitional period when a young person separates from his or her parents, yet still lacks the maturity and independence of adulthood (Arnett, 2010; Baxter, 2008; Mish, 2008). Rapid physiological changes occur, sexual feelings develop, personal identity is being formed, and thinking becomes more abstract and less concrete. They have not yet mastered the ability to think flexibly but still typically think in black-and-white terms (Feinstein, 2009; Kessler, 2010). The emotional system remains immature. Feelings can change quickly and be extreme, often resulting in an overreaction to seemingly small situations. Because of this, their behavior can sometimes be unpredictable or erratic (Feinstein, 2009; Kessler, 2010). One can see how all of these concepts are relevant in the treatment process.

IF YOU BUILD IT, THEY WILL TALK

Merriam-Webster's Collegiate Dictionary defines rapport as "relation, especially a relation marked by harmony, conformity, accord, or affinity" (Mish, 2008, p. 1031). Rapport is the art of establishing a relationship. This definition describes what must be achieved before an adolescent will truly allow an adult into his or her world. Teenagers bring with them a vast amount of baggage including betrayal, doubt, fear, helplessness and shame (Finkelhor & Browne, 1985; Mather & Debye, 1994). Too often a therapeutic rapport is assumed to be established just by the perfunctory interchange of the first few sessions. This expectation will likely make them feel vulnerable. When teens feel vulnerable they react defensively and this may also cause the effects of the trauma to be even more pronounced in their lives (Mather & Debye, 1994; van der Kolk, 1994). Trust and respect must be earned and given. The therapy setting is a perfect place to model and teach this important life lesson. Establishing a healthy therapeutic relationship is a process that takes . . . well, as long as it takes.

MEET THEM WHERE THEY ARE: THE POWER OF EQUALITY

The teen client prominently displayed bright pink hair, torn black T-shirt, pink and black polka dot hose under torn denim shorts, piercings in her ears, eyebrow, and nose, and scar upon scar from years of self-injury.

After being told she could sit wherever she wanted, this teen quickly determined which chair she believed belonged to the therapist. With great flourish she plopped into that chair and flung her legs over the arm wearing a smile that would make the Cheshire cat jealous.

What could have become a power struggle about who sits where became an opportunity to make a dent in this teen's defenses with humor. So without hesitation the therapist laid down on the couch, stating she was glad the teen chose the chair. The Cheshire cat smile turned into an open-mouthed stare of surprise. Eyes met, smiles returned, and a little laughter filled the room. Allowing the teen to feel a little bit of control helped with the building of rapport.

This teen's action might be seen as an act of defiance or resistance. It was certainly a power play, an effort for this teen to gain control over an uncomfortable situation. An important developmental task of the teen is to become independent and confident. This struggle for power and control can be exacerbated when abuse is a part of a teen's background. Teen survivors are often facing the unfortunate trauma-induced thinking error that if they had only exerted their power and control during their abuse they could have prevented their own victimization (James, 1989; Mather & Debye, 1994; Vieth & Smith, 2010). Consequently, if they let go of *any* power and control now, they may mistakenly believe they will be victimized again, even within the confines of a therapy session.

When the therapist takes a step back and recognizes the teenager's underlying apprehension, fear, guilt, shame, and trauma, it becomes easier to understand most of these protective behaviors as reactions to trauma (van der Kolk, 2010). Yet teens are still so often misunderstood even within therapy. Sometimes therapists try bulldozing over a teen's defenses. The struggle for power ensues and the teen's walls of protection become higher, wider, and less penetrable. They might be labeled as resistant and termination or referrals may follow. The teen then becomes more firmly convinced that no one can help, and that no one is willing to wait patiently to gain respect and trust and be invited into the client's world. Resistance in therapy can usually be interpreted as the teen's way of telling the therapist he or she is just not ready yet.

TRAUMA AND ADOLESCENTS

Critical to the successful treatment of sexual abuse victims is a comprehensive, extensive, and constantly updated understanding of all aspects of trauma, as well as proficiency in using the most current and effective treatment modalities. Children with posttraumatic stress disorder (PTSD) symptoms likely have a history of traumatic experiences such as witnessing domestic violence, experiencing physical abuse, or experiencing sexual abuse (Luthra et al., 2009). Those experiences may or may not create long-term trauma symptoms. Whether the abuse is processed as traumatic, or as a less negative experience, can vary based on the nature of the abuse, the child, particularly the age at the time of the abuse, and may change as the child moves from one developmental stage to another (Brown, 2005; Hindman, 1989; James, 1989). This is equally true whether they were abused during adolescence or at a younger age (Kendall-Tackett, Williams, & Finkelhor, 1993).

In some children the impact of the trauma shows up later in life, and at the time of the abuse they may appear asymptomatic (Dominguez, Nelke, & Perry, 2002). These children are sometimes overlooked because they seem to be fine, and appear to have no lasting effects from the sexual abuse. But as children mature, sexual abuse traumas are continually reprocessed and take on a different meaning for teens. These are some of the reasons why a thorough trauma assessment is an important step in the treatment process.

The effects of trauma in teens sometimes reflect their developmental differences. Rather than having language that is only concrete and simple, adolescents can think and communicate in much more abstract terms. They have the capacity to think ahead, and to imagine what might take place based on what choices they make. Adolescents often try to anticipate, manage, and manipulate outcomes. However, teens can frequently misperceive that they are omniscient. They tend to underestimate what they do not know or understand, and make decisions based on these inaccurate assumptions. Teenagers tend to avoid admitting their gaps in knowledge, often misjudging long-term effects of their decisions and choices. This includes what they choose to reveal and withhold from professionals trying to intervene on their behalf, even if that continues to put them at risk (Finkelhor & Browne, 1985). Perhaps that is one reason for the unfortunate finding that about 86% of sexual assaults of adolescents go unreported, according to an account from the National Institute of Justice (Ashcroft, Daniels, & Hart, 2003).

Traumagenic factors from sexual abuse including betrayal, powerlessness, stigmatization, and traumatic sexualization may be observed in teens in a variety of ways (Finkelhor & Browne, 1985). Teen victims generally distrust people, particularly adults, and this includes the therapist. This dynamic is sometimes seen in a willingness to share abuse information with a trusted peer but not with any adult attempting to intervene positively on their behalf. An example of this phenomenon is a girl who disclosed sexual abuse by an uncle to two female friends, and a boy she only knew through the Internet, then swore them to secrecy.

Another week went by before she finally decided to tell her father what happened to her. He was dismayed that she kept her victimization a secret from him but shared it with persons who could not effectively help her. Yet this dynamic is common and can also impact what a teen will reveal to their therapist (Sorenson & Snow, 1991; Summit, 1983).

Traumatic sexualization issues may emerge in several different ways. There can be extreme avoidance of sexuality through actions such as poor hygiene, gaining weight, or dressing in unattractive baggy clothes. The apparent opposite may occur where sexuality and sexual behaviors are used in an attempt to meet nonsexual needs. There may be multiple inappropriate and often risky sexual encounters or relationships where even more episodes of victimization occur. Sexual abuse can cause confusion about sexual and/or gender identity (Maltz & Holman, 1987). Distorted beliefs about healthy sexuality are common. Teen survivors may believe that sex must be painful. Teens may also believe that they have no right to their own bodies, cannot say no to unwanted sexual contact, or set limits (Maltz & Holman, 1987). Survivors often believe they will never have a healthy, positive, and mutually respectful sexual relationship. Compensation for feelings of powerlessness combined with sexual traumatization can even lead to sexual exploitation of others, repeating the abuse cycle (Arata, 2002). Exploring beliefs about sexuality and helping teens to establish healthy sexual boundaries are important components of treatment. Therapists who treat adolescent survivors of CSA must become comfortable discussing these topics.

Severe levels of traumatization can lead an adolescent victim to use avoidance as a primary coping mechanism. They will frequently try to prevent reexperiencing powerful emotions that can accompany traumatic memories. Understanding this avoidant coping pattern can help clinicians plan initial interventions in the therapy process. If in a teen's first session they are asked to describe in detail what happened to them, it is likely the session itself could induce further trauma. By overlooking the difficulty in sharing traumatic experiences without first establishing true rapport and healthy coping skills, the therapist may inadvertently show the teen that he or she may not be safe in the therapist's hands. Pushing too soon in treatment may have iatrogenic effects.

It is essential to develop and effectively utilize a wide variety of healthy coping strategies to manage and regulate emotions *prior to* addressing any traumatic details or memories through the retelling, and thus a reliving of their trauma, even for survivors whose response to the trauma is less severe (Cook et al., 2005; Goodyear-Brown, 2010; Mather & Debye, 1994). Promising treatment approaches that pay attention to brain-based interventions may help calm the neurological triggering of trauma reactions during and outside of the therapy session (Levine, 1997; Perry, 2000; Stein & Kendall, 2004; van der Kolk, 1994, 2010). Helping teenagers learn ways to greatly reduce these powerful trauma-related emotions will improve their ability to examine and process their trauma issues at the appropriate time. It will also significantly reduce the level of interference these hyperarousal symptoms may cause in their daily lives.

DEVELOPING COPING STRATEGIES

The development of healthy coping skills is so essential that it should be considered one of the cornerstones of therapeutic trauma work. Skill development for coping with emotional distress and feelings such as anger, anxiety, depression, guilt, fear, panic and shame should occur early and continue throughout the entire therapeutic process (Deblinger & Heflin, 1996; Goodyear-Brown, 2010; Kenney-Noziska, 2008; Mather & Debye, 1994). Healthy coping skills help to manage and reduce the symptoms that could otherwise overwhelm the teen survivor (Mather & Debye, 1994; McGee & Holmes, 2008; Ross & O'Carroll, 2004).

Each person, including trauma therapists, develops certain ways of coping with the stressors of life, some healthy and some unhealthy. The more powerful the stressors the more important our coping habits become. Typically the main goal during emotional distress is to feel better as soon as possible. Because unhealthy coping skills tend to block the uncomfortable and generally unwanted emotions and trauma reactions, it is often easier to acquire maladaptive, unhealthy coping skills. The difficulty in challenging unhealthy coping skills is that they work, at least initially. Alcohol, drugs, numbing, purging, and self-harm are just a few of the unhealthy methods abused adolescents may turn to. Substance abuse is an issue to examine with all teenagers, but especially with teen survivors. Some nonabused adolescents may experiment with alcohol or drugs as a rite of passage, but survivors often quickly discover that it temporarily numbs their dysregulated emotions. Self-harm is also a fairly prevalent maladaptive coping behavior in teens. As with substance abuse, it is important to assess whether self-harm is present, and to learn how to properly address this issue (Conterio, Lader, & Bloom, 1998; Hollander, 2008; Klonsky, 2007; Plante, 2007; Weierich & Nock, 2008).

Though unhealthy coping skills may work, their effectiveness is usually temporary and often results in other problems. Unaddressed feelings go underground just waiting for an inconvenient time to resurface. Each time they do the feelings become stronger and often more overpowering. This requires more intense use of unhealthy coping skills with little to no positive long-term results. Teens are left with emotions more powerful than they have ever been and more resistant to all the methods they are using to deal with them. This can create frustration and confusion because they do not understand why the things they have used to cope in the past are no longer effective. Sometimes this will increase internalization of emotions, resulting in a teen who appears detached and/or unaffected by almost anything. The opposite can also occur where a teen seems overly affected by everything, even relatively minor situations (Kessler, 2010; Mather & Debye, 1994; Pipher, 1994). This emotional dysregulation, not the trauma specifically, may actually be the presenting issue that eventually lands a teen in therapy.

With coping skills, whether healthy or unhealthy, it is important to discuss and explore them without judgment. If an unhealthy coping skill is revealed by teens and they perceive judgment or criticism they likely will not reveal anything else and will simply withhold information. Life-threatening or dangerous behaviors should be handled in an appropriate, professional, and therapeutic manner. In other situations, it is important to help the client develop a healthy coping skill to replace the maladaptive one prior to encouraging the teen to stop using the unhealthy coping skill. Otherwise the teen is left vulnerable with no way to deal with the overwhelming emotions inside (Mather & Debye, 1994; McGee & Holmes, 2008). Remember this rule of thumb: replace do not erase.

One technique we use is simple. Take a sheet of colored paper and markers, and on one side write all the healthy coping skills the teen uses. This list may be short initially. On the other side write all the unhealthy coping skills the teen uses now or in the past. Remember, no judgment, just writing. We want the teen to feel safe putting it out there. Processing and hopefully eventual elimination of the unhealthy ones will come in due course.

After the list is made we provide a handout containing a compilation of healthy coping skills, which we constantly expand based on the teen client's input. Knowing this list is from other teens seems to make it more acceptable. When teens see a list of healthy coping skills and realize they already use some of them it is a powerful and empowering cognitive technique. Healthy coping strategies commonly used by teens such as art, music, and talking to friends are on the handout. We also encourage them to think outside the box and consider things such as: blowing bubbles, cloud watching, crossword puzzles, martial arts, mindful breathing (yoga breathing), popping bubble wrap, rocking, swinging, or even vacuuming. Something monotonous can be soothing to the mind and things that have a positive end result such as vacuuming or cleaning produce positive feelings. One teen recently discovered she likes how she feels when she cleans up the kitchen and puts everything away. For her it has become symbolic of her mentally putting things in their place.

Once both lists are complete and a good therapeutic relationship has been established, a deal can be struck between the therapist and teen. The deal we work toward is having the teen agree to use at least three to five healthy coping skills whenever he or she faces overwhelming situations or emotions before he or she can use any unhealthy coping skill. With more traumatized teens, we may ask them to agree to only three, so they do not feel pushed too hard. What typically occurs is the healthy coping skills reduce the symptoms, resulting in teens having no need for their unhealthy coping skills. However, because we have not taken away those old unhealthy coping skills they still provide a safety net, and a realization that the therapist truly does understand the importance of those other coping skills, even if they are unhealthy. Even just reading the list engages the cognitive, language-based side of their brains, which alone can help slightly reduce the level of emotion (van der Kolk, 2010). As teens work through difficult times and emotions with their new healthy coping skills, their reliance on unhealthy coping skills decreases and their confidence in their ability to handle their own emotions increases.

One caveat about music is how important it is for therapists working with teens to be familiar with their music. Music might be a teen's most prevalent coping skill, which on the surface seems harmless and positive. However, it depends on the music. If therapists do not know what their teen clients are listening to, it is difficult to know whether a specific playlist is positive or negative. Some teens have playlists including music that is dark, depressing, fatalistic and negative overall (Greenwald, 2003). The predominance of this type of music increases in teens who have suffered trauma. Encourage them to limit their use of these darker songs until their emotions become more balanced and to add a few positive, more upbeat selections. Consider keeping a well-stocked teen playlist on your computer and/or MP3 player to help make suggestions to teens about songs to add.

ENCOURAGING THE DEVELOPMENT
OF CRITICAL THINKING SKILLS

Another key ingredient in the treatment of trauma is helping teens develop better critical thinking skills, commonly referred to as CT. The term we use in treatment is *thoughts over feelings* (TOF). Incorporating cognitive behavioral concepts teaches teens to be aware of how subjective their emotions can be. It also fosters the opportunity to view feelings in a different light and test their accuracy. One inaccurate belief teens sometimes share is the notion that if you believe something strongly and feel deeply about it, then the belief must be accurate. Actually, many irrational beliefs are deeply felt, and this is one of the reasons they are difficult to challenge and change (Murdoch & Lewis, 2000). Another popular misconception about emotions is the belief that being excessively rational will cause a person to become emotionally detached, almost robotic. In truth, cognitions and affect influence one another in determining our beliefs and our behavior. The goal is to strive for an accurate, healthy balance between our cognitive processes and our emotions. Teens are generally lacking in all aspects and understanding of CT or TOF. Trauma amplifies this disconnect. We maintain a focus on cognitive change in a variety of ways, including sending home props as reminders to put thoughts over feelings. Educating teens about how the mind works and the importance of practicing self-discipline with these issues can help them learn to take charge of their thinking and underlying emotions (Elder & Paul, 2001).

We teach that feelings are not positive or negative, as they are frequently classified. Instead, we use terms such as comfortable and uncomfortable, or feelings we like to feel and feelings we do not like to feel (McGee & Holmes, 2008). For example, the feeling of fear does not automatically have to be debilitating, nor should it be ignored as meaningless. Fear is a warning to pay attention, process information, and choose how to respond effectively. If we view fear as only negative it becomes difficult to see how it is actually beneficial and helpful (Rothschild, 2000). Of course, if a teen feels fear because they smell an aftershave associated with their perpetrator, the goal is to determine the source of the fear and if there is actual danger. It may simply be the association of a sensory experience coming from a perfectly neutral party. CT or TOF encourages teens to accurately understand their feelings when processing events, situations, or traumatic experiences in light of the current reality. Then they can make a decision about how to respond instead of just reacting.

BOUNDARIES AND LIMITS

Many aspects of a teen's life intersect with boundaries such as issues with phone usage, academics, sexuality, parties, clothing, relationships, curfews, use of the Internet, and many other areas of functioning (Townsend, 2006). Close work with parents will be necessary to ensure that they are fulfilling their parental role of establishing and maintaining healthy boundaries and setting appropriate limits with their abused teens. Often because of the abuse parents may have slipped into friendship roles.

When parents abdicate their parental role and give authority to the child it creates a feeling of insecurity in the child. This insecurity often manifests itself in the form of anxiety. This shifting of parental rules/ boundaries in response to the trauma may inadvertently give additional power to the traumatic situation. This, too, can increase symptoms including acting-out behavior.

It is not uncommon for parents of an abused teen to try to make up for the abuse by being more lenient. The opposite also occurs where parents mistakenly believe that being a stricter more authoritarian parent will keep their child safe so the rules and consequences become more severe. Neither approach is fruitful, as teens need both firm boundaries, and an opportunity to work through their developmental challenges. Therapists can help reinforce to parents and teens that the limits, rules, and expectations should not change because of their abuse. Therapists can also help parents separately address and overcome their own internal struggles, which may be influencing their parenting in a negative way. Helping the parents ultimately helps the teen.

There will likely be occasions when the therapist may need to establish clear boundaries within the therapy setting itself. Being able to tolerate a great deal of out-of-the-box behavior is preferable when working with teens, but therapists will need to know their own limits even if those limits mean they are not well suited for working with teen clients. The therapeutic relationship should model and mirror a healthy relationship with boundaries and limits and a clear understanding of the nature of the relationship (Skuka, 2010). Clinicians should maintain an attitude of friendliness without becoming a friend to their teen clients.

This work also includes helping teens develop and/or clarify their personal boundaries. When abuse occurs personal boundaries are trampled over if they were ever allowed to exist. In traumatized teens this lack of boundaries can manifest itself in things such as provocative or inappropriate dress, sexual acting out, risky relationships, and a lack of awareness of the predatory behaviors of others. These teens are particularly vulnerable to what is known as "emotional grooming" (McGee & Buddenberg, 2003, pp. 1–2). This is the process of using emotions to gain power over someone. Seduction and control are utilized in order to manipulate emotions. These predators will often pretend to have deep feelings for a teen when essentially they are artfully coercing the teen into a relationship that typically becomes sexually abusive and controlling (McGee & Buddenberg, 2003). With absent, weak, or unhealthy personal boundaries teens become easy targets for this type of predator, and may fall prey to additional victimization. The probability of this happening can be reduced when teens learn what healthy personal boundaries are and how to establish them.

INTEGRATING PLAY AND EXPRESSIVE THERAPIES

Play and expressive therapy techniques are well suited for helping to process abuse issues and are easily incorporated into Trauma-Focused Cognitive-Behavioral Therapy (TF-CBT), allowing for creativity and flexibility (Cavett, 2009). But like adults, teens may be a little more reluctant to participate in anything referred to as play therapy. Research suggests, and our experience supports, that teens have a willingness to participate in playful and other expressive therapies when rapport and trust have been established and a teen feels emotionally safe and not judged (Green, 2010). One way to approach play and expressive therapy is to include aspects from each without making teens feel like they are being treated as children. Begin by using activities that focus more on abstract skills such as sand play, artwork, journaling, guided imagery, and dream work (Green, 2010). These more creative approaches are very effective with teen survivors and also raise motivational levels and increase involvement in the therapeutic process.

TREATING EMOTIONAL DYSREGULATION: REDUCING ANXIETY AND DEPRESSION

Many survivors of child sexual abuse have experienced the trauma of multiple incidents of victimization by someone they trust, over an extended period of time (Cicchetti & Toth, 1995; Cloitre, Cohen, & Scarvalone, 2002). One of the primary clusters of symptoms in trauma includes the issue of emotional dysregulation, whether based on the existing diagnosis of PTSD (American Psychiatric Association, 2000) or the proposed additional category of Complex Trauma in Children and Adolescents (Cook et al., 2005). Research suggests that repeated trauma can even impact a child's developing brain causing it to grow in a different manner than that of a child who has not been exposed to trauma (De Bellis, Keshavan, & Shifflett, 2002; Kaufman, Plotsky, & Nemeroff, 2000; Perry & Pollard, 1998; Schore, 2001; Siegel, 1999; Teicher, Andersen, & Polcari, 2002). Therefore, adolescent survivors of multiple sexual abuse traumas can have powerful neurological reactions that evoke strong emotions when trauma memories are triggered. Often it is these dysregulated emotions including anxiety-based symptoms, and depression, not the abuse itself, which may result in a referral to a therapist (American Psychiatric Association, 2000).

Consequently, teen survivors may also be more at risk for developing symptoms of depression than younger child survivors (Browne & Finkelhor, 1986). Teenagers who have low self-esteem and are highly self-critical, with little sense of control over negative events, are especially vulnerable to problems with depression. Possible complications that accompany depression are low energy levels, feelings of hopelessness, negative self-speech, and suicidal ideations. Suicide attempts among American teenagers have risen dramatically in the past 15 years. In fact, suicide is now the third leading cause of death for persons in the United States between the ages of 15 and 24 (National Institute of Mental Health, 2010). Many factors, such as loss, insufficient family support, and hopelessness, play a role in U.S. teens' suicidal thinking. However, a history of sexual abuse is also one of the factors (Dube et al., 2001; Morano, Cicler, & Lemerond, 1993). It is important for therapists to be proactive in talking with teens about suicidal ideations. Teens likely will not introduce the topic, but therapists should specifically ask about it in a format that encourages an open dialogue.

Boys in our culture are taught to be tough and brave and to ignore their feelings (Gartner, 2005; Holmes, Offen, & Waller, 1997; Sorsoli, Grossman, & Kia-Keating, 2008). The expression of feelings of fear, confusion, and helplessness runs completely counter to what our culture teaches boys. However, avoiding awareness of underlying feelings can result in depressive symptomatology. Although these core issues need to be approached gradually in treatment, they need to be addressed.

Some teens may attempt to deal with their symptoms by trying to disconnect from their past. However, life-changing events leave semipermanent neurological equivalents (NEs) in our brain (Murdoch & Lewis, 2000). NEs refer to neurological pathways present for all the mental events, including thoughts, beliefs, opinions, and actions that exist and once activated will produce those mental activities. The strength of NEs is increased by repetition and by the emotional impact of that mental event. Thus, trauma experiences, especially repeated trauma experiences, leave NEs that typically last a lifetime (Murdoch & Lewis, 2000). Healing from the trauma of sexual abuse will not come from the fading out of the NEs underlying trauma memories. Healing comes from producing new NEs that are empowering and health promoting,

Identity continues to be formed throughout life. But it is during childhood and adolescence that the process of identity formation is more dominant and the foundation of identity is laid (Briere, 1992; Josselson & Lieblich, 1995; Lieblich, McAdams, & Josselson, 2004). Shame caused by abuse often results in serious problems with self-esteem and can develop into a flawed identity. Identity is formed not only by what teens themselves think about who they are, but also by what they believe others think about them. Therefore, as sexual abuse survivors reach adolescence, they must make sense of their experiences in a manner that coincides with identity formation. Their internal dialog is typically negative and can make teens vulnerable to depression. Therapeutic activities should include cognitive-behavioral approaches to change the teen's negative self-speech because it strongly influences moods, and impacts ongoing identity formation (Bonner, Walker, & Berliner, 1993; Cohen, Mannarino, Berliner, & Deblinger, 2000; Lieblich et al., 2004; McGee & Holmes, 2008).

It is important to assess for anxiety in teen survivors entering treatment. Teens often believe they are crazy because of trauma symptoms like anxiety. Education about PTSD and the mechanisms that reinforce anxiety can normalize their experience. It will also provide an opportunity to learn to combat their anxiety. Asking teenagers what their bodies feel they need to do when anxiety is present will provide clues about the best coping skills. If they feel the need to run, then a more physically exerting activity involving movement of the body along with deep breathing and positive self-talk may be the best technique. If they feel the need to remain still or retreat, having them sit down, relax, and take a deep breath will be helpful along with positive self-talk. Relieving the symptoms of anxiety and utilizing effective coping skills to work through it empowers the teen as they address their trauma issues.

WHEN TEENS WHO ARE ABUSED ABUSE OTHERS

Unfortunately, in some cases, teen survivors of sexual abuse develop sexual behavior problems with other children (Letourneau, Schoenwald, & Sheidow, 2004; Porter, 1986; Rogers & Terry, 1984). Possible reasons for this include reactions to the traumagenic factors of powerlessness and traumatic sexualization (Finkelhor, 1984). Aspects of this behavior are relevant when working with teen survivors. Research indicates that adolescents commit a substantial percentage of the sexual abuse of children, especially sexual abuse of young children (Davis & Leitenberg, 1988; Snyder & Sickmund, 1999). However, it is important to note that most adolescent offenders do not meet the criteria for pedophilia, and most do not have a deviant sexual arousal pattern with frequent deviant sexual fantasies (American Psychiatric Association, 2000; Becker, Hunter, Stein, & Kaplan, 1989; Hunter, Goodwin, & Becker, 1994). In addition, sexually reactive adolescent survivors are more amenable to treatment efforts, and less likely than adult offenders to indefinitely continue a pattern of offending throughout adult life (Association for the Treatment of Sexual Abusers, 2000). It is also possible for a teenage survivor to have a pattern of delinquent thinking and behaving that might include inappropriate sexual behaviors as just one part of a more general pattern of rule-breaking behavior. In such cases, the risk of re-offending sexually is still substantially lower than for adult offenders, and they are still appropriate for some type of treatment program, often in the community. In addition, not all sexual behavior problems result in violations of criminal statutes, but still warrant specific clinical attention. Consequently, as treatment providers we need to ask questions about sexual behaviors in victims, and be sure to include these issues in our treatment plans, when relevant.

The worlds of survivor treatment providers and offender treatment providers have not always involved the same professionals working from the same perspectives. However, there is now a push to get victim- and offender-treatment specialists to collaborate more effectively (Friedrich, 1993; Goodyear-Brown, 2008; Holmes & Whitson, 2007). Within this collaboration comes the question of who is qualified to treat teenage survivors with sexual behavior problems. We would suggest that the answer involves the specific training of the therapist, and the specific treatment demands of the individual adolescent being considered. The training a professional needs in order to appropriately complete a psychosexual assessment is extensive and may be determined by state law, but generally is addressed by the practice standards of the Association for the Treatment of Sexual Abusers (2004) and by using guidelines from "Understanding juvenile sex offending behavior: Emerging Research, Treatment Approaches, and Management Practices," from the Center for Sex Offender Management (2010). See Chapter 21, this volume, for more information on adolescents with illegal sexual behavior. All of these factors are important to consider in the overall treatment planning when working with teen survivors of sexual abuse.

TEEN SURVIVORS AND THEIR RISKY HIGH-TECH TOYS

We live in a rapidly changing high-tech world. Teenagers tend to be on the cutting edge with new technologies. Unfortunately, this includes technology-based ways that sexual abuse can occur. In addition we live in a world that has become much more sexualized (Anderson, 2007; Cooper, 2002; DeAngelis, 2007). One term used to describe the current sexual cultural climate in the United States is *pornified* (Paul, 2005). Is it any surprise that more and more new cases of sexual offenses involving teens include computers, cell phones, and other high-tech devices?

The National Center for Missing and Exploited Children now reviews over 18 million child pornographic images found in a year. Eighty percent of child pornography is produced by people that the child knows and trusts and 39% of child pornography is produced by family members (National Center for Missing and Exploited Children, 2010). This means that investigators sometimes find sexual images of minors prior to that child or youth making a disclosure about this illegal use of media. The knowledge of the existence of these images can be overwhelming to a teen victim. Not only are these technology-based devices used by perpetrators to sexually exploit teens, a growing number of kids are producing and distributing their own sexual images through activities such as sexting due to the "easy access of technology" (Vieth & Smith, 2010). When teens have voluntarily engaged in sending sexual images of themselves, often as a result of a lack of personal boundaries caused by their own victimization, they may be even more reluctant to report any photos and/or videos taken by a perpetrator. These factors can cause the line between victim and participant to become harder to determine. The possibility of teens engaging in risk-taking behavior through activities such a sexting with or being victimized by perpetrators using these technologies should not be overlooked, but explored during therapy with caution and care in order to provide the most comprehensive treatment.

TEENS SPEAK FOR THEMSELVES

Because this chapter focuses on how to help adolescent survivors of abuse we felt it was appropriate to ask teens to speak for themselves. We asked them to imagine they were asked to talk to a group of therapists in training. Most teens expressed similar thoughts. This is a small sampling.

> Take it slowly, get to know us first. Sometimes we just want to talk, but not about what happened. Try not to ask "So how does that make you feel?" so much. It's stereotypical therapist and we don't always know how we feel. Some teens can take things very personally and we all respond in different ways. Please, make us feel comfortable. This may sound rude but when we aren't comfortable with a situation we don't tell the truth and/or we don't tell you everything.
>
> —*Sarah, age 15*
>
> Trust and respect must be earned no matter what age or who you may be. Always be teachable.
>
> —*M. Jet, age 14*
>
> Please don't say I know how you feel or what you are going through. You have NO IDEA what we've gone through. Be patient and above all tell the truth. Teens are going to throw tests out there to see what a therapist is made of so just be honest with them. We are called young adults so think how you would treat a newly planted flower. That is what a teen is, all grown on the outside but SCARED to death on the inside.
>
> —*James D., age 18*

Please take time to get to know me. Make me comfortable, get on my level so we're on the same ground, like sitting with me on the sofa AFTER you ask me if it's okay. It's easier to talk then. Don't tell me what to do but give me options. Listen to me; adults are really bad at listening.

—Paige, age 16

Do not be condescending to us. Listen. Find ways to make it easier for us to talk like art or taking a walk. Be creative.

—Cassie, age 15

CONCLUSION

The developmental tasks of adolescence must be understood when planning treatment for adolescents who have been sexually abused. Boundary issues, identity formation, the way in which initial rapport is built and nurtured, the involvement of parents in treatment, the expansion of healthy coping, and the reduction of problematic cognitions must all be addressed through a lens that honors the particular developmental dilemmas that face adolescent survivors of child sexual abuse in order to ensure positive long-term outcomes for this population.

REFERENCES

American Psychiatric Association. (2000). *Diagnostic and statistical manual of mental disorders* (4th ed., Text rev., *DSM IV-TR*). Washington, DC: American Psychiatric Association.

Anderson, C. (2007, March). *Marketing, technology, pornography, & hypersexualized pop culture: Countering the normalization & harm.* The 23rd Annual Symposium on Child Abuse, Prevent Child Abuse Georgia, Atlanta, GA.

Arata, C. (2002). Child sexual abuse and sexual revictimization. *Clinical Psychology, 9,* 135–164.

Arnett, J. (2010). *Adolescence and emerging adulthood: A cultural approach, 4/E.* Upper Saddle River, NJ: Pearson.

Ashcroft, J., Daniels, D., & Hart, S. (2003). Youth victimization: Prevalence and implications. Washington, DC: National Institute of Justice.

Association for the Treatment of Sexual Abusers. (2000). *The effective legal management of juvenile sexual offenders.* Position paper. Beaverton, OR: ATSA.

Association for the Treatment of Sexual Abusers. (2004). *ATSA practice standards and guidelines for evaluation, treatment and management of adult male sexual abusers.* Beaverton, OR: ATSA.

Baxter, K. (2008). *The modern Age: Turn-of-the-century American culture and the invention of adolescence.* Tuscaloosa: University of Alabama Press.

Becker, J., Hunter, J., Stein, R., & Kaplan, M. (1989). Factors associated with erection in adolescent sex offenders. *Journal of Psychopathology and Behavioral Assessment, 11,* 353–363.

Bonner, B., Walker, C., & Berliner, L. (1993). *Children with sexual behavior problems: Assessment and treatment.* Washington, DC: National Center on Child Abuse and Neglect, Administration for Children Youth and Families, DHHS.

Bradley, A., & Wood, J. (1996). How do children tell? The disclosure process in child sexual abuse. *Child Abuse & Neglect, 20,* 881–891.

Briere, J. (1992). *Child abuse trauma: Theory, and treating of the lasting effects.* Newbury Park, CA: Sage.

Brown, N. (2005). *Blame my brain: The amazing teenage brain revealed.* London, England: Walker Books.

Browne, A., & Finkelhor, D. (1986). Impact of child sexual abuse: Review of the research. *Psychological Bulletin, 99,* 66–77.

Bruckner, D., & Johnson, P. (1987). Treatment for adult male victims of childhood sexual abuse. *Social Casework, 68*(2), 81–87.

Cavett, A. (2009). Playful trauma-focused cognitive behavioral therapy with maltreated children and adolescence. *Play Therapy, 4*(3), 20–22.

Center for Sex Offender Management (CSOM). (2010, July 25). *Understanding juvenile sex offending behavior: Emerging research, treatment approaches, and management practices.* Retrieved from www.csom.org/pubs/juvbrf10.pdf

Cicchetti, D., & Toth, S. (1995). Developmental psychopathology and disorders of affect. In D. Cicchetti & D. Cohen (Eds.), *Developmental psychopathology, volume 2: Risk, disorder and adaptation* (pp. 369–420). New York, NY: John Wiley & Sons.

Cloitre, M., Cohen, L., & Scarvalone, P. (2002). Understanding revictmization among childhood sexual abuse survivors: An interpersonal schema approach. *Journal of Cognitive Psychotherapy, 16*(1), 91–111.

Cohen, J., Deblinger, E., & Mannarino, A. (2004). Trauma-focused cognitive behavior therapy for sexually abused children. *Psychiatric Times, 21*(10), 1–2.

Cohen, J., Mannarino, A., Berliner, L., & Deblinger, E. (2000). Trauma-focused cognitive-behavioral therapy for children and adolescents: An empirical study. *Journal of Interpersonal Violence, 15*(11), 1202–1223.

Conterio, K., Lader, W., & Kingston-Bloom, J. (1998). *Bodily harm: The breakthrough healing program for self-injurers.* New York, NY: Hyperion.

Cook, A., Spinazzola, J., Ford, J., Lanktree, C., Blaustein, C., Cloitre, M., . . . van der Kolk, B. (2005). Complex trauma in children and adolescence. *Psychiatric Annals, 35*(5), 390–398.

Cooper, A. (2002). *Sex and the internet: A guide for clinicians.* London, England: Brunner-Routledge.

Davis, G., & Leitenberg, H. (1988). Adolescent sexual offenders. *Psychological Bulletin, 101,* 417–427.

DeAngelis, T. (2007). America: A toxic lifestyle. *Monitor on Psychology, 38*(4), 51.

De Bellis, M., Keshavan, M., & Shifflett, H. (2002). Brain structures in pediatric maltreatment-related posttraumatic stress disorder: A sociodemographically matched study. *Biological Psychiatry, 52,* 1066–1078.

Deblinger, E., & Heflin, A. (1996). *Treating sexually abused children and their non-offending parents.* Thousand Oaks, CA: Sage.

Dominguez, R., Nelke, C., & Perry, B. (2002). *Child sexual abuse. Encyclopedia of crime and punishment, 1* (pp. 202–207). Thousand Oaks, CA: Sage.

Donker, T., Griffiths, K., Cuijpers, P., & Christensen, H. (2009). Psychoeducation for depression, anxiety, and psychological distress: A meta-analysis. *Directory of Open Access Journals, 7*(1), 1–3.

Dube, S., Anda, R., Felitti, V., Chapman, D., Williamson, D., & Giles, W. (2001). Childhood abuse, household dysfunction, and the risk of attempted suicide throughout the life span: Findings from the adverse childhood experiences study. *Journal of the American Medical Association, 286,* 3089–3096.

Elder, L., & Paul, R. (2001). Critical thinking: Thinking with concepts. *Journal of Developmental Education, 24*(3), 42–43.

Feinstein, S. (2009). *Secrets of the teenage brain: Research-based strategies for reaching and teaching today's adolescents.* Thousand Oaks, CA: Corwin Press.

Finkelhor, D. (1984). *Child sexual abuse: New theory and research.* New York, NY: Free Press.

Finkelhor, D., & Browne, A. (1985). The traumatic impact of child sexual abuse: A conceptualization. *American Journal of Orthopsychiatry, 55*(4), 530–541.

Friedrich, W. (1993). Sexual victimization and sexual behavior in children: A review of recent literature. *Child Abuse & Neglect, 17,* 59–66.

Gartner, R. (2005). *Beyond betrayal: Taking charge of your life after boyhood sexual abuse.* Hoboken, NJ: John Wiley & Sons.

Gil, E. (1996). *Treating abused adolescents.* New York, NY: Guilford Press.

Goodyear-Brown, P. (2008). Sexual behavior problems. *Mining Report.* Clovis, CA: Association for Play Therapy.

Goodyear-Brown, P. (2010). *Play therapy with traumatized children: A prescriptive approach.* Hoboken, NJ: John Wiley & Sons.

Green, E. (2010). Jungian play therapy with adolescents. *Play Therapy, 5*(2), 20–23.

Greenwald, A. (2003). *Nothing feels good: Punk rock, teenagers, and emo.* New York, NY: St. Martin's Griffin.

Gries, L., Goh, D., & Cavanaugh, J. (1996). Factors associated with disclosure during child sexual abuse assessment. *Journal of Child Sexual Abuse, 5*(3), 1–19.

Hall, L., & Lloyd, S. (1993). *Surviving child sexual abuse: A handbook for helping women challenge their past.* London, England: Falmer Press.

Hindman, J. (1989). *Just before dawn: From the shadows of tradition to new reflections in trauma assessment and treatment of sexual victimization.* Ontario, OR: AlexAndria.

Hollander, M. (2008). *Teens who cut: Understanding and ending self-injury.* New York, NY: Guilford Press.

Holmes, C., & Whitson, S. (2007, March). *Therapy outside the box: Creative and practical techniques for group therapy for adolescent males with sexual behavior problems.* 23rd National Symposium on Child Abuse, Huntsville, AL.

Holmes, G., Offen, L., & Waller, G. (1997). See no evil, hear no evil, speak no evil: Why do relatively few male victims of childhood sexual abuse receive help for abuse-related issues in adulthood? *Clinical Psychology Review, 17,* 69–88.

Hunter, J., Goodwin, D., & Becker, J. (1994). The relationship between phallo-metrically measured deviant sexual arousal and clinical characteristics in juvenile sexual offenders. *Behavior Research and Therapy, 32,* 533–538.

James, B. (1989). *Treating traumatized children.* Lexington, MA: Lexington Books.

Josselson, R., & Lieblich, A. (1995). *Interpreting experience: The narrative study of lives.* Newbury Park, CA: Sage.

Kaufman, J., Plotsky, P., & Nemeroff, C. (2000). Effects of early adverse experiences on brain structure and function: Clinical implications. *Biological Psychiatry, 48,* 778–790.

Kendall-Tackett, K., Williams, L., & Finkelhor, D. (1993). Impact of sexual abuse on children: A review and synthesis of recent empirical studies. *Psychological Bulletin, 113,* 164–180.

Kenney-Noziska, S. (2008). *Techniques, techniques, techniques: Play-based activities for children, adolescents, and families.* Conshohocken, PA: Infinity.

Kessler, L. (2010). *My teenage werewolf: A mother, a daughter, a journey through the thicket of adolescence.* New York, NY: Viking Press.

Klonsky, E. (2007). The function of deliberate self-injury: A review of the evidence. *Clinical Psychology Review, 27*(2), 226–239.

Letourneau, E., Schoenwald, S., & Sheidow, A. (2004). Children and adolescents with sexual behavior problems. *Child Maltreatment, 9,* 49–61.

Levine, P. (1997). *Waking the tiger, healing trauma.* Berkeley, CA: North Atlantic Books.

Lieblich, A., McAdams, D., & Josselson, R. (2004). *Healing plots: The narrative basis of psychotherapy.* Washington, DC: American Psychological Association.

Luthra, R., Abramovitz, R., Greenberg, R., Schoor, A., Newcorn, J., Schmeidler, J., . . . Chemtob, C. (2009). Relationship between type of trauma exposure and posttraumatic stress disorder among urban children and adolescents. *Journal of Interpersonal Violence, 24,* 1919–1927.

Malloy, L., Lyon, T., & Quas, J. (2007). Filial dependency and recantations of child sexual abuse allegations. *Journal of the American Academy of Child & Adolescent Psychiatry, 46*(2), 162–170.

Maltz, W., & Holman, B. (1987). *Incest and sexuality: A guide to understanding healing.* Lexington, MA: Lexington Books.

Mather, C., & Debye, K. (1994). *How long does it hurt: A guide from incest and sexual abuse for teenagers, their friends, and their families.* Hoboken, NJ: Jossey-Bass.

McGee, K., & Buddenberg, J. (2003). *Unmasking sexual con games: Helping teens avoid emotional grooming and dating violence* (3rd ed.). Boys Town, NE: Boys Town Press.

McGee, S., & Holmes, C. (2008). *Finding sunshine after the storm: A workbook for children healing form sexual abuse.* Oakland, CA: New Harbinger.

Mish, F. (Ed.). (2008). *Merriam Webster's Collegiate Dictionary: Tenth Edition.* Springfield, MA: Merriam-Webster.

Morano, C., Cicler, R., & Lemerond, L. (1993). Risk factors for adolescent suicidal behavior: Loss, insufficient family support, and hopelessness. *Adolescence, 28,* 851–865.

Murdoch, B., & Lewis, S. (2000). *Psychology for life*. Macon, GA: Fore (In) Sight Foundation.

Nagel, D., Putnam, F., Noll, J., & Trickett, P. (1997). Disclosure patterns of sexual abuse and psychological functioning at a 1-year follow-up. *Child Abuse & Neglect, 21,* 137–147.

National Center for Missing and Exploited Children. (2010, July 25). *What is child pornography?* Retrieved from www.missingkids.com/missingkids/servlet/PageServlet?LanguageCountry=en_US&PageId=2451

National Institute of Mental Health. (2010, July 25). *Suicide in the U.S.: Statistics and prevention.* Retrieved from www.nimh.nih.gov/health/publications/suicide-in-the-us-statistics-and-prevention/index.shtml

Paine, M., & Hansen, D. (2002). Factors influencing children to self-disclose sexual abuse. *Clinical Psychology Review, 22*(2), 271–295.

Paul, P. (2005). *Pornified: How pornography is in our lives, our relationships, and our families.* New York, NY: Holt.

Perry, B. (2000). Traumatized children: How childhood trauma influences brain development. *Journal of the California Alliance of the Mentally Ill, 11*(1), 48–51.

Perry, B., & Pollard, R. (1998). Homeostasis, stress, trauma, and adaptation: A neurodevelopmental view of childhood trauma. *Child & Adolescent Psychiatric Clinics of North America, 7,* 33–51.

Pipher, M. (1994). *Reviving Ophelia: Saving the selves of adolescent girls.* New York, NY: Ballentine Books.

Plante, L. (2007). *Bleeding to ease the pain: Cutting, self-injury, and the adolescent search for self.* Westport, CT: Praeger.

Porter, E. (1986). *Treating the young male victim of sexual assault.* Syracuse, NY: Safer Society Press.

Rogers, C., & Terry, T. (1984). Clinical interventions with boy victims of sexual abuse. In S. Greer & I. Stuart (Eds.), *Victims of sexual aggression: Men, women, and children* (pp 91–104). New York, NY: Van Nostrand Reinhold.

Ross, G., & Carroll, P. (2004). Cognitive behavioral psychotherapy intervention in childhood sexual abuse: Identifying new direction from the literature. *Child Abuse Review, 13,* 51–64.

Rothschild, B. (2000). *The body remembers: The psychophysiology of trauma and trauma treatment.* New York, NY: Norton.

Schore, A. (2001). The effects of early relational trauma on right brain development, affect regulation, and infant mental health. *Infant Mental Health Journal, 22,* 201–269.

Sgroi, S. (1988). *Vulnerable populations: Volume 1.* Glencoe, IL: Free Press.

Siegel, D. (1999). *The developing mind: Toward a neurobiology of interpersonal experience.* New York, NY: Guilford Press.

Skuka, R. (2010). The rationale and principles of effective limit setting in child-centered play therapy, filial therapy, and parenting education. *Play Therapy, 5*(2), 10–14.

Snyder, H., & Sickmund, M. (1999). *Juvenile offenders and victims: 1999 national report.* Washington, DC: Office of Juvenile Justice and Delinquency Prevention.

Sorenson, T., & Snow, B. (1991). How children tell: The process of disclosure in child sexual abuse. *Child Welfare, 70*, 3–15.

Sorsoli, L., Grossman, F., & Kia-Keating, M. (2008). "I keep that hush-hush": Male survivors of sexual abuse and the challenges of disclosure. *Journal of Consulting Psychology, 55*(3), 333–345.

Stein, P., & Kendall, J. (2004). *Psychological trauma and the developing brain: Neurologically-based interventions for troubled children.* New York, NY: Haworth.

Summitt, R. (1983). The child sexual abuse accommodation syndrome. *Child Abuse & Neglect, 7*, 177–193.

Teicher, M., Andersen, S., & Polcari, S. (2002). Developmental neurobiology of childhood stress and trauma. *Psychiatric Clinics of North America, 25, Special Issue: Recent advances in the study of biological alterations in post-traumatic stress disorder*, 397–426.

Townsend, J. (2006). *Boundaries with teens: When to say yes, how to say no.* Grand Rapids, MI: Zondervan.

Ullman, S. (2003). Social reactions to child sexual abuse disclosures: A critical review. *Journal of Child Sexual Abuse, 12*(10), 89–122.

van der Kolk, B. (1994). The body keeps score: Memory & the evolving psycho-biology of post traumatic stress. *Harvard Review of Psychiatry, 1*(5), 253–265.

van der Kolk, B. (2010, February). New frontiers in trauma treatment. Workshop presented in Atlanta, GA.

Vieth, V., & Smith, S. (2010, July). *Understanding the dynamics of child sexual abuse, and the role of these dynamics in a case of child pornography.* Savannah, GA: When Words Matter Conference.

Weierich, M., & Nock, M. (2008). Posttraumatic stress symptoms mediate the relation between childhood sexual abuse and non-suicidal self-injury. *Journal of Consulting and Clinical Psychology, 76*, 39–44.

CHAPTER 21

Understanding and Treating Adolescents With Illegal Sexual Behavior

SUSAN R. SCHMIDT, BARBARA L. BONNER, and MARK CHAFFIN

INTRODUCTION

T HE SEXUAL ABUSE of children is recognized as a major social problem in the United States. Statistics from a 2008 report showed that approximately 89,000 females were the victims of rape (U.S. Department of Justice [USDOJ], 2009) and more than 70,000 children were sexually abused (U.S. Department of Health and Human Services [USDHHS], 2010). It is of significant concern that youth under age 18 account for more than one-third (35.6%) of the cases involved with the police for sex offenses against minors (Finkelhor, Ormrod, & Chaffin, 2009). This statistic has been consistent over the past 20 years, indicating that juveniles are responsible for a large number of sexual assaults against minors every year. Male adolescents are predominantly the aggressor in these cases, with female adolescents accounting for approximately 6% of juveniles who commit sex offenses (USDOJ, 2004).

Adolescents with illegal sexual behavior are defined as girls and boys from age 13 to 18 who have committed a sexual act that is illegal in the jurisdiction where the behavior occurred. The term *juvenile sex offender* is a broader label that includes all youth under age 18 with illegal sexual behavior. The label *adolescent sex offender* has long been used for youth ages 13 to 18 in treatment programs, research, and the literature on this population. More recently, professionals working with these adolescents have recommended the term *sex offender* not be used with this population as it ties the youth too closely to adult sex offenders, a population shown to be substantially different from adolescents. Terms currently being used to describe these youth are *adolescents with illegal sexual behavior (AISB)* or *juveniles with sexually abusive or sexually harmful behavior.*

The research on this group of problematic youth extends back more than 50 years. Fortunately, in the mid-1980s, interest in addressing AISB from a more scientific approach developed (Chaffin, Letourneau, & Silovsky, 2002) and the research base has continued to grow, with more than 200 articles currently available. In recent years, research on AISB has focused on identifying group characteristics, establishing AISB typologies, developing methods for assessing risk for reoffense, and evaluating treatment methods.

AISB CHARACTERISTICS

Research has documented that adolescents with illegal sexual behavior are a heterogeneous group with differences in several characteristics including: victim age, gender, and relationship to the adolescent (Fehrenbach, Smith, Monastersky, & Deigher, 1986; Finkelhor et al., 2009); level of violence (Hunter, Hazelwood, & Slesinger, 2000); history of abuse (Veneziano, Veneziano, & LeGrand, 2000); and risk for recidivism (Kemper & Kistner, 2007; Parks & Bard, 2006). The Association for the Treatment of Sexual Abusers (ATSA, 2000) has adopted a position, stating,

> Recent research suggests that there are important distinctions between juvenile and adult sexual offenders, as well as the finding that not all juvenile sexual offenders are the same. There is little evidence to support the assumption that a majority of juvenile sexual offenders are destined to become adult sexual offenders. Moreover, the significantly lower frequency of more extreme forms of sexual aggression, fantasy, and compulsivity among juveniles than among adults suggests that many juveniles have sexual behavior problems that may be more amenable to intervention.

In comparison to adult sex offenders, AISB have fewer numbers of victims (Miranda & Corcoran, 2000), are less driven by deviant sexual interests (Becker, Hunter, Stein, & Kaplan, 1989; Hunter & Becker, 1994; Hunter, Goodwin, & Becker, 1994), rarely engage in sexually predatory behaviors or meet the criteria for pedophilia (APA, 2000), and seldom have long-term tendencies to commit sexual offenses (Caldwell, 2007). In addition, juveniles are more likely than adult offenders to commit illegal sexual behavior in groups (U.S. Department of Justice, 2004), suggesting that peers may be as influential in the commission of juvenile sexual delinquency as they are in nonsexual delinquency (Finkelhor et al., 2009).

A study of 13,471 juveniles by the U.S. Department of Justice (2004) revealed the following information about adolescents with illegal sexual behavior histories. Although about 75% of youth acted alone, approximately 25% had one or more offenders involved. The juveniles sexually involved family acquaintances (63%), family members (25%), strangers (2.5%), and about 9% of the victims were not identified. The most common offense was fondling a child (49%), but rape (24%) and sodomy (12.5%) accounted for a significant number of offenses. The remaining offenses were sexual assault with an object (4.7%) and a nonforcible sex offense (9.5%). The offenses were most often against female children (79%), occurred in a home (69%), and happened throughout the day: morning (27%), afternoon (43%), evening (25%), and night (5%). In this study, 30% of the cases involved an arrest of the youth.

Several typologies have been developed to define subtypes of adolescent males with illegal sexual behavior, from a clinically based model by O'Brien and Bera (1986) to a research based approach by Hunter (2006). The typologies can be used to understand the differences in the etiology of the behavior, case management, level of supervision needed, responsiveness to treatment, and risk for recidivism. For example, differences have been found in adolescents who assault peers and those who molest younger children, that is, those who molest children are younger in age, less socially competent, have less peer sexual activity, and fewer conduct problems (Krauth, 1998). Hunter (2006) has proposed that adolescents who molest young children, type Adolescent Onset-Nonparaphilic, are likely to have psychosocial inadequacies, expect ridicule and rejection from their peers, prefer the company of younger children, and typically abuse young females. This subtype of behavior is viewed as experimental and opportunistic, as opposed to repetitive and planned in nature. A second group, Lifestyle Persistent, engage in oppositional and aggressive behavior as youngsters, offend against young and adolescent females, and have the highest rates of arrests for nonsexual offenses post treatment. A third group, Early Adolescent Onset-Paraphilic, is seen as developing paraphilic interests, with more young male victims and the highest rates of arrests after treatment for sexual re-offenses.

To date, Mathews and colleagues (1997) have provided the only typology to differentiate between subgroups of female AISB. Based on a sample of 67 girls, they identified three subgroups. The first group included adolescent girls motivated by sexual curiosity who commit a limited number of offenses against nonrelated children. They were described as naive and sexually inexperienced. The second group was comprised of adolescent girls with personal victimization histories who abuse younger children in a manner similar to their own victimization. They had moderate histories of abuse and personal difficulties but appeared to be functioning relatively well interpersonally. The third group included adolescent girls who engaged in more frequent and extensive illegal sexual behavior with children. They had more severe individual and familial dysfunction and significant early personal victimization histories. More comprehensive studies are needed to further evaluate the applicability of this typology within the larger population of female AISB.

RECIDIVISM AND RISK ASSESSMENT

Professionals working with AISB, including mental health providers, probation officers, judges, and district attorneys, have been concerned with the level of risk AISB present after treatment (Worling & Langstrom, 2006). Instruments to assess risk for sexual reoffense have been developed and are in the process of establishing validity and reliability (Prentky, Harris, Frizell, & Righthand, 2000; Prentky & Righthand, 2003; Worling & Curwen, 2001). The following instruments are under development to assess risk in AISB:

- *Estimate of Risk of Adolescent Sexual Offense Recidivism-2 (ERASOR-2)* (Worling & Curwen, 2001). The ERASOR-2 is a 25-item checklist designed to assess the short-term risk of sexual re-offense by youth ages 12 to 18. There are five scales: Sexual Interest Attitudes, and Behavior; Historical Sexual Assaults; Psychosocial Functioning; Family-Environmental Functioning; and Treatment; both static ($N = 9$) and dynamic ($N = 16$) factors are assessed. The initial data documented the reliability of the item composition of the original ERASOR (Worling, 2004) and research continues on this instrument. The authors state that this instrument is under development and should not be utilized to predict recidivism at this time.
- *Juvenile Sex Offender Assessment Protocol-II (J-SOAP-II)* (Prentky & Righthand, 2003). This is a 28-item experimental instrument divided into four scales: Sexual Drive Preoccupation (8 items), Impulsive/Antisocial Behavior (8 items), Intervention (7 items), and Community Stability/Adjustment (5 items). The items are scored from (0) absence of the risk factor to (2) clear evidence of the trait as described in the manual. Acceptable reliability and validity data are based on an earlier version of the J-SOAP (Prentky

& Righthand, 1998), and item modifications were made in 2003. It is noted that the predictive validity of the instrument has been limited by the low base rates of sexual recidivism by adolescents.

Another instrument that has been used to predict recidivism in adolescents is described below.

- *Psychopathy Checklist: Youth Version (PCL-YV)* (Forth, Kosson, & Hare, 2003). This is a 20-item instrument designed to measure traits that may contribute to the development of adult psychopathology. It is divided into four scales: Interpersonal (4 items), Affective (4 items), Behavioral (5 items), and Antisocial (5 items) and two additional items. The Psychopathy Checklist-Revised (PCL-R, 2nd edition; Hare, 2003) is used with youth aged 12 to 18 and the items are scored from (0) absence of trait to (2) trait is present. It is recommended that the clinical application of the PCL-YV be based on a file review and a clinical interview. The PCL-YV has been used for research purposes (Gretton, McBride, Hare, O'Shaughnessy, & Runka, 2001; Murrie & Cornell, 2002) and the manual reports data showing associations between the PCL-YV results and adolescent recidivism (Forth et al., 2003).

The current literature on AISB provides limited information on the assessment and treatment of adolescent girls. At present, there is no scientifically validated risk assessment system designed for use with this population. Although the risk-assessment tools previously described are being developed for use with male AISB, these instruments will require further validation to determine their applicability to adolescent girls. Caution is suggested in the use of these tools as they may overestimate the relevance of certain risk factors in girls and may underestimate or fail to identify factors that may be unique to recidivism with female AISB.

Contrary to common societal perceptions, the overall sexual recidivism rate for AISB who receive treatment is low in most U.S. settings as compared to adults. Two recent studies on recidivism of institutionalized adolescents aged 12 to 17 (Parks & Bard, 2006) and 12 to 19 (Kemper & Kistner, 2007) compared three subgroups: adolescents who had illegal sexual behavior (a) with children, (b) with peers or adults, and (c) with both or mixed type offenses. The data reflected the youths' sexual and nonsexual recidivism rates. Kemper and Kistner found that mixed type offenders were less likely to successfully complete treatment, but this group did not differ in recidivism from the other two subgroups. After approximately five years, the sexual recidivism rates for the three groups were 8.16% for AISB against children, 1.32% against peers/adults, and 4.76% for mixed type offenses, for an average recidivism rate of 4.74%. The nonsexual recidivism rates were much higher, reflecting previous findings. For adolescents with illegal sexual behavior with children, the re-offense rate for nonsexual illegal behavior was 38.78%, with peers/adults, the rate was 44.74%, and against both types of victims, 38.01%, for an average of 40.5%.

Parks and Bard (2006) found that the average of the three groups' recidivism rates was 6.4% for sexual offenses and 30.1% for nonsexual offenses. Using the J-SOAP-II and the Psychopathy Checklist: Youth Version (PCL:YV) (Forth et al., 2003), the authors found significant differences among the three subgroups. The mixed type adolescents consistently had higher scores on risk factor items compared with the other two groups. The Impulsive/Antisocial Behavior scale on the J-SOAP-II and the Interpersonal and Antisocial factors on the PCL-YV were found to be significant predictors of sexual recidivism. The results of these recent studies underscore two findings that have been consistent in the research literature: (a) sexual recidivism rates for AISB are typically below 10%, and (b) the risk for nonsexual recidivism is significantly higher than for future illegal sexual behavior in adolescents. Although adolescents treated for sex-offending behavior do not appear to re-offend sexually with high frequency, they do have a high rate of involvement in other types of delinquent behavior such as shoplifting, drug/alcohol abuse, nonsexual assault, operating a motor vehicle without a license, and so on.

TREATMENT

Current professional consensus regards community placement and out-patient treatment as appropriate for most adolescents who have engaged in illegal sexual behavior. With appropriate adult supervision, the majority of AISB can safely live in the community, participate in out-patient treatment and attend public school with minimal risk to society. Currently, there are many AISB who are attending public schools and participate in school activities, such as sports, the band, and school clubs without jeopardizing the safety of other students. There may be cases in which school personnel need to have information about the offense, and in fact, there are states that require schools to be notified. However, some AISB may require residential, inpatient, or incarcerated placements that can provide more intensive supervision and treatment. These adolescents pose higher societal risks due to factors such as having committed extensive or violent sexual and/or nonsexual offenses, possessing more focused and pervasive illegal sexual interests, re-offending after treatment participation, or having significant comorbid mental health diagnoses requiring more intensive treatment. The decisions about where a youth is placed to receive treatment should be made on a case-by-case basis and depend on community safety and the treatment needs of the adolescent.

During the mid- to late 1980s, AISB treatment programs began to develop and to proliferate rapidly. Early treatment programs for adolescents were often based on adult sex offender models, with the assumption that adolescents with illegal sexual behavior shared the same etiology, motivation, and pathology as adults. These approaches are easily recognized by their focus on deviant internal sexual factors (such as sexual fantasies, sexual arousal patterns and distorted thinking, use of behavioral conditioning techniques); their emphasis on long-term management of enduring or compulsive tendencies (such as "cycles" or relapse prevention, or long-term lifestyle restrictions); their distrust of self-report (such as use of routine polygraph examinations or regular confrontation); and their conceptualization of the behavior as highly planned and pathologically motivated. Many AISB treatment programs based on the adult deviancy model share the perspective that treatment needs to be long-term (i.e., several years) and often require some period of confinement, although for AISB confinement is typically in a residential facility rather than an adult prison.

A wide variety of clinical treatment approaches for AISB have been described in the literature, including behavioral conditioning approaches (Kaplan, Morales, & Becker, 1993; Weinrott, Riggan, & Frothingham, 1997), pharmacological approaches (Bradford, 1993; Galli, Raute, McConville, & McElroy, 1998), family systems approaches (Bentovim, 1998), rational-emotive therapy (Whitford & Parr, 1995), music and art therapy (Gerber, 1994; Skaggs, 1997), "cycle" based approaches (Ryan, Lane, Davis, & Issac, 1987), cognitive-behavioral approaches (Becker & Kaplan, 1993; Kahn & LaFond, 1988), relapse prevention approaches (Gray & Pithers, 1993; Steen, 1993), and ecological multisystemic approaches (Swenson, Schoenwald, Randall, Henggeler, & Kaufman, 1998).

Many current treatment programs are group-based cognitive-behavioral interventions lasting from 8 to 28 months. These approaches focus on changing attitudes and belief systems in areas such as victim empathy and cognitive distortions or thinking errors. Cognitive-behavioral approaches may also focus on increasing social skills, improving anger management, and teaching self-control techniques. In some programs, these may be combined with a relapse prevention approach along with behavioral approaches focused on changing arousal patterns where this is indicated.

Treatment is often carried out in a peer group environment (i.e., outpatient therapy, group homes, specialized residential units), although some findings have raised concerns that programs which aggregate delinquent youth together may have negative effects due to the risks associated with increased delinquent peer influences and socialization into delinquent behavior and belief patterns (Chamberlain & Reid, 1998).

A number of diverse treatment programs have published single group outcome data, but there are currently no published studies comparing the outcomes for AISB randomly assigned to treatment versus no treatment conditions. The available scientific evidence cannot determine whether treatment is helpful, harmful, or inert. However, there is evidence that AISB who complete treatment fare better than a comparison group of those who do not, who drop out of treatment, or who are expelled from treatment (Worling & Curwen, 2000). Low re-offense rates are the rule across a range of treatment approaches. This consistency of fairly positive outcomes across a diversity of approaches stands in contrast to the common opinion that only highly specialized and intensive approaches are effective and to the general prognostic pessimism evident in some policies and practices with AISB.

The evidence-based practice philosophy, which continues to gain momentum across service settings, is an effort to move practice toward those interventions with sound empirical support. The evidence-based philosophy relies on first testing interventions in highly controlled randomized trials to determine if they are efficacious, then testing their effectiveness in field dissemination trials before taking the models to scale in large-scale field settings. Because of its reliance on clinical trial methodologies, the evidence-based approach emphasizes many features found more often in research settings than in field settings—sticking to a specific protocol, assuring high protocol fidelity, using targeted interventions based on a specific theory or model, and stringently evaluating hard outcomes, such as recidivism rates over time.

Several evidence-based delinquency interventions have been developed and disseminated over the past decade (Muller & Mihalic, 1999). For example, multisystemic therapy (MST), a community-based treatment model developed in the early 1990s, was one of the first delinquency interventions to demonstrate efficacy in a series of randomized trials. Other approaches, such as functional family therapy (FFT), and Chamberlain's Treatment Foster Care (TFC) model have strong evidence supporting their efficacy. Many current evidence-based models are quite distinct from the traditional deviancy-focused sex offender treatment model on which many AISB programs are based. First, most are far shorter term, even those designed for severe delinquents. Second, most current evidence-based models do not limit their focus to intra-individual factors, but rather focus more broadly on the youth's family and social environment (e.g., parental supervision, school engagement, peer group affiliations, parent-child communication).

These types of models are increasingly drawing the attention of AISB treatment providers for several reasons. First, it is clear that sexual behavior and sexual offense recidivism are not the sole problems for many of these youth. Across numerous treatment outcome studies, it is clear that nonsexual delinquent behavior is vastly more prevalent than sexual recidivism among AISB. Also, many AISB present with multiple problems in addition to their sexual behavior, including learning disabilities, social isolation, ADHD, drug or alcohol problems, family instability or conflict, school or academic problems, delinquent peer affiliations, limited social or courtship skills, or general difficulties with judgment and self-control. The youth's illegal sexual behavior should be a significant component of therapy, but other areas may be of equal importance, such as treatment for PTSD, depression, or substance use. For example, an empirically validated abuse-focused clinical intervention, such as Trauma-Focused Cognitive-Behavioral Therapy (TF-CBT) (Cohen, Mannarino, & Deblinger, 2006), should be incorporated into the treatment plan of AISB experiencing posttraumatic symptomatology related to childhood victimization.

A growing body of research suggests that multisystemic therapy (MST) (Henggeler & Borduin, 1990; Henggeler, Schoenwald, Borduin, Rowland, & Cunningham, 1998), a broad ecologically focused delinquency intervention, is effective with AISB (Henggeler et al., 2009; Letourneau et al., 2009). MST is an evidence-based treatment intervention for youth with chronic delinquency or substance abuse problems. The intervention targets the improvement of caregiver supervision and parenting skills through the provision of therapeutic services in the family's natural environment such as the home, neighborhood, or school setting. The recent effectiveness trial by Letourneau and her colleagues (2009) compared an adapted version of MST to community-based cognitive-behavioral group interventions. The adaptation includes addressing youth and caregiver denial about the offense, safety planning to minimize the youth's access to potential victims, and the promotion of age-appropriate and normative social experiences with peers. Compared to youth in the community group programs, youth participating in MST demonstrated significant reductions in sexual behavior problems, delinquency, substance use, externalizing symptoms and out-of-home placements. Approaches such as MST appear to be especially promising for AISB who have multiple problems including both sexual and nonsexual behavior problems in combination with general delinquency.

In sum, many AISB have general behavioral problems, not solely or even predominately the specialized sexual problems often assumed by the traditional deviancy-oriented model. Consequently, AISB treatment is increasingly taking a holistic or ecological approach, focusing on broad and general areas and including sexual and nonsexual treatment content. This might include greater involvement of parents or parent substitutes and families in treatment; less focus on the sexual offense; and increased focus on general behavior, decision making, and on developing specific social, behavioral, and interpersonal competencies. Given the variability of AISB, it is recommended that treatment and placement decisions are made on a case-by-case basis to best meet the needs of each adolescent (Mathews et al., 1997).

CONTROVERSIAL PRACTICES

Ethical issues arise in many areas of mental health practice. The problems are often magnified when professionals are working with children and adolescents and increase significantly when working with youth who are court-ordered to treatment. In providing services to adolescents with illegal sexual behavior, mental health providers become involved in issues not dealt with in a typical practice. They are often expected to collaborate with the juvenile justice system; be involved in making decisions affecting the day-to-day lives of adolescents and their families; address concerns about community safety; and handle highly sensitive legal information. Clinicians who provide treatment to adolescents with illegal sexual behavior need to be aware of accepted practices and interventions with this population and the limits of the available knowledge.

Providers need to know that many of the methods currently used in the treatment of AISB are based on work with adult sex offenders, including intrusive treatment techniques that have not been empirically tested with youth aged 13 to 18. Second, as noted earlier, there are no instruments currently available with established validity and reliability to predict the risk of future illegal sexual behavior in adolescents. Further, only one treatment approach has been evaluated for effectiveness (Letourneau et al., 2009) and there is not a strong scientific basis that one treatment approach is superior to another for an individual adolescent. Based on these limitations of the current knowledge base, clinicians should be cautious in stating that specific treatment approaches are recommended over other approaches, predicting the risk of recidivism, and utilizing highly intrusive assessment or treatment techniques.

Several areas that present ethical concerns when working with adolescents with illegal sexual behavior are addressed below along with suggested practices (Hunter & Chaffin, 2008).

- *Clinical competency*: It is recommended that mental health providers be licensed to provide mental health services and have specific experience and knowledge to work with this population. This includes extensive training and experience in working with adolescents in general, knowledge of adolescent development and expectations, and specific expertise in working with AISB. If a state has a certification process for clinicians working with this population, the provider should be licensed and certified. For trainees or clinicians beginning to provide treatment to AISB, it is recommended that they provide services only if they are closely supervised by an experienced licensed professional who has expertise in this area.
- *Limits of confidentiality*: Clinicians should understand and clearly explain, verbally and in writing, their role and the limits of confidentiality to adolescent clients and their parents/guardians before conducting any form of interview, administering assessment instruments, or initiating treatment. Clients should understand that, based on each state's mandatory reporting laws, confidentiality will *not* be maintained if previously unknown or unreported abuse or neglect is disclosed. Clients need to be fully informed of the clinician's legal duty to report suspected maltreatment and duty-to-warn requirements.

  The adolescent and parents/guardians should give written consent for the clinician to communicate freely and openly with juvenile justice personnel and any other individuals approved by the family, such as a grandparent who may provide supervision or the adolescent's attorney. For all other individuals, such as school personnel, victims, or family members, confidentiality will be maintained unless a release of information is signed by the family.
- *Gender issues*: The research on adolescent females with illegal sexual behavior is quite limited. The extant literature and clinical observations suggest that the development of illegal sexual behavior in females may be different from males and this should be taken into account when conducting an assessment or planning a treatment approach. To date, there is no test or instrument with scientific validity and reliability to determine the level of risk of recidivism for female AISB. The instruments developed for males (J-SOAP II, ERASOR 2, PCL-YV) may overestimate the applicability of certain

factors in predicting recidivism for females and their use is not recommended. Current clinical observations suggest that male and female AISB may have different treatment needs based on victimization history, sexual health, and the development of relationships (Grayston, Mathews, & DeLucy, 1999).

- *Conducting clinical assessments for treatment*: Providers may be requested to conduct a clinical assessment of an AISB. The assessment can utilize a clinical interview of the youth and family members and psychological testing to determine the youth's cognitive and general psychological functioning, the youth's and family's amenability to treatment, the necessary level of care and supervision, and the youth's treatment goals. The recommended time for this evaluation is *after* adjudication by the court but *before* disposition. The information from the assessment can be useful to the court in making decisions about the appropriateness of outpatient treatment, placement in the home, need for residential care, and so on. Caution should be used when conducting assessments for treatment planning *prior* to adjudication, particularly when an adolescent has not made a statement regarding guilt, as the assessment may elicit information that could be used against the youth in court.

  Clinical assessments should not, and in fact cannot, be used to determine whether an adolescent is guilty or not guilty of any particular charge.

- *Conducting risk assessments for recidivism*: As described earlier, there are instruments under development. However, to date there is no risk assessment procedure that can validly predict whether a specific adolescent is at significant risk to reoffend sexually. All risk assessment reports should include explicit language that documents the current limitations of the accuracy of risk prediction for adolescents. Providers should use caution when making judgments about a particular adolescent's level of risk for reoffending sexually, particularly when their opinion will be used to determine the youth's placement and treatment intervention. It is imperative that clinicians remain up-to-date with the developing research and assessment instruments in order to provide ethically sound services to this population.

- *Use of intrusive assessment or treatment procedures*: The use of intrusive procedures, such as aversive conditioning, masturbatory reconditioning, a plethysmograph assessment, and a polygraph examination, should be used with caution, on an individual basis, and only after a careful review of the limited research using these techniques with adolescents. It is recommended that adolescents and their parents/guardians sign a specific consent form to provide approval for the use of intrusive assessment or treatment procedures. The form should clearly describe the potential risks and benefits of the procedures and the availability of conventional or less intrusive procedures that could be used.

The use of a polygraph is not part of customary mental health treatment. Therefore, specific ethical issues, such as informed consent, should be considered when using this examination technique. It is recommended that the procedure be used only with the knowledge of the court and full informed consent of the adolescent and the parents/guardians. Although half of all U.S. treatment programs for AISB use the procedure (McGrath, Cumming, Burchard, Zeoli, & Ellerby, 2009), the validity of the polygraph is not scientifically established (Chaffin, 2010). When considering the ethical issues, this is, beneficence, nonmaleficence, respect for autonomy and justice, in relation to using the polygraph with AISB, this practice is viewed with substantial concern and is, consequently, not used in our clinical practice. Future research may clarify the ethical concerns related to requiring adolescents to take polygraph examinations. Clearly, it is considered unethical to offer, or of more concern, require treatments that do not deliver benefits, and the validity and benefits from polygraph use with AISB have not been established.

Plethysmograph assessments are a highly intrusive technique and should be restricted to a limited number of adolescents who are older, have a history of repetitive sexual offending, or who have shown highly unusual sexual behaviors. There are no norms established for the results of a plethysmograph assessment with AISB. There are less-intrusive techniques available that use visual reaction time to assess sexual interest patterns, which may be useful with adolescents.

CONCLUSION

In summary, clinicians working with adolescents with illegal sexual behavior are faced with numerous problems in providing ethical, effective treatment and services to these youth. As this is a developing field, it is recommended that clinicians stay current on the literature regarding assessment and treatment of the population, utilize treatment approaches that are considered best practices with adolescents, and be aware of the ethical concerns that exist in this treatment field.

REFERENCES

American Psychiatric Association (APA). (2000). *Diagnostic and statistical manual of mental disorders* (*DSM-IV-TR* 4th ed.). Washington, DC: Author.

Association for the Treatment of Sexual Abuses. (2000). *The effective legal management of juvenile sexual offenders*. Retrieved from http://atsa.com/ppjuvenile.html

Becker, J.V., Hunter, J., Stein, R., & Kaplan, M. S. (1989). Factors associated with erectile responses in adolescent sex offenders. *Journal of Psychopathology and Behavioral Assessment, 11*, 353–362.

Becker, J. V., & Kaplan, M. S. (1993). Cognitive behavioral treatment of the juvenile sex offender. In H. E. Barbaree (Ed.), *The juvenile sex offender* (pp. 289–319). New York, NY: Guilford Press.

Bentovim, A. (1998). A family systemic approach to work with young sex offenders. *Irish Journal of Psychology, 19*, 119–135.

Bradford, J. (1993). The pharmacological treatment of the adolescent sex offender. In H. E. Barbaree (Ed.), *The juvenile sex offender* (pp. 289–319). New York, NY: Guilford Press.

Caldwell, M. (2007). Sexual offense adjudication and sexual recidivism among juvenile offenders. *Sexual Abuse: A Journal of Research and Treatment, 19*, 107–113.

Chaffin, M. (2010). The case of juvenile polygraphy as a clinical ethics dilemma. *Sexual Abuse: A Journal of Research and Treatment*. Retrieved at ATSA October 15, 2010, from sax.sagepub.com on

Chaffin, M., Letourneau, E., & Silovsky, J. F. (2002). Adults, adolescents, and children who sexually abuse children: A developmental perspective. In J. E. B. Myers, L. Berliner, J. Briere, C. T. Hendrix, C. Jenny, & T. A. Reid (Eds.), *The APSAC handbook on child maltreatment*, (2nd ed., pp. 205–232). Thousand Oaks, CA: Sage.

Chamberlain, P., & Reid, J. (1998). Comparison of two community alternatives to incarceration of chronic juvenile offenders. *Journal of Consulting and Clinical Psychology, 66*, 624–633.

Cohen, J. A., Mannarino, A. P., & Deblinger, E. (2006). *Treating trauma and traumatic grief in children and adolescents*. New York, NY: Guilford Press.

Fehrenbach, P. A., Smith, W., Monastersky, C., & Deisher, R. W. (1986). Adolescent sexual offenders: Offender and offense characteristics. *American Journal of Orthopsychiatry, 56*, 225–233.

Finkelhor, D., Ormrod, R., & Chaffin, M. (2009). Juveniles who commit sex offenses against minors. *Juvenile Justice Bulletin*. www.ojp.usdoj.gov/ojjdp

Forth, A. E., Kosson, D. S., & Hare, R. D. (2003). *The psychopathy checklist: Youth version*. Toronto, Ontario, Canada: Multi-Health Systems.

Galli, V. B., Raute, N. J., McConville, B. J., & McElroy, S. L. (1998). An adolescent male with multiple paraphilias successfully treated with fluoxetine. *Journal of Child and Adolescent Psychopharmacology, 8*, 195–197.

Gerber, J. (1994). The use of art therapy in juvenile sex offender specific treatment. *Arts in Psychotherapy, 21*, 367–374.

Gray, A. S., & Pithers, W. D. (1993). Relapse prevention with sexually aggressive adolescents and children: Expanding treatment and supervision. In H. E. Barbaree (Ed.), *The juvenile sex offender* (pp. 289–319). New York, NY: Guilford Press.

Grayston, A. D., Mathews, R., & DeLuca, R. V. (1999). Female perpetrators of child sexual abuse: A review of the clinical and empirical literature. *Aggression and Violent Behavior, 4,* 93–106.

Gretton, H. M., McBride, M., Hare, R. D., O'Shaughnessy, R., & Kumka, G. (2001). Psychopathy and recidivism in adolescent sex offenders. *Criminal Justice and Behavior, 28,* 427–449.

Hare, R. D. (2003). *The Hare psychopathy checklist-revised* (2nd ed.). Toronto, Canada: Multi-Health Systems.

Henggeler, S. W., & Borduin, C. M. (1990). *Family therapy and beyond: A multi-systemic approach to treating the behavior problems of children and adolescents.* Pacific Grove, CA: Brooks/Cole.

Henggeler, S. W., Letourneau, E. J., Chapman, J. E., Borduin, C. M., Schewe, P. A., & McCart, M. R. (2009). Mediators of change for multisystemic therapy with juvenile sexual offenders. *Journal of Consulting and Clinical Psychology, 77, 3,* 451–462.

Henggeler, S. W., Schoenwald, S. K., Borduin, C. M., Rowland, M. D., & Cunningham, P. B. (1998). *Multisystemic treatment of antisocial behavior in children and adolescents.* New York, NY: Guilford Press.

Hunter, J. A. (2006). Understanding diversity in juvenile sexual offenders: Implications for assessment, treatment, and legal management. In R. E. Longo & D. S. Prescott (Eds.), *Current perspectives: Working with sexually aggressive youth and youth with sexual behavior problems* (pp. 63–77). Holyoke, MA: NEARI Press.

Hunter, J. A., & Becker, J. V. (1994). The role of deviant sexual arousal in juvenile sexual offending: Etiology, evaluation, and treatment. *Criminal Justice and Behavior, 21,* 132–149.

Hunter, J. A., & Chaffin, M. (2008). *Ethical issues in the assessment and treatment of adolescents with illegal sexual behavior.* National Center on Sexual Behavior of Youth www.NCSBY.org

Hunter, J. A., Goodwin, D. W., & Becker, J. V. (1994). The relationship between phallometrically measured deviant sexual arousal and clinical characteristics in juvenile sexual offenders. *Behavior Research and Therapy, 32,* 533–538.

Hunter, J. A., Hazelwood, R. R., & Slesinger, D. (2000). Juvenile-perpetrated sex crimes: Patterns of offending and predictors of violence. *Journal of Family Violence, 15,* 81–93.

Kahn, T. J., & LaFond, M. A. (1988). Treatment of the adolescent sexual offender. *Child & Adolescent Social Work, 5,* 135–148.

Kaplan, M. S., Morales, M., & Becker, J. V. (1993). The impact of verbal satiation of adolescent sex offenders: A preliminary report. *Journal of Child Abuse, 2,* 81–88.

Kemper, T. S., & Kistner, J. A. (2007). Offense history and recidivism in three victim-age-based groups of juvenile sex offenders. *Sexual Abuse: A Journal of Research and Treatment, 19*(4), 409–423.

Krauth, A. A. (1998). A comparative study of male juvenile sex offenders. *Dissertation Abstracts International*, 58, 4455B.

Letourneau, E. J., Henggeler, S. W., Borduin, C. M., Schewe, P. A., McCart, M. R., Chapman, J. E., & Saldana, L. (2009). Multisystemic therapy for juvenile sexual offenders: 1-year results from a randomized effectiveness trial. *Journal of Family Psychology*, 23, 89–102.

Mathews, R., Hunter, J. A., & Vuz, J. (1997). Juvenile female sexual offenders: Clinical characteristics and treatment issues. *Sexual Abuse: A Journal of Research and Treatment*, 9, 187–199.

Miranda, A. O., & Corcoran, C. L. (2000). Comparison of perpetration characteristics between male juvenile and adult sexual offenders: Preliminary results. *Sexual Abuse: A Journal of Research and Treatment*, 12, 179–188.

McGrath, R. J., Cumming, G. F., Burchard, B. L., Zeoli, S., & Ellerby, L. (2009). *Current practices and emerging trends in sexual abuser management: The safer society 2009 North American survey*. Brandon, VT: Safer Society Press.

Muller, J., & Mihalic, S. (1999). *Blueprints: A violence prevention initiative* (OJJDP Fact Sheet #110). Washington DC: U.S. Department of Justice, Office of Justice Programs, Office of Juvenile Justice and Delinquency Prevention.

Murrie, D. C., & Cornell, D. G. (2002). Psychopathy screening of incarcerated juveniles: A comparison of measures. *Psychological Assessment*, 14, 390–396.

O'Brien, M. J., & Bera, W. (1986, Fall). Adolescent sexual offenders: A descriptive typology. *Preventing Sexual Abuse*, 4, 1–4.

Parks, G. A., & Bard, D. E., (2006). Risk factors for adolescent sex offender recidivism: Evaluation of predictive factors and comparison of three groups based upon victim type. *Sexual Abuse: A Journal of Research and Treatment*, 18, 319–342.

Prentky, R. A., Harris, B., Frizzell, K., & Righthand, S. (2000). An actuarial procedure for assessing risk with juvenile sex offenders. *Sexual Abuse: A Journal of Research and Treatment*, 12(2), 71–93.

Prentky, R. A., & Righthand, S. (1998). *Juvenile sex offender assessment protocol manual*. Unpublished Manuscript.

Prentky, R. A., & Righthand, S. (2003). *Juvenile sex offender assessment protocol-II manual*. Unpublished manuscript.

Ryan, G., Lane, S., Davis, J., & Isaac, C. (1987). Juvenile sex offenders: Development and correction. *Child Abuse & Neglect*, 11, 385–395.

Skaggs, R. (1997). Music-centered creative arts in a sex offender treatment program for male juveniles. *Music Therapy Perspectives*, 15, 73–78.

Steen, C. (1993). *The relapse prevention workbook for youth in treatment*. Brandon, VT: Safer Society Press.

Swenson, C. C., Schoenwald, S. K., Randall, J., Henggeler, S. W., & Kaufman, K. L. (1998). Changing the social ecologies of adolescent sexual offenders: Implications of the success of multisystemic therapy in treating serious antisocial behavior in adolescents. *Child Maltreatment*, 3, 330–338.

U.S. Department of Justice, Federal Bureau of Investigation. (2004). *National Incident-Based Reporting System, 2004*. Compiled by the U.S. Department of

Justice, Federal Bureau of Investigation. ICPSR04468-v1. Ann Arbor, MI: Inter-university Consortium for Political and Social Research, 2006–09–20. doi: 10.3886/ICP SR04468.

Veneziano, C., Veneziano, L., & LeGrand, S. (2000). The relationship between adolescent sex offender behaviors and victim characteristics with prior victimization. *Journal of Interpersonal Violence, 15*, 363–374.

Weinrott, M. R., Riggan, M., & Frothingham, S. (1997). Reducing deviant arousal in juvenile sex offenders using vicarious sensitization. *Journal of Interpersonal Violence, 12*, 704–728.

Whitford, R., & Parr, V. (1995). Uses of rational emotive behavior therapy with juvenile sex offenders. *Journal of Rational-Emotive & Cognitive Behavior Therapy, 13*, 273–282.

Worling, J. R. (2004). The estimate of risk of adolescent sexual offense recidivism (ERASOR): Preliminary psychometric data. *Sexual Abuse: Journal of Research and Treatment, 16*(3), 235–254.

Worling, J. R., & Curwen, T. (2000). Adolescent sexual offender recidivism: Success of specialized treatment and implications for risk prediction. *Child Abuse & Neglect, 24*, 965–982.

Worling, J. R., & Curwen, T. (2001). *The "ERASOR": Estimate of risk of adolescent sexual offense recidivism, version 2.0.* Unpublished manuscript. Toronto, Canada: Ontario Ministry of Community and Social Services.

Worling, J. R., & Langstrom, N. (2006). Risk of sexual recidivism in juveniles who sexually offend: Correlates and assessment. In H. E. Barbaree & W. L. Marshall (Eds.), *The juvenile sex offender* (2nd ed., pp. 219–247). New York, NY: Guilford Press.

U.S. Department of Health and Human Services (USDHHS) (2010). *Child maltreatment 2008.* Washington, DC: U.S. Government Printing Office.

U.S. Department of Justice. (2009). *Crime in the United States. 2008.* Washington, DC: U.S. Government Printing Office.

U.S. Department of Justice, Federal Bureau of Investigation. (2004). *National incident-based reporting system, 2004.* Compiled by the U.S. Department of Justice, Federal Bureau of Investigation. ICPSR04468-v1. Ann Arbor, MI: Inter-university Consortium for Political and Social Research, 2006–09–20. doi: 10.3886/ICPSR04468.

CHAPTER 22

Cultural Issues in Child Sexual Abuse Intervention and Prevention

LISA ARONSON FONTES and CAROL A. PLUMMER

INTRODUCTION

IN THIS CHAPTER we introduce ideas about how to work with culturally diverse individuals and families on issues of child sexual abuse (CSA). We define "culture" here as the pattern of values, beliefs, behaviors, and attitudes that are shared by a group of people. In this chapter we focus on issues related to ethnic cultural differences in prevalence, reporting and disclosure, abuse dynamics and prevention. We focus most closely on cultural issues in psychotherapeutic intervention because we believe the topic of how to intervene effectively in situations of child sexual abuse with victims, families, and adult survivors from culturally diverse groups has been neglected in the professional literature.

COMPARATIVE PREVALENCE

People often wonder if the rates, types, and dynamics of abuse vary by ethnicity or culture. Certainly, different cultures present different risk and protective factors for children being sexually abused (Fontes, 1995; Plummer & Njunguna, 2009). For example, in cultures in which a girl child is devalued and left unsupervised for many hours while working to help support her family, she will be at increased risk for abuse by nonfamilial abusers. In another culture where children have little contact with adults outside their families, they may be unusually vulnerable to CSA by family members. In families with extreme poverty, financial incentives and bribes carry more influence. In situations of homelessness, war, and natural disaster, the usual protective mechanisms may falter, exposing children to predatory adults. In cultures where alcohol use is more acceptable, given the strong relationship between substance abuse and child abuse, children may be at additional risk (Sharpe, Abdel-Ghany, Kim, & Hong, 2001). In addition, differences may occur based on opportunity, levels of oversight, types of extended family networks, and the independence allowed children, as well as roles and expectations of male and female children. Thus far there are few methodologically sound studies that allow us to compare rates of prevalence in the United States or in other countries, in part because although it is possible to pose the same question to people from different backgrounds, it is difficult to determine whether the questions will be interpreted or answered in the same way. For example, most studies indicate relatively low incidence rates for child abuse in Asian societies and cultures; however, these conclusions have been questioned, in part due to different levels of willingness to discuss or report abuse (Fontes & Plummer, 2010; Hahm & Guterman, 2001). Taken altogether, there are mixed results regarding cultural differences in incidence and prevalence and we believe it is too early to make definitive statements about these.

The relationship is complex between widespread cultural subjugation and individual acts of deviance such as child sexual abuse. Colonization, war, and other shared traumas influence individuals, families, and communities and can contribute to a legacy of CSA. For instance, Native American children were often torn away from their families and subjected to sexual abuse in boarding schools (Evans-Campbell, 2008; Smith, 2007; Whitbeck et al., 2004). African slaves, including children, were subject to the sexual whims of the slave masters. Vietnamese, Salvadoran, Congolese, Burundian, Somali, Liberian, and other refugees to the United States often endured sexual assault in their countries of origin or in the refugee camps where they fled. We cannot calculate how the history of these traumas reverberates over the decades in affected communities. They may or may not lead to higher rates of prevalence, but they almost certainly shape the experiences of safety and danger and feelings about sexuality, abuse and receiving "help" in the affected communities (Fontes, 1995; Steele, 2004).

The broad ethnic and racial categories that are often used to sort people in the United States may mask more information than they illuminate, which also makes it difficult to compare incidence rates among groups.

This is perhaps clearest in the Hawaiian Islands, where one quarter of the population is of mixed ethnic ancestry and where blended cultures predominate. Further, the histories of the multitude of peoples who fall under the categories of "White," "African American," "Latino," "Asian," or Native American, respectively, lead to highly different risks for CSA; but when lumped into the broader categories, these intragroup differences disappear. Malley-Morrison and Hines (2004) concluded from seven studies of CSA that the rates among Native Americans as a whole reflect those of the larger society, but that CSA rates differ from tribe to tribe. Official government figures show Native American and Alaska Native children in the United States had a sexual victimization rate of 16.5 per 1,000, while the rate for White Non-Hispanic children was 10.8 per 1,000 children (United States Department of Health and Human Services [USDHHS], 2007). One retrospective study found that 49% of women in one Southwestern tribe had been sexually abused as children (Robin, Chester, Rasmussen, Jaranson, & Goldman, 1997). Where higher abuse rates have been identified among particular Native American tribes, these are thought to be partially attributable to the heightened risk and limited social control that result from centuries of marginalization (Dunkerley & Dahlberg, 1999; Fontes, 2005; Steele, 2006).

Questions of comparative prevalence among and within groups remain unanswered, but it is clear that some children are victimized in all cultures. Those children and families affected by CSA deserve a conscientious and culturally competent professional response.

CULTURE AND ABUSE DYNAMICS

Child sexual abuse typically has certain similarities across cultures: secrecy, shame, trauma, and the possible involvement with outside systems, among others. However, different cultural contexts can also shape how children become vulnerable, who is most likely to prey upon them, and what kinds of protective mechanisms are available to them. These may shape both the abuse that occurs and how victims and their families respond.

Patriarchy, which is found in varying degrees across most cultures, seems to be interpreted by certain men as according them a "right" to take advantage sexually of the women and girls whom they believe they control. In traditional Anglo-American families, the father is seen as having both the responsibility and the entitlement to rule over his family (Schmidt, 1995), which some men exaggerate into abusive practices. The Latino concept of *respecto* (respect) emphasizes that children should be respectful to elders and particularly to older male relatives

(Comas-Díaz, 1995); this may encourage children to go along with—rather than defy—the sexual requests of their elders.

A given culture may also provide settings in which abuse could occur that are simply unavailable in other cultures. For instance, the aura of infallibility accorded to Catholic priests and the way they have operated in most countries beyond the rule of law created a climate in which the sexual abuse of children could flourish unchecked. Only by changing aspects of Catholic institutional culture and making the church aware of its responsibility to report crimes to lay authorities will this rampant sexual abuse of children be halted within institutions of the Catholic Church. Abusive clergy from other faith backgrounds have also often enjoyed the trust and protection of their congregations (Neustein, 2009).

It is important to note that people who offend sexually against children will use any and all explanations to justify or excuse their actions, including a version of "My culture made me do it." For example, in 2008 a teacher who had served as guardian for a boy whom he forced to perform sexual acts over a period of years made the claim in court that these acts were a traditional aboriginal cultural practice (Maud, 2008). We have known abusers who claimed that their abusive acts were normative for their cultural group—these acts ranged from inappropriately invasive touch that was masked as hygiene (Fontes, 1993a) to sodomy and intercourse. Any "cultural" explanations for CSA should be investigated carefully by holding confidential conversations with others (especially professionals) from the culture, and not simply accepted at face value. Importantly, even if a given practice has some kind of cultural origin, if the practice is harmful to children and/or illegal in the country where it occurs, children must be protected from it. For instance, although the practice of genital cutting of girls does have cultural origins for many (but not all!) families of Muslim backgrounds, it is considered an illegal assault in most countries of the world (United Nations Population Fund [UNFPA], 2007). Most forms of genital cutting of girls have the potential to produce dire physical and psychological harm; girls must be protected from it and the perpetrators stopped and held accountable.

REPORTING AND DISCLOSURES

As noted in one study of 125 nonabusive mothers, over half sensed a problem and sought to understand it prior to learning conclusively that their child had been sexually abused (Aronson & Plummer, 2006). This finding indicates that prior to any official systems intervention, in coming to learn of sexual abuse and in considering actions to take once it is suspected, families make decisions both within and outside formal structures. A similar finding was found in a replication study with Hispanic mothers (Plummer, Eastin & Aldaz, 2010). This desire to handle problems themselves is likely to be especially true for cultures where distrust of authorities and previous negative experiences with police and other officials are prevalent. For example, in forensic situations Latino children are usually asked to recall and explain emotionally charged sexual abuse events in a way that seems credible to non-Latino professionals and also meets the needs and expectations of the criminal justice system. This is not likely to be the same way the children might define or recall the event themselves, nor the way that is most comfortable for them—particularly for those children who are less acculturated to the dominant culture. Although disclosing and recounting abuse can be difficult for any child, it is particularly hard for children who have little experience with the definitions of truth, time, abstraction, and habits of storytelling that characterize the criminal justice system (Steele, 2008). These cultural differences and others may contribute to the great reluctance of some interviewees when meeting with a culturally different interviewer (Fontes, 2008).

Regardless of cultural background, most sexually abused children do not reveal the abuse during childhood (London, Bruck, Ceci, & Shuman, 2005). Rarely does a child simply make a straightforward report after the first incident of abuse (Alaggia, 2004). Children who are part of a minority culture in the United States, or who are recently arrived here from another country, may be even less likely to reveal abuse to authorities.

When considering reporting abuse to authorities, both adults and children weigh the costs of disclosing; and sometimes they decide these costs offset any possible benefit. Unfortunately, disclosing does not necessarily result in increased safety for a child. When adults hear a disclosure of CSA, they may respond in ways that upset the child or they may misinterpret the situation by either exaggerating or minimizing its significance (Jensen, Gulbrandsen, & Mossige, 2005; Staller & Nelson-Gardell, 2005).

The role of culture in formal disclosure has been examined in several studies, and researchers believe that culture can affect disclosure in a number of ways. Children from minority groups face culture-specific barriers to disclosure that could contribute to delays or denials (Dunkerley & Dalenberg, 1999; Elliott & Briere, 1994; Fontes, 1993; Olafson & Lederman, 2006). For example, groups holding relatively strong prohibitions concerning sexual behaviors, and those emphasizing family preservation and independence from government regulation, are likely to inhibit disclosure (Fontes 1995). In some cultures it is considered improper or dangerous to discuss personal matters with outsiders (Fontes, 2005).

Members of marginalized cultures who suffer from discrimination, instability and poverty are likely to have lower rates of disclosure as well because the risks of disclosure may seem greater (Fontes & Plummer, 2010; Fontes, 1993b). Children vary in their degree of being bicultural; children who have more experience with the dominant culture and are more comfortable with it may be more willing to disclose painful personal and family issues to authorities (Fontes, 2005).

Most sexual abuse is perpetrated by an adult who is from the same family and community as the child victims, so minority children who have been abused may feel in their interviews as if they are being asked to betray not only a family member, but also their cultural group. We know that the closer the relationship between a child and an abuser, the longer it typically takes the child to disclose (Ullman, 2007). In some cultures, children have more people within their intimate network, which might make it more difficult for a child to disclose abuse perpetrated by any of these of individuals. For instance, among Latinos, godparents, cousins, aunts and uncles are often considered part of a child's immediate, rather than extended, family. Native American families often blur the distinction between parents and other caregivers (Cross, Earle, & Simmons, 2000), creating more relatives and nonrelatives in the child's personal network who would have a close familial connection and against whom it might be difficult for a child to make a disclosure. The presence of many caring adults is usually a protective factor, of course, unless one of these adults happens to be a person who would abuse a child sexually.

What is the relationship, then, between disclosing and ethnic culture? Details of how the abuse happened and how secrecy is maintained may be distinctive based on culture. Some studies show that Hispanic victims may be more likely to live with their perpetrator (Rao, DiClemente, & Ponton, 1992), or to be abused by a parental figure (Feiring, Coates, & Taska, 2001), than are non-Hispanic whites or African Americans. In a study comparing Hispanic and African-American families ($n = 159$), Hispanic girls experienced more abuse incidents, waited longer to disclose, and were significantly more likely to be abused by fathers and stepfathers than were the African-American girls (Shaw, Lewis, Loeb, Rosado, & Rodriguez, 2001). Apparent differences in ethnicity or culture in reporting, therefore, may be more related to differences in these abuse characteristics among groups than to cultural differences per se. One study found more of a correlation between acculturation level and reporting of child sexual abuse than with ethnicity itself and reporting (Katerndahl, Bruge, Kellogg, & Parra, 2005).

Certain issues that present differently and are weighted heavily in various cultures may silence disclosures of child sexual abuse. These issues include shame, taboos and modesty, sexual scripts, virginity, women's status, obligatory violence, honor, respect and patriarchy, among others (see Fontes & Plummer, 2010, for further discussion). Shame also may be a strong predictor of post-abuse adjustment (Feiring, Coates, & Taska, 2001). Shame can be related to the topic, the involvement of the authorities, and the possible perceptions of neighbors and friends. Additionally, religious taboos around even talking about sex can inhibit disclosures (Fontes, 2007). In addition to general silence on the topic of both sex and sexual abuse, a "gender struggle" model of sexuality, where males pursue sex and females are taught to avoid it, can make situations where males prey upon younger females seem normal. This model can also make abuse of boys by women seem unimportant or impossible.

The notion that females need to control male sexual aggression through their dress or behavior is also stronger in some cultures than in others. One South African girl described hiding her body even from family members: "When my father, my uncle or my brother is there I don't wear [tight trousers] because if they rape me, I can't blame them" (Jewkes, Penn-Kekanna, & Rose-Junius, 2005). If they cannot blame their male assailants, girls blame themselves, further hindering their disclosure of abuse.

The centrality of girls' virginity in some communities also impedes disclosure of unwanted sexual contact of children. According to Yuksel (2000), virginity is a strong value within the Muslim population in Turkey. A real or perceived loss of virginity may mean that a young woman loses her chance for marriage. "If the situation is known, she loses her prestige within the family [just] as the family loses it in their close neighborhood. The first reaction of the non-offending parent and other relatives is to take the child or young girl for an examination of her virginity when they find out about the abuse. If the hymen is left intact, the sexual abuse cannot be proved, and this makes the denial easier for the family" (p. 157). In some Arab communities, if a child is rumored to have been abused sexually, it may hurt the marriage prospects of not only the victim but also of all of the child's siblings (Baker & Dwairy, 2003). Female victims in some cultures are seen as having disgraced the family, making them vulnerable to violent assault or murder by family members, in an attempt to restore the family name and honor. The prospect of such an assault naturally makes it harder for girls to disclose their victimization.

An additional fear in some cultures may be that retributive violence could harm other family members. Franco (2006), who studied Mexican American families, and Fontes (1993b), who studied Puerto Rican families, both found a tendency for mothers to advise their children to protect their fathers from knowledge of the abuse, for fear of his possible angry and violent response. Franco also found that girls were advised to keep secret their victimization so as not to shock or hasten the death of elderly or infirm relatives.

Girls in India gave the following reasons for not disclosing sexual abuse, starting with the most common: wanting to forget, fearing what people would think, self-blame, distrust, minimizing its importance, feeling guilty for experiencing pleasure, fearing being disbelieved, feeling she had been a willing participant, threats and bribes, and feeling confused or not knowing whom to tell (Gupta & Ailawadi, 2005).

While all children face barriers to disclosure, these may be especially intense for children from marginalized groups: "Children who have been marginalized because of discrimination related to race, ethnicity, and poverty may feel too disempowered to tell about abuse" (Alaggia, 2004, p. 1216). Given a background of historical and contemporary trauma, marginalized child victims and their families may simply avoid authorities (Brave Heart, 2000). If children and family members perceive that the justice system is neither effective nor acting legitimately in the interests of their group or tribe, child victims and their adult supporters would be unlikely to participate in the justice process (Evans-Campbell, 2008).

No mainstream religion advocates the sexual abuse of children, but a wide variety of religious norms and expectations may make disclosure of sexual abuse difficult. For instance, Catholic women and girls may be expected to suffer sexual abuse in silence, with the abuse seen as a cross that they simply have to bear. The relevant terms for this in Spanish are *aguantarse, resignarse,* and *sobreponerse,* meaning, respectively, enduring, resigning oneself, and overcoming adversity (Comas-Díaz, 1995). Catholic children may pray for the abuse to stop and accept their abuse as "fate" if it continues (Kennedy, 2000). Buddhists may believe that abuse is Karmic retribution for a misdeed committed in a previous life, thereby stigmatizing victims and their families. In an article on rape in Taiwan, Luo (2000) writes, "This belief system suggests that any negative life event, such as rape, is caused by the individual's karma from previous lives and revenge (e.g., punishment of the rapist) should not be sought to avoid a karmic vicious cycle." In this way, victims and their families are encouraged not to proceed with prosecutions, so they can end the cycle of negative karma in this lifetime, rather than extending it into the next lifetime.

Jewish religious proscriptions to honor one's parents can make children believe they should not fight off assaults or disclose. *Lashon Hara*, a prohibition against speaking ill of others, is also often referred to as the reason why abusers cannot be publicly named (Silberg & Dallam, 2009). However, the Jewish Talmudic legal tradition offers exemptions that allow rejection of parents when they have committed abusive acts against the child and justifications for speaking out against abusers (Dorff, 2003).

CHILD PROTECTION SERVICES, DISPROPORTIONALITY AND CULTURE

Ample research has demonstrated disproportionality by race, ethnicity, and income level in child protection cases (Hill, 2007) throughout the United States. Experts disagree as to what extent this disproportionality is due to differences in income, neighborhood factors, or biases in people and policies throughout the child welfare system. Further, cases may be handled differentially according to race, with African American and Native American caretakers more likely to receive punishment than concrete help (Roberts, 2002), and their families less likely to be reunited. Federal and state child welfare systems are much more likely to remove Native American children from family control (USDHHS, 2006) and Native children are three times more likely than non-Native white children to be placed in out-of-home care (Hill, 2007). African American children are at particular risk of being removed and remaining separated from their families for long periods or having parental rights terminated, once they are removed (Ehrle & Green, 2002). In fact, mothers of all ethnicities have, in the recent past, enumerated insensitive and unhelpful services from the "system" designed to help their abused child, pointing to the need for increased training that includes cultural competency (Plummer & Eastin, 2007a; Plummer & Eastin, 2007b).

However, disproportionality is only one issue among several regarding child protection services and culture. Cultural competence is an important factor throughout the process. Those who make mandatory reports of abuse, especially school and medical personnel, must be educated about cultural differences so they do not either over-report cultural practices that they are not familiar with as abuse, nor fail to intervene when families need assistance in avoiding abuse. When CPS is assessing a family, this assessment must be conducted in a fair way, based on a body of evidence rather than personal impressions, which are prone to bias. We believe Structured Decision Making (Johnson, 2004) is especially promising in this regard. And once families are involved with CPS, interventions must be fair and must fit well with the families' cultures. From the first conversation to the last, agency policies and worker practices must welcome, understand, and handle fairly families from diverse cultural groups (Fontes, 2005). Family group decision making can sometimes be helpful in this regard, but we are skeptical about using it before the risk to a child has been thoroughly assessed, and especially in cases of sexual abuse. Where foster care or even adoption is found to be necessary, every attempt should be made to place children in homes where they will be well taken care of and loved, and have as few disruptions as possible. Members of a child's extended family or community are often the best candidates in this regard.

CULTURE AND CLINICAL INTERVENTION

It is important to avoid seeing members of any cultural group as monolithic. The differences among members of a particular group are apt to be vast, and often more significant than differences between groups. For instance, a recent undocumented immigrant girl from Hong Kong who was sexually abused during the process of immigration may have more in common with a recent undocumented immigrant from El Salvador who has been similarly exploited than she does with a fifth-generation Chinese American girl—although the girl from Hong Kong and the Chinese girl would both fall into the category of Chinese American. Similarly, two neighboring families with father/daughter incest in an upper middle-class gated community in Florida may have a great deal in common—although one sees itself as white and the other as Black. Identity is complex and multifaceted for many individuals and families; whatever group characteristics we have learned to expect are just as likely *not* to apply with any particular family.

Clinical approaches to child sexual abuse rarely take into full account the culture of the recipient of services. Hays (2007) outlines the ADDRESSING model for assessing the different factors in a person's identity. The acronym ADDRESSING is a mnemonic for Age (effects of generation), Disability (born and acquired), Developmental (individual development and stage of life), Religion and spirituality, Ethnic identity, Social class (including occupation, education, income, rural or urban, current and former class status and especially the influence of childhood social class status), Sexual orientation, Indigenous heritage, National origin (immigrant, refugee, international student, native born), and Gender (biological sex and gender roles). Ideally, a clinician would take into account all of these factors in shaping work with a client affected by CSA. Some of these identity characteristics will be more salient for particular individuals than for others. Brown (2008) offers suggestions for applying the ADDRESSING model to clinical work with people impacted by trauma.

Building Trust and Rapport

Many clients—especially immigrants and people from lower socio-economic groups—may not understand psychotherapy, thinking using such services means they are "crazy." They may not understand how psychotherapy works, how long it may take, or what is expected of them. They may not endorse abstract goals such as *insight* and are likely to expect rapid relief from their troubling emotions and symptoms. It is extremely important, therefore, for clinicians to explain as much as they can about the setting and expectations, so clients do not feel inadequate or uncomfortable. With adequate orientation and continued cultural competence, psychotherapy and counseling can be of tremendous help to those affected by CSA.

Members of groups who are historically marginalized and oppressed may be slower to confide in an authority, and less inclined to acquiesce to treatment protocols that appear to require giving up control, such as hypnosis. They may need a long period of getting to know the therapist before they are even willing to disclose personal information, let alone speak about the sensitive topic of child sexual abuse. Reticent clients may also decline to mention child sexual abuse unless it is asked about directly. Because abuse is often disguised as affection and is confusing to children, it is best to ask in a way that does not require clients to label their experience as "abuse." A psychotherapist could say, for instance, "Many of the people I work with have had sexual experiences or experiences with their bodies that were upsetting or confusing to them. Have you had some experiences like that?" Even if these kinds of questions are posed during an intake, they may need to be repeated several sessions beyond the intake appointment, when the client is more apt to trust the provider. Psychotherapists, therefore, have to tread carefully. Frequent check-ins with the client may be helpful, including questions such as, "How are we doing here? How do you feel about our work together? Is there anything more you'd like me to know?" Assessment, as well as treatment, must be congruent with cultural attitudes and beliefs of the family and community (Eamon, 2001).

Members of oppressed groups who are in psychotherapy with a person from another cultural group often fear further stigmatization if they discuss "bad" things that happened inside their families, such as CSA. Telling an outsider is considered "washing one's dirty laundry in public." African Americans, for instance, may hesitate to discuss sexual abuse for fear that it "will be used in some damnable way to further exclude African Americans from the American mainstream" (Abney & Priest, 1995, p. 11). Jews' hesitation to reveal problems to people from outside the culture is revealed in the Yiddish expression, *shandeh fur die Goyim*, which roughly means a shameful situation that non-Jews might use as a weapon against Jews. In minority cultures, the act of sharing personal matters with people from outside the inner circle may be seen as leading to unwanted and threatening attention that might jeopardize family and community integrity. A therapist would need to proceed slowly, and address these concerns with a client as they occur. Shame is virtually universal for victims of CSA—members of oppressed cultural groups often carry the additional shame derived from discriminatory encounters with peers and authorities.

LANGUAGE COMPETENCE

Language competence is central to cultural competence because most major approaches to child sexual abuse involve conversations about the abuse and its aftermath. Providing services in the client's preferred language is essential to adequate communication (Perez Foster, 1999). Particular languages make certain concepts and feelings more easily available to speakers than do others. In addition, people who are asked to do psychotherapy in their nonpreferred language may find themselves reaching for words and trying to keep up a good impression—which is a serious distraction to the work (Fontes, 2008). Finally, the feelings of being unable to express oneself adequately in English might elicit from the client feelings of powerlessness and infantilization, which echo the childhood abuse.

Psychotherapy around CSA with someone who prefers speaking a language other than English is best achieved through a clinician who speaks the client's preferred language fluently. Second best is to engage the services of a professionally trained interpreter. It is rare, however, to find an interpreter who knows how to handle the exigencies of a clinical mental health session, especially for a sensitive topic like child sexual abuse. Perez Foster (1999) and Fontes (2005, 2008) offer suggestions for working effectively with interpreters, and for conducting sensitive discussions with clients in their non-native language. Some clients who are not fluent in English prefer working without an interpreter, even if there are limitations to the discussion, because of concerns regarding confidentiality or a simple preference to speak with the therapist directly without a third person intervening. In this case, the client's wishes should be respected. However, accommodations will need to be made to overcome the challenges this presents.

It is important that family members, and especially children, are not used as interpreters. Family members are apt to have their own perspective on events and have an interest in the outcome. This introduces interference in the clinical process. Children who are asked to interpret in sensitive situations may be exposed to material that is beyond their years, blamed if the outcome is not to the liking of the parents, and find they are unable to explain complex concepts, thus either "editing" or not sharing the intended message.

TREATMENT EFFECTIVENESS

Most CSA treatment research in the United States has been conducted on the majority dominant culture (Euro-American) and even there, evidence of successful treatment for many problems is sparse or only addresses those subsets of the groups who fit the research protocol criteria. Unfortunately, best practices, and particularly evidence-based approaches, have been even more difficult to measure in minority, immigrant, and indigenous communities, where potential participants may question the motives of researchers and even respond differently to research instruments and procedures than people from the dominant culture (Fontes, 2004). Therefore, little is known about what truly works for recovery from CSA with members of different groups. Indigenous communities in particular have criticized the "evidence-based" focus for ignoring different ways of knowing what works, in some cases abandoning traditional healing methods because they either have not yet undergone research, or are not amenable to standard empirical methodologies (Weber-Pillwat, 2004).

While the jury is still out on some approaches to CSA, we are optimistic that Trauma-Focused Cognitive-Behavioral Therapy (TF-CBT) is a viable option to treat culturally diverse victims of CSA. Although a thorough discussion of TF-CBT is beyond the scope of this chapter, its key elements are: child, parent, and conjoint sessions; telling the trauma story; psychoeducation; cognitive coping skills; and relaxation. These would seem to be adaptable cross-culturally and effective in alleviating mental health symptoms in victims of CSA (Cohen, Mannarino, & Deblinger, 2006). Of course, like other approaches, TF-CBT should be implemented by culturally competent psychotherapists. In addition to TF-CBT, which is promising cross-culturally, clinicians may find that culturally specific interventions are helpful with particular groups, and should, after refinement, be tested with experimental designs to ascertain their usefulness.

Many indigenous groups are exploring "different ways of knowing" and their efforts at designing and evaluating programs based on traditional cultures offer some promise.

ALTERNATIVE TREATMENT POSSIBILITIES

It is often wise for clinicians to ask new clients about the resources and practices they have drawn on successfully in the past when facing difficulties. Understanding key coping mechanisms can be an important part of the clinical intake for CSA, and these previously successful practices may offer ideas for our work with clients in overcoming the trauma of CSA. When treating child victims, remember that the entire family is suffering and parents and siblings may also need support or professional assistance (Plummer et al., 2010).

When clients mention non-Western cultural practices, such as consulting with clergy or faith healers, engaging in traditional rituals of purification or healing, clinicians need to decide how closely their own work will be intertwined with the traditional healing. Most importantly, if the client raises these issues, the clinician should be comfortable enough to explore how and if these should be supported.

Moodley and West (2005) suggest that traditional healing practices may be helpful as long as the client has faith in the system used. Much traditional healing is based on decades, centuries, or even millennia of practice, shared beliefs between the healer and the client, and faith in the healer. Traditional healers rarely differentiate between healing the mind or body or spirit. Partnering in some way with a traditional healer, therefore, may help Western trained practitioners influence some of the bodily symptoms resulting from the trauma of CSA—symptoms that may be slower to respond to Western psychotherapy.

The different stances a clinician might take can be labeled parallel, consultative, collaborative, and integrative. A clinician who chooses a *parallel* stance toward traditional healing might ask if the client thinks any traditional resources might be helpful, and then encourage the client to pursue these independently. The clinician could ask about them periodically, but would not try to become involved in these directly in any way. For instance, a clinician who supports a Jewish client in accessing traditional resources might learn that the client has chosen to do a *mikvah* or ritual bath so she can feel clean again after the abuse (Featherman, 1995). In another example, a client who uses incense or smudging for purification might be encouraged to consider developing a related ritual around sexual abuse to enact alone or with friends. Clinicians who are unfamiliar with or not comfortable with the religion or beliefs of the client, or who do not believe these have a place in psychotherapy, may choose this parallel stance.

A clinician who takes a *consultative* stance might consult a clergy member or traditional practitioner from the client's culture and ask for information and suggestions about working with a client from that culture on CSA, while maintaining confidentiality, of course. For this, we must be aware of traditional healers in our communities who are knowledgeable about CSA and who could offer us advice regarding our clients. A *collaborative* stance would require clinicians to find, or ask the client to find, a traditional practitioner from the culture, with whom they would work to design healing rituals and practices. Using a collaborative stance, a traditional healer might be brought into a psychotherapy session. And finally, an *integrative* practitioner might find ways to incorporate aspects of the client's traditional culture and healing practice within the session without bringing an additional person into the session. Rituals often provide turning points in more traditional psychotherapy (Imber-Black, Roberts, & Whiting, 2003). This makes sense in a setting where a client has purposely sought out psychotherapy with a given cultural overtone, such as in a pastoral counseling center, or a clinic that advertises itself as "Afrocentric" or has the name of a tribe in its title.

Even where the psychotherapist and the client are from the same cultural group, we urge caution in integrating cultural practices into the therapy session, particularly using the closer collaborative, or integrative stances. Dangers here include: the possibility that the traditional healer not only does not understand the dynamic of CSA but may blame the client for what has occurred or for speaking about it, thus increasing the client's shame. It is also possible that the traditional healer will discourage the client from continuing with psychotherapy related to the CSA. Clinicians must also be careful that they do not unwittingly push clients into engaging in practices that are either alien to them, or which they have abandoned. For instance, a Muslim who was abused within the context of an Islamic religious school may actively reject traditional Islamic healing practices and may be offended by the clinician who suggests engaging in them. A clinician might also be seen as a kind of poseur if he or she suggests a traditional healing practice that is not part of his or her tradition. For instance, if a non–American Indian psychotherapist were to suggest to an American Indian client that he or she consider smudging to feel pure again, the client might consider this suggestion a form of stereotyping. To avoid this, the clinician would do better to *ask* the client if there are any traditional practices that he or she might find helpful. We must also remember that people accept and reject aspects of the culture they grew up in to different extents and in different ways. Just because a person grew up in a particular culture does not necessarily mean that person would find comfort in practices from that culture in his or her adult life. In fact, in one study female survivors of CSA were *more* likely than others to convert to a different religion as adults (Russell, 1987).

PREVENTION

We must begin by assessing the community we wish to reach, just as we would assess an individual client. This assessment includes conducting a thorough mapping of assets and assessment of cultural protective and risk factors (Plummer & Njunguna, 2009). Even within one country, an approach that was found to be successful in a given community may not be a good fit in another. In Western societies, where prevention programs have been characterized by both child- and adult-focused educational efforts, too often prevention has been "adapted" for culture by simply translating materials or enlisting community members as trainers. Unfortunately, this simplistic view of cultural congruence, while a starting place, is far from adequate. Adaptations need to be made for the following four reasons, among others:

1. Sexual abuse may occur differently in this community.
2. Specific aspects of the culture may themselves protect children from CSA or, alternatively, may subject children to additional risks related to this danger.
3. Communities must "own" their programs, to reach the targeted audiences and achieve desired outcomes, especially if they are to be sustained and maintained over time.
4. Research or evaluation done on excellent programs may have little relevance to this population.

There are two kinds of culturally competent prevention programs: *multicultural* and *culture specific*. Multicultural programs are meant to reach *diverse* groups, such as a school-based program that uses examples relevant to a variety of cultures or a general public service announcement that is not targeted to any particular group but has multiculturally inclusive images. Culture specific programs target the needs of specific cultural groups. Examples include a public service announcement about CSA on a Spanish-language television station in the United States targeting Latino viewers, or a Reservation-based CSA prevention program targeting the needs of that American Indian community.

Culturally specific and multicultural approaches to CSA are in place at a variety of organizations throughout the U.S. and the world. Unfortunately, there is no central clearinghouse or repository for effective program descriptions or materials. This lack of coordination inhibits agencies from pooling their resources, and increases the likelihood that various organizations will find themselves "reinventing the wheel." Multiple agencies have undoubtedly translated and retranslated the same or similar forms and brochures—even within the same city.

Deborah Daro (2003), who has focused her distinguished career on child abuse prevention, reminds us that "prevention is often about building a relationship, not simply about delivering a product" (p. 4). Key relationships between community members and prevention professionals will form *only* when people are approached in ways that fit their culture and circumstances. Establishing links with cultural communities requires careful planning. Some possible steps include: waiting to be invited into a community, allowing the community to set its own agenda and priorities, speaking with community leaders and elders before initiating a program, becoming aware of community divides or factions, and handling these political issues with care. Once a program has begun, it can be important to allow extra time for activities so that cultural variations can be incorporated. All this is usually dependent on the strength of the relationships built by prevention advocates within the communities they hope to serve.

It can be difficult for "outsiders" to gain the trust of people from small ethnic communities. Establishing trust in ethnic communities is time consuming, especially when the work is focused on issues of sexuality. It is crucial to partner with community leaders and agencies that are already trusted by the ethnic communities, and to build efforts that make true sense within the ethnic context. These local agencies and leaders are more apt to know the needs and habits of the community than would an agency "from outside." However, we cannot assume that leaders in the community hold views about issues of child sexual abuse that will promote prevention or recovery. We may need to begin by tactfully educating those service providers, leaders, and elders who hold the respect of the community.

It might be advisable first to assess the naturalistic prevention approaches that currently exist, and lend support to enhance these, rather than "importing" strategies that may seem foreign and ill-suited to a given community. Designing prevention programs that build upon naturalistic prevention strategies requires an intimate knowledge of the community. Ideally, prevention professionals would offer leaders from ethnic communities "flexible, empirically based criteria for building their own prevention programs" (Daro, Cohn, & Donnelly, 2002, p. 440). By providing existing community organizations with the resources and training they need to establish their own programs, professionals avoid the ethnocentrism likely when "outsiders" try to impose their preformed ideas with insufficient knowledge of community values.

CONCLUSION

To prevent child sexual abuse, enhance children's ability to disclose, and provide high-quality intervention, professionals need to tune in to our own cultures and assumptions and continually learn about the backgrounds and needs of the diverse people in our communities. While frequently mentioned, cultural differences are seldom sufficiently considered when planning prevention, or assessing and treating people affected by CSA. In an increasingly global environment, with culturally diverse families bringing their languages and customs to communities where they have never before lived, we cannot afford to remain complacent. Children's safety and wellbeing is at stake.

REFERENCES

Abney, V., & Priest, R. (1995). African Americans and sexual child abuse. In L. Fontes (Ed.), *Sexual abuse in nine North American cultures: Treatment and prevention* (pp. 11–30). Thousand Oaks, CA: Sage.

Alaggia, R. (2004). Many ways of telling: Expanding conceptualization of child sexual abuse disclosure. *Child Abuse & Neglect: An International Journal, 28*(11), 1213–1227.

Aronson, J., & Plummer, C. A. (2006). The discovery process: What mothers see and do in gaining awareness of the sexual abuse of their children. *Child Abuse & Neglect, 30*(11), 1227–1237.

Baker, K. A., & Dwairy, M. (2003). Cultural norms versus state law in treating incest: A suggested model for Arab families. *Child Abuse & Neglect, 27*, 109–123.

Brave Heart, M.Y.H. (2000). Wakiksuyapi: Carrying the historical trauma of Lakota. *Tulane Studies in Social Welfare, 21*, 245–266.

Brown, L. S. (2008). *Cultural competence in therapy: Beyond the flashback.* Washington, DC: American Psychological Association.

Cohen, J. A., Mannarino, A. P., & Deblinger, E. (2006). *Treating trauma and traumatic grief in children and adolescents.* New York, NY: Guilford Press.

Comas-Díaz, L. (1995). Puerto Ricans and sexual child abuse. In L. A. Fontes (Ed.), *Sexual abuse in nine North American cultures: Treatment and prevention* (pp. 31–66). Thousand Oaks. CA: Sage.

Cross, T. L., Earle, K. A., & Simmons, D. (2000). Child abuse and neglect in Indian country: Policy issues. *Families in Society, 81,* 49–58.

Daro, D. (2003). Child abuse prevention: Accomplishments and challenges. *APSAC Advisor 15*(2), 3–4.

Daro, D., & Cohn Donnelly, A. (2002). Child abuse prevention: Accomplishments and challenges. In J. Myers, L. Berliner, J. Briere, C. T. Hendrix, C. Jenny, & T. A. Reid (Eds.), *The APSAC handbook on child maltreatment* (2nd ed., pp. 431–448). Thousand Oaks, CA: Sage.

Dorff, E. (2003). Jewish law and tradition regarding sexual abuse and incest. In R. Lev (Ed.), *Shine the light: Sexual abuse and healing in the Jewish community* (pp. 46–60). Boston, MA: Northeastern University Press.

Dunkerley, G. K., & Dalenberg, C. J. (1999). Secret-keeping behaviors in black and white children as a function of interviewer race, racial identity, and risk for abuse. *Journal of Aggression, Maltreatment, and Trauma, 2,* 13–35.

Eamon, M. K. (2001). Antecedents and socioemotional consequences of physical punishment on children in two-parent families. *Child Abuse & Neglect, 6,* 787–802.

Ehrle, J., & Green, R. (2002). Kin and non-kin foster care: Findings from a national survey. *Children and Youth Services Review, 24*(1–2), 15–35.

Elliott, D. M., & Briere, J. (1994). Forensic sexual abuse evaluations of older children: Disclosures and symptomatology. *Behavioral Sciences and the Law, 12,* 261–277.

Evans-Campbell, T. (2008). Historical trauma in American Indian/Native Alaska communities: A multilevel framework for exploring impacts on individuals, families, and communities. *Journal of Interpersonal Violence, 23,* 316–338.

Featherman, J. (1995). Jews and child sexual abuse. In L. A. Fontes (Ed.), *Sexual abuse in nine North American cultures: Treatment and prevention* (pp. 128–155). Thousand Oaks, CA: Sage.

Feiring, C., Coates, D. L., & Taska, L. S. (2001). Ethnic status, stigmatization, support and symptom development following sexual abuse. *Journal of Interpersonal Violence, 16,* 1307–1329.

Fontes, L. A. (2008). *Interviewing clients across cultures: A practitioner's guide.* New York, NY: Guilford Press.

Fontes, L. A. (2007). Sin vergüenza: Addressing shame with Latino victims of child sexual abuse and their families. *Journal of Child Sexual Abuse, 16,* 61–82.

Fontes, L. A. (2004). Ethics in violence against women research: The sensitive, the dangerous and the overlooked. *Ethics and Behavior, 14,* 141–174.

Fontes, L. A. (1995). *Sexual abuse in nine North American cultures: Treatment and prevention.* Thousand Oaks, CA: Sage.

Fontes, L. A. (1993a). Culture and oppression: Steps toward an ecology of sexual abuse. *Journal of Feminist Family Therapy, 5,* 25–54a.

Fontes, L. A. (1993b). Disclosures of sexual abuse by Puerto Rican children: Oppression and cultural barriers. *Journal of Child Sexual Abuse, 2,* 21–35.

Fontes, L. A., & Plummer, C. (2010). Cultural issues in disclosures of child sexual abuse. *Journal of Child Sexual Abuse, 19,* 491–518.

Franco, E. M. (2006). Intrafamilial childhood sexual abuse and a culture of silence: Experiences of adult Mexican survivors with disclosure. *Unpublished master's thesis*. School for Social Work, Smith College, Northampton, MA.

Gupta, A., & Ailawadi, A. (2005). Childhood and adolescent sexual abuse and incest: Experiences of women survivors in India. In S. J. Jejeebhoy, I. Shah, & S. Thapa (Eds.), *Sex without consent: Young people in developing countries* (pp. 171–202). New York, NY: Zed Books.

Hahm, H. C., & Guterman, N. B. (2001). The emerging problem of physical child abuse in South Korea. *Child Maltreatment, 6*(2), 169–179.

Hays, P. (2007). *Addressing cultural complexities in practice* (2nd ed.). Washington, DC: American Psychological Association.

Hill, R. 2007. An analysis of racial/ethnic disproportionality and disparity at the nation, state, and county levels. *Casey-CSSP alliance for racial equity in child welfare*. Seattle, WA: Casey Family Programs.

Imber-Black, E., Roberts, J., & Whiting, R. A. (Eds.). (2003). *Rituals in families and family therapy* (revised). New York, NY: Norton.

Jensen, T. K., Gulbrandsen, W., Mossige, S., Reichelt, S., & Tjersland, O. A. (2005). Reporting sexual abuse: A qualitative study on children's perspectives and the context for disclosure. *Child Abuse & Neglect, 29*, 1395–1414.

Jewkes, R., Penn-Kehanna, L., & Rose-Junius, H. (2005). "If they rape me, I can't blame them." Reflections on gender in the social context of child rape in South Africa and Namibia. *Social Science & Medicine, 61*, 1809–1820.

Johnson, W. (2004). *Effectiveness of California's child welfare structured decision-making (SDM) model: A prospective study of the validity of the California Family Risk Assessment*. United States Department of Health and Human Services Administration for Child & Family. Accessed on November 15, 2010, www .nccd-crc.org/crc/crc/pubs//ca_sdm_model_feb04.pdf

Katerndahl, D., Burge, S., Kellogg, N., & Parra, J. (2005). Differences in childhood sexual abuse experience between adult Hispanic and Anglo women in a primary care setting. *Journal of Child Sexual Abuse, 14*(2), 85–95.

Kennedy, M. (2000). Christianity and child sexual abuse: The survivor's voice leading to change. *Child Abuse Review, 9*, 121–141.

London, K., Bruck, M., Ceci, S. J., & Shuman, D. W. (2005). Disclosure of child sexual abuse what does the research tell us about the ways that children tell? *Psychology, Public Policy, and Law, 11*(1), 194–226.

Luo, T. Y. (2000). He was responsible but was she to blame?: Attrition of responsibility and blame toward date rape among Taiwanese adolescents. *Proceeding of the National Science Council, 10*(2), 185–200.

Malley-Morrison, K., & Hines, D. A. (2004). *Family violence in a cultural perspective: Defining, understanding, and combating abuse*. Thousand Oaks, CA: Sage.

Maud, J. (2008). Child sexual abuse, the law and culture. Culture matters. Accessed on September 27, 2010, at: http://culturematters.wordpress.com/2008/02/19/child-sexual-abuse-the-law-and-culture/

Moodley, R., & West, W. (Eds.). (2005). *Integrating traditional healing practices into counseling and psychotherapy*. Thousand Oaks, CA. Sage.

Neustein, A. (Ed.). (2009). *The tempest in the temple.* Lebanon, NH: Brandeis University Press.

Olafson, E., & Lederman, C. (2006). The state of the debate about children's disclosure patterns in child sexual abuse cases. *Juvenile and Family Court Journal, 57*, 27–40.

Perez Foster, R. (1999). *The power of language in the clinical process: Assessing and treating the bilingual person.* New York, NY: Jason Aronson.

Plummer, C. A., & Eastin, J. (2007a). System Problems in Cases of Child Sexual Abuse: The Mothers' Perspectives. *Journal of Interpersonal Violence, 22*(6), 775–787, DOI: 10.1177/0886260507300753

Plummer, C. A., & Eastin, J. (2007). The Effect of Child Sexual Abuse Allegations on the Mother/Child Relationship. *Violence Against Women, 13*(10), 1053–1071.

Plummer, C. A., & Njunguna, W. (2009). Cultural protective and risk factors: Professional perspectives about child sexual abuse in Kenya. *Child Abuse & Neglect, 33*(8), 524–532.

Plummer, C. A., Eastin, J., & Aldaz, S. (2010). Hispanic mothers of sexually abused children: Experiences, reactions, concerns. *Social Work Forum, 42/43*, 55–75.

Rao, K., Diclemente, R., & Ponton, L. (1992). Child sexual abuse of Asians compared with other populations. *Journal of the American Academy of Psychiatry, 31*, 880–886.

Roberts, D. (2002). *Shattered bonds: The color of child welfare.* New York: Basic Books.

Robin, R. W., Chester, B., Rasmussen, J. K., Jaranson, J. M., & Goldman, D. (1997). Prevalence and characteristics of trauma and posttraumatic stress disorder in a southwestern American Indian community. *American Journal of Psychiatry, 154*, 1582–1588.

Russell, D. E. H. (1987). *Incest in the lives of girls and women.* New York, NY: Basic Books.

Schmidt, L. K. (1995). *Transforming abuse: Nonviolent resistance and recovery.* Gabriola Island, BC: New Society.

Sharpe, D. L., Abdel-Ghany, M., Kim, H., & Hong, G. (2001). Alcohol consumption decision in Korea. *Journal of Family and Economic Issues, 22*(1), 7–24.

Shaw, J. A., Lewis, J. E., Loeb, A., Rosado, J., & Rodriquez, R. A. (2001). A comparison of Hispanic and African American sexually abused girls and their families. *Child Abuse & Neglect, 25*, 1363–1379.

Silberg, J. L., & Dallam, S. (2009). Out of the Jewish closet: Facing the hidden secrets of child sex abuse and the damage done to victims. In A. Neustein (Ed.), *Tempest in the temple: Jewish communities and child sex scandals* (pp. 77–104). Waltham, MA: Brandeis University Press.

Smith, A. (2007). Soul wound: The legacy of Native American schools. *Amnesty.* Accessed on May 22, 2009, at www.amnestyusa.org/amnestynow/soulwound .html

Staller, K. M., & Nelson-Gardell, D. (2005). A burden in your heart: Lessons of disclosure from female preadolescent and adolescent survivors of sexual abuse. *Child Abuse & Neglect, 29*, 1415–1432.

Steele, P. (2004). *Analysis of case characteristics, decision-making, and outcomes of child sexual abuse cases in Madison County, Alabama.* Washington, DC: U.S. Department of Justice, Office of Juvenile Justice and Delinquency Prevention.

Steele, P. (2006). *Comments concerning revision and reauthorization of S.1899, the Indian child protection and family violence prevention act before the 109th Congress, Senate Indian Affairs Subcommittee, March 15.* Congressional Record, S. Hrg. 109–478: 35–37, 81–106: Washington, DC: U.S. Government Printing Office.

Steele, P. (2008). Responding to child sexual abuse in the United States: Facing challenges in the civil and criminal justice systems. *Forum on Public Policy, 4,* 41–56.

Ullman, S. E. (2007). Relationship to perpetrator, disclosure, social reactions, and PTSD symptoms in child sexual abuse survivors. *Journal of Child Sexual Abuse, 16,* 19–36.

United National Population Fund. (2007). A holistic approach to the abandonment of female genital mutilation/cutting. New York, NY. Author. Accessed on October 6, 2010, at www.unfpa.org/public/publications/pid/407

United States Department of Health and Human Services. (2006). *The AFCARS (Adoption and Foster Care Reporting System) report.* Washington DC: United States Government Printing Office.

United States Department of Health and Human Services, Administration for Children and Families. (2007). *Child Maltreatment 2005.* Washington, DC: United States Government Printing Office.

Yuksel, S. (2000). Collusion and denial of childhood sexual trauma in traditional societies. In A. C. McFalane, R. Yehuda, & A. Y. Shaley (Eds.). *International handbook of human response to trauma* (pp. 153–162). Dordrecht Netherland: Kluwer Academic Publishers.

Weber-Pillwat, C. (2004). Indigenous researchers and indigenous research methods: Cultural influences or cultural determinants of research methods. *Pimatisiwin: A Journal of Aboriginal and Indigenous Community Health, 2*(1), 77–90.

Whitebeck, L. G., Adams, D., Hoyt, and Chen, X. (2004). Conceptualizing and measuring historical trauma among American Indian people. *American Journal of Community Psychology, 33,* 119–130.

CHAPTER 23

Working With Survivors of Child Sexual Abuse

Secondary Trauma and Vicarious Traumatization

MICHELE M. MANY and JOY D. OSOFSKY

INTRODUCTION

C HILD SEXUAL ABUSE (CSA) not only traumatizes the child, but may also negatively impact the helpers and evaluators called in after the incident to learn more about and make sense of what happened, why it happened, and what can be done to help the child and affected family. The literature has shown that working with survivors of child sexual abuse places the helper at increased risk for the development of a spectrum of traumatic responses (Brady, Guy, Polestra, & Brokaw, 1999; Chouliara, Hutchison, & Karatzias, 2009; Etherington, 2009; Pearlman & Mac Ian, 1995; Perron & Hiltz, 2006; Schauben & Frazier, 1995). After a sexually abused child's initial outcry, the child will come in contact with many different people and professionals, all of whom are trying to help. These can include police, medical personnel, forensic interviewers, child protection caseworkers and supervisors, therapists, judges and other court personnel, attorneys and court-appointed special advocates. Some will have received specialized training in working with survivors of sexual abuse and ongoing professional supervision. Others will have received little training in working with survivors of CSA or may be provided limited or no professional support. Indeed, some helpers may think it a sign of weakness to ask for help in dealing with the feelings of anger and frustration that often arise during investigations and treatment of sexual abuse.

Those who work with survivors often are confronted with events that can trigger strong negative feelings that may not be responded to supportively by colleagues. The following case illustrates one example of this frustration. A clinician worked with a young child who had been repeatedly raped by an adult male relative. Only when the perpetrator focused on another child in the family did the client disclose the abuse in the hopes of protecting the younger child. The perpetrator was not prosecuted due to a lack of physical findings. The clinician later heard that, after the perpetrator was made to leave the family home, he moved next to an elementary school. The clinician expressed her feelings of fury and helplessness at this failure of the system. Similar scenarios occur frequently in CSA work and are too often dealt with by emotional distancing from the victims and cynicism about the perpetrators, the responding systems, and sadly, even sometimes about the victims. Those who work in this field will be able to recall callous remarks made by colleagues or by others involved in a case, persons that one knew to be dedicated, caring professionals, yet who had become hardened over time with continual exposure to heart-wrenching cases. Although individual vulnerabilities play a role in the difficulties that helpers encounter while working with CSA survivors, equal attention should be given to professional and systemic issues.

Many different factors play a role in how helpers will respond. For example, frequency of contact may influence the effects of CSA work on any of these responders. Most of the helpers called on to assist an abused child are tasked with responding to allegations of child sexual abuse, and thus will be exposed repeatedly to variations of the same scenario with numerous survivors over their career. Hearing the abuse each child endured may cause secondary trauma, prompting symptoms of avoidance, hyperarousal and intrusive recollections (Figley, 1995). Empathically engaging with the child's abuse experiences may vicariously traumatize the helper, causing changes in the helper's perceptions of safety, control, and intimacy (McCann & Pearlman, 1990). Some helpers will assist many survivors at any given time and some may have only minimal contact with each child, leaving unanswered questions as to how each fared as the investigation continued. The helper's continual exposure to survivors' traumatic material, with no evidence of resolution may result in distortions in the helper's worldview. For other helpers there may be ongoing contact with each child for months or even years. Often these helpers will be carrying caseloads that include many abused children. Bearing witness to the long-term impact of sexual abuse on these children and their families, and working primarily with those survivors with the most pervasive and severe symptoms can cause these helpers to feel overwhelmed by the scope of the problem, distorting their worldview as well.

Systemic issues may also play a role in the impact of working with CSA survivors on helpers. Limited resources, excessive caseloads, delays in prosecutions, poor coordination between multidisciplinary team (MDT) members and system members with a poor understanding of the dynamics of trauma may result in increased burnout for helpers. At times helpers may struggle against a system that does not value their work.

In this chapter we discuss secondary traumatic stress (STS), vicarious traumatization (VT), countertransference, and burnout. These concepts are related, but they are different constructs, all useful in understanding and addressing the emotional, professional, and systemic costs of working with childhood trauma survivors. We first discuss each concept and their interrelationships. This is followed by a brief review of the literature on STS, VT, and burnout in those who work with child sexual abuse survivors. We close with an overview of interventions that may attenuate the impact of STS, VT, and burnout.

DEFINITION OF TERMS

Since the 1980s, the related concepts of burnout (Freudenberger, 1980; Maslach, 1982; Pines & Aronson, 1988), secondary traumatic stress, later called *compassion fatigue* (Figley, 1995), and vicarious traumatization (McCann & Pearlman, 1990) were hypothesized and defined, and a wealth of literature researching and refining these concepts was produced (Baird & Kracen, 2006; Jenkins & Baird, 2002; Pearlman & Mac Ian, 1995). Countertransference has a longer history, having been identified in the early development of psychoanalytic theory and practice. These concepts overlap, but it is important to understand each as a distinct process that may affect trauma workers.

COUNTERTRANSFERENCE

Countertransference has been defined as a situation in which "an analyst's feelings and attitudes toward a patient are derived from earlier situations in the analyst's life that have been displaced onto the patient" (Moore & Fine, 1990, p. 47). It is essentially viewed as the therapist's reaction to the patient's transference. Analysts debated whether countertransference consisted only of negative or harmful reactions on the part of the therapist, or if it encompassed all of a therapist's feelings toward his or her patient, positive and negative. Nevertheless, if therapists were able to identify and explore their own countertransference, it was considered to potentially enrich the client's treatment. If unacknowledged, countertransference posed a threat to the value of the therapeutic relationship. Countertransference is thought to arise only within the context of the therapeutic relationship and does not apply to other kinds of helping relationships. Countertransference is briefly discussed here only to acknowledge its similarities to and overlap with STS and VT. However, this chapter focuses specifically on burnout, VT, and STS as they impact those who work with sexually abused children.

BURNOUT

Freudenberger (1980) first conceptualized burnout as stress related to conditions in the workplace. He proposed that employees could become vulnerable to "a state of fatigue or frustration brought about by devotion to a cause or relationship that failed to produce the desired results" (p. 13). Maslach (1982) continued to study the phenomenon, looking specifically at those who worked in direct services, bringing them into contact with others. Maslach defined burnout as "a syndrome of emotional exhaustion, depersonalization, and reduced personal accomplishment that can occur among individuals who do people-work of some kind" (p. 3). In burnout the individual becomes "overly involved emotionally, overextends himself or herself, and feels overwhelmed by the emotional demands imposed by other people" (p. 3). Early studies found that burnout was prevalent among the helping professions (Farber, 1991; Pick & Leiter, 1991; Pines & Maslach, 1981), supporting the relationship between service-oriented interpersonal interactions and burnout.

Over time, Maslach and her colleagues broadened their views, returning to Freudenberger's original concept of burnout as a systems problem. Although burnout was common in helping professionals and service workers, Maslach and Leiter (1997) asserted that it resulted from organizational dysfunction, not from poor coping on the part of the individual. Burnout consists of three components: (1) exhaustion, (2) depersonalization/cynicism/distancing, and (3) inefficacy. Exhaustion was most widely reported of the three, and was thought to prompt the development of detachment as a negative coping mechanism. Inefficacy was seen as more directly resulting from systems problems (e.g., lack of resources), whereas exhaustion and depersonalization were thought to result from interpersonal conflict and unrealistic work demands (Maslach, Schaufeli, & Leiter, 2001). Outcomes of burnout include reduced job productivity, depression, poor physical health, increased absenteeism and turnover, and more interpersonal conflict (Kahill, 1988). Burnout can also result in staff perceiving clients less favorably (Corcoran, 1986) and has been linked with substance abuse. (Maslach et al., 2001).

VICARIOUS TRAUMATIZATION

Vicarious traumatization describes disruptions in the helper's schemas of self, other, and the world as a result of empathic exposure to the survivor's traumatic material. It was originally identified in trauma therapists, specifically in mental health professionals who served incest survivors and survivors of sexual abuse (McCann & Pearlman, 1990; Pearlman & Saakvitne, 1995). VT impacts several areas of schema: safety, trust, esteem, intimacy, and control (Pearlman & Saakvitne, 1995). In order to function effectively in the world, we must believe that we are safe, and that we govern our lives. However, when this belief in the fundamental safety of the world and in a person's ability to control his or her life is compromised, the individual's ability to enjoy life is also affected. For example, when forensic interviewers or police officers repeatedly hear the disclosures made by CSA survivors, their schema of the world as a safe place for themselves and for their children is compromised.

An example of the interrelatedness of our beliefs in fundamental safety and our own enjoyment of life outside of our professional roles is illustrated in this experience related to us by a colleague:

A therapist who worked in a forensic interviewing agency expressed her difficulty in going out to eat with her husband. She talked of looking around the restaurant, wondering which of the children present in the restaurant had been molested. She had stopped these "dates" with her husband, much to his confusion. She could not explain her concerns to him, but did bring them to her supervisor to process.

When her schema or her belief in the world as a place in which most children are happy and safe was disrupted, her ability to function effectively in the world, one aspect of which was to maintain a healthy, mutually enjoyed relationship with her husband, was compromised.

Secondary Traumatic Stress/Compassion Fatigue

Secondary traumatic stress (STS), later called *compassion fatigue*, was defined by Figley (1995) as "the natural consequent behaviors and emotions resulting from knowing about a traumatizing event experienced by a significant other—the stress resulting from helping or wanting to help a traumatized or suffering person" (p. 7). Figley proposed that helpers, after exposure to the traumatic material of trauma survivors, could develop a symptom cluster nearly identical to that seen in posttraumatic stress disorder (PTSD), including hyperarousal, reexperiencing, and avoidance (American Psychological Association, 2000). Positing STS as a mirror to PTSD, he named this symptom cluster "Secondary Traumatic Stress Disorder" (Figley, 2002).

A feature of STS is its focus on symptomatology and rapid onset, as distinct from vicarious traumatization (VT), which stresses cognitive shifts and deemphasizes causation (Jenkins & Baird, 2002). A colleague recently shared an experience with our team that highlights the difference between VT and STS. Having worked for several years in New Orleans post-Hurricane Katrina, she remarked to us one day that she could not watch the news coverage of the Haitian earthquake. She said that the plight of the Haitians too closely resembled that of the clients whose stories, anxiety, and grief she had "held" for years. Our colleague had engaged empathically with her clients, bearing witness to their traumatic material or narratives and had developed a distortion of her schema of safety and control (VT). This resulted in her current avoidance of a trauma reminder (STS) represented by the news coverage of the Haitian earthquake.

VT represents the purely cognitive effects of exposure to traumatic material. STS is a broader concept, encompassing a spectrum of symptoms mirroring PTSD including avoidance, reexperiencing, and hyperarousal. These could certainly be triggered by disruptions in cognitive schema, but would extend beyond those disruptions. Additionally, while VT generally results from repeated exposure to traumatic material over time, STS can occur after a relatively short exposure (Baird & Kracen, 2006). STS can impact helping professionals who work with survivors of trauma, and also the loved ones of the survivors (Figley, 1983). VT was associated with the cumulative effects felt by mental health professionals who engaged empathically with survivors of trauma (Pearlman & Saakvitne, 1995).

THE IMPACT OF CHILD SEXUAL ABUSE ON HELPERS

Working with CSA survivors places helpers at risk for STS, VT, and burnout. Pearlman and Mac Ian (1995) reviewed a number of studies looking at VT/STS impact on therapists treating survivors of child sexual abuse, rape survivors, and sexually traumatized clients, noting, "The trauma-specific literature tells us that doing trauma therapy can affect therapists negatively and that its effects are different from those related to doing general psychotherapy" (p. 559). In their review of the literature, Chouliara et al. (2009) found a consensus about the negative impact of CSA and sexual violence work on mental health providers, including avoidance and intrusive thoughts, schema disruptions, negative emotions (anger, sadness, horror), rescue fantasies about their clients, and high levels of burnout. They also found that although many clinicians reported a personal trauma history of maltreatment, sexual assault, and CSA, most studies failed to find statistically significant differences in VT and belief disruption, coping or burnout in CSA/sexual violence counselors and a variety of comparison groups. However, several of the comparison groups were in fields that could be vulnerable to STS including psycho-oncology professionals, child welfare workers, palliative care workers, and those who work with sex offenders. Since only symptoms of VT and burnout were explored in two of the three studies reviewed, STS may have been overlooked. Variables associated with increased VT and STS were younger age, increased exposure to sexual trauma work, and less professional experience whether general or specific experience working with sexual violence (Brady et al., 1999; Pearlman & Mac Ian, 1995; Schauben & Frazier, 1995).

A primary risk factor for the development of STS among clinicians treating CSA relates to caseload. Schauben and Frazier (1995) found that the percentage of sexual violence survivors in the therapist's caseload was correlated with increased PTSD symptomatology. The findings of Brady et al. (1999) were consistent, showing that "(w)omen psychotherapists who have more sexual abuse clients in their caseloads or see a high number of survivors over the course of their careers are more likely to exhibit trauma symptoms themselves" (p. 390) but not disruptions of cognitive schema.

Police are often the first to interact with children who have reported sexual abuse. Confronted with a child who has been victimized in this way, police in their role as protectors may feel pulled to intervene and rescue the child from the victimizer. However, their job is to document the information provided, gather relevant evidence, and escort the child to his or her forensic interview or medical examination. The desire for immediate and decisive action is redirected into the pragmatics of protocol, paperwork, and investigation.

Although limited research has been done into the effects of child abuse investigations on police officers, Martin, McKean, and Veltkamp (1986), in their study of 53 police officers, found that 26% exhibited clinical symptoms of PTSD related to their work with crime victims. The primary symptoms identified were intrusive thoughts and memories. Respondents noted that there was no ability to avoid the trauma reminders due to the nature of their work. Another study of PTSD symptoms in police officers as a precursor to STS found that the killing of a fellow officer in the line of duty and aiding victims of serious crime markedly increased the risk of developing trauma symptoms (Violanti & Gehrke, 2004). Interestingly, gender differences were found related to trauma risk. Female officers are at higher risk after working with abused children, and male officers are at higher risk after shooting incidents where officers were involved. The authors concluded that greater frequency and type of traumas could eventually lead to emotional compassion fatigue. Follette, Polusny, and Milbeck (1994) found in their study of law enforcement professionals tasked with CSA investigations that they "were significantly more distressed than mental health clinicians" (p. 279) working with the same population. Follette et al. theorized that one reason for this finding was that many more therapists (59.1%) than police (15.6%) reported participating in some form of therapy, which could serve as a protective factor. For police, stress, personal trauma history, and negative responses to investigation of CSA were predictive of trauma symptoms.

There are few studies that look at the psychological impact of CSA work on forensic interviewers. Perron and Hiltz (2006), in their online survey of 66 forensic interviewers affiliated with advocacy centers in the United States found no substantive evidence of STS or burnout associated with forensic interviewing or with any personal characteristics studied. An inverse association was identified between self-efficacy and both disengagement and STS. They hypothesized that the reason for the lack of correlation between interviewing and STS symptoms was the kind of relationship required. Forensic interviews are semi-structured and interviewers are trained to avoid any strong emotional connectedness to the child being interviewed. Perron et al. posited that, because STS is the result of hearing traumatic material from a significant other (Figley, 1995), that is, within the context of emotional connectedness, it would be less likely to occur where such connectedness is neither sought nor achieved. The relationship between self-efficacy and both a higher level of engagement and fewer STS symptoms is intuitive. The literature supports the notion that increased perceptions of autonomy correlates with job satisfaction (Maslach et al., 2001).

It should be noted that other members of a child advocacy center team who face varying degrees of exposure to the traumatic material elicited in the forensic interviews may be impacted in similar ways.

The physicians who conduct forensic examinations, the coordinators who set up the interviews, greet the family and attempt to make the child feel welcome and safe at their center, and directors who conduct multi-disciplinary conferences in which details about the abuse of numbers of children are reviewed all are subject to the stressors of helping trauma-tized children.

Child protection workers may be most at risk for developing STS, VT, and burnout. They work long hours for low salaries, carry heavy case-loads (averaging 24 to 31 children, far above the recommended 12 to 15 child caseload), and routinely cope with aggressive and angry clients and threats of violence (Alliance for Children and Families [ACF], American Public Human Services Association [APHSA], & Child Welfare League of America [CWLA], 2001; Friedman, 2002). In one study of 205 child protection workers, 77% reported having been assaulted or threatened while on the job (Cornille & Meyers, 1999). In addition, they struggle with administrative burdens (with CW workers spending an estimated 50% to 80% of their time on paperwork), limited supervision and insufficient training (U. S. General Accounting Office [USGAO], 2003). A 2004 survey conducted by the National Association of Social Workers (NASW) of the 716 members of their Child Welfare Specialty Practice Section reported that the most challenging aspects of their work were as follows: the issues facing their client families, caseload, paperwork, salary, media portrayal, working conditions, court appearances, safety and lack of train-ing. By contrast, the most satisfying aspect of their job was "successes with children and families" (p. 12). This highlights the fact that most do this job because they want to help children, a motivation that increases their vulnerability to STS. In order to be effective in their jobs, they must be able to engage with each child, gain the child's trust and listen to each child's story of deprivation and/or abuse. To be effective advocates for the child they may be required to read, write, and recite the details of these traumas many times to their supervisors, in court, to police, CASAs, health-care providers, and more, exposing themselves again and again to the harm inflicted on the vulnerable children in their care.

The workers' empathic engagement with the terrible stories of abuse that these children share with them increases their risk of developing the distorted schemas that are the hallmarks of VT. Their exposure to the trauma history of the children in their care, and the workers' repeatedly frustrated desires to help these children places workers at risk for developing STS. Indeed, Cornille and Meyers (1999) found that 37% of child protective workers in their study exhibited "clinical levels of emotional distress associate with STS" (p. 1). Organizational issues are thought to contribute to burnout. These may include low wages, limited resources, excessive caseloads, unsafe working environments, poorly defined roles, lack of autonomy, and long working hours. Other problematic organizational issues include excessive and redundant paperwork, unclear hierarchies, and gaps in services. When the state budget is reviewed each year, the demands on workers may change dramatically from one month to the next in response to budget cuts that reduce or discontinue much-needed supportive programs and services for their clients. Collins (2009) found that of workers at New York City's Administration for Children's Services, surveyed one week after their self-identified most distressing work-related experience, 60% reported clinically significant PTSD symptoms. Half of that group continued to experience these symptoms for an average of two years later.

Another group of professionals at risk for VT, STS, and burnout is juvenile and family court judges who must listen dispassionately to the stories of abuse and neglect that children in custody have endured (Osofsky, Putnam, & Lederman, 2008). They are tasked with determining the child's best interest as regards placement, hearing multiple stories of abuse and neglect each day, and often must weigh the law against the harsh realities faced by their charges. Results from a focus group conducted by the National Child Traumatic Stress Network, with juvenile and family court judges, revealed that 53% had received no training regarding the assessment and treatment of child trauma (2008). Respondents also described the building blocks of burnout in their careers including heavy dockets, and no opportunity to discuss or process the painful stories they listen to daily. Mistrust among judges was identified as an obstacle to peer support. Symptoms of VT were also found in criminal, family, and juvenile court judges in a study by Jaffe, Crooks, Dunford-Jackson, and Town (2003). They were noted to experience sleep disruptions, lack of concentration, irritability, depression, isolation, loss of spirituality and somatic complaints.

Criminal attorneys who prosecute child sexual abuse cases face different challenges. They must advocate aggressively for the survivor, heightening their empathic engagement with the child and eliciting the trauma narrative again and again, through the investigation, in deposing and preparing witnesses and finally in the court hearings. They must read police reports and medical records detailing the crime in ways the child cannot. They may endure watching pornographic videos of the perpetrator grooming or even abusing the child. Prosecutors' empathy and their repeated exposure to the child's trauma increases their vulnerability to STS and VT. A small study of prosecutors who worked primarily with CSA cases found that 41% demonstrated signs of work-related VT. Although they did not find a correlation between caseload and levels of VT, this was explained by the moderate caseloads most respondents reported (Russell, 2010).

WHAT WORKS? POLICY AND PRACTICE RECOMMENDATIONS

Research has delineated the ways in which those who work closely with survivors of CSA may be negatively impacted. In a natural progression, having identified risk factors for burnout, VT, and STS, more recent studies have examined interventions designed to address and/or prevent them. This section will provide a brief overview of these studies, highlighting those interventions that were found to be most effective in reducing or preventing burnout, STS, and VT.

SYSTEMIC INTERVENTIONS

For those who work with sexually abused children, burnout, vicarious traumatization, and secondary traumatic stress remain occupational hazards. The interplay among these three conditions requires interventions that address each. For example, Johnson and Hunter (1997) found elevated levels of emotional exhaustion and greater use of escape/ avoidance coping in their study of sexual violence (SV) counselors as compared to non-SV counselors. Emotional exhaustion is a central characteristic of burnout, and escape/avoidance coping is symptomatic of STS (Figley, 1995; Maslach et al., 1997). Ongoing empathic engagement with survivors' traumatic material may result in distortions of the helper's schema regarding safety, trust, intimacy and control, symptomatic of VT. Research has shown that, while personal interventions may be helpful, systemic interventions may be even more important in the prevention of burnout, VT, and STS (Hernandez, Gangsei, & Engstrom, 2007; Maslach, 2003; Phelps, Lloyd, Creamer, & Forbes, 2009). Unaddressed STS, VT, and burnout are associated with long-term negative consequences including cynicism, increased absences from work, high employee turnover, decline in interpersonal relationships, depersonalization, avoidance, numbing, hyperarousal, powerlessness, decreased self-efficacy, and alterations of the helper's ability to trust, feel safe, and to sustain intimacy (Dunkley & Whelan, 2006; Figley, 2002; Maslach & Leiter, 1997; Pearlman & Mac Ian, 1995).

Sadly, many systems have not responded to this information, pointing to the urgent need for intervention at the policy level. The Child Welfare League recently reviewed the organizational-level prevention/intervention practices in child welfare agencies in 32 states. They found that most states had no protocol in place to address STS/VT, but only provided debriefings after a major crisis and employee assistance programs. Some states reported one-time trainings on STS with no follow-up. Only a few states indicated they were developing a more systemic and top-down, multileveled approach to STS/VT education/prevention/intervention (Collins, 2009). The recognition of the importance of systemic responses is long overdue. For many years recommendations regarding preventing and intervening in burnout, STS and VT were primarily directed at the individual, ignoring systemic issues which are often at the heart of these phenomena. Indeed, recent studies indicated that the use of individual preventative strategies, in the absence of organizational interventions, were largely ineffective.

In their study of the effectiveness of commonly recommended self-care strategies for trauma therapists, Bober and Regehr (2006) found that the therapists' beliefs in and use of such strategies was not correlated with lower traumatic stress scores. However, higher trauma scores were related to increased hours per week spent working with traumatized clients, while increased schema disruption was related to cumulative years of exposure to such clients. This supports the notion that organizational, rather than individual interventions would be more efficacious in preventing burnout, STS, and VT. Bober and Regehr concluded that, while the clinical community has advocated that trauma survivors not be blamed for their victimization, "when addressing the distress of colleagues, we have focused on the use of individual coping strategies, implying that those who feel traumatized may not be balancing life and work adequately" (p. 8). Phelps et al. (2009) asserted that, "with growing awareness of the links between work stress, stress-related conditions and mental health disorders, employers have a duty of care to protect the well-being of their personnel as much as possible" (p. 322).

Researchers have explored the risk and protective factors associated with VT and STS at the personal, professional and organizational levels. In Baird and Kracen's (2006) research synthesis, risk and protective factors identified in several studies of trauma therapists and child welfare workers were compared. Results indicated that there was evidence to support trauma history, coping style, and supervision experiences as predictors for VT. There was also evidence to support exposure to traumatic material and personal trauma history as predictors of STS. In their review of the literature, Chouliara et al. (2009) found relationships between size of caseload and symptoms of STS and VT, and between lower levels of professional experience and increased risk of developing VT. While helpers are often encouraged to do appropriate self-care, it is on the organizational and professional levels that much prevention work can be done.

INTERVENTIONS TO CHANGE POLICIES

The wealth of literature supporting the importance of top-down preventive measures to address burnout, STS, and VT suggests the urgent need to review and revise current policies regarding the workplace as it relates to those who work with CSA survivors. Although individuals may implement their own wellness and self-care plans, it is essential that there is a culture of concern at the organizational level. In the many self-care talks the authors have given and attended, there have been abundant anecdotal reports regarding a pattern of agencies apparently promoting self-care through workshops and posters, but not following through with improved policies regarding smaller caseloads, effective use of medical, vacation, and personal leave and substantive support through modeling by supervisors and administrators, peer-support opportunities, and ongoing reflective supervision. Helpers have expressed their frustration at being told how important self-care is, but being shown through example that self-denial and stoicism is the demonstrated agency policy. If true change is to take place, it must first take place at the policy level, and be modeled consistently by administrators and supervisors.

Preventing Burnout Maslach and Leiter (1997) outlined the steps that organizations can take to minimize the risk of burnout among their staffs. They proposed that burnout was "an important barometer of a major social dysfunction in the workplace" and stressed that "it's not the individual but the organization that needs to change" (p. 21). They described six factors as the "critical factors" that "either contribute to exhaustion or sustain the energy that people bring to their work" (p. 148): (1) sustainable workload; (2) feelings of choice and control; (3) recognition and reward; (4) a sense of community; (5) fairness, respect, and justice; and (6) meaningful and valued work. They stressed that establishing and maintaining a supportive and productive work environment was attainable only through the collaborative efforts of the organization and the employee.

Trauma Informed Systems The National Child Traumatic Stress Network (NCTSN) is spearheading the movement to create trauma–informed child serving systems. They propose to collaborate with child-serving systems to:

- Increase public awareness and knowledge about the impact of traumatic stress and the range of effective trauma assessment strategies and interventions which exist.

- Build strategic partnerships with national organizations that can assist with the dissemination of information, products and tools.
- Provide trauma-focused education and skill-building for front-line staff, clinicians and administrators within and across key child-serving systems in order to change practice (NCTSN, 2007).

To this end they have developed basic informational briefs for a variety of systems including child welfare, health care, juvenile justice, law enforcement/first responder and mental health systems. In addition, a few organizations have developed pilot programs to address burnout, STS, and VT among their staff. In a collaboration between the Administration for Children's Services (ACS) and the Mount Sinai School of Medicine (MSSM) the MSSM Children's Trauma Institute in New York City, an NCTSN member, developed a comprehensive pilot program to address STS in child welfare workers (Tullberg & Chemtob, 2009). The resilience-based, skills-focused intervention provided four training units each to both an intervention group and a control group of child welfare workers and their supervisors. Six months of follow-up sessions were provided to the intervention group, while the control received only a one-time secondary trauma training. Findings indicated that intervention participants had greater optimism, improved stress-management, greater job satisfaction, less burnout, lower attrition rates in new workers and fewer overdue cases as compared to controls.

The Connecticut Department of Children and Families' Training Academy and the Division of Special Reviews and Staff Support developed a multilevel training and support program to address STS in their staff. At the organizational level, workers are assigned balanced caseloads, a team-oriented working environment is provided with a focus on competency, safety and trust, and flexible scheduling including the use of adequate vacation and sick leave and the use of personal time for stressed workers. This organization also supports professional self-care by providing on-site supports. For example, regular supervision is provided, and the ABCs of professional care are stressed: *Awareness* of STS as an occupational hazard and focusing their empathy on client strengths and resilience, *balancing* work and home lives, and *connection* with professional supports including supervisors and peers (Collins, 2009). Model programs like those mentioned earlier offer options for struggling agencies as they tailor programs for their own employees.

Those helpers who work within a response team can also be a source of support for those who work with traumatized clients. Team members can monitor each other for signs of stress and provide mutual support.

They can normalize the strong responses members may have after working with a client. Teams provide the opportunity for informal "debriefs" after a potentially traumatic event or session. They can be a "holding" environment for a traumatized helper, creating a safe space in which the helper can heal.

PRACTICE INTERVENTIONS TO ATTENUATE STS AND VT

Although the literature points to change at the policy/organizational level as the most effective in mitigating the impact of burnout, STS, and VT, a full discussion should include those practice interventions that have been deemed as helpful adjuncts to organizational supports. Some clinicians in small or private practices may only require interventions at the practice level. In those cases, the importance of regular professional supervision and peer support, and the use of positive coping strategies to provide a strong line of defense against STS and VT are strongly indicated.

Clinicians and other professionals who work with CSA survivors require adequate training and supervision in order to perform their duties responsibly and to maintain longevity in the field, yet few perceive they are receiving enough. Follette et al. (1994) found that "(a)pproximately 96% of mental health professionals and 93% of law enforcement officers reported that educating themselves about sexual abuse was an important way of coping with difficult sexual abuse cases" (p. 281). In those studies that looked at the impact of burnout, STS, and VT in trauma therapists and child welfare workers, a consistent theme was the need for advance training to prepare clinicians and workers for the risks associated with treating survivors of trauma (Harrison & Westwood, 2009; NASW, 2004; Pearlman & Mac Ian, 1995). Training in general trauma, in the impact of working with survivors of CSA, and in effective coping skills (including mindfulness techniques and self-care) were suggested.

A supportive work environment and ready access to continuing education throughout a helper's career have also been recommended. Professional supervision and peer consultation are integral parts of a supportive work environment. Given the vulnerability of younger and less experienced clinicians, adequate amounts of supervision on a regular schedule and based on level of experience could beneficially impact retention and longevity in trauma work. Pearlman and Saakvitne (1995) recommend a minimum of one hour of supervision weekly for more experienced clinicians and more frequent supervision for beginning clinicians. Consistent and ongoing professional supervision has been identified as a protective factor regarding the development of STS and VT (Etherington, 2009; Pearlman & Mac Ian, 1995; Phelps et al., 2009; Pistorius, Feinauer, Harper, Stahmann & Miller, 2008). It can benefit helpers by providing ongoing education in the helper's profession, supportive responses to address the negative feelings experienced by the helper, guidance in identifying and maintaining healthy professional boundaries with clients and monitoring for signs of STS and VT. Indeed, the provision of regular supportive consultation and supervision was cited most frequently across professions as a protective factor (Chouliara et al., 2009; Collins, 2009; Etherington, 2009; Harrison & Westwood, 2009; NASW, 2004; Pearlman & Mac Ian, 1995; Pistorius et al., 2008).

Monitoring caseloads to ensure clinicians are carrying appropriate numbers of clients and that there is not a disproportionate representation of severe trauma cases in any single clinician's caseload is recommended as well (Maslach & Leiter, 1997; Schauben & Frazier, 1995). Attention to balancing workload, including assigning fewer and less severe trauma cases to inexperienced clinicians is indicated as a preventative to burn-out, STS, and VT (Baird & Jenkins, 2003; Brady et al., 1999; Pearlman & Mac Ian, 1995). Ideally this should occur at the organizational level, but helpers may be required to advocate with their agencies for more balanced workloads. Supervisors should support their supervisees by advocating for them and promoting systemic changes in practices regarding case assignments. With paced increases of caseload in relation to experience and with consistent professional supervision, the helper's capacity to take on more challenging cases will steadily increase and their capacity to cope with the stressors this creates will be improved. Indeed, studies demonstrated that while inexperienced clinicians were more susceptible to VT and burnout, more experienced clinicians showed no such vulnerability (Baird & Jenkins, 2003; Way, Van Deusen, Marin, Applegate, & Jandle, 2004).

PERSONAL INTERVENTIONS

Some personal characteristics may play a role in the development of burnout, STS and VT, but others may play a role in its prevention. For example, although personal trauma history was correlated in studies with increased VT in trauma therapists and child welfare workers, a personal history of sexual trauma was *not* predictive of VT in therapists treating sexual assault survivors (Chouliara, et al., 2009; Dunkley & Whelan, 2006). Clinician's negative coping responses and level of personal stress were correlated with increased VT and STS (Follette et al., 1994). Schauben and

Frazier (1995) found that positive coping strategies (e.g., exercise, healthy diet, reframing difficulties, problem solving and seeking personal and professional support) were found to be correlated with fewer STS, VT, and burnout while negative coping strategies (e.g., disengagement, alcohol use and denial) were associate with greater symptomatology.

Thus the literature appears to support the notion that traditional self-care techniques may reduce some symptoms of burnout, STS, and VT. A synthesis of the most commonly recommended personal interventions follows: maintain exercise and a healthy diet; get adequate sleep; have realistic expectations of oneself and of others; maintain healthy boundaries both professionally and personally; identify one's own unique "red flags" of increased stress; find relaxing hobbies; use social supports, including friends and family; engage in a meaningful spiritual practice; participate in personal therapy; and use stress-management techniques. Additional strategies include the use of mind-body techniques such as massage, mindfulness, meditation, or yoga. These may be effective in concert with organizational and professional supports, but we caution against the notion that individual interventions in isolation will attenuate burnout, STS, or VT symptoms.

CONCLUSION

Much of the literature has focused on the negative impact of working with CSA and other trauma survivors. However, researchers are currently making a case for the concept of *vicarious resilience* as a result of their interviews with therapists who worked with survivors of political violence and kidnapping (Hernandez et al., 2007). Vicarious resilience (VR) is defined as a "resilience process" that "is characterized by a unique and positive effect that transforms therapists in response to client trauma survivors' own resiliency" (p. 237). Hernandez et al. contend that therapists may gain resilience as readily as they may become wounded by empathically engaging with the client's trauma material. They identified the key elements in the development of VR:

> witnessing and reflecting on human beings' immense capacity to heal; reassessing the significance of the therapists' own problems; incorporating spirituality as a valuable dimension in treatment; developing hope and commitment; articulating personal and professional positions regarding political violence; articulating frameworks for healing; developing tolerance to frustration; developing time, setting and intervention boundaries that fit therapeutic interventions in context; using community interventions; and developing the use of self in therapy. (p. 238)

This may be an area of great promise for professional development among helpers who work with trauma as it builds on a wealth of literature on resilience and strengths-based interventions, turning the lens of intervention from the client to the helper.

Helpers who work with survivors of CSA are uniquely vulnerable to symptoms of burnout, secondary traumatic stress, and vicarious trauma. Although individual helpers may benefit from personal self-care strategies, research suggests that burnout, STS, and VT are more effectively addressed through top-down, organizational interventions. However, much work remains to be done in promoting effective policy change and in identifying best practices in this arena, including research to determine what interventions show the most promise, and coordinated education though professional organizations, regarding promising practices.

REFERENCES

Alliance for Children and Families, American Public Human Services Association & Child Welfare League of America. (2001, May). *The child welfare workforce challenge: Results for a preliminary study.* Paper presented at Finding Better Ways, Dallas.

American Psychological Association. (2000). *Diagnostic and statistical manual of mental disorders* (4th ed., Text rev.). Washington DC: American Psychiatric Association.

Baird, S., & Jenkins, R. J. (2003). Vicarious traumatization, secondary traumatic stress and burnout in sexual assault and domestic violence agency staff. *Violence and Victims, 18,* 71–86.

Baird, K., & Kracen, A. C. (2006). Vicarious traumatization and secondary traumatic stress: A research synthesis. *Counselling Psychology Quarterly, 19*(2), 181–188.

Bober, T., & Regehr, C. (2006). Strategies for reducing secondary or vicarious trauma: Do they work? *Brief Treatment and Crisis Intervention, 6*(1), 1–9.

Brady, J. L., Guy, J. D., Polestra, P. L., & Brokaw, B. F. (1999). Vicarious traumatization, spirituality and the treatment of sexual abuse survivors: A national survey of women psychotherapists. *Professional Psychology: Research and Practice, 30*(4), 386–393.

Chouliara, Z., Hutchison, C., & Karatzias, T. (2009). Vicarious traumatisation in practitioners who work with adult survivors of sexual violence and child sexual abuse. *Counselling and Psychotherapy Research, 9*(1), 47–56.

Collins, J. (2009, March/April). Addressing secondary traumatic stress. *Children's Voice,* 10–14.

Corcoran, K. (1986). The association of burnout and social work practitioners' impressions of their clients: Empirical evidence. *Journal of Social Service Research, 10,* 57–66.

Cornille, T. A., & Meyers, T. W. (1999). Secondary traumatic stress among child protective service workers: Prevalence, severity and predictive factors. *TRAUMATOLOGYe* 5(1), 1–17, at www.fsu.edu/~trauma/contv5i1.html

Dunkley, J., & Whelan, T. A. (2006). Vicarious traumatization: Current status and future directions. *British Journal of Guidance & Counselling, 34*(1), 107–116.

Etherington, K. (2009). Supervising helpers who work with the trauma of sexual abuse. *British Journal of Guidance and Counselling, 37*(2), 179–194.

Farber, B. A. (1991). *Crisis in education: Stress and burnout in the American teacher.* San Francisco, CA: Jossey-Bass.

Figley, C. (1983). Catastrophes: An overview of family reactions. In C. R. Figley & H. I. McCubbin (Eds.), *Stress and the family: Vol. 2. Coping with catastrophe* (pp. 3–20). New York, NY: Brunner/Mazel.

Figley, C. (1995). *Compassion fatigue: Coping with secondary traumatic stress disorder in those who treat the traumatized.* New York, NY: Brunner/Mazel.

Figley, C. (2002). Compassion fatigue: Psychotherapists' chronic lack of self care. *Psychotherapy in Practice, 58*(11), 1433–1441.

Follette, V. M., Polusny, M. M., & Milbeck, K. (1994). Mental health and law enforcement professionals: Trauma history, psychological symptoms and impact of providing services to child abuse survivors. *Professional Psychology: Research and Practice, 25*(3), 275–282.

Freudenberger, H. J. (1980). *Burn out: How to beat the high cost of success.* New York, NY: Bantam Books.

Friedman, R. (2002, Winter). The importance of helping the helper. Best practice, next practice, a publication of the national child welfare resource center for family-centered practice. *Trauma and Child Welfare,* 16–21.

Harrison, R. L., & Westwood, M. J. (2009). Preventing vicarious traumatization of mental health therapists: Identifying protective practices. *Psychotherapy Theory, Research, Practice, Training, 46*(2), 203–219.

Hernandez, P., Gangsei, D., & Engstrom, D. (2007). Vicarious resilience: A new concept in work with those who survive trauma. *Family Process, 46*(2), 229–241.

Jaffe, P. F., Crooks, C. V., Dunford-Jackson, B. L., & Town, M. (2003). Vicarious trauma in judges: The personal challenge of dispensing justice. *Juvenile and Family Court Journal, 54*(4), 1–9.

Jenkins, S. R., & Baird, S. (2002). Secondary traumatic stress and vicarious trauma: A validational study. *Journal of Traumatic Stress, 15*(5), 423–432.

Johnson, C. N. E., & Hunter, M. (1997). Vicarious traumatisation in counsellors working in the New South Wales sexual assault service: An exploratory study. *Work and Stress, 4,* 319–328.

Kahill, S. (1988). Symptoms of professional burnout: A review of the empirical evidence. *Canadian Psychology, 29,* 284–297.

Martin, C. A., McKean, H. E., & Veltkamp, L. J. (1986). Post-traumatic stress disorder in police and working with victims: A pilot study. *Journal of Police Science & Administration, 14*(2), 98–101.

Maslach, C. (1982). *Burnout: The cost of caring.* Englewood Cliffs, NJ: Prentice-Hall.

Maslach, C. (2003). Job burnout: New directions in research and intervention. *Current Directions In Psychological Science, 12*(5), 189–192.

Maslach, C., & Leiter, M. P. (1997). *The truth about burnout.* San Francisco, CA: Jossey-Bass.

Maslach, C., Schaufeli, W. B., & Leiter, M. P. (2001). Job burnout. *Annual Review of Psychology, 52,* 397–422.

McCann, L., & Pearlman, L. A. (1990). Vicarious traumatization: A framework for understanding the psychological effects of trauma work on trauma therapists. *Journal of Traumatic Stress, 3,* 131–149.

Moore, B., & Fine, B. (1990). *Psychoanalytic terms and concepts.* Binghamton, VT: Vail-Ballou Press.

National Association of Social Workers. (2004). *"If you're right for the job, it's the best job in the world": The national association of social workers' child welfare specialty practice section members describe their experience in child welfare.* Washington, DC: NASW.

National Child Traumatic Stress Network. (2007, July). Creating trauma informed child-serving systems. *NCTSN Service Systems Briefs,* V1, n1. NCTSN.org

National Child Traumatic Stress Network. (2008, August). Judges and child trauma: Findings from the national child traumatic stress network/national council of juvenile and family court judges focus groups. *NCTSN Service Systems Briefs,* V2, n2. NCTSN.org

Osofsky, J. D., Putnam, F., & Lederman, C. (2008). Vicarious traumatization and compassion fatigue: How to maintain emotional health when working with trauma. *Juvenile and Family Court Journal, 59,* 91–101.

Pearlman L. A., & Mac Ian, P. S. (1995). Vicarious traumatization: An empirical study of the effects of trauma work on trauma therapists. *Professional Psychology: Research and Practice, 26*(6), 558–565.

Pearlman, L. A., & Saakvitne, K. W. (1995). *Trauma and the therapist: Counter-transference and vicarious traumatization in psychotherapy with incest survivors.* New York, NY: Norton.

Perron, B. E., & Hiltz, B. S. (2006). Burnout and secondary trauma among forensic interviewers of abused children. *Child & Adolescent Social Work Journal, 23*(2), 216–234.

Phelps, A., Lloyd, D., Creamer, M., & Forbes, D. (2009). Caring for carers in the aftermath of trauma. *Journal of Aggression, Maltreatment & Trauma, 18,* 313–330.

Pick, D., & Leiter M. P. (1991). Nurses' perceptions of the nature and causes of burnout: A comparison of self-reports and standardized measures. *Canadian Journal of Nursing Research, 23,* 33–38.

Pines, A., & Aronson, E. (1988). *Career burnout: Causes and cures.* New York, NY: Free Press.

Pines, A., & Maslach, C. (1981). Characteristics of staff burnout in mental health settings. In A. Briggs & A. Agrin (Eds.), *Crossroads: A reader for psychosocial therapy* (pp. 110–114). Rockville, MD: American Occupational Therapy Association.

Pistorius, K. D., Feinauer, L. L., Harper, J. M., Stahmann, R. F., & Miller, R. B. (2008). Working with sexually abused children. *American Journal of Family Therapy, 36,* 181–195.

Russell, A. (2010). Vicarious trauma in child sexual prosecutors. *Center Piece: The Official Newsletter of the National Child Protection Training Center, 2*(6), 1–7.

Schauben, L. J., & Frazier, P. A. (1995). The effects on female counselors of working with sexual violence survivors. *Psychology of Women Quarterly, 19,* 49–64.

Tullberg, E., & Chemtob, C. (2009). Implementing trauma informed system change within child welfare. At www.nctsn.org/nctsn_assets/pdfs/CTI_111408.pdf

U.S. General Accounting Office (GAO). (2003). *Child welfare: HHS could play a greater role in helping child welfare agencies recruit and retain staff.* Washington, DC: Author.

Violanti, J. M., & Gehrke, A. (2004). Police trauma encounters: Precursors of compassion fatigue. *International Journal of Emergency Mental Health, 6*(2), 75–80.

Way, I., Van Deusen, K. M., Marin, G., Applegate, B., & Jandle, D. (2004). Vicarious trauma: A comparison of clinicians who treat survivors of sexual abuse and sexual offenders. *Journal of Interpersonal Violence, 19,* 49–71.

CHAPTER 24

Preventing Childhood Sexual Abuse

An Ecological Approach

SANDY K. WURTELE and MAUREEN C. KENNY

B ASED ON THE magnitude of the problem and its association with a range of health outcomes, childhood sexual abuse (CSA) has been identified as a significant public health challenge by the Centers for Disease Control and Prevention, and its prevention has been listed as a priority concern (Hammond, 2003). Several experts have recommended using a public health approach to CSA prevention (e.g., Anderson, Mangels, & Langsam, 2004; Kaufman, Barber, Mosher, & Carter, 2002; Krugman, 1998; McMahon & Puett, 1999; Mercy, 1999). A public health model portrays sexual abuse as a *disease* and attempts to alter the interaction between agent (perpetrator), host (victim), and environment (community, society). With this approach, the problem is defined, risk and protective factors are identified, prevention strategies are developed and evaluated, and effective strategies are then adopted.

The public health approach also advocates a focus on primary prevention strategies. With respect to CSA, primary prevention efforts are aimed at the general population for the purpose of stopping abuse before it occurs. Services are offered to everyone, regardless of risk status (i.e., universal prevention efforts). Primary prevention also includes modifying conditions in the environment or ecology that promote or support the sexual victimization of children.

Researchers, health educators, and other health-care professionals have become aware of the necessity of adopting ecological perspectives when examining influences on health outcomes (Salazar et al., 2009). An ecological approach emphasizes that behaviors happen within a context, and examines the bidirectional transactions between human beings and the systems in which they interact. Increasingly, prevention is moving from individual-focused programming to community-based models. These efforts are based on Bronfenbrenner's ecological model, which promotes intervening at the individual, relationship, community, and cultural contexts (Bronfenbrenner, 1977; Zielinski & Bradshaw, 2006). Bronfenbrenner identified four specific environmental systems as influencing the individual: the micro-, meso-, exo-, and macrosystems. This chapter reviews the impact of two of those environmental systems on the incidence of CSA: micro- and macrosystem. The microsystem refers to the most immediate settings containing the developing child, and this chapter focuses on the microsystems of the child's home and youth-serving organizations. The macrosystem refers to cultural beliefs and values that influence all the other systems.

An ecological approach is highly compatible with a public health framework. In the public health field, consensus has emerged that the etiology of many health problems arise from multiple levels, and, therefore, interventions focused on a single level of influence are limited (Wandersman & Florin, 2003). Applying this heuristic to CSA, preventing the occurrence of child sexual victimization can be done by educating parents, children, schools, and the community at large about CSA. Previous efforts to prevent CSA have primarily focused on educating children, less frequently on informing parents/caretakers, and infrequently on modifying environments in which CSA occurs. This chapter reviews primary prevention efforts directed at these three targets (i.e., youth, parents, and community). The need for prevention efforts is demonstrated, and empirical findings about effectiveness are presented. Challenges to comprehensive prevention efforts are described, and suggestions for expansion of interventions are offered.

CHILD-FOCUSED PREVENTION EFFORTS

In response to the growing body of knowledge regarding the scope and consequences of CSA, many prevention programs were developed in the late 1970s and widely disseminated in the early to mid-1980s. In contrast to prevention programs for physical abuse or neglect of children, which focus on modifying caregiver behavior, the primary focus of CSA prevention efforts has been to equip children with the knowledge and skills they need to respond to or protect themselves from sexual abusers. Group-based instruction on personal safety has usually been conducted in educational settings.

School systems evolved as the obvious choice for teaching children about sexual abuse, given that their primary function is to inform and educate, and also because of their ability to reach large numbers of diverse children in a relatively cost-efficient fashion. A universal primary prevention approach of this nature also eliminates the stigma of identifying specific children or families as being at risk for sexual abuse, and thus avoids costly and intrusive interventions into family privacy.

One of the earliest programs designed for children was the Child Assault Prevention Program developed by Women Against Rape in Columbus, Ohio. Shortly thereafter, the "good touch–bad touch–confusing touch" continuum was created by Cordelia Anderson and was later produced in a play. Stimulated by federal funding allocated through the National Center on Child Abuse and Neglect, several books, films, plays, and structured prevention education curricula targeting children began appearing. Many children participated in these educational programs. In fact, in 1990 more than 85% of U.S. school districts surveyed offered CSA prevention programs (Abrahams, Casey, & Daro, 1992). In 1993, a telephone survey of 2,000 young people between the ages of 10 and 16 found that 67% of respondents reported having participated in a school-based CSA prevention program (Finkelhor & Dziuba-Leatherman, 1995). Current rates of school-based program implementation are unknown, although one study found that 60% of public elementary schools in Texas reported implementing a CSA program (Lanning, Ballard, & Robinson, 1999).

Most child-focused personal safety programs share common goals, including: (a) helping children *recognize* unsafe situations or potential abusers; (b) teaching children to verbally *refuse* inappropriate requests by saying no; (c) encouraging children to physically *resist* by removing themselves from the potential perpetrator; (d) encouraging children to *report* previous or ongoing abuse to a trusted authority figure; and (e) helping children understand that the secret or inappropriate touching is never the child's fault—it's always the abuser's *responsibility* (Wurtele, 2008, 2010). Thus, classroom-based curricula emphasize training in these five "R's" (Recognize, Refuse, Resist, Report, and Responsibility). Programs typically cover various concepts to help children better recognize the abusive context (e.g., perpetrators can be both strangers and people they know). Some programs also teach children the correct terminology for the genitals, so they can effectively communicate experiences of inappropriate touching.

Need for Child-Focused Education

In general, children report minimal knowledge of sexual abuse and self-protection skills (Wurtele, 1998). Research clearly shows that children, especially young ones, have difficulty recognizing potential perpetrators (Kenny & Wurtele, 2010). In one study of 406 children ages 3½ years to 5½ years, only 38% correctly recognized inappropriate touch requests; instead, the majority regarded sexual touching as acceptable (Wurtele & Owens, 1997). Furthermore, half of the children believed that abuse was the child's fault, and few participants thought that children should report secret touching. Few children were willing to tell anyone about the abusive incident, and even fewer knew how to report.

Other research has found that although almost all preschool children know the correct terms for their nongenital body parts, very few know the correct names for genitals (Kenny & Wurtele, 2008; Wurtele, 1993; Wurtele, Melzer, & Kast, 1992d). Knowing the correct terminology for genitals facilitates helpful responses to children's disclosures of abuse. In contrast, children who make disclosures using incorrect and idiosyncratic terminology (e.g., "She touched my muffin") may not be understood and, consequently, may not receive a positive, supportive response. As a result, adults may be less likely to report abuse and child protection agencies may be reluctant to investigate reports perceived as difficult to substantiate.

Empirical Findings About Effectiveness

Evaluations have documented that both school- and preschool-aged children demonstrate enhanced knowledge about CSA prevention concepts following program participation. After participating in personal safety classes, children have demonstrated increased ability to: (a) recognize potentially abusive situations, (b) resist potential lures, (c) report abusive situations, (d) blame the perpetrator, not the child, and (e) report positive feelings about their bodies and genitals (Kenny & Wurtele, 2009; Wurtele & Owens, 1997). In their meta-analysis of CSA prevention evaluation studies, Berrick and Barth (1992) reported large effect sizes for both preschool-aged children ($d = .86$) and elementary school-aged children ($d = .98$). Knowledge gains have been shown to be maintained for up to one year (Briggs & Hawkins, 1994).

Research also shows that preschool- and school-aged children can learn certain preventive skills. In their meta-analysis, Rispens, Aleman, and Goudena (1997) found a significant and considerable mean post-intervention effect size for skill gains ($d = .71$), and concluded that victimization prevention programs are successful in teaching children sexual abuse concepts and self-protection skills. Zwi and colleagues (2007) also concluded that school-based educational programs result in significant improvements in both knowledge and protective behavior measures. Programs that were delivered over four or more sessions produced the highest effect sizes. A review of reviews on the effectiveness of universal child maltreatment interventions concluded that "school-based interventions to prevent child sexual abuse are effective at strengthening protective factors against this type of abuse (e.g., knowledge of sexual abuse and protective behaviors)" (Mikton & Butchart, 2009, p. 354). Finally, in his review of child-focused educational programs, Finkelhor (2007) concluded that "the weight of currently available evidence shows that it is worth providing children with high-quality prevention-education programs" (p. 644).

What constitutes a "high-quality" program? Ample research concludes that programs that incorporate modeling (i.e., demonstrating the skill to be learned) and rehearsal (e.g., role-plays) are more effective than programs that primarily rely on individual study or passive exposure. For example, the U.S. General Accounting Office's (1996) summary of CSA educational programs concluded that concepts and skills are better grasped when taught with active participation (e.g., modeling, role-playing, or behavioral rehearsal techniques) than with more passive methods (e.g., films or lectures). A similar conclusion was reached by Finkelhor and Dziuba-Leatherman (1995) who asked 2,000 youth about their experiences with and responses to actual or threatened sexual assaults. Children were more likely to use self-protection strategies if they had received comprehensive prevention instruction, which included opportunities to practice the skills in class (Finkelhor, Asdigian, & Dziuba-Leatherman, 1995). Likewise, Roberts and Miltenberger (1999) concluded that "a behavioral skills training approach to prevention results in the greatest improvement in sexual abuse knowledge and prevention skills relative to approaches involving plays, films, lecture/ discussion, and written materials" (p. 85). In their meta-analysis, Rispens et al. (1997) found that resistance skill scores were higher when children participated in active-learning programs that provided multiple opportunities for children to practice the skills during the program. In another meta-analysis, Davis and Gidycz (2000) concluded that "programs that allowed physically active participation and made use of behavioral skills training such as modeling, rehearsal, and reinforcement produced the largest changes in performance level" (pp. 261–262).

SUMMARY AND IMPLICATIONS FOR CHILD-FOCUSED PREVENTION

In summary, ample empirical evidence exists attesting to the importance of behavioral skills training for teaching children self-protection skills (see also Hazzard, Webb, Kleemeier, Angert, & Pohl, 1991; Poche, Yoder, & Miltenberger, 1988; Wurtele, 2008). The National Center for Missing and Exploited Children (NCMEC, 1999) has published guidelines for CSA prevention programs (available at www.ncmec.org). These guidelines suggest that prevention programs: (a) be developmentally appropriate with regard to language, content, and teaching methods; (b) use behavior rehearsal, role-playing, and feedback to teach skills; (c) occur on multiple occasions over several years and include periodic reviews and supplemental sessions to reinforce skills; and (d) include homework and active parental involvement.

Despite empirical evidence and NCMEC recommendations to employ behavioral approaches to teach personal safety skills, a survey of 87 CSA prevention programs found that only 37% of programs used role-play activities for the children to practice the skills (Plummer, 2001). Instead, children were much more likely to be shown movies or videos (74%) and the majority (63%) of programs used one-time sessions to educate youth. Inadequate programming may be due to limited resources; a problem reported by over 70% of the programs surveyed. The lack of effective programming may also be driven by the pressures on schools for academic accountability, which may leave less time for implementation of "social-emotional programs" (Zins, Weissberg, Wang, & Walberg, 2004). CSA prevention programs also compete for limited time during the school day with prevention programs targeting other social problems (e.g., bullying, dating violence, sexual harassment).

PARENT-FOCUSED PREVENTION EFFORTS

Consistent with NCMEC (1999) guidelines that recommend active parental involvement in CSA prevention efforts, experts have encouraged schools to enlist parents as "partners in prevention" (Wurtele & Miller-Perrin, 1992). There are many advantages to partnering with parents to help prevent CSA. One role a parent plays in prevention efforts is to support their child's participation in a school-based program. Parents who have concerns about these programs or believe they may endanger or harm their children may refuse to allow them to participate. By consenting to have their children participate in school-based programs, parents indirectly support prevention efforts. Parents can also be enlisted to provide more direct support in the role of adjunct teacher of personal safety. When parents are trained to be prevention educators, then their children receive repeated exposure to prevention information in their natural environment, thus providing booster sessions to supplement classroom presentations. Involving the family in the educational process may help reduce the secrecy surrounding the topic of CSA and can stimulate parent-child discussions about sexuality in general. Encouraging parents of preschool-aged children to discuss this topic at home may help prevent abuse that begins at early ages, before the children have an opportunity to participate in a school-based program. Educated parents would also be better able to identify child victims and respond appropriately to victim disclosures.

Another advantage of targeting parents is that parents can make the home environment safer for their children and they also have the ability to limit the access of potential perpetrators to their children. Many of the factors that heighten a child's risk for sexual exploitation relate to the home environment (i.e., lack of supervision or privacy, presence of unrelated males, restricted parent-child communication about sexuality, high frequency use of babysitters). Parent-directed educational programs have the potential to build assets in the home and reduce the child's risk for being sexually abused (Fieldman & Crespi, 2002). There are many other parent-tailored strategies to limit access of potential perpetrators to children. Parents could be trained to do safety screening on potential babysitter candidates, households in which their children play, and youth-servicing community programs (Kaufman, Mosher, Carter, & Estes, 2006; Wurtele, 2010; Wurtele & Berkower, 2010). According to the situational prevention model for CSA (Smallbone, Marshall, & Wortley, 2008), parents can create safer environments for their children by modifying their home environments to reduce the risk of sexual abuse, eliminate interactions between potential perpetrators and their children, and increase the supervision of their children. Parents are also key players in the prevention of sibling sexual abuse. As can be seen in Table 24.1, there are many risk factors for CSA in domestic settings and parents need to be informed about ways to decrease the risk factors and increase the protective factors within the child's home.

NEED FOR PARENT-FOCUSED PREVENTION EFFORTS

Preliminary research provides support for parental involvement in personal safety education. Several surveys of parents have shown that the majority of parents strongly support the education of children on this topic and that parents are receptive to learning more about CSA (e.g., J. Chen & D. Chen, 2005; Elrod & Rubin, 1993; Olsen & Kalbfleisch, 1999;

Table 24.1

Risk and Protective Factors Associated With CSA

Component	Risk Factors	Protective Factors
Perpetrator (Male)	Objectifies children (willing to use children sexually)	Respects and values children (no interest in using children sexually)
	Early attachment failures, frequently anxious attachments	Secure attachment patterns in infancy/childhood
	Early (before 10) and extensive use of pornography	Has someone who cares about/praises/loves him and who child trusts/admires
	Early (before 11) onset of masturbation	
	History of victimization and/or victimizing others	If past history of victimization, has received counseling and does not blame self
	Witnessed abuse/intrafamilial violence	No history of witnessing abuse/DV
	Empathy deficits (lack of empathy for child victims)	Empathy for, sensitivity to others
	Impulse control problems	Good decision-making and coping skills
	Cognitions/beliefs or fantasies supporting sexual contact with children	Absence of deviant cognitions or fantasies involving sex with children
	Creates or takes advantage of situations affording privacy and control over child	Knows adult-child sex is immoral and illegal
	Exhibits intrusive behaviors with children (insists on hugging, touching)	High self-esteem; good coping abilities
	Lacks respect for child's privacy and personal boundaries	Respects others' privacy and boundaries
	Prefers company of child(ren)	Healthy, nonexploitive relationships with adults
	Need for power and control over others (intimidates)	Equitable power relationships with others
	Sense of entitlement/narcissistic traits (cunning, conniving)	
	Sexual attraction toward children	Sexually attracted to adults

Table 24.1
(*continued*)

Component	Risk Factors	Protective Factors
	If parent, noninvolvement in early parenting	If parent, involvement in early parenting
	History of sexual activities with animals during childhood	
	Uses alcohol/drugs to lower inhibitions	
	Feelings of inadequacy, loneliness, vulnerability, dependency	
	Poor interpersonal skills	Good interpersonal skills
	High stress (e.g., unemployment)	
	Blames others, doesn't take responsibility	Takes responsibility for own behavior
	Depressed, socially isolated	Emotionally stable; good social supports
	Psychopathic characteristics (insincerity, antisocial behavior)	
Child	Lacks knowledge about appropriate and inappropriate sexual behavior	Knowledgeable about appropriate and inappropriate sexual behavior
	High need for attention or affection	Secure with self
	Low self-esteem, lacks confidence	High self-esteem and self-competence
	Emotionally neglected/insecure attachments	Secure attachments to caregivers; has support people
	Passive, unassertive, blindly obedient; need to please others	Assertive; willing to disobey authority figures
	Poor decision-making or problem-solving skills	Good problem-solving, decision-making skills
	Lacks knowledge about and understanding of sexual development	Knows about and understands sexual development
	Age-inappropriate sexual knowledge and behaviors	Age-appropriate sexual knowledge and behaviors

(*continued*)

Table 24.1
(*continued*)

Component	Risk Factors	Protective Factors
	Does not respect or set appropriate personal boundaries	Respects and sets appropriate personal boundaries
	Cognitive/physical disabilities	
	Early attachment failures	Secure attachment history
	Experienced abuse/neglect/ previous sexual abuse	No history of victimization
Child's Home	Caregivers not involved in child's life	Caregivers spend time with, are involved in, child's life
	Inefficient or sporadic supervision	Efficient supervision and monitoring
	Child's use of Internet not monitored	Child's use of Internet carefully monitored; Internet safety regularly discussed
	Family characterized by secretiveness, poor communication	Open climate; good communication patterns
	Over- or undersexualized home	Healthy sexual boundaries; healthy parent-child communication about sexual development
	Single parent home or presence of step-father or boyfriend	
	Families characterized by parental discord, divorce, violence	Supportive parent(s)
	Lack of privacy; household crowding	Adults and children respect each other's privacy
	Family history of drug/alcohol use	No substance abuse present
	Parent-child role reversal (inappropriate expectations regarding child's responsibilities)	Children are not expected to assume adult responsibilities
	Self-protective behavior not modeled by parents, children not taught personal safety	Importance of personal safety stressed in home; parents model safety behaviors and teach children body-safety rules
	Socially or geographically isolated	Good social supports

Table 24.1
(*continued*)

Component	Risk Factors	Protective Factors
	Power imbalance in marital dyad	Positive parental relationships (mutual, symmetrical)
	History of abuse in either parent	
	Inappropriately close or distant parent-child relationships	Appropriate boundaries between adults and children
	Children are exploited to meet parents' needs	Children are valued, loved, and respected
	Children are abused or neglected	Affectionate parent-child relationship, in which child's self-esteem is promoted
	Substitute caregivers not carefully chosen/screened	Substitute caregivers carefully chosen/screened
	Caregivers adhere to common myths about perpetrators	Caregivers are informed about perpetrators and the grooming process
	Caregivers demand that children obey authority figures	Children are empowered to refuse to obey authority figures when they make unsafe requests
	Caregivers insist that children give and receive physical affection	Caregivers allow children to choose how they demonstrate affection
Other Child-Serving Micro-systems	Background checks and screenings not conducted on staff or volunteers	Background checks and rigorous screenings done on all employees and volunteers who have contact with children
	Environment has high-risk situations where children can be sexually exploited	Environment set up to reduce the likelihood that a child could be sexually exploited
	Allows one-on-one interactions between adults/children	Prohibits one-on-one interactions between youth and adults
	No education/training in childhood sexual abuse	Staff members and volunteers receive education/training on what constitutes sexual misconduct and how it can be identified and prevented

(*continued*)

Table 24.1
(*continued*)

Component	Risk Factors	Protective Factors
	No rules about toileting, diapering, showering, or cleaning children	Has set rules about these intimate activities
	No policies prohibiting adult-child interactions outside of organization-sanctioned events	Has policy prohibiting private adult-child interactions outside of organization-sanctioned events
	Lack of policy statements regarding sexual misconduct	Clear and unequivocal policy statements that reflect zero tolerance for sexual misconduct
	Lack of policies and protocols for documenting disclosures and reporting sexual abuse	Clear policies for documenting and reporting sexual misconduct
	No provision of age-appropriate education on personal safety	Students receive age-appropriate education on sexual abuse/harassment
	Lack of sexuality education in educational system	Provision of comprehensive sexuality education
	No information/education regarding sexual misconduct provided to parents	Information/education regarding sexual misconduct available to parents
	Lack of community support/ services for families	Community support/services for families
Macro-Systems (society)	View children as possessions and commodities, and youth are not valued or viewed negatively	Culture opposed to deriving sexual satisfaction from children. Youth are highly valued, viewed as assets rather than problems, with child-protection policies to protect them from harm.
	People fail to recognize CSA as a public health problem	Media campaigns to enhance public awareness of CSA and to send message that it is wrong and illegal to use children sexually. Media coverage includes a "what to do about the problem" component.

Table 24.1
(*continued*)

Component	Risk Factors	Protective Factors
	Erotic portrayal of children in media and advertising (sexualization of children)	Zero tolerance for sexualizing children in media and advertising. Media portrays healthy sexual relationships.
	Reluctance of legal system to prosecute and punish offenders	Quick prosecution and consistent punishment of offenders by legal system
	Patriarchal-authoritarian subcultures	Cultural emphasis on equality between males and females
	Belief that children should always obey adults	Support for children's rights to refuse to obey authority figures
	Lack of CSA education in the curriculum in medical, educational, and mental health fields	Inclusion of CSA education in medical, educational, and mental health fields.
	Strong masculine sexualization (females viewed as inferior, under-represented in positions of power and influence)	Cultural emphasis on equality between males and females
	News media focuses on sensational cases of child abduction and rape	Media accurately reports on the less sensational but more frequent cases of CSA occurring in homes and youth-serving institutions.
	Media portrays offenders as "monsters" or "predators"	Media accurately describes offenders (as known acquaintances, respected members of the community, adolescents)
	Sexually explicit images of children available in media and on the Internet	Actively working to eliminate child pornography
	Few Internet-based interventions for parents and youth	Accurate, age-appropriate information about sexual health and CSA readily available on the Internet
	Community lacks treatment programs for offenders, victims, and family members.	Community has treatment programs available for victims, family members, and offenders

Reppucci, Jones, & Cook, 1994; Tutty, 1993; Wurtele, Kvaternick, & Franklin, 1992c). It is also clear from these surveys that parents have much to learn about CSA. There are many myths about CSA held by the public in general and parents in particular, myths that may affect a parent's willingness to allow his or her child to participate in a personal safety program. For example, parents who believe that their children are at low risk for sexual exploitation (Collins, 1996; Tang & Yan, 2004) or are too young to understand the topic (Wurtele et al., 1992c) may not support their children's personal safety education.

Despite adults' fears of sex offenders and parents' worries about child molestation (Kernsmith, Craun, & Foster, 2009; Levenson, Brannon, Fortney, & Baker, 2007), few parents report discussing CSA with their children (Deblinger, Thakkar-Kolar, Berry, & Schroeder, 2010; Tutty, 1997; Wurtele et al., 1992c). What parents *do* tell their children is often inaccurate. Child molesters are often described as "dirty old men" (Morison & Greene, 1992) or most frequently, as "strangers" (Berrick, 1988; Calvert & Munsie-Benson, 1999; J. Chen & D. Chen, 2005; Chen, Dunne, & Han, 2007; Deblinger et al., 2010; Wurtele et al., 1992c). Few parents accurately describe perpetrators (i.e., as being family members, substitute caregivers, teenagers, or authority figures), and they also tend to omit topics including the types of ploys that perpetrators use to lure children, such as tricks, bribes, and threats. Instead, parents tend to talk to their children about kidnapping or not taking candy or accepting rides from strangers.

Parents need to be informed about how to identify potential offenders, the types of ploys and manipulations they use to gain the trust and acceptance of the parent(s) and child, and how to talk to their children about this threat (Wurtele, 2010; Wurtele & Berkower, 2010). Given the potential for children to be abused via cyberspace through online sexual solicitation and access to pornography (Dombrowski, Gischlar, & Durst, 2007), it is critical that parents also be informed about safe Internet use. Parents should begin to educate their children about personal safety on the Internet as early as possible (see Willard, 2007; Wurtele & Kenny, 2010, for guidelines).

EMPIRICAL FINDINGS OF PARENT-FOCUSED EDUCATION

One way parents have been involved in CSA education is when schools inform parents about personal safety programs being implemented in the classroom. Schools commonly invite parents to view the materials before program implementation. A few programs distribute handouts to parents, describing the skills and concepts their children are learning.

In 1995, Finkelhor and Dziuba-Leatherman reported that only 11% of programs sent materials home to parents. According to Plummer's (2001) review of 87 child-focused programs, about half provided take-home educational materials. The depth and effectiveness of these parent-focused efforts are unknown. However, the value of including parents in prevention efforts is supported by Finkelhor's telephone interview study (Finkelhor et al., 1995). Programs that prompted parent-to-child discussions were more likely to result in children using the skills taught in the program.

Research also suggests that when provided with teaching materials, parents can effectively teach their children to recognize, resist, and report CSA (Wurtele, Currier, Gillispie, & Franklin, 1991; Wurtele, Gillispie, Currier, & Franklin, 1992a; Wurtele, Kast, & Melzer, 1992b). Studies have also demonstrated that preschoolers retain more knowledge about correct genital terminology when taught by parents as compared to teachers (Deblinger, Stauffer, & Steer, 2001; Wurtele et al., 1992d). In another study, parents viewed a commercially produced educational video ("What Do I Say Now?"; Borch, 1996), which portrayed parents talking to their children about sexuality and explaining to them how to resist unsafe touches. Compared with control parents, parents who viewed the video were more likely to report that they felt capable of discussing CSA with their children and reported greater intentions of talking to their children about CSA. At follow-up, parents who had attended the workshop reported having had significantly more discussions about CSA with their children compared with control parents (Burgess & Wurtele, 1998). Seeing parent actors demonstrate the skills proved effective in enhancing parents' self-efficacy beliefs, intentions to discuss CSA, and subsequently their CSA-related parenting behaviors.

More recently, Wurtele, Moreno, and Kenny (2008) evaluated a three-hour educational workshop designed to inform parents about CSA, promote parent-child communication about the topic of CSA, and help parents create safer environments for their children. A pretest–posttest design found that parents significantly increased their knowledge about the characteristics of perpetrators and reported increased parent-child communication about CSA.

CHALLENGES TO PARENT-FOCUSED PREVENTION EFFORTS

Although there are many advantages of having parents talk to their children about CSA, there are several challenges to developing a full partnership with parents. Home-based educational approaches would be difficult to implement with families experiencing abuse and/or dysfunction. Children in these homes not only need personal safety education at school, but finding a way to intervene with the parent(s) should be a priority. Additionally, school-sponsored workshops for parents tend to be poorly attended. Attendance at informational meetings has been quite low (e.g., 21% of parents in Tutty, 1997; 20% in Hébert, Lavoie, Piché, & Poitras, 2001), and fathers rarely attend (Elrod & Rubin, 1993; Tang & Yan, 2004; Tutty, 1993). Reviews of CSA prevention programs have found that parents often cited scheduling conflicts or lack of time as barriers to attending programs (Babatsikos, 2009; Wurtele & Kenny, 2010). Other factors found to influence parents' decisions to attend prevention programs include interest, qualifications of presenters, source of referral, time to attend, and location and time of program.

More research is needed to identify predisposing factors for parent participation in CSA prevention programs (e.g., Chasen-Taber & Tabachnick, 1999; Collins, 1996; Tang & Yan, 2004). Research is also needed to determine more effective ways of reaching parents, especially fathers (e.g., through the media, employer- or health-care sponsored workshops, in homes, faith-based institutions, libraries). The effectiveness of parent guidebooks on keeping their children safe from sexual abusers needs to be determined (e.g., Salter, 2003; Van Dam, 2001, 2006; Wurtele, 2010; Wurtele & Berkower, 2010). Internet-based interventions (IBIs) may be especially useful for parents, yet few existing IBIs are aimed at parent-child dyads (Amstadter, Broman-Fulks, Zinzow, Ruggiero, & Cercone, 2009). A few online educational programs about CSA exist (e.g., STAND for the Protection of Children and Youth at www.childsafeeducation.com) but their effectiveness has yet to be established. Web-based interventions can reach a large population at relatively low cost, and can be accessed privately and conveniently from the home—a plus for parents who may be reluctant or unable to attend school-based meetings.

COMMUNITY- AND SOCIETY-FOCUSED PREVENTION EFFORTS

As noted in the introduction, prevention experts have drawn attention to the need to create safer environments in addition to creating safer individuals. In this third and final section of the chapter, we suggest strategies that may be used to eliminate CSA in youth-serving institutional settings (i.e., microsystems) and at the broader societal level (i.e., macrosystem).

YOUTH-SERVING ORGANIZATIONS

These settings are establishments, organizations, and clubs that serve children for various purposes. They include schools, youth groups, faith-based institutions, and recreational or sporting clubs. As noted by Trocmé and Schumaker (1999), "participation in these activities provide children with important protective factors against sexual abuse including increased self-esteem and skills development, relationships with adults outside the home who may act as role models and confidants, and relationships with peers" (p. 631). Many of these organizations promote close and caring relationships between youth and adults outside the family, but this same closeness can provide opportunities for abuse to occur. Organizations must balance the need to keep youth safe with the need to provide them with beneficial adult mentoring and both adult and youth companionship. Although many more children are sexually abused in homes by parents, siblings, and relatives, a significant enough number of children are abused by staff in youth-serving organizations to warrant developing strategies to address this problem.

CSA in institutional settings has been recognized as a global problem. Research in the United States has revealed widespread sexual abuse of children by Catholic priests (John Jay College Research Team, 2004) and by teachers or others employed in school settings (Shakeshaft, 2004; Shoop, 2003). Recently, the Boy Scouts of America were ordered to pay $18.5 million in punitive damages for allowing troop leaders or volunteers to continue working with children even after the Scouts had received complaints that they had committed sexual abuse (Yardley, 2010). In 2001, *Seattle Post-Intelligencer* reporter Ruth Teichroeb exposed the unchecked sexual abuse plaguing state-run residential schools for deaf children across the country. Sexual abuse in formal and informal day care facilities in the United States has been reported (e.g., Finkelhor & Williams, 1988; Margolin, 1991). McAlinden (2006) reviewed several tragic cases of institutional abuse in England, Wales, and Ireland. In Canada, Trocmé and Schumaker (1999) reported on cases of CSA in educational and recreational settings and Moulden, Firestone, and Wexler (2007) described child care providers who sexually offended against youth. Others have reported on the sexual abuse of pupils by female and male teachers in Zimbabwean schools (Nhundu & Shumba, 2001; Shumba, 2004). In the United Kingdom, there have been numerous cases of the physical and sexual abuse of children in residential child-care facilities (Colton, Roberts, & Vanstone, 2010; Green, 2001) and in youth-serving community settings including schools and voluntary organizations (Gallagher, 2000). Sexual abuse occurring within competitive sports has been documented in several countries including the United States (Crosset, Benedict, & McDonald, 1995), United Kingdom (Brackenridge, 2001; Hartill, 2009), Germany (Palzkill, 1994), and Australia (Leahy, Pretty, & Tenenbaum, 2002).

Sullivan and Beech (2002) refer to sex offenders who use their employment to target and sexually abuse children as "professional perpetrators." In the following section, we will examine institutions and organizations where professional perpetrators have seized opportunities to sexually exploit children. Like others (e.g., Smallbone et al., 2008) we approach abuse in organizations through the lens of situational prevention theory (Tonry & Farrington, 1995). Situational prevention theory shifts attention from an exclusively individual-level focus to the context in which the potential offender and potential victim interact. Situational prevention of CSA depends on a thorough understanding of abusers' characteristics, how they select their victims, their strategies (modus operandi) for gaining victims' cooperation and maintaining their silence, and the characteristics of the settings that might contribute to abuse.

In the vast majority of accounts of CSA occurring in institutions or organizations, perpetrators obtain a trusted role or position where they have access to and power and authority over vulnerable children. Perpetrators are trusted by other staff members, parents, and children. They often have an appearance of being "above reproach." For example, Ralph Morris, principal of a residential school for behaviorally disturbed boys, was able to persuade others that "he could not possibly be an abuser because he was a middle class, heterosexual pillar of the local community" (Green, 2001, p. 14). Dr. Robert Shoop, author of *Sexual Exploitation in Schools*, describes how this coach gained the trust of parents: "I don't drink. I don't smoke. I don't do drugs and the parents knew this, they thought 'this individual is ok with my child'" (p. 30). In a study of clergymen who had sexually abused children, researchers Saradjian and Nobus (2003) quoted one priest who said, "I will never be suspected because I am a concerned, hardworking, and good priest. Should a complaint ever be made, the children wouldn't be believed" (p. 918). Abusers are sometimes described as charismatic (e.g., [Abuser] was a "powerful personality who made friends easily and commanded natural respect"; Green, 2001, p. 16). Perpetrators misuse their authority, control, trust, and reputation to take advantage of children's natural dependency, willingness to obey, desire to please, and naiveté about sexual activities.

There have been several studies aimed at understanding the strategies used by (male) sexual offenders. It appears that an offender's relationship with a victim has an impact on his modus operandi. For example, Leclerc, Proulx, and McKibben (2005) found that the modus operandi of 23 apprehended sexual offenders who worked with youth (e.g., as teachers, sports coaches) depended on their position of trust in relation to their victim. They used primarily noncoercive strategies to achieve victim compliance. To gain victims' trust, they spent a lot of time with the children, told them personal things, and gave them a lot of love and attention. They gained victims' cooperation in sexual activity by desensitizing victims through nonsexual touching and saying loving, caring things to them. Threats or coercive strategies were not needed to get victims involved in sexual activity because victims liked and trusted them. Few offenders used any strategies to maintain victims' silence (e.g., saying that the offender would go to jail or get in trouble if they told anyone). Leclerc et al. (2005) suggest that some offenders may believe that they do not need strategies to maintain victim silence due to the close relationship they have with the child. This may also be "due to the fact that their victims became so attached to them that they did not want to lose their friendship, love, affection or their special status" (p. 193). Using this and other studies of strategies used by sexual offenders, the following implications for prevention strategies are offered.

IMPORTANT COMPONENTS OF CSA PREVENTION FOR YOUTH-SERVING ORGANIZATIONS

The following section offers suggestions for how organizations can protect their youthful members from being sexually victimized. It covers various risk-management strategies including screening employees and volunteers, implementing policies to reduce high-risk situations, and establishing procedures for monitoring interactions between staff and youth. As no studies have tested these interventions, these suggestions remain speculative.

Screening and Selecting Staff   The most obvious prevention strategy for youth-serving organizations is to screen out potential perpetrators from obtaining positions in these institutions. And indeed, most youth-serving organizations conduct criminal background checks on all employees and volunteers. Although screening out known CSA offenders makes common sense, criminal record checks will not identify most sexual offenders because the majority of people who commit sex offenses do not get caught, let alone convicted. For example, Smallbone and Wortley (2000) found that more than three-quarters of their sample of CSA offenders did not have previous sexual offense convictions. Kendrick and Taylor (2000) suggest that although criminal checks are not the sole answer, they can act as a deterrent.

We recommend that programs use rigorous selection procedures and multiple methods to screen staff. Those methods might include the use of personality tests (e.g., Minnesota Multiphasic Personality Inventory; MMPI) or instruments assessing potential for abusing children (e.g., Child Abuse Potential Inventory; CAPI), although research into the effectiveness of using these instruments to screen for abuse potential has produced ambiguous results (e.g., Herman, 1995). In-depth personal interviews are also critical, asking applicants about their motives for wanting to work with children, along with previous histories of sexual offenses, violence against youth, substance abuse problems, attitudes toward control and punishment of children, and past rule-breaking or (nonsexual) criminal activities. Saul and Audage (2007) suggest that interviewers describe possible scenarios that involve personal boundary issues or youth protection policy violations in order to gauge the applicant's response. Because sexual offenders prefer to spend a lot of time with their victims (Leclerc et al., 2005), organizations need to determine if the applicant prefers the company of children over that of similar-age peers. Personal reference checks are also critical. Informal Internet searches of an applicant, which can be conducted free of cost, may reveal legal involvement or news stories related to sexual (or nonsexual) crimes.

Childhood victimization expert David Finkelhor argues that organizations should, along with background checks, do "foreground checks," meaning that the topic of child protection be brought to the "fore" in recruitment and hiring. He urges organizations to inform all applicants about the importance of child protection (Finkelhor, 2008). Saul, Patterson, and Audage (2010) recommend requiring an applicant to sign a document that describes the agency's commitment to protecting children and its expectation that employees will abide by this policy. Likewise, the guidebook *Preventing Child Sexual Abuse Within Youth-Serving Organizations* (Saul & Audage, 2007) recommends informing applicants about an organization's policies and procedures relevant to CSA prevention. An organization's obvious commitment to children's safety may encourage unidentified offenders to seek victims elsewhere. By emphasizing child protection it sends a very clear message: Children in this organization are off limits to sexual abusers (Wurtele & Berkower, 2010).

Protecting Youth in High-Risk Situations   The sexual victimization of a child requires privacy. The perpetrator needs to be alone with a child. Gallagher (2000) found that 92% of cases of institutional CSA involved lone perpetrators. As noted by Moulden et al. (2007), professional perpetrators are difficult to detect due to their "unsupervised access to victims and the trust that is bestowed upon them" (p. 397).

One strategy to prevent CSA in institutions, therefore, is to minimize opportunities for staff to be alone with children. Some organizations have a policy limiting one-on-one interactions between youth and adults.

For example, Boy Scouts of America (BSA) has a "two-deep leadership" policy, which requires that at least two adults be present on all trips and outings (BSA Youth Protection, n.d.). Furthermore, BSA prohibits one-on-one contact between adults and youth members. In situations that require personal conferences, the meeting is to be conducted in full view of other adults and youths. Some activities, such as traveling in a vehicle, overnight trips, bathing, changing clothes, and nighttime activities pose greater risks for CSA. Many codes of conduct prohibit youth workers from transporting children alone in a vehicle (e.g., BSA, n.d.). In sports activities, coaches should not be permitted to go to competitions or on trips alone with individual athletes, or to use the athletes' changing room or shower (Brackenridge, 1998). Depending on the mission of the organization, prohibiting or restricting such activities may be advisable when it is not possible to implement other risk-management procedures.

Another high-risk situation is when staff has contact with youth outside the context of the program. Organizations should limit contact between staff and youth to organization-sanctioned activities. Some organizations require that if a teen or adult employee/volunteer wishes to be in contact with a youth outside of organization-sponsored events, it must be with the knowledge and consent of the parents, and the staff member's supervisor must also be notified. Another way to control interactions between individuals is to institute a buddy system, where youth are required to travel with a peer and never alone.

Limiting Physical Contact   Some experts have recommended that adults avoid any kind of physical contact that could be misconstrued as sexual (e.g., hugging a child). Yet many positions require physical contact with children, and nurturing touch is vital to a child's development. And sometimes it is unclear if a behavior is appropriate, inappropriate, or harmful. As pointed out by Saul and Audage (2007), "hugging may be appropriate and positive in some circumstances, but it can also be inappropriate if the child is not receptive, if the employee/volunteer is hugging too often or for too long, or if the contact is romanticized or sexually intimate" (p. 10). It is important that organizations identify behaviors that fall into the categories of appropriate, inappropriate, and harmful, and carefully describe them in their codes of conduct.

Monitoring Interactions Between Staff and Youth   Organizations should develop a monitoring protocol defining inappropriate or harmful behaviors or boundary violations, which might indicate a potential perpetrator is grooming a child. All employees and volunteers should be informed about the monitoring protocol and clear about their roles and responsibilities regarding reporting inappropriate or harmful behavior. A well-designed supervisory plan can reduce the risks of sexual misconduct.

Managing Inappropriate Sexual Behavior Between Children There is increasing evidence of the problem of the sexual abuse of children by other children in residential child care (Kendrick & Taylor, 2000). Spencer and Knudsen (1992) found that in 10 out of 15 cases of sexual abuse in hospital settings, the perpetrator was another child rather than a staff member. Peer-to-peer abuse is not limited to residential settings as there are other situations where unsupervised youth can abuse other youth. When children participate in camps or sports activities that require showering or changing clothes and there is a policy preventing adults from being present, this situation can increase the possibility of youth abusing one another. As suggested by Saul and Audage (2007), a potential solution would be to adopt a policy requiring at least two adults present at all times.

Facilitating Children's Disclosures of Abuse It is essential that there are easily accessible ways for children to disclose abuse. Along with establishing formal complaints procedures, organizations should provide telephone and Internet help lines for children to express their concerns. Something as simple as a drop box for students to submit concerns may provide a confidential way for staff to find out about abusive situations.

Designing Safe Environments Opportunities to abuse may be reduced through physical redesign of the environment. Certain physical features of the setting can make children vulnerable to manipulation and exploitation. Isolated places should not exist in settings where adults work with children or, at least, be kept to a minimum. Spaces where children congregate should be open and visible to multiple people. To increase visibility, identify secluded areas and consider locking areas not being used for program purposes (e.g., closets), install windows in doors, and institute a "no closed-door" policy (Saul & Audage, 2007). In addition, multiple entry/exits should be staffed or monitored to check on individuals coming and going. Organizations should develop policies and procedures for reducing risk during activities such as toileting, showering, and changing clothes. In addition, parents should be encouraged to visit and observe their children at any time, with no area or time being off-limits. Some facilities install monitoring devices (e.g., video cameras). We recommend that settings where adults are working with children have zero-tolerance for sexual conduct between adults and children and children with each other (Kenny & Wurtele, 2009).

Training About CSA Prevention Adult education is the cornerstone of any CSA prevention plan. It is critical that in-service training programs be offered to all employees and volunteers to raise their awareness of CSA in youth-serving organizations. Indeed, Schirick (1998) describes education and training of staff as the "second line of defense" (after criminal background checks) against the risks of sexual misconduct. He notes that a solid training program will give those individuals who may have slipped through the screening process a heightened awareness of an organization's commitment to and intolerance of inappropriate behavior. Trainees need opportunities to discuss ethical principles underlying their care of youth, particularly the need to maintain professional boundaries, knowing what constitutes sexual misconduct, and acknowledging the potential for exploiting their greater status and power. Training should also be provided to staff on how to recognize and respond to questionable behaviors exhibited by fellow staff members, like when a coworker has a special or intimate relationship with a particular child, gives a particular student excessive attention, is seen touching the child in questionable or inappropriate ways, or communicates with a child (via e-mail, text messages, letters) about personal or intimate issues. When all employees adhere to the code of conduct they may be more willing to intervene in potentially unsafe situations (e.g., Bringer, Brackenridge, & Johnston, 2002).

Saul and Audage (2007) offer suggested content for education of employees/volunteers, caregivers, and youth. In addition, we recommend that parents whose children are enrolled in these organizations be educated about the characteristics of sexual offenders along with their grooming techniques, be informed about high-risk situations, and be encouraged to partner with the organization in keeping children safe from CSA. Encouragingly, Internet-based training interventions are beginning to appear.

When abuse has occurred in youth-serving organizations and litigation follows, the legal case often alleges that there was negligent hiring, supervision, or retention (Saul et al., 2010). Essentially, victims or their families claim that organizations did not adequately fulfill their duties of screening or supervising staff or failed to take decisive action when problems surfaced. Agencies are urged to continuously monitor their prevention and risk-reduction plans, perhaps with the professional aid of someone with program evaluation expertise (Kaufman, Hayes, & Knox, 2010).

CHALLENGES TO CSA PREVENTION IN YOUTH-SERVING ORGANIZATIONS

Saul and Audage (2007) describe some of the challenges that organizations face in preventing CSA. Certain beliefs can hinder CSA prevention (e.g., that CSA never happens in "my organization"). Particular fears or concerns can also thwart prevention efforts (e.g., fears of uncovering CSA cases; reluctance to talk about healthy sexuality and CSA). Then there are structural issues that hinder CSA prevention, including lack of resources, poor employee/volunteer retention, and problems with internal communication. This report offers many helpful ideas for overcoming these barriers and the interested reader is encouraged to refer to this document.

MACROSYSTEM INFLUENCES ON CSA

Thus far we have considered how CSA might be prevented by targeting potential victims, parents, and the settings in which CSA occurs (youth-serving organizations). We now turn our attention to how CSA might be prevented by targeting prevention efforts at the overarching macrosystem (society). In the next section we describe some of the more salient macro-level factors that support and even condone the sexual exploitation of youth (see Table 24.1 for a more complete list of macrosystem influences).

Cultural Attitudes About CSA   The United States is one of the few countries (along with Canada and Australia) to have extensive laws regarding child abuse (Mathews & Kenny, 2008). The laws established in the U.S. are intended to detect cases of abuse and neglect at an early stage, protect children, and facilitate the provision of services to children and families. Yet these laws exist within a society where fewer than half of U.S. citizens believe that CSA is a significant problem. A recent study by Stop It Now! (2010) found that only 44% of a large sample ($N = 5,241$) reported that CSA was a major problem in their community. Only 8% of the respondents knew of another adult who was probably sexually abusing a child in the past year. The authors of the report suggest, "We either do not recognize behaviors that should raise concerns about abuse or choose not to see them" (p. 8).

Sexual Socialization   Sexual socialization is defined as the process by which knowledge, attitudes, and values about sexuality are acquired (Ward, 2003). According to the American Psychological Association (APA, 2007), sexualization occurs when a person is sexually objectified—made into a thing for others' sexual use, a person's value comes only from his or her sexual appeal or behavior, and a standard is applied, which equates physical attractiveness with being sexy. For children, messages about sexuality come from family members, peers, school, church, and increasingly from the media, television, Internet, and magazines.

Entertainment Media   Rapid advances in technology—the Internet, cell phones, e-mail, text messaging—have made sexual images and information available to everyone, including children and teenagers. The American Psychological Association Task Force on the Sexualization of Girls (APA, 2007) concludes that, "virtually every media form studied provides ample evidence of the sexualization of women, including television, music videos, music lyrics, movies, magazines, sports media, video games, the Internet, and advertising" (p. 1). In her review of entertainment media in the sexual socialization of American youth, Ward (2003) concludes that frequent and involved exposure to sexually oriented genres such as soap operas and music videos is associated with greater acceptance of stereotypical and casual attitudes about sex, and occasionally with greater levels of sexual experience. Embedded in these sexualized images is the dangerous message that it is socially acceptable to view children as sexual objects and to use them sexually for personal or financial gain.

Given the content of some television programming and the extent to which most children view television (approximately two hours a day; Christakis, Ebel, Rivara, & Zimmerman, 2004), parents are encouraged to screen shows for sexual content and talk to their children about it when there is sexual content. Media education should also be incorporated into the school curriculum, starting in the elementary grades. Media literacy education enables youth to understand, analyze, and interpret media messages, and to expose the hidden agendas and manipulation. In addition, media literacy should be a part of every sex education and health education curriculum (Levin & Kilbourne, 2008).

Internet   An article in *Newsweek* (Norland & Bartholet, 2001) declared that the Internet is directly responsible for an increase in child pornography and other forms of child sexual abuse. The Supreme Court of the United States also recognized this when Justice Scalia acknowledged that the Internet has allowed child pornography to proliferate despite legislative efforts (Rogers, 2009). To demonstrate this point, in 1988 there were 35 people charged with child pornography offences but in 2002 this figure rose to 6,500 people who had accessed Internet pornography as part of one sting operation (Carr, 2004). Baker and Krebs-Pilotti (2006) note how the proliferation of personal computers and easy access to the Internet have made it possible to distribute and receive sexually explicit images of children quickly and cheaply. In addition, the Internet provides anonymity and unlimited opportunities to view such images and removes some of the obstacles of the past (i.e., it was an expensive, risky, and a difficult endeavor). This proliferation is alarming because many experts consider use of indecent images of children as a precursor to other sexual offenses against children (Baker & Krebs-Pilotti, 2006; Community Care, 2004). Bowker and Gray (2005) argue that offenders who use the Internet have a sense of validation from one another, as they see many chat rooms and websites catering to their sexual interests, thus reinforcing their deviant behavior and perhaps "emboldening them to commit acts, such as sex with a child, in the real world" (p. 14). Pedophiles also show children these indecent and obscene images to lower children's inhibitions and desensitize them to sexual acts (Rogers, 2009). The Internet also makes pornography instantly available to youth users, contributing to the pornographic attitude toward sex that dominates our culture today, and gives teenagers the idea that children are sexual objects, to be used at their disposal (Levin & Kilbourne, 2009).

Positive Uses of Media   Although the mass media has been widely used in the health promotion field, little is known about its effectiveness in preventing CSA. Public health campaigns that educate parents and the general public are of critical importance. Primary prevention efforts to educate the public are sorely needed. Although the media have been used effectively to promote sexual responsibility in other countries for decades, few such opportunities have been seized in the United States (Keller & Brown, 2002). National media campaigns involving television, radio, educational entertainment, billboards, and print ads are needed to raise awareness of this public health problem. These public information initiatives need to stress the clear and consistent message that the sexual exploitation of children is morally and legally wrong. In addition, efforts are needed to ban ads that sexually objectify children, messages that sexually degrade or violate children, and "sex sells" messages involving children.

Role of Parents in Countering Sexualized Childhoods   Given the importance of caregivers and family members in a child's life, much prevention work needs to be targeted at the home environment and values reflected therein. Parents who allow their children to appear in a sexualized manner (e.g., in beauty contests; advertisements; entertainment media) need to consider how this involvement promotes the sexualization of children. Parents also need to be critical consumers of product advertising. Protests can be effective ways to garner media attention and increase awareness of the issue. For example, in 2003, there was widespread public backlash to the quarterly catalog of Abercrombie & Fitch, a popular teenage and young adult clothing company, due to the sexual content and nudity, forcing the company to remove the magazine from circulation. A group of 13- to 16-year-old girls protested Abercrombie & Fitch T-shirts printed with the slogan, "Who needs a brain when you've got these?" and got national news attention with their "girl-cott" (Levin & Kilbourne, 2008).

CONCLUSION

Clearly, CSA is a multifaceted social problem that will require broad solutions, involving all facets of society, not just individuals, to eliminate. The ecological framework provided in this chapter emphasizes the need for change at both the individual and community levels, understanding both risk and protective factors. Encouragingly, substantiated cases of sexual abuse have decreased an estimated 62% over the past 15 years (Wurtele, 2009). Although this decline cannot be definitively attributed to the sexual abuse prevention movement (see Finkelhor & Jones, 2006, for other explanations), prevention efforts have most likely played a role.

Conceivably, with more focus on including parents as an integral part of the prevention process, primary prevention efforts have the potential to prevent the sexual victimization of the most vulnerable members of society and to achieve the overall objective of eliminating this serious public health problem. Applying situational prevention theory to youth-serving organizations also has the potential to reduce sexual victimization of the youthful participants.

Although the task of preventing CSA seems daunting, as Saul, Patterson, and Audage (2010) remind us, other fields have lacked the same evidence and resources, have met with the same resistance to the problem, but have persisted in their efforts to gain public support, financial resources for prevention and evaluation, and have gathered evidence of success. Prevention interventions that modify both the individual and the environment hold the most promise for eradicating CSA. The time for implementing multicomponent, coordinated prevention interventions is now. Children cannot wait.

REFERENCES

Abrahams, N., Casey, K., & Daro, D. (1992). Teachers' knowledge, attitudes, and beliefs about child abuse and its prevention. *Child Abuse & Neglect, 16,* 229–238.

American Psychological Association. (APA). (2007). *Report of the APA task force on the sexualization of girls.* Washington, DC: American Psychological Association.

Amstadter, A. B., Broman-Fulks, J., Zinzow, H., Ruggiero, K. J., & Cercone, J. (2009). Internet-based interventions for traumatic stress-related mental health problems: A review and suggestion for future research. *Clinical Psychology Review, 29*, 410–420.

Anderson, J. F., Mangels, N. J., & Langsam, A. (2004). Child sexual abuse: A public health issue. *Criminal Justice Studies, 17*, 107–126.

Babatsikos, G. (2009). Parents' knowledge, attitudes and practices about preventing child sexual abuse: A literature review. *Child Abuse Review, 19*, 107–129.

Baker, J. A., & Krebs-Pilotti, M. (2006). Internet pandemic? The not-so-secret and expanding world of child pornography. *Federal Lawyer, 53*, 50–56.

Berrick, J. D. (1988). Parental involvement in child abuse prevention training: What do they learn? *Child Abuse & Neglect, 12*(4), 543–553.

Berrick, J. D., & Barth, R. P. (1992). Child sexual abuse prevention: Research review and recommendations. *Social Work Research & Abstracts, 28*, 6–15.

Borch, P. (1996) *What do I say now?* [Motion picture]. (Available from Committee for Children, 568 First Avenue South, Suite 600, Seattle, WA, 98104–2804)

Bowker, A., & Gray, M. (2005). The cybersex offender and children. *The FBI Law Enforcement Bulletin, 74*, 12–17.

Boy Scouts of America (BSA). (n.d.). *Youth protection.* Retrieved July 17, 2010, from www.scouting.org/Training/YouthProtection.htm

Brackenridge, C. (1998). Healthy sport for healthy girls? The role of parents in preventing sexual abuse in sport. *Sport, Education and Society, 3*(1), 59–78.

Brackenridge, C. H. (2001). *Spoilsports: Understanding and preventing sexual exploitation in sport.* London, England: Routledge.

Briggs, F., & Hawkins, R.M.F. (1994). Follow-up data on the effectiveness of New Zealand's national school based child protection program. *Child Abuse & Neglect, 18*, 635–643.

Bringer, J. D., Brackenridge, C. H., & Johnston, L. H. (2002). Defining appropriateness in coach-athlete sexual relationships: The voice of coaches. *Journal of Sexual Aggression, 8*, 83–98.

Bronfenbrenner, U. (1977). Toward an experimental ecology of human development. *American Psychologist, 32*, 513–530.

Burgess, E. S., & Wurtele, S. K. (1998). Enhancing parent-child communication about sexual abuse: A pilot study. *Child Abuse & Neglect, 22*, 1167–1175.

Calvert, J. F., Jr., & Munsie-Benson, M. (1999). Public opinion and knowledge about childhood sexual abuse in a rural community. *Child Abuse & Neglect, 23*, 671–682.

Carr, J. (2004). *Child pornography, child abuse, and the Internet.* London, England: National Children's Home. Retrieved March 21, 2011 from http://www.make-it-safe.net/esp/pdf/Child_pornography_internet_Carr2004.pdf

Chasen-Taber, L., & Tabachnick, J. (1999). Evaluation of a child sexual abuse prevention program. *Sexual Abuse: A Journal of Research and Treatment, 11*, 279–292.

Chen, J. Q., & Chen, D. G. (2005). Awareness of child sexual abuse prevention education among parents of Grade 3 elementary school pupils in Fuxin City, China. *Health Education Research, 20*(5), 540–547.

Chen, J. Q., Dunne, M. P., & Han, P. (2007). Prevention of child sexual abuse in China: Knowledge, attitudes, and communication practices of parents of elementary school children. *Child Abuse & Neglect, 31,* 747–755.

Christakis, D. A., Ebel, B. E., Rivara, F. P., & Zimmerman, F. J. (2004). Television, video, and computer game usage in children under 11 years of age. *The Journal of Pediatrics, 145*(5), 652–656.

Collins, M. E. (1996). Parents' perceptions of the risk of CSA and their protective behavior: Findings from a qualitative study. *Child Maltreatment, 1,* 53–64.

Colton, M., Roberts, S., & Vanstone, M. (2010). Sexual abuse by men who work with children. *Journal of Child Sexual Abuse, 19,* 345–364.

Crosset, T., Benedict, J., & McDonald, M. (1995). Male student-athletes reported for sexual assault: A survey of campus police departments and judicial affairs offices. *Journal of Sport and Social Issues, 10*(2), 126–140.

Davis, M. K., & Gidycz, C. A. (2000). Child sexual abuse prevention programs: A meta-analysis. *Journal of Clinical Child Psychology, 29,* 257–265.

Deblinger, E., Stauffer, L., Steer, R. (2001). Comparative efficacies of supportive and cognitive behavioral group therapies for children who were sexually abused and their nonoffending mothers. *Child Maltreatment, 6*(4), 332–343.

Deblinger, E., Thakkar-Kolar, R., Berry, E., & Schroeder, C. (2010). Caregivers' efforts to educate their children about child sexual abuse. *Child Maltreatment, 15*(1), 91–100.

Dombrowski, S. C., Gischlar, K. L., & Durst, T. (2007). Safeguarding young people from cyber pornography and cyber sexual predation: A major dilemma of the Internet. *Child Abuse Review, 16,* 153–170.

Elrod, J. M., & Rubin, R. H. (1993). Parental involvement in sexual abuse prevention education. *Child Abuse & Neglect, 17,* 527–538

Fieldman, J. P., & Crespi, T. D. (2002). Child sexual abuse: offenders, disclosure, and school-based initiatives. *Adolescence, 37,* 151–160.

Finkelhor, D. (2007). Prevention of sexual abuse through educational programs directed toward children. *Pediatrics, 120,* 640–645.

Finkelhor, D. (2008). *Childhood victimization: Violence, crime and abuse in the lives of young people.* New York, NY: Oxford University Press.

Finkelhor, D., Asdigian, N., & Dziuba-Leatherman, J. (1995). Victimization prevention programs for children: A follow-up. *American Journal of Public Health, 85,* 1684–1689.

Finkelhor, D., & Dziuba-Leatherman, J. (1995). Victimization prevention programs: A national survey of children's exposure and reactions. *Child Abuse & Neglect, 19,* 129–139.

Finkelhor, D., & Jones, L. M. (2006). Why have child maltreatment and child victimization declined? *Journal of Social Issues, 62*(4), 685–716.

Finkelhor, D., & Williams, L. (1988). *Nursery crimes: Sexual abuse in day care.* Newbury Park, CA: Sage.

Gallagher, B. (2000). The extent and nature of known cases of institutional child sexual abuse. *British Journal of Social Work, 30*(6), 795–817.

Green, L. (2001). Analysing the sexual abuse of children by workers in residential care homes: Characteristics, dynamics and contributory factors. *Journal of Sexual Aggression, 7*(2), 5–24.

Hammond, W. R. (2003). Public health and child maltreatment prevention: The role of the Centers for Disease Control and Prevention. *Child Maltreatment, 8*(2), 81–83.

Hartill, M. (2009). The sexual abuse of boys in organized male sports. *Men and Masculinities, 12*(2), 225–249.

Hazzard, A., Webb, C., Kleemeier, C., Angert, L., & Pohl, J. (1991). Child sexual abuse prevention: Evaluation and one year follow up. *Child Abuse & Neglect, 15*, 123–138.

Hébert, M., Lavoie, F., Piché, C., & Poitras, M. (2001). Proximate effects of a child sexual abuse prevention program in elementary school children. *Child Abuse & Neglect, 25*, 505–522.

Herman, K. C. (1995). Appropriate use of the child abuse potential inventory in a big brothers/big sisters agency. *Journal of Social Service Research, 20*(3/4), 93–103.

John Jay College Research Team. (2004). *The nature and scope of the problem of sexual abuse of minors by Catholic priests and deacons in the United States: A research study conducted by the John Jay College of Criminal Justice.* New York: City University of New York. Retrieved from www.usccb.org/nrb/johnjaystudy

Kaufman, K., Barber, M., Mosher, H., & Carter, M. (2002). Reconceptualizing child sexual abuse as a public health concern. In P. A. Schewe (Ed.), *Preventing violence in relationships: Interventions across the lifespan* (pp. 27–54). Washington, DC: American Psychological Association.

Kaufman, K., Hayes, A., & Knox, L. A. (2010). The situational prevention model: Creating safer environments for children and adolescents. In K. L. Kaufman (Ed.), *The prevention of sexual violence: A practitioner's sourcebook.* Holyoke, MA: NEARI Press.

Kaufman, K. L., Mosher, H., Carter, M., & Estes, L. (2006). An empirically based situational prevention model for child sexual abuse. In S. Smallbone & R. Wortley (Eds.), *Situational prevention of child sexual abuse, crime prevention studies* (Vol. 19) Monsey, NY: Criminal Justice Press.

Keller, S. N., & Brown, J. D. (2002). Media interventions to promote responsible sexual behavior. *Journal of Sex Research, 39*(1), 67–72.

Kendrick, A., & Taylor, J. (2000). Hidden on the ward: The abuse of children in hospitals. *Journal of Advanced Nursing, 31*(3), 565–573.

Kenny, M. C., & Wurtele, S. K. (2008). Preschoolers' knowledge of genital terminology: A comparison of English and Spanish speakers. *American Journal of Sexuality Education, 3*(4), 345–354.

Kenny, M. C., & Wurtele, S. K. (2009). A counselor's guide to preventing childhood sexual abuse. *Counseling and Human Development, 42*, 1–14.

Kenny, M. C., & Wurtele, S. K. (2010). Children's abilities to recognize a "good" person as a potential perpetrator of childhood sexual abuse. *Child Abuse & Neglect, 34*, 490–495.

Kernsmith, P. D., Craun, S. R., & Foster, J. (2009). Public attitudes toward sexual offenders and sex offender registration. *Journal of Child Sexual Abuse, 18,* 290–301.

Krugman, R. D. (1998). It's time to broaden the agenda. *Child Abuse & Neglect, 22,* 475–479.

Lanning, B., Ballard, D. J., & Robinson, J. (1999). Child sexual abuse prevention programs in Texas public elementary schools. *Journal of School Health, 69*(1), 3–8.

Leahy, T., Pretty, G., & Tenenbaum, G. (2002). Prevalence of sexual abuse in organised competitive sport in Australia. *The Journal of Sexual Aggression, 8*(2), 16–36.

Leclerc, B., Proulx, J., & McKibben, A. (2005). Modus operandi of sexual offenders working or doing voluntary work with children and adolescents. *Journal of Sexual Aggression, 11*(2), 187–195.

Levenson, J. S., Brannon, Y. N., Fortney, D., & Baker, J. (2007). Public perceptions about sex offenders and community protection policies. *Analyses of Social Issues and Public Policy (ASAP), 7*(1), 137–161.

Levin, D. E., & Kilbourne, J. (2008). *So sexy so soon: The new sexualized childhood and what parents can do to protect their kids.* New York, NY: Ballantine Books.

Margolin, L. (1991). Child sexual abuse by nonrelated caregivers. *Child Abuse & Neglect, 15,* 213–221.

Mathews, B., & Kenny, M. (2008). Mandatory reporting legislation in the United States, Canada and Australia: A cross-jurisdictional review of key features, differences and issues. *Child Maltreatment, 13*(1), 50–63.

McAlinden, A. M. (2006). "Setting'em up": Personal, familial and institutional grooming in the sexual abuse of children. *Social & Legal Studies, 15*(3), 339–362.

McMahon, P. M., & Puett, R. C. (1999). Child sexual abuse as a public health issue: Recommendations of an expert panel. *Sexual Abuse: A Journal of Research and Treatment, 11,* 257–266.

Mercy, J. A. (1999). Having new eyes: Viewing child sexual abuse as a public health problem. *Sexual Abuse: A Journal of Research and Treatment, 11,* 317–321.

Mikton, C., & Butchart, A. (2009). Child maltreatment prevention: A systematic review of reviews. *Bulletin of the World Health Organization, 87*(5), 353–361.

Morison, S., & Greene, E. (1992). Juror and expert knowledge of child sexual abuse. *Child Abuse & Neglect, 16,* 595–613.

Moulden, H. M., Firestone, P., & Wexler, A. F. (2007). Child care providers who commit sexual offences: A description of offender, offence, and victim characteristics. *International Journal of Offender Therapy and Comparative Criminology, 51*(4), 384–406.

National Center for Missing and Exploited Children (NCMEC). (1999). *Guidelines for programs to reduce child victimization: A resource for communities when choosing a program to teach personal safety to children.* Available from NCMEC, 9176 Alternate A1A, Suite 100, Lake Park, FL 33403-1445.

Nhundu, T. J., & Shumba, A. (2001). The nature and frequency of reported cases of teacher perpetrated child sexual abuse in rural primary schools in Zimbabwe. *Child Abuse & Neglect, 25,* 1517–1534.

Norland, R., & Bartholet, J. (2001, March 19). The web's dark secret. *Newsweek, 137,* 44–51.

Olsen, M. E., & Kalbfleisch, J. H. (1999). A survey of pregnant women's knowledge about sexual abuse. *Journal of Pediatric and Adolescent Gynecology, 12,* 219–222.

Palzkill, B. (1994). Between gym shoes and high heels: The development of a lesbian identity and existence in top class sport. *International Review for the Sociology of Sport, 25*(3), 221–234.

Plummer, C. A. (2001). Prevention of child sexual abuse: A survey of 87 programs. *Violence and Victims, 16,* 575–588.

Poche, C., Yoder, P., & Miltenberger, R. (1988). Teaching self-protection to children using television techniques. *Journal of Applied Behavior Analysis, 21,* 253–261.

Reppucci, N. D., Jones, L. M., & Cook, S. L. (1994). Involving parents in child sexual abuse prevention programs. *Journal of Child and Family Studies, 3,* 137–142.

Rispens, J., Aleman, A., & Goudena, P. (1997). Prevention of child sexual victimization: A meta-analysis of school programs. *Child Abuse & Neglect, 21,* 975–987.

Roberts, J. A., & Miltenberger, R. G. (1999). Emerging issues in the research on child sexual abuse prevention. *Education & Treatment of Children, 22,* 84–102.

Rogers, A. (2009). Protecting children on the internet: Mission impossible? *Baylor Law Review, 61*(2), 323–356.

Salazar, L. F., Bradley, E.L.P., Younge, S. N., Daluga, N. A., Crosby, R. A., Lang, D. L., & DiClemente, R. J. (2009). Applying ecological perspectives to adolescent sexual health in the United States: Rhetoric or reality? *Health Education Research, 25,* 552–562.

Salter, A. (2003). *Predators, pedophiles, rapists and other sex offenders: Who they are, how they operate, and how we can protect ourselves and our children.* New York, NY: Basic Books.

Saradjian, A., & Nobus, D. (2003). Cognitive distortions of religious professionals who sexually abuse children. *Journal of Interpersonal Violence, 18*(8), 905–923.

Saul, J., & Audage, N. (2007) *Preventing child sexual abuse within youth-serving organizations: Getting started on policies and procedures.* Atlanta, GA: Center for Disease Control and Prevention, National Center for Injury Prevention and Control, Retrieved August 20, 2009, from www.cdc.gov/ncipc/dvp/PreventingChildSexualAbuse.pdf

Saul, J., Patterson, J., & Audage, N. (2010). Preventing sexual maltreatment in youth-serving community organizations. In K. L. Kaufman (Ed.), *The prevention of sexual violence: A practitioner's sourcebook* (pp. 449–464). Holyoke, MA: NEARI Press.

Schirick, E. (1998). *Risk management: Managing the risk of sexual misconduct.* Retrieved July 17, 2010, from www.acacamps.org

Shakeshaft, C. (2004). *Educator sexual misconduct: A synthesis of existing literature* (U.S. Department of Education Document No. 2004–09). Washington, DC: U.S. Department of Education.

Shoop, R. (2003). *Sexual exploitation in schools: How to spot it and stop it.* Thousand Oaks, CA: Corwin Press.

Shumba, A. (2004). Male sexual abuse by female and male perpetrators in Zimbabwean schools. *Child Abuse Review, 13,* 353–359.

Smallbone, S., Marshall, W. L., & Wortley, R. (2008). *Preventing child sexual abuse: Evidence, policy and practice.* Portland, OR: Willan

Smallbone, S., & Wortley, R. (2000). *Child sexual abuse in Queensland: Offender characteristics and modus operandi.* Brisbane: Queensland Crime Commission.

Spencer, J. W., & Knudsen, D. D. (1992). Out-of-home maltreatment: An analysis of risk in various settings for children. *Children and Youth Services Review, 14,* 485–492.

Stop It Now. (2010). What do U.S. adults think about child sexual abuse? Measures of knowledge and attitudes among six states. Retrieved from www.StopItNow.org/rdd_survey_reportfrt

Sullivan, J., & Beech, A. (2002). Professional perpetrators: Sex offenders who use their employment to target and sexually abuse the children with whom they work. *Child Abuse Review, 11,* 153–167.

Tang, C. S., & Yan, E. C. (2004). Intention to participate in child sexual abuse prevention programs: A study of Chinese adults in Hong Kong. *Child Abuse & Neglect, 28,* 1187–1197.

Teichroeb, R. (2001). Abuse and silence: Examining America's schools for the deaf. *Seattle Post-Intelligencer, 11/27/2001.* Retrieved 11/20/2007 from http://seattlepi.nwsource.com/national/48233_deaf27.shtml

Tonry, M., & Farrington, D. (1995). *Building a safer society; Strategic approaches to crime prevention.* Chicago, IL: Chicago University Press.

Trocmé, N., & Schumaker, K. (1999). Reported child sexual abuse in Canadian schools and recreational facilities: Implications for developing effective prevention strategies. *Children and Youth Services Review, 21*(8), 621–642.

Tutty, L. M. (1993). Parent's perceptions of their child's knowledge of sexual abuse prevention concepts. *Journal of Child Sexual Abuse, 2,* 83–103.

Tutty, L. M. (1997). Child sexual abuse prevention programs: Evaluating who do you tell. *Child Abuse & Neglect, 21,* 869–881.

U.S. General Accounting Office (1996). *Preventing child sexual abuse: Research inconclusive about effectiveness of child education programs.* Washington, DC: U. S. Government Printing Office.

Van Dam, C. (2001). *Identifying child molesters: Preventing child sexual abuse by recognizing the patterns of the offenders.* New York, NY: Haworth Press.

Van Dam, C. (2006). *The socially skilled child molester: Differentiating the guilty from the falsely accused.* New York, NY: Haworth Press.

Wandersman, A., & Florin, P. (2003). Community interventions and effective prevention. *American Psychologist, 58,* 441–448.

Ward, M. L. (2003). Understanding the role of entertainment media in the sexual socialization of American youth: A review of empirical research. *Developmental Review, 23*(3), 347–388.

Willard, N. E. (2007). *Cyber-safe kids, cyber-savvy teens: Helping young people learn to use the Internet safely and responsibly*. San Francisco, CA: Jossey-Bass.

Wurtele, S. K. (1993). Enhancing children's sexual development through child sexual abuse prevention programs. *Journal of Sex Education and Therapy, 19*(1), 37–46.

Wurtele, S. K. (1998). School-based child sexual abuse prevention: Questions, answers, and more questions. In J. R. Lutzker (Ed.), *Handbook of child abuse research and treatment* (pp. 501–516). New York, NY: Plenum Press.

Wurtele, S. K. (2008). Behavioral approaches to educating young children and their parents about child sexual abuse prevention. *Journal of Behavior Analysis of Offender and Victim Treatment and Prevention, 1*(1), 52–64.

Wurtele, S. K. (2009, August). *Preventing sexual abuse of children in the 21st century: Challenges and opportunities*. Workshop presented at the 10th National Conference on Child Sexual Abuse & Exploitation Prevention, New Orleans, LA.

Wurtele, S. K. (2010). *Out of harm's way: A parent's guide to protecting young children from sexual abuse*. Seattle, WA: Parenting Press.

Wurtele, S. K., & Berkower, F. (2010). *Off limits: A parent's guide to keeping kids safe from sexual abuse*. Rochester, VT: Safer Society Press.

Wurtele, S. K., Currier, L. L., Gillispie, E. I., & Franklin, C. F. (1991). The efficacy of a parent implemented program for teaching preschoolers personal safety skills. *Behavior Therapy, 22*, 69–83.

Wurtele, S. K., Gillispie, E. I., Currier, L. L., & Franklin, C. F. (1992a). A comparison of teachers vs. parents as instructors of a personal safety program for preschoolers. *Child Abuse & Neglect, 16*, 127–137.

Wurtele, S. K., Kast, L. C., & Melzer, A. M. (1992b). Sexual abuse prevention education for young children: A comparison of teachers and parents as instructors. *Child Abuse & Neglect, 16*, 865–876.

Wurtele, S. K., & Kenny, M. C. (2010). Preventing online sexual victimization of youth. *The Journal of Behavior Analysis of Offender and Victim Treatment and Prevention, 2*(1), 63–73.

Wurtele, S. K., Kvaternick, M., & Franklin, C. F. (1992c). Sexual abuse prevention for preschoolers: A survey of parents' behaviors, attitudes, and beliefs. *Journal of Child Sexual Abuse, 1*, 113–128.

Wurtele, S. K., Melzer, A. M., & Kast, L. C. (1992d). Preschoolers' knowledge of and ability to learn genital terminology. *Journal of Sex Education & Therapy, 18*, 115–122.

Wurtele, S. K., & Miller-Perrin, C. L. (1992). *Preventing child sexual abuse: Sharing the responsibility*. Lincoln: University of Nebraska Press.

Wurtele, S. K., Moreno, T., & Kenny, M. C. (2008). Evaluation of a sexual abuse prevention workshop for parents of young children. *Journal of Child & Adolescent Trauma, 1*(4), 1–10.

Wurtele, S. K., & Owens, J. S. (1997). Teaching personal safety skills to young children: An investigation of age and gender across five studies. *Child Abuse & Neglect, 21*, 805–814.

Yardley, W. (2010, April 23). $18.5 million in liability for scouts in abuse case. *New York Times*. Retrieved 7/25/2010 from www.nytimes.com/2010/04/24/us/24scouts.html

Zielinski, D., & Bradshaw, C. (2006). Ecological influences on the sequelae of child maltreatment: A review of the literature. *Child Maltreatment, 11*, 49–62.

Zins, J. E., Weissberg, R. P., Wang, M. C., & Walberg, H. J. (Eds.). (2004). *Building academic success on social and emotional learning: What does the research say?* New York, NY: Teachers College Press.

Zwi, K. J., Woolfenden, S. R., Wheeler, D. M., O'Brien, T. A., Tait, P., & Williams, K. W. (2007). School-based education programmes for the prevention of child sexual abuse (Review). *Cochrane Database of Systematic Reviews, 3*, Art. No.: CD004380. DOI: 10.1002/14651858.CD004380.pub2

Author Index

Subject Index